MW01012954

SURVIVOR

Drawing by Steve Callahan

Survivor

By Michael Greenwald

Edited by

Steve Callahan and Dougal Robertson

Blue Horizons Press, San Diego

Blue Horizons Press, Box 60778, San Diego, CA 92166 619-222-8254

© 1989 By Michael Greenwald. All rights reserved.
Published 1989. First Edition.   Reprints 1992, 1994. Revised fourth printing 1995
Printed in The United States of America
2000   99 98 97 96 95   5 4 3 2 1

Library of Congress Cataloging in Publication Data
  Greenwald, Michael,
    1. Survival, Marine (Shipwrecks, etc.)   2. Boating safety   363.123

Bibliography: pp. 583-587
Includes index
1. Survival, Marine   I. Title
Library of Congress Catalog Card Number: 89-50291   1989
ISBN 0-931297-02-8.
ISBN 0-931297-03-6 pbk.

The following publishers or agents have generously given permission to use extended quotations pho-tos, or illustrations from copyrighted works: Antheneum Publishers, Inc., New York, *Lost*, by Thomas Thompson, 1985; A.M. Heath & Co. Ltd. (Agent) for Ann Davison, *Last Voyage* , published by Grafton Books; 1988; A & C Black (Publishers) Ltd., *117 Days Adrift (Staying Alive)* by Maurice and Maralyn Bailey, 1988 reprint; Houghton Mifflin Co. *Adrift,* by Steve Callahan © 1986 by Steve Callahan; Grafton Books, a Division of Collins Publishing Group, *Survive the Savage Sea*, by Dougal Robertson © 1973 by Dougal Robertson; Consumer Reports, *1989 Buying Guide*, © 1988 by Consumers Union of the United States; K.S. Giniger Co., New York and Greenhill Books/Lionel Leventhal, London, *Safety and Survival at Sea*, by E.C.B. Lee and Kenneth Lee © 1980, 1971; William Morrow & Co., Illustra-tions from *Rage to Survive*, by Jaques Vignes © 1975 English Translation by William Morrow & Co.; Museum National D'Histoire Naturelle, Laboratoire d'Oceanographie Physique (agent), charts from *Descriptive Regional Oceanography* by P. Tchernia, published by Permagon Press, Oxford; Rijksmuseum Van Natuurlijke Historie, Leiden, *European Atlantic Turtles*, Zool. Verh 121, by L.D. Brongersma, 1972, Simon & Schuster, *Kon Tiki*, by Thor Heyerdahl, 1950.

MICHAEL GREENWALD holds a 100-Ton Master's license, Power and Sail. He has 55,000 miles of cruising experience, including nine crossings of the At-lantic Ocean, two crossings of the Pacific, and has crossed both the Atlantic and the Pacific Oceans solo. He was a combat medic in the USA and USAR. He is an aircraft pilot with experience in Central and South America. He has made several canoe voyages through the Canadian Arctic and has traveled extensively in North and Central Africa. He lives aboard his 36-foot sloop in Southern California.

I have known the sea too long to believe
in its respect for decency.

Joseph Conrad

Table of Contents

CHAPTER I
CHOREOGRAPHY OF DISASTER. 1
Loss of Yacht RHINOCEROS 3
Hurricanes and Killer Storms 6
Collision...18
Navigation Errors 31
Fire 32
Capsizing, Pitchpoling 35
The Right Boat..39
CHAPTER II
THE WILL TO SURVIVE. 43
Bombard Story by Alain Bombard 43
Sailing With a Loose Cannon: *Lost* by Thomas Thompson 53
CHAPTER III
THE SURVIVAL CRAFT. 63
About Life Rafts 63
Using a Dinghy as a Lifeboat 95
Rigging a Dinghy as a Survival Craft 99
Using an Inflatable Boat as a Lifeboat 102
CHAPTER IV
ADRIFT ON TROPIC SEAS. 103
Special Problems of the Tropics 103
Sudden Disaster in Tropic Seas 106
Survive the Savage Sea by Dougal Robertson 106
Adrift by Steve Callahan 118
Staying Alive/117 Days Adrift by Maurice and Maralyn Bailey 130
Rule No. 1: Never Abandon Ship 'til the Ship Abandons You 140
Rage to Survive by Jaques Vignes 141
CHAPTER V
SURVIVAL FISHING. 151
Pelagic Fish...151
Turtles 160
Plankton 169
CHAPTER VI
ABOUT SHARKS. 175

CHAPTER VII
  MAROONED ON A TROPIC ISLE. 188
  Crusoe of Caroline Island 189
  Food from the Reef and Lagoon 197
  Food from the Island...204
  Making a Fire..212
  Signals from Land 213
CHAPTER VIII
  FOOD AND WATER. 215
  The Physiology of Water Loss 215
  The Symptoms of Dehydration...217
  Problems of Ion Deficiency 219
  The Water Ration..221
  Collecting Water 224
  Reverse Osmosis Water Purifiers 227
  Food Rations 234
  Selecting Survival Food...237
CHAPTER IX
  DISASTER IN COLD WEATHER. 241
  Almost Too Late by Elmo Wortman 241
  Hypothermia 249
  Cold Weather Clothing 255
CHAPTER X
  ABANDON SHIP!. 265
  Making a Disaster Contingency Plan 265
  Making a Survival Plan 266
  Assessment of the Damage: Rule No. 2: The Buttocks Rule 267
  Good Reasons to Abandon Ship 270
  The Psychology of Survival 277
CHAPTER XI
  EMERGENCY MEDICINE FOR CASTAWAYS. 283
  Preparation and Planning for a Medical Emergency 285
  Treatment of Medical Emergencies 287
  Wounds 297
  Fractures 300
  Burns...305
  Infection 311
  Common Survival Craft-Related Disorders 333
  Reef-Related Disorders..337
  Medical Kit for Survival Craft..345

CHAPTER XII
> **LIFEBOAT NAVIGATION.** 349

CHAPTER XIII
> **LAND FALL.** 361
> Signs of Land 361
> The Wind and Water Near Shore 363
> Landing through Surf..373
> Landing on a Windward Shore 378
> Lifeguard or Beach Patrol Signals 382

CHAPTER XIV
> **RADIO TRANSMISSIONS AND SURVIVAL.** 372
> Preparing Radio Equipment for Emergencies 372
> Emergency Transmissions 2.182 MHZ 376
> Emergency Transmissions 4-22 MHZ 376
> Sending an Emergency Transmission..377
> Special Case Emergency Signals 381
> Radio Help for Medical Emergencies 383
> Receiving Weather Warnings by Radio 390

CHAPTER XV
> **OCEANS AND SURVIVAL.** 393
> What is Weather?..394
> Fronts 405
> Frontal Systems 411
> Killer Storms..414
> Ocean Currents 420
> Birds Encountered at Sea..428
> Bird Classification 430
> Sea Birds 433
> Offshore Birds 444
> Coastal Birds 449
> Land Birds 451

CHAPTER XVI
> **SIGNALS.** 453
> History of Pyrotechnic Signals 453
> Rule No. 3: Signals Are Like Blessings 455
> Day Signals 459
> Night Signals 465
> Emergency Radios 469

CHAPTER XVII
> **THE SURVIVAL PACK.** 470

CHAPTER XVIII
    MAN OVERBOARD!. 481
    The Risk of Loss and Difficulty of Recovery 481
    Boat Safety Features 482
    Personal Safety Gear 484
    Man Overboard Equipment 494
    Rescue without a Search 498
    Overboard Search Strategy 503
    Search Patterns 504
    Nighttime Procedures 512
    Bringing a Swimmer Aboard 513
CHAPTER XIX
    SEARCH AND RESCUE. 517
    SAR Organization...517
    Assistance for Disabled or Distressed Vessels 524
    Coast Guard SAR Aircraft 540
    AMVER Alert...550
    A Classic Rescue 551
    The Yacht SPIRIT Affair 556
CHAPTER XX
    SURVIVAL AND THE LAW. 568
    CONCLUSION. 582
SAFE HARBOR. 584
BIBLIOGRAPHY. 585
INDEX. 590
ABOUT THE ARTISTS. 601

List of Illustrations

Loss of the TITANIC by Richard DeRosset 1
Final Voyage by Jim Sollers 20
Collision Course by Rafael Monroy 22
Running Lights for a Tug-in-tow by Rafael Monroy 23
Tug-in-tow by Rafael Monroy 24
Death in the Night by Richard DeRosset 26
Engineroom Fire by Jim Sollers 33
Sea Anchor by Rafael Monroy 35
The Right Boat by Jim Sollers 38
Cartoon by Gary Larson 41
The Survival Craft by Richard DeRosset 62
The Weak Link by Rafael Monroy 65
Righting an Inverted Raft by Rafael Monroy 67
Givens Buoy Life Raft by Rafael Monroy 68
Fish-eye View of Avon Raft from *Staying Alive* 69
Deployed Sea Anchor by Rafael Monroy 76
Viking Sea Anchor, Icelandic Type by Rafael Monroy 77
Switlik Coastal Raft by Rafael Monroy 79
Coastal Raft Internal Sleeves by Rafael Monroy 80
Sole Survivor of a "Four-man" Raft by Rafael Monroy 87
Raft Plugs by Rafael Monroy 88
Raft Hole Clamps by Rafael Monroy 89
Survival Dinghy by Jim Sollers 95
Rigging a Dinghy as a Survival Craft by Jim Sollers 99
Adrift on Tropic Seas by Steve Callahan 102
Killer Whales by Rebecca Thomson 108
Usual Disposition of Bodies in the Raft at Night by Pam Littlewood 111
EDNAMIR Towing the Life Raft by Pam Littlewood 112
Usual Disposition of Bodies in EDNAMIR by Pam Littlewood 112
Gaffs by Pam Littlewood 116
Two Views of RUBBER DUCKY III by Steve Callahan from *Adrift* 120
Self Portrait by Steve Callahan from *Adrift* 128
Detail Map of the Galapagos Area from *Staying Alive/117 Days Adrift* 135
Bailey Fish Trap by Rafael Monroy 139
Becalmed from *Rage to Survive* 147
Illustration from *Rage to Survive* 149
Survival Fishing by Steve Callahan 150
Flying Fish by Rebecca Thomson 152

Triggerfish by Rebecca Thomson 153
Dorados by Rebecca Thomson 154
Emergency Spears by Rafael Monroy 156
Assorted Lures by Rafael Monroy 157
Make-shift Trap by Rafael Monroy 158
Green Turtle and Hawksbill Turtle from *European Atlantic Turtles* 162
Loggerhead Turtle from *European Atlantic Turtles* 164
Ridleys Turtle from *European Atlantic Turtles* 165
Copepods by Rafael Monroy 170
Plankton Net Made from Panty Hose by Rafael Monroy 173
Homer's *Gulf Stream* by Rebecca Thomson 174
The Great White by Richard DeRosset 176
Tiger Shark by Rebecca Thomson 179
Bull Sharks by Rebecca Thomson 181
Mako Shark Attacking a Swordfish by Rebecca Thomson 183
Hammerheads around a Life Raft by Rebecca Thomson 187
Gary Mundell and his Wrecked Boat by Richard DeRosset 188
Hatian Fish Trap by Rebecca Thomson 198
Carolina Hanging Snare by Rafael Monroy 205
Baited Trigger Deadfall by Rafael Monroy 206
Coconut Opening Stick by Rafael Monroy 208
Breadfruit Tree and its Leaves by Raoul Reys 209
Taro Plant by Raoul Reys 210
Distilling Fresh Water from Sea Water by Rafael Monroy 210
Making a Fire by Rafael Monroy 212
Offshore View of Rescue Signals by Rafael Monroy 213
The Water Ration by Jim Sollers 214
Chart: Winds and Rain, January-February-March 230
Chart: Winds and Rain, April-May-June 231
Chart: Winds and Rain, July-August-September 232
Chart: Winds and Rain, October-November-December 233
Cartoon by Gary Larson 239
Disaster in Cold Weather by Jim Sollers 240
Chart: Immersion Time by U.S.C.G. 251
Dressing in Layers by Rafael Monroy 256
Assume Fetal Position by Rafael Monroy 256
Immersion Suit by Rafael Monroy 260
Caught in the Rigging by Jim Sollers 269
Pressure Points by Raoul Reys 286
Applying a Tourniquet by Rafael Monroy 288
Tying Off a Blood Vessel by Rafael Monroy 289
Tracheotomy Procedure by Rafael Monroy 293

Different Types of Wounds by Rafael Monroy 297
Applying a Triangular Bandage by Raoul Reys 304
Location of Lymph Nodes by Rafael Monroy 312
How to Give an Injection by Rafael Monroy 316
Anesthetizing a Wound by Rafael Monroy 328
Place First Suture by Rafael Monroy 329
Tie Several Square Knots by Rafael Monroy 330
Continue Running Suture by Rafael Monroy 331
Tie with Several Square Knots (II) by Rafael Monroy 332
Pacific Puffer by Rafael Monroy 340
Stonefish by Rafael Monroy 341
Lion Fish by Rafael Monroy 342
Polaris and Cassiopaiae by Rafael Monroy 357
Southern Cross by Rafael Monroy 358
Compass Card as an Astrolabe 359
Surf Mechanics by Raoul Reys 365
Body surfing technique by Raoul Reys 367
Wind Near Cliffs by Raoul Reys 369
"This is the best place to land" by Rafael Monroy 371
"Landing here is very dangerous" by Rafael Monroy 371
Illustration from *Rage to Survive* 391
Clouds by Raoul Reys 392
Cumulonimbus Convection Cell by Rafael Monroy 395
Cartoon by Gary Larson 399
Chart: Atlantic and Mediterranean Summer Winds and Pressures 400
Chart: World Summer Winds and Pressures 401
Chart: World Winter Winds and Pressures...403
Cold Front by Rafael Monroy 407
Warm Front by Rafael Monroy 409
Frontal System by Raoul Reys 412
Hurricane Tracks by Rafael Monroy 414
High Latitude Storm, Hurricane Showing their Most Dangerous Areas........417
Buys Ballot's Law by Rafael Monroy 418
Vessel Positioned Directly in Hurricane's Path 419
Cartoon by Gary Larson 421
Chart: Surface Currents, Northern Summer 422
Chart: Surface Currents, Atlantic Ocean Winter 423
Turtles by Karon Harrod..424
Tropic Bird by Rebecca Thomson 429
Food from the Skies by Steve Callahan...431
Brown Pelicans by Rebecca Thomson 432
Sea Birds by Rebecca Thomson 434

Head Shapes of the Fulmar Family by Rebecca Thomson 437
Fulmar in Flight by Rebecca Thomson 438
Storm Petrels at Sea by Rebecca Thomson 439
Shearwater in Flight by Rebecca Thomson 441
Kittiwakes by Rebecca Thomson 442
Phalaropes by Rebecca Thomson 443
Magnificent Frigate in Flight by Rebecca Thomson 444
Boobies by Rebecca Thomson 446
Skua or "Sea-eagle" by Rebecca Thomson 447
Terns by Rebecca Thomson 448
Common Gull by Rebecca Thomson 450
Blue Heron by Rebecca Thomson 451
Flares Seen at Different Distances by Raoul Reys 457
Smoke Signal by Rafael Monroy 459
Clothing Used as a Signal by Maurice Bailey 461
The Heliograph by Rafael Monroy 462
Heliograph Made from Can Lid by Rafael Monroy 464
Cutaway of a Parachute Signal by Rafael Monroy 467
How to Launch a Flare by Rafael Monroy 468
Man Overboard! by Richard DeRosset 480
Typical Type I-V Flotation Devices by Rafael Monroy 485
Man Overboard Pole with Equipment by Rafael Monroy 495
M.O.M. Deployed by Rafael Monroy 496
Crash Stop for Sailboats by Rafael Monroy 499
Expanding Square Pattern by Rafael Monroy 509
Parallel Search by Rafael Monroy 510
How to Enter a Parallel Search Using the Wind by Rafael Monroy 511
Boarding a Swimmer by Rafael Monroy 514
Helicopter Rescue by Richard DeRosset 516
Monkey's Fist and Messenger Attached to a Line by U.S.C.G. 527
Unmanned Life Raft by U.S.C.G. 528
Towing Bridle by U.S.C.G. 531
Wrenching a Grounded Vessel by U.S.C.G. 532
Maximum Safe Towing Speeds for Displacement Hulls by U.S.C.G. 534
Lowering a Dewatering Pump by Richard DeRosset 539
Basket Hoist by U.S.C.G. 549
Stokes Litter by U.S.C.G. 550
Cartoon by Gary Larson 567

List of Photographs

Alain Bombard 42
Photo Taken in the English Channel by Maurice & Maralyn Bailey 45
Viking Life Raft..71
Photo of LUCETTE Survivors 117
AURALYN Sinking from *Staying Alive* by Maurice & Maralyn Bailey 131
Seaman from the WEOLMI Helps Maralyn Bailey 140
Verkade Survival Ration 236
Hypothermia Victim by Andrew Besley 254
Aligning a Fracture from *Advanced First Aid Afloat* 302
Foul Weather Gear Being Used as a Signal by Maurice Bailey 461
"Core" Size Survival Pack Container with Positive Flotation 471
How Far Could a Head Be Seen in this Photo? 483
Dead Man in a Life Jacket 487
Packaged Emergency Throwing Line...497
Rip Currents by Willard Bascom..361
The R.N. Penlee Lifeboat SOLOMON BROWNE by Andrew Besley 517
Wreck of the UNION STAR by Andrew Besley 518
The Wessex Helicopter with Body of Capt. Richards by Andrew Besley 519
R.N. Lifeboat from St. Ives by Andrew Besley..522
41' Utility Tow Boat, U.S.C.G. 525
44' Self-righting Motorized Lifeboat 526
The U.S.C.G. Falcon Jet..541
"Bomber" Trench Dropping a Life Raft 542
HH52A Helicopter, U.S.C.G. 543
Dolphin Helicopter Hoisting One of Five Fishermen from the Sea 545
The Doomed 482-foot KOMSOMOLETS MIRGIZII 546
Dolphin Helicopter Hoisting Survivor of THE PRIDE OF BALTIMORE ...555
SPIRIT under Full Sail 557
SPIRIT at Anchor in French Polynesia 559
Raft Containing Durel Miller and Nancy Perry by Bruce Collins 561
Portrait of Bruce Collins by Jim Ahola 564
Cutter CAMPBELL Approaching Bruce Collin's Raft................................567

Preface

Since everyone knows that sailing is the slowest way to travel, many people persistently ask why and why not? Why sail? If you must go somewhere, why not fly? Why not join a travel club? Why not "do" Europe by train? Why not fly to Tahiti and catch the inter-island freight boat? After all, it's obvious one can get there faster, spend more time enjoying the place, live like kings (and queens) and return to the comfort of one's own snug home for about what it would cost to buy a new life raft.

The answer, of course, is that a small boat voyage is an inward trip and only incidentally involves green islands and beautiful native girls. It is a voyage of discovery, but the things we wish to discover are about ourselves. Our increasingly complex society surrounds us with a variety of safeguards. We no longer have to fight the Indians or the wolves. We have hospitals to protect our health, welfare, unemployment and social security to provide funds, the police, the fire department and the armed services to shield us from violence. We are sheltered from womb to tomb, and this is good. But along the way we have lost contact with a part of ourselves.

There is no longer any simple way to know what kind of people we are, whether we are brave, stoic or moral. Bravery may mean facing your boss and asking for a raise, not pulling an oar in a 36' whaling canoe. Being stoic may involve saving money for your children's education, not standing in a tree with a bow waiting for a deer. Everyone wants to know what kind of person they really are inside. That's why people climb mountains and skydive. Another way to find out is to buy a boat and head for the blue water.

There is a slight risk of death associated with sailing small boats across oceans which cannot be eliminated. One can be experienced, have good equipment, sail in the right season and still end up in a life raft or dead. Knowing this, not denying this, is your ticket of admission to the inward voyage and to all the sweet, green islands which lie beneath the wind. It's the price you pay.

Sinking in a small boat is fundamentally different from sinking aboard a ship. Ships usually (but not always) sink slowly. There is more time for an orderly abandonment, and there is a reasonable presumption that a distress message will be sent. Ships usually carry large lifeboats or rafts which, because of their size and price, are better built and equipped than a small boat's life raft. Last, but not least, a ship usually goes down in a shipping lane, which makes a speedy rescue even more likely. Sailboats go where the wind takes them, and that is often far from the shipping lanes. Boats (usually, but not always) sink in one to three minutes. There is rarely time to transmit a distress message. All of this implies that there are important differences between the two types of disasters. This book has been written to improve the chances of surviving a boat disaster.

There is no substitute for thinking about disaster before it happens. Dougal Robertson's 43', 19-ton schooner LUCETTE was hit by a killer whale in the South Pacific in June, 1972 and the boat went down in exactly one minute. He, his crew and his family spent 37 days adrift under the most desperate conditions. Although he was an experienced sailor, his boat was not equipped with a survival pack, and he had a life raft only by the merest of coincidence—an old one given to him as a gift by a friend. No plan been made for such a disaster.

Believe me, I am not faulting Dougal Robertson. I have sailed many thousands of miles with a life raft I would now not recommend for a child in a pool, without a survival pack, in a tiny boat with neither a radio or motor, with kerosene running lights that often went out, trusting my fate and that of my love to pure white light, karma and the fickle goddess of the sea. I call her the Lady with the Green Eyes. She can be sweet, but there is always a surprise behind her smile. She did her absolute best to eat me.

Over the years, a number of my friends have gone. The Lady with the Green Eyes took them and they disappeared. I, too, have paid my dues in various lifeboats, have had contemplative periods floating alone in a life jacket, rowed for my life toward a distant beach and have even had a few delightful moments swimming after a boat that did its best to sail away from me. In short, I have been a pure fool. This is the reason I have written *Survivor*, so that others may learn from my hard-won wisdom.and from the deaths of my friends. And that, I am sure, is why Dougal Robertson wrote his book, *Sea Survival, A Manual*. As he said in its preface:

Information is a major factor in successful survival, and although survivors can learn much from their own mistakes, death may intervene before the learning can be applied to a second chance.

Foreword

By Steve Callahan

About a year ago I was reviewing a manual by Martyn Forrester that was primarily oriented towards land survival. In my reply to him, I mused, "I wish someone would write a text as thorough on ocean survival." Ironically, soon thereafter I got a call from Michael Greenwald. The result, here, is just what the doctor ordered. Ocean survival manuals have come and gone, but none is as thorough as this one, and I suspect it will be the standard for a long time.

As I found out first hand, ocean survival is not a simple subject. All of us who venture upon the sea must resist the urge to push the subject to the back of our minds. I was lucky to survive about two and a half months in a rubber ducky on the wild blue wilderness. Since returning in 1982, at least one person whom I've known or met has disappeared each year. Of course, my life is sailing, so it is somewhat like a race car driver knowing many people who met their maker in car crashes. Still, water-related accidents are the number four accidental killer in this country and number two for children. It is serious business.

Trying to sell survival, be it equipment, training, or books, is a tough business. It's rather depressing, after all. It requires you to spend time and money you hope you'll never use. Mr. Greenwald has done an admirable job, with his easy writing style, to make the subject fun. I have always found survival case histories fascinating, and he includes enough of them here to bring theoretical and esoteric aspects of survival alive.

The fact is, you can gain more from learning about survival than from getting yourself out of a pinch. While you are sailing the world's greatest wilderness, you are exhilarated by the feeling of total freedom. Ironically, total freedom requires total, ultimate responsibility. Man is very vulnerable in the wilderness. There is no guarantee that anyone will bail you out of the mess that you have gotten yourself into. Alain Bombard's intentional survival voyage in 1952 proved that survival is not a passive undertaking--you're not likely to make it by lying about, hoping someone else will save you. Survival requires a psychological and philosophical approach, as well as nuts and bolts survival skills. The author here has successfully mixed these together. The skills that make someone a survivor are the same as those which make a successful person in other walks of life: versatility, creativity, the ability to act reasonably under stress and make tough decisions.

The most difficult aspect of survival preparation is the unique character of each situation and the limit of that for which one can prepare. Cold is the greatest problem for some; for others, it's dehydration. The problem of the moment may shift with the weather. I found that every aspect of every situation presented a paradox. When the wind blew hard, I moved well towards landfall and safety, but it made fishing difficult, cut water production and kept me wet, so saltwater sores multiplied. On hot, windless days, I could dry out, fish more easily and produce more water, but I required more water and food and got no closer to salvation. Each choice was a dilemma as well.

If I chose to fish, I might receive immediate hunger relief, but spearing large, powerful fish put the raft and equipment at risk, and I didn't know how long I would be out there. Should you use another flare on a passing ship, or write that one off and save the flare for another vessel that will hopefully keep a better watch? You must ration not only food and water but also equipment use, energy, everything. No manual or piece of equipment can make these decisions for you, but books such as this one will help you make an educated guess. Beyond that, you can only do what I constantly did: remind yourself that you are doing the best you can.

Ideally, when your boat sinks, it would be grand to step off onto another just like it. That's a little impractical, of course. Survival equipment can not possibly cover every eventuality and must compromise ideal design with weight and space restrictions. Even the best survival equipment standards, such as those suggested in SOLAS, limit the weight of equipment. Manufacturers can only try to cover the bases as best they can. In my opinion, there is no ideal piece of gear. Like every design decision, all entail compromise. Debates over the best way to achieve raft stability, what type of water producer is best, and so on, will likely never die. Herein you will find as reasonable arguments and wide variety of options as I've found anywhere.

Items we ignore in everyday life can become valuable raw materials from which to fashion survival equipment. In many cases, a sheet of plastic and a bit of string is more valuable than an expensive bit of specialized equipment, for the string and plastic can be fashioned into a solar still, rain catcher, fish trap, or whatever. Survival requires the survivors to be creative and determined. We take our lessons from men like Dougal Robertson and the Baileys, without whom I would not be alive. These survivors shaped not only my survival voyage, but my voyage in everyday life, for they demonstrated the value of survival skills in solving everyday problems, enhancing the enjoyment of that great wavy wilderness and the freedom it gives us, if we are willing to submit to its rule.

Survival, in strange and often horrible ways, presents us with great gifts. Through my own suffering, I found strength I never knew I had, saw incredible beauty in a living hell. I was confronted with the difference between needs and wants and found that most of our modern lives are made of the latter, rather than the former. I got a new appreciation for the luxury of normal existence. In that luxury of hindsight, I have no regrets, although I hope never to have to live through anything like it again.

Survival training and prepraration need not be depressing or a waste of time. If you put on a survival suit and jump into an icy harbor, you're likely to find it fun. I once put a group of survival students into a raft and capsized it. They soon turned the intimidating problem into a game and learned to right the thing without even getting out. What's more, skills learned will assist you in jury rigging failed gear afloat or ashore and will help you approach problems with common sense.

You can put together a ditch kit largely from inexpensive items which are easy to obtain. There's alot of good gear and good information out there, and in these pages. It is true that cost is a consideration, but I have little patience with those who take no responsibility for themselves and are poorly equipped, who complain when safety gear isn't perfect or when the authorities have not saved them. One must question the priorities of those who think nothing of spending thousands for new sails, yet complain that a full set of safety gear might cost as much.

Use this book and embark on a fun, informative and utilitarian voyage, beginning with survival skills and interesting stories, then proceed to risk assessment, the appreciation of life itself and the enjoyment of freedom at sea. If you do embark on this voyage of survival preparation and ever find yourself in a tight spot, you will not despair, but will see yourself as caught in a time warp, a nautical cave man, surrounded by piles of raw materials, yet possessing the technical skills and knowledge of the twentieth century.

Voyaging entails risks and may lead to a horrible survival situation, but risk is part of any fulfilling enterprise, and with proper preparation, you may be able to face survival as just another leg of the adventure. It will be tough and very risky, but after you have survived (never _if_ you survive) it will remain one of the most important events of your life. There are no real guarantees in life, but follow this road and I will guarantee you more confidence afloat, a much better chance to survive and thrive in that great wilderness that covers two thirds of the earth and from which all of the creatures of the land first crawled.

Foreword

By Dougal Robertson

The subject of human survival after shipwreck has been portrayed in harrowing detail by story tellers over the centuries since writing began, and before that in legendary tales, passed down by word of mouth in epic poems and breathtaking sagas, doubtless losing nothing in the passage of time. If we are to search for a code of behavior in those tales of survival at sea, which can be recommended to survivors who, for whatever reason, find themselves castaway on a survivor craft, then it has to be certain that the information used for that purpose is genuine, and verifiable in the accounts of ordeals which are cited. It is therefore worth taking a look at a cross sample of people who write these accounts and their motives for doing so.

First, there is the formal account from hardheaded, professional seamen, given in a dispassionate statement of facts which, while authentic, often conceal important details of a physical and emotional nature. Then there is the colored version which could well be from the same source, but with an eye to emphasizing extenuating circumstances to evoke a sympathetic response. A third variety comes from the secondhand account, written by journalists or appointed storytellers who are often commissioned to present an engaging and absorbing story for public consumption, or to portray an unpleasant feature of survival practice as an unavoidable consequence of the survivor's circumstances. Fourthly, there is an ever-increasing body of knowledge emanating from dedicated research establishments whose contributions in the construction of life-supporting craft, protective clothing, treatment for acute hypothermia in varying degrees, sophisticated search and rescue systems, and improved distress communication, play an ever-increasing role in recommended minimums for survival living.

Finally, there is the anthologist who, like Michael Greenwald has the unenviable task of sifting fact from fiction, so that he can present, in conjunction with expert's recommendations, a survivor's guide to life. Not an easy undertaking, but worthwhile if it sounds a note of caution for those who seek business or pleasure in deep water.

To my mind, there are two basic views of survival living at sea. There is the survivor's view of survival and there is Officialdom's view of survival. I once asked a high-ranking naval officer why his Navy's survival manual stopped short at the sixth day, by which time, if the survivors had obeyed instructions, they would have consumed the whole of the allocation of water and emergency rations provided for them. He replied, *"If Search and Rescue had not discovered the survivors by that time, they would be"* he looked around sharply and lowered his voice *"written off"*. In confirmation of this view, a publisher asked another Navy if it would be interested in helping to produce a waterproof edition of my book *Sea Survival , a Manual*, to be supplied to all survival craft as standard equipment. The request was rejected on the grounds that the Navy did not expect any of their survivors to be at risk long enough to make use of a book on long term survival. This confident attitude conceals a grim and gristly paradox which castaways will ignore at their peril. It is that if the search part of Search and Rescue fails, the rescue part cannot function and by this time, those at risk become aware of this failure it will coincide with the discovery that the only thing left to sustain life is the much vaunted "will to survive." Which brings us face to face with the survivor's view of survival.

The "will to survive" is a phrase coined by survival 'experts' to explain why, against considered professional opinion, people who ought to be dead still cling to life. This inexplicable refusal to die can operate with equal facility in a hospital, concentration camp or survival craft and, being a state of mind rather than body, it is an attitude which is very difficult to instill into someone who doesn't already possess it, especially at the drop of a survival raft. Whether the survivor at sea possesses the "will to survive" or not, the continuing process of survival will largely depend on the survivor's "fitness to survive" which, make no mistake, is also a state of mind rather than of body. The 'fitness to survive' is the capacity to act with cautious restraint or immediate resolve when occasion demands, not so much with the successful conclusion of the ordeal in mind but simply to avoid the imminent disaster which threatens. The 'fitness to survive' takes into consideration the minute by minute, hour by hour, day by day requirements to sustain life, with a cussed tenacity which borders on fanaticism. There is nothing particularly heroic about survivors. The risks they take are compulsory, their endurance a necessity and their restraint, not so much born of self-denial, as a recognition that self-indulgence is punishable by death. There is no safety in survival, only the continuity of life on the razor's edge, between exhaustion and collapse, where the survivors live in a world of civilized people's nightmares, their sleep is a snatched moment of oblivion. They awaken instants later to another crisis, or an agonized contact with another boil-infested fellow survivor.

If there is one characteristic which can strengthen the survivor's will and fitness to survive, it is a sustained sense of the ridiculous. How else can one view the timidity of huge, man-eating sharks, the miniscule pieces of food which constitute the daily ration, the sip of that heavenly liquid called rain, the cockleshell of a survival craft in which two is a crowd, but with six, an inch of space is luxury. It may seem paradoxical to write of survival and luxury in the same sentence, and it would be ridiculous to suggest that a survival pack should include the luxury of a reference library, but accurate information becomes a critical factor in the struggle to survive. When a castaway is thrown back on the reserves of knowledge contained, with pitiful inadequacy, in the brain's memory bank, there arises a desperate need not only to confirm that one's actions will benefit the survival situation, but also that they will not jeopardize it.

In the same way that desire can nurture belief, dislike can foster rejection. Castaways have to make enormous concessions to uncivilized living in order to survive, and for some, as in the ordeal of the SPIRIT's castaways, adjustment seemed particularly difficult. For some, to whom such a change is beyond the psychological barrier of acceptance. I recommend the attitude of my thirteen year-old son who, travelling back to England on an ocean liner a month after our rescue said to me one bright sunny day, *"Dad, I'm bored stiff. I wish I were back on the raft!"*

To complement this collection and analysis of ordeals at sea, Michael Greenwald has compiled a valuable addition to the techniques of distress communication, the recovery of overboard personnel and the lore of desert island living, all subjects which should exercise the minds of those who may find themselves at one with the lonely sea and sky--and no boat. *Survivor* is not exactly a reference library, but it's probably as close as you will get to one between the covers of a single book.

The author would like to thank the following
individuals whose, advice, counsel, editorial contributions,
and consideration have helped make this book possible:

CONTRIBUTING EDITORS

Steve Callahan, Ellsworth, Maine
(Author of *Adrift*)

Dougal Robertson, St. Denis de Pile, France
(Author of *Survive the Savage Sea* and *Sea Survival, a Manual*)

SECOND PRINTING EDITOR

Marcy Raphael, San Diego, California

AND THE FOLLOWING

Ellen Ahola, San Rafael, California; Maurice and Maralyn Bailey, Everton, Lymington, England; Willard Bascom, Long Beach, California; Andrew Besley, St. Ives, Cornwall, England; Sandy Becker, San Diego, California; W. Robert Buxtom, San Francisco, California; Michael and Nancy Daniels, Ernest Carson, San Pedro, California; Bruce Collins, Stockton, California; Poul Gensen, Viking Life Raft Company, Miami, Florida; Gertrude Greenwald, Coral Gables, Florida; Captain Stephan B. Lewis, MD, USN, Bethesda, Maryland; Donald Meier, Sea Mate Marine, San Diego, California; Kathy Massimini, Ellsworth, Maine; Douglas Moore, San Francisco, California, Gary Mundell, Nome, Alaska; Werner Siems, Commandant, U.S.C.G., Washington, DC; Deanne Sclar, Santa Barbara, California; Captain A. L. Steinman, U.S.C.G., Washington, DC; Lt. JG. John Sullivan, U.S.C.G., San Diego, California; Cilla Thomson, Evergreen, Colorado; California, Derrick Van Loan, Sausalito, California.

Overleaf: *Death of the TITANIC* by Richard DeRosset

For

My friends,
whom the sea has taken.

CHAPTER I: CHOREOGRAPHY OF DISASTER

Disaster Can Happen Any Time

Everyone remembers the description of the doomed TITANIC, slipping beneath the waves, with the men standing around looking dignified in their tuxedos, while the band played Auld Lang Syne. Boats never sink like that. The TITANIC was a ship, and even though she had a rather large gash in her side below the waterline, it took many tons of water and a considerable amount of time to fill her up. If there had been enough life boats, all might have survived.

Because they are so much smaller and usually lack double bows, collision bulkheads and sealable compartments, boats often sink in little more than a minute. If you're trying to hold your breath, a minute seems like a long time; but when your boat is going down, a minute hardly gives one time to think. Steve Callahan, (see Chapter IV), making a solo passage across the Atlantic, was asleep when his boat struck—something. His terrifying experience certainly typifies that of anyyone who has gone down suddenly at sea:

> BANG! A deafening explosion blankets the subtler sounds of torn wood and rush of the sea. I jump up. Water thunders over me as if I've suddenly been thrown into the path of a rampaging river. Forward, aft—where does it come from? Is half the side gone? No time. I fumble with the knife I have sheathed by the chart table. Already the water is waist deep. The nose of the boat is slipping down, down! From *Adrift* (Pg. 21)

Anyone who ventures into the blue water is vulnerable to the little tricks which the Lady with the Green Eyes can play. People out for a few quick turns around the sea buoy, who had planned to be back at the yacht club for Happy Hour, suddenly find themselves in a survival situation which was totally unanticipated. You may spend just a few hours in a survival craft—or longer—and nothing can ruin your day like having to jump into the water with just a life jacket between you and eternity. When these things happen to me I always say,*"God, get me out of this one and I'll be good forever."*

The common factor in all disasters is that they are all unique. There is no such thing as complete preparation for all the mean things the sea can do—or all the disasters we can get into by ourselves without any help at all. In some cases, one incredible, devastating blow, from—something—crushes the hull and sends her down. In other cases, a combination of disaster, bad luck, and man-made screw-ups combine and ultimately sink the boat:

A shroud parts, the mast goes over the side, punches a hole in the hull and fouls the prop. The boat drifts sideways with the mast to leeward (it usually falls to leeward as it being pushed in that direction by the wind). The boat smashes into it again and again, relentlessly increasing the damage before the mast can be cut away. The bilge pumps might have held the leak in check, but one of them had a frayed wire that was long on the "fix-it" list. It failed. The manual pumps are manned, but this is an extremely exhausting activity and it soon becomes apparent that she's going down—all because of a little broken piece of stainless steel wire. It hardly makes any sound at all when it fails.

My own experience, fortunately aboard someone else's boat, is a fine illustration of how a variety of small omissions can combine to create a really first-class disaster.

A shuddering crash followed by bumping and scraping sounds brought me suddenly out of a deep sleep. Moonlight and a balmy Atlantic breeze slid through the open forward hatch of the 54' ferrocement ketch, RHINOCEROS, (name changed to protect the foolish). The boat continued to heel, driven by a gentle ocean wind. What lingers in the memory is that during those first few moments after the collision everything seemed so normal. No klaxons, no call for "all hands on deck," no overwhelming sounds of rushing water. The RHINOCEROS continued on, bashing through the waves in her brutish way.

A few moments went by. At first I thought it might have been a dream. I lay back and prepared for sleep, then there was one of those little twangs of fear, far down in the gut, a delicate little twang to which every prudent sailor listens. Where was the boat hit? I didn't know. She was built like a tank, but a good ferrocement job is an art. I decided to see what was happening on deck. Besides, I thought I could faintly hear running water and an electric motor. Go check it out. Later it occurred to me that the motor must have been the single bilge pump, deep underwater in the sump, trying to stem the flood.

When I finally swung my legs out of the bunk they immediately plunged almost to the knee into a small portion of the Atlantic Ocean. At that moment I must confess, the poetic Muse failed me completely. A profuse sheet of profanity slid easily off the tongue. It was clear that unless everyone aboard did some really fancy footwork, we would soon be swimming rather than sailing.

Slogging my way aft through the rapidly rising flood, I climbed the companionway ladder to spread the alarm. Having just waded through foaming salt water I was acutely aware that gravity was rapidly replacing buoyancy as the principal force acting on the boat. No visions of childhood raced through my mind, but the scene on deck made me realize that my death might be imminent.

The helmsman was still at the wheel, a beer in one hand. He had on a set of earphones and was dancing to the music. He obviously had no idea of what was going on and could not feel the rapidly increasing sluggishness of the boat. "Scratch one fool from the survival effort," I thought to myself.

The owner and his wife were on the foredeck shining flashlights into the water, trying to see if there was any damage. The impact of whatever we hit must have hardly been felt on deck. They had no idea of what was coming down. The boat, a massive beast which sailed and handled like the name I have given it, obviously had a few small defects; perhaps a few thin spots where the bow met the keel, far beneath the water line, through which the sea was now rushing with rip-tide determination.

The moonlight, the sweet breeze, the obvious air of unconcern on deck, created a surrealism that made me think for a moment that it might have all been a dream. But there was no question that the vessel was sharply down by the bow. A shuddering rather than rolling motion was becoming increasingly evident and the RHINOCEROS was no longer springing back when she heeled. I don't remember what things I said, but whatever they were, everyone was immediately convinced that their plans for the weekend had changed.

An abandon-ship plan had not been made. There was no survival pack. The "life raft" was one of the cheap ones mentioned in Chapter III. It was a "six-man" raft, weighing perhaps 20 pounds, the approximate size of a stuffed cat. It would not inflate or even whimper. The water jug had a crack. It was empty. The life jackets were in the forward compartment, neatly packed beneath everything, and all of those everythings were floating in a confused mass in the pitch-black interior. The flares and signals were, alas, with the life jackets.

The "ship's boat" was a 12 foot double-hulled skiff. It had been stored upright on deck and a small crack in the inner hull had admitted rain water. The drain plug had been glassed over. The air space between the hulls was completely full of water. The boat was heavy as lead and our combined efforts could not move her. We were not even sure the skiff would float if we could get it unglued from the deck.

The VHF radio was mounted beneath the chart table. It was rendered inoperative by water almost immediately. The owner plunged into the cabin to try and send out a "Mayday" on the long range, SSB radio, but it was an amateur (Ham) rig. It needed to be warmed up, the frequency selected, and the antenna tuned. Before the call could be sent, the set became wet, rewarding the owner with a series of shocks that made him jump like a frog.

The owner's wife, with great courage and presence of mind, unhesitatingly plunged below and began diving for cans of food and drink, which she stuffed into garbage sacks. Her job was not made any easier by the darkness, the floating debris, and the ominous feeling that the RHINOCEROS would sink suddenly, without warning.

We were unquestionably in deep trouble. The "good news" was that we were about 40 miles east of the Bahamas and a gentle SE breeze was blowing us toward land. But the skiff was ominously low in the water. Just a few inches of freeboard separated us from eternity. The slightest rogue wave would instantly send us down. In desperation I took a pocketknife, and by gouging over the same lines again and again, finally succeeded in cutting a hole through the inner hull big enough to admit a bailing cup. With the between-hull air space bailed dry, we had about a foot of freeboard.

The sunrise was our most precious gift. We succeeded in blowing up the "life raft" by mouth. The "bellows" was inoperative. The raft had a single flotation chamber whose cheap inflator mechanism looked like something from a fire extinguisher. It consisted of an aluminium lever secured to the steel gas bottle with a brass pin. It was completely corroded. The raft contained nothing but a corroded, useless knife which broke when we tried to open it, a bailer, and two sponges. The flotation chamber and the floor both leaked. There was no question that we were better off in the skiff.

Our assortment of cans was wet, and the labels had come off. We had no can opener and the only knife was my pocketknife. We had two oars but no sea anchor, no sailing rig, no fishing equipment, life jackets, or a compass. The only way to determine our direction of drift was with the sun and the presumption that the breeze was a steady SE.

We tried rowing, but after about ten minutes, it became painfully apparent that the skiff was indeed "son of RHINOCEROS." It lay uneasily in the swell, so we used the half deflated, sodden "life raft" as a stern drogue. It may have slowed us down, but it kept the stern to the sea and, despite its poor quality, no one wanted to jettison it.

Our sole signal device was a 25 mm flare pistol which unfortunately was packed in the cocked position. The spring had therefore lost its tension and the gun would not operate. The "signal kit" contained two meteor shells and a parachute flare. All of the shells were corroded and out of date. We discovered the gun's shortcoming when a small island freighter passed about three miles away, paralleling the island chain. The meteor shell wouldn't fire, and by the time we figured out the problem, the ship was almost abeam. We then hit the gun's hammer with a shoe which fired the shell's charge, but the meteor failed to ignite. By the time all this occurred, the ship had passed, and we decided to not risk the remaining two shells.

Despite the failed rescue, the passing ship tremendously buoyed our hopes. We told each other that many ships would pass as we drifted closer to the islands. In addition, the weather remained pleasant. We felt certain that we would make land in a day or two, even if a ship did not rescue us. It seemed wise to encourage this attitude, since it would do no good to dwell on the slimness of the thread by which our lives hung.

The sun was hot, and late in the day, we decided to open a quart can of juice. The job proved harder than anticipated, for the can was made of steel. The only tool we had was my knife, and we were afraid we might break the blade. We tried bashing a hole with an oar lock but this just succeeded in deforming the can. Finally, as thirst prevailed, we tapped a small hole in the lid with the knife, then enlarged it with someone's house key. We tried to ration the juice, but the can didn't want to stay upright and in the crowded skiff it was knocked over several times.

The denuded cans provided our moment of comic relief. We wanted peaches and shook a bunch of cans to find them, but got pickled beets instead. We had a hell of a time getting the can open with the knife, which was no longer sharp. We half cut, half tore the lid off and had a feast. The beets were really tart, but they tasted pretty good and afterward we all had a sip of juice. We also split a pack of soggy jelly beans.

A gorgeous sunset and moonrise left us unimpressed. Our clothes were wet and the trade wind breeze made us cold. The owner and his wife were really straight and didn't appreciate the suggestion that we snuggle together for warmth. The center thwart of the skiff was part of the hull, so we couldn't stretch out beneath it. The owner and his wife stayed on one side and I ended up in the bow with the crewman. Having fled from my bunk, I was wearing just a T-shirt and shorts, so I was really cold. To make matters worse, the kid next to me was even colder, and bony.

Just before midnight, another ship passed about five miles away. We weren't optimistic about being seen, but fired the second meteor flare anyway. The flare worked, but the ship did not alter course. We decided not to use the parachute flare, hoping that we would have a better opportunity later in the night. We didn't.

The sunrise was gorgeous, but it just wasn't the same without my espresso. About 2 p.m. we sighted land, and about an hour later a small fishing boat responded to the noise of our parachute flare being fired. The flare itself failed to ignite. We made it to land by Happy Hour, only to discover that we had landed on a "dry" island. Fortunately, one of the residents had a "medicinal" bottle of cheap brandy (awful stuff), but we drank it anyway and toasted the god of fools, drunks and sailors.

Hurricanes and Killer Storms

Some accidents may be prevented by an alert lookout, by a sound boat, good equipment and good navigation. At other times, there can be no other conclusion than that the Bird of Misfortune has flown over one's head and dropped a malicious gift. Certainly foremost among these misfortunes is a collision with a whale or submerged object. Other disasters are preventable. Among these is loss due to sailing in the bad weather season or when bad weather is predicted.

Foolish indeed is the fool who heads for the blue water when bad weather is forecast. At the very minimum, everything which has not been properly stowed will fly around and break if it can break. Crew who haven't got their "sea legs" or "sea stomach" will wish they were elsewhere. The boat, its contents and the crew will not have the opportunity to become a coordinated unit. That's if you are lucky. If you are unlucky, the forecast will be just a bit incorrect, the depression will prove deeper than anticipated and instead of a summer gale you will get a great killer storm—the kind that eats birds and fish and ships and men in an immutable, relentless way.

The only rational reasons for putting to sea in bad weather are espionage, piracy, or to sea-trial a boat. An experienced hand would know that a boat should be sea-trialed in the worst weather one can find. The best place to find a boat's faults before a sea voyage, to bend or break a boat, is close to home, not out of sight of land. Break it and drown your sorrows in the nearest cafe, not 1000 miles from shore.

Since yachtsmen can pick their sailing weather, one would assume that pleasure craft would not often fall victim to storms. But sailors have a way of ignoring the warnings, and Mother Nature has a way of trapping the unwary. The wise long-distance sailor picks his season above all other considerations, waits for excellent conditions before setting sail, then heads for the blue water in a boat which is ready for the worst that the sea can offer. After all, God may protect fools, drunks and sailors, but Mother Nature favors only the prepared.

The Caribbean hurricane season straddles the summer months but the fine, settled summer weather is a continuous temptation. In addition, the prevailing SE trade wind drops considerably and becomes variable, making passages to the Islands and Central America much more pleasant. The hurricane season is, in fact, just about the best time of year to head south—except for the hurricanes.

The prudent Caribbean sailor must adopt an ironic strategy. He must keep his boat in or near the confines of a sweltering harbor during the summer months until the hurricane season has passed, sometime in late October. At that point, the SE trade winds have returned with a vengeance, making the voyage down-island a beat dead into the wind. Our prudent sailor therefore waits for the first winter weather pattern to appear before departing.

The first indication of the "Norther" cycle is a wind shift to the south. The boat is then headed east, through the Bahamas, into the Atlantic. During the next three or four days the wind goes through a clockwise shift, finally blowing hard from the north and northeast. When the SE Trades return, the boat is then headed SW, hopefully toward the island of choice. The other alternative is to sail in the hurricane season.

In the bad old good old days, before long range radio, weather satellites, the National Weather Service and hurricane hunter aircraft, the first indication of an approaching hurricane was the short, heavy swell coming from the direction of the storm, the shifting wind, the distant sighting of the first squall bars and the horrifying, pumping, steady drop of the barometer, indicating that one's ship was directly in the hurricane's path. Today a global network consisting of weather satellites and ground stations provides an early warning of bad weather, undreamed of fifty years ago. As a result, some sailors have come to believe that it is safe to sail during hurricane season, relying on data transmitted by Radio Weather Warnings. **Radio station WWV (Fort Collins, Colorado) and WWVH (Hawaii),** Weather FAX, U.S. Coast Guard frequency warnings to mariners on SSB, VHF, and AM frequencies, which give early warning of an approaching storm. People have been lured into a false sense of security by the glitter of modern technology. They have forgotten about Mother Nature and the relationship between caution and survival.

The 48 foot, 30-ton Bahama ketch, ISLAND PRINCESS, built by William H. Aubury at Man-O-War Cay, Abaco Island, was a strong, extremely well-equipped boat, being delivered by a paid captain, Barry Gittelman, and three crewman: Bob Harvey, 47; Mathew "Doc" St. Claire, 36; and Mike Munroe, 34. Their intended voyage was from Marathon, Florida, to Belize. The captain was well aware that August was the heart of the hurricane season. He had planned a route through the Bahamas and the Windward Passage which would take the vessel past a number of "hurricane holes," harbors which offer protection from cyclonic storms. The strategy might have been good, but Hurricane Allen had a few surprises in store for the ISLAND PRINCESS.

ISLAND PRINCESS departed Marathon, Florida on July 27, 1980 and headed through the Bahamas, toward the Windward Passage between Cuba and Haiti. On Sunday, August 2nd, radio station WWV reported that a tropical depression had become Hurricane Allen, and was heading west, probably passing south of Jamaica. Indications were that the hurricane was deteriorating back into a tropical depression. The ISLAND PRINCESS, more than 400 miles to the north, seemed in no immediate danger. Two days later the ISLAND PRINCESS had passed through the Windward Passage into the Caribbean Sea with a potential stop in nearby Jamaica, on the final leg of the voyage to Belize. Hurricane Allen had been down-graded and it continued in an westerly direction. What neither the crew nor the hydrographic office knew was that, at that very moment, the storm had intensified back into a hurricane, speeded up, and taken a jog to the north, precisely in the area of recurvature, at about 15° N, just SE of Jamaica, where hurricanes sometimes change their direction from NW to NE—a jog which would place the ISLAND PRINCESS directly in its path and in the dangerous semicircle of the storm.

At 10 a.m. on the 5th of August, the crew sighted the outer squall bars of the approaching hurricane, which they first mistook for a local depression. The seas were running 20-25 feet, but Jamaica was in sight, and they thought Port Antonio would provide safe refuge from any gale. They were wrong. Port Antonio is not only on the lee shore but has a shallow bar at its entrance. When the mouth of Port Antonio harbor came into view, their hearts sank. The outer bar was a maelstrom of white, breaking water through which they could not pass. They would have to weather the "gale" at sea. ISLAND PRINCESS turned North, away from Jamaica's reef-bound coast.

The wind and seas increased with amazing suddenness. The crew started to reef the mainsail, but before the reef could be put in, the wind became so strong that the mainsail had to be dropped. Torrential rain and howling wind, followed by calms battered the boat. It was then that they began to suspect the awful truth. By midnight, the storm forestaysail had blown to pieces and the wind had increased to an estimated 160 knots. Thirty five foot seas, their tops blown off by the raging wind, surged around ISLAND PRINCESS but the thirty ton vessel still felt stable, motoring slowly into the steep seas. Mike Munroe grabbed the Captain's arm and said, *"You scared yet, Barry?"* The skipper managed a sickly smile and said, *"Nope! Not yet. It can't get any worse!"* *"Well,"* Mike said, *"when you do get scared, let me know!"*

By 2 a.m. ISLAND PRINCESS was being tossed off the tops of waves, sailing through the air, landing in the troughs with a thundering crash, assaulted by winds exceeding 200 miles per hour. The wind was so strong the captain was blown out of the cockpit and was saved by his safety line. The crew finally managed to pull him back aboard. When Gittelman could speak he said *"Mike, now I'm scared."* Mayday transmissions by Bob Harvey on the VHF brought no response. Shortly thereafter ISLAND PRINCESS took her first major knockdown. Matthew "Doc" St. Claire, making his first blue water passage, was seasick down below when the boat broached. He climbed on deck to find a horrifying scene:

The heavy, leaden sky was a brilliant orange from unremitting sheet lightning which illuminated the ghastly scene despite the heavy rain and spray. The captain was hanging from the boom gallows screaming to the crew, who clung desperately to the high side of the mizzenmast, surrounded by trailing lines and debris. His was a futile gesture, as the noise of the storm had passed into the realm of pure nuclear sound. Rain beat against the terrified crewmen like shot gun pellets. The wind blew so hard it was difficult to breathe. Brilliantly lit orange crests, sheared off their waves by the force of the wind, flew horizontally through the air. Huge waves, without pattern or interval, assaulted the boat from every side. After a series of knockdowns the boat's lead internal ballast shifted. ISLAND PRINCESS lay on her beam, shipping water with every passing wave.

St. Claire cut the lashings of their heavy Givens Buoy life raft. The wind instantly picked it up and smashed it against him, breaking a number of his ribs. He pulled the painter and the raft instantly inflated—and just as quickly was whisked away by the wind, to be brought up at the end of its painter. Two of the four men abandoned ship into their six-man life raft and tried desperately to keep it away from the wildly flailing mizzenmast, which smashed at them every time the ISLAND PRINCESS rolled on her beam ends.

The captain, obviously in a state of shock, doggedly continued to steer the boat, even though it was almost completely under water. He, too, leaped to safety just as ISLAND PRINCESS made her final plunge. The boat went down so fast that only a quick slash at the connecting line kept the raft from being pulled beneath the waves. Bob Harvey had become trapped in debris and could not detach his safety harness from the sinking boat. At the last moment, before being sucked under, he was able to unclip his end at the harness and leap for the raft, but it was too late. The raft was already beyond his reach and moving rapidly away. With quick insight, Munroe jumped in after him, but remembered to hold onto the heaving line attached to the raft. It looked for a moment like Harvey was doomed, but at the final moment their fingers touched. Munroe got a grip on his friend and managed to pull him to the raft

Caught in the heart of the hurricane, with a night-time leaden sky made brilliant with lightning, assaulted from every side by huge waves, wind driven spray hitting the raft canopy like buckshot, the four survivors struggled for life. The Givens Buoy life raft has a water-ballasted stabilization chamber which hangs like a big bag beneath the raft. Once the ballast chamber filled, the raft stabilized and refused to capsize. The four felt secure despite the huge waves which fell on the raft, pushing it so far beneath the surface that the men's ears popped. They stood inside the raft, straining for air, and pushed with so much force that the raft's tubes began to separate. Sometimes, they had to hold their breath for 20-30 seconds before they came back to the surface. They were constantly up to their necks in water, with fish swimming around them.

Suddenly, without warning, the wind subsided and the men could see patches of night-time sky. They had entered the eye of the hurricane. For five or ten minutes they sat, looking at each others strained, drawn faces in total silence. Then the opposite side of the eye fell upon them *"with the noise of a thousand freight trains"*. But no-one knew what the eyewall looked like because no one volunteered to open the raft door and look out. Finally, at 6 a.m. St. Claire peeked and later said he wished he hadn't.

> Waves were collapsing on top of waves that were collapsing on top of waves. Everything was grey and white and screaming. It was insanity. From *Total Loss* (Pg 80)

By daylight the captain and one of the crew started vomiting blood. Nothing could be done to help them. The raft was well equipped and contained an EPIRB, but the device had a separate battery pack whose wires had been damaged. It was inoperative. They tied the separated flotation tubes together with line.

By Thursday morning the wretched castaways were in bad shape. All were hallucinating and the face of Munroe began to assume the mask of death. He became incoherent, with sunken eyes, and continued to vomit blood, apparently from stomach ulcers. At that moment, a ship was spotted. Four red rockets were fired and a hand flare lit. One of the crewmen who knew Morse code began to signal with a flashlight.

Aboard the 1,200 foot Norwegian tanker JASTILLA the second mate spotted a pinpoint of red, then saw the blinking signal. He tried the radio, then the radar. Nothing. It had to be a raft. Within a week the four castaways were home in Key West. Afterwards Captain Gittelman said:

> It has played on our minds, sure; but we are sailors, and it won't keep us from going back to sea. What we'll do is go back with a few lessons learned. We learned about life rafts, about survival, and we learned about what it takes to sink a boat—but most of all we learned where not to be when. We learned to stay the hell out of the Caribbean during hurricane season. From: *Sail Magazine* (Feb. '81)

THE DANGER OF RACING FEVER

Sailboat racing is a kind of madness. After all, allegedly sane, mature men spend hundreds of thousands of dollars and tremendous amounts of time trying to make a vehicle designed to go just eight miles per hour go ten. There is a mental preparation, a "psyching up," which is part of preparing for any contest. It may be important, but it seems to dull that little pang of fear and caution in the stomach to which wise sailors always listen. That is just the sort of opportunity for which the Lady with the Green Eyes is waiting. And after all, one must never forget that in a contest at sea, the ultimate race is always the race with Death.

The RTL-TIMEX, a 16.3 meter (53.5 foot), sloop-rigged, center-cockpit racing trimaran with a fiberglass foam sandwich hull left Bermuda on April 4, l979 with a crew of five Frenchmen. The captain, Alain Gliksman, age 46, was extremely experienced as were all members of the ship's permanent crew. They were all in their twenties, young enough to be his sons, and, in fact, Denis Gliksman, age 22, was just that. The least-experienced crew member was Nicolas Angel, a Parisian journalist from Radio Luxembourg who joined the vessel as a correspondent at the last moment and who wrote the tale of their terrifying tribulations in *Capsize* .

The object of the voyage was to sail first to New York, then attempt to break the transatlantic speed record established in 1905 by the Yacht AT-LANTIC. The RTL-TIMEX was therefore not exactly in a race from Bermuda to New York or across the Atlantic. But another French boat, KRITER IV, was in New York, preparing for a similar attempt, and the crew of the RTL-TIMEX wanted to race with them to vie for the record.

As is so often the case with contenders, they were gripped by **racing fever** and sailed out of port into forecasted conditions which were less than ideal. This is not to imply that the RTL-TIMEX was incapable of facing bad weather. Any vessel rigged for the blue water should be able to laugh at a summer gale. RTL-TIMEX was well built, recently overhauled, upgraded for the stress of ocean racing, and sailed by experts. Nevertheless, why begin a voyage with less than optimum conditions? More than one well-found boat has sailed from Bermuda's safe haven into deteriorating bad weather—and been seen no more.

A cold front with gale force winds was predicted to pass through the area within two days. But rather than lie safe within the pleasant confines of St. George's harbor, the crew of the RTL-TIMEX pressed on, hoping to catch up with the KRITER IV before she sailed. A few days later, while in the teeth of the gale, the men aboard RTL-TIMEX were delighted to hear that the port of New York was closed due to the bad weather. KRITER IV could not sail.

These men were gripped by racing fever. They weren't listening to what the sea was trying to tell them. It was only later that they learned KRITER IV had also foundered in a storm on the transatlantic run about the same time that RTL-TIMEX went down. The crew of KRITER IV had been picked up by a Norwegian ship just two days before the rescue of the men from RTL-TIMEX.

Within a half-hour of leaving port, the wind was gusting to 40 knots and the vessel beat to windward with two reefs in the mainsail. Conditions did not improve and by the next day, the mainsail had to be taken in. The wind continued at gale force and by the third day, the vessel was beating with a tiny storm jib into a wild and confused sea. Rather than lie to the sea anchor at this point, the crew added extra sail whenever the wind dropped off, in order to increase their chances of catching up with KRITER IV in New York.

The barometer began to drop ominously and, by the third day, the wind had built to a steady 45 knots with gusts to 60. It was now clear that the weather was worse than anticipated and the Coast Guard forecast predicted force 10-11 conditions, a forecast which was soon to prove entirely accurate. By the next afternoon (Saturday), winds with gusts of 70 knots and cross seas from the back side of the front started to overwhelm the vessel.

At 6:30 p.m. Captain Gliksman decided to heave to with the sea anchor. If he'd made the decision five minutes earlier, the disaster might never have occurred. As the crew in the main salon was passing the sea anchor gear up from below deck, the boat mounted a huge wave, heeled incredibly, the port pontoon caught the wind, the starboard pontoon caught the crest, dug in, and in a second the RTL-TIMEX was lying upside down, lashed by the raging sea.

Each member of the crew had his own prismatic perspective of the ensuing and terrifying pandemonium. Every loose object in the boat fell to the overhead (which had suddenly become the floor), pelting the bewildered occupants and compounding their confusion. Water rushed into the upturned hull through every open orifice: through the main companionway, dismembered hatches, and shattered portholes. The fading light of day was suddenly replaced with the dark, unearthly aquamarine hues of the ocean depths.

Each man frantically labored like a dream dancer for survival—confused, mired in the rising water and swirling debris, fearful not only for his life but for the lives of the others. The captain, standing in the cockpit, watched horrified as one crewman was swept into the sea. He felt certain that, in addition to the man lost overboard, two others in the stern cabin had been drowned. The two men trapped in the stern cabin did not die, but had to swim through a night-marish, darkened grotto formed by an air bubble in the cockpit to reach the main cabin, then struggle with an escape hatch in the bottom of the boat, designed to permit access to the outside in just such an emergency. Finally, through a combination of miracles and determination, the entire bedraggled crew reached the relative safety of the "survival capsule," a portion of the main salon designed to sustain life should just such a capsize occur.

To compound their other difficulties, the vessel, designed to be unsink-able should a capsize occur, began to sink, dragged down by a waterlogged pontoon. By the next morning it was clearly time to abandon ship, despite the fury of the storm.

Weather conditions were still terrible. The wind was so strong it was necessary to scream to be heard, and the lunging motion of the doomed vessel made the simplest task a feat of coordination. The ship carried no survival pack, and some essential items were lost in transit from the wreck to the raft. Essentials were hard to find in the half-flooded vessel and confusion reigned. Important food items and clothing were lost during the capsize and some fell into the water and sank during the abandoning of the ship. The items successfully transferred included:

A box of flares   A distress radio
10 gallons of water in 2 jugs   A few lemons, onions
A compass, sextant, and tables (wet)   Some clothing
A first aid kit in a zip-lock bag (wet)

The dazed, wave-lashed crew succeeded in entering the raft only to find it trapped between the pontoon and the hull. It was necessary for them to get out and flounder about half in and half out of the water, struggling to pull the raft over the pontoon crossbeam, while survival items and odd bits of clothing which were not secured washed out of the raft and sank. The men finally succeeded, but the connecting line between the raft and the boat had become fouled, and further efforts to clear it had to be made.

Captain Gliksman wanted to stay attached to the wreck. He hoped to salvage more equipment if the storm abated before the boat sank. In addition, the upturned hull with its extended centerboard made them more visible to rescue craft. Unfortunately, this sensible idea frequently does not work. A life raft is quite light, with considerable windage. It is blown to the end of its tether, which acts as a sort of vicious spring, bringing the raft up short, threatening to tear it apart with every surge and breaking wave. A very long (as long as possible) nylon line can sometimes be used successfully as a tension buffer if one is available, but the raft painter alone is too short. In addition, the raft is quickly blown down wind, and the wreck, even though waterlogged, has a tendency to surf toward it on the crest of the waves. The sight of the overturned hull rushing at them like a berserk monster made the terrified crew of the RTL-TIMEX quickly release their connecting cord and abandon themselves to the sea.

A six-man life raft containing five big men and some survival equipment is, despite its "six-man" rating, completely overloaded. USCG approved rafts have just four square feet of sitting space per person and Offshore class rafts frequently have less. The five thoroughly soaked, frozen men could never avoid lying or sitting on each other or being tossed, one upon the other by wild seas. This persistent problem became more maddening with every passing day. It made any sort of restful sleep impossible and forced them to constantly toss about, draining their strength. Last, but certainly not least, the crowded conditions made raft maintenance and repair almost impossible. They were lucky indeed that a ship found them in just eight days.

The raft's sea anchor, at first thought to be toy-like in quality, was deployed, but was not completely effective. But wild, breaking seas smashed at the raft, occasionally overturning it, throwing its occupants and loose equipment into the sea. During one of these episodes the journalist, Nicolas Angel, began to experience the strange, euphoric effects of hypothermia:

> The water's warm *[not true]* . . . It would be a dream to stop moving, stop thinking, give up completely. For what seems like an eternity I allow myself to be overcome by this sense of well-being. I'm not drowning in the middle of the Atlantic, I'm floating somewhere . . . I'm rocked gently, in a cradle, perhaps. Besides, I feel sleepy and I'm going to sleep. I savor the moment; I even have impressions of giving little sighs of satisfaction. From *Capsize* (Pg 55)

The captain's frantic call made Nicolas open his eyes to discover that he had already drifted away from the other struggling men.

Their initial experience in capsizing made them realize that it was necessary to "trim" for every breaking wave; that is, shift their weight to the upside of the raft, like movable ballast. As soon as the lookout spotted an oncoming breaker, he would shout, everyone would lean into the swell and the lookout would throw himself atop the others. Since the roar of breaking waves occurred about every six minutes for the next eight days one can easily imagine the energy which was used to prevent a capsize.

On Tuesday, during a relatively calm moment, the sodden contents of the raft equipment pack were examined, to the dismay of everyone. Their raft contained the universally inadequate "survival knife," in this case a small, dull, floating knife, with a rounded point and a tiny blade, not more than a few inches long, barely capable of cutting the painter line which connected the raft to the wreck.

Next came the "fishing kit," more useful for minnow fishing at a children's camp than for capturing the larger, combative fish that linger near life rafts. There may be exceptions, but every life raft equipment pack I have examined had one of these cruel jokes aboard, containing (at best) a few tiny hooks, thread-like line without leader, a few tiny weights, a spinner, and a line holder that could be easily concealed in the palm of the hand. They give the distinct impression that their designer gained his experience by fishing for bluegills in a mountain lake rather than in a life raft at sea. These kits are invariably more useful as sources of levity, to break the tension of a frightened, demoralized crew than for the sustaining of life.

The RTL-TIMEX's fishing kit was even less luxurious than the one described above. The line *"wouldn't hold out against a struggling sardine."* The fishhooks *"wouldn't catch a Mackerel in the Channel,"* Nicolas said. If one wants to try life raft fishing it is certainly clear one must make separate preparations. The crew of the RTL TIMEX felt that the kit had been put aboard to keep them occupied while awaiting rescue rather than to help them catch fish.

Other items in the "survival kit" brought further ribald comments:

> The bailer is the shape and size of a baby's bottle . . . The first aid kit wouldn't please a kiddie who wanted to play at "doctors". It contains a tube of ointment for sprains, another for burns or infections, a pair of round-tipped scissors, a tiny strip of gauze and some seasickness pills. A sales girl in a department store could just about wrap up a present with the two bits of "string" which moor the sea anchor and the grab rope which is supposed to help recover a man overboard. As for the torch, which obviously should be waterproof, it's already mouldy and useless. From: *Capsize* (Pg 60)

Cynical as it may seem, this cruel reality is experienced over and over again by the terrified, demoralized survivors of many a shipwreck. Whether the manufacturer of the RTL-TIMEX' life raft was merely ignorant or consumed by greed is not clear. What is certain is that your life is in your own hands. You can either believe 'it will never happen to me' or prepare to survive with your own equipment.

Fortunately one of the two lights in the raft canopy, which operated on saltwater-driven batteries, functioned for a few days, giving the men light during the dark, stormy nights.

In addition, the kit contained three kilos (about seven pounds) of survival rations, which included glucose wafers and vitamin-enriched biscuits, but the one kilo packets, once opened, could not be closed, so much of the food became contaminated and mushy with sea water. Only one lemon survived the sea's assault and it had been so badly squashed underfoot that it, too, was thrown into the sea.

A few hours after abandoning ship the total possessions of the desperate survivors consisted of:

3 kilos of food	2 sponges
1 measuring cup	1 polyester film survival blanket
1 canvas bucket	1 signal mirror
2 parachute flares	6 hand flares
1 raft repair kit	2 can openers
1 compass	some sugar syrup

12 gallons of water (2 gallons in the equipment pack)
 1 fishing line and two hooks (the "fishing kit")
 1 first aid kit (completely wet)
 1 flashlight, 2 batteries (wet, moldy, useless)
 1 distress radio (broken)
   flares salvaged from the wreck

This included the items salvaged from the wreck and the contents of the raft equipment pack. The thoughtless inadequacy of the raft equipment pack made the men laugh at the time—but not later.

The sextant and some of the clothing had been lost. The crew was woefully short of clothing, foul weather gear, and boots. Bermuda is surrounded by warm Gulf stream water, but the RTL-TIMEX sank more than a hundred miles to the north, and the water was unquestionably that of the North Atlantic, still freezing cold from the winter. The raft had an inflatable floor which offered some insulation as well as protection from fish attacks, but the flap sealing the life raft door failed almost immediately, and sea water washed freely through the opening, keeping everything wet and cold. Constant bailing was necessary.

The distress radio, an early type designed to transmit and receive on VHF channel 16 (but not on aircraft emergency frequencies), had lost its antenna. The men improvised another from wire. Unfortunately the length of an antenna is rather precise and is a function of the transmitter's wave-length. The antenna of a tiny, low-powered transmitter must be extremely efficient to radiate any sort of signal, and it is extremely doubtful that the makeshift repair fulfilled this need. It gave the crew some hope, but none of the five ships which passed saw their signals or replied to their calls. The radio was eventually added to the collection of materials used as a sea anchor.

As the days passed, the cramped conditions aboard the raft, accentuated by sores and raw, chafed skin, made every moment pure hell. Each man reacted to it in his own way. Denis, the captain's son, was the most fragile, a thin young man lacking protective fat. The least weight applied to his ankles, shins, or shoulders caused him to cry out in pain. The captain found having his leg stepped on to be most painful. Nicolas Angel would hold his breath until the pain was unendurable, then start gasping for breath. Alain Gouedart complained the least, giving no sign of his agony. Olivier would silently contort his face into a mask of pain, then politely say, *"Would you mind moving your leg a little?"*

This polite attitude nearly cost Olivier his life. He politely refused to mention that he was virtually naked beneath his foul weather gear and was slowly freezing to death. This fact was only discovered days later when he entered the dreamlike stages of intermediate hypothermia. Very little could be done to help him at that point except to sandwich him for warmth between the other men's bodies.

The weather began to improve during the second day adrift. The seas remained large and confused, but increasing sunlight warmed the men, improved their spirits and allowed them to dry some of their wet clothes. The slightly reduced threat of being capsized came as a welcome relief even though the lookout had to be on constant guard against breakers. A passing ship produced feverish activity: the men launched flares and sent out a distress call, but the ship failed to stop.

By the third night, the infamous salt water boils, familiar to all castaways, began to appear, making the men's existence even more unendurable. Their backsides, elbows, and ankles became chafed and sore. The tube of antiseptic ointment reduced the pain but the thumb-sized tube was soon exhausted.

A cold night was followed by a sunny day—Friday the 13th. During the day the sea anchor was lost and an assortment of items had to be used to replace it, including the useless radio, empty tins, and the emergency flare container. The aggravating effort to replace the sea anchor took the entire day. Several other ships passed without responding to their flares.

The bad weather would just not let go. A series of fronts kept the sea agitated and sapped the men's strength. By the sixth night, it was clear that the raft was drifting to the northeast, across the Atlantic, rather than toward land. The raft started to show signs of wear: The canopy sagged so much it had to be propped up with a paddle. The emergency blanket fell apart. The raft started to leak and had to be pumped frequently. The small amount of remaining food had become moldy and contaminated by salt water. Lady Luck seemed to have deserted them. Fortunately, the water supply proved adequate and the cold weather at least reduced dehydration. Another ship passed them by. On the seventh day, a thunderstorm with vivid lightning terrified them but allowed the collection of some fresh rainwater.

During the eighth day, Olivier's chronic hypothermia was finally discovered. The others noticed that he had fallen into a stupor from which he was not easily aroused. Chafing and slapping, followed by more (wet) clothing volunteered by the others did little to bring him around. All that could be done was to make a sort of bed out of the two water jugs and try to keep him warm with body heat. Of course, his immediate need added to the maddening discomfort of the others.

Fortunately, at 3:05 a.m. the 120,000 ton Liberian Chemical Carrier AFRAN DAWN virtually ran them down, and a flare, possibly tossed onto her deck, caught the attention of the ship's crew. For an incredible moment it seemed that this ship, too, would pass by, but as it sped into the night the sound of the motors changed, the vessel turned and started searching for them with a light. Another flare caught their attention and the huge tanker hove to 200 yards away. With sudden energy which none knew they possessed, they paddled like madmen to the ship's side and mounted the bosun's ladder. Even Olivier suddenly found enough strength to save himself.

To the disinterested observer, the AFRAN DAWN was nothing special to look at, but to the castaways of the RTL-TIMEX she was the most beautiful ship in the world.

Collision

COLLISION WITH SHIPS

When collisions between ships and boats occur, the boat crew are sometimes killed or are rescued promptly, and subsequent life raft adventures are rare. But big ships sometimes hit small craft without realizing it, or, in bad conditions, assume they have hit a log and continue on their way. That kind of experience could definitely ruin your whole trip. Sometimes they hit you, know it, and still don't stop. Go sue.

First, one must survive the delightful experience of having one's boat ground against perhaps a thousand feet of ship's hull and, incredible as it may sound, a number of boats have done so, to sail again. If that was all that happened, it would be good luck, relatively speaking. You could merely limp to port or sink with dignity. Unfortunately, many ships ride high when in ballast with their props barely underwater. So, the bad luck would be getting sucked into a dance with the ship's propeller, which often weighs considerably more than the boat. After that, if there was an "after that," one's life raft adventures could begin. Collision avoidance is further discussed in this chapter.

THE REAL RULES OF THE ROAD

Regardless of what you have learned about rules of the road, there is but one rule at sea: LET THE SMALLER VESSEL BEWARE. Foolish indeed is the sailor who presses on, into the face of danger, protected only by the rules of the road. When nautical push comes to shove, the big guy always wins, and the little guy's heirs settle out of court.

There is no question that some ships are poorly operated and that some run on auto pilot without adequate watch, barreling along at full speed, an accident waiting to happen. Some have a single man on the bridge who spends most of his time monitoring automatic equipment, rather than acting as a lookout. Other ships are well manned by men who aren't fools and who act accordingly. Yet one must never forget the crushing monotony of the hours spent on watch, day after day, month after month. So there is, even on the most disciplined bridge, the irreducible human element.

I was once on watch on a clear, moonlit, calm night. I walked out on the bridgewing, swept the horizon with my binoculars, walked to the opposite side and did the same, looked around with my naked eyes and assured myself that all was well. I then went into the wheel house, poured myself a cup of coffee and looked up just in time to see a freighter cross my stern, considerably less than a quarter of a mile away. It was painfully obvious that neither lookout saw the other ship. It was so terrifying, and the magnitude of my folly was so painfully obvious that I could not even tell this story for many years. When a ship is bearing down on you, there is no way to judge this human element or whether the crew is alert. It's much safer to assume you haven't been seen and act accordingly.

THE ABILITY OF A SHIP TO MANEUVER AND STOP

Most small boat operators have never spent time on a ship's bridge and do not understand the limitations under which a ship operates. A smallish Very Large Crude Carrier, say 200,000 tons, for example, fully loaded and running at 20 knots generates about seven billion foot-pounds of kinitic energy, and it doesn't turn or stop like the family car. Prompt action may get it halted in half an hour and nine or ten miles; but in many cases, eighteen to twenty miles and forty to sixty minutes from full ahead to dead in the water is more realistic.

A fishing boat engaged in trawling is particularly restricted in its ability to maneuver and is a "sitting duck." This watercolor was completed just after the loss of the JACK JR., a 73' dragger, whose chilling, frantic, MAYDAY, made just seconds before impact, was heard by many vessels in the area north of San Francisco, including the author's. The ship which cut her down did not stop, initially denied fault, but part of a fishing net, wrapped around the tanker's bulbous bow and paint scrapings, discovered later by divers—led to as yet unresolved homicide charges against the ship's captain. See *National Fisherman*, December, 1986. Art by Jim Sollers.

The ability of large ships to make sudden turns is equally discouraging. Their rudders are relatively small, and the momentum of a fully loaded ship is absolutely awesome. If the bow of a ship starts to swing, this by no means indicates an effective course change. The beast will often continue for five to eight miles on its original course before an actual course change begins to occur.

Like a car motor, a ship's engine does not like to go into reverse suddenly, from full ahead, and an emergency attempt to reverse under such conditions may result in a stall. A ship with a stalled engine is a ship out of control. Ships, like boats have a minimum rudder speed, below which the rudder no longer functions. For a small boat that speed may be a half knot, but for a large ship it may be anywhere up to nine knots. Below that speed, the helmsman has no control over the vessel, it goes where it wishes and you had better not get in its way.

These few facts should make one realize that a big ship has about as much maneuverability as a lead sled, and you better <u>give it a wide berth</u>. This is particularly true in restricted waters, such as in straits, approaches or channels where currents and bottom effect alter the ship's maneuverability in unpredictable ways. A ship's master or pilot may actually decide that collision with a small craft is less hazardous than attempting to stop and losing rudder control, or to turn and risk plowing into another ship or running aground.

Boat operators often do not realize that they are on a collision course with a ship until too late. Align the ship with a point on the boat, for example, a winch. Your eye and the winch form a sight. If the ship moves ahead or falls behind the sight line, you will pass correspondingly behind or ahead of the ship. But if the angle doesn't change (without your moving, and your boat on the same course) a collision is imminent. In other words, <u>a collision will occur when the bearing of an oncoming ship does not appreciably vary as the range decreases</u>.

MAKING OBVIOUS ALTERATIONS OF COURSE AND SPEED

Even when you think a ship has seen you, get out of the way. Don't freak those guys out with fancy footwork and don't wait for the rules of the road to prevail. Make <u>one</u> great big, definite turn so that even a one-eyed myopic on the ship's bridge can see what you're doing, if he sees you at all. Then, as the ship passes, slowly swing back to your original course. NEVER turn to run closely parallel with a ship. You may be caught by the ship's bow wave, or the helmsman may misinterpret your intent and turn into you.

MANMADE CONDITIONS WHICH OBSCURE A BOAT

Visibility from the deck of a boat is different than from the bridge of a ship. The view from the bridge may have blind spots caused by cargo or gear. The blind spot may be unnoticeable in ship-ship meetings but can completely obscure a boat, particularly when the ship is overtaking.

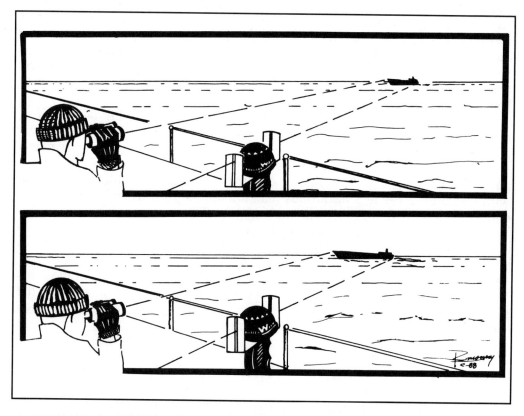

Align your eye with something on the boat. When bearing remains the same, and range decreases, you're on a collision course.

NATURAL CONDITIONS WHICH OBSCURE A BOAT

Rain, sea smoke, light haze, ground fog, sunlight reflection and heavy seas can also cause differences between what a boat operator or a castaway sees six feet above the water and what is seen from a ship's bridge sixty to one hundred feet higher. Adverse conditions can completely obscure a boat, while the boat operator enjoys complete visibility.

One question boat operators rarely ask is: **"Can I be seen?"** White is probably the most popular color for sailboats and for their sails. But white is also a very common sea color (as in whitecaps), so a white boat may be much harder to spot than you realize. Bridge personnel viewing an area within three or four miles of their vessel are looking AHEAD, at the horizon, not DOWN at the sea surface. In bad weather a white boat might look like any other breaking wave.

Iridescent orange, green, and red, such as one sees on buoys, are the most visible colors. Some carriers paint their vessels these colors for the express purpose of safety, and sailboaters should consider brightly striped sails for the same reason. Unfortunately, boat hulls aren't exactly chic in buoy green, for example.

The running lights for a Tug-in-Tow and a vessel with Restricted Ability to Maneuver.

THE DANGER OF TUGS-IN-TOW

A similar problem exists when encountering tugs with a stern tow. Ocean-going tugs use their heavy towing cable as a sort of spring to reduce the shock of rough seas. The longer the cable, the more slack (called the catenary) hangs down below the ocean surface. Really heavy tows require a tremendous length of cable. You must see one to really appreciate how long, long can be. Would you believe 2000 feet, or more?

Tug operators sometimes have the idea that they are delivering someone else's barge and are therefore not responsible for the barge's running lights. If the barge lights are dim, dirty, full of water or inoperative, they may not correct the problem as they would if it were aboard their tug. Passing behind the tug, a boat would hit the cable, then be swept beneath the barge and at that point, there wouldn't be anything the tug could do about it. The tug might not even be able to stop to pick up survivors. So BEWARE.

Memorize the running light pattern for a tug-in-tow and keep clear when you see them. A tug with a long tow has three vertical white masthead lights in addition to running lights. When the tow is really cumbersome and the tug is <u>restricted in its ability to maneuver,</u> it may also show a vertical set of red-white-red lights. The corresponding day shape is a vertical ball-diamond-ball configuration. This is a subtle method of telling you that you should get any idea about rules of the road out of your head and <u>stay clear</u>. A yellow light is shown over the white stern light at night. So if you get behind a ship and see a yellow over white, there's trouble just out of sight—and you better do some fancy footwork—fast.

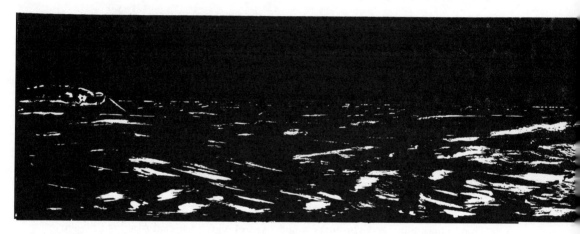

An unwary skipper might fail to realize that there is a cable connecting these two vessels

Heavy weather is a dandy time to hit something. Big waves and deep troughs make wonderful places for submerged objects to hide. It is absolutely amazing how close something really big, like a ship, can get before it is noticed. If a ship can get close under those conditions, imagine how close a cargo container can get. You are on the crest and it is in the trough. Then you are in the trough, and it's hidden behind the crest. Then, BANG!

The world, and particularly its oceans, is becoming increasingly polluted, not only with chemicals, but with all kinds of junk. When something falls off a truck, the road maintenance people pick it up and cart it off. When something like a log or a cargo container falls off a ship, it stays in the sea, as deadly to a boat as a mine, until it sinks or breaks up—and that may take years. All kinds of amazing things float around, seemingly as immortal as material things can be. Thousands and thousands of steel drums are out there, some heavy with chemicals. At least they eventually rust and sink. Huge logs can and do fall off ships and also wash down the great rivers such as the Mississippi and the Amazon. They tend to sink into a vertical position and bob up and down in the swell. In the Puget Sound area, they call them "deadheads". Sometimes they will oscillate up and down ten feet. We're talking about an object that weights tons and if one came up under your boat. . . . I have seen refrigerators, Navy targets, fishing trawl doors, pianos and wrecked boats, all floating at or just below the surface, accidents waiting to happen. A sharp lookout may see them in time or may not. It is obvious that it is even harder to see them at night. Defend yourself against them with a strong hull, waterproof bulkheads—and Lady Luck.

COLLISIONS WITH WHALES

Whales, unfortunately, are an illiterate lot. They have never read the *International Rules of the Road*, don't know about right of way, never show running lights or emit fog signals. Unlike a submarine, they never fire surfacing signals, and it is known that they often keep a poor watch. They have on occasion attacked boats and ships as is recounted in *Moby Dick*, *Staying Alive* and *Survive the Savage Sea* (See Chapter III), but as a rule they are inoffensive to men and ships. Hitting them is like hitting a water-logged tree or a submerged freight container—it's just bad luck that is virtually unavoidable. In addition, they're becoming more numerous because of the general moratorium on whaling. An alert lookout might see them in time—or it might not. The only way to minimize the extent of this type of disaster is to have the right boat in the first place.

RICHARD DeROSSET

Until recently, small craft radar was bulky, expensive, power consumptive and frequently inoperative. These conditions have changed. A radar is an excellent safety device, not only because of the picture it supplies but also because it acts as a warning beacon to oncoming ships. The ship radar picks up the transmission scatter from the boat's radar much more easily than the return image from a radar reflector. It "sees" the boat's radar transmission as a large, sharp target. Such scatter is sufficient to activate an oncoming vessel's radar alarm. The ship's crew, assuming they are approaching another ship, will be more motivated to avoid it. In addition, radar is extremely useful when approaching land at night or in obscured conditions. The land may not be where the chart says it is or position data from other aids to navigation may not be available at the critical moment.

NIGHTTIME DANGERS

Ships don't slow down at night and protect themselves against collision with a radar alarm and a lookout. Feel free to presume that the lookout is alert, out cold, or nonexistent, as the mood moves you. Feel free to believe that this ship's radar is nonexistent or broken. Fiber glass and wooden boats make bad radar targets at best and **a boat without a radar reflector is almost invisible**. Even a radar reflector provides a very small target but it is designed to return all of the radar signal which hits it. A radar reflector, held aloft on an oar creates as bright an image as a 50' boat, broadside to the oncoming ship. A boat with a radar reflector may very well provide a sharper return than a much larger steel vessel, which is approaching head-on. This of course does not mean that a radar reflector will invariably activate an oncoming ship's radar alarm, if it has an alarm.

People who place complete faith in radar reflectors are making a mistake. Sea surface conditions, particularly when the sea is rough, cause false returns, and a radar operator can use the machine's anti-clutter control to tune out these false echos, which activate the alarm. Some lookouts, annoyed by the radar alarm, abuse this procedure and desensitize the unit so that it will only show the echo of a large ship, leaving the boat operator in the dark.

There is also the "x-factor" which means "no-one knows why the damned thing don't work" or "this shouldn't be happening." I once had a canvas cylinder hung in the rigging of my fifty-foot sailboat that allegedly had a radar reflector inside. People used to ask me what it was, and I always said it contained either a radar reflector or a ham sandwich. One day, I was sailing across the Atlantic and met a drifting Farber Line container carrier with engine

FACE PAGE: *Death in the Night* By Richard DeRosset

problems. I asked them if they wanted to be taken in tow. They politely de-
clined, so I asked them if they were interested in buying some fresh fish. Alas,
no. When I asked them if they could "see" my radar reflector, they said no. So
there it was. I concluded that the cylinder in fact had a ham sandwich inside
(stale by this time), and threw it over the side. I have hailed ships in mid-ocean
many times, using VHF channel 16, and asked them if they could see me on
radar. The results were always mixed.

Radar has been used aboard ships since World War II but it is still not a
fully developed technology. Radars can and do provide false returns, ghost images, image dissipation, and, of course, they often break down and can't be repaired at sea.

I once transited the Panama Canal on a brand-new German ore carrier.
The German crew was very, very German indeed, with crisp, white uniforms,
sharp haircuts, and a ship so clean one could eat off the decks. Every officer
had his sextant and cap on a little shelf in the bridge made exclusively for this
purpose. This was the very embodiment of how a ship should be run. When I
asked if they could pick up a sailboat on radar they laughed. Both radars and the
depth sounder were broken. They relied on an alert helmsman and a bow lookout. In fog—well. . . .

THE IMPORTANCE OF BRIGHT RUNNING LIGHTS

A boat with dim running lights is as unsafe as one without a radar reflector. Think of what a fifteen-watt bulb looks like five miles away when viewed
against a lighted shore line or in a rain squall.

**Bright running lights may do more than anything else to
save your life.** A masthead mounted strobe, used for emergencies, can produce 350,000 candlepower and is visible up to twenty miles away. Spreader
lights, a searchlight, a white parachute signal (80,000 candelas), or a white hand
flare are also powerful position identifiers, but they must be used when the ship
is far enough away to take evasive action. If you have to shine a searchlight UP
at a ship's bridge, you have waited too long, far too long.

HORN SIGNALS

Fog has the strange ability to absorb, alter, and redirect horn signals.
When an oncoming vessel is far away its location by fog horn is clear but, as it
approaches, the fog scatters the signal in a confusing way. Old-timers used to
roll up a chart to make a funnel and stick it in their ear. They would then sweep
around with this "ear trumpet" to locate the direction of the foghorn. The same
technique can be used for locating breakers. The only other thing you can do

when a ship is approaching in fog is to STOP, make fog signals (not very effective with a standard boat horn), and hope the other fellow sees you on radar.

Fog is terrifying to the small boat operator caught in a shipping lane. There is no experience quite like having a ship suddenly appear about arm's length away, pushing a huge bow wave, clipping along at fifteen knots, unwinding past you like a huge steel snake which disappears as it appeared, suddenly and silently, making you wonder if it wasn't some terrible dream.

INTERPRETING RUNNING LIGHTS

In addition to running lights, ships carry white lights fore and aft, called range lights: the aft light is the higher of the two. Cruise ships and some freighters burn hundreds of other lights and often look like small cities clipping along at sea. One can spot their loom beyond the horizon. But tankers often show only the required lights, which may burn out or become obscured. Boat operators often fail to understand how large these vessels can be. A typical Very Large Crude Carrier may displace 400,000 tons, be 1,220-1,400 feet long and draw 90-100 feet of water. A BIG one such as the SEAWISE GIANT displaces more than 564,000 tons.

When fully loaded, these dark-hulled monsters lie very low in the water. If they have been loaded beyond their legal limit, the only portion of the vessel which shows a silhouette at night is the superstructure. Their sheer immensity can be extremely confusing, particularly on a dark and stormy night. More than one sailor has seen the fore and aft range lights of a low-lying tanker—concluded they were TWO ships, and tried to sail between them.

For some reason, boat operators often fail to use the most obvious of all safety devices at their disposal—the VHF radio. ALL ships are expected to monitor channel 16, and ships running along the coast often monitor channel 13 as well. If your course is converging with a ship, call by location and direction *"calling south-bound ship one mile west of Point Reyes."*

MORE ABOUT THE X-FACTOR

One morning, I was making the approach to Cape Conception, sometimes called the "Cape Horn of California." We were motoring at four knots, in fog so thick you couldn't see the bow. We were running on Sat/Nav and RDF bearings. My fix showed us far offshore. The depth sounder showed no bottom. You can imagine my dismay when I began hearing a land-type foghorn (not a ship signal) from the direction of land. That did nothing for my self-confidence, and fog in itself creates uncertainty. Then, eerily, out of the mist, appeared a small city of boats and equipment consisting of an oil drilling platform and moored attending vessels. We were already among them before they came into view. Good thing we weren't driving in a gale! My chart was brand new, but these "vessels" were not on it because they were moored, not permanent fixtures, and were therefore not shown on the chart.

I started to hail the rig on the VHF to give them a piece of my mind but they weren't interested in me. They kept calling a a vessel appearing as a big blip on their radar screens. The vessel was coming at then out of Los Angeles, doing eighteen knots. They kept saying things like *"Vessel forty miles NW of Los Angeles, you are standing into danger."* And things like *"Vessel passing Cape Conception you are standing into danger. Turn hard to port, turn hard to port!"* My theory was, if they were concerned, I should be concerned.

The rig radio operator left his microphone "open" once, and more of the tale became clear. The drilling rig was held in place by cables which extended, just beneath the surface to buoys, as far as two miles away. The buoys were chained to massive moorings. Obviously, I had sailed over one or more of them already, without a friendly warning from the rig's crew. Hadn't they seen me on radar? A radar aboard my boat would certainly have turned my part of the problem around!

I could guess, from the increasing anxiety in the controller's voice, that something terrible would happen if the ship hit one of those cables. I heard someone in the background say they were going to "swing out the boats," presumably meaning: prepare to abandon the rig. They clearly weren't happy and I, in their midst, felt the same. I had visions of this monster ship hurtling at me out of the fog, cables flailing from its bow. If the people on the rig were afraid, I should be afraid! I called all hands on deck, had them get into their float suits and life jackets, turned on my masthead strobe and spreader lights, throttled back to "dead slow" and told God, again, that I'd be good forever if he'd get me out of this one.

The controller then ordered one of the rig's fast boats to go out and reconoiter. Finally, the captain called back and said, *"It went past me in the fog like a shot. I couldn't keep up. All I could read on the stern was the word 'HYUNDAI'."*

So the controller started calling, *"HYUNDAI, HYUNDAI, HYUNDAI, danger, danger danger. You are on a collision course! Turn hard to port. Turn left, turn left!"* The controller then sent out another boat and told the captain to fire a flare at the ship if he saw it. At that point, someone who <u>thought</u> they were speaking English came on the radio. I could not understand a single word he said. But the controller started speaking the "universal language." He let forth with a combination of pleas, obscenities, and suggestions, his voice obviously filled with great fear. If he was that scared, I had better be just as scared, and I was, I was. Finally, the captain of the boat called *"I see him!"* But the controller said *"It's too late, he's in the field."* The captain said, *"No! He's turning!"* Then he said, *"He missed the float by about fifty feet."* No one said a single word on the VHF after that.

In conclusion, never forget the "x-factor;" never for a moment think you are protected by the rules of the road. Never conclude that a ship has seen you Give ships a wide berth; be afraid and, when you lose your fear, sell your boat and buy a chicken farm because, my friend, the sea is going to eat you.

Navigation Errors

In the days before chronometers, position estimation was an art. One might run for days in bad weather without a "fix." One could easily sail right onto the beach without seeing it. In this day of electronic navigation, it is surprising that navigators allow their boats to hit hard, immovable objects such as land, rocks or reefs—but they do. Buy long-distance electronic aides to navigation such as a GPS receiver and use it but do not be lulled into a state of complacency by the assurance they seem to offer.

Some navigators fall in love with their electronic gadgets and are lured into a false sense of security by them. They incorrectly plot a fix or set courses to pass too close to a danger and learn in an abrupt way that objects aren't always where they appear to be on the chart. Others fail to develop the habit of consulting other aids such as depth sounders and neglect to take bearings to confirm their position. Do not neglect bearings. If you take a bearing and it doesn't jive with your plotted position one of three things is wrong: the chart; the fix or the bearing. You may therefore conclude that you are uncertain about where you are and you had better be afraid. Do not let the contest between man and the sea become obscured by state-of-the-art technology. Remember, if you hit the rocks your GPS won't cry, and it won't pay. All it will do (if you're lucky) is float.

The navigator should rely on logic. A boat traveling about five knots for five hours in a normal current didn't run ten miles and didn't run fifty. If your fix disagrees with your logic, you may safely conclude that you are lost and you had better do something about it. If you arc not surc of your position (lost) and are running at night or in bad weather, heave to or shorten sail until you know where you are. The best way to get safely from A to C without hitting B is to always run scared, take many fixes, many bearings, watch the depth sounder and listen to that twinge of fear that originates in the pit of the stomach. Do all those things, and you will live to sail far and enjoy the life of adventure.

Fire

Everyone knows that most fires and explosions are caused by carelessness, so it doesn't do much good to say "Be careful." A well-planned fire extinguishing system is the best defense against total loss by fire. An automatic extinguisher in the engine compartment is essential and a smoke detector located next to it may give warning that something is amiss—before the extinguisher is activated.

There are three varieties of extinguishers that are useful on boats. The standard **powder type** is the cheapest and the one most commonly found aboard yachts. The powder is a mixture of dry chemicals designed to smother a fire and prevent its access to oxygen. The small ones (TYPE B-I) contain two pounds of dry chemical, which is a burst of five seconds or less, although they are officially rated to have a longer duration, so have a clear idea of what you wish to accomplish before you act. The powder is very fine and, believe me, it coats the entire inside of a boat. You emerge looking just like Kris Kringle. It is extremely hard to remove, it's corrosive, particularly to electronics and electric motors, it discolors cloth and ruins finishes. The single virtue of the powder extinguisher, aside from its price, is that it provides a definite barrier between the inflammable material and the air. In other words, once the fire goes out, it is likely to stay out.

Halon and CO_2 are both gases designed to deprive the fire of oxygen. Carbon dioxide also fights the fire by cooling it, but is <u>extremely toxic in a confined space</u>. The advantage of these gases is they are clean, relative to dry chemicals, but are more expensive and, once dissipated, the fire may rekindle. For this reason <u>engines and blowers should be stopped immediately after using gas-type extinguishers, to keep the gas from being vented off</u>. Gas-type extinguishers are the first line of defense but powder units should be on hand.

Halon extinguishers are available with automatic discharge valves which are activated by high temperature (212°F.). They are ideal for engine rooms, where they can put out a fire before it spreads. The better models have a pressure gauge mounted on the bottle and an indicator lamp which can be installed on a boat's control panel, to show that the system is armed. Even the

Engine room Fire by Jim Sollers. Note extinguisher mounted where it cannot be reached in case of fire. Only an automatic extinguishing system capable of flooding the entire compartment with Halon or Carbon Dioxide gas could turn this problem around.

smallest units are capable of completely flooding most boat engine compartments with gas. Halon is particularly useful in engine compartments big enough to enter, since it will not kill you if you are trapped inside when it goes off as will CO_2. More than one mechanic has accidently activated a CO_2 system while working on an engine—and died.

Gas type extinguishers have another overwhelming advantage. They can displace oxygen in entire living compartments (if the unit is large enough), even if the source of the fire is not known. In many cases where a vessel has been lost to fire, the source of the flames were concealed in an inaccessible area or hidden by thick smoke. The terrified crew discharged the ship's powder extinguishers into the area which they believe was burning, without success. They were kept at bay by the smoke which, in a boat, is particularly deadly because it comes from the combustion of plastics and resins.

When installing a manually operated extinguisher, do not place it close to the intended area of use, but in a location where the crew would retreat should a fire break out. For example, an extinguisher is useless for a galley fire if it is placed next to the stove. That area may be enveloped in flames, preventing access to the extinguisher. A hand-operated unit is similarly useless mounted inside the engine compartment.

Keep in mind that Coast Guard requirements for firefighting equipment are minimum requirements. The absolute cheapest insurance a wise captain can buy are extinguishers, particularly automatic ones for the engine compartment. If a fire does start aboard a boat, minimum equipment may very well yield minimum results.

People often underestimate the potential explosive capability of in-flammable materials. It may be obvious that chemicals like gasoline and alcohol burn, but their vapor and that of chemicals such as paint, solvents, engine starting fluid, to name a few, explode violently with a force similar to that of dynamite. Very little vapor is needed to make a glorious bang. Ventilation is the name of the game. Gasoline vapor is of course extremely explosive and I would guess that just a half cup of vaporized gasoline could destroy a boat, if touched off. The wise captain of a gasoline-driven vessel shuts off the gas at the tank- then runs the engine dry. In addition, a partly filled gas tank contains vapor, which is a potential source of danger. Gas tanks are best kept full.

I had a friend who owned a big racing boat with a little gasoline engine. The motor was only to help the boat into the slip. The gas tank held just two gallons. When the engine was not in use, my friend carefully turned the fuel off at the tank. Unfortunately, the sump beneath the engine was deep and was not ventilated. This captain had one bad habit. When he worked on the engine he put his cigarette on the manifold.

For years and years, everything went right, but one day a cigarette rolled off the manifold and fell into the sump. In about one second, the entire boat was burning. It was a miracle that the crew was able to inflate the life raft before the vessel was consumed by flames. My friend always used to joke around and say, *"Women and dogs first into the lifeboat."* The ship's dog, who normally hated water, didn't wait for instructions. He was first into the raft. Think of what a nice, big, automatic fire extinguishing system could have done to turn this problem around.

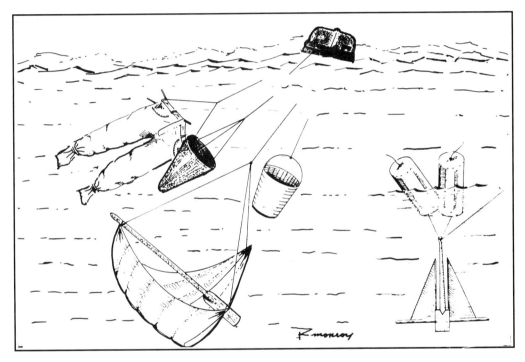

A sea anchor is an essential part of survival craft equipment. If you don't have one, make one.

Capsizing, Pitchpoling and Broaching

The first thing to ask yourself when encountering really bad weather is why you went out in that damned fool boat instead of catching a plane. After that, a good strategy for many boats, when encountering really bad weather, is to **heave to, lie to a sea anchor, stream warps** or **lay ahull.**

Many sailors instinctively run with bad weather, and there are certain circumstances where this may be the dreaded last alternative. This is particularly true when sailing a lightly built boat or one with a big cockpit such as a racer, which may not be able to stand up to a breaking wave. Never go to sea in a marginal boat.

Even with all sails furled, a boat running before the wind can be instantly overwhelmed. The rudder can fail; the helmsman, who is fatigued, can make a mistake, allowing the ship to broach; a particularly strong gust can hit the vessel's superstructure, bowling it over by brute force; the vessel can also suddenly accelerate in a strong gust, driving it into the back of a wave or over the crest. In all these cases, the sea will eat you and the vessel in one gulp. The disaster occurs so rapidly that, once begun, virtually nothing can be done to stop it. For this reason, it is safer to heave to or lie ahull.

Until relatively recently, sea anchors were made in the form of a cone, held open by a wire hoop. Three or more stout lines attached the hoop to an anchor rode. A lighter "trip line" was attached to the pointed end of the cone, so that the pointed end could be pulled toward the vessel. This type of sea anchor was often used effectively, but it had some faults. If the wind droped (and for other, unclear reasons) this type of sea anchor had a tendency to dive. The cone tended to rotate, fouling the trip line with unpredictable results. At best, it would not trip when needed, making it necessary to winch the anchor aboard. It can also cause a premature trip, just when you need the sea anchor most.

I met a man who needed to do some masthead work while single-handing across the Atlantic. He didn't want to use the classic four-part block and tackle to hoist himself up the mast. He hit on the novel idea of attaching his sea anchor to a halyard. He reasoned that as the boat drifted backwards, the sea anchor would pull him up, and when he was done, he would just use the trip line to let himself down. It was, alas, a better idea on paper than in reality. He got everything ready, then tossed the sea anchor overboard.

He said the damned thing took him up so fast it sucked him out of his shoes. He hit the spreaders on the way up and broke his leg. Then the trip line fouled and tripped the sea anchor. He fell onto the life lines, breaking several of his ribs. He was just lying there, congratulating himself on being alive when the trip line released, the sea anchor re-engaged and took him up again. God knows how he made Bermuda. I bet he never tried that trick again.

Today, a variety of different sea anchors is available. It is impossible to recommend a specific type, since each vessel behaves differently when hove to a sea anchor. If you purchase a sea anchor, be sure you try it out and experiment with it, so that you will know how to obtain best results when it is needed. Some boats just don't like sea anchors. I had one that did its best to sail away with every sea anchor I threw at it. Test your rig before you hit the blue water.

Stream oil if the seas are breaking. In the days of sail, oil-impregnated fiber or rags were contained in a cloth bag (called an oakum bag) attached to the sea anchor. The oil oozed through the cloth and spread an oily film on the water. If you have an oil bag, use it. If not, boats may stream oil from the galley sink. This technique, used effectively by sailors for centuries, has fallen into disrepute. It has come to be regarded as an old seaman's tale and has been scorned by a variety of marine writers, some of whom tested the technique and saw it fail. The reason is, all oils are not equally effective. The most readily available oil, motor oil or diesel fuel, in fact all petroleum products, are the least effective. Fish oil works best. Used while lying ahull or hove to, spreading oil is a useful technique and may save the vessel.

Unlike the drifting boat or the breaking part of a wave, oil has a tendency to remain in the area where it was disbursed, while the water passes beneath it. It resists being driven by the wind. The oil spreads out to windward in a vast, extremely thin film. It changes the surface viscosity of the sea and any wave which is not already breaking will not break when it hits the oil. As the film becomes thinner, its strength <u>increases</u>. The vessel rides in a relatively calm slick, surrounded by a world of breaking waves. Blown spray is also reduced, making visibility better.

The old-time method of letting the oil dribble from a bag attached to the sea anchor was a good one. It kept the oil away from the ship and spread it where it was needed most—to windward, not next to the hull, where it has a tendency to be blown onto the decks. If you don't have an oakum bag, an ice pick hole in the bottom of a can left sitting in the sink produces the desired rate. A quart per three hours will usually suffice. In this procedure, less oil—a thinner film—is more effective than a heavy one. An additional advantage of fish oil is that it is more easily cleaned off the hull than petroleum products.

PORTHOLES AND HATCHES

Boats whose portholes and hatches are sound (and closed) can't fill up with water. Properly ballasted sail boats, **with firmly secured internal ballast, if any,** usually right themselves. A storm may roll the boat, dismast her, even destroy the interior without damaging the integrity of the hull. It is truly terrifying to roll your boat but a rolling does not have to mean a sinking. Don't let fear paralyze you. Go on deck (crawl if necessary) and set a sea anchor. If you don't have one, create one. A sail lashed to a spinnaker pole, bumpers, a sun awning, or flotation cushions can be combined to make a sea anchor. After the sea anchor is set, stay inside as much as possible, keep pumping, and tell God you'll be good forever if He'll just get you out of this mess.

The Right Boat (author's humble opinion).   (1) Antennae, radar and overboard pole mounted on an independently stayed mizzenmast. (2) Man Overboard Module (3) Horse shoe ring with line (4) Jacklines (5) Plexiglas covers on large ports. (6) Water jugs with lanyards and snap shackles (7) Triple life lines (8) Safety rail (9) Traction pads. (10) Sea anchor. (11) Life raft and survival pack. Recommended hull material: steel. Art by Jim Sollers

THE RIGHT BOAT

The Right Boat is the safest boat, a boat with at least <u>three compartments which have heavy bulkheads</u> which can be isolated from each other by closing strong doors. The forward and aft compartments must be large enough to keep the boat afloat if the center portion is holed. This makes a boat just about unsinkable, or at least as unsinkable as the TITANIC. In other words, nothing is complete proof against what Mother Nature and bad luck can do, and, if safety is an ultimate concern, stay in bed—although people have been known to die there, too.

More than one boat has sunk because the windows popped out during a knockdown, allowing water to flood the interior. Weak or open hatches or doors can do the same thing. Pieces of heavy Plexiglas LARGER than the window should be fitted for a sea voyage, hopefully in such a way that they can be easily removed in port. Doors or washboards should be critically examined. After all, if the boat capsizes and all openings are strong there is a great likelihood that the boat will right itself, not fill up with water and sink.

A well-secured interior: Ask yourself "What will happen to my boat if it were suddenly turned upside down and given a good shake?" If, for example, you think your engine just might tear loose and rip out the stern bearing, or that your batteries might come free and drop through a window or the overhead, you're on the right track. If your boat has internal ballast, will it shift? What would about a ton of lead falling on the inverted cabin top do to it and to the boat's stability? What would that lead do to you if you were asleep down below? Ask yourself these hard questions and, if you don't like the answers, ACT.

Mizzenmasts are really marvelous things and not just because they hold up mizzensails. Mizzenmasts are great places to hang mizzen staysails, fisherman topsails, radars, VHF, SSB, Sat Nav antennas and radar reflectors. If they are independently stayed, not connected to the main mast by a wire (the triatic stay) at the top, they will continue to stand if the main mast falls. At that point one, might be particularly happy to have one's antenna system still standing. In addition, there is nothing which satisfies the soul like a sea anchor-mizzen storm sail combination. The mizzen helps the sea anchor keep the boat into the wind, makes it ride easier, yaw less, and reduces the chance of a knock down. The boat drifts less and rolls less. In storm conditions the storm jib and reefed mizzen balance the boat and allow the main sail to be dropped and lashed.

Electronic aids: The right boat has at least a **radio direction finder (RDF)** aboard. RDFs are cheap and can usually be found secondhand. There is no excuse for not having one and even less excuse for not having batteries to make it operate. After that, let your pocketbook be your guide.

A blue-water boat without a good **sextant** is a bay boat. A bay boat in the blue water is an accident waiting to happen. Electronic aids to navigation are wonderful until they fail. Count on that happening. But a sextant is no good without **tables, a current almanac**, and someone who can step on deck, take a sight, go below, reduce it, and make a mark on a chart which (hopefully) indicates your position. Learning to use a sextant includes a great deal of practice. Someone who just went to class, learned, wrote it down, and put the notes with their sextant is not a navigator. A navigator is someone who, as a result of dozens or even hundreds of repetitions can whip through a sight reduction problem as easily as a chandler can total your bill. Buy an artificial horizon and practice, my friend, practice.

The right boat has the right **survival equipment**. The survival pack is discussed in Chapter XVIII. A boat which goes into the blue water without a life raft or survival dinghy, a survival pack, life jackets, a man overboard pole, flotation cushions, and life rings is being operated by a fool. Fools die.

THE TIME OF GREATEST DANGER—IS ANY TIME

There are no statistics that prove which time of day or night or a specific season is the most dangerous. One can hit a cargo container or a log or a whale in broad daylight on a sunny day or in the middle of the night. A boat can sink in a spring gale, a summer hurricane, or a winter storm. There are, however, times to be particularly vigilant. Night time, especially the grey hours of the false dawn when visibility is poor and lookouts are tired is a time of great danger. It is a wise captain who reserves these hours for his own watch. Oddly enough, clear nights with full moons are also dangerous. In the Caribbean some sailors (who work mostly at night) call the full moon a "smuggler's moon" because it is a time when the uninitiated think visibility is increased and are therefore less vigilant.

From *The Far Side* © Universal Press Syndicate
Reprinted by Permission. All rights reserved.

Alain Bombard, next to a French Sailor, in 1953 after his triumphant reuturn from a
Transatlantic passage in his inflatable, *L'Hérétique*. *AP Wide World Photo*.

CHAPTER II: THE WILL TO SURVIVE

The Bombard Story : By Alain Bombard

Some people have been castaways and lived to be survivors; some have written about their experiences so that others might survive. But there are just a few, like Alain Bombard, a 27-year-old French doctor, who purposely cast himself adrift in a 15' inflatable boat of his own design—a design so successful that it was later adopted by Zodiac and Avon. He tested his theories about survival; first by drifting with a companion for two weeks in the Mediterranean sea, and then, when people still did not believe him, by crossing the Atlantic Ocean alone, from Tangier to Barbados, living on the resources of the sea.

Dr. Bombard noted that many castaways, adrift without water or food, died in as few as three days, even though a person can live for more than six weeks without food and ten days without a drop of water. Bombard concluded that, having neither food nor water, believing death was inevitable, they died of despair. Today, we would probably conclude that these people died of exposure. Regardless of whether this conclusion was correct, Bombard was the first person to address questions regarding both the physiological and the psychological effects of shipwreck. Today, we know that it is possible to "wish for death" and, to a certain degree, induce it or permit to happen. The **"will to survive"** may be the most important tool a castaway can possess.

In 1952 Bombard put forth the incredible theory that the sea was not cruel but abundant, not a watery desert in which to die, but a sort of gigantic soup in which the castaway was floating. To survive, all one had to do was stretch forth one's hand and partake of the vitamins, fats, proteins—and water—which are an arm's length away. He wanted to prove that a castaway adrift without water or food was not in a hopeless condition and need not die.

It was clear from past experience that when castaways were saved those who had drunk seawater were always in worse shape that the others—if they even lived to tell the tale. Bombard did not dispute this but reasoned that these poor souls had only drunk saltwater as a last resort, when their bodies were already dehydrated and most susceptible to the debilitating effects of the salts in seawater. He believed that small amounts of saltwater could be drunk, about 1,5 pints per day, particularly in the first few days after the disaster, until other water sources including fish juices could be found. He insisted that saltwater-induced nephritis (kidney inflammation) does not become really acute for five days.

While this may be true, undiluted seawater contains so much salt that more water is required to excrete it than is gained. Scientists were aware of this in the early 1950s and refused to endorse Bombard's theory.

Bombard and a companion decided to make a test run in the Mediterranean Sea, using an inflatable boat of his own design as a survival craft. It was 15 by 6 feet and was similar to modern hard-floored sport inflatables. By today's standards this boat was not suitable as a life raft. It had a "tent" but no canopy, a "single doughnut" tube, a small sail with a stubby, six-foot mast, a set of leeboards instead of a keel, no venting valves, and no ballast bags. Those things did not exist in 1952. Bombard was well aware of what others thought about his ideas, so he named the inflatable L'HÉRÉTIQUE (THE HERETIC).

His preliminary voyage was made to test his equipment, but the whole affair deteriorated into a media event, complete with interviews, photos of Bombard kissing his wife, and the incredible installation of a radio transmitter in the raft, a transmitter which was completely unprotected against saltwater and, needless to say, never uttered a squawk. It was even suggested that he eat his crew if death by starvation should occur. The whole sorry mess did much to make Bombard look like an opportunistic fool and set the stage for the troubles that followed.

After numerous screw-ups, false starts, and comic episodes, Bombard and his companion, Jack Palmer, were towed away from Monte Carlo, Monaco, during the afternoon of May 24 amid great fanfare (which somewhat muted the clacking of tongues) and cast adrift. Their goal was to reach the Balearic Islands, off the coast of Spain. May and June are kind months in the Mediterranean and the next day, beneath sunny, windless skies the pair set several fish lines and replaced the sea anchor with a plankton seine. In about an hour the seine had collected about two tablespoons of "pap," not very appetizing to look at, but filling and palatable.

The two started drinking seawater on the second day. They supplemented it with dew sponged from the raft's floor. They caught a fish and ate part of it, extracted and drank the juice, then sun dried the rest for "lunch." Everything was going according to plan.

During the third day two ships saw and greeted the crew of L'HÉRÉTIQUE but none of the other numerous craft Bombard and Palmer saw seemed to notice them, even though some passed quite close to the raft. Dolphins saw them, whales saw them, turtles saw them. The crew of L'HÉRÉTIQUE began to experience what many a castaway has learned to their anguish—a raft is incredibly hard to see from the bridge of a ship.

Just 72 hours after their departure, they saw the coast of Minorca and slept that night in the certainty that they would reach land by the next day. Unfortunately, the weather deteriorated, a contrary wind sprang up, fog and confused seas plagued them, a huge albino whale terrified them, a ship almost

This photo, taken in the English Channel by the Bailey's (see Chapter IV) gives some idea of how difficult it is to see a life raft, which, in this case, is slightly left of center. The camera is about 500 yards from the raft. From *Staying Alive* by Maurice and Maralyn Bailey.

ran them down, and Bombard developed an abscessed gum. Although he had penicillin in his sealed rations, he decided that a castaway would not—so he cut the abscess open with a pocketknife, an excruciating job, and let the wound drain naturally. Last, but not least, there were no fish.

On the eleventh day the weather cleared, leaving the men exhausted and starving, but confident enough to resist opening the emergency rations, which had been sealed by the Monaco Customs as proof that they had not been used. A tuna was speared, but escaped. Three more days passed without solid food. They drank saltwater and sustained themselves by eating plankton, although it was increasingly disgusting to their palates

A ship passed and they tried to attract it with the heliograph but, as unbelievable as it seemed to them, no one saw their signal. The next day, Saturday, June 7, 1952, induced by several rockets and a smoke flare, the SIDI FERRUCH reluctantly stopped. The captain, a Frenchman, said *"What do you want? . . . Come on, we have no time for experiments."* He obviously knew all about Bombard and disapproved of his theory. The captain reluctantly gave them a small sack of provisions and departed. The SIDI FERRUCH then radioed the position of L'HÉRÉTIQUE—and mentioned the sack of provisions.

The following Tuesday, the 14th day of the adventure, L'HÉRÉTIQUE made a landfall on the island of Minorca. The fact that Bombard and his partner had lived for ten days on dew and seawater, and four days on fish juices and plankton, meant nothing to the public. The fact that they had made this preliminary voyage just to test their equipment and learn also meant nothing. What meant everything was the sack of provisions from the SIDI FERRUCH.

The public scoffed, backers deserted him, and Bombard had to go begging to accumulate the few humble provisions he needed to continue his voyage, but in the end, he prevailed. L'HÉRÉTIQUE departed the Balearic Islands without fanfare, without crowds, without a radio, without assistance and also without luck, for head winds drove them right back to the island from which they had departed. Bombard began to realize that that if his experiment were to be conducted at all, speed was of the essence. He needed to begin his Atlantic drift, or the opportunity would be lost.

He hastily traveled to France looking for funds. We're not talking about money for a new space shuttle; we're talking about cash for a new inflatable boat. He had to beg. In the end, Bombard succeeded in obtaining a new raft but little else. His partner, Jack Palmer, lost his enthusiasm because of the delays. A false start, aborted because of rough seas and head winds, forced them to land. Jack Palmer's will to continue had disappeared. He went to town on an errand and never returned to the boat. Finally, Bombard decided to leave without him. He rowed alone into the mouth of the Strait of Gibraltar, alone on his flimsy raft, surrounded by strong winds and the terrifying full sweep of the mighty Atlantic.

An east wind carried him into turbulent, confused seas, but after being nearly driven back into the Strait of Gibraltar by in-rushing currents, the Cape Spartel light, on the NW tip of Africa disappeared astern. Bombard sailed down the coast toward his next destination, Casablanca.

The North Atlantic provided far better fishing than the Med. The raft was soon loaded with fish. His food and liquid problems were solved. Bombard also decided that it might be best if he learned how to navigate, something he had formerly left to his partner. Seven days later, without incident, Bombard rowed L'HÉRÉTIQUE into the Casablanca Yacht Club.

Even at this point, people continued to think of Bombard as a lunatic and some continue to do so to this day. The commodore of the yacht club told members that their membership would be rescinded if they so much as gave Bombard a tow from the dock. The newspapers scoffed, but four days later L'HÉRÉTIQUE was adrift once more, hopefully headed for the Canary Islands.

By this time Bombard had become hardened to the rigors of being a professional castaway. A passing ship offered him food, which he refused. He caught plenty of fish. He drank seawater and claimed that Atlantic water was less salty and better tasting than that of the Med. Bad weather demoralized and exhausted him but 11 days after leaving Casablanca, Bombard made his landfall on the island of Gran Canarie. His voyage from Tangier to Gran Canarie had taken a total of 18 days, but the distance covered represented just 20% of the total crossing which he had planned.

A lesser man would have stopped right there. Jack Palmer, his former associate, said that it would be pure madness to continue and God knows, one doesn't cast one's self adrift without questions arising regarding one's sanity. In addition, people warned him that fish would be much less plentiful beyond the continental shelf. These comments, of course, made Bombard even more determined to prove that a castaway could survive the open sea. On October 19, 1952, Bombard departed Gran Canarie Island and began his solo crossing of the vast Atlantic.

During the first few days, fishing was poor and Bombard drank seawater to sustain himself. A gale swamped the boat repeatedly, ripped his sail, and forced him to bail for hours. His advice to castaways, *"be more obstinate than the sea and you will win."* By the morning of October 24th, he had repaired his sail and restored his equipment. The water resistant radio receiver, given to him so that he could receive a time signal for navigation purposes, continued to function. Unfortunately, Bombard made a navigation procedural error at this point that caused a consistent 600-mile error in his "fix," making him think he was progressing at great speed. He correctly calculated his latitude by taking the noon sight, the simplest of all celestial observations to determine, not dependent on the correct time. But when determining longitude, time must be converted mathematically into arc and, somehow, Bombard got this all wrong. The error was, without question, a result of his lack of experience with a sextant. *"Navigation is by no means a simple affair,"* he said. An experienced navigator would have noticed a discrepancy between estimated and plotted position. This mistake caused Bombard much anguish later, when his calculations erroneously indicated he had reached the Antillies.

Its sail repaired and rehoisted, L'HÉRÉTIQUE started to sail once more. Bombard had a fishing packet such as one would find in a life raft, but he decided as an experiment to try bending his pocket knife and lashing it to an oar to make a spear. He speared several fish which escaped but finally succeeded in landing a fine dorado that not only provided food and liquid but bait as well. He removed the bone behind the gill cover and used it as a hook.

From this point on, Bombard always had an abundance of fresh fish. In addition to his success with the spear, his light-colored sail lured numerous flying fish during the night. He usually found 5-15 of them in the boat at first light. So many flying fish came aboard that Bombard became very selective and only ate the largest. He used the rest as bait, trolling them when the raft was moving or casting them out and skidding them across the surface of the sea. The fish he had unsuccessfully speared never took his bait and never came close enough to be speared again. They stayed with the raft all the way across the Atlantic and Bombard became quite fond of them, giving each a name. As the weeks and months passed L'HÉRÉTIQUE's bottom became foul and this attracted a huge shoal of fish.

Bombard celebrated his 28th birthday by having sea bird tartare, without the tartare sauce. He was trolling a hook with a piece of flying fish and a shearwater snatched it from above. Bombard hauled it in. The bird vomited all over him, then passed out, probably from fear. Bombard broke its neck and skinned it. He recommended skinning instead of plucking because the skin contains rich fat that may be sucked from the inside. He ate half of the bird immediately, commenting that it tasted strongly of fish, then hung the rest up to dry. He awoke during the night to find the remaining half of the shearwater glowing so strongly from phosphorescence that it illuminated the sail.

Bombard fought his isolation by establishing a rigid routine. He would wake up, collect his flying fish, then troll for an hour, which invariably resulted in enough food for the day. He would separate his catch into a liquid supply, a lunch and a dinner supply. He then minutely inspected the raft for chafe and wear, unquestionably his greatest enemies. After that, he exercised for a half hour, then the **plankton seine** was towed until he had collected and eaten the two tablespoons he considered essential to prevent scurvy (a vitamin deficiency disorder that takes 5-8 weeks of vitamin C deprivation to occur). Flying fish also contain these essential vitamins. The time between 11 a.m. and noon was reserved for celestial observations. The afternoon was the hottest part of the day and Bombard lay beneath the tent, devoting himself to reading, writing in his journal, and to his medical studies. He then gave himself a physical check-up and made notes about his condition. He had dinner after dusk and listened to music on the radio for a few hours.

Bombard began to experience classic symptoms of being a castaway. Despite the abundance of fish and plankton, he lost weight and started to dream about food. He had always been chubby, and the loss of fat made sitting or lying down a painful experience. He was easily fatigued. The nail on his small toe fell off, and a rash, the precursor of saltwater boils, appeared on his hands.

Strong trade winds kept everything constantly wet. He disliked the constant soaking, but was cheered by his rapid progress. This, of course, was an illusion caused by his erroneous position estimate. He now regretted having no companion and had to fight the depression caused by solitude. By the tenth day adrift, the full immensity of his commitment had become clear:

> . . . I was suddenly overwhelmed by the thought of the grave situation I was in. . . It was impossible for me to stop or turn around, there was not the slightest possibility of help. I was a drop in the ocean, a part of the world not measured in human terms. From: *The Bombard Story* (Pg. 139)

Larger fish were attracted to the raft as time passed. The fish that Bombard landed were so big that it was only necessary to cut slits in them and suck the juice, so his technique of squeezing the flesh in a cloth was abandoned. His skin eruptions plagued him, and he refused to unseal the medical kit, since other castaways would not have access to penicillin. He had become fond of sitting and lying on a small air cushion because of this painful rash. On November 4th, it fell overboard and Bombard, a strong swimmer, impulsively dove in after it. As he swam toward the cushion he noticed, to his horror, that the raft was rapidly sailing off. The sea anchor must have tripped. He abandoned the cushion and swam for the raft. In his weakened state, only the sudden re-engagement of the sea anchor allowed him to catch up with the raft and wearily pull himself aboard.

Confusion about his position started to drive Bombard crazy. By November 5th, nineteen days from the Canaries, he thought he was halfway across the Atlantic. In reality he was not far from the Cape Verde Islands, off the coast of Africa. The discrepancies between his observations and the phenomena listed in the Nautical Almanac was completely baffling and only served to create doubt. Early in the voyage Bombard's watch had quit. On November 8th, his radio also failed, making position determination even more of a guess. Alain Bombard was totally lost—like many a castaway.

Despite the abundance of fish and the liquid they provided, Bombard dreamed of fresh water and beer. During the morning of November 11th rained and he was able to have a wash, drink his fill and store 3-4 gallons in his air mattress, a 35 to 42 day supply. During the following days it rained several more times and Bombard was able to collect a considerable amount of fresh water, enough, he thought, to last the entire voyage.

Bombard considered sharks cowardly creatures and drove them off by hitting them on the head with an oar. A more aggressive shark, not easily discouraged was killed with the spear he had made from his knife and an oar. But an incident with a swordfish thoroughly terrified Bombard. Swordfish use their sword as a sort of hunting tool. They swim through schools of small fish or squid, slashing with their sword, turning and consuming the injured ones. But swordfish also know how to use their sword as a weapon, and on occasion they have attacked sport fishing boats. Sometimes, the sword hits the boat's hull hard enough to penetrate it and break it off. It is easy to imagine what such a weapon could do to a rubber raft.

On November 11th, after the rain stopped, the raft's rudder was given a violent blow, and Bombard found himself confronted by an enraged swordfish. It had raised its sail and followed the dinghy as though about to attack. Bombard fumbled with his spear to defend himself and in his haste incredibly dropped it over the side! He quickly lashed his spare knife to an oar and prepared to defend himself. The fish rushed to attack the raft several times but always veered off at the last moment. Bombard spent twelve miserable hours in a state of constant fear before the fish disappeared.

The next week was relatively uneventful, with occasional bad weather, rain, skin ulcers, and irritations taking up most of the space in Bombard's log. By November 25th, he became convinced he was just sixty miles from land and should make his landfall in less than a week. This was of course completely wrong. He was actually about six hundred miles from land.

Bombard's most serious medical problem occurred on November 30th, an unexplained attack of diarrhea, rectal bleeding, and exhaustion which continued for two weeks, interspersed with massive rectal discharges that left him weak, exhausted, and gasping with pain.

Since some of the Caribbean islands can be seen for thirty or more miles away on a clear day, he spent endless hours searching the horizon, vexed by light winds and becoming increasingly irritated. The days stretched into weeks of calms and torrid heat. Bombard, confused because of his position error, thought he was close to land. Its refusal to appear drove him increasingly mad. By December 6th, completely defeated, he wrote his Last Will and Testament. He was succumbing to the very despair which he had originally declared as the prime enemy of the castaway. He saw birds that did not venture far from land, he saw a fly, but never any land.

After twenty days of calms he was at his wits' end, but kept his sense of humor enough to dream of the dinner he would have, at the expense of an associate who bet he would never reach land: a *paté de fois* with truffles, a roasted duck with steamed potatoes, assorted cheeses followed by a dessert omelette and fruits marinated in champagne—or perhaps it should be lobster Thermidore and a dozen Crêpe Suzettes. Then there was the wine. Certainly a Muscadet, a rich Pommard '28, a glass of Vosne-Romanee '30, a vintage Mouton-Rochschild '47 and of course the fabulous Chateau-Yqem '29—all followed by a fine cigar.

After 53 days at sea, the 7,000 ton freight boat ARAKAKA came out of nowhere, responded to his heliograph and hove to along side. Bombard raised his French Tricolor, and the ARAKAKA dipped the Union Jack in salute, just as though they were two warships meeting in the open sea. The experience with the SIDI FERRUCH was fresh in his mind—Bombard asked only for his correct position. It was then that he learned he was exactly 600 miles, or 10 degrees from his estimated position.

The captain offered to pick Bombard up. He refused. The Captain offered him provisions. Bombard refused. He had been 53 days adrift and wasn't going to blow it now. The captain offered him a freshwater shower. It would have taken a man of steel to refuse this offer. Bombard accepted. He also accepted a 1953 Almanac and a tiny dinner consisting of a fried egg, a piece of liver, a spoonful of cabbage, and some fruit—a meal he subsequently regretted as it caused the worst case of what he termed "heartburn" he ever had. Perhaps his sparse diet and ingestion of seawater had caused ulcers or colitis. He also gratefully accepted new batteries for his radio.

Realizing that he faced at least another twenty days at sea, Bombard asked the Captain to transmit his position and ask the BBC to please play Bach's Brandenberg Concerto #6 for him on Christmas Day. He then climbed down the Jacob's ladder, settled himself in L'HÉRÉTIQUE, and watched the ARAKAKA pull away.

Bombard awoke to find another ship just passing him a few days later. He fired a flare and when the ship turned around, he asked how they had passed so close to the raft without seeing him. The captain replied that they had seen the raft and in fact circled it, but seeing no one they had continued on their way. God help the half-dead castaway, too weak to raise a signal, Bombard concluded.

The next morning at 12:30 a.m., he spotted the Barbados light, 16 miles away. After a harrowing day negotiating the reefs and seaward cliffs Bombard found a sandy beach. Before he could even reach land, some native fishermen came aboard and started to loot the raft. It was only with difficulty that Bombard dissuaded them. When the raft reached the shore, the problem became even more acute. Bombard had the presence to find a policeman, a teacher, and a preacher to certify that his emergency rations were still sealed. He then distributed this food to the crowd—as a Christmas present, for it was the day before Christmas. Dr. Bombard slept well that night, then turned on his faithful radio receiver the next morning to hear the BBC play the Brandenberg Concerto #6 and wish him Godspeed.

Alain Bombard had drifted alone across the Atlantic in a tiny rubber boat, armed with knowledge, creativity and the will to survive. He lost 55 pounds, which he attributed to his lack of carbohydrates. His weight loss of nearly a pound per day is typical of many castaways. Chubby when he started his voyage, Bombard looked a bit baggy, but healthy, when he arrived. He also started out in a state of exceptional health and vigor, which certainly improved his chance of survival. He had a temporary case of anemia. He had two weeks of severe diarrhea, rectal bleeding, and discharge. He had fits of weakness and blurred vision. He had lost several toenails, suffered temporary blurred vision during the voyage, and been plagued with a painful skin rash. He had had nothing to drink but seawater and fish juices for the first 23 days of the voyage. A test of his blood showed no problems caused by lack of vitamins. He said in conclusion:

> To hope is to seek better things. The survivor of a shipwreck, deprived of everything, must never lose hope. . . my brother castaway, if you remain firm in belief and hope, you will see, as Robinson Crusoe on his island, how your riches increase from day to day. And now I trust there is no further reason for you to lose hope. From: *The Bombard Story* (Pg. 213)

Despite the example of Bombard, one must remember that he was a very unusual, extremely fit man who set out to prove his theories. It is clear that a man would have to powerfully believe in such ideas to undertake such a risky venture. The powerful motivation, plus the psychological preparation for the trip made him different from a typical castaway. It would be difficult, under such circumstances, to be scientifically objective about results. One could say that, because he lived, his theories were proved, but others have survived longer, and drank no seawater.

Following Bombard's successful voyage, several people became ill from drinking saltwater and strict instructions are still given in almost every life raft manual to never drink it. In addition to its potentially negative effects if consumed in controlled amounts, it becomes psychologically harder and harder to stop drinking seawater, once begun. The British Board of Trade, Marine Division, in their March, 1968 Merchant Shipping Notice said:

> A belief has arisen that it is possible to replace or supplement fresh water rations by drinking seawater in small amounts. This belief is wrong and DANGEROUS. Drinking untreated seawater does a thirsty man no good at all. It will lead to increased dehydration and thirst and may kill him.

To drink or not to drink, that is the question. It is a core controversy with highly polarized proponents on both sides and no end to the argument is in sight. His radical theories and sensational voyage made Bombard a focal point of controversy that continues to this day. Dougal Robertson, who now lives in France, said this about Bombard's theory regarding the drinking of saltwater:

> False information can kill, so that where basic survival practice is concerned, any quick-fix solutions to age old problems should be fully documented and approved by competent research establishments which monitor survival technique. In this respect the Bombard experiment does not measure up to the stringent rules under which medical research is carried out, and the fact that spurious support for his theory has to be exposed as such from time to time, lends much weight to research findings that seawater drinking has no place in sea survival technique . . . . Bombard seems to have dominated French survival

thinking for a span of years but has now lost credence to a considerable extent. The French Navy advises 1/7th part saltwater to 6/7 fresh water and this with considerable reservations. (editorial letter 5/88)

Regarding Bombard's theories about "death from despair": more than one weary castaway has longed for death, usually after many days or weeks of unendurable agony, suffering from every mean thing the sea can do. It is, on the other hand, unlikely that healthy sailors, hardened to the rigors of the sea, will *"give up and die within three days, believing death is inevitable,"* as Bombard claimed. They may die from hypothermia, from thirst or from wounds, but I think most people would try to hang on longer than three days, and literature is full of stories about people who have doggedly endured ultimate survival situations even though the possibilities of survival were infinitely slim.

It is not unreasonable to theorize that people hasten their own demise by longing for it, and a fatal languor, a symptom of "disaster syndrome" where the victim does little to help himself, can certainly contribute to death. This attitude must be fought with an unremitting "will to survive." It is also clear that many people, perhaps the majority of castaways, know when death is near and arm themselves with a fatalistic despair which is, in fact, a realistic attitude.

Sailing With a Loose Cannon:
Lost By Thomas Thompson

Never have theories regarding the "will to survive" been so well demonstrated as they are in the book *Lost* by Thomas Thompson which, in fact, contains a foreword by Dr. Bombard. Food, water, a good survival pack are all important to the shipwrecked castaway. Of even greater importance is cooperation, the will to live, and an aggressive attitude about survival. This anthology is full of stories about people who have spent months in leaky life rafts, desperately short of food and water, with little more than their determination and their courage to keep them alive. In some cases they were reduced to a mere spoonful of water per day. Some had to suck fish eyeballs and backbones to sustain themselves. Some were suddenly cast into the most hostile environments lacking not only food and water but even clothing. They often possessed little more than their <u>fierce determination to survive</u>.

The crew of the capsized trimaran, TRITON, were infinitely better supplied than many castaways. They had a large, rigid (admittedly overturned) survival platform and the entire contents of their capsized vessel to work with. Some of the equipment and gear was lost during the capsize but, relative to the equipment in a life raft, a capsized vessel contains a whole world of items, presumably enough to make survival a likelihood. And yet it seems as though everyone, particularly the captain, must have an energetic, determined attitude about surviving, or the advantages are lost.

The captain as the <u>recognized authority figure</u> must take definite and immediate action to prevent his shocked companions from falling into a lethal state of despair. If he can't do the job, someone else must take charge. But how does one take authority away from a captain? What is mutiny under these circumstances and how is the new authority established? How does one resist the infectious quality of despair and lethargy which overwhelmed the old captain? There is no simple way to answer these questions. Nevertheless, the accounts in this anthology demonstrate over and over again that the <u>will to survive is one's most important tool</u>. If in doubt, do <u>something</u>.

The crew of the TRITON was hindered by the religious fanaticism of the captain and the alienation of his crew. There are, of course, always two sides to such a sad story, and it is possible that we might have gained another perspective had all players lived to recount their version of the truth. But only one lived to tell this tale, and we must, therefore, be content with the perspective of the sole survivor.

The TRITON, a 31-foot trimaran, departed Tacoma, Washington, in July, 1973 for a coastal cruise to Costa Rica. The captain, Jim Fisher, a devout Seventh-Day Adventist, had accepted a position to proselytize and convert Costa Rican youth. He decided to take his home-built vessel with him. The boat was sound, but multihulls, in general, and this design in particular, sometimes pitch-pole (capsize) under certain conditions.

The TRITON had provisioned for fifty days, with fresh food to be purchased during the stops. The trip, although billed as a coastal cruise, was in fact a blue water passage more than forty miles offshore. Sometimes it's amazing how long a mile can be, but there were good reasons for an offshore passage. Better wind could be found there and they would be out of the coastal shipping lanes. The strategy was sound, but the concept was disastrously wrong, for there are two and only two types of sailboats in the world: those which are ready for the blue water, and all the other ones. The TRITON was, unquestionably, in the second category.

The Fishers didn't have much money, and the boat, used as a weekender in Puget Sound, was minimally equipped. There was apparently no life raft, dinghy, survival pack, or rescue-locater radio. The engine had just <u>one battery</u>, so the boat lacked the "start-up reserve" that many sailors consider essential. There were apparently no water tanks. Water was stored in one-gallon plastic jugs, stowed in the pontoons.

Jim also had no crew. He asked his brother-in-law, Bob Tininenko, and Bob's wife, Linda, to sail with him. The Tininenkos were, philosophically and religiously, the antithesis of Jim Fisher, enjoying the more worldly pleasures of life. They made a handsome pair: he was dark, muscular, and bright; she was a beautiful Japanese-American, 24 years old, with long black hair, gentle and charismatic. Bob had renounced the Adventist religion, but he was known as a good sailor, and Jim needed crew. He was also hoping that Bob would "see the light" during the cruise and return to the faith.

The TRITON had never been rigged for ocean cruising, and Bob Tininenko knew it. The boat lacked both navigational equipment and a radio. The navigation equipment was no problem, but Adventists do not listen to the radio, watch TV, or go to the movies for the sake of amusement. Bob insisted, as a condition for his services, that a long-range radiotransmitter and the necessary permits be obtained. His brother-in-law promised to buy good communication equipment and did so.

When the Tininenko's arrived in Tacoma, they found the TRITON equipped with a receiver, a VHF, and an amateur single sideband radio. The new Hallicrafter Ham transceiver and antenna system cost almost $1,000, which may seem expensive to the uninitiated. Marine radios are considerably more expensive and operate only on marine frequencies, but once you have paid, a license is easily obtained, merely by completing an FCC registration form.

A ham radio license is considerably more difficult to obtain. Amateur frequencies are reserved for people who are interested in the technology of radio communication. It is necessary to pass a variety of examinations, including several written tests, in order to obtain a "Ham" general license. In addition, one must be proficient in Morse code, know how to tune an antenna, select optimum frequencies, and do many other things. The whole licensing procedure usually takes months, but for amateurs, getting there is half the fun.

For someone who is busy equipping a boat for a long voyage, a Ham license might be more of a pain than a pleasure to obtain. After the TRITON had been at sea several days, when Linda asked to call her parents, they learned that Jim had not obtained a license which permitted voice communication.

On July 10th, the TRITON ran into a gale about 40 miles off the coast of Northern California. The gale increased in fury, and it was necessary to run before the wind, streaming sea anchors from the pontoons to prevent a capsize. Bob, the better sailor, manned the helm all night. Toward daybreak, the weather had not improved and a vicious cross swell made it difficult to steer.

Huge waves swept over the tiny TRITON, and it was clear that they were in considerable danger. Why the vessel was not hove to is unknown, but heaving to or lying ahull is often the best strategy in a storm. Bob asked Jim to call the U.S. Coast Guard. He was exhausted and did not think that Jim could steer under the harsh conditions created by the gale.

Jim did "get on the horn" and was connected via a Ham telephone patch to the Coast Guard through a Ham station in San Carlos, just south of San Francisco. When Jim reached the Coast Guard, his courage failed. <u>It is a crime to transmit on amateur frequencies without a license</u> and a few people have actually been prosecuted. On the other hand, if one's life is on the line, logic would clearly dictate a creative attitude about call letters. In addition, international law clearly states that any frequency may be used to attract attention in the event of an emergency. Jim apparently kept thinking of the possible $10,000 fine and/or two years in jail for transmitting without a license. When asked if the vessel was in distress, Jim told them, *"Negative. Do not need assistance at this moment . . . . We are becalmed."* When Bob inquired about the call, Jim told him that a plane was being sent.

By the time Bob finally pried the truth out of Jim, the damage was done. The battery was too low to transmit another call or even to start the engine. Shortly thereafter, at 9:18 a.m. on July 11th, with Jim at the helm, the TRITON capsized. Bob and Linda had been asleep in their bunk. They had to dive through the open hatchway into the freezing North Pacific Ocean to escape the water that was flooding into the main hull.

Think of the shocking situation into which the three desperate souls had been cast. Barely clothed, clinging to wreckage in the freezing water, (the current in this area descends from Alaska), trying to maintain a tenuous grip on the slimy, upturned bottom of the capsized vessel, the three terrified people struggled for life against the storm.   After three hours in the water, Linda went into shock, collapsed, stopped breathing, turned blue, then revived in a paranoid state and frantically pushed the men away, screaming:

"I know what you want . . . . You want to kill us. I won't let us kill us."
"Us?" said Jim, puzzled.
But Bob understood. He looked at his young wife, he saw the way she pressed her hands against her stomach, and he knew, in an instant of revelation, that Linda was pregnant. From: *Lost* (Pg. 54)

The storm began to abate that afternoon, but the wretched survivors realized they would not last through the night without shelter. In desperation, Jim removed a buckle from his life jacket and used it to saw a hole in the hull, through which they crawled.   The water inside was waist deep with just eighteen inches of air space, but by wedging debris into narrow places they were able to make crude platforms and partially escape from the freezing water. They found a single can of root beer and shared it. It was all that sustained them through the night.

The next morning, having somewhat recovered from their ordeal, Bob spent the day making a sleeping platform inside the main cabin while Jim searched for supplies. The full enormity of Jim's religious dementia was revealed that night. While Bob had been making the sleeping platform, Jim had spent the day finding food and equipment—and throwing it away. Only four pounds of food remained. When confronted, Jim said:

"We'll be rescued when God is ready for us to be rescued. . . . There's nothing that we can do to bring on that moment. I don't see any need for us to make plans and ration food and lie around saving energy." From: *Lost* (Pg. 70)

A few days later they learned that he had also thrown away their solar still kit.

"Maybe it is the will of God that we no longer have the kit . . . If we made water ourselves, then we would just congratulate ourselves and perhaps live a long time and believe that we did it all. I believe it is God's will that the kit is gone. We must be dependent on the Lord." (Pg. 89)

It's hard to say how one would react under the circumstances. Perhaps Bob believed it was bad luck to kill a crazy man, and, after all, Jim was his brother-in-law. But the offender's head might have been whacked a few times, just to loosen the log jam. In any event the damage was done. The captain was not harmed. But the die was cast.

Bob found some paint and painted the blue bottom of the TRITON white with a large "HELP" sign prominently displayed. He took the ship's orange curtains and the extra life jackets and nailed them prominently around the up-turned hull.

By the eighth day after the capsizing, having nothing to drink except the liquid from their few cans of food, Linda had weakened to the point where she could no longer eat solids. Her legs were badly ulcerated with saltwater boils. Big bruises, incurred during the capsize, oozed and festered, refusing to heal. A wall of hostility had grown between the two men, fueled by Jim's prayers:

"Dear Jesus, we come to you tonight with understanding in our hearts. We know now that one of us is not ready for Your coming . . . One of us on board has not consecrated his life to you. And we know that when this person does these things, when he accepts Your power, dear Jesus, when he gives You his heart, then you will rescue us . . . ." (Pg. 94)

The sea had calmed enough for Bob to dive into the pontoons to search for the water jugs which had been stored there. On the first dive, he found his brother-in-law's diving gear, which he brought to the surface. Jim used the gear to dive into one of the pontoons where he found a gallon jug of water. Bob urged him to continue the search but Jim said:

> "There's no water, Bob. It won't do any good to look. I told you how I feel about interfering with the Lord's will." (Pg 97)

Yielding to a combination of pleas and threats, Jim continued his search of the pontoons and found a total of thirteen gallons of water in plastic jugs. Linda was immediately started on a liquid diet of powdered milk and eggs. This, plus a double ration of water, sustained her, but she was never able to join the men when they consumed their tiny ration of solid food.

A combination of bad luck and other factors continued to plague them. They fished, but lost their hooks one by one until all were gone. They never succeeded in landing a single fish. Several attempts to spear fish failed. The schools of minnows which swam through the wreck by the thousands eluded them. No mention was made of sighting sea turtles or trying to catch birds. The capsized trimaran was not a good trap for flying fish.

During the 73 days of their ordeal, not a single bite of food was taken from the sea. An aircraft and ship passed nearby, but did not see them. Settled summer weather prevailed, there was no rain, and their water supply dwindled. The TRITON drifted slowly to the West, into the trackless Pacific.

It seemed as though the captain's determination not to interfere with the will of God prevailed, robbing the group of the creative spark essential for their survival. They had found the ship's tool chest and had a boatload of materials to work with but the captain, an excellent carpenter, did nothing. Certainly some sort of tower with a signal flag could have been constructed. They found paint and other combustible materials but made no smoke signals, despite the passing of many ships.

By August 5th, Linda was no longer able to take even liquid nourishment. She slowly drifted into a raving coma, a dying Ophelia, twisting her fingers in her hair, her mind *"dancing with a macabre gleefulness across the sweet part of her life "* (Pg 13). The next day she rallied for the last time. Her face took on the <u>look of death</u>. Her eyes were hollow, opaque and filmy. She was so weak that her husband had to put his ear next to her mouth to hear her last words:

> "Bob, . . . unless rescue comes pretty soon, I have to go . . . . Haven't we had the best marriage?"
> "I'm so sorry it has to end this way. . ."
> "I'm sorry too, I do love you so," Bob replied. (Pg 155)

A few minutes later, Linda died. The men gave her mouth-to-mouth respiration for a long time, without success. One can only guess the cause of her death. She had been given enough water to sustain a healthy person, up to four cups per day toward the end, but her symptoms indicate the possibility of kidney failure. Perhaps they started to fail at the beginning of the disaster, when water was scarce. It is also possible that she miscarried some time during the ordeal. Perhaps the fetus' death hastened her own. Bob wrapped her body in turn after turn of the anchor chain, then dropped her into the depths.

So many people spend their lives looking for love and never finding it. Some find it, but the love somehow dribbles away through their fingers and is gone. To find love and have it torn from you is a terrible thing, a wound that never heals. The survivor is indeed a castaway, adrift on the raft of life, surrounded by an ocean of despair which has no shore. Bob Tininenko was therefore doubly adrift at sea, remembering his wife's body sinking into the blackness. At the very moment the two men were committing Linda's body to the sea, two cargo ships passed, less than a mile away. Neither ship saw the wreck.

Two gallons of water and a small quantity of food were all that remained. One gallon would last five days. The captain seized the open jug and said:

"Listen to me! I make you this promise. There's enough water in this container to last five days—according to your rationing. Five days! But if we believe, if we give our hearts to Christ, if we commit these five days to nothing but Him, then Jesus will send rescue. At the end of the fifth day, when the last drop of water is gone, then we will be delivered." (Pg 166)

Jim asked Bob to commit himself to Belief, and Bob decided, what the hell, give it a try.   They prayed earnestly for five days, and on the evening of the fifth day, they drank their last drop of water from the jug. As darkness approached, they sat on the overturned hull, waiting, waiting. Finally, Bob went below to sleep but Jim remained topside, waiting for God. God did not come, nor did any ship.

The next day was August 13, 1973. Jim's faith was destroyed. He remained in a fetal position for several days and seemed to grow noticeably older. Bob realized that Jim would soon die, which would leave him alone. This fear of the upcoming solitude surpassed his hatred for his brother-in-law. Finally, he said:

". . . . I 'm sorry God didn't come through for us, but, like you said, He has His own game plan. Maybe you pushed him too hard." (Pg 177)

Bob then recounted the story of Job, which, not surprisingly, brought Jim around. On August 14th, the weather started to deteriorate and Bob convinced Jim to help build a rain collection funnel. Jim decided that it was all right to collect God's bounty so a funnel was built, more than a month after the disaster. It was the first decisive, positive step that the castaways had taken to save themselves since the TRITON had capsized. A small amount of rain fell the next day, their fortieth day at sea. They managed to collect almost a cup.

The next day, an entire fishing fleet of five ships passed them. One ship coming within a few hundred yards of the wreck. The two men screamed, flashed mirrors and waved their life jackets—in vain. Nothing they could do attracted attention and the ships disappeared over the horizon. During the next ten days, three more ships were seen but they passed far from the wreck.

Jim had fallen into the habit of donning his wet suit and diving beneath the boat for a short swim. On September 1st, while diving, his safety line fell off unnoticed. Jim found himself a hundred yards from the wreck, which was drifting away at a rapid rate. He screamed for help but Bob was asleep inside the hull and did not hear him.

Jim fought his way back to the wreck, but the effort drained the last of his energy and will to live. It seemed as though his God had abandoned him. He collapsed on his bunk, refused food, and lapsed into periods of incoherence. His face began to assume the look of death. He seemed indifferent, resigned to his fate. He confessed that he had jettisoned the mast stub, sails, and other gear during the first day of the disaster. He said he didn't want to interfere with the will of God. He also admitted taking an extra sip of water and some peanut butter. Then he shut his eyes and waited for death.

Bob seems to have decided he would rather be adrift with a madman than with no one at all. But what could be done to make this stubborn fellow fight for his life? Obviously he had given up. His lack of will was going to kill him more surely than starvation. When someone gives up, what can be done?

Bob decided to curse the righteous. He called Jim every foul name and cursed him. Jim begged him to stop and finally promised to live. His confession and preparation for death had been besmirched. In addition, someone had to live to hear Bob's last confession and purge his sins.

The two lived on the edge of death for more than two weeks, with just a quarter cup of water and a half-teaspoon of food per day. Occasional small quantities of rainwater supplemented their tiny supply. Jim never recovered from his swimming ordeal. His will to live had vanished. He demanded his five-day ration of water (about one cup), drank it in a single gulp, then lay down to die. Dried blood caked his lips. He could not speak. He slept constantly, barely breathed and was wracked by occasional spasms. He drifted in and out of a coma. He awoke once and tried to commit suicide by hanging himself with a piece of fishing line. Bob cut him down. Twelve ships had passed them. They had been adrift for 73 days

That morning the S.S. BENALDER, a 58,000 ton container ship nearly 1,000 feet long spotted the wreckage almost 1,000 miles West of Los Angeles, saw the flag and noted the message on the upturned hull. But there were no visible survivors. The castaways were beyond the ability to keep a watch. This information was radioed to the U.S. Coast Guard, in San Francisco and, at their request, the huge ship was turned around. A lifeboat was launched.

The two survivors were taken in the lifeboat, which was raised by pulleys to the ship's deck. Bob looked at the TRITON, less than 500 yards away. It was just a tiny speck on the sea, her flag and markers somehow blending with sunlight and shadows. It was now obvious how difficult the wreck had been to see. How different their fate might have been if they had been able to use the mast stub as a tower for their flag!

The BENALDER was ordered to Midway Island, five days away. The two survivors were airlifted from Midway to Honolulu. Bob made a rapid recovery, ate solid food the day after his rescue, and was soon able to walk. Jim never recovered from the ordeal. He suffered kidney failure in the hospital and, on October 2nd, nearly three months after the capsizing, he died.

CHAPTER III: THE SURVIVAL CRAFT

About Life Rafts

A life raft is the ultimate back-up system for a boat, and since it is designed exclusively for survival, it differs from an inflatable boat or a dinghy in many ways. It is not a form of transportation; it usually goes slowly and erratically from Disaster to Nowhere until the survivors are rescued. Its favorite—and only—direction of travel is downwind and/or down current. It has no maneuverability and about as much elegance as a wet sponge. It is an extremely uncomfortable way to spend one's vacation, since the sea causes it to constantly undulate. It is usually wet inside and out, is either roasting hot or freezing cold. It never comes in designer colors and is never equipped with patio furniture or cold beer.

Life rafts fall into three classes: **ocean, offshore** and **coastal**. These classes refer to the distance offshore in which the vessel normally operates. The **ocean-class** raft meets USCG or SOLAS (Safety of Life at Sea) convention requirements and they are found on all **inspected vessels**, ocean-going ships and commercial fishing vessels. They may look identical to offshore rafts, but don't let their appearance fool you. Most of their construction, the quantity of food and water and the items in the equipment pack are proscribed by law and international convention. They are more expensive than offshore or coastal-type rafts, but you get what you pay for. Offshore and coastal rafts are usually used on boats, although a boat operator could in fact buy an ocean-class raft.

The words **offshore** and **coastal** imply that a life raft adventure in them will be brief. The food (if any), water, and equipment have been provided with this in mind. The overwhelming majority of boaters do not venture far from the harbor, and it is well known that of the few who do sink, the great majority are found within a few days. The equipment pack inside the offshore raft is designed with this in mind. These packs, sometimes called "D" or "E" packs, were conceived by the British Board of Trade for racing or coastal cruising.

When sailors buy life rafts, they are invariably annoyed by the extremely high price of an item they never expect to use. You will notice that cost is mentioned over and over again in this chapter, because cost is a major consideration for both the seller and the buyer and enters into every decision the manufacturer makes.

Face Page: Painting by Richard DeRosset

A life raft is a completely expensive nuisance, unless it is needed. It is bulky, heavy, inelegant, and requires yearly doses of additional cash to pay for inspections. One can never invite a date over to see one's life raft as would be possible with an etching or piece of sculpture of comparable value. The darn thing just sits there, taking up money and space.

As a result, raft manufacturers are caught in a conflict between utility, size and price. A captain who buys a cheap or "economy" raft selling for a fraction of the cost of other rafts is just kidding himself. A life raft is just a tool. There are good and bad ones. Knowing how to select, use, and survive in one is what this book is all about.

One American manufacturer whose motto must be "dead men tell no tales" produces a raft so cheap and of such incredibly poor quality that it just might not be safe for use in a pool. The owners of this company must either be atheists or not believe in an afterlife. Incredible stories of misadventures resulting from the use of their products abound. I have never found a life raft certification center that would touch one of their products for fear of being sued, presumably by the crew's heirs. Their only virtue, that which sells so many of these beasts, is the price.

At the other end of the spectrum, other U.S. manufacturers produce the Cadillac of rafts—but one could just about buy a nice, slightly used Cadillac for the same price. The adage "you get what you pay for," certainly applies to survival equipment.

FUNCTION

The raft's main function is to keep its occupants from drowning. Its secondary function is to protect the survivors from dying of exposure, hypothermia in cold weather or dehydration in tropic seas. Its third function, far down on the list, is to provide food, water and equipment to sustain life. This implies that there isn't much food, water or equipment packed in an "off-the-shelf" raft, and this invariably is the case.

A life raft prevents its occupants from dying in two ways: It keeps them afloat and reduces the possibility of their being pitched out. A life raft is a womb-like vehicle designed to keep its occupants inside in the event of bad weather. The whole affair has a low center of gravity and profile to prevent capsizing. **Ballast bags** and a **sea anchor** or **drogue** (described later), reduce the threat of a capsize. If a raft does capsize (and many do) the **canopy arch-tube** prevents a bottom-up position and makes the raft, relatively speaking, easier to right.

INFLATION

For a raft to save lives it must inflate. Good-quality, frequently inspected rafts almost always inflate. In other words, the bottle contains gas and the valve works. It is extremely rare for an inflator mechanism to fail. <u>A boat-launched life raft is always thrown into the water and inflated there to avoid tearing the raft material on sharp objects</u>. The **painter**, a line extending from the raft pack, is attached near the gas bottle to the **lanyard**, a short piece of stainless steel wire which fires the inflator mechanism. The painter is also connected to a **strong point** on the raft. The painter is anywhere from 30-100 feet long and it is important to know how much you've got. If it's short, and your boat has alot of freeboard, the raft may end up hanging from the painter. If it's long, it must be pulled out of the container before the lanyard is activated.

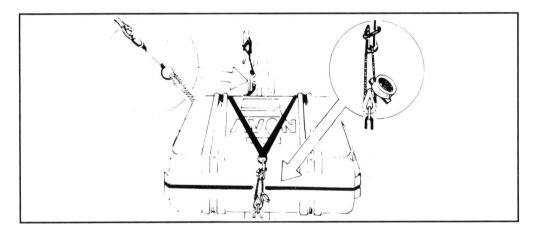

A "weak link" (left) in the painter line and a hydrostatic cutting device (right).

The painter is connected to the raft at one end and a strong point on the boat via a **weak link.** <u>The weak link is a piece of lighter wire or line, designed to break before the raft is pulled under with the sinking boat</u>. The "weak link" is a safety device, to prevent loss of the raft in an <u>extremely sudden sinking</u>. It should not be used during an orderly abandonment, since it is weaker than the painter**.** It is extremely important to secure the painter to a strong point on the boat BEFORE the raft is inflated. What a pity it would be to forget this detail .

A **hand pump** is provided in the raft equipment pack, and it is possible to inflate the raft by hand (or foot), but trying to open a raft and pump one up by hand while floating in the water is extremely difficult. A lever must be applied to force the cannister apart. It's no easy job on land, let alone afloat.

The gas used to inflate the raft is a **carbon dioxide/nitrogen mixture.** The amount of gas needed to inflate a raft is, of course, determined by the raft's size and also by air/sea temperature. In cold weather the gas contracts and more is needed to inflate the raft. The cylinder therefore contains a considerable excess of gas as a safety precaution. Excess gas is vented-off by spring-actuated **relief valves**, which are very noisy when in operation, making terrified castaways think that the raft is defective.

The raft inflates automatically when the lanyard is pulled. Under certain circumstances, such as when both the survivors and the raft are already in the water, the painter must be pulled rather sharply to activate the inflator mechanism. Several types of release mechanisms have been designed to automatically deploy the raft in the event of a cataclysmic sinking. They may be either standard or optional equipment. <u>Be sure your raft has both</u>. The first is a pressure actuator which makes the raft inflate automatically if the boat sinks. Automatic disconnect devices called **hydrostatic release mechanisms** are available. They cut the hold-down straps in the event of an extremely rapid sinking. The depth at which the mechanism functions is adjustable. Many deck-mounted cannisters are well-secured to prevent their loss in bad weather. They cannot break free without the help of a hydrostatic release mechanism.

Modern life rafts, when deployed, usually (but not always) inflate in the upright position. Rafts with a canopy arch tube cannot really rest in an upside down position as the arch tube prevents this from happening. Nevertheless, if the raft opens "upside down," some brave soul may have to jump into the water, grasp the righting handle on the raft bottom and flip the beast into the upright position—no easy job for the unitiated. The term "brave soul" is used because boats rarely sink in ideal weather conditions. A man in the water is a man at risk.

Righting an inverted raft. 1. Stand on gas bottle and grasp righting handle. 2. Pull handle and push down with feet. 3. Move away as the raft rights. Inset: Use a belt if no handle is available. Art by R. Monroy

Once a raft is inflated, a **boarding ladder** automatically deploys. This may appear to be a toy-like affair but it is stronger than it seems and is important. A survivor, properly dressed in warm clothes, foul weather gear, boots and a life preserver, is one wet, heavy critter. Some rafts have an inflatable boarding step which is a valuable added feature, since it is easier to use than a ladder.

BALLAST BAGS/STABILITY POCKET

One or more ballast bags hang beneath the raft. They are designed to make the raft more stable and to lower the center of gravity when the raft is lifted by waves, to reducing the risk of capsizing. Theories differ from manufacturer to manufacturer on the optimum size, shape, and location of these bags, but it is becoming increasingly clear that large ballast bags save lives. The USCG proposed regulations which called for 3.4 cubic feet or 217.6 pounds of water ballast per person but this regulation was never implemented. If it had been, a six man raft would have 1,305.6 pounds of water ballast. There are only two life rafts manufactured today which meet this high standard, despite the fact that the relationship between ballast weight and stability has been known for more than a decade. The argument revolves around whether a raft should achieve stability through ballasting or through a combination of ballast, shape, canopy contour, and use of the sea anchor. The Givens Buoy life raft, described on the next page has the largest ballast chamber of any life raft currently manufactured.

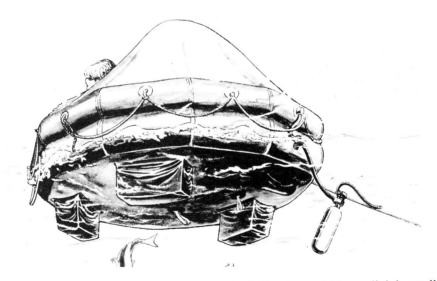

A fish-eye view of a late 1970's Avon raft showing its ballast bags which are slightly smaller than those in current production. In this ilustration the gas bottle has slipped from its pocket. The sea anchor line extends to the right. From: *Staying Alive* by M. & M. Bailey, by permission of A. & C. Black Ltd. London

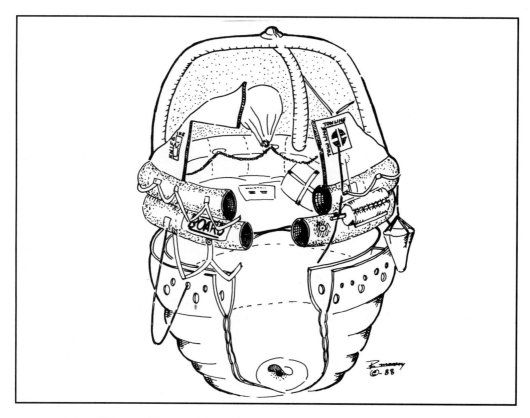

The **Givens Buoy life raft** (above) deploys a patented ballast bag which is unique and superior. Water enters the large **hemispheric bag** which hangs from the lower "doughnut," and completely covers the raft's bottom. In addition to providing ballast, the bag also prevents fish from butting the raft's floor, an important feature. A flapper valve allows water into the lower chamber but retards its exit. Baffles facilitate drainage into the bag as the raft tilts, increasing stability and making the raft **self-righting** (once the bag is filled), an important feature. The hemispheric bag makes this raft relatively deep-drafted, preventing wind from undermining and flipping it. The bag, containing more than a ton of water, prevents capsize up to 110° tilt.

An upper-**toroidal ballast ring** supplements the hemispheric bag. The ring fills rapidly through numerous entry holes, to provide stability before the bag fills. Because of the heavy ballast, a Givens raft drifts less rapidly than others. The bag must be "tripped" (with the line provided) to increase drift. The "ride" in a Givens raft is rather uncomfortable because of the heavy ballast, but superior performance compensates for this.

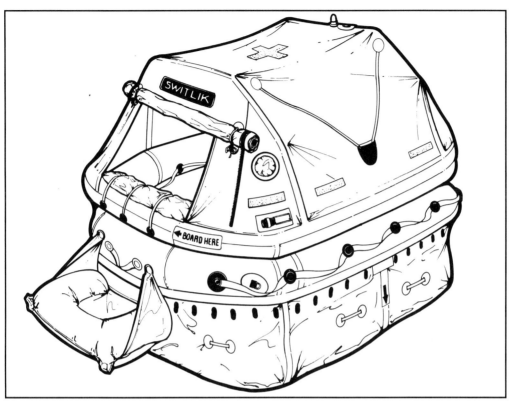

The Switlik S.O.L.A.S./Coast Guard Approved, ocean class raft (selected for personal use by the author and also by editor Steve Callahan), showing its large toroidal ballast chamber, inflatable boarding step and double door, designed to withstand breaking waves.

The only other manufacturer whose rafts meet the proposed USCG recommendations regarding ballast capacity is the **Switlik Parachute Company**. Their ballast chamber provides a pound of water ballast for every pound of floatation buoyancy. This equals 217-250 pounds of ballast weight per person. Their six person USCG approved ocean class raft has a doughnut-shaped "**toroidal stability device**" (TSD) which allows water in, but retards its ability to escape. It contains 1,302 pounds of water. The TSD is compartmentalized to prevent water movement, so that ballast cannot slide to the low side when the raft tilts. The TSD of the Switlik raft fills rapidy, providing essential stability in the critical first minutes after deployment. Because the toroidal chamber is not as deep drafted as the Givens hemispheric bag, the Coast Guard uses the Switlik Search and Rescue life raft as a sort of tender, to reach vessels grounded in shallow water (illustration on pg. 528) and this is one of several reasons why most coastal USCG vessels carry Switlik rafts.

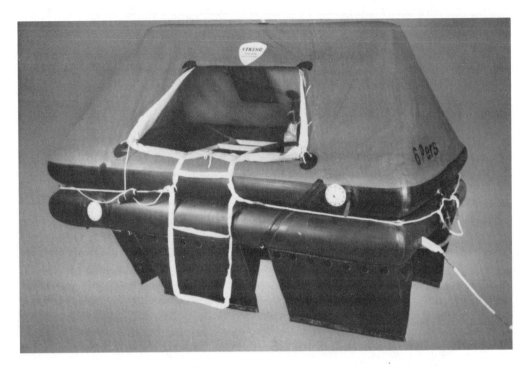

A rectangular Viking life raft, showing its deep Icelandic-type ballast pockets.

Viking Life Saving Equipment Company makes a classic, high-quality raft which has ballast pockets containing a total of 75 gallons of water (about 600 lbs.) ballast (for the six-man raft), which were designed as a result of tests conducted by the government of Iceland. Rafts ballasted this way achieve stability in rough seas by combining water ballast weight and the stabilizing properties of a sea anchor. The anchor must be deployed to achieve stability.

Other raft manufacturers have been less responsive to the need for proper ballasting. Many of the rafts sold today originally had flat bottoms, and it is painfully clear that the "ballast pockets" hanging from them are an afterthought, possibly an easily accomplished design modification of an existing product. Superficial examination of them often reveals a capacity of less than 200 lbs. ballast. Flat-bottomed rafts, with or without ballast pockets, are easily undermined and flipped by the wind. A properly deployed sea anchor usually reduces this tendency. Capsizing is a potentially deadly occurrence. In addition to being drenched, the crew must expend energy righting the raft, which rarely rights itself.

Ballast bags provide stability and prevent capsizing, but they also create drag and deter the raft from moving with the wind. Some people have cut the bags away to gain speed and this is wrong. If it is desired to increase speed, it is far better to run lines beneath the raft (if you have the line) and tie the bags against the floor, or leave them alone rather than cutting them away.

FLOTATION CHAMBERS

The flotation chambers of a life raft are segmented so that a hole in one chamber will not deflate the other. The two chambers and the arch tube are connected by one-way valves which allow air to be added but not escape. If the lower chamber deflates, the upper chamber and arch tube remain inflated. If the upper chamber deflates, it usually takes the arch tube with it. If the arch tube deflates, the flotation chambers are unaffected. The pressure needed to keep the raft firm is rather low, 2-3 lbs. per square inch. This makes it possible to keep the raft inflated with the hand pump and <u>maybe</u> by mouth if the pump fails. In any event, the Robertsons (see Chapter IV) did it by mouth and preferred it to drowning. The flotation chambers should be kept filled to capacity at all times.

The international SOLAS system for rating a life raft is based on the ability of **one** flotation ring to hold a specific number of people. A six man raft must hold six large men with one of the two "doughnuts" deflated. The volume of the flotation chamber is therefore rather specific, and so is the number of feet of seat room allocated for each person. Since these rules do not apply to offshore rafts, some manufacturers are rather creative about these two important features. Some rafts are too small to contain the rated number of persons. Flotation chambers can be designed to produce a round (doughnut shaped), hexagonal, or rectangular raft. There are various small advantages of one over the other. Round or hexagonal rafts are considered the most stable. A rectangular raft has the distinct advantage that survivors can more easily stretch out and lie down in it.

THE CANOPY

All marine life rafts should have a canopy. It and the inflated **arch tube** are of critical importance in sustaining life. The tube serves the double function of supporting the canopy and preventing a "bottoms-up" position after a capsizing . The canopy serves the triple function of keeping the survivors inside the raft when the sea is rough, shielding them from the elements and collecting rain for drinking purposes. The canopy also keeps waves from filling the raft. High-quality (SOLAS) rafts usually have double (inner and outer) canopies which offer even more thermal insulation and protection from water. A good canopy is colored international orange on the outside and fitted with **retro**

reflective tape for visibility at night. Some rafts came with a **metalized canopy** designed to reflect radar signals. This proved to be ineffective. The inside of the canopy should be a "cool" color, which is easier on the eyes, more restful and reduces seasickness. All rafts are designed so that you may jump directly onto the canopy and arch tube when entering the raft

Canopy lighting: Modern life rafts have an inside and outside **canopy light, visible at least 2 NM** which is powered by a seawater activated lithium battery. These lights are designed to help survivors find the raft during a nighttime sinking and to help them get initially organized. The battery does not last more than a few days, at best. These lights are dim and not intended for rescue.

A **flashlight** is usually provided in the equipment pack and, if the raft has been serviced regularly, the batteries will be fresh. Unfortunately, the flashlight, if not a USCG—or SOLAS-recommended type, is <u>not always waterproof</u> and even rubber-coated ones which seem to be waterproof, often are not. Really waterproof flashlights are expensive. The flashlight should therefore be hung up immediately, kept as dry as possible and used only for emergencies. If the supply of flares and signals becomes wet or exhausted the flashlight may become the sole remaining nighttime signal device. In addition, a rescue vessel alerted to the presence of a life raft in the area may not be able to spot it at night. A flashlight or strobe flasher from a homemade survival pack may be all that saves you.

DRINKING WATER

Water is unquestionably the item in shortest supply in a life raft equipment pack, often being insufficient to last two days, even with severe rationing. This may seem horrifying, but the manufacturer is faced with weight and size limitations which cannot be ignored. If, for example, a four-man life raft contained just five gallons (40 lbs.) of water, the size and weight of the raft pack would increase by more than 30%, making the raft difficult to store or deploy. In other words, if you want sufficient water in your life raft, you better take your own or pack a desalinator in the equipment pack.

Water is packed in cans of varying size or plastic bags called **sachets**. Sachets are small (about 1/4 pint) and are designed to be completely consumed after opening. The cans, if supplied with a lid, can be saved. Cans can also be used for water-collection purposes after their initial contents have been consumed.

EQUIPMENT PACK

Food, water, and hardware in the equipment pack are of critical importance for sustaining life in a raft. In many instances the vessel sinks so suddenly that only the raft and its contents are available to the survivors. Regardless of type, the packs are designed to sustain life for a week or less. Most rescues come within that time. SOLAS rafts, for inspected vessels, contain equipment packs which are specified by regulation to contain food, water and equipment sufficient to sustain life for a week. Offshore and coastal rafts usually contain packs similar to those specified by the British Board of Trade, but this is a British standard and has no counterpart in American law. The British "E" pack, common in offshore rafts, is designed for short-term survival.

The most important hardware, flares and signals, are in short supply. An "off-the-shelf" raft might have none in the equipment pack, so check the packing list. The contents of a life raft equipment pack are usually listed in the raft literature or affixed to the exterior of the cannister.

Signal devices are of critical importance, and a separate chapter has been devoted to them. Parachute flares are the best of all long distance night signals but they are very expensive—and no-one ever sold a life raft because it was luxuriously stocked with flares. I once opened the cannister of a six-man life raft made by a reputable manufacturer, that had been recently inspected and passed. It had no contents list, with good reason. The "survival pack" lacked a few items one might normally expect to find in a life raft:

MISSING ITEMS

fishing kit	sponges
flashlight (and batteries)	cups
food	first-aid kit
patch kit	smoke signals

THE KIT DID CONTAIN

2 rockets	1 set of instructions
3 flares (red)	1 sea anchor
2 paddles	1 bailer
1 pump	2 pints water in bags
1 heliograph	1 set hole stoppers

Castaways afloat in this raft would have been in deep, deep trouble. Even a contents list may not provide all of the information one needs to get a clear picture of what's going on. An item listed as a "fishing kit" does not tell you how much fishing the manufacturer envisions. Only a serious kit will help to land the large, combative fish which usually follow rafts. A "first-aid kit" undoubtedly does not contain much, if anything, in the way of prescription drugs, and the manufacturer's idea of what a first aid-kit is, might differ significantly from yours. "Survival rations" are sometimes found in a raft pack, but the quality of these rations is never discussed. What all this implies is that a prudent captain, who is investing thousands of dollars in a life raft, should make a considerable effort to find out exactly what he is getting.

Solar stills, extra parachute flares, and an EPIRB are undeniably expensive. Solar stills, discussed in chapter VIII, are almost never found in a life raft equipment pack. New ones are prohibitive in price and surplus ones are often too old to function properly. Including a surplus solar still in a raft pack would leave the raft manufacturer open to lawsuit and new ones would substantially increase the cost of the raft. Desalinators are also never sold as standard equipment.

Solar stills, EPIRBS, extra flares and other equipment, should be added to new rafts by special order or placed in a separate survival pack. Most cannisters are designed to fit very snugly around a raft, to prevent chafe. It is quite impossible to put more than a few small items into them. When purchasing a new raft, or when an old one needs inspection, it is possible to ask for a larger cannister or valise, and extra equipment may be packed inside (which adds not only to the size but to the gross weight). This alone vastly increases one's chances of survival since the survivors, the raft, and a reasonable amount of equipment all end up in the same place at the same time. Almost invariably people who must suddenly rely on the contents of a standard yacht life raft equipment pack are completely horrified by its skimpy contents and immediately despair.

Editorial note by Steve Callahan:

I suggest three basic bailout packages (to distribute weight, water and supplies.):

(1) The raft, standard equipment pack, EPIRB, at least a pint of water per person, etc.

(2) Full ditch kit with a water _producer_ , 2nd EPIRB, more flares & redundant equipment as would be needed around the boat in case of an emergency. Tie this one very securely with a long painter to the life raft so that if you need to bail out you can dump both the bag and the raft into the water together.

(3) Five-gallon water jug and food, etc, set up similarly to package #2.

THE SEA ANCHOR

When a raft deploys, castaways will usually find inside it a small conical bag with a light line attached and wrapped around it. This is the sea anchor, sometimes called a **drogue**. It is usually stored separately from the equipment pack and is tied down in a spot where it is easily seen. The reason is that this piece of equipment, although often toy-like in appearance, is a crucial item which may make the difference between life and death, particularly with lightly ballasted rafts. As is true with life rafts, there are good and bad sea anchors.

The raft sea anchor works the same as those used on boats but has additional functions. A sea anchor "digs into" the sea, its forward motion deterred by drag, while the raft, with little underwater resistance and considerable windage, skates along on the surface. The sea anchor therefore moves more slowly than the raft, slowing it down. Secured to the side of the raft <u>opposite the door</u>, it keeps seas from sloshing into the raft. It slows the raft, reducing the chance that it will plane off the face of a wave into the air. It also aligns the raft with the wind, preventing a rotating motion which drives the

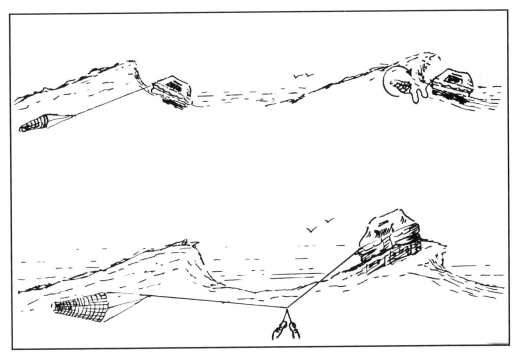

A properly deployed sea anchor decreases a raft's tendency to capsize. Upper left: Line of proper length. Right: Short line allows anchor to drive forward, reducing its efficiency. Lower: Using weighted shoes to create a catinary, which reduces slack. Drawing by Rafael Monroy

passengers crazy. Last, but most important, the sea anchor, firmly planted in the sea, keeps the windward edge of the raft from lifting, thereby reducing the chance of an end-over-end pitchpole in heavy weather.

There are a variety of different sea anchors of dissimilar quality. The least effective (for a raft) look like a little parachutes and are connected by a swivel to a light line (anchor rode). The swivel indicates that this type of sea anchor rotates and this increases line wear at the swivel, even though the swivel is designed to prevent this. New, high quality sea anchors built to Icelandic (and SOLAS) requirements are made of plastic mesh. They have a wire hoop mouth (to keep them open). Sea anchors are conical, and slightly stiff so that they retain their shape. They do not rotate and so a swivel is unnecessary. Some, such as the Viking sea anchor, are designed to prevent foreign objects, such as wood, from entering and damaging the cone. The same design also prevents the

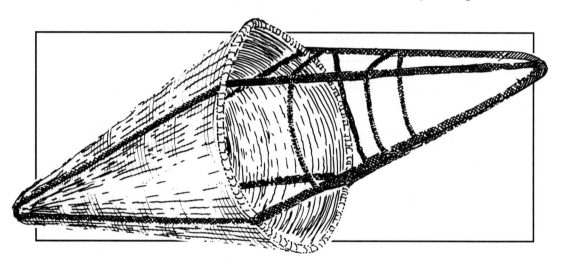

A Viking sea anchor, Icelandic type. Note the webbing around the bridle, which prevents the drogue from tumbling through itself in rough seas and prevents the entrance of foreign objects.

cone from getting half-pushed through the hoop. A good sea anchor increases raft stability tremendously. A spare sea anchor is recommended in the survival pack. The sea anchor is, undoubtedly, the most active part of the raft unit and the forces of chafe and wear are extremely active at the anchor line's connecting points. Check them several times per day. One is often informed that the sea anchor has been lost by a capsizing—and that can ruin one's whole day.

NAVIGATION EQUIPMENT

Life rafts are virtually unnavigable, following the wind and current. The tiny, ping pong-like paddles, provided in the raft, are designed only to help move the raft away from the sinking vessel. If a raft were just ten miles offshore, it would be extremely unlikely that even a fresh, determined crew could paddle that distance. As a result, life rafts never contain position-locating devices. Knowing where you are does not really help you get where you want to go. Life raft charts, if any, are tiny, to be used only for reference. Some survivors take sextants and charts with them when abandoning ship but I have never heard of this equipment affecting the outcome of a life raft adventure. They are not even of much help in gauging rationing since raft movement is erratic, even close to shore, but knowing where you are is a moral-builder.

COASTAL AND OFFSHORE RAFTS

Smart sailors buy "double doughnut" or offshore rafts, which means that there are two complete sets of inflation chambers, one on top of the other. If one of the chambers is holed, the survivors are supported by the other. Some rafts are made with a cost-saving "single doughnut" and are designed for coast-wise use. In addition to the single "doughnut" the raft is usually more lightly built. A loose-fitting sheet is sometimes the "canopy," which may have to be erected manually or with a paddle. This makes a coastwise service raft cheaper and smaller. In other words, you get what you pay for. The term *coastal* or *coastwise* is used to imply that a life raft adventure near a coast will be less severe and a brief one. Unfortunately a coast is also the place where an ocean begins, and an offshore breeze might turn into an offshore gale, making a life raft adventure far more than a coastal adventure. Read the tragic misadventure of the Davisons in the following section on "survival platforms." Their disaster began against a cliff, which is about as close to land as a boat can get.

Coastal rafts (and survival platforms), since they are small, light and cheaper, are useful on small boats and yachts which operate in sheltered waters or close to shore in heavy traffic areas. A coastal raft is intended for use within twenty miles of shore and if you are certain you can arrange to sink within twenty miles of land, buy one. Regardless of what the advertising literature implies, these rafts are usually more lightly constructed than offshore rafts.

The coastal class single-doughnut offshore life raft shown on the next page costs and weighs about half that of the six-person offshore life raft. It is made of a high quality urethane-coated nylon and has a short-term equipment pack. It lacks the toroidal stability device, but the ballast chambers contain more than twice the ballast of Icelandic pockets found on European life rafts. It also lacks parachute signals, water, food and a rainwater collector. An extended range survival pack is optional. Its canopy is firmly attached to the buoyancy tube, and there are two arch tubes to support it. The canopy has strong closures and it can be opened several different ways to suit existing conditions. One configuration allows the castaway to use the canopy as a sail, to sail down wind. In addition, the ballast pockets are furlable. When the pockets are furled, the raft sails more easily. The coastal raft comes with an optional seperate inflatable floor, hydrostatic release mechanism and EPIRB.

The Switlik coastal life raft buoyancy tube has two chambers separated by two internal sleeves. Should the tube be holed, both sleeves would extend in the direction of the hole. The buoyancy tube would lose half its air, but would not collapse, dumping the castaways into the water. The remaining good side can then be inflated using the hand pump, and the result provides as much buoyancy as the original. Repairs on the damaged side can then be made.

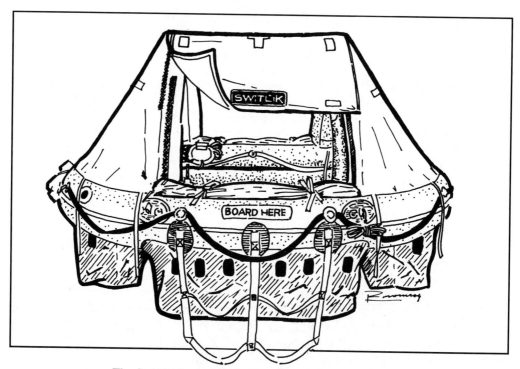

The Switlik Coastal Raft. Drawing by Rafael Monroy.

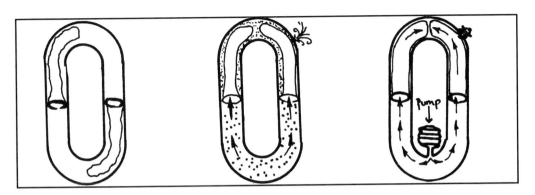

The internal sleeve mechanism of the Switlik coastal raft. Illustration by Rafael Monroy

THE LOSS OF SIBONY

After all the unkind things just said about coastal rafts, keep in mind that a good quality coastal raft is light years better than the best life jacket, much safer than a survival platform, an inflatable boat, and most dinghies. If Denial is the name of your game, buy a coastal raft rather than a pair of water wings and a bible. Bill Butler sailed for twenty-two years without a life raft. He had 35,000 miles of cruising experience, had beached his 38-foot cutter SIBONY during a typhoon in the South China Sea, traveled far in her, and understood ocean's merciless quality, but he was among those who believed "it will never happen to me." Bill yielded to his wife Simone's wish for a life raft when they decided to make the Pacific crossing together in 1989. He bought a Switlik four-person coastal raft at the Miami Boat Show. The coastal raft was selected for all the classic reasons: it was lighter, smaller, and cheaper than the equivalent offshore model, although even its name *coastal life raft* indicated that it was not designed for blue water use. *"Hell, I'll never need the damned thing anyway,"* Bill said as he paid for the raft.

A few months later, 1,200 miles off the Pacific coast of Central America, exactly seventeen years after editor Dougal Robertson's vessel was attacked, SIBONY was also attacked by whales—in about the same location. The Butlers' frantic MAYDAYs, transmitted on several frequencies, brought no response. SIBONY'S bilge pumps were unable to stem the flood. A few minutes after the first whale struck their boat, Bill and Simone were alone in their coastal raft, watching SIBONY slip beneath the waves. To make matters worse, the raft's only buoyancy tube had snagged on the self-steerer mechanism during the abandonment, creating a four-inch tear. Fortunately, the internal sleeves provided enough buoyancy and maintained the shape of the raft to prevent the Butlers from drowning until Bill was able to repair the damage.

Although the Butlers had only a coastal raft which lacked a survival pack, they had been fortunate enough to take some food and equipment with them before abandoning ship:

8 cans of food and juice	1 log book	1 partial box of cookies
1 box of crackers	1 EPIRB	1 fishing rod
1 jar peanut butter	6 gal. water	1 Survivor 35 Desalinator

Bill activated the EPIRB expecting, like so many other desperate castaways, that help would soon arrive. Unfortunately, the location of the disaster was not within the COSPAS/SARSAT satellite area of coverage (see pg. 387), so their emergency signal was not received. The sinking also occured more than 250 miles from commercial aircraft routes, along which the overwhelming majority of transoceanic aircraft regularly fly. At 4 p.m. a huge freighter came over the horizon and headed straight toward them. Bill and Simone were certain that the ship was responding to their distress call, but the couple had no flares and could only signal by waiving and shouting. The ship was not responding to their distress message, did not see them, did not stop, nearly ran them down, and continued on its way. The Butlers soon came to realize that they were on their own, in one of the most deserted and trackless places on earth.

"The worst thing were the sharks" Bill later said. Thirty to forty of them circled the raft constantly, bashing it with their heads and tails, day and night. One shark hit the raft floor hard enough to tear it. Others tore the ballast bags. The Butlers were able to repair the damage to the floor, but they could not repair the ballast bag. A five-foot shark eventually became caught in the torn chamber and struggled so frantically to escape that the terrified couple thought the raft would be destroyed. It seemed incredible to them that the raft was able to take this sort of punishment week after week.

After twenty days, the meager rations salvaged from the wreck were gone. Bill had no bait with which to fish, so he straightened his fishing hook and lashed it to one of the raft's paddles to make a spear. Unfortunately, the fish were too fast for him and the spear was too short. Occasional birds landed upon the raft, but Simone begged Bill not to catch them *"They are so beautiful— they're our only company—you can't kill them"* she said weakly. Simone had been sinking deeper and deeper into despair, but despite the potential food and bait which the birds would have provided, Bill honored her wishes and refrained from killing them.

Numerous turtles had passed the raft and Bill looked longingly at them, but they were huge creatures, far too large for him to catch in his weakened state. Finally a smaller one came within grabbing distance. He caught it and slit its throat. They ate almost half of the carcass for lunch. *"It was the best meal I ever had"* Bill said. Using turtle meat for bait, Bill was able to catch several hundred pounds of triggerfish during the ensuing weeks. He ate 11-12 raw fillets daily, about 2 pounds, and forced Simone to eat 2-3, despite her protests. She was becoming weaker and more despondent daily and didn't like raw fish. *"Think of your family—you have so much to live for!"* Bill would remind her. Then she would eat

The raw fish slowed their deterioration from starvation but unquestionably their Survivor 35 Desalinator (in addition to their raft) was what saved them. It produced all the water they could drink. (Read more about desalinators on p. 227.) As a result of a sufficient water supply, they did not develop the horrible salt water sores which are so common among life raft survivors.

On their thirty-sixth day adrift, they sighted Cocos Island. The raft drifted to within five miles of the shore. Simone wanted to swim for it, but Bill realized that they were unquestionably too weak to reach shore and would probably be devoured by the numerous sharks which swam around the raft. They drifted off. To make matters worse, the fishing had turned bad and they had not eaten for several days. Triggerfish stole their last bait.

The next day, fortune smiled upon them. A school of dolphins began feeding around the raft. Small fish, frantic to escape, jumped into the air. Bill was able to catch four of them before the frenzy was over. Reprovisioned with food and bait, Bill was able to catch a steady supply of fish thereafter.

On their fifty-sixth day adrift the Butlers sighted the coast of Central America, but the current which had been carrying them toward land now began to parallel the coast. Occasional views of the land would tantalize them, but the raft came no closer. The current swept them relentlessly toward the northwest. A point of land seemed their last hope but the current swept them farther and farther offshore. Bill paddled most of the day trying to reach land, but in his weakened state he was unable to make it. The point slid past a few tantalizing miles away. The gaunt castaways had reached the limits of their endurance. Exhaustion made them move like dream dancers in a nightmare, fleeing through heavy mud, pursued by the swift, winged riders of the Apocalypse. Death hovered at their shoulders. Their food was gone. Bill had lost 49 of his 176 pounds. Simone had lost 58 pounds. It seemed as though the end was near, that they would sink down and be devoured by the ever-present sharks.

August 19th, an incredible 66 days after the sinking, was wonderfully fair and clear. A summer gale had come and gone, taking its tole in blood, yet one could say it was a perfect day for a rescue. The Costa Rican Coast Guard patrol boat PUNTA BURICA was about five miles offshore, near Golfito, searching for a missing shrimper. They had searched fruitlessly for days, running down the wild blue valleys of the sea like a mother hunting for her lost children. They never found them. They found the Butlers instead.

AIRCRAFT RAFTS

Private aircraft rafts are not the same as marine type rafts, either in design or intent. Weight is a critical factor in aircraft safety equipment, and an assumption is made that the pilot will succeed in sending out a "Mayday," with a location, before ditching. The implication is that help will arrive within hours. Private aircraft rafts are usually "single-doughnut" types without canopies, similar in to survival platforms. Most do not contain an equipment pack.

Since rafts kept in aircraft are not exposed to saltwater or the marine environment, the inflator mechanisms are occasionally made of dissimilar metals which become electrolytically active and corrode when exposed to a sea-salt environment. The overwhelming virtue of an aircraft life raft is its price. Since it contains so much less, it costs so much less. These rafts are occasionally sold in marine stores and through mail order houses. They are not what you want.

SURVIVAL PLATFORMS

A survival platform is a single-doughnut raft with neither a canopy nor any equipment. It is better than nothing at all and better than floating in a life jacket, since it does get one out of the water. A graphic example of how unsafe a survival platform can be is vividly described in **Last Voyage, by Ann Davison** (A Grafton Books reprint, 1988), recounting the tragic loss of the Yacht RELIANCE in 1949. Ann Davison and her husband Frank were motor sailing at night, a few miles off Devonshire, England. While trying to clear a rocky point named Portland Bill, the sail suddenly blew out and the ancient engine quit. The Davisons considered dropping an anchor, but the boat, caught by a fierce current, had drifted into an area of towering cliffs, which dropped steeply into the sea. The water was too deep to anchor. A big, old boat, an unreliable engine and the cruel sea had sealed their fate. Their survival craft consisted of a cork float, the WW II equivalent of a "survival platform."

[Frank] said, "We'll have to look to ourselves. . . . " Quickly, he got the paraffin and as I handed him a bundle of garments for a flare, he hesitated —"Won't you want these again?"—and laughed shortly and soaked them in paraffin.

The flare cast an orange glow over the deck and by its weird light we unlashed the float and moved it over to the lee side, ready for launching.

We were putting on life jackets, Frank grumbling he couldn't work in one, when she struck. Lightly at first, then harder and harder. We were in front of the wheel house. He shouted, "Hold tight!" and we grabbed the mainsheet. Jolting and bumping on the bottom, louder and louder she crashed. Each crash the knell for our hopes and beliefs. Sounding the end of all for which we had laboured and endured. . . .

Frank yclled, "Float!" and we heaved it over the side. . . .

Our queer little craft was a lozenge-shaped ring of cork, or some other unsubmergible substance, canvas bound and painted red and yellow. The ring was woven about with an intricate system of lifelines. . . .

We sat on the ring and paddled. . . . Sometimes the water swept across our laps. The float swooped gamely to the top of a wave and dived down into the trough. Frank said she was a good little craft, but wet. We were very cold. . . .

As we paddled along the coast, careening up and over the waves, we saw terrific activity burst out on the cliff-tops. A rocket shot up with a bang [a maroon], leaving a white trail against the night sky. Torch, bicycle and car lights appeared and ran about in a purposeful manner. An organization was going into operation. We visualized telephonings, shouts, orders; a lifeboat launched, coast guards in action. . . because of a ship in distress. . . . Our ship. . . .

By now we realized that the fierce current that had wrecked RELIANCE was turning and carrying us out to sea. . . .

We could see the masthead light of the lifeboat rising and falling. Then it moved close inshore, and passed us.

We yelled at the top of our voices and waved the torch. The torch went out irrevocably, and our shouts were drowned out in the tumult of wind and water. . . .

When daylight came, they did not see us. Nor by then could we see them. Only from the wave-crests could we see land at all. The seas were tremendous and very steep. From the top we looked down into impenetrable depths, from the troughs we gazed, awestruck, at the huge wall of water. The cold was intense.

The current took us into the very center of Portland Race. The sea was white with intense rage. . . . Towering pinnacles of water rushed hither and yon, dashing into one another to burst with a shrapnel of foam—or to merge and grow enormous. . . .

Dizzily, the float tore up and down, swinging and swaying. Tensely we watched the advance of each white-headed mountain. Frank had lost his paddle in the last upset and we could not even make a pretense of fighting.

Then we were flung into the sea again. And this time, we saw how it happened. Saw with slow-motion clarity how the float was sucked up under a great overhanging crest, and thrown over backwards in the boiling tumult as the wave broke. . . .

Hours dragged out in immeasurable misery as the sea struck with a sledgehammer to kill a pair of gnats.

No longer buoyed by the slightest hope of rescue we sank into an apathy of endurance, huddled together, heads on the ring, hands grasping lifelines with the prehensile, immovable grip of the newborn. Or the dying. Passively fighting for the lives which were a little less living after every blow. In a comparative lull, from a wave-top, I glimpsed land, Portland Bill, thin and attenuated in the distance. Pointed to it. Frank slowly stood up and called in a whisper for help.

It was such a pitiful travesty of his usual stentorian bellow [that] I was inexpressively shocked, and with a surge of protective energy reached up to pull him down, dreading a recurrence of the horror of the other night. . . .

He did not speak. He put out a hand, pressed mine, reassuringly, smiled at me. And gradually, the smile fixed and meaningless and terrible, faded into unconsciousness, into a slow delirium when, blank-eyed, he tried to climb out of the float. I held onto him and feebly tried to rub his hands, my own unfeeling.

A monster wave rose above the rest. Fury piled on fury. Curling foaming crest.

Sweeping down on us. Inescapable. I threw an arm around Frank, leant forward. The little float drove into the wall of water and was lost within it. When it broke free, Frank was dead.   From: *Last Voyage* (pp 229-34)

The tide eventually turned, carrying Ann Davison, her husband's dead body and the float back to an area of cliffs not far from where the boat sank. By sheer luck, she was tossed onto a small cave-like ledge from which she was able to climb the cliff. A survival platform is an extremely minimal safety device best used on waterways, bays, lakes and swimming pools.

THE INFLATABLE FLOOR

Modern life rafts can be purchased with an optional inflatable floor which has an important life-saving quality of far greater value than the extra cost implies. The manually inflated floor insulates the raft's occupants from the energy-draining quality of cold water. In addition, the rigid floor somewhat insulates the castaways from fish attacks. Having one's ass bitten every five minutes may not be life threatening—but it certainly is a—pain in the ass. Inflatable floors usually require less pressure to deploy (1lb.) than the flotation chambers. They are usually designed so that small quantities of water run off to collection points, which must be sponged dry. An air matress can also be used.

SURVIVAL RATIONS

The quality and quantity of survival rations in a life raft vary tremendously, and a section of this book has been devoted to them. Generally speaking, the quantity of food found in "off-the-shelf" survival packs is sufficient for about a week and survivors who have spent a week or less in a raft have experienced very little weight loss. Since people do not starve to death in a week, the value of the ration is as much psychological as physical. Good-quality rations are high energy, low residue, vitamin enriched, and easily assimilated. Some of the biscuits or tablets should be easily dissolved so that they can be made into a sort of soup which can be fed to a badly injured crewman. Select your rations carefully. You might have to eat them.

RAFT FABRIC

The single-most expensive part of any life raft is the fabric from which it is made. The previous generation of rafts (WW II) was made from natural rubber that was bonded to cotton cloth. The main disadvantage of these rafts was their limited life. Some, stored under ideal conditions, would last a decade or more but others would develop rubber cancer, especially if exposed to heat or moisture. Rubber cancer, sometimes called **"copperization,"** is a chemical decomposition of raft material. There is some copper in the inflator mechanism and other metal parts, and if they are exposed to saltwater, copper sulfate results. Copper sulfate corrodes raft fabric. The decomposing material emits a gas that causes water soluble, cancerous spots to appear. Once the process has begun, it is usually irreversible, and repairs ultimately fail. Moisture can enter a cannister, as condensation or travel along the painter line, if the line has not been treated with an inhibitor. If a raft is not serviced regularly, copperization results.

Life rafts manufactured today are made of a variety of different materials designed to fulfill different functions. Some, such as Nitrile-Butadine, resist oil and are useful on tankers. Rafts made of fluorinated hydrocarbons perform well under a variety of conditions but are quite expensive and short lived. Neoprene, used in both rafts and inflatable boats, is less expensive but gets stiff in extreme cold. Silicone or natural rubber rafts are less subject to cracking in extreme cold but don't last as long under some conditions. Natural rubber, laminated on synthetic cloth, performs well over a wide temperature range, but can and does deteriorate. The table which follows, supplied by Viking Life Saving Equipment Company, describes the characteristics of life raft materials.

Characteristics of Various Elastomers

Type	NR	IR	SBR	CR	NBR	BR	IIR	EPOM	CSM	PUR	MVQ
Hardness	25-100	40-100	40-100	40-95	30-100	45-80	30-100	40-90	50-95	70-98	30-85
Tensile Str.	25-30	25-28	25	25	25	15-20	20	25	18	40	8
Resilience	1	1	2	3	3	1	6	4	4	3	3
Str. Stabil.	1	1	4	3	4	4	3	4	3	1	4
Abras Resist	2	2	2	2	2	1	3	3	2	1	4
Temp. Range	-60/120	-60/120	-40/130	-35/140	-40/130	-90/130	-30/150	-35/180	-50/180	-40/100	-90/180
Res. Aging	4	4	3	2	4	4	2	1	1	3	2
Water	3	3	2	4	2	3	2	3	4	4	3
Alkalis	3	3	3	3	3	3	2	3	2	5	4
Acids	3	3	3	3	4	3	2	3	2	5	4
Oil	6	6	6	3	1	6	6	6	3	1	3

Rubber Type

NR- Natural rubber; IR Isoprene, Synthyetic; SBR Styrene-Butadine; CR Chloroprene; NBR- Nitrile- Butadine; BR- Butadine; IIR- Butyl; EPOM- Ethylene Propylene; CSM Chlorosulfonyl Polyethylene;   PUR- Polyurethane; MVQ Silicone;   Rubber types: 1=excellent; 6= very poor Max. Tensile Strength in N/m sq. Temp.=Operational Temp. Range

Most boat life rafts are made of natural rubber or Neoprene (chloroprene). Some high quality boat rafts are made from the same material as commercial ship life rafts but others are constructed from cheaper materials. High-quality raft material is made of rip-stop fabric. This quality can be seen by wetting the material and looking for a pattern of tiny bumps in the fabric. Concerning raft fabric, "heavy" means "good," and "heaviest" means "best." The highest-quality rafts are made of several layers of different material laminated together to produce both airtightness, waterproofing, and chafe resistance.

INSPECTION, CERTIFICATION, AND APPROVAL

Moisture kills rafts and their contents. Moisture may take the form of rain, saltwater, or condensation. A completely watertight—and vapor-proof package does not exist. The only way to be sure the raft will function is to have it inspected annually or at least every eighteen months. Raft inspectors should be factory-certified and licensed. There is no law requiring this, so it might be a good idea to see if the man who has your life in his hands has a factory-approval certificate on the wall—for YOUR brand of raft.

The condition of the raft material, the gas cylinder, inflator mechanism, and the contents of the raft pack should be inspected. The raft is inflated, pressure tested, allowed to stand a long time, then retested for leaks. Some items, such as flashlight batteries, must be replaced annually. Other items, including medications in the first aid kit are replaced on a schedule. Cylinders are removed and hydrostatically tested about every five years or to meet manufacturers' specifications. Special service and equipment updates are also made in accordance with manufacturer and Coast Guard requirements. There is absolutely no substitute for annual recertification which can be obtained in every major port city in the world. Don't consider recertification expensive, consider it as a sort of rider on your life insurance policy.

Life raft inspectors are trained and certified. But they are also human and make mistakes. One raft I examined, inspected and certified by a licensed repacker, lacked batteries for the canopy lights. The boarding ladder was not deployed. The equipment pack was not secured, a serious error of great importance. The painter is usually moisture-proofed at the entry point to the cannister, and a rubber grommet, through which the painter must pass, further deters the entry of water. This is to prevent the painter from becoming a "wick." The grommet was not positioned properly and the cannister contained water. The water had attacked not only the raft material but the gas cylinder, which was badly rusted. Nothing makes a raft deteriorate faster than standing water.

One couple I met had their raft recertified on one of the small islands in the Pacific. When they returned to the States and took it in for recertification, all they found inside the cannister was—a sack of sand. The raft had been stolen. What all this means is that the prudent mariner will be present when his raft is packed, have a check list of what must be done, and personally inspect the inflated raft for abrasions and rubber cancer. If a certification center doesn't like your being present, find another. After all, your life is at stake.

A raft that is not USCG approved does not mean it is disapproved. It also does not mean it is a quality product. It's all up to you to determine what you're getting. Examine life raft samples at boat shows. Get on the Survival Technologies Group mailing list and receive its tabloid, NEWSWAVE. The Safety of Life At Sea convention (SOLAS) has a list of equipment recommendations for (ship) life rafts, which is a standard throughout Europe. USCG requirements for Ocean-class rafts closely follows SOLAS recommendations, but the USCG does not provide recommendations for offshore rafts.

RATINGS AND CAPACITY

Offshore and coastal-class rafts are rated by the manufacturer (not the USCG) for their man-carrying capacity. SOLAS recommends 200% buoyancy for each person of rated capacity for "double-doughnut" rafts. The manufacturers of cheap, killer rafts are often creative about this point. One, when confronted with the fact that four people could not possibly fit in his four man raft, responded by saying,*"Four people don't have to be in it all of the time to survive. . . .they can take turns hanging on the outside."* One four-man-rated U.S. manufactured raft was so small and floated so low in the water that it constantly swamped, and capsized several times, when occupied by three young men. It had a single doughnut, no canopy and was hardly adequate for two men. Two of the three souls fell out and died within 24 hours. The third was saved. The illustration on the next page is a tracing of a poor photo taken by a crewman at the moment of rescue. Could four men fit into this raft?

If you want a seat in your raft, take a look at an inflated sample of what you are going to buy. A six-man life raft should hold twelve rather heavy men without sinking. This does not, even for a moment, consider how comfortably six will remain afloat, andit is completely safe to say that all six will survive in complete agony, discomfort, and misery, even in a quality raft. The inability to move around in a fully loaded raft is so severe that it rapidly becomes life-threatening. It is almost impossible to make repairs with so many people in the way, and the cramped conditions make rest impossible. Exhaustion and despair

The sole survivor of a "four-man" raft. Tracing (from a photo) by Rafael Monroy.

are among the survivors' greatest enemies. A wise captain will provide a six-man life raft for not more than four persons and a rich captain will be even happier with an eight man raft for four castaways.

PACKAGING

Life rafts are packed either in a **soft valise** or a **hard fiberglass cannister**. The valise makes it possible to store the raft in a locker or on a bunk and the raft is protected from the elements. A hard container is usually deck-mounted with some sort of quick-release mechanism. The advantage of deck mounting is that the raft is already outside "at hand" if the boat explodes or sinks rapidly. In addition, rafts which are stored in lockers are invariably placed or end up on the bottom of the locker, with additional contents piled upon them. The seconds lost freeing the raft and getting it on deck may be very precious seconds indeed. In addition, the deadly smoke of a fire may make it impossible to reach the raft, and this is another good reason to deck-mount it.

CHAFE

Chafe is a rubber raft's enemy, and the No. 1 strategy to prevent chafe is to <u>keep the raft rigid with air</u>. Raft material is designed to last at least 30 days at sea, and if the raft is not destroyed by cuts or chafe, it will undoubtedly last much longer. But if the raft is allowed to get soft, it will begin to flex and rub against itself, and that must be avoided at all costs. Sunshine warms a raft, causing air to be vented off, and cool, nighttime temperatures cause the remaining air to contract. Even the best fabric is not completely airtight. Wave action and movement by the occupants within the raft also cause air venting. All of these things cause the raft to soften. As a result someone, usually the person on watch, must regularly examine all of the air chambers and pump them as necessary. If the pump fails, the tube must be cut from it and the raft inflated by mouth.

Chafe is also a great enemy of the sea anchor. The sea anchor and its connecting line should be examined in great detail. One should "freshen the nip" frequently, meaning that the points on the line connecting the sea anchor and to the raft should be changed to prevent failure. If sufficient line is available a "lazy" back-up line—meaning a slack line, should be tied to it, which will prevent loss of the sea anchor, should the anchor line break.

THE PATCH KIT AND RAFT PLUGS

Sharp objects may create holes, and chafe holes appear, despite efforts to prevent them. As time passes, the raft bottom becomes foul, and fish occasionally nibble holes into it. They rub their abrasive skins upon it and scrape it with sharp spines. These holes must be repaired promptly to avoid exhausting labor at the pump.

A patch kit comes with the raft, consisting of patches, glue and a piece of sandpaper to clean the site. For an unknown reason, the patch-kit glue is the type which only works when the site is dry. This seems to be a grave oversight, since a variety of underwater glues are now available This patch kit would work wonderfully in the desert, but on a raft?   In addition to a patch kit, the equipment pack usually contains several plugs. They are for large holes or to fill spots worn-out by chafe. Learn to use them. Unfortunately, there are only a few plugs with each raft and new ones are difficult to make from materials at hand. Therefore the plugs should be kept in reserve, to be used only where patches are totally impractical.

A high-quality patch-clamp is available and sold as standard equipment with some rafts. One plate is slipped through the tear, then secured to the other plate with a wing nut. The tear is sandwiched between the plates. Air is prevented from escaping by rubber gaskets.

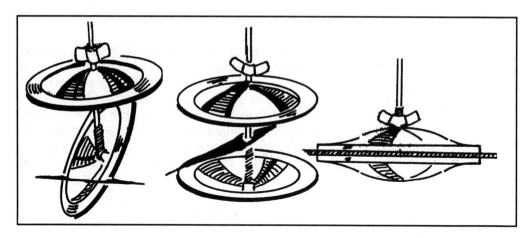

The clamp, used for reapiring large holes. Left to right: (1) The clamp is inserted through the tear. If the tear is too small to admit the plate, enlarge it. (2) The plates are positioned (3) The wing nut is screwed tight. Drawing by Rafael Monroy.

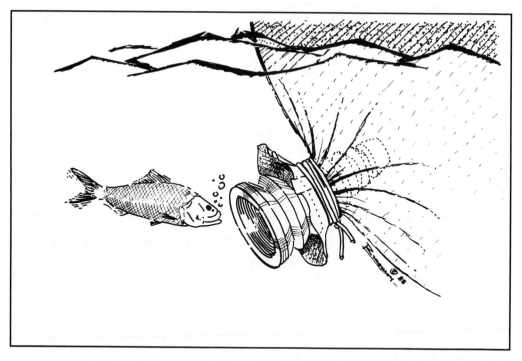

A cone-shaped plug for small holes. Drawing by Rafael Monroy.

OPERATIONAL LIFE

According to USCG and SOLAS requirements, life rafts are designed to have a <u>minimum useful life of thirty days</u>. This is one case where manufacturers almost invariably exceed these minimum requirements by a considerable margin. The Bailey's raft (see Chapter IV) lasted 117 days and was in good condition when they were rescued.   Most life raft fabric, while often lighter than that of inflatable boats, is incredibly tough and is highly resistant to deterioration caused by sunlight. The chambers and arch tube are usually well connected, and it is extremely rare that a raft fails along its seams because of poor design. The best rafts have seam tape inside and out. The worst are just overlapped and glued. Watch out for them. Raft fabric is just about as saltwater resistant as anything can be and one might guess its test life in saltwater to be measured in years. The question of "How long will a life raft last" is therefore not really one regarding materials or design, but about individual events which vary from disaster to disaster.

Tiny mollusks burrowing under the seams are a considerable source of concern if the raft is in the water more than a few weeks. Older rafts are particularly vulnerable to this problem. Free swimming, larval clams looking for a place to attach, often choose places where the seam is not perfectly glued. Over a period of weeks they grow, enlarging the separation. Crush them.

BUYING A SECOND-HAND RAFT

It is extremely rare that one finds a used raft in good condition at the right price. The owners, having paid thousands of dollars for something that they never used (and probably never saw), think the raft should be worth at least half of the original value. They do not realize that the raft deteriorates just sitting in the canister, that the gas bottle must be inspected every five years and that expensive items such as flares, must be replaced at least every three years. If a life raft has been dry-stored in a desert, it is possible that it will remain in factory condition for 10-15 years. But a raft that is stored on a boat, particularly in a deck-mounted canister, has a much shorter life. It is therefore unwise to even consider a second-hand raft which costs more than 25-30% of its original value.

A second-hand raft should be inspected at a certification center and pronounced certifiable before any money changes hands. If the raft requires a new canopy, a new floor, or more than 25% of any one panel has rotted, the end of its life is approaching. Invariably these repairs exceed the raft's repaired value. My personal rule is never buy a raft more than three or four years old, and only if it is in great condition.

INTERNATIONAL CONVENTION FOR THE SAFETY OF LIFE AT SEA (SOLAS) 1974, 1983

The International Governmental Maritime Consultative Organization (IMCO) adopted a series of recommendations for the prevention of loss of life at sea at a series of conventions beginning in 1960. Periodic meetings have added to the body of suggestions, which become local law only if individual states create suitable legislation. The United States has generally amended or modified its requirements for inspected vessels to conform with SOLAS convention. Since most boats are uninspected, the Ocean-class raft is not required. An offshore-class raft is usually purchased, which is cheaper and looks similar but is not, in fact, the same. Nevertheless, it is possible to buy four, six, eight and ten-man SOLAS-type rafts, but they are generally not available off the shelf in most marine stores. In addition to less equipment, an offshore raft may be made of lighter material, and this is not immediately apparent. Ask.

SOLAS REQUIREMENTS FOR OCEAN LIFE RAFTS:

1. When inflated in an upright position, the life raft must be stable in a seaway.
2. It must be able to drop (unopened) into the water from a height of 60 feet without damage to the raft or its equipment.
3. It must have a canopy, colored for high visibility, which includes a rain-catcher, seawater battery driven lights, inside and out.
4. It must have a painter and life lines, inside and out.
5. It must be easily righted by one person if it inflates in the inverted position.
6. It must have a boarding ladder.
7. Each raft must be fitted with a protective valise or container which is both durable and buoyant.
8. The buoyancy compartments must be able to support twice the number ofpersons for which the raft is rated.
9. The (25-man size) raft cannot weight more than 400 pounds.
10. The number of persons a raft is rated to hold is a specific ratio of men to displacement of the buoyancy tubes and interior space.
11. The raft floor must be both waterproof and insulated.
12. The inflation gas must be noninjurious to people; inflation must be automatic and easily accomplished, as with a lanyard; a topping-up pump must be included in the equipment pack.
13. The raft material must be capable of withstanding 30 days of sea use.
14. An ocean-class raft must be able to hold a minimum of 6 and a maximum of 25 people.
15. The raft must be able to operate in temperature ranges from -22° to 150° F..

16. The raft must be stowed so that it is readily available. It must be able to float freely, inflate and break freely of the vessel if it sinks.

17 The raft must be capable of being towed (as by a lifeboat).

EQUIPMENT REQUIRED FOR A SOLAS '86 RAFT (REGULATION 17)			
CONTENTS	4 Person	6 Person	8 Person
Parachute Rocket Signals	4	4	4
Hand Flares	6	6	6
Signal Flashlight	1	1	1
Spare Batteries	2	2	2
Spare Bulb	1	1	1
Whistle	1	1	1
Signal Mirror	1	1	1
Emergency Ration (kg)	2	3	4
Drinking Water (liters)	6.5	9.5	12.5
Safety Tin Opener	3	3	3
Fishing Tackle	1	1	1
Medicine Box	1	1	1
Seasickness Tablets	24	36	48
Bailer	1	1	1
Sponges	2	2	2
Instruction for Survival	1	1	1
Sea Anchor	1	1	1
Scissors	3	3	3
Smoke Signals	2	2	2
Seasickness Bags	4	6	8
Rescue Bags*	2	2	2
Operating Instructions	1	1	1
Drogue and Cord	1	1	1
Buoyant Safety Knife	1	1	1
Paddles	2	2	2
Repair Kit	1	1	1
Bellows	1	1	1
Rescue Quoit and Line	1	1	1
Water Bags, Sets	1	1	1

* 1989 requirement, otherwise known as thermal protection bags or "suits"

Courtesy of Viking Life Saving Equipment Co. Inc.

QUESTIONS TO ASK WHEN PURCHASING A LIFE RAFT

 1. What kind of material is used in the raft?
 2. How are the tubes reinforced? Is the material rip-stop?
 3. How many air chambers and "doughnuts" does the raft contain?
 4. Is there an inflatable floor?
 5. Are there sea anchors? How many? What type?
 6. Exactly what items are contained in the survival pack? Does the pack meet SOLAS standards? What kind of signals are included?
 7. Can you show me a sample equipment pack?
 8. Is a video available to show me how to operate the raft?
 9. How is the canopy supported? What is its inside color?
10. Does the raft have ballast bags? What type? How much water do they hold?
11. Are there interior, exterior life lines, a boarding ladder, lights?
12. Is there a hydrostatic inflation and release mechanism? How does it work?

QUESTIONS TO ASK ABOUT THE RAFT EQUIPMENT PACK

 1. What kind of rations are in the pack?
 2. How much water is in the pack and how is it packaged?
 3. What kind of and how many signals are in the pack?
 4. What is in the medical kit? Is it in a waterproof valise?
 5. What kind of patch kit and how many plugs are there?
 6. Is a delux-kit available?
 7. Can I see a sample of the equipment pack?

Using a Dinghy as a Lifeboat

A lifeboat is a special-purpose vessel used as a survival craft aboard a ship. It is usually not less than 28 feet long and is obviously far too large to carry aboard a boat. In addition to its size, it is different from a dinghy in a number of ways. A lifeboat is first and foremost designed for maximum carrying capacity, not for speed and maneuverability. It is unsinkable and achieves this with sealed positive flotation tanks, located fore and aft and frequently under the seats. The loss of interior space to the flotation tanks is compensated for by greater beam and freeboard. These also reduce the possibility of capsizing. A lifeboat is double-ended to defend against overtaking

Face page: A dinghy with positive flotation and proper equipment. Drawing by Jim Sollers

waves and to facilitate maneuvering in both directions. Handrails are affixed to the outside of the hull at the water line, and grab ropes are attached to the gunwales. Special compartments or tie-down points, usually beneath the seats, exist for emergency provisions. Older versions have oars, oarlocks, or a hand-powered propeller and occasionally a sail. The most modern lifeboats are completely enclosed with a hard top and often have small engines.

During World War II, lifeboats could and often did travel great distances to reach land. During peace, a lifeboat usually tries to maintain position near the shipwreck or its oil slick, assuming that a distress message or EPIRB signal will bring rescue craft to the vicinity. International Maritime Law requires that a ship have a lifeboat seat for every passenger and crew person. Does your dinghy have the same capacity?

A dinghy is another type of special-purpose boat, but it is not a lifeboat and is selected for different reasons. First and foremost, it is, of course, selected for its size, which is a function of the place where it will be stored. If it is less than, say, 12 feet long, it will invariably be a rowboat, hopefully strong enough to take a low-powered outboard engine. Larger dinghies are often high speed, planing hulls and their carrying capacity is sacrificed for speed. All dinghies have little freeboard, relative to that of a lifeboat, and are designed to carry passengers to and from a boat at anchor or for limited coastal excursions. Needless to say, they are not intended for ocean passages. On the other hand, a well-designed, 14- to 16-foot, self-righting boat, with positive flotation and a sailing rig, prepared with emergency equipment, would make a good survival craft with a number of advantages (discussed later) over a life raft. It would make an excellent survival craft, and if your vessel can carry something this size, it is worth considering.

Safety of course, is a major consideration when selecting a dinghy, whether it is used for its intended purpose or as a lifeboat. Unquestionably, the most important built-in safety feature of a dinghy is positive flotation, whether it is created by foam-sandwich construction, flotation tanks, foam blocks or a double hull with an air space. Double-hulled boats are usually quite comfortable, since the inner hull is usually molded with seats, bait wells, etc. But if either hull springs a leak, it is impossible to bail the between-hull space, and one ends up in a sodden, unmaneuverable heavy, unseaworthy craft which the slightest wave will instantly sink.

Since a typical dinghy is not designed as a lifeboat, it is not as safe as one, and also not as safe as a life raft. Life rafts are more easily deployed, more stable and offer better protection than a dinghy from exposure and surf. A dinghy is more maneuverable and durable. Let's talk about some more about its virtues. Since a dinghy is hard, it offers protection against shark attacks and the constant harassment of fish. It will of course resist sharp objects and is immune to chafe. The seats get one up out of the water in good weather, so the skin has a better opportunity to dry. When it rains, everyone can get a wash and also spread emergency blankets to capture rain. As a result, there is less chance of developing the classic, horrible saltwater boils and skin eruptions common aboard life rafts. Last but certainly not least, a dinghy can sail if it has a sail, or if a sail can be improvised, and it can even go in a direction other than downwind. Without a doubt, a dinghy rows light-years better than a raft and a desperate crew might very well be able to row many miles to shore, something well nigh impossible with a raft. This is a big advantage if you go down near a coast where fickle currents and wind could carry a life raft farther offshore. In addition, a life raft and dinghy may be used in combination and a number of survivors have used this combination successfully, see Chapter IV.

Despite a life dinghy's virtues, foolish indeed is he who goes to sea without a life raft. No one knows how many have bitterly regretted this error, for the sea holds its secrets and dead men tell no tales. An incredible few, because of luck and good seamanship, have managed to defy death in their hard dinghies or the ship's boat, in some cases sailing incredible distances before being saved. Certainly Captain Bligh's boat adventure must head this list, although the loss of the BOUNTY was caused by a collision of personalities rather than a collision with a submerged object. The crew of the HORNET (1866) survived the loss of their vessel and a 43-day, 4,000 mile lifeboat voyage. Dougal Roberston's incredible voyage with five other souls in a 9-foot dinghy is another monument to courage, skill—and luck (see Chapter IV).

Peter Tangvald was another lucky, lucky man. He left Cayenne, French Guinea, sailing solo, aboard his 32-foot Bermuda cutter, DOROTHEA, on March 7, 1967, and during the night of March 12th, hit a submerged object which sank the boat. Having no abandon ship equipment, he had to use his flimsy, plywood seven foot dinghy as a life boat. The closest land was Barbados, some forty miles away, but it was dead to windward, so his nearest practical landfall was in the Grenadines, some 55 miles downwind (fortunately for him). He hastily gathered provisions for the voyage which included:

2 bottles water, 2.5 gals. each	1 dinghy folding anchor and line
1 gaff	1 chart and compass
1 sail bag of clothes	1 life jacket
1 awning and rope	sail bag partially filled with food
2 flashlights and spare batteries	ship's documents

Tangvald had been cooking dinner at the time of the collision and, as an afterthought, took the cooked food as well, but in his haste, he forgot to take a knife. As soon as he entered the dinghy, it became immediately apparent that it was grossly overloaded and shipped water with every passing wave. He hastily threw overboard the anchor, one water bottle, and the life jacket, then emptied half of the remaining water over the side. The weight reduction made a tremendous difference, as it had for Captain Bligh. It is, Tangvald reasoned, better to sail with few supplies than to swim with none.

Without a knife it was necessary for him to tear the awning with his teeth in order to make a sail, but the line wouldn't "chew through", so the whole affair had to be constructed with one continuous piece of line. He made the gaff into a yard and one of the oars into a mast, reserving the other oar to use as a rudder. The dinghy sailed beautifully, and Tangvald settled down in the stern for a long voyage.

The night was cold and lonely, but daylight brought the best reward of all—land! It was, unfortunately slightly upwind, and the dinghy could not beat toward it. More islands soon appeared, the tropical sun warmed Peter and he was able to determine his position on the chart. As he closed on another island (one of the Grenadine group), he stood up to get a better view, a disastrous error because the destabilized dinghy immediately filled with water and nearly swamped. He immediately threw the mast, rig and the remaining water over the side to gain buoyancy, then bailed the tiny boat dry.

The island, Canouan, had high cliffs on its north coast. The southern sandy beaches were guarded by breaking reef. It would have been more sensible to sail into the island's lee, but exhausted by his ordeal, Peter decided on the direct approach. A native spotted him from the cliff and tried to warn him away, but seeing that his warning was disregarded, the man hastened to the beach and pointed to the best spot, where the breakers were the least dangerous.

Peter Tangvald expected to be swamped in the breakers but, at the critical moment, the dinghy shot ahead on the crest of a wave and was carried into calm water. The islander who had seen him jumped into a boat, rowed out and helped this lucky survivor ashore. (From: *Hard Chance in a Nutshell*, *Yachting World*, September, 1967. Also, the book *Total Loss*).

One is forced to wonder how well Tangvald would have fared had the weather been rough or an island had not been conveniently located down-wind. Perhaps the experience of Keith Douglas Young might be more typical. He was a crewman aboard the 43-foot Bermuda sloop, MERLAN, which ran onto a reef north of Tasmania :

> On the cabin top was a small plywood dinghy. Though none too optimistic about its chances of supporting us in the waters swirling over the reef, we did hope it might carry us some way. It did—about six feet. We had barely left the stricken MERLAN when our cockleshell dinghy was swamped, and we were left struggling in the powerful rip tide. From: *Yachting*, [Oct. 1950]

By a combination of desperate swimming and good luck the crew managed to pull themselves up onto an exposed part of the reef where they were picked up by a lifeboat.

Other sailors have managed to sail or row hard dinghies safely to land but the ones who failed are invariably silent. Superb seamanship and considerable luck may save the day, but one is reminded yet again that the sea remorselessly exploits every small error. Someone who has decided not to buy a life raft because they are convinced they have the skill to "make it" in a typical dinghy has already committed the ultimate, fundamental error of incorrect mind-set.

Rigging a Dinghy as a Survival Craft

If financial or space considerations make the purchase of a life raft unsuitable, a well-designed "life-dinghy" can be built or a hard dinghy can be made into a survival craft. First, the dinghy should be as large and have as much freeboard as possible, with positive flotation in the form of foam sandwich construction, or sealed, foam-filled containers fore and aft. Boat fenders can also be used to supplement built-in flotation. In theory, there should be enough foam to allow the swamped dinghy and its contents, but not necessarily its passengers, to ride with the gunnels slightly above the water line. This makes the boat much easier to bail. Ideally a survival dinghy should have enough floor space for several people to stretch out and sleep, so avoid flotation under the 'midship's seat. The area beneath the seat should be used for survival equipment specifically intended to turn the dinghy into a survival craft.

"LIFE-DINGHY" EMERGENCY "DAY PACK":

2 qts water	1knife	1 screwdriver
1 pair of pliers	1bailer	1lb. of survival rations,
1 fishing kit	1 set of oars	1 sea anchor, anchor, and line
1 heliograph	1 bx signals	1 flashlight and batteries in a
1 canopy with zipper and snaps		sealed pack

The proposed kit is not intended to replace a life raft equipment pack. In addition to its use in a sinking situation, this pack may save your life if, for example, the dinghy is swept out of an anchorage in a sudden squall. The "day pack" should stay in the dinghy at all times, whether it is on deck or in use.

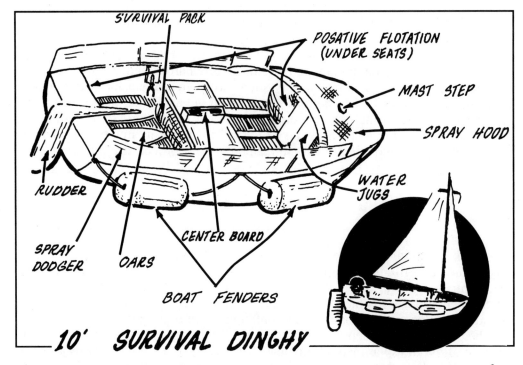

SURVIVAL PACK

POSATIVE FLOTATION
(UNDER SEATS)

MAST STEP

SPRAY HOOD

WATER
JUGS

RUDDER

SPRAY
DODGER

OARS

CENTER BOARD

BOAT FENDERS

10' SURVIVAL DINGHY

Certainly, a mast, boom, sail, centerboard and rudder are a great plus. They provide propulsion and also can be used to support the canopy. All of these items, should be securely lashed inside the dinghy before a voyage. The dinghy, including extra water and the ADDITIONAL survival pack should be tried in calm, shallow water prior to the voyage. Include the ENTIRE crew. If you cannot make it around the bay without getting into trouble, your dinghy is sending you a message.

USE OF A DINGHY AT SEA

The tendency of a dinghy to capsize influences every action. When entering the dinghy, everyone should be dressed for survival and be wearing a life jacket. All items not in use must be lashed down to prevent losing them in the event of a capsize.

Trimming with body weight is a major consideration, particularly in rough weather. It requires constant vigilance, an exhausting task. The best strategy is to have as many of the crew as possible lie on the bottom of the dinghy while one person both steers and trims. As starvation and thirst begin to make themselves felt, it gets harder and harder to continue this dance and inevitably, a misstep must occur.

During bad weather, the crew should stand by in life jackets, secured by a lanyard to the boat. It may be necessary for them to suddenly jump overboard to lighten the boat in the event of swamping if the craft does not have sufficient positive flotation to support the crew and the load of water. If that occurs, it may be necessary for one or more crew members to quickly jump over the side to lighten the boat. The remaining crew then bail for their lives. One can imagine both the necessity and the terror of this act. It would take no small bit of courage to jump into a raging sea, possibly at night, as a last desperate attempt to save one's life. Perhaps, when contemplating this delightful thought, you will consider saving to buy a nice life raft or having the old one inspected.

USING AN INFLATABLE BOAT AS A LIFEBOAT

An inflatable boat is not a life raft, although some of them have some of the same features. It has no advantages over a life raft as a survival vehicle, but space and financial considerations may make it necessary to count on the boat's inflatable raft. Like a coastal life raft, an inflatable is "single doughnut," but lacks the coastal life raft's inflatable inner sleeve. It does have three or more separate compartments, so if one fails the craft does not sink, but the holed chamber would fill with water and drag. One would certainly be in the hurt locker—the chances of survival would go way down.

An inflatable is blown up with a foot pump, but can be inflated by mouth. Since most boats sink quickly, a considerable number of those precious seconds would be spent pumping—pumping and pumping fast—one's foot would be just a blur. Even if the inflatable were kept partially filled, one would still have to pump and pump, with the water rising around one's knees. Several companies make an inflatable boat equipped with a gas bottle and a venting system but people who try to adapt something like a diving tank to this use are playing with their lives, and the word "play" is emphasized. A life raft has a series of venting valves to release excess gas. A standard inflatable boat does not. In the terror and confusion of a sinking, God help the person who over-inflates an inflatable boat which lacks these valves. The tubes will rupture.

An inflatable boat also lacks an arch tube and a canopy. The arch tube, in addition to supporting the canopy, makes it harder for a life raft to turn completely upside down. The canopy performs the absolutely essential function of reducing hypothermia or dehydration. A tent or cover can certainly be made for an inflatable boat and supported with flexible battens. But if the boat overturns, the canopy then becomes a giant ballast bag or keel, making it extremely difficult to right the craft. An inflatable boat lacks ballast bags or chambers. The fact that virtually every life raft manufactured today has these chambers indicates that they have become universally accepted as a life-saving feature.

Art by Steve Callahan

CHAPTER IV: ADRIFT ON TROPIC SEAS

Special Problems of the Tropics

HYPOTHERMIA

People always dream of sailing on tropic seas, with dolphins playing in the bow wave, surrounded by the gentle trade winds. If one must sink, certainly a tropic sea is the place to do so, since the relatively warm water and wind provide the least hostile marine environment on earth. But tropic seas are still well below body temperature and are therefore capable of causing chronic hypothermia which can be serious over a period of time. It may seem odd to be warning the mariner first and foremost about hypothermia in a chapter about tropic seas, but, in fact, <u>hypothermia is the greatest single enemy of the survivor under all circumstances</u> (see chapter IX for more information).

A life raft environment is almost constantly wet and therefore almost constantly cold. Waves wash into the raft, spray flies everywhere and condensation is an invariable nighttime phenomena. One may roast in the tropic heat, but without proper clothing and an **inflatable raft floor,** the nights will be cold, leaving the weary survivor weak and stiff in the morning.

For this reason, it is essential to dress for survival before abandoning ship. Proper clothing for abandoning ship is discussed in Chapter VIII . One must remember that clothing sufficient to keep you warm in a life raft is different from the clothes worn on deck, even in bad weather.

At least two synthetic **emergency blankets** should be included in the boat survival pack for each crewman. The blankets are cheap, compact and easily dried. They efficiently reflect escaping body heat. In addition, most emergency blankets are made of **metalized mylar** or other plastic, and the metal on the film is **radar reflective**. Hoisted as a sail or flag, they make the raft more visible to a ship's radar. **Thermal protection suits** made of a similar material are even more effective. Both the blankets and the suits are designed to reflect and trap body heat.

Penetrating cold is a problem at night because of the damp sea air condenses on the cooling raft, so the interior of the raft should be dried as much as possible at dusk. The lookout should not only watch for ships, but should keep the raft pumped rigid as the air in its chambers cools and condenses. In addition the lookout should constantly wipe the raft floor and try to keep it and the emergency blankets dry.

DEHYDRATION

In the bitter, ironic world of the life raft survivor, it seems appropriate to discuss broiling heat immediately after the comments about penetrating cold. The nights may be cold, but the days of light winds and flat calms are hot, increasing loss of body fluids. Nothing protects the survivor from dehydration and sunburn as much as the raft canopy. The better rafts have a **double canopy** with an air layer between which acts as insulation. If the raft or lifeboat has no canopy, **emergency blankets** may be used to form a personal protective shield from the sun and heat. In addition space blankets may be tied over the raft canopy, to create a shield that reflects the sun. This shield will keep the canopy cool.

Seawater is often used to cool hot survivors, and it is very refreshing. But seawater leaches body oils from the skin, making it more susceptible to saltwater ulcers, boils and rashes. A greasy sunscreen, insoluble in water, not only protects the survivor against sunburn, it reduces the loss ofskin oil. Creams that contain vitamins A and D replace body oil and also promote healing.

A normal person consumes about 1.5-3 quarts of water per day, but survivors have lived on far less for weeks at a time. A survival ration of **600 ml (a bit more than a pint) of water per day is considered a minimum.** Water requirements and sources are discussed in Chapter VIII. Any sort of exertion, such as rowing, may triple this requirement. If water is in short supply, **rowing should be done in the cool of the night if possible.**

People who are hot always consider taking a dip in the sea, but the numerous sharks which are never far from the raft make this risky. Even the smaller fish often rush up and nibble the swimmer, causing lacerations which are not apparent at the time but are painful and often become infected. It is far wiser to dip a rag in the sea and use it as a turban for the head, which is a highly vascular area.

SUNBURN

Sunburn is extremely dangerous to the survivor. **Damaged skin weeps, increasing fluid loss**. Saltwater attacks damaged skin and prepares the site for infection. Salt on a sunburn is painful and may cause **saltwater sores,** which are painful and slow to heal. These sores are more than uncomfortable, they are excruciating and life threatening. They reduce the ability of the victim to fish, bail, pump and even sleep. Stay under the canopy or **wear protective clothing** and a hat. Make sure that the tops of the hands, noses, and necks are protected with clothing or cream. **Reduce exposure to the sun**. Save main-tenance jobs for the twilight hours if possible.

RAFT DETERIORATION DUE TO SUNLIGHT

The bright sunlight of the tropics not only bakes the survivors, it attacks and deteriorates the canopy fabric or the paint on it, particularly of older rafts. The canopy's outer surface sometimes flakes away, destroying its water-proofing and making collected rain unpalatable <u>but not poisonous</u> due to tiny flakes in the run-off. The canopy and the raft's occupants are best protected from this problem by making a "fly" or cover from an emergency blanket, sail, or piece of plastic. Washing the canopy with saltwater prior to rain collection is recommended.

FISH "ATTACK"

A raft in tropic waters may be "attacked" by fish such as the dorado or mahi-mahi, which constantly bite or bump the raft's bottom. Some think the fish are trying to get at the survivors, eat small organisms on the raft bottom or "scratch" themselves against the raft to rid their bodies of parasites. These attacks begin within a few days after the disaster, as soon as big fish find the raft. The bumps occur every few minutes day and night. Sometimes the effect is mild but Captain Warren Whitlock, a survivor of the JANETTE BELCHER, which sank in the Gulf of Mexico on April 17, 1982, said the fish hit

". . . hard enough to make you think you'd been punched by a 200 pound man."
From: *The National Fisherman*, Dec. '83 (Pg. 31)

In his book, *Adrift*, Steve Callahan described the attacks like this:

> Quick, hard punches batter my back and legs. It is not a shark, but a dorado. I am not surprised. Their nudging has grown more violent, like a boxer's jab. Time and again they hit where my weight indents the floor of the raft. Perhaps they are feeding on barnacles. The projection makes it easy for them to get at the little nubs of barnacle meat that have begun to grow under me. . . . My feet, butt and arms are beaten, as if I'm being mauled by a gang of hoodlums. For a time I drive them off with a spear, but they always return. Time and again they strike, more and more joining in. (Pg. 66-70)

Survivors in rafts with single-layer floors or with floors that are not protected by ballast chambers are the most seriously affected victims. Rafts that have torroidal ballast chambers or skirts offer some protection. The attacks are annoying and unrelenting. As time progresses the survivors become more emaciated and covered with ulcers. With the body so debilitated and less protected by fat, each bump becomes an agony. Some people speculate that suspending a sail, blanket ,or plastic sheet beneath the raft floor will reduce the effects of these attacks. The fish hit the sail instead of the raft floor The hemispheric chamber beneath a Givens raft protects survivors against fish attack.

Sudden Disaster in Tropic Seas

The suddenness of boat disasters is the constant theme of this book. Two classic cases are beautifully described in Dougal Robertson's *Survive the Savage Sea* and Steve Callahan's *Adrift*.

Survive the Savage Sea By Dougal Robertson

After fifteen years of "ungentlemanly living" on an English dairy farm, Dougal Robertson was thoroughly sick of milking cows. Life had come full circle for him. He had spent twelve years at sea, gaining his Master Mariner's Certificate, met and married a nurse named Lyn, then fulfilled the sailor's dream of buying a piece of land and settling down to raise a family. Why he chose a dairy farm is unknown. Old salts usually dream of chicken ranches.

Fifteen years of dream fulfillment was apparently enough. The dangers and hardships of the sailor's life seemed far preferable to the financial burdens, the hard routine of farm labor and the crude realities of economic necessity. And then there was the sea, beckoning. Some say that once you've tasted the bitter salt, the sea never lets you go. They sold the farm, bought a 50-year-old, 19-ton, 43' schooner named LUCETTE and, in January, 1971, pointed her bow toward the west.

Aside from the usual gale off Finisterre, the Atlantic run was uneventful. The family cruised the Caribbean, then stopped in Florida, where they purchased a 9' fiber glass dinghy, which they named EDNAMAIR. Lyn commented at the time that their lives might someday depend on it.

The LUCETTE reached the Galapagos Islands in early June and provisioned for the transpacific run to the Marquesas Islands, 3,000 miles to the west. The crew consisted of Dougal's three children: Douglas, 18; the twins, Niel and Sandy, age 12; Dougal's wife, Lyn; and a Welsh college graduate, Robin Williams, age 22. Despite Lyn's vehement protests, the LUCETTE departed the island of Espinosa on June 13th, a decidedly unlucky date for all souls aboard.

At 9:58 a.m. on June 15th, everything was going just fine, with a fresh trade wind, dropping seas and a thin overcast, slowly giving way to blue skies. At 9:59 a.m. Dougal Robertson was down below, working out the morning position when:

> . . . sledgehammer blows of incredible force struck the hull beneath my feet, hurtling me against the bunk, the noise of the impact almost deafening my ears to the roar of incoming water I heard Lyn call out, and almost at the same time heard the cry of "whales!" from the cockpit. My senses reeled as I dropped to my knees and tore up the floorboard to gaze in horror at the blue Pacific through the large splintered hole punched up through the planking between two of the grown oak frames. From *Survive the Savage Sea* © Dougal Robertson 1973 (Pg. 23)

The LUCETTE, hit by three killer whales from a pod of about twenty, went down like a pole-axed ox. Orcas usually cruise at 10 knots but can sprint to thirty. They can inhale a 10-pound fish or take on a ninety-ton blue whale with the same efficiency and the same inevitable result. Although there is little recorded data to indicate a taste for human flesh, there are correspondingly few who have lived to tell the tale. And any creature which can generate more than thirteen million foot-pounds of force commands considerable respect.

The LUCETTE was not prepared for disaster. The water jugs lacked an air space, to make them float high, and disappeared with the vessel. The life raft, an old, but recently serviced model in a canvas pack, had seen better days and was in fact an offering from the fickle finger of fate. It had been an afterthought, a gift from a friend. There was no time to think, or make a plan, not even time to select provisions. At 10 a.m., one minute after the attack,

Killer Whales. Drawing by Rebecca Thomson.

the **six castaways** found themselves alone, crammed into a 10-person life raft, surrounded by the vast Pacific. The extra flares and the water had not been tied down and were lost.

Aside from the contents of the life raft survival pack, the only items salvaged from the wreck were:

10 oranges	1 knife	EDNAMAIR (the dinghy)
12 onions	1 sail	A sailing guide
6 lemons	1 lb. biscuits	200' fishing line, 100 lbs. test
1 sewing kit	8 oz. glucose candy	3 gal. gasoline

Their situation was clearly desperate. The Galapagos Islands, was less than 200 miles to the east was the closest land, but the wind and current pushed them relentlessly northward, toward the equator and the doldrums, into the most isolated and trackless part of the Pacific Ocean. There was no way back.

The life raft survival pack was opened and found to contain:

1 bailer	18 pts. water
4 fish hooks	1 fishing line (25-lb test)
1 signal mirror	1 flashlight
1 first aid kit	1 bellows (which didn't work)
3 paddles	2 sea anchors
2 sponges	1 lure (spinner and trace)

Bread and glucose tablets for 20 man-days
(less than four day's rations for the six).
8 flares (2 rockets, 6 hand-held signals)
1 raft knife with rounded point (tiny, dull and useless)
1 raft patch kit (but the patching glue was dried up)
1 instruction kit (containing little useful information)

Even with the strictest rationing, their water could not last more than 10 days. June was the heart of the dry season and they had no way to make fresh water. This was same time and place depicted by Coleridge in his poem, *The Rhyme of the Ancient Mariner:*

> Water, water, everywhere/And all the boards did shrink
> Water, water everywhere/Nor any drop to drink.

Thirst would quickly kill them. The children, with their greater metabolism and larger surface-to-mass area, would die first. Rain was their only hope for survival.

Fortune had placed a floating spool of heavy line within their grasp as the LUCETTE sank; otherwise they would have had to rely on the puny 25-lb. breaking-strength line provided in the "fishing kit." Line that light, lacking steel leader, would have proved no match against the large, combative dorados which surrounded the raft.

The area where the LUCETTE sank, far from major shipping lanes, is known for its isolation. The great circle route from Panama to Tahiti lies 300 miles to the south, the Panama-New Zealand track 400 miles to the north. Sailboats often travel for weeks in this area without sighting a single ship. They were as in the middle of nowhere as one could get. It would be generous to say that the lives of LUCETTE'S crew hung by a thread.

On their first night as castaways, they dined sumptuously, relative to future meals. The appetizer was one orange, shared by all six survivors, followed by the main course—a half-inch piece of biscuit per person, then a candy each for dessert. A single sip of water had to suffice. The water was in such short supply it was not considered possible to issue a ration. Dougal Robertson recently told me:

> At the minimum of one pint per day, the water would have been finished in three days. For this reason water was restricted on a voluntary basis, easch person taking as little as they felt necessary to carry on, from a communal glass jar. In practice, this amounted to an average of 1/3 pint per day, some having less than that, others more (the children, and Robin, when seasick).

The exhausted crew slept fitfully the night because of fish attacks:

> As we turned and twisted around seeking ease for our aching limbs, we began to experience curious bumps and sharp nudges through the inflated floor of the raft; at first I thought something sharp had wedged under the raft and worried lest it should puncture the flotation chambers, then I heard Lyn give a faint shriek, as she too was nudged from below. (Pg. 35)

Sunrise revealed further difficulties. The raft had gone soft during the night and they discovered that the bellows pump did not work. It was necessary to remove the bellows hose and inflate the raft by mouth, a laborious and exhausting process that had to be repeated many times every day. The 10- man Elliot raft had an inflatable floor and was divided into two sections by a central transverse flotation chamber. A tiny pinhole in the raft floor constantly admitted seawater. As a result the area within the raft was constantly half wet, requiring continuous sponging and bailing.

EDNAMAIR, tethered by its painter line was floating half-submerged, supported by flotation material beneath the seats. It was bailed out, and a sail saved from the wreck was cut down to make a square sail. The steel luff wire made a fine painter, connecting the dinghy to the raft. A mast and rig were constructed from paddles and line. The dinghy was rigged to sail backwards, thereby reducing the chance of its being swamped by overtaking seas.

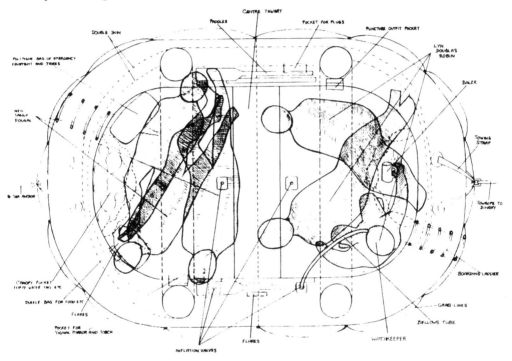

The usual disposition of bodies in the raft at night. Drawing by Pam Littlewood. From *Survive the Savage Sea* by Dougal Robertson © 1973, by permission of Granada Publishing

When the sail was hoisted, EDNAMAIR gave a great lurch and took off. The dinghy, sailing stern first, began to tow the heavy raft. The rig could only sail downwind. Both wind and current pushed this strange "tug and tow" to the NNW, first toward the equator, then into the doldrums, to find rain. After that, if there were an "after that," would be South America.

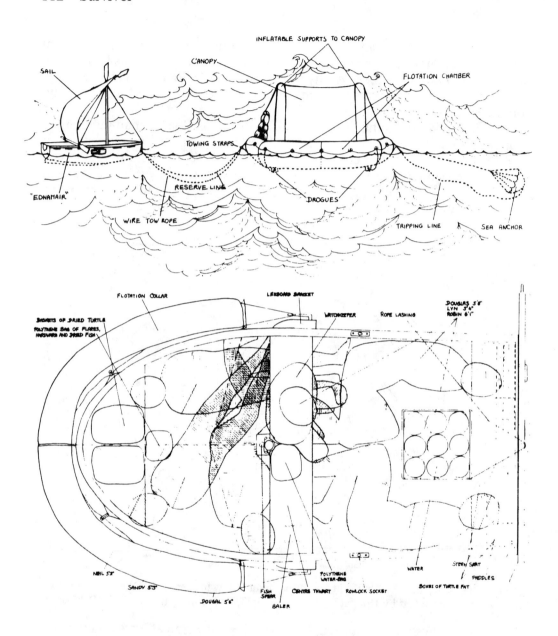

EDNAMIR towing the life raft (Top). The usual disposition of bodies in EDNAMIR.
(bottom). Art by Pam Littlewood. From *Survive the Savage Sea* by Dougal Robertson ©
1973, by permission of Grafton Books, a Division of Collins Publishing Group Ltd.

Sunrise of the third morning provided a pleasant surprise. During the night a small flying fish had hit the sail and fallen into the dinghy. It was marinated in lemon juice and eaten for breakfast, one mouthful for each person. The arrival of such tidbits from the sea did little to satisfy their raging appetites.

The patter of rain on the raft canopy was greeted with enthusiasm but the canopy was old and the run-off, which was a sickly yellow color and foul smelling, proved too badly contaminated to drink. Bad luck plagued the initial attempts at fishing. The first hook was bitten off, and when Dougal cast the spinner, it and the line sailed out of the raft and disappeared into the sea. He had forgotten to secure the line's loose end. Dougal made a lure from some foil and one of the three remaining hooks but an exhausting hour of casting around the raft yielded not a single bite.

To make matters worse, the raft was wearing out before their eyes. The air chambers needed reinflation two or three times per hour. The patch kit was useless because the glue had dried out and the few plugs supplied in the repair kit did not suffice. Various make-shift plugs were devised but the paper-thin fabric was clearly losing the race against chafe.

Just six pints of water, including the contaminated run-off were all that remained. Several flying fish and a dorado had fallen into the dinghy but fishing had proved fruitless. Luckily, a torrential rain shower replenished their meager supply and permitted everyone to drink their fill.

Between rain showers, they saw a ship. It passed less than three miles away but did not see them despite the use of two rockets and three hand flares. Only three hand flares remained. It was a grim reminder that many ships keep a poor watch in the untraveled areas of the sea, steering with their autopilot, relying on their radar alarm to warn of oncoming traffic.

One would think that the failed rescue would have caused the castaways to be miserably depressed, but just the opposite occurred. Having drunk their fill, the chronic depression and lethargy associated with dehydration had vanished. The group was flooded with a fierce determination to survive. Dougal decided:

> If those poor bloody seamen couldn't rescue us, then we would have to make it on our own and to hell with them. We would survive without them, yes, and that was the word from now on, "survival" not "rescue," or "help," or dependence of any kind, just survival. I felt the strength flooding through me, lifting me from the depression of disappointment to a state of almost cheerful abandon. I felt the bitter aggression of the predator fill my mind. This was not our environment and the beasts around us would eat us if we failed. We would carve a place for ourselves amongst them; they had millions of years of adaptation on their side, but we had brains and some tools. We would live for three months or six months from the sea if necessary and we would do it ourselves if there was no other way. (Pg. 68)

As though a capricious Neptune had decided to give them a break, a turtle became tangled in the sea anchor line. The huge beast was first secured by its hind flippers, then pulled to the dinghy. Hauling its eighty pound bulk into EDNAMAIR, thrashing and snapping, was no easy job. Once it was aboard, Dougal cut the beast's throat. The raft was becalmed, so fearing sharks, the blood and offal were left in the dinghy.

It took hours to dress out the big turtle with a small knife but the reward was more than 20 pounds of meat and *"a golden cascade of a hundred or so yellow egg yolks,"* Dougal said. The limp, raw, bloodstained flesh looked unappetizing but:

> Neil grinned and sank his teeth into a piece of steak. "Good" was all he said, and we all fell to with a will. We swallowed egg yolks, bursting them like yellow plums inside our mouths and allowing their creamy richness to permeate our taste buds, enjoying the flavor of raw food as only starving people can. (Pg 72)

Seven days of hardship had transformed this farmer and his family from "civilized folk" into a bunch of happy, blood covered savages, feasting on the kill. Their hunger and thirst momentarily sated, they were gripped by a fierce determination to survive. Turtle and dorado flesh festooned EDNAMAIR'S rigging, drying in the sun. The water tanks had been topped. The most pressing need was to repair the raft, which was going to pieces beneath them. Everything possible was used as a plug. Despite their best efforts the leaks increased, keeping someone constantly on watch with the bellows tube and a bailer. It was becoming increasingly obvious that the raft's days were numbered.

Their skin, constantly wet, soon became wrinkled and lumpy with infections. **Saltwater boils** plagued them. Sitting or lying on the boils was painful but it was impossible to stand because of the raft's motion. The constant bumps of the dorados against inflamed skin areas was pure agony. To add to his misery, Dougal had an incredibly sunburned behind, acquired while cleaning a turtle. He had to lay on his stomach because sitting was too painful to endure.

They steadily lost weight. Their diet of turtle and fish filled them, but it was deficient in fats and carbohydrates. The few remaining glucose tablets and fortified bread rations were reserved for the children and even then only for emergencies. The crew dreamed and talked about food, and even decided to open a restaurant when they reached land. It would be named *Dougal's Kitchen*. The menu was a constant source of discussion. Famished visions filled their minds of pasties containing meat or cheese, rich soups, salads, shish kebab, Stroganoff, shrimp curries, stews, porridge, steak and kidney puddings, of melons full of fresh fruit topped with ice cream then covered with a lemon sauce.

The crew of the LUCETTE became hollow-eyed sacks of skin and bones. The energy demanded by bailing and blowing up the flotation chambers exceeded their caloric intake. Their mouths became raw from using the bellows tube. The demands of the dying raft were killing them.

Their fifteenth day started out well, with a refreshing rain shower that added 3.5 gallons to their water supply. Shortly afterward, Douglas, who was on watch, cried out, *"Dad, the dinghy's gone!"* Both the stainless steel luff wire from the sail and the safety line securing the dinghy had broken. The dinghy, upon which their lives ultimately depended, was 60 yards from the raft, sailing away for all it was worth.

Dougal immediately dove in after it, painfully aware of the numerous sharks which surrounded the raft. Even sailing backwards, the dinghy could move faster than a man could swim. It seemed entirely possible that both Dougal and EDNAMAIR would disappear forever, leaving the others to their fate. Just when Dougal was ready to dispare, a wave made the dinghy yaw, and its sail collapsed. Dougal swam furiously, closing the distance to just 30 yards, then the dinghy yawed back and the sail refilled. Dougal later said:

> I felt no fatigue, no cramped muscles, my body felt like a machine as I thrashed my way through the sea only one thought now in mind, the dinghy or us. Then I was there; with a quick heave I flipped over the stern of the dinghy to safety, reached up and tore down the sail before my knees buckled and I lay across the thwart trembling and gasping for breath, my heart pounding like a hammer. (Pg 93)

As he recovered his strength, Dougal glanced into the sea to find the sharks circling just beneath him. He concluded that they must have already had breakfast. While repairing the dinghy tow lines, Lyn noticed that there was an accumulation of rainwater mixed with turtle blood in the bottom of the dinghy. It was undrinkable but could be consumed rectally, introduced by enema, with absorption through the intestinal membrane. A piece of rubber tubing from the raft ladder was combined with a funnel, and the crew had a hilarious time "drinking" in this fashion. They were each able to absorb 1 to 2 pints of water, more than their shrunken stomachs could have held.

They decided to abandon the raft on the 17th day. If their situation had been desperate before, the limited space and lesser stability of the dinghy made their survival even more tenuous. The raft was cut apart to make foul weather gear, a spray cover and a buoyancy bag to support the bow. Most of the raft disintegrated as they worked. The flotation chambers had become paper thin and tore at the slightest touch. The nine-foot dinghy, fully loaded with six persons and their gear would not have been considered safe in a swimming pool, let alone in the open sea.

Less than six inches of freeboard separated them from the ever-present sharks. One would think of this time as among the darkest of moments, yet the health and prospects of the group actually improved. Determined to eat the creatures that wanted to eat them, Dougal decided to "have himself a shark." They hooked and played a five-foot Mako, hauled it aboard, jammed a paddle into its mouth, then hacked it to death. The hunted had become the hunters.

A burst of creative activity produced a number of startling improvements. They learned how to render turtle oil from the fat by crushing and skimming it. The oil could be combined with undrinkable fresh water and used as an enema to relieve bowel congestion. It could be rubbed into raw skin and over sea ulcers, to promote healing. It could be used as oil spread on the water to calm rough seas.

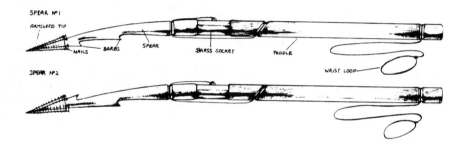

Gaffs improvised by the crew of the LUCETTE. From *Survive the Savage Sea* by Dougal Robertson © 1973, by permission of of Grafton Books, a Division of Collins Publishing.

A creation of even greater magnitude was the **jerk spear**, actually a gaff. Dougal lashed his last large hook to the broken end of a paddle and connected several lengths of heavy fish line to the hook's eye. He would then hang the spear in the water and wait until one of the smaller dorados swam by. With a sudden upward jerk, the fish was gaffed from beneath and simultaneously pulled into the dinghy. The jerk spear proved hugely successful. Soon the rigging of EDNAMAIR was full of drying fish steaks.   There was enough fresh liquid in the fish eyeballs and vertebrae to partially sustain them in times of drought.

Photo of LUCETTE survivors, looking remarkably fit, taken by TOKA MARU II crewman. From *Survive the Savage Sea* by Dougal Robertson © 1973

As the result abundant rain, fish and turtles, the health of the survivors began to improve. Since they were no longer sitting on the raft floor, the nagging skin ulcers and boils began to heal. Their bowls began to function. They had dried a considerable quantity of fish and turtle meat (a two week supply). Having sailed an incredible 800 miles in their tiny craft, the group began planning their landfall on the coast of Central America (300 miles away).

During the afternoon of the thirty-eighth day at sea, Dougal looked up to find a Japanese ship, the TOKA MARU II bearing down upon the dinghy. He stood on the thwart, aware that an error could still place them among the sharks and fired one of the two remaining hand flares. The ship immediately altered course, and soon the crew of the LUCETTE was safely aboard the TOKA MARU II. Unquestionably they could call themselves SURVIVORS in every way

ADRIFT By Steve Callahan

Of all the many desperate castaways described in this book, Steve Callahan was the best prepared for disaster. His self-built, 21-foot plywood sloop, NAPOLEON SOLO, smaller than most lifeboats, was fully equipped with survival gear, including a six man life raft, two survival packs, and a neoprene survival suit. Steve had read Dougal Robertson's *Sea Survival a Manual* and had a copy in his kit. This gave him a tremendous advantage in the "race to survive." The only small fault with his planning was that the equipment was not mixed together. If any of the packs failed to make it aboard the raft, all of that type of survival gear would be lost. Nevertheless, Steve Callahan planned to be a survivor in the event of a sinking and prepared accordingly. Unfortunately, the sea also had its plans.

Steve raced his tiny craft from Newport to Bermuda in the Spring of 1981, then sailed to England to begin a single-handed transatlantic race, the Mini-Transat. The contest began ominously. Two boats were lost and one man was killed while en route to England. In addition, it was the week of the autumn equinox, a time of gales. During the first leg of the race to La Coruna, Spain, one boat sank, two were hit by ships and one lost its rudder. NAPOLEON SOLO was nearly among those lost. Steve awoke during the night to find the boat taking on water and sinking after apparently hitting debris. A long crack in the hull, just under the deck, was the cause. Only quick repairs and luck saved the vessel. Considering what happened later in the voyage, some might call the near-disaster an omen.

Steve succeeded in making port, but the race was over for NAPOLEON SOLO. A month of repairs left him broke, with little choice but to head for the Caribbean in order to find a job. He sailed from Portugal to the Canary Islands where he made still more repairs. On January 29, 1982, NAPOLEON SOLO's anchor was stowed and her bow was pointed toward Antigua.

Since the time of Columbus, ships have sailed the friendly Trade Winds which are found south of the Canary Islands. NAPOLEON SOLO ran with the wind under twin jibs on a calm sea, sparkling with sunlight.   After a week of perfect sailing, the weather deteriorated into a gale. The night of February 4, 1981, while Steve was asleep, disaster struck, without warning.

"BANG! A deafening explosion blankets the subtler sounds of torn wood and rush of the sea. I jump up. Water thunders over me as if I've suddenly been thrown into the path of a rampaging river. Forward, aft—where does it come from? Is half the side gone? No time. I fumble with the knife I have sheathed by the chart table. Already the water is waist deep. The nose of the boat is slipping down, down! From *Adrift* (Pg. 21)

What had NAPOLEON SOLO hit? Or what hit the boat? Was it a whale, a cargo container, a floating log, some sort of man-made debris? Never mind! All that was important was SURVIVAL! His survival pack was secured next to him. It was only necessary to cut the lashings and heave it on deck. But a raging sea thundered into the bow compartment, forcing him to leap for his life, abandoning the precious package.

In seconds, NAPOLEON SOLO had been turned into a smashed wreck, ready for her final plunge. With Death hovering at his shoulder, Steve Callahan released and inflated his six-man Avon life raft. The boat had sunk to the point where sea began to suck hungrily at his legs as he struggled to release the raft. A cold, indifferent moon cast shadows on the wave-swept deck.

NAPOLEON SOLO seemed ready to make the final plunge at any moment, but as she rolled over in the heavy swell her bow came up, out of the water. Steve chose that moment to dive below and force the sodden, heavy survival pack up the companionway. A sleeping bag, a cushion, part of a sail, the boat's man-overboard pole and its line, some water and a few other items were also saved, but the bags which contained thirty days of food, clothes, ten gallons of water in jugs and his incredibly precious survival suit were in other areas of the boat, which had sunk below the surface and could not be reached.

Before Steve could return from the raft and dive for these supplies the painter line broke, separating the raft and the doomed NAPOLEON SOLO forever. His last sight of her was a sad one, with her starboard side under water, temporarily kept afloat by her waterproof compartments and the small amount of air trapped in the main salon.

Despite his excellent preparations, sheer bad luck had tossed Steve Callahan into the most desperate situation. He was suddenly alone in his tiny raft (which he named RUBBER DUCKY III, since it was his third inflatable), assaulted by the gale, with just three pounds of food and eight pints of water. He was 450 miles from the nearest shipping lane and an awesome 1,800 miles from the nearest possible landfall. He was isolated on a lonely sea, as hostile and relentless as any Sahara; his struggles, his courage and his desperation, witnessed only by nomadic birds and the fish who would eat him if he failed to survive.

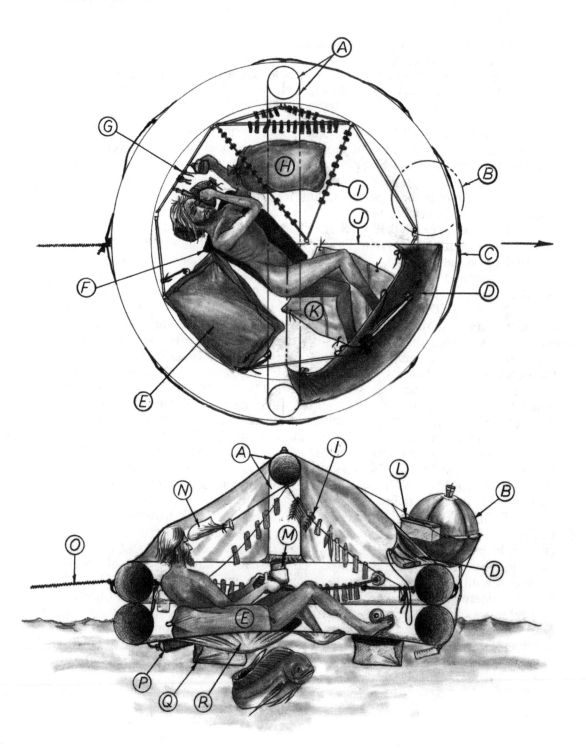

Face Page: Two views of *Rubber Ducky III*.   In the profile view I am shown grasping the air pump, which is plugged into one of the valves.   *Rubber Ducky III* has an upper and an arch tube inflation chamber and a bottom-tube chamber.   The wind is from the left in these views, pushing *Ducky* to the right. (A) *arch tube:* supports the canopy; (B) *solar still:* bridled in place.   The distillate drainage tube and bag hang down and under the raft; (C) *exterior handline:* runs all around the outside of the raft; (D) *spray skirt or bib:* across the entry opening, keeps some waves out and provides a shelf for spear gun; (E) *equipment bag:* salvaged from *Solo,* contains the bulk of gear; (F) *cushion:* made from two-inch thick closed-cell foam, which does not absorb water.   This helps to cushions blows from sharks and fish under the raft; (G) *interior handline:* serves as an anchor for all the equipment.   Fish are strung up between the anchor points.   In the plan view the arrow points to the water bottle, sheath knife, and short pieces of line, in position for instant access;   (H) *raft equipment bag:* supplied with the raft when purchased.   It contains standard equipment such as the air pump and it is secured to an anchor point on the floor.(I) *clothesline: to hang fish in the "butcher shop."*   Strung between the handline anchor points and up to the canopy arch tube; (J) *entry opening* (shown by the phantom line): kept on the forward right corner of the raft away from the wind and approaching waves; (K) *sailcloth;* salvaged from *Solo* , folded and tied.   Helps to cushion fish blows and to protect the raft from damage from the spear tip when fish are landed; (L) *Tupperware box:* wedged in the solar still bridle where it catches rain   Later on it will be positioned on the top of the canopy arch tube on its own bridle, and then inside under the leaky observation port; (M)   EPIRB (Emergency Position Locating Beacon) sends a signal on two frequencies monitored by commercial flights; (N) *observation port:* leaks badly and must be tied up since it is on the windward side.   Eventually a water collection cape will drain through this opening into the Tupperware container; (O) *painter to the man-overboard pole;* trails astern, and serves as a speedometer.   It also keeps the raft aligned properly and prevents capsize.   The pole increases my visibility.   The line gives a good surface for the growth of barnacles, on which I and the triggerfish feed; (P) *gas cylinder;* inflated *Rubber Ducky*.   Its vulnerable position is always a worry; (Q) *ballast pocket;* four pockets on the bottom fill with water to prevent capsizes; (R) *sagging floor;* typical where any weight pushes down.   Water pressure otherwise forces the floor to arch upward slightly.   The bumps pushing downward make good targets for fish, such as the dorado shown aiming for my left foot   From *Adrift* (pgs 34-5) by Steve Callahan, © by Steve Callahan, 1986, Reprinted by permission of Houghton Mifflin Co.

Having survived the storm-swept night in his cold, sodden, sleeping bag, dawn brought Steve his first glimmer of hope. He opened the raft survival pack and found:

6 pts. water with 2 lids	2 paddles
3 red hand flares	2 parachute flares
2 sponges	2 can openers
2 solar stills	2 smoke flares
1 medicine cup (broken)	1 rubber basin
1 first-aid kit	1 raft patch kit
1 heaving line, 1/8" x 100'	2 signal mirrors
2 charts, protractor, eraser, pencil	1 flashlight
1 fishing kit (a miserable one, as usual)	
1 radar reflector but no pole to mount it on.	

Steve's personal survival pack contained :

1 protractor	3 red meteor flares	wooden plugs
2 knives	10 oz. peanuts	sail twine
16 oz. baked beans	3 solar stills	hooks
10 oz. corned beef	1 EPIRB	codene
1 space blanket	2 pts water	plastic bags
10 oz. raisins (wet)	1 Very pistol	light line 3/16"
100 ft. heaving line 1/8"	1 short spear gun	wood cutting boards
100 ft. line 1/4"	1 white hand flare	assorted stainless shackles
2 orange smokes	3 red hand flares	
2 pintles, gudgeons	12 red parachute flares	

writing materials and *Sea Survival, a Manual* by D. Robertson

The only other food he was able to save were several cabbages. None of the water in jugs was saved, and the few pints in the life raft emergency pack were woefully inadequate for the difficulties which lay ahead.

Steve activated his EPIRB. Stories flashed through his mind of incredible rescues which occurred because of them. Unfortunately, NAPOL-EON SOLO had sunk in a particularly trackless part of the Atlantic, far from both shipping and aircraft lanes and the EPIRB-locating satellite system in use today had not yet been built. The radio ran until the 30-hour battery was exhausted—without bringing help.

The gale and the sudden loss of his boat made Steve acutely aware of exactly how uncomfortable a life raft can be. Even in a boat as small as NAPOLEON SOLO, you are protected from the elements when you go below during a gale. But his raft of just five and a half feet inside diameter with less than two feet of freeboard offered little more than the breath of life, an infinitely minute separation from every cruel thing the sea can do.

The thin floor of the raft jumped and rolled, a bizarre water bed assaulted by mad kangaroos, robbing him of any semblance of rest. The howling wind and crashing waves flung themselves unhindered through the madly flapping door, whose seal could not resist the gale. When he kneeled or sat the raft floor sagged, and cold seawater ran into those spots which he had to continuously bail. Occasional larger waves would fall upon the raft like cannon shots. They swamped the interior, making it into an inflated children's pool filled with numbing 65-degree water, which sucked away his strength.

During the three days of gale conditions, continuous saltwater immersion took its tole. Hundreds of saltwater boils erupted all over his body and the bruises incurred during the sinking became oozing, putrid sores. His psychological wounds were equally serious:

I may just reach the shipping lanes where I will have a remote chance of being spotted. Dehydration will take its toll by that time. My tongue will swell until it fills my mouth and then will blacken. My eyes will be sucked deeply into my head. Death will knock at the door to my delirious mind. Desperation shakes me. I want to cry, but I scold myself. Hold it back. Choke it down. You cannot afford the luxury of water wept away. (Pg 44)

Four days after the sinking, the gale began to abate. By dropping crumpled paper from his log book into the water and measuring the time it took to float past the man overboard pole, Steve calculated his progress to be just 17 miles per day, including drift. He pulled in the raft's sea anchor and increased his speed to 25-30 miles per day, estimating that his arrival at the nearest shipping lane would be in 22 days. The only question was, would the water last?

Deployment of the solar stills brought another crushing disappointment. The first one failed to hold air. The second one inflated but produced only saltwater. The third and last still had to be constantly attended, but at last began to produce a half-pint of salty semi-drinkable water per day. Hunger and thirst, the castaway's twin demons, had come to plague him.

Calm weather and a scorching sun did nothing to relieve his thirst, but did cause most of the saltwater boils to dry up and disappear. By the 11th day, schools of triggerfish appeared. Dorados and an occasional shark had come and gone, but attempts to spear them had failed. The life raft fishing kit, as usual, contained too few hooks, no steel leader, and ridiculously light line through which large fish could easily bite. In his desperation for food, Steve spent more and more time kneeling at the raft's door, speargun poised, waiting for a target.

Driven by hunger and obsessed by the tempting food supply just beyond his reach, Steve began to have hallucination-like daydreams about the fish:

> The dorados remain, beautiful and alluring. I ask one to marry me. But her parents will hear none of it. I am not colorful enough. Imagine, bigotry even here! However they also point out that I do not have a very bright future. It is a reasonable objection. (Pg. 56)

Constant thirst was an obsession. Rationed to a single medicine cup of water per day, with daytime temperatures of 80 degrees, hours, minutes, seconds were spent dreaming about the next precious sip.

Each day seemed to bring another defeat and cause for despair. On the eleventh day adrift, his remaining solar still was damaged by the waves and became inoperable. He took one of the non-functional units apart and discovered two problems. The still had to be fully inflated at all times to prevent the black inner bag containing saltwater from touching the balloon walls. In addition, rough seas caused saltwater to spray from the wick into the distillate compartment. Steve patched one of the defective stills, then floated it next to the raft. The unit still failed to produce fresh water. Finally, by securing it to the raft's canopy it was coaxed into life. Success! As the precious drops of distillate began to accumulate his hopes surged. The still was finally coaxed into producing up to 20 ounces per day. There was a chance to survive, after all!

SHARKS

One afternoon, a shark attacked the raft:

> A flat, gray, round-headed beast scrapes its hide across the bottom as it lazily swings around for another bite . . . . he slowly swims around to the stern and slides under. Rolling over, belly up, he bites one of the ballast pockets, quaking the raft with his convulsive ten foot torso . . . . should I take a shot and risk losing the spear? He cruises out in front of me just below the surface. I thrust, and the steel strikes his back. It is like hitting stone. With one quick stroke, he slithers away. (Pg. 59)

By rationing himself to a half-pint of water per day, Steve Callahan was able to slowly build up his drinking water reserve. But his attempts to catch fish were unsuccessful. Hunger constantly gnawed at his belly, and his body drained of fat reserves, began to waste away. The raft bottom, now covered with barnacles, was constantly nibbled by the schools of trigger fish that swam maddeningly just a few feet from his hand. He finally speared one on the 13th day.

> I yank the impaled fish aboard. Its tight round mouth belches a clicking croak. Its eyes roll wildly. The stiff, rough body can only flap its fins in protest. Food! Lowering my head I chant, "Food, I have food" . . . Powerful thrusts with my knife finally penetrate the trigger's armored skin. Its eyes flash, its fins frantically wave about, its throat cracks, and finally it is dead. My eyes fill with tears. I weep for my fish, for me, for the state of my desperation. Then I feed on the bitter meat. (Pg. 62)

Even for a starving man, a triggerfish is no feast. They are numerous because even sharks find them disgusting. Just a glance at the "fillet" of the creature makes one consider dining out. The skin, considering its thickness is tougher than rhino hide; the flesh is tough, stringy, and bitter, even the eyeball and backbone liquid is eminently disgusting. The only truly "palatable" parts of the creature are the organ meats and the eggs. The triggerfishe's main redeeming quality is that they hang around life rafts in great quantity. In other words, they're there.

The next day Steve had better luck. He speared his first dorado. It's hard to say who was more amazed. Steve hauled the violently struggling creature aboard, dividing his energy between killing the fish by severing its backbone and keeping the spear from ripping the raft. Steve had noticed that many of the dorados travel in pairs. The captured fish's mate now attacked the raft with unmitigated fury. He cut the 15 pounds of flesh into strips and hung them in the sun to dry. The head and bones were flung as far from the raft as possible, to avoid attracting the sharks.

A few nights later another shark attacked the raft with even greater determination:

> The raft is lifted and thrown to the side as if by a giant's boot. A shark's raking skin scrapes a squeak from it as I leap from slumber. . . . A fin breaks the water in a quick swirl of phosphorescent fire and darts behind the raft, circling to strike again. A flicker of light in the black sea shows me he is below and I jab with a splash. Nothing. Damn. The shark smashes into the raft with a rasping blow. I strike at the flicker. Hit! The water erupts, the dark fin shoots out and around and then is gone. Where is he? My heart's pounding breaks the silence. It beats across the still black waters to the stars. I wait. (Pg. 60)

But the shark did not return. Fortunately, it bit only the ballast bags of the raft, not the air chambers.

That night, February 18, the fourteenth day adrift, a small freighter passed four miles off. Steve fired several parachute shells and a hand flare. He was so sure the signals had been seen that he started packing his belongings in preparation for abandoning the raft. But the ship continued on its way, oblivious to his signals. Another passed even closer on February 21 during a flat calm, bright, sunny day, equally oblivious to his flare and smoke signal. Another passed on the 25th of February. Only two meteor, two smoke and two parachute flares remained from his originally ample supply.

The blazing sun and light wind baked him and started to destroy the raft. The canopy waterproofing began to flake away early in the voyage, contaminating the runoff from occasional squalls. The tiny flakes made the water taste like vomit but, unlike the crew of the LUCETTE, he had no way to give himself an enema using the disgusting liquid. His thirst was maddening. The beauty of the ocean, the shimmering, bioluminescent glow of the fish at night and the brilliant starry sky were apparent, but, according to Callahan, it was like "looking at Heaven from somewhere in Hell."

On February 22, Steve speared his second dorado. He ate the heart and liver, sucked the liquid from its eyes, ate the gelatinous material from between its vertebrae and cut his water ration to a half-pint per day from his reserve supply of 6.5 pints. The raft, his sleeping bag and all other gear became a mass of encrusted salt, that had been baked by the searing sun.

His mind became dazed, his body lethargic, a mass of withered flesh and torn scabs. His life revolved around repairing the raft, his solar stills, his equipment, and hunting for fish and dreaming in a near schizophrenic state about food and the comforts of the land. Hot sherried crab in flaky pie crusts bedded on rice pilaf with toasted almonds floated in his mind's eye. Thoughts about fresh muffins with melted butter, hot pies, brownies, chilly mounds of ice cream danced through his starved brain. Soft fabrics caressed his skin. The smell of food filled his nostrils, he dreamed of the sweet times in his life, which became more real than the hell which was in fact his reality.

The raft, the equipment and Steve Callahan's body deteriorated a little more each day. It took more and more effort to repair the damage, longer and longer to force his failing body, spinning head and brain to function. On the 26th day adrift, the strap on his spear gun failed. He turned the gun into a spear, lashing the extended shaft to the stock to increase its length. Hours were spent motionless, leaning over the side, poised and immobile, waiting for a fish to come within reach. The large, combative dorados became more and more difficult to spear, land, and subdue, as his body became increasingly emaciated. The lack of starches, sugars, and vitamins caused bodily deterioration which no amount of raw fish could arrest.

The searing heat and light winds gave way to a gale on the 30th day. The raft was assaulted again and again by huge waves, that filled it with freezing water which its exhausted occupant was too exhausted to remove. Two days later, the gale dropped sufficiently for him to catch his third triggerfish and fourth dorado, but damp weather prevented the dorado from drying, and it became inedible. A triggerfish bit a hole in one of the precious solar stills: six ounces of water, a half-day's ration—lost. A few days later the second still just fell apart and could not be repaired.

With one of the solar stills inoperative, the second damaged and rain run off contaminated by the deteriorating canopy water became a maddening imperative. Steve managed to repair the still and set up a Tupperware box to collect rain water.

On the 43ed day adrift, that which Steve Callahan feared the most finally occurred. A speared dorado, struggling to escape, not only damaged his spear but succeeded in driving the tip through the raft's lower inflation chamber, creating a horrendous, four-inch tear. With the lower tube gone, only three inches of freeboard remained. Even the smallest swells now flowed freely into the raft. Surviving with one buoyancy tube was a life of slow torture Steve later told me:

> It was like walking in rubber quicksand with my legs poking down to be bitten by fish (and sharks?); The raft dragged through the water, slowing progress to a standstill. The raft wobbled so badly it was impossible to fish and difficult to tend the [solar] still.

It was horrifyingly clear that unless the damage could be repaired, Steve Callahan would not last long. Nothing seemed to work. The plugs supplied with the raft were never designed to repair such a massive hole. A piece of closed-cell foam from a seat cushion inserted as a larger plug proved equally ineffective. All through the next day Steve frantically struggled to create a working patch. In addition, it was necessary to repair the spear in order to hunt for food. The remaining tube had to be pumped more frequently and the solar still had to be tended. The extra labor and the fight against panic made even further demands on his emaciated body.

Using a variety of materials, a somewhat effective patch was created. The lower tube remained inflated, but only if the raft were pumped forty times every hour, about 1,000 times a day. The extra labor pushed Steve to the limit of his endurance.

More bad luck plagued him. Another speared dorado neatly spiraled away, unscrewing the spear's tip. He replaced it with a knife blade, but the blade frequently bent, allowing fish to escape. He took it apart and lashed two knives in place, making a more effective tip. The knives represented the last pieces of metal he had with which to make spear repairs.

Self portrait of the author. From *Adrift* by Steve Callahan © 1986, reprinted by permission of Houghton Mifflin Co.

Because of the constant demands made on his energy by the leaking patch, it was not always possible to keep the tubes properly inflated. Day and night it was necessary to labor at the pump. Small waves that washed aboard kept the raft constantly wet, and collapsed it around the weary survivor's feet, making it difficult to move. Robbed of sleep, a slave to the pump, Steve Callahan's body continued to deteriorate.

The plug failed a few days later. It was repaired and failed again. Steve repaired it again. Once more it failed. Death seemed near:

An immense energy pulls at my mind, as if imploding within my body. A dark pit widens, surrounding me. I'm frightened, so frightened. My eyes well with tears, pulling me away from the emptiness. Sobbing with rage, pity, and self-pity, clawing at the slope, struggling to crawl out, losing grip, slipping deeper. Hysterical wailing, laments, lost hope. I scrape to catch hold of something, but nothing is there. Darkness widening, all around me, millions of faces, whispering, crowding in, calling "Come, it's time." (Pg 149)

At the height of his despair, realizing death from exhaustion was imminent, Steve suddenly conceived a brilliant plan to make a patch by using a fork and light line. With his body at the edge of physical collapse, it took a half day to do what a healthy person could have accomplished in an hour but, in the end, SUCCESS. A glorious 12 hours passed before it was necessary to labor at the pump.

The ordeal left its mark. It was not possible for Steve Callahan to recover from the strain. Ten days after the damage occurred he still felt like he had been "hit by a locomotive." His strength was at a new low, without reserves to cope with another disaster. Emotionally exhausted, the smallest difficulty sent him into rage or depression. His body was hardly able to follow his mind's commands. He could barely lift his sodden sleeping bag onto the arch tube in an attempt to dry it. The deteriorating solar still required constant repair. It needed hourly attention to function, and deflated every night.

On the 58th day adrift, one of the blades used as a spear point broke off. The remaining butter knife blade remained. Steve's lifeboat navigation placed him about 450 miles from Antigua, with a forward drift of 17-25 knots per day. The wind and current had assumed a more NW'ly direction and. If the raft were forced above 18°N it would take much longer to reach land for the Caribbean chain begins to run more east-west at that point.

One day the raft apparently drifted into an eddy littered with trash and Sargassum weed. It provided a variety of food in the form of barnacles clinging to the trash, and small edible organisms which lived in the weed. New birds and fish appeared. Three birds landed on the raft arch tube and were immediately seized and devoured. The water became lighter and more sparkling. Steve was convinced he had reached the edge of the continental shelf. A jet passed overhead and Steve instantly turned on his EPIRB, but no help came from the sky.

On April 17th another freighter did not respond to an orange smoke signal. But the ship passed a few miles away, heading west. Land MUST be nearby! Rather than succumb to depression, Steve spent the day rigging a new water collector.

On his 75th night adrift, Steve Callahan sighted land. LAND! A distant lighthouse cast its loom from beyond the horizon, indicating that the end of the ordeal was in sight. A celebration! He immediately consumed two pints of water, more delicious than the finest champagne. By the next day, the overwhelming panorama of green islands, spread more lushly than any artist's dream greeted Steve's weary eye. A flat-topped island, directly in the raft's path lay 5 to10 miles away.

Aware of the dangers involved in making a landfall, Steve began making mental preparations for the dangerous moments ahead when the virtually unnavigable raft would have to land through surf. He planned to cut away the canopy and use the material as a sort of protection against being cut.

The sound of a boat engine interrupted Steve's plans for a beach landing. A small, roughly made 20 foot native fishing craft roared up. Steve waved to them. They waved back. This lucky SURVIVOR had found himself a boat.

Ironically, Steve Callahan's ordeal was not quite over. The fishermen wanted to fish for the numerous dorados which had accompanied the raft for thousands of miles. Steve encouraged them:

> . . . I'm O.K. I have plenty of water. I can wait. You fish. Fish! Plenty of fish, best fish in the sea!   Plenty of fish here, you must fish! (Pg 211)

They gave him an incredibly delicious piece of raw coconut-covered with sugar to eat while they fished. The fishermen roared around, catching the dorados that had followed the raft for thousands of miles. Shortly thereafter our lucky, lucky SURVIVOR was taken to the tiny island of Marie Galante, near Guadeloupe.

Staying Alive/117 Days Adrift
By Maurice and Maralyn Bailey

Maurice and Maralyn Bailey probably hold the endurance record for pig-headed cussedness, refusing to die in a life raft. When it comes to making long passages in small boats, there is no combination quite like two people who love each other. The same elements of love and devotion make survival in a life raft a greater likelihood. The Bailey's worked together and survived to sail again. Their second book, *Second Chance* (1977), describes the fulfillment of the dreams they shared while adrift in their life raft. Their 31-foot sloop, AURALYN, was struck by a wounded sperm whale on March 4th, l973, while the couple were enroute to the Galapagos Islands. The Baileys believe the whale had been wounded by a whaling ship which they saw working with lights during the night. They theorized that the wounded, enraged beast either followed them or encountered them by chance at dawn and took revenge upon the boat.

AURALYN did not sink immediately after the accident. An attempt was made to save her by lowering a sail over the side to block the hole. This method, called "foundering a sail," was used in the Age of Sail with mixed

Yt. AURALYN sinking in the South Pacific. From *Staying Alive* By Maurice and Maralyn Bailey © 1974, by permission of A. & C. Black (Publishers) , Ltd.

success. Old ships had more rounded hulls than those of modern boats, and the rounded bottom made it more likely that the sail would be sucked into the hole. It was rare, even long ago for a vessel to be saved by foundering a sail, and a twin-keeler like AURALYN, was particularly unsuited for this procedure.

When the sail didn't work, blankets were jammed into the 12-by 18-inch opening, but the water continued to rise. Perhaps other, unseen damage had been sustained. It is certainly possible to second-guess the situation and speculate on whether the damage could have been repaired under water, although the underwater design of AURALYN (twin bilge keels) made such repairs particularly difficult. Maurice Bailey later speculated that no matter what happened, the boat was doomed.

The AURALYN took almost an hour to sink. Sunshine and flat seas made the task of abandoning ship easier. The Baileys had a four-man life raft whose inside 4.5 feet in diameter and a 9-foot inflatable dinghy. They had an emergency kit and two sail bags of food and gear, that were salvaged from the wreck before it sank. All of the boat's water containers were transferred to the raft before it went down.

Because of their hour's grace period, the Baileys were almost as fully equipped for a life raft adventure as one can be. On the other hand, few boats, let alone a life raft, are prepared for a 117-day voyage adrift. The gear which was saved included:

1	box matches	1	flashlight
1	camera	1	mallet
1	Tilly lamp	1	scissors
1	waste basket	1	binoculars
2	bowls, plates mugs	2	sail bags
2	sets utensils	1	box glucose tablets
2	buckets	2	sets foul weather gear
2	compasses	2	books
2	cushions	2	towels
2	diaries	1	knife/marline spike
2	dictionaries	1	Camp Gaz stove
2	saucepans	1	bag clothes
1	gal. kerosene	2	toothbrushes
1	gal. alcohol	2	canteen-type plastic bottles
1	penknife	1	first-aid kit
1	sextant, watch, tables, log		clothes hangers
6	flares		water (unknown amount)
1	felt-tip pen		toothpaste, soap, comb

In their haste, they failed to take fishing equipment, having forgotten to repack it with the survival gear in Panama. It was easy to appreciate the magnitude of this omission—later on.

But in other ways, they were rich. Their food consisted of approximately 22 tins, a bag or 2 of nuts and dates, a bottle of vitamins, plus 4 packs of biscuits and one cake. They estimated sufficient supplies for 20 days.

The ship went down 300 miles east of the Galapagos Islands in the doldrums, ninety miles north of the equator—an area of light, variable winds perfectly designed to take a weary survivor nowhere very slowly. AURALYN sank near a shipping lane, so the Bailey's had hope that they would soon be rescued. But no ship passed, and it soon became apparent that the raft would drift to the north of Culpepper Island, the most northwesterly of the Galapagos group.

Realizing how important it was to reach land, Maurice Bailey decided they must row ten miles south every night, in order to neutralize the northern component of their drift. Their goal was San Cristobal Island. Unfortunately a rubber dinghy does not row well and a rubber dinghy towing a life raft rows hardly at all. They labored to exhaustion with blistered hands for three nights, eight hours per night, in two-hour shifts but made only ten miles of southing.

Even doubling their water consumption of a pint per day did not compensate for what was lost during their labors. At the end of the fourth night, it became obvious that no matter how hard they rowed, they would still pass to the north of Culpepper Island. The currents in the area would never take them to land but would lead them instead on a drunken, deadly dance to the northwest, into the trackless sea. Their only hope was to find a ship.

Their eighth day in the raft was a gloomy one. A ship passed, did not see them, and they wasted three of their six flares attempting to attract its attention. There had been no rain. It would soon be necessary to cut their water ration in half. They were assailed by a blazing sun hot as liquid iron in a shimmering sky, with a second, reflected sun, to further sear the eyes.

Almost immediately after the sinking, the raft was visited by amorous turtles so intent on mating with the raft that even beating them off with a paddle proved ineffective. Turtles are famous for being determined lovers. In Jamaica they sometimes dry the beast's penis, and boil bits of it in tea as a love potion. The turtles which the Bailey's encountered bumped the raft bottom hard enough to bruise its occupants. Afraid the huge beasts would damage the float chambers, the Baileys finally solved the problem by permanent *coitus interuptus*, catching and eating the suitors.

Turtle meat is tender and delicious, but getting at it is no easy task. Maurice realized that the marine turtle's head does not retract completely into the shell, so he first stunned the beast by beating its head with a paddle. The thick, rubbery skin proved to be a new dimension in toughness. The knife supplied with the raft was incapable of cutting cold cheese. The sheath knife salvaged from the wreck was dull but they sharpened it by honing it on the leather sheath. Then they started hacking away. The poor beast suddenly regained consciousness before it could be dispatched. They finally succeeded in killing the flailing animal by hacking through a vein in the throat. Maralyn performed the gristly job while Maurice held the head.

Turtle blood, considered quite delicious by other castaways, is initially not very inviting stuff. The Baileys dumped it over the side the first time and were amazed to see hoards of scavenger fish rush to devour the coagulating droplets. Seeing this huge food source literally beneath their feet Maralyn remembered that the first-aid kit contained safety pins. She fashioned several fish hooks from them, perfectly designed for the triggerfishe's tiny mouths.

The tiny hooks proved remarkably effective. The turtle meat itself made poor bait as it was soft and easily torn from the hook. But a bit of membrane from the intestines worked well. Once the fish started taking the bait, the ravenous beasts were induced into a feeding frenzy. It was no longer necessary to use bait. The hook alone sufficed.

The majority of the catch was triggerfish. These ugly, purple-grey, disgusting creatures are never served in the better restaurants. They taste even less delicious, if possible, when eaten raw. Triggers range in size from six inches to a foot, have skin tougher than leather and are equipped with two dorsal and one ventral spine that locks into place. A typical trigger weighs less than a ten pound although a really big one may weigh as much as 10 pounds. The spines are sharp and covered with a mucus which causes pain and infection if they pierce the skin. These fish don't take well to being caught and, for a fish with a small mouth, they have a mean bite.

Triggers are normally considered reef fish and, when taken on a Pacific reef, are often poisonous. The fish contain a powerful chemical agent called tetrodotoxin which raises havoc with the human body. If the poison does not kill within 24 hours, one is sick and weak for weeks. Yet triggers have often been all that sustained many a castaway. The Baileys estimated that they ate more than 1,000 of them before being rescued, and caught up to 100 triggers per day. Fortunately the pelagic (deep water) variety do not seem to be poisonous. If they were, this anthology would be much shorter.

Triggerfish and turtles became the Bailey's main food source. They ate the fillets, livers, roe, milt, and heart. The eyeballs were sucked for the liquid they contained. Scraps were always saved to be used as bait.

Boredom is a real problem when you have nothing to do for, say, four months except eat raw fish and drift across an empty sea. The Baileys were fortunate that they had books, which they read aloud to each other, and a diary in which they made daily notes. They also used the diary to make paper dominos and a pack of playing cards. When they got tired of paper games, they played word games, made drawings of AURALYN— and the new boat they were going to build when they reached the land.

It seems difficult in this age of black leather and lace panties to think of a life raft as a sex object, but a raft seems to have a magnetic attraction for a variety of sea creatures. It is a well-known fact that whales have tried to force their amorous attentions on sailboat hulls, to the distress of all aboard. One could argue that there is a similarity between a boat's shape and that of a whale. Perhaps the leviathans involved were young and inexperienced. But a raft??

On their 10th day adrift, a huge sperm whale surfaced near the raft and spent more than 10 minutes trying to elicit a friendly response. Was this just curiosity or romance? Having never seen a sperm whale engaged in *flagrante delicto,* the extent of its capabilities must remain speculative, but I once saw a dead whale on the beach that had a relaxed organ more than 10-feet long.

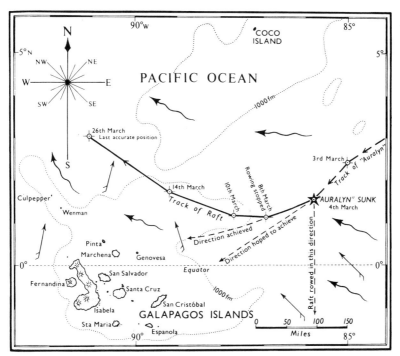

Detail map of the Galapagos area showing the position of the sinking and the track of the raft in the few days thereafter. Feathered arrows show prevailing winds. Wavy arrows show currents. From *Staying Alive /117 Days Adrift,* by Maurice and Maralyn Bailey © 1977, by permission of A. & C. Black (Publishers), London.

Despite their inactivity and a supply of fish, turtle meat, and tinned food, the Baileys became locked in a losing race with starvation. Within three weeks they were gaunt and emaciated. A chronic lack of water certainly contributed to this problem. Because of their low fat, water and carbohydrate diet, the bruises they incurred while abandoning ship refused to heal. Their bodies were chafed raw from contact with the raft material, but the raft floor did not leak, and they were not plagued by boils or saltwater sores as were other survivors.

Starvation proved a great stimulus for turtle catching and consumption. They ate the flesh, drank the blood (which proved better than anticipated), consumed the heart, liver and kidneys with a Bolognaise sauce (while it lasted) but rejected the membranes. They particularly treasured the greenish fat, an indication of the fat shortage in their diet. As they became weaker, hauling the huge beasts aboard became an ever more difficult task.

On their 25th night at sea a ship passed but did not see their flare or an SOS message, signaled with the flashlight. To add to their bad luck, a hand flare failed. On the plus side, the weather turned rainy and for two weeks there was more water than they could drink or store. Turtles were numerous, so they ate only the smaller ones. On a whim they caught a huge male and tied him by his rear flippers to the raft. To their astonishment the beast started towing the raft with considerable speed toward the Galapagos Islands. Reasoning that additional turtle power was what they needed, they caught another male and added him to the team. Unfortunately, this turtle was not a team player. He took off in the other direction.

On April 10th, their 37th day adrift, a third ship passed them less than a half mile away during the night. They had no flares and waved their foul weather jackets to no avail. Determined to improve their chances of being seen in the future, Maurice made three hand flares by wrapping cloth strips around an opened hanger. The plan was to dip them in kerosene and touch them off with an alcohol primer. A smoke signal was made out of a cake tin into which had been placed paper and strips of cloth.

Two days later, when yet another ship (the fourth) heading south ran towards them on a choppy, windy sea, the smoke flare was set up in a turtle shell and touched off, but the wind whipped the smoke away. It appeared as though the ship did see them, for it stopped and turned in a number of directions, then sat motionless in the water. Finally, it continued to the south and was soon out of sight.

Rough weather plagued and exhausted the pair during the middle part of April and a fifth ship passed them at midnight on April 18, their forty-fifth day at sea. The flares they had made from cloth strips failed to ignite and their flashlight batteries were almost dead. When they examined the kerosene fuel used on the torch it was discovered that it had become badly contaminated with water. The flares were useless.

Despite their desperate position, the Baileys spent much of their time dreaming about the exciting places they would visit in their new boat. It was certainly clear that they had the mentality of survivors! Not only did they design their future vessel, they eventually did realize their dream—to sail the coast of Patagonia.

On April 28, their 55th day at sea, the two castaways awoke to find the lower tube of the raft deflated. Perhaps a fish had punctured it with its dorsal spines. Their attempts to glue a patch over the holes failed, and there were apparently no plugs in their patch kit. The loss of the lower tube made life immeasurably more difficult. It lowered the raft's freeboard, allowing even small waves to splash inside. The surviving tube had to be pumped every 20 minutes. If it became soft the raft slowly collapsed, enveloping them. The constant pumping exhausted them, and their health began to decline. The loss of the lower tube increased their discomfort and made it more difficult to sleep. Their skin, already chafed raw from constant contact with the raft, now began to develop saltwater ulcerations that would not heal. They began to discuss their deaths with weary resignation.

Even though the Baileys were eating up to 40 triggerfish per day, plus turtles and occasional milkfish, weight loss continued to plague them. Their once-healthy bodies became emaciated, and their muscles slack and wasted. They moved painfully, because of aching joints. By the end of the adventure they had both lost about 40 pounds. Women have a bit more fat on their bodies than men, and therefore are slightly more resistant to starvation. Maralyn, correspondingly, remained stronger than Maurice.

Sickness plagued them during the month of May. Their drinking water had become a slimy green color and made them ill. They had no choice but to drink it and the resulting dysentery plagued them intermittently for weeks. To their horror, they finally realized that all but two gallons were undrinkable and had to be discarded. A piece of fish left uneaten overnight went bad and made them ill. Maurice slowly developed an apparent case of pleurisy, with a dry, hacking cough, chest pains and pains in his limbs. He became feverish, slept constantly and had trouble moving because of pain. He lost his appetite, and eating became an ordeal. He was unable to help Maralyn fish or clean turtles. There was no medicine in their first-aid kit for pleurisy. Fortunately, Maurice slowly recovered. Another ship passed them 1.5 miles away but did not stop. The canopy of the life raft deteriorated and leaked. Despite the constant fish and turtle supply, the wretched pair were obsessed by thoughts of food. Their tinned food reserve dwindled away

On May 30, a pack of sharks appeared and began to strike the underside of the raft. They had been visited by sharks almost daily, but the beasts swam contentedly among the shoal of fish that hovered near the raft and showed no interest in the turtle blood or jettisoned offal. In a pack, the sharks' mentality seemed to change. They charged the raft again and again, bumping the bottom with great force (but not attempting to bite it), bruising the occupants' ulcerated bodies, making them cry out in pain. There was no way to drive them off. The attacks continued for days, and were repeated throughout the rest of the ordeal, causing severe bruises that healed slowly.

June in the doldrums is the rainy season and it poured buckets almost every day. The fresh water even made it possible to wash, but the abundance of fresh water increased their raving hunger. When it rained, or the seas kicked up, they had to bail, immersed in water up to their thighs, the deteriorated canopy admitted rain like a fast mist. During bad weather, waves would overturn the dinghy. The supplies lashed to the overturned craft were heavy, and righting the nine-foot craft exhausted them.

On June 10th, their 98th day adrift, a blue-footed booby landed on the raft. Sea birds eat tremendous amounts of fish, in order to fuel their high metabolisms—and create tremendous amounts of shit. Annoyed by the load being deposited in their dinghy, Maurice gave the bird a wack with a paddle to drive it off. With a surprised squawk, the booby plopped into the water and regurgitated four whole flying fish before flying off—a fine supplement to the Baileys' supper.

Since they had been able to catch a constant supply of fish, the Baileys drove off the birds which landed on the raft. On their 100th day at sea they decided to start eating them. The foolish creatures showed absolutely no fear and were easy to grab. The birds' flesh was sweet and a pleasant change from the constant diet of fish. Unlike Alain Bombard, they had no complaints about the fishy taste. In addition, the wing tips, when dipped in the water, were attacked by the voracious triggerfish which held on tenaciously, even when the wing was removed from the water. Three or four fish at a time could be caught this way.

A week of bad weather left the castaways with neither food nor bait. Maralyn spotted a small shark swimming around the raft, and she impulsively grabbed it by the tail. Maurice, aroused from sleep, quickly wrapped the head in a towel, then killed the beast. In a matter of minutes they had landed two more. Shark meat, high in urea, should not be eaten when water is scarce, but water was plentiful at that time. While they were cleaning the sharks, a blue-footed booby landed on the dinghy just two feet away. It was an easy matter to reach out and wring its neck. Before the feathers had settled, another bird landed in the same spot and was similarly dispatched. A few minutes later a white booby started diving for fish near the raft. When it surfaced nearby, Maralyn reached out and grabbed its wing. Instead of starving that day, they had a feast, eating shark liver and 1 1/2 birds apiece.

The Bailey fish trap, a successful design borne of desperation. Drawing by Rafael Monroy

Toward the end of June, turtles became so numerous it was necessary to drive them off by beating on their heads with a paddle. The supply of safety pin fish hooks dwindled, but Maralyn invented the "Bailey fish-trap". It consisted of the one-gallon kerosene container with one side removed. A baited line was run through the spout hole and out through the missing side. When this was lowered into the water, the triggerfish were suspicious at first, but their greed overcame all caution. They lunged for the bait, which was then slowly drawn into the container. When the fish entered, the trap was lifted from the water. During calm weather, it was easy for the Baileys to catch their fill, without risking their last hook.

On June 30, their 118th day at sea, a small, white, very rusty Korean fishing boat , WEOLMI 306 approached, from the west. It was the first boat they had seen in 43 days. At first, having become so aclimated to their enviornment, they thought to "let it pass," but finally, they waved their jackets

A seaman from the WEOLMI holds the ladder while Maralyn prepares to climb aboard. Even though emaciated from her ordeal, Maralyn Bailey is still strong enough to climb by herself, after 117 days adrift. Photo from *Staying Alive !117 Days Adrift*.

mechanically, without hope, and the ship passed by. Then, in disbelief they watched as the ship stopped, turned around and pulled along side. *"We've made it!"* Maurice said. *"Now for AURALYN II—and Patagonia!"* Maralyn replied.

Rule No.1: Never Abandon Ship 'til the Ship Abandons You

This rule is rule No.1 because it is the most important rule. More than one survivor has made it to shore, after having nearly croaked in a life raft, only to find his boat either lying high and dry on the beach or tied up at some customs dock. Several Fastnet sailors had this happen to them. Merely abandoning ship, particularly in bad weather, is extremely dangerous, and people have been lost jumping from the doomed vessel to a survival craft. In addition, a survival craft is less comfortable and poorly equipped, compared to even a damaged boat which is still afloat. A damaged boat is more visible to other vessels than a tiny life raft and, while awaiting rescue, it is possible that emergency repairs can be made.

Lucine Schlitz, twenty-five year-old captain of the NJORD, would very likely be a strong supporter of Rule No. 1. Lucien was not an extremely experienced sailor when he bought the NJORD, and his girlfriend, 19-year-old Catherine Plessz, had no sailing experience at all. But after all, how does one gain experience if one doesn't take the risk, head for the blue water, and become experienced? It's called "paying your dues." Unfortunately the sea has no mercy for the young or the inexperienced. Their story of near doom is chillingly told in *Rage to Survive*.

Rage to Survive By Jaques Vignes

Sailors often call the Mediterranean sea "The Lake" because it looks rather small on a chart when compared to the Atlantic ocean. But the Med can be a killer lake, and its relatively small size can create a false sense of security. Bad weather comes up suddenly and creates short, viscous seas in just a few hours. The Gulf of Lyons is particularly bad that way. Cold air moving south through central Europe becomes trapped by the Pyrenees and the Alps, like water in a bowl. When the bowl is filled, the cold air spills over the mountains and flows into the Gulf of Lyons in violent gusts, creating very sudden clear-weather gales (or storms) called mistrals or tramontanes. The wind veers back and forth as it roars down the mountain passes creating some marvelous cross seas to increase the sailor's delight.

The NJORD, a 26-foot, steel-hulled Colin Archer double-ender, was well built and rigged for long-distance cruising. Like every Colin Archer she was round-bilged with a long keel and had a tendency to roll. She displaced seven tons, a weight more typical of a larger boat. One could say that she was strongly built or one could say that she was overbuilt. Colin Archer originally designed this type of boat as a sail-driven rescue craft and she was, in theory, capable of taking whatever the Med could dish out. But the NJORD was also an old boat and this has many implications.

Many inexperienced sailors, particularly men, see an old boat and fall in love with her. I say "particularly men" because it is the unfortunate short-coming of the human male to fall in love at first sight, based purely on physical beauty. Some say that a boat is like a woman, but this is not so. If a man gives a woman all his time and all his love and all his money, it is possible that the woman will continue to love him if he runs out of money. A boat will abandon him immediately.

In addition to the charm of old boats, they often further tempt one by virtue of their price. There is invariably a reason why a bargain boat is a bargain, and a bargain isn't really a bargain if the bargain wants to kill you. Colin Archers go cheap because no one wants them, and in this case, all those no ones are sending a message. Experienced sailors know that old boats, no matter how beautiful, are past their prime and often belong in museums. If one wants a boat from the "Age of Sail", it is perhaps better to buy a new one built from old plans rather than to attempt a restoration. In the end the restoration always costs considerably more than originally estimated, and even then, there is no guarantee that the boat is fit for the blue water.

What all this implies is that, like a lover, an old boat reveals its beauty immediately but its faults later, a little bit at a time. A great deal of time and effort and money may correct these faults, or it may not. In the case of the NJORD, her owner gave her all the time and effort any boat could ask for. But he did not have all the money the NJORD needed. He did not have the cash for new sails and the old ones—particularly the storm sails, failed when he needed them most. NJORD needed a new life raft but got instead an old one. Last, but not least, the hull of the NJORD might have been strong but her wooden rudder was old and weak.

The NJORD departed Beaulieu, Southern France on September 13, 1972, bound for Spain's Balearic Islands. After a day and a night of light winds, while still within view of the coast, the mistral came to get them. The storm came from the land, and with a heavy boat and an inoperative outboard engine, there was no going back—the NJORD could not beat against the gale. By 2 a.m. the NJORD was running to the SW under bare poles, rolling heavily. Later in the day they had had enough. The captain rigged a sea anchor and lay the boat to it, stern first with about 60 yards of line. That old rudder did not like being exposed to those seas and had quite a bit to say about it later on.

Sea anchors often function better in theory than in fact. Each boat lies to a sea anchor differently. Boats with mizzen sails can set them to help hold the stern downwind, but single-masted boats do not like to cooperate with a sea anchor. Wind pressure on the mast pushes the bow off. The boat wallows rather than rides. The NJORD did not lie stern to the wind but at a considerable angle, and this made her roll. The cold mistral had created vicious cross seas which the heavy, round-bilged boat disliked. The waves crashing against a steel hull are always noisy and become quite deafening during a storm. It's extremely demoralizing, particularly if you are not used to it. At 5:30 p.m. the boat was knocked on its beam ends and, in the classic manner, every single item in the boat went flying through the air, including the terrified crew who were lying below.

By 7 p.m., the boat was running under bare poles once more, but the seas continued to rise and eventually, a huge wave swept the boat. The crew were not wearing safety harnesses, there were no life lines around the cockpit and the two were instantly swept into the sea. They somehow managed to drag themselves back aboard, only to find a horrible sight. The rudder was smashed, the entire contents of the boat below decks was washing back and forth in several feet of water and the boat was drifting sideways through the storm under completely bare poles—the seas had even stripped away the furled storm sails.

At this point, the exhausted and terrified crew of the NJORD violated Rule No. 1. The NJORD was damaged, but the steel hull was intact. A knock-down or two does not a sinking make. The boat had water inside but that is why God created bilge pumps—and buckets. Colin Archer did not design boats that sink in mistrals. The NJORD did not in fact sink. She was found adrift weeks later and taken in tow.

The crew had a secondhand life raft. It was British and, being British, was therefore suspect in France and for sale at a bargain price. Remember bargains? None of the French chandleries sold or serviced it. Only God knew when it was last inspected, if ever. Lucien was absolutely sure it would not inflate. He set the container on deck and pulled the lanyard. The raft immediately inflated and just as immediately did its level best to take off like a bird into the gale.

Now they were faced with another question. Where does one put an inflated life raft on a 26-foot boat? There is only one answer—in the water. But as soon as the raft hit the water, it wanted to do what all rafts want to do when attached to a boat—it wanted to be detached. There is no way a raft in a gale will form a lasting relationship with a boat, and after all, a life raft and a boat are specifically designed to be divorced.

From this point on, there was great psychological pressure to enter the raft. Fear and fatigue had taken their toll and the time for cold logic had passed. So things happened very fast. Lucien gathered some supplies, while Catherine struggled to hold the tether, not an easy job. Lucien found some tinned food, the distress signals, two five-gallon jugs of water, a compass and their documents. The water jugs were full, lacking both float lines (an air pocket) and safety lanyards. These items were tossed into the raft but not secured and this would have disastrous consequences later on. A few moments later they were in the raft. Catherine said, *"As soon as we were in [the raft] I felt safe."* She wasn't. They wanted to stay attached to the boat, but the raft did not, and in a few moments, the mooring ring ripped out, separating them forever from the NJORD.

The castaways were just about as in the middle of nowhere as one can get in the Gulf of Lyons. They were about a hundred miles from Spain, France, and the Balearic Islands, the closest landfalls. If the wind held steady for any length of time, they would undoubtedly have been blown somewhere. But the wind in the Gulf of Lyons is variable. Their only real hope was to find a ship. One would think that in a "lake," especially so close to France, Spain, and the Balearic Islands, one would certainly find a ship. The following days of hardship and near-death are a reminder of how hard ship-catching can be.

Their first concerns were a great deal more immediate than finding a ship. The raft was deflating. The arch tube and the upper doughnut were becoming soft. They found the non-functioning interior light on top of the arch and, mistaking it for an inflation orifice, they spent a great deal of time trying to inflate the raft through the socket. It may seem amusing in print but, if you are sinking in the night in the middle of the Lake in a mistral, it is considerably less than amusing.

The sheer terror of the situation must really be experienced to be fully appreciated. The roaring night had enveloped them like a tomb. A bitter wind howled and boomed around their flimsy tent and the breakers stalked them like deadly beasts. Huge breaking waves bore down with the noise of berserk locomotives and fell upon the raft, completely submerging it or flinging it high onto the crests, to hurtle with sickening uncertainty into the bottomless troughs. The monstrosity went on and on and on. Every sound, every motion implied death, to be sucked into the blackness, to struggle and fail, to drown and sink down into the endless depths.

Shortly thereafter a huge wave caught the raft and caused it to capsize. In the darkness they had not found the sea anchor. Had it been deployed the chance of capsizing would have been highly reduced. Fortunately Lucien was near the door and was able to pull it open, permitting the two to escape. The water was quite warm and they were able to climb onto the raft's bottom. They apparently did not notice the righting handle at the center of the raft's bottom, but by waiting for a wave to tilt the raft, they were able to right it by standing on the life line and pulling on the ballast pockets.

The capsizing had virtually emptied the provisions from the raft. All that remained were:

1	air pump	1	tin corned beef
1	signal rocket	1	jug with 2 gallons of water
3	hand flares	1	document and money pouch

One jug of water had been completely full. Since the jug contain so little air, it floated very low in the water. It either drifted away or was pushed further underwater, out of view. The other jug had a loose cap. Most of the water had leaked out, but the resulting air pocket kept it afloat.

In the small hours of the morning, the raft capsized again. The two had dozed off and were caught completely by surprise. The arch tube had deflated while they slept, making the canopy into a shroud. In the confusion and total darkness, it was not possible to find the door. Lucien, wildly thrashing about, finally kicked open the flap and dove through. When he surfaced, Catherine was not to be found. By half diving, half reaching into the submerged opening, he caught hold of her foul weather jacket and pulled her free.

Hypothermia and exhaustion had considerably reduced their energy reserves. In addition, the partially deflated arch tube made it much more difficult to right the raft. After several unsuccessful attempts they finally pulled themselves aboard, completely exhausted. They then noticed, through their exhaustion, the lights of a ship bearing down upon them. Lucien sized the signal rocket and fired it aloft. The rocket was not launched at a proper angle to the wind and did not achieve optimum altitude, but it did ignite, slightly burning Lucien in the process. The ship saw the signal and initiated a search, using its powerful spotlight. Lucien ignited the remaining hand flares, burning himself each time, but in the storm-swept darkness, despite a four-hour search, the ship failed to find them. What a difference additional flares, a radar reflector, a hand-held VHF, or even a flashlight would have made!

Without warning, the raft capsized once more. Only their life jackets kept the exhausted couple afloat. They were completely invisible to the ship, now just a few hundred yards away. Gripped by hypothermia, it was easy to relax and drift with the overturned raft. Lucien started to fall asleep but finally jerked himself awake. Righting the raft had become a Herculean job. The arch tube was almost completely deflated, and the upper doughnut had also lost most of its air. The canopy had filled with water and acted as a sort of keel, making the righting of the raft even more difficult.

Dawn brought no hope. The ship had drifted more than two miles from the raft during the night. The ship's captain had apparently decided to wait for dawn to see what it might reveal. Seeing nothing, the ship continued on its way.

The two castaways were able to find the inflation valves and pump the arch tube and the upper doughnut rigid. A sip of water, some corned beef from their remaining tin, and the hope that they had been reported (not true) sustained them through the day. The raft capsized again. They righted it with ever-increasing effort only to discover that the canopy had been torn away. The loss of the canopy was an extreme disaster whose magnitude was revealed only in stages. Every passing wave now filled the raft, and they had no bailer. The womb-like quality which the canopy provided was gone, exposing them to the full force of the elements. Last but most terrible of all, the canopy was orange, a color quite visible at sea, but the raft was black and it is possible that no better color could be chosen—for complete invisibility.

With the canopy gone, it was easier to watch for breaking waves and occasionally prevent the raft from capsizing, by shifting weight. But waves continuously filled the raft, and they had absolutely nothing with which to bail. When the water would reach about knee-high, the water-logged beast would capsize, and there was nothing they could do to prevent it. Their only defense was to become adept at righting the raft, which capsized so many times they lost count.

The mistral began to decrease during the second night, leaving angry cross seas that did not permit the exhausted castaways to rest. The raft continued to fill with water and capsize until the desperate couple realized that they could use a pair of foul weather pants, knotted at the feet as a sort of bucket. When the raft was bailed almost dry, the inflation pump was then used to complete the job. The pump also had to be used to re-inflate the upper doughnut and arch tube every three hours.

By late afternoon, the weather turned pleasant. There was no food, but the remaining jug still contained water. Although hungry and miserable, the castaways were able to sleep in snatches that night, while water continuously leaked into the raft. They often awoke chilled to the bone and had to bail. The next morning, during a glassy calm, they discovered a dreaded tear in the raft floor. They had nothing with which to patch it. In addition, the doughnuts and the arch tube leaked ever more persistently. The "bargain" raft was, after all, an old one, well past its prime.

The settled weather continued and Lucien tried to make a sort of sail using the remnants of the canopy and the arch tube. He later dove below the raft and cut off the ballast pockets to increase their speed. This is another big no-no. Ballast pockets can be tripped, but they are of vital importance for raft stability and should never be cut away. Urination became an increasing problem. It seems clear that the two were not rationing their water as strictly as possible because they continued to void regularly and in large quantities. While they had been in the storm, continuously wet, they had merely urinated in their pants. But numerous castaways have discovered to their anguish that urine is extremely caustic, particularly when passed by someone who is dehydrated. It burns the skin and causes saltwater pimples, the predecessor of saltwater boils. The burns are so painful that it is preferable to undress rather than wet one's pants.

A torrential downpour during the fifth night raised their hopes and allowed them to collect about three gallons of water by pumping it from the raft floor into their jug. Light variable winds gave way to strong breezes, rain squalls and constant cold which sapped their strength and made the ensuing days

Becalmed. Illustration from *Rage to Survive* by Jaques Vignes © 1975, by permission of William Morrow & Co., Inc.

a blur. Several ships passed them, but they had neither signals nor a heliograph with which to attract attention. One ship almost ran them down, missing the raft by just a few yards.

Lucien sighted land on Sunday, their ninth day adrift. The land was probably the north coast of Majorca, about twenty miles away. A friendly wind carried them toward it, and it seemed most likely that they would be ashore by nightfall. An hour later the wind died. The raft was a mere twelve miles from land. It soon became clear that the current would drift them past the island. In desperation, Lucien attached a line to his body, leaped into the sea and attempted to tow the raft toward the land. Minutes later, he was exhausted, and forced to stop. By nightfall the raft was totally becalmed with the island a tantalizing dozen miles away. The next morning the island was still there, the friendly breeze returned once more. Suddenly, the island was enveloped in a fog bank, a contrary wind sprang up and the island was seen no more.

The next day, their 11th day adrift, Catherine and Lucien were completely defeated. The loss of the island had been a great shock. They were covered with saltwater sores caused by their constant exposure to breaking waves. Sitting or lying on these inflammations was a constant agony. They were forced to live from minute to minute with the pain. Their weight loss had been considerable and they dwelled in a sort of half life, a trance-like torpor, from which they roused themselves only to speak of death. Lucien had become resigned to his fate. Having neither signals, a heliograph nor the strength to wave, he felt that death was inevitable. He began to succumb to the classic despair which Bombard claimed was so fatal. Lucien's mind began to wander and he dreamed that they had been saved, that he had been fed and soon would take a shower. Catherine still believed in miracles. She tried to make Lucien believe, but in the end it didn't seem to matter much. In their dream-like state the other person was no longer important. It was each for himself, each retreating into an ultimate confrontation with the mysteries of death.

Boats passed them, the sun rose from the rim of the sea and descended into night. A pale moon rose and died. The two desperate voyagers had become phantom shadows whose every move was slow and clumsy. In their exhausted state, every action became an impossible feat. Catherine was too weak to operate the air pump, and the hungry raft made its constant demands. Lucien's burns, caused by the flares, had been further inflamed by the sea. He could operate the pump only by falling upon it with his chest.

They talked about whether it would be right for the survivor to eat the corpse of the one who died first. Lucien had a repetitive dreadful dream of landing on a beach with Catherine's half-consumed body. He wanted to run, to avoid being caught with the savaged corpse. He decided that his only chance was to cut it up and drop it in the sea. He then destroyed the raft to hide the bloodstains. Afterward he fled to the forest and fed himself by stealing food. He would then awaken and frantically check to see that Catherine was still alive. They had been reduced to a state of human debris flickering with a tenuous flame of life. Hunger, thirst and pestilence, three of the dreaded four horsemen of the Apocalypse, beat upon their dying brains.

At 2 p.m., September 26, 1972, on their 12th day adrift, the ABLE TASMAN, a 720-foot, 10,000-ton freighter of Australian registry, clipping along at 23 knots, almost ran the raft down, passing just a few yards away. The officer on watch spotted them and brought the ship around. The sea was not calm and the castaways could not maneuver their frail craft. It is not easy to maneuver a huge ship to within a few feet of a raft, but after several attempts, the stern of the ABLE TASMAN stopped within inches of the raft, and two heaving lines were tossed to the castaways. The ship's carpenter slid down one of the lines. The crew dropped a harness over the side, then winched aboard Catherine and Lucien, two lucky survivors.

It was clear from photos taken at the time of the rescue that the two survivors had lost weight, but they looked nothing like concentration camp victims. In the photo taken of 19-year-old Catherine before the rescue she looked just a bit chubby and at the moment of rescue, she looked rather—cute. But her image of herself, as she was being undressed in the rescue ship's infirmary, was at odds with the photo taken by one of the ship's passengers;

> I looked at my body and it frightened me. Next to those healthy beings [the ship's crew] I suddenly realized that I had become a dying skeleton, covered with wounds and whose skin, where it was intact, was a strange reddish color. From *Rage to Survive* (Pg 184).

The couple made a rapid recovery. Catherine was able to explore the rescue ship two days after being saved. Lucien's feet had become swollen. He needed a week in the hospital to recover.

Illustration from *Rage to Survive.* by Jaques Vignes © 1975, by permission of William Morrow & Co., Inc.

Survival Fishing by Steve Callahan

CHAPTER V: SURVIVAL FISHING

Every castaway who has spent more than a few days at sea has tried to catch fish or other seafood to survive. The wise captain prepares a small but efficient fishing kit, which supplements the "fishing kit" sold with the raft. Catching a fish can mean the difference between life and death. After all, fish not only provide food; they provide essential liquid—the very stuff of life. It is rare that the kit provided with the raft is adequate for conventional fishing, let alone the special requirements of survival fishing. One of the main reasons is that successful survival fishing involves gaffing, trapping and spearing. Hook-and-line techniques work only under special circumstances.

The raft is a "floating island" in the sea, and within a few days becomes a miniature ecosystem. Certain species of fish and phytoplankton become associated with it while others are never seen. Some marine animals attach themselves to this environment and travel thousands of miles with it. Others are just passersby. Regardless of what they do, they represent just one thing to the castaway: FOOD AND WATER. If you can not catch them you cannot eat them and if you do not eat them they very well may end up eating you.

Pelagic Fish

The fish species predominantly associated with survival craft in the tropical latitudes are the **triggerfish, flying fish, shark and dorado** (also known as the **mahi mahi or the dolphin-fish**, which is not to be confused with the marine mam-mal of the same name). In the Caribbean the male dorado is known as the "bull head" or "bull dolphin" because of its blunt face. Other species, including the **milkfish** and the **mackerel** are also caught on occasion but these creatures are passersby and do not become part of the life raft ecosystem. **Tuna** and various bill fish also pass near the raft but these species are only attracted to rapidly trolled baits or lures and the raft just moves too slowly for them.

Flying fish. Drawing by Rebecca Thomson.

Flying fish have sustained many a castaway. They are small (often less than a pound) quite good eating, and their carcasses make the finest lures. Flying fish are attracted to light-colored objects at night. A white sail or reflective emergency blanket makes a fine lure when there is moonlight. When larger fish such as dorados are caught, it is wise to examine their stomaches, as they frequently contain partially digested, but edible flying fish. Flying fish make the best bait to catch dorados. A lure made from a flying fishhead and tail usually drives them nuts. Flyers are a basic food source, like phytoplankton. The big game fish eat them. Sea birds also delight in following above a school of feeding game fish, picking off the flying fish as they flee.

Sharks are ever present, but most castaways try to avoid catching them because of their ferocity. Small ones are, of course, the most desired, but there is no way of knowing which shark will end up speared or hooked. Sharks take bait but rarely lures. They require a three-foot wire leader as they tend to to gulp small bait. Shark flesh smells of ammonia but this smell diminishes by the next day. The liver is tasty and full of vitamins. One can get vitamin poisoning

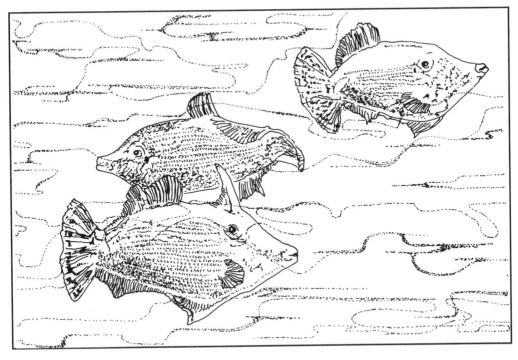

Another view of the ill-tasting but edible triggerfish. Drawing by Rebecca Thomson.

by eating large quantities of shark liver, but a single meal is safe. The meat is not esteemed by castaways, and there is no liquid in shark vertebrae. The meat should not be eaten in times of water shortage, since it is high in urea.

Fish may not be able to read and write but this does not mean they're stupid. Once you have speared or hooked a fish and it escapes, a learning process occurs. It is extremely unlikely that you will succeed in catching that fish by the same method. As a result, the ever-increasing number of fish associated with a raft may not in fact represent the same number of possible dinner entrees. Those "old timers" must be induced to lose their caution, as often occurs during a **feeding frenzy**, or they must be hunted in a way different from that to which they have been exposed.

TRIGGERFISH

Triggerfish are probably best caught using the method developed by the Baileys. One needs a **scoop and some bait,** but finely chopped fish skin, entrails, turtle intestine or coagulated blood (chum) are sufficient to make this method effective. Chum must be used with discretion to avoid attracting sharks.

Bait fishing for triggerfish beneath the raft also works, but their mouths are tiny, requiring a very small hook (#6-9), the size used for trout. The triggers' mouths may be small but their jaws are powerful, and so require a steel leader. If a feeding frenzy is induced, triggers can be hooked and landed without their friends becoming aware of what's happening. Otherwise, the fish see what is going on and hold back.

Night fishing for triggerfish takes advantage of the fishes' natural curiosity. A flashlight may be shined into the water if you have power to spare; a heliograph or reflective emergency blanket can be used to reflect moonlight. Fish can be speared or gaffed as they approach the light.

Bait fishing for dorados requires a larger piece of bait, cast well away from the ravenous hordes of triggerfish that surround the raft. Dorados are cautious and rarely hit any old bait. They are much more interested in a bait-lure made from the head and tail of a small fish, such as a flying fish, which should be given a few convulsive jerks as soon as it hits the water. Dorados, like triggerfish, have sharp teeth and powerful jaws. It is very important to use

Dorado, also called Dolphin-fish or Mahi-Mahi. Drawing by Rebecca Thomson

a steel leader. If leader material is not available, it may be wiser to save large hooks to use as a gaff, rather than risk them bait fishing. Some fish, such as bill fish, initially hit a bait, then turn and swallow it head first. As a result one should not strike instantly, but wait for the fish to swallow its meal. Dorados may be stunned by a blow to the head and killed by severing the spine behind the gill cover. One must be careful not to puncture the raft while doing so.

The Spear Gun

The most effective tool for catching fish from a survival craft and well worth its space in a survival pack is a spear gun, as large as possible, with extra spears, spear heads and rubbers. A double rubber gun with a safety lock and positive flotation is ideal. Spearhead selection is important. Small fish such as the triggers are best caught using a multi-pronged head, sometimes called a **"paralyzer."** There is a good chance you will land the fish even if only one of the barbs hit. Larger fish should be hunted with a detachable head. The spear hits, penetrates, and then the shaft falls away, connected to the raft by a separate lanyard. The shaft remains undamaged and cannot damage the raft. The head penetrates the fish and turns at right angles to the body line, reducing the chance of holing the raft. The fish is able to dash about, exhausting himself at the end of a stout line. After that, grab it around the root of the tail with a rag to ensure your grip. Heave it aboard spear head side UP.

The range of a spear gun may be 10 to 15 feet, but the effective distance of the gun when fired from a survival craft is much less. It is unwise to attempt anything but a certain shot, since a wounded fish becomes a very, very cautious fish. In addition, every time one takes a shot, there is the risk of damaging the equipment or losing a spear. Moving fish must be "led" with a spear gun. Refraction makes it difficult to aim accurately. The effects of refraction are minimized by aiming straight down. Since one often spends hours lying motionless on a flotation chamber, it is a good idea to pad this area if possible.

Big fish move quickly and it is not easy to hit them, let alone select the perfect spot to strike. Ideally, a chance shot just behind the gill cover may break the spine, killing the fish instantly. It is also an area rich in blood vessels and nerves.   Correspondingly, the tail is the worst spot to hit and if you shoot a game fish there, the next few minutes won't be dull since the fish will struggle violently to escape.

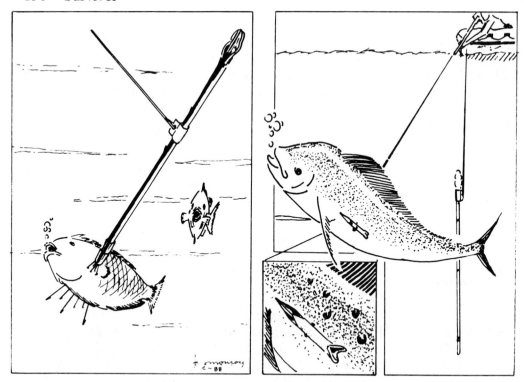

Emergency spears. Left: A "paralyzer" head, used on small fish. Right: Detachable head, rigged to separate from spear, for large fish. Drawing by Rafael Monroy

Emergency spears, made from oars, etc. are much less effective than a spear gun, and it is unquestionably better, if possible, to attempt fabricating a gaff from the same materials. The heart of any spear system is the head, which must be capable of penetrating and holding the prey. The head must either detach, or an effective barb must be made. A knife is one of the logical implements to use as a spearhead, but it is an extremely valuable object and its potential loss should be considered. In addition, a knife attached to a wounded, desperate fish is a dangerous object to people and to the raft.

A **gaff** is almost as useful as the spear gun, but the fish become wise very quickly and only newcomers wander within range. The gaff's simplicity is it's virtue. All that is required is a stout hook, a pole, such as an oar, and some lashing line. The gaff is hung over the side and when something comes close enough the gaff is jerked upward, carrying the fish right into the raft.

The ideal place to gaff a fish is in the area behind and slightly below the gill covers. The strike should be made with enough force to gaff the fish and pull it into the raft in one smooth motion.

The constant danger of bait fishing is that sharks often take the bait, hook and line, particularly at night. Their razor-sharp teeth usually sever the leader or whatever gets in their way. They can cut a hooked dorado in half or take the whole thing, including your tackle. Land every fish quickly. Do not play them, if possible.

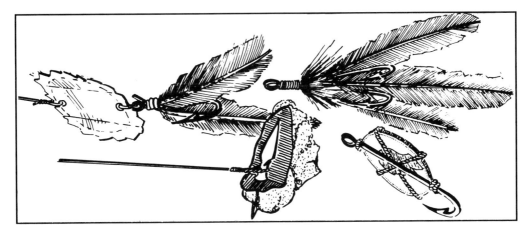

Assorted lures. A gorge, imbeded in meat is second from left. Drawing by Rafael Monroy

Lures and Bait

Lures are the least effective of all baits, but sometimes you have to go with what you've got. Lures do not work well, because they have to get going faster than about five knots to be effective. At slower speeds caution always seems to overcome hunger in the big fish. The advantage of lures is that they require no bait. They can be made from materials on hand and debris scavenged from the sea.

Bird feathers, coins, cigarette pack foil, can tops, unlayed line, a "skirt" of light line or even human hair can be used to make a lure. Hooks may be constructed from a variety of items. If all else fails, make a gorge, as illustrated above. Keep in mind that Polynesian natives used **gorges** successfully for millennia. It's a proven method that works. Wire leader vastly increases the chance of success or at least reduces the chance of losing one's hook. Look for usable metal around the raft, inside flashlights, etc.

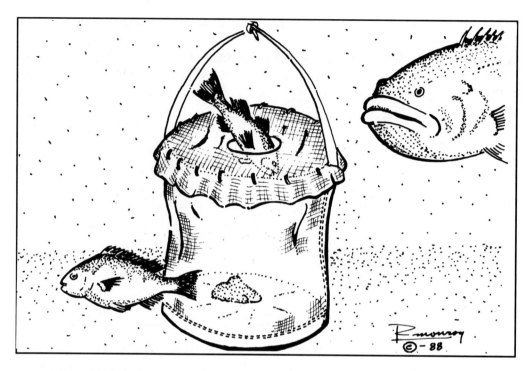

Make-shift bait-fish trap, useful only when becalmed. Drawing by Rafael Monroy

Fish Traps

Fish traps can also prove quite effective for catching small fish that can be eaten or used for bait. Making the trap is easy, sacrificing the materials to make it may be the most difficult part. A mesh sack, stiffened with floating debris, etc., baited if possible, makes a fine trap.

Traps can be made out of canvas buckets, large cans, fishing net or anything large enough to enclose a square foot or two of space. The material has to create a barrier; it does not have to be strong. Plastic sheeting, for example, can be made into a trap.

GRABBING SHARKS

Some survivors have resorted to the desperate expediency of grabbing sharks. Small sharks can be taken this way, and their rough, non-slimy skin is much easier to hold than that of a scale fish. If one must resort to shark grabbing, hold them by the root of the tail, pull them up, encircle the body just behind the head to keep the terrified creature from turning and biting, jam a plug in its mouth, then cover its eyes. Keep in mind that a shark suddenly hauled from the water may be too amazed to act for a moment, but is completely aware that its life is at stake. It will struggle violently if given the chance. Sharks may be killed by stabbing through the eye or severing the spine just behind the gills. Sharks are capable of taking a reflex bite out of you long after they are "dead," so BE CAREFUL.

Killing and Cleaning Fish

A blow to the head, a knife driven behind the eye or into the backbone just behind the gill cover are the most effective ways of killing ocean fish. Large fish first may be stunned with a blow on top of the head at eye level, then, when they start to shudder, a knife may be hammered through the backbone. If a fish thrashes and cannot be clubbed, cover its eyes. This usually calms them.

Large fish should be bled into a container to improve the keeping quality of the flesh and to keep the raft from being fouled. The blood should be drunk or allowed to stand until it coagulates before being thrown away. Blood and all the offal which is not useful should be thrown as far as possible from the raft, hopefully in one load, to avoid exciting the sharks.

Large fish can be landed on the raft canopy to minimize the chance of their spines penetrating the raft. If you choose that route, climb onto the canopy yourself to reduce the chance of losing them. All spines are potentially dangerous. A spine wound is painful and heals slowly. Cut the spines off before cleaning, if possible.

Drawing by Karen Harrod

Turtles

Turtles are marine creatures whose principle diet is jellyfish, shellfish, sponges, crabs or whatever they can find. They are not aggressive, but have dull claws on their powerful front flippers which cause dirty wounds that are slow to heal. They also have a bite powerful enough to crush a conch shell and breath bad enough to paralyze an ox. Barnacles live on their tongues. They NEVER brush after meals.

The most common, the hawksbill, ridley, loggerhead and green turtles, spend their entire lives at sea, except during the egg-laying season, which runs from summer through fall. In addition to man, cats, rats, pigs, raccoons, and other animals often find the nests and take the eggs. Their numbers are further decimated as the young scurry down the beach from the nest to the sea, pursued by hoards of ravenous birds, crabs, and animals.

Aside from man, the adult turtle's major enemy is the shark. Small turtles are often consumed whole. True to their legendary voracity, large sharks often bite adult turtles in half, shell and all. Mature turtles are frequently found with flippers and parts of their shell missing, lost to a shark. Conversely, turtles hate sharks and attack them relentlessly whenever they can, which is not often.

The turtle may achieve an amazing 2,000% weight-gain during its lifetime. Freshly hatched turtles weigh just a few ounces. Those which survive predation may grow to weigh hundreds of pounds and lay thousands of eggs during their lifetime. Some mature turtles are so large that a castaway must think twice about trying to catch them, regardless of need. Turtle meat is considered quite delicious. The carcass usually contains a quantity of fat which can be used as food, body oil, or as a lubricant.

The marine turtle population has been reduced to a pitiful remnant by man, and they should never be hunted, except to save one's own life. The beaches, to which an immutable God has decreed they must return again and again to procure their young, have been turned into tinsel-draped condominiums, possessed by hordes who can hardly comprehend the magnitude of their folly. One day, when the last turtle is dead and its clean bones are gone, we will dimly remember them as desperate castaways, for which there was no sweet shore upon which to land.

Generally, the female is the preferred sex for the castaway to catch, because she may be carrying eggs. The male has a longer tail and a concave lower shell, called the plastron, which allows him to mount the female during mating. A large female may have more than a hundred eggs in various stages of development. They are nutritious, full of protein and fat.

Male turtles have huge penises, are aggressively horny but myopic, and often try to copulate with survival craft. Hold them by their rear flippers (if you do not want to keep them) or beat them with a paddle to discourage them, but turtle love is a rough game and they are not easily discouraged.

THE GREEN AND HAWKSBILL TURTLES

The green and hawksbill turtles are similar in habits and range. The Green turtle is found from 35°N to 35°S. The hawksbill, named for its pointed, overhanging beak, likes warmer waters, from 25°N to 25° S. The green feeds on marine grasses, snails and shellfish, found in shallow beds 50-75' deep. They graze in weed beds, in bays, inlets or lagoons, always near shore. The Green turtle is fond of sleeping under ledges, in shallow, quiet waters. It migrates from rich feeding grounds for distances as great as 1,400 miles to nesting grounds located on isolated beaches. A rich algae grows on the shells of these creatures while they are on the feeding grounds.

The Green turtle (above) and the Hawksbill. From *European and Atlantic Turtles,* by L.D. Brongersma. Courtesy of Rijksmuseum van Natuurlijke History, Leiden.

The green turtle is found all over the world, within its latitude range, but the hawksbill is a Caribbean and Southern Florida creature, and where the ranges of these two species overlap, they often nest on the same beaches.

The hawksbill turtle has a magnificent shell, prized as tortiseshell, and its beauty has resulted in the hawksbill's near extinction. The shell is amber colored, with reddish brown or black streaks. The green turtle's shell is black to brown with streaks of yellow. The shell is less beautiful, but the meat more desired, so the green turtle is also on the endangered species list.

The hawksbill, a culinary opportunist, will eat whatever it can catch, including Portuguese man-of-war, sponges, crabs, snails, even mangrove fruit. Their opportunistic diet makes the hawksbill less esteemed for its meat. It sometimes mistakes plastic bags for jellyfish, and the meal is invariably fatal.

The females of both species have a two-to four-year laying cycle and, as they approach the beach to deposit their eggs, something unpleasant awaits them, or possibly even your raft. The sex-crazed males lie just offshore and copulate so strenuously that the poor ladies often arrive broken and bleeding on the beach. They dig their 18" deep nests, already impregnated for their next nesting, years away. Female turtles deposit their 70 to 200 eggs in the sand at night, high on the beach or under bushes. Sometimes a female will start a nest, then change her mind and abandon it, returning the next night to try again. Both species nest from spring through late fall, with the maximum rush in early summer. The eggs hatch in 30 to 72 days.

A green turtle weighing 850 pounds with a shell five feet long was once caught, but 150-pound adults, four feet long, 10 to 16 years old are common. A Hawksbill rarely weighs more than 165 pounds or is longer than three feet.

THE LOGGERHEAD TURTLE

The Loggerhead is distinguished from the green and hawksbill turtles by its uniformly colored black or dark brown shell. It is both shorter and wider shaped than the others. A few big ones have been caught that weighed 800 pounds and thought to be 35 years old. Large adults usually attain a maximum length of three and a half feet and a hefty weight of 350 pounds. It ranges the Atlantic from 38° N to 38° S but are occasionally found well beyond these latitudes.

Loggerheads are the most opportunistic feeders. They will eat whatever they can catch, including grasses, small fish, stingrays, squid, sponges, crabs, jellyfish, barnacles, shellfish large, and small, tennis balls, plastic floats, foam rubber and styrofoam cups. They are very aggressive feeders and can be extremely vicious.

The loggerhead turtle. From *European Atlantic Turtles* by L.D. Brongersma, Courtesy of Rijksmuseum van Natuurlijke History, Leiden

Loggerheads migrate over distances of a thousand miles or more and breed from late spring through midsummer. They lay about one hundred eggs. Their nesting and mating habits are similar to green turtles. The flesh of the loggerhead is less desired that that of green turtles because it is sinewy, but it is just as delicious if the sinews are picked out.

RIDLEY TURTLES

There is an Atlantic (Gulf of Mexico to Cape Hattaras) and Pacific species. The Pacific species also ranges into the Indian ocean. The two types look very similar with a rounded shell, which is dark colored with occasional olive tones. They are the smallest of the marine turtles discussed, and they rarely exceed two feet in length. They feed along shore, but are seen migrating in large groups. They are bottom dwellers, and spend time between the reef and the shore. The Pacific species (the olive ridley) feeds on grasses, mollusks, urchins, and snails. The Atlantic (Kemp's) Ridley prefers crabs and shellfish.

The Ridleys turtle. From *European Atlantic Turtles,* by L.D. Brongersma. Courtesy of Rijksmuseum van Natuurlijke History, Leiden.

Ridleys nest from late spring through early summer. They have rather specific breeding locations and gather offshore to mate, then nest by the hundreds, often digging up and destroying the nests of other turtles in their frenzy. They repeat this process two or three times, at 28-day intervals.

Turtles do not have particularly good hearing, but they are sensitive to vibration. They are usually oblivious to a quiet approach but erupt into amazing action as soon as they are touched. It is important to have a plan of approach.

In a recent conversation, Dougal Robertson recommended the following technique for landing and killing a turtle:

Turtles are best brought into a small craft by grasping the hind flippers and bringing them aboard on their backs. Place a knee on each forward flipper, grasp beak (closed) by one hand, leaving the knife hand free for the "coupe de grace". Arteries close to the neck bones can be severed and blood directed into receptacles.

The turtle is most defenseless on its back, but is still capable of flailing around with its flippers, which are extremely powerful and can do a raft and its occupants much damage. Since biting is their main weapon, it is best to jam something like a piece of wood into their mouths. Whatever you use as a mouth plug should be dispensable, as the turtle will probably mangle it.

When the beast's throat is cut, a bowl should held to collect the copious blood which is not salty and very nutritious. A large turtle may yield several quarts of blood, which should be drunk immediately, before it coagulates. The weakest crew members should be favored when it is distributed.

Coagulated blood, when cut up, releases its serum, which is easily separated, and drunk. The coagulated material can be mixed with turtle eggs, fish organs or roe to make a "sauce" for meat or fish. All marine flesh, including turtle meat, contains a considerable amount of fluid which may be sucked out or squeezed in a cloth. The squeezed flesh may then be dried and eaten later. When the meat is first collected, let it drain into a container and drink the juice.

CATCHING TURTLES ON LAND

Sea turtles are most easily caught and killed on the beach at night. They usually come in on the night high tide, particularly spring tides, to make a nest and lay eggs. Sea turtles become very involved in the egg-laying process, becoming almost trance-like, and are less cautious when laying. Look for their tracks by walking the beach just above the surf line, so that the breaking surf masks the sound of your approach. If one finds tracks in the morning, walk the beach after dark, armed with a light, hatchet, knife and some line. The sign of one turtle is a strong indication that others will appear.

Turtles return to the beach of their birth to lay eggs. Signs of a completed nest does not mean that they will not return. Turtles have a two week laying cycle and return again and again to the same beach as batches of eggs mature. Turtles frequently make nests, but lay no eggs. Test the nest for eggs by poking around in it with a stick. Listen for digging sounds above the highest tide line. Approach the beasts quietly from the seaward side because turtles turn toward the sea to escape. Dazzle them with a light, if available, and flip them over.

Turtles, unlike their cousins, the tortoises (the land animal), are unable to retract their heads into their shells. As a result it is possible to render them unconscious with a powerful blow to the head. Anyone who has looked at a turtle skull can easily see that it is as thick as a knight's helmet and almost impossible to actually fracture, unless one has a hatchet or hammer. If you cannot flip the creature over, stop its advance by beating its head. After it has been stunned, stab it multiple times in the neck, churning the knife to sever the major arteries. Bleeding kills the beast and improves the flavor and preserving quality of the meat.

These creatures have a tremendous amount of vitality, so trying to kill one by stabbing it in the only accessible area, the neck, does not result in an instantly dead turtle but in a frantic beast determined to reach the sea.

Turtles small enough to flip without stunning may be kept alive in this inverted position for weeks or months if they are shaded and occasionally rinsed with saltwater. Greens are completely helpless in this position. Other species occasionally do right themselves and must be staked down with rope. This inhumane method is, unfortunately, an ideal way to have an assured reserve food supply.

CATCHING TURTLES UNDERWATER

Turtles sometimes do not return to the deep water after laying their eggs but sleep under ledges in the lagoon. They make easy prey during this time as they are drugged with sleep and unwary. If the turtle is small enough, it may be seized by the top of the shell at the front and back, guided to the surface and dumped into the dinghy or onto the beach.

SPEARING TURTLES IN THE WATER

Sea turtles use their front flippers for locomotion, so spearing through the front flipper will cause it to swim in circles. A spear with a detachable head is the best weapon, since the struggling creature would undoubtedly bend a spear shaft. If a float or raft is attached by a line to the spearhead, the beast will exhaust itself towing the float around. It may then be guided to the beach or hauled into a dinghy. Try not to kill turtles in the water because they bleed profusely and attract sharks.

COOKING TURTLE MEAT

Like most reptiles, turtles are mild tasting and delicious. Hawksbill turtles have a stronger flavor than Green turtles, but the meat can be improved by boiling in several changes of fresh water. Steaming or boiling keeps the flesh from toughening. Cutting into small pieces and frying in turtle fat is a second choice. Turtle meat can be roasted on a stick but tastes tough and dry this way.

Like most seafood, turtle flesh can be cut into strips and hung in the sun for several days to dry. Store in a cloth sack or ventilated container. Examine each piece before storage. Discard any fly-blown or moldy pieces. Re-examine frequently and redry in the sun as often as necessary.

TURTLE EGGS

You have to acquire a taste for turtle eggs, whether cooked or raw. They are extremely popular among island people. Let hunger be your guide. They are rich in protein and fat and are therefore quite nutritious. Freshly laid eggs do not solidify when cooked. Eggs less than a week old do not have much of an exterior membrane—as the egg matures, the membrane thickens.

TURTLE LIVER AND ORGANS

Turtle liver is sweet, delicious, and completely edible either raw or cooked, as are all of the internal organs. Turtle liver is full of vitamin-rich oil. If the survivor's diet consists of large quantities of fish, shark and turtle liver, the risk of vitamin poisoning exists. The livers should be crushed, the oil skimmed and used as a skin oil or lubricant. The liver, eggs, coagulated blood, brain, and sweetbreads may be mixed and used as a sauce with meat or fish.

USE OF BODY PRODUCTS

Turtle fat, found in copious quantities around the intestines, can be crushed and the oil skimmed off. The oil makes a fine body lotion and can be used as an enema to relieve constipation.

The internal organs, including the brain, make a tasty change from a monotonous diet. They are all completely edible. The liver, like all marine liver, is rich in vitamins and should be eaten in moderation to prevent vitamin poisoning.

Turtle intestines are full of partially digested material which makes wonderful chum, and this chum can be used to induce a feeding frenzy. The intestines can also be used for bait, but make poor eating.

A turtle shell may prove useful if one has a place to store it. A shell can be used as a bailer or to hold inflammable, signal-making materials. Conversely, if space does not permit, all offal from the carcass can be placed in the shell which is then jettisoned when the raft is moving. As is true with any catch, do not wash bloody hands or spread blood around the raft. Do not wipe blood on the raft or do anything that would attract a shark, looking for wounded fish.

CATCHING SEA BIRDS

Sea birds sometimes land on a raft and can be caught by hand. If opportunity permits, try to wrap the hand and arm in a cloth, since some birds are can inflict a nasty bite. South Sea natives tie a piece of cloth to a pole and slowly wave it back and forth when a bird is nearby. Some species, such as boobies, are very curious and may be attracted, almost mesmerized by the motion. When the bird gets close to the pole, flail around with it, in the hopes of hitting the creature. Birds are quite fragile and even a slight blow may bring them down.

When a bird is caught, pull its head off and drink the blood. Skin, rather than feather it and suck the inside of the skin for fat. Save an assortment of feathers and the feet to make lures. Suck the eyeballs for liquid. Eat the liver and organs first. Crack the skull to get at the brain. Sea bird flesh often tastes of fish but is completely edible. Since sea birds eat fish which eat phosphorescent plankton, the bird's flesh often glows at night. This does not mean that glowing birds or fish are inedible. Read more about birds in Chapter XV.

Plankton

For the blue-water yachtsman, particularly the solo sailor, the ocean often appears to be a vast, lonely desert, visited only by a few solitary, nomadic creatures such as himself. We know that beneath our keels there is some life on the unlit, freezing cold ocean floor and that a few fish such as the dorado and the tuna dwell in the desert-like expanse of the upper sea. But few realize that the ocean is, in fact, as Alain Bombard described it, a sort of "gigantic, very diluted soup", consisting of tiny organisms called plankton. **Plankton** consists of vegetation (**phytolankton**) and animals (**zooplankton**). The plankton biomass is greater than all other life on earth combined. To give some idea of what this really means, consider that a mature blue whale weighing 100 tons is equal in weight to 10^{20} or 100,000,000,000,000,000,000 zooplankton animals.

The **diatom**, a one-celled algae just visible to the naked eye, is the most common of all plankton species and is at the bottom of the food chain. The diatome and its relatives represent almost all of the organic life in the sea. Diatoms are live in highly ornamented, sparkling, transparent, pill box-like shells made of silicon dioxide. In other words, they live in glasshouses. Like all

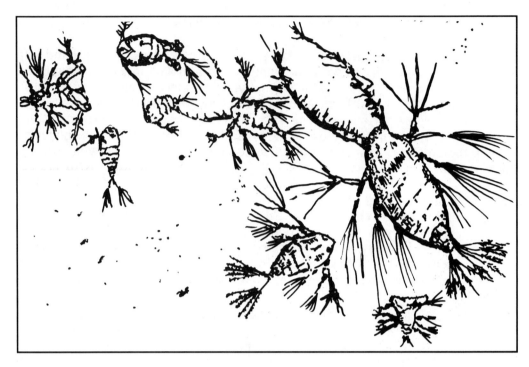

Copepods. Drawing by Rafael Monroy

plants, the diatoms and all phytoplankton need sunlight and therefore live in the upper sea. Phytoplankton concentrate their food in the form of organic oils, which help support the heavy shell. Those which escape being eaten eventually die and sink to the ocean floor, taking their oil reserves along. It is this oil which eventually becomes petroleum, a product which, when refined, is used to fuel stinkpots. An intermediate group of creatures, neither plant nor animal are called **dinoflagellates**. These sweethearts cause the red tide, certain types of fish poison, and some produce their own light, called **bioluminescence**.

Zooplankton can be found at much greater depths than phytoplankton, although they often concentrate closer to the surface at night. The smallest animals in the sea are such a basic life form that the main difference between them and the diatoms they eat are a lack of chlorophyll and that they do not live in glass houses. The shells of phytoplankton which have died through the millennia form a basic substrata of the ocean floor hundreds of feet thick in some places, and which are called **ooze**.

An intermediate-sized zooplankton animal, the **copepod** (1-10 mm) are sometimes called sea-fleas because of their ability to "jump". They are probably the most numerous creatures on earth visible to the naked eye. They exist in every habitable part of every ocean. They bear eggs which hatch into one-eyed larvae. Copepods are ravenous eaters. They consume half their own weight every day. The larvae and young adults eat plankton. Mature adults eat their own young and anything else that does not eat them first. Copepods are almost the exclusive diet of the world's largest fish, the basking and whale sharks.

At the top of the plankton chain are small shrimp-like creatures called **krill.** An adult could sit on a thumbnail—if it would sit still. Krill are so abundant in some parts of the sea that blue whales feed upon them as their main food source. Other organic material, such as fish eggs, tiny crabs, and various larvae including coral polyps, are also plankton-size although they become much larger as adults. We will consider them all phytoplankton for our purpose.

In his book *Kon Tiki* , Thor Heyerdahl had much to say about plankton:

> It is certain that there must be very nourishing food in these almost invisible plankton, which drift about with the current on the oceans in infinite numbers. Fish and sea birds which do not eat plankton themselves live on other fish or sea animals which do, no matter how large they themselves may be. . . .What they cannot offer in size they can offer in numbers.

> In good plankton waters, there are thousands in a glassful. More than once, persons have starved to death at sea because they did not find fish large enough to be speared, netted, or hooked. In such cases, it has often happened that they have literally been sailing about in strongly diluted, raw fish soup. If, in addition to hooks and nets, if they had had a utensil for straining the soup they were sitting in, they would have found a nourishing meal — plankton. Some day in the future, perhaps, men will think of harvesting plankton from the sea to the same extent as now they harvest grain on land. A single grain is of no use, either, but in large quantities it becomes food.

> The marine biologist Dr. A. D. Bajakov told us of plankton and sent us a fishing net which was suited to the creatures we were to catch. The "net" was a silk net with almost three thousand meshes per square inch. It was sewn in the shape of a funnel with a circular mouth behind an iron ring, eighteen inches across, and was towed behind the raft. Just as in other experiments the catch diminished as the sea grew warmer, farther west, and we got the best results at night, because many species seemed to go deeper down into the water when the sun was shining.

> If we had no other way of whiling away time on board the raft, there would have been entertainment enough in lying with our noses in the plankton net. Not for the sake of the smell, for that was bad. Nor because the sight was appetizing, for it looked a horrible

mess. But because, if we spread the plankton out on a board and examined each of the little creatures separately with the naked eye, we had before us fantastic shapes and colors in unending variety.

Most of them were tiny shrimp-like crustaceans (copepods) or fish ova floating loose, but there were also larvae of fish and shellfish, curious miniature crabs in all colors, jellyfish, and an endless variety of small creatures which might have been taken from Walt Disney's Fantasia. Some looked like fringed, fluttering spooks cut out of cellophane paper, while others resembled tiny red-beaked birds with hard shells instead of feathers. There was no end to Nature's extravagant inventions in the plankton world; a surrealistic artist might well own himself bested here.

Where the cold Humboldt Current turned west south of the Equator, we could pour several pounds of plankton porridge out of the bag every few hours. The plankton lay packed together like cake in colored layers — brown, red, gray, and green according to the different fields of plankton through which we had passed. At night, when there was phosphorescence about, it was like hauling in a bag of sparkling jewels. But, when we got hold of it, the pirates' treasure turned into millions of tiny glittering shrimps and phosphorescent fish larvae that glowed in the dark like a heap of live coals. When we poured them into a bucket, the squashy mess ran out like a magic gruel composed of glowworms. Our night's catch looked as nasty at close quarters as it had been pretty at long range. And, bad as it smelled, it tasted correspondingly good if one just plucked up courage and put a spoonful of it into one's mouth. If this consisted of many dwarf shrimps, it tasted like shrimp paste, lobster, or crab. If it was mostly deep-sea fish ova, it tasted like caviar and now and then like oysters.

The inedible vegetable plankton were either so small that they washed away with the water through the meshes of the net, or they were so large that we could pick them up with our fingers. "Snags" in the dish were single jelly-like coelenterates like glass balloons and jellyfish about half an inch long. These were bitter and had to be thrown away.. Otherwise everything could be eaten, either as it was or cooked in fresh water as gruel or soup. Tastes differ. Two men on board thought plankton tasted delicious, two thought they were quite good, and for two the sight of them was more than enough. From a nutrition standpoint they stand on a level with the larger shellfish, and, spiced and properly prepared, they can certainly be a first-class dish for all who like marine food. From *Kon Tiki* pp 138-141, by Thor Heyerdahl, 1950, with permission from Simon & Schuster Co. Inc, Anglewood Cliffs, NJ

Since fourty years have elapsed since Dr. Heyerdahl's adventure, it might be prudent to look for and remove tar balls and plastic spicules, in addition to the little jellyfish, before the repast.

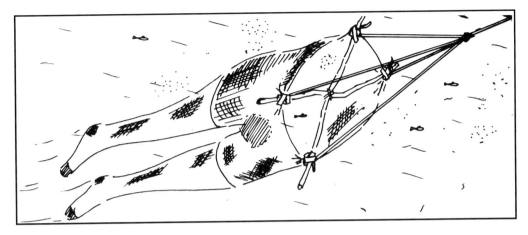

A plankton net made from pantyhose. Drawing by Rafael Monroy.

In 1948, two Harvard scientists, George Clark and David Bishop conducted tests to see if phytoplankton could be used as food for castaways. They concluded that the plankton had a mildly pleasant taste, being somewhat reminiscent of shrimp or oysters. They also said that no one in the test group could eat more than a quarter pound per sitting, and that it did seem to linger in the stomach, undigested, for several hours (doubtless because of the indigestible plant material it contained). Areas where cold, dense,up-welling currents carry nutrients to the surface are rich in plankton. Other places have much lower concentrations. In conclusion, if you are a castaway, get out your pantyhose and give it a try.

William Beebe, the famous American naturalist, towed a one-yard wide net for one hour at two knots (in a rich part of the ocean), then counted 1/150th of the catch. He found 271,080 edible organisms. That's, uh, about 40.6 million edible beasties per hour. So plankton are out there and it's a whole lot easier to catch than a dorado. Scientists use a 3,000 mesh/inch conical net. You can use a pair of heavy support pantyhose, with reinforced toes and a hoop or a couple of sticks. If you include pantyhose in your survival pack, take several pair, they do not last long. If you forget your pantyhose in the boudoir, a shirt or pair of pants, knotted at the legs is better than nothing.

Fish for plankton at night, when the zooplankton are closer to the surface. Experiment at different depths and only use the plankton net when the survivalcraft is moving. Last but not least, take several pairs of pantyhose.

Overleaf Homer's *Gulf Stream* by Rebecca Thomson

CHAPTER VI: ABOUT SHARKS

We've shot the tiger, poisoned the wolf, made the bear into rugs and the crocodile into handbags, but the world's last great man-eater, the shark, roams over two-thirds of the earth's surface unchecked. None of these animals ever killed as many people in reality as were killed in the movies. In addition, more people die every year from lightning or bee stings (but not at sea) than from shark bite. That does not interest the one being eaten, of course, and does nothing to lessen the shark's image as a monster.

The shark is, after all, a superb killing machine. Solid muscle, covered with a hide tougher than rhino skin. It possesses a variety of sense organs designed to help it find prey—rows of razor sharp teeth to tear and devour it, and a small forebrain with about as much capacity as a $20 calculator.

Of the 350 shark species, all but the whale and the basking sharks eat meat. This is not to imply that every shark is a potential man-eater. Just a few species are really dangerous, and they are quite sufficient. In the discussion below, several shark species, particularly those well known as man-eaters are mentioned. But any shark, large or small, may take an experimental bite or two out of you. Their unpredictability is the problem, and they must all be treated with great care, even small ones. As a result, this discussion is general in nature and does not give details about every shark known to attack man.

Sharks may not be smart enough to recite Shakespeare, but what they do, they do extremely well. They have excellent hearing, acute black and white vision, and an incredible sense of smell. Just one or two molecules of blood in the water, as little as <u>one part per hundred million,</u> will make them instantly veer and race toward the injured creature. If you are "it", you are in big trouble.

In addition to their amazing sense of smell, sharks have taste cells in their skin, in the area of their snout. This is why they often bump their victims before attacking, to see if the creature is easy prey and to take a "taste" before they take a bite. Under normal circumstances, like most wild animals, sharks are terribly afraid of being hurt. An injury, even a small one, can result in death by starvation or being eaten by their own kind. When they bump something (or someone) and it does not fight back, they take an experimental bite. The sensory system in shark skins, located all over their bodies, make them perhaps the most sensitive and responsive hunter in the world. They can also detect pressure waves—such as a ship being torpedoed, or the struggles of a swimmer—miles away. To a shark, a swimmer "feels" much like an injured, dying fish. Those happy splashings at the beach mean just one thing to a shark—**FOOD**.

RICHARD DeROSSET

Contrary to popular opinion, sharks spend most of their time being placid, timid fish, easily frightened, ready to flee at a moment's notice. Sharks have been known to swim for hours around castaways floating in life jackets, held at bay by kicks and shoves. Each year, there are only about fifty shark attacks on people, ten of which are fatal attacks. Four times as many people die from bee stings. But any living thing within sensing distance of a shark is a potential meal. The slightest trace of blood, vomit, the smell of fear and struggling noises transform these placid, stupid beasts into determined killers whose exploits usually exceed even a writer's imagination. This is why injured, struggling survivors from sunken ships are so often attacked by sharks.

Sharks are scavengers and opportunists. They eat the dead and the dying, regardless of species. By eating and digesting the dead they return their nutrients to the pool of life. Sharks do not mind rotten meat. They are capable of unhinging their upper jaw to get a bigger bite and are perfectly designed to consume their prey in extremely large gulps. Sharks love to eat rays and other sharks, including members of their own species. Some, dissected, have been found to contain partially digested whole sharks half their length, apparently eaten with a single gulp. Only during the mating season does a temporary truce seem to be declared.

A shark's multiple rows of razor sharp teeth fall out easily and are readily replaced. Shark's are therefore content to gnaw on things that cause considerable tooth loss (like boat hulls) without apparent discomfort. They seem willing to give anything a bite or two, just to see if it's edible.

The shark's skin is covered with "scales" which are in fact more similar to their teeth than to a fishes' scales. These dermal denticles or tooth-like plates are shaped just like shark teeth. Shark skin makes good sandpaper. If a swimmer is bumped by a shark these sharp plates usually cause abrasions which bleed—and galvanize the creature into action. This is but another good reason to jump for a life raft—well clothed.

No one knows why sharks pick out an individual swimmer to attack. Invariably, of course, anyone who is bleeding is at the top of their list. When a victim is selected, the sharks concentrate their attack on that person, often bumping aside or swimming between the legs of other people nearby. This is the reason why courageous souls who have rushed to the aid of a shark victim are so often spared. The shark(s) can only think of one kill at a time, it seems.

Like man-eating tigers, individual sharks can develop a taste for human flesh. "Rogue" sharks have been known to attack numerous bathers over a period of time and when they are caught, the limbs from different persons are

Overleaf: *The Great White.* Painting by Richard DeRosset

The Tiger Shark. By Rebecca Thomson.

often found in their gut. The most feared are coastal sharks, and the **Great White** is unquestionably the King of Mean. It is used to taking seals and sea lions in the surf, but occasionally devours boats. It takes bathers in knee-deep water but is also found far out at sea.

The mass of a Great White really must be seen to be appreciated. A rather ordinary, 18-foot Great White shark just scratching his back on a becalmed 48 foot sloop I was delivering made every timber of the vessel shake. Standing on deck, I could see both ends of this monster at the same time as he passed beneath the keel. He had an eye as big as a saucer and when he looked up, I knew he was thinking of me.

The sheer size of the Great White makes a tuna, a sea lion—or a man—look like hors d'oeuvres. Great Whites may weigh as much as two tons and reach 27 feet in length. Fortunately the Great White is among the least numerous of the sharks.

As huge and terrifying as the Great White may be, it is the tiny cousin of a really serious monster called **megalodon**, a fifty-foot shark with a mouth containing hundreds of razor sharp, six-inch-long teeth, bigger than a man's hand. Its maximum weight is unknown, but a 50-foot whale would weigh about 25 tons. It undoubtedly could take on a boat or a small ship and would be about as unstoppable a critter as a malicious god could produce. Fortunately megalodon seems to be extinct, although its teeth are frequently dredged up from great depths—and they aren't always fossilized!

Tiger sharks are famous man-eaters and have the nasty habit of hanging around bathing beaches. They are very indiscriminate eaters. Their name comes from the pronounced vertical stripes on their sides, not from their eating habits. Some sharks have a preferred food. Makos, for example, prefer swordfish and bluefish. But Tiger sharks aren't fussy at all. They are among those most prone to try munching a boat. One attacked a 28 foot motor boat and sank it on the spot. They can weigh a ton and grow to 18 feet. Monsters this size can easily gulp down a diver, tanks and all—and there are photographs of them doing so. They are probably the most dedicated man-eaters.

Young Tigers have stripes, but they fade as maturity is reached. The adult is easy to identify. It had a very broad head, almost square when seen from above. It also has pronounced nostrils close to the end of its snout. If you have the bad luck to get close enough to see its teeth, they are serrated and razor sharp.

The **bull shark** is another man-eater, 6-7 feet long, weighing a paltry 300 pounds. Try not to think of them as pigmies. A bull shark that size can easily eat a man. They have made their reputation by attacking bathers close to

Bull sharks. Drawing by Rebecca Thomson.

shore. They are also capable of swimming in fresh water, up rivers and into lakes. Bull sharks have attacked swimmers in Lake Michigan and Lake Nicaragua. More than one religious Indian has been eaten while bathing in the Ganges.

Whaler sharks got their name from following whaling ships and devouring the dead carcasses of abandoned whales, but their notorious reputation comes from attacks in shallow water, particularly in Australia. Whaler sharks run 10-12 feet and 700-1,000 pounds depending on variety. The quotation in this chapter from *Moby Dick* (pg. 184) unquestionably refers to Whaler sharks.

White tip sharks. Drawing by Rebecca Thomson.

Pelagic or deep-water sharks are usually larger than their coastal cousins. Certainly among the most ferocious is the **White Tip**, a surface-feeding, warm-water, yellow-brown killer weighting up to 1,000 pounds and reaching 13 feet in length. They are probably the most numerous shark in the ocean and some scientists say it is the most numerous large fish in the world. The White Tip is ugly, has small, beady eyes and swims with a jerky motion. It is usually timid and easily discouraged but when aroused, presses home its attack slowly, almost lethargically, but unrelentingly. Even shooting this shark elicits little reaction. Either you kill, it or it kills you. Jaques-Yves Cousteau calls this creature *"Lord of the Long Hands"* because of its long, white-tipped pectoral fins. Its other fins are also white-tipped. They make the animal easy to identify.

A Mako shark attacking a swordfish.   Drawing by Rebecca Thomson.

Makos and hammerheads are two more very large offshore species. Makos are famous as game fish. Ernest Hemingway held the Atlantic rod-and-reel record with a Mako that tipped the scales at 786 pounds. Much larger ones (1,300 lbs) have been taken commercially. Makos are famous jumpers and have occasionally pursued people who have fled from the water by jumping onto the beach. They attack swordfish for food, and leap into the air to escape the swordfish' attacks. **The hammerhead**, an aggressive shark weighting up to a ton, it has the nasty habit of swimming in packs, although where there is any possibility of food numerous sharks of any species always appear.

Sharks are fearful enough creatures by themselves, but become even more terrifying in groups, when induced into a feeding frenzy. Oddly enough, sharks do not become frenzied when there is a really large amount of dead food, such as a whale to be had. They are often seen patiently waiting their turn to scoop out bucket-sized mouthfuls of the dead beast's flesh. But blood, struggling sounds, and fresh meat drive sharks wild. It seems as though each becomes afraid it won't get its share. All rules, and certainly all decorum, go out the window. At the height of the frenzy they will eat anything—steel barrels, pieces of wood, packets of shark repellant, and, of course, other injured sharks. The harrowing descriptions of sharks' frenzied attacks on shipwreck victims provides more than adequate food for thought.

Herman Melville, a veteran sailor, had a few words to say about the feeding frenzy and although *Moby Dick* is fiction, Melville had "paid his dues" at sea and knew whereof he spoke:

> When in the Southern Fishery, a captured Sperm Whale, after long and weary toil, is brought alongside late at night , it is not, as a general thing at least, customary to proceed at once with the business of cutting him in [removing the blubber]. But sometimes, especially upon the Line in the Pacific, this plan will not answer at all; because such incalculable hosts of sharks gather round the moored carcass that were he left so for six hours say, at a stretch, little more than a skeleton would be visible by morning. From: *Moby Dick, The Shark Massacre* by Herman Melville (Pg. 435)

When this occurred, the harpooners would stab at the swarming creatures, in an attempt to drive them off:

> But in the foamy confusion of their mixed and struggling hosts, the marksmen could not always hit their mark [the brain]; and this brought new revelations of the incredible ferocity of their foe. They viciously snapped, not only at each other's disembowelments. . . but bit their own; 'til those entrails seemed swallowed over and over again by the same mouth, to be oppositely voided by the gaping wound. (Pg 437)

Small boat sinkings are different from ship disasters, because there is, of course, so much less noise, less blood, and fewer struggling men in the water. From the details mentioned above, life raft strategy should be clear. Get everyone out of the water and into the raft as quickly as possible, bleeding people first. If a crewman is bleeding, bind up the wounds immediately and throw bloody bandages as far as possible from the survival craft. Don't splash about, and, if you must swim, do a sidestroke or any style which does not require a lot of splashing—as does the crawl. Stay in the raft, don't go for a swim!

If seafood is caught, disposal of the blood and offal should be carefully considered before any action is taken. Don't dispose of it if the raft is becalmed, as you will just create the equivalent of a giant neon sign that says "Eat at Joe"'s." Wait until the raft is moving, preferably at night, then fling the offal as far ABEAM as possible. Try to dump the bloody water in one or two loads into the sea—don't create a trail for sharks to follow.

During World War II, aviator's life raft equipment packs often contained packets of "shark repellant," a combination of chemicals believed to irritate the shark, mask odors, and reduce the shark's vision with an opaque dye. Later research failed to support this theory. Researchers have had success firing a strong detergent into a shark's mouth, and a squeeze bottle of strong detergent might work at close range—too close for me! Experiments with a shark-repelling toxin, exuded from a species of flounder, are still being conducted. No commercially available repellant now available is highly effective.

It is not known how many life raft survivors have been eaten by sharks, for once a raft is bitten it's usually gone—and dead men tell no tales. One lucky group of survivors, drifting off the coast of Colombia in two Viking six-person rafts were attacked by sharks. They tore the ballast bags and bit through one of the lower doughnuts. Fortunately, the sharks were frightened off by the rush of escaping bubbles.

Numerous survivors have been exposed to sharks and have succeeded in driving them off. The most effective way seems to be a blow on the snout, eyes, or gills. This seems much safer than stabbing or spearing one as there is absolutely no telling what a wounded, enraged shark may do. One account describes a huge tiger shark, speared in the shallows, that sped off, threw the spear, then charged back up and onto the beach, completely out of the water, jaws snapping, trying to attack its attacker.

Despite the numerous tales about sharks ferocity, many castaways have treated them with cautious contempt. Alain Bombard's attitude is typical :

I was being visited more frequently by sharks, but I had become quite used to them and treated them with complete disdain. They seemed a cowardly lot. A smart rap on the snout and they were off in a flash. They often came to prod the floats with their noses, and when I picked up an oar and clouted them on the head they never waited for more but plunged out of sight immediately. From: *The Bombard Story* (Pg. 151)

Occasionally Bombard found it necesary to defend himself against shark attack:

During the night of Thursday, 6th November [1952],I was again attacked by a shark. He seemed a particularly tough customer and I could not keep him off. He must have acquired a taste for human flesh. I fixed my knife to the end of an oar while he butted away at the floats. . . the next time he turned on his back to attack at an angle, I stuck the knife in him and slit him from throat to tail. The sea burned a blackish color around him and I saw his entrails spilling out. My dolphins [dorados] pounced on them. (Pg. 153)

Rafts, fortunately, are big, bulky items and sharks are unfamiliar with them. Because of their size and shape, rafts aren't easy to bite and fortunately sharks do not seem to realize how flimsy they are. In addition, if a shark is not provided with the attack stimuli (blood, fear, vomit, or struggling sounds), they approach much more cautiously. When they bump the raft to taste it, they get no stimuli that it is an animal. They therefore get no clear picture of what's going on or how capable this raft-creature is of defending itself. A well-placed blow may drive them off. This of course does not make the experience any less terrifying. Steve Callahan experienced just such a heart-stopping episode:

The raft is lifted and thrown to the side as if kicked by a giant's boot. A shark's raking skin scrapes a squeak from it as I leap from slumber. "Keep off the bottom!" I yell to myself as I pull the cushion and sleeping bag close to the opening . . . A flicker of light in the black sea shows me he is below, and I jab with a splash. Nothing. Damn! Again the fin cuts the surface. The shark smashes into the raft with a rasping blow. I strike at the flicker. Hit! The water erupts, the dark fin shoots out and around and then is gone. Where is he? My heart's pounding breaks the silence. From: *Adrift* (Pg. 60)

Dougal Robertson had an all-too-intimate encounter with a shark which he mistook for a dorado (at night):

I was tense and ready [to catch it by hand] when the fish jumped for the third time.; It landed against the side of the raft just under my right arm. I hooked my right arm under it and grabbed quickly with my left hand, then feeling the unslippery skin looked down at the white belly and U-shaped mouth of five foot shark lying docile in my arms like a baby. . I dropped it like a red-hot poker. It snapped its savage jaws, struck the raft a blow with its tail and was gone. From: *Survive the Savage Sea* (Pg. 84)

In conclusion, sharks are lean, mean killing machines but many life raft survivors have learned to live with them and drive them off. On their own turf, under their own rules, with a defenseless person in the water at their mercy, they represent the ultimate terror. If one sees a shark while floating in a life jacket one's hours are numbered, although many lucky survivors have succeeded in keeping them at bay by striking them.

While researching this subject, I have come across numerous suggestions from those who had obviously never seen the business end of a shark up close, and to lighten the somewhat heavy nature of this chapter I would like to share the two best with you: 1. Knock two stones together to frighten them (be sure to attach two stones to each life jacket). 2. Climb onto the shark's back and stick your fingers in its eyes. I love that one the most and I'm sure it would work—if the shark would let you .

A pack of hammerheads around a liferaft. Art By Rebecca Thomson

Gary Mundell and his wrecked boat. Painting by Richard DeRosset.

CHAPTER VII: MAROONED ON A TROPIC ISLE

There is just a small chance that one will be shipwrecked, and on a world populated by three billion people, there is an infinitely small possibility one will be cast up on a deserted island, rock or atoll. There are few places in the Atlantic or Mediterranean seas where one would find an unpopulated place or one that was not visited weekly by fishermen.

There is, however, a general depopulation of small islands as the natives migrate toward the cities. Islands with a population too small for a school are primary candidates. The people are forced to send their children away for an education. The children like the action of the larger place and stay. Eventually the island population consists of old people, and the community fails.

So there is an increasing, rather than decreasing, chance that one might encounter a truly deserted place somewhere in the Pacific, the Indian Ocean and the waters of Indonesia, including the Arafura, Banda, Celebes and Molucca seas. Most of these places were abandoned because they were geographically isolated, small, and lacked air strips or ports. Atolls with no passage or a shallow lagoon are first on this list. Being cast up in such a place is no joke but is certainly less life threatening than drifting in a raft. The principle problems consist of finding food and water and preventing illness. One must also have a shelter and create signals to attract passing vessels. All of these subjects will be discussed in this chapter.

Crusoe of Caroline Island

Gary Mundell once told me he had only been frightened at sea three times: when he sailed alone into Puget Sound, when he first sailed by himself out of sight of land and the night he hit Caroline Island. Our last time together before the loss of his Cape Dory 27, PETRAL, was in Bora Bora during the final days of August 1985. We were both preparing for solo passages to Hawaii, something not lightly undertaken. We talked then about fear, its mastery, and how the two were the yin and yang of courage. If one is never afraid, one can never be courageous. Fear and its mastery are a part of the ship's equipment: a combination, like anchors and sails, complimentary yet opposite, both essential to making the vessel complete.

The sun was so bright the day we parted, and in the calm air one could hear the ocean crashing on the distant reef. The lushness of the land, the smell of flowers and the smiles of the native girls surrounded us. In a way it seemed incredible that we should be moving on, but I guess there were still things we needed to learn that only the sea could teach us. We accepted the beauty of Bora Bora and stored it away, speaking in quiet tones not of the native girls but about oceans, currents and reefs. I believe my last words to Gary were *"You should buy a Sat/Nav and an EPIRB"*. *"I will"*, he said, *"as soon as I get to Hawaii."*

A week later PETRAL was lying high and dry on South Caroline Island. Gary's dead reckoned position had been in error. Light winds and a contrary current misled him. He thought he was well past the island by midnight when in fact it lay directly in his path 10-12 miles away. He was asleep when the boat hit the reef at 4:30 in the morning. PETRAL grounded gently. Her heavy glass hull remained intact.

Gary awoke suddenly when PETRAL jolted to a stop and heeled to starboard. The seas were calm and the boat did not pound. Still drugged by sleep and confused, he automatically donned his safety harness and stumbled on deck.

The sails were aback, and he freed them. Still not understanding the situation, Gary could not comprehend why PETRAL continued to heel. Was it some sort of weird current? Why was the water around the boat all white? Then he saw the distant coconut trees. He stared at them for a full 30 seconds and was shocked with understanding. He realized then that he was aground on Caroline island, an uninhabited atoll seven miles long, one mile wide, consisting of about 40 islets (called motus) and a shallow lagoon to which there is no entrance. Located at 150° W, 10° S, it is one of the most isolated pieces of real estate in the world, in one of the most trackless parts of the South Pacific Ocean.

The boat was in water only eighteen inches deep. Gary took an anchor, waded to the edge of the reef and planted it. There was still a chance, he thought, to kedge her off. But PETRAL was small and had no anchor windlass. She was also heavy (almost four tons), and there was no way he could get her unglued. He waded ashore in the false dawn to look for help but there was no help. The island was uninhabited and looked as though it had always been so. By the time he climbed back aboard PETRAL it was dawn.

Gentle but persistent seas had moved PETRAL even further onto the reef. Each wave of the rising tide pushed her 6-8 feet closer to shore. Gary took one look at her, knew she was doomed and understood completely the trouble he was in. Then he said the magic words: *"I'm afraid, but I'm a SURVIVOR and I'll live through this."* We spoke of that promise in San Diego, a year after the accident. He said:

> "I'm from Alaska and you have to learn to be tough in a cold place like that. When things get tough, I always consider it a sort of personal challenge. I've always thought of myself as a survivor and I knew I could make it. But it's a good thing I didn't know how long I was going to be on that island!
>
> Ninety percent of being a survivor is in the head. It's common sense and attitude. After all, the difference between an adventure and an ordeal is attitude. Some people just give up. Why? I can't understand that. I mean I knew I was in trouble but in some ways I never felt so alive. I just took a good, hard look at my needs versus my wants. I needed food and water, and I had them. I wanted toothpaste and toilet paper and cold beer. But I could live without them. When the ship rescued me, the first thing they did was give me a shower and a cold beer. Boy was that good.
>
> Sometimes things were tough, and in the beginning I didn't know if I was going to make it. But I just said to myself 'you're OK today, and we'll take care of tomorrow tomorrow'."

The water between the wreck and the shore was wading depth but it was full of large spiny urchins and some of the most aggressive (but fortunately not large) black-tip sharks. They charged Gary as soon as he set foot in the water. The god of fools, drunks, and sailors had protected him on his first trip ashore, but in the daylight, it seemed prudent to blow up his small inflatable.

A search of the motu confirmed that he was indeed alone. The only foot-prints in the sand were his own. Numerous glass fishing floats, plastic floats, countless SANTORI (Japanese) whiskey bottles and glass jugs littered the beach. He also found a 10-foot ACHILLIES inflatable marked YACHT HOWQUA. Countless terns, frigates, boobies and shearwaters wheeled overhead, crying, crying, casting their calls to the wind. Coconut crabs scurried into the bush. Clouds of mosquitoes and no-seeums surrounded him, and coconut rats fled from his advance. A survey marker at the southern tip of the island, left just three months before, confirmed that he was indeed on Caroline Island.

Despite his misfortune, Gary was lucky to have the entire contents of his boat with which to survive. When his VHF MAYDAY calls brought no response he began ferrying supplies to the beach. His first load consisted of the gear he considered most essential:

4-man Avon life raft	sails
10 gals. water	line

An emergency grab bag containing:	A signal pack containing:
diving goggles	10 red hand flares
candy	4 orange smoke flares
compass	1 flare gun, 25 mm
fishing kit	15 shells, red meteor
Gator Aide	8 shells, red parachute
pole spear with spare heads	
solar stills (2)	

On his second trip, Gary broadcast more Maydays, again without success, then returned to the island with most of the boat's canned goods, his fishing and diving gear, and a butane stove. Eventually he salvaged everything from the wreck including the boat's water tanks. Sea water finally washed onto the VHF making it inoperative.

A grove of coconut palms close to the beach seemed a good place for a camp. It was quite close to the wreck and had a 270° view of the sea to the south. Gary stretched a sail between the trees for an awning and used another for a floor. He inflated his life raft to use as a bed. At $2,500, the raft was undoubtedly the most expensive bed in the South Pacific! Inside the raft was the inevitable, totally inadequate "fishing kit;" three good parachute flares with a 90 second burn; a flashlight that worked; the inevitable, totally useless raft knife; and a small heliograph; as well as the usual pump, oars, first aid kit, bailer, patch kit, and sponges. He set up his kerosene cooker and the back-up propane burner nearby.

Except for the canned goods, his food supplies had become water-logged and useless. The vegetables, eggs and a plastic can of rice had survived. He ate the fresh food while it lasted and used the cans as a reserve. A 27-foot boat doesn't hold much food or water in the first place, and it was clear that the situation was not good. Gary psyched himself up for the ordeal and repeated over and over to himself *"I'm a SURVIVOR."* He collected trash from the beach and made a huge S.O.S. signal.

Despite his predicament, it was impossible to not appreciate the pristine beauty of the place. Countless palm trees chattered in the wind. The crash of the surf and the cries of the sea birds drifted on the ocean breeze. Tiny wavelets chuckled up a white coral beach to disappear in the sand. To the north the shallow, crystal clear lagoon sparkled in the sunlight. A thousand images of what the world was like when it was young danced before his eyes. It was, except for smiling native girls, the very image of paradise.

But coral atolls invariably lack one essential to make them a paradise— water. Coral rock is porous. Fresh water percolates through it and disappears. There isn't a single natural formation on an atoll which holds rain. Since there is no hard rock, to channel and collect subterranean water, there are never any springs. The plants which live there are specialized. All of them are, of course, highly resistant to salt. They have shallow root systems which cling to the coral rock since deep, penetrating roots would reach only salt water. Some, such as the coconut palm, have sponge-like interiors which hold fresh water. Other plant systems, such as mangrove, absorb sea water and excrete the salt. Still others, like glasswort, send out numerous tubers which act as a superficial root system, capable of absorbing rain and dew. Of these few species, the only one of interest to Gary Mundell was the coconut palm.

The first night ashore was hot and windless. Gary decided not to sleep in the raft but lay naked on a sail. He awoke with a start during the night to find a huge coconut crab crawling on him. It seemed as though the creature intended to devour Gary's most tender parts. In revenge, he killed it and had it for breakfast. All South Pacific islanders know that coconut crab is one of the area's greatest delicacies and is in fact the main export from many remote islands. The first crab proved to be entirely delicious as did the second, third, tenth, and hundredth. Gary never lost his taste for them and feasted on one aboard ship a few days after his rescue.

Gary made a coconut picker by lashing his spinnaker pole, boat hook, and fish gaff together using hose clamps. There were plenty of coconuts in the trees, but the rats and coconut crabs immediately devoured any which fell. He was able to drink as much coconut juice as he wished but coconut meat is a powerful laxative. If he ate more than a coconut or two per day he inevitably got cramps and diarrhea.

There was no rain during the first week, and Gary went on short rations. Normally a mellow, even-dispositioned man, he could not understand why he became extremely depressed a few days later. Consulting his medical guide, he learned that one of the effects of dehydration is depression. He immediately drank his fill, reminding himself that he had plenty of water and, also to "worry about tomorrow tomorrow." To his amazement the depression vanished almost as soon as he finished drinking.

Gary was afraid to dive for food because of the aggressive sharks and hesitated to eat the fish because many reef fish occasionally are poisonous (see Reef and Lagoon Fishing). He could have caught rats by suspending bait over a partially buried bucket. Rats make good food. That may seem disgusting but this is pure prejudice. Keep in mind that these were not city rats. They lived in an isolated, pristine environment and were certainly not contaminated. In many areas of the world, such as southeast Asia grain rats are regularly hunted and sold in the market place. They are sold skinned, but their tails are kept intact to show that they are not city rats. Coconut crabs were numerous and quite delicious—the idea of rat *en brochette* never occurred to him.

Gary did regret that he was unable to dive for lobster which are invariably quite numerous in lagoons. Later he learned that they are often trapped simply by dropping a piece of gill net (frequently found as flotsam along the beach) onto a grassy patch in the lagoon. The lobster, which wander along the grass flats at night, become trapped by their spines and are retrieved at dawn. Lobster traps, made from coconut fronds and a large tin can are also quite efficient. Coconut meat or dead fish make an excellent bait.

The coconut crabs and an occasional can of food became his entire diet. He caught rain using his sails and, after the first rain, never had to ration water again. By the time he left the atoll he had accumulated 60 gallons of water, having filled every tank and jar he owned. When it rained hard, Gary filled his inflatable and had a bath. The limitless quantity of empty jugs and whiskey bottles that littered the beach would have further increased his supply but Gary felt that 60 gallons would suffice.

Days turned into weeks. A month went by and neither ship nor plane passed by. Gary went to his lookout spot every half hour during the day and during the evening hours until it was time to sleep. He had decided to try attracting the attention of ships during the night, but not yachts, lest they become trapped by the low-lying reef. He often considered attempting to sail the ACHILLIES raft to Penrhyn island, 460 miles to the west. But such a voyage would have been extremely risky and this low-lying land would have been easy to miss. Once he departed Caroline Island, there would be no turning back. Since he had abundant food and water, he decided to "stay put."

When time hung heavy on his hands or he became frustrated, Gary would work on a "sail away" plan. "If you don't know what to do, do something. Keep busy, it does you a world of good." He made a square sail and mast for the inflatable and a list of what he would take with him. He salvaged his radio receiver from the wreck and was able to rig a long wire antenna, which pulled in Radio Australia quite well. He had a few magazines and books and fell into a routine.

He would awake with the sunrise, make coffee and then beachcomb. He eventually explored all of the motus, but they were small and barren. During the heat of the day, he would read beneath the awning or dictate notes into his cassette recorder. He would listen to the radio in the evening and then seal himself into his life raft in order to avoid the mosquitos, no-seeums and coconut crabs during the night.

Gary celebrated his thirtieth day as a castaway with a feast of ham and rice, a curry sauce and seed sprouts. He took a bath in the lagoon, cut his hair and beard and felt pretty good. His month of isolation had brought subtle character changes; he had learned to live entirely for the moment and not worry about the future. He became less emotional and was able to view the world without passing judgment upon it. Having no human contact, he had become totally absorbed with the activities of the world around him—the habits of the birds, the nocturnal wanderings of the crabs, the changes of the tide.

Through, or perhaps because of his ordeal, Gary had achieved the trans-cendental state. He came to realize the most important lesson of all: that happiness is in the mind. One doesn't need to be surrounded by possessions or even friends to be happy. It was sufficient to simply be alive, refreshed by the clean sea air and entertained by the cries of the sea birds. Beer is wonderful but so is fresh rain water. Steaks and ice cream are delicious, but so is fresh crab. Gary Mundell had become a happy man. Every day, in subtle ways, his bounty increased. He had no bank account, but also no taxes. He had only a sail for a roof and a life raft for a bed, but he also had no mortgage. There was neither television nor movies to entertain him but somehow he had learned to become content with the sunset, the moon-rise, the subtle workings of the world.

On the morning of the 45th day, while beachcombing, Gary spotted turtle tracks. The next day he found more tracks and a nest. The hole was huge, three feet deep and five wide, but he was unable to find any eggs. He concluded that he had dug in the wrong place. The hole had been created to cover the eggs which he thought were probably on the seaward side of the hole. The next evening he found turtle tracks that went up the beach, made a U-turn and went back into the sea. Gary decided to return that night and see if he could catch the beast on the beach.

He quietly walked the beach that night and heard the turtle digging a nest. He finally spotted a huge green turtle, weighing more than 250 pounds, flinging sand with its flippers at the edge of the beach. Gary didn't want to kill the creature but he was hungry. He had lost about 25 pounds and that turtle represented a huge amount of meat. He had a huge, double-edged dirk, what he calls an "armchair commando knife"—which he stabbed deep into the turtle's neck. He jerked his hand away, fearful of the turtle's bite. The turtle instantly made a U-turn and headed for the sea with the knife in his neck. Gary was finally able to pull out the knife and stab it again. The turtle hit him with a blow from its flipper that sent him flying.

With a huge effort Gary managed to flip the creature onto its back. He then returned to camp, got a hatchet, and tried to kill the beast with it, but the turtle's neck was so thick the hatchet wouldn't penetrate it. Gary finally used a piece of coral rock and the commando knife to sever its vertebrae. He opened the carapace and found 20-30 eggs, some in the unformed state. He concluded that the turtle had been making trips ashore to lay the eggs as they matured.

He took the eggs and the hind quarters, which weighed 20 pounds apiece, back to camp. Unlike some life raft castaways, Gary found the eggs disgusting, but the meat was delicious and a welcome change from crab. He returned the next day and took the front quarters back to camp. They weighed 40-50 pounds apiece. After cleaning, Gary had more than 100 pounds of fresh meat. He sliced it and hung it up to dry. At night he packed it away from the damp air. It was quite dry within two days and he felt rich.

On his 50th day, Gary busied himself collecting rain water. Between squalls, he saw a small ship three miles east of his island. Since he had seen no other vessel during his whole time on the motu, he made quite sure that the crew saw him, by firing a number of 12-gauge parachute and meteor flares, 2 orange and several red hand signals, and flashing his heliograph. He had prepared a smoke fire on the beach and he hastily dumped some kerosene on it and set it ablaze. He later learned that the crew had seen every signal but that made by the heliograph. The ship answered with its search light. Gary had been seen.

The CORIOLIS, a French oceanographic research vessel, then maneuvered to a place where the chart showed a pass through the coral and fired a green and a white rocket, a signal which means "We will attempt to land here." Gary frantically dumped the rain water out of his dinghy and began loading it with gear. He put on a red shirt so the crew would see him, collected his documents and paddled toward the ship which was in the process of launching an 18-foot outboard-powered runabout.

Unfortunately the charted pass no longer existed. It had become a mass of coral and there was in fact no break in the reef. The ship's crew spent almost a hour looking for a way to enter the lagoon, then tried to float a buoyed line through the surf, without success. Gary finally had to swim for it. The surge knocked him back a few times and he was cut by the coral but he at last succeeded in reaching the boat. Once aboard the CORIOLIS, the captain asked Gary if he wanted a cold beer. "You bet!" replied this lucky survivor.

The CORIOLIS spent several days at Caroline Island, during which the crew retrieved most of Gary's gear. In addition they discovered that Caroline island is more than 15 miles east of its charted position, an error more than sufficient to catch the boat of a tired single-hander.

Crab and lobster traps. Drawing by Rafael Monroy.

Food from the Reef and Lagoon

Crabs, octopus, shell fish and lobster are edible, and commonly found in all of the unpopulated areas where a castaway might come ashore. The white meat of land and beach crabs (intertidal zone crabs) is safe and edible and, because crabs are most easily caught, they usually are the first item on the castaways' menu.

TRAPS

Fish, crab, and lobster traps are labor-effective, easy-to-make and to use. The secret which makes these traps effective is the construction of the entrance, which permits the prey to enter but not escape. Fish traps utilize the fact that fish have eyes on the sides of their heads and therefore lack depth perception, particularly if they have to lie on their side and look upward, so trap doors should always point downward. The trap is designed to take advantage of this weakness. The fish easily perceive the entrance to the trap from the outside, but, without depth perception, cannot find their way out. The mouth's sharpened prongs, pointing inward, also deter escape.

Crab and lobster traps take advantage of the fact that the animals being trapped cannot actually swim (the crab species that can swim escape). A smooth entrance, made from a tin can or plastic jug (as are found washed up on beaches) makes it possible for the creatures to drop into the trap but offers no claw-hold when attempting to escape.

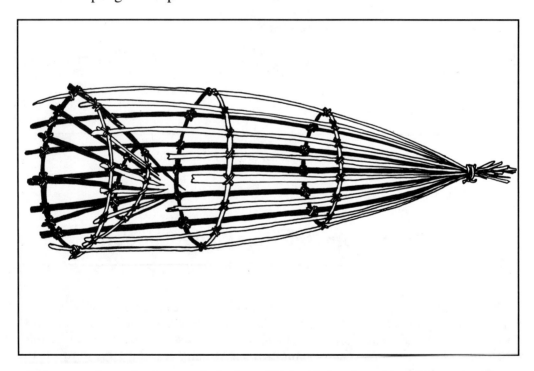

This trap can be made of coconut leaf spines. The fronds (not shown) can be woven together into a cage. The conical mouth has sharpened spines pointing inward to deter escape. The trap must be weighted. A piece of coconut meat can be added for bait. Art by Rebecca Thomson

Fish traps may be baited, but there is no positive evidence that the bait is what attracts fish. The bottom line is that fish are curious creatures and enter the trap to see what's inside. In some areas, items like broken china, tin cans or anything shiny are used to entice them.

Crabs and lobsters are scavengers, and the smell of carrion attracts them, especially at night. A dead bird carcass or fish flesh makes great bait but there is no evidence that spoiled flesh is preferred.   The traps are dropped on grass flats if possible, as these creatures scavenge the flats at night. Baits should be protected by wire mesh or a tin can to prevent the bait from being eaten. Traps can be made from any combination of coconut fronds, fish net, sticks, or line in some combination to make a cage. Several illustrations show successful traps that are in common use.

Traps must be weighted with rock because marine animals hesitate to enter objects that appear to be unstable or moving. Predatory animals such as sharks, octopi, and rays like to eat some or all of the trapped animals, so drop the traps in the evening and pull them up at first light.

THE LEAF SWEEP

This seemingly unlikely method is in reality an effective way of trapping fish   Groups of natives use the leaf sweep like a net to encircle fish but the survivor must operate in a different way, utilizing the sweep to trap fish in tide pools. Coconut fronds are tied or woven together to make a psychological barrier. The crude affair is placed in such a way as to block or impede the exit of fish from a tide pool as the tide falls. The fish could of course dart through the leaves but they have a tendency to retreat into the deepest end of the pool. The sweep is placed in position at high water and secured with coral rock anchors. The fisherman may also stand in the area and beat the water with a stick, shake the leaf sweep, or throw rocks to add to the effectiveness of the barrier. When the tide falls, the trapped the fish are then poisoned and/or speared.

SPEAR FISHING

Hunting for seafood with a spear is conducted in three ways: the spearing of surface fish, working tide pools, and diving. Diving is invariably productive, if one has goggles, but the dangers—coral cuts, fish attack, and drowning—should be considered. Natives in many areas have become extremely adept at spearing surface fish such as mullet.   The preferred technique is the first to

Spear heads can be made from a variety of materials. Left-to-right: stingray barbs, bamboo, stick and nail, fire-hardened stick with barbs, notched bamboo, bamboo with open jaws for minnows. Illustration by Rafael Monroy.

separate a fish from the school, keeping between it and the deep water. After the fish has jumped about seven times, or made a corresponding number of runs, it becomes fatigued and slows down. The spear is thrown at a shallow angle just ahead of the fish. The problem is that this technique requires considerable practice and is not labor-efficient unless the hunter is skilled.

Spear fishing in tide pools, especially if the pools have first been poisoned is quite effective. If one wades in a pool, it is extremely important to protect the feet and legs. Spears can be made from a variety of materials, including stingray spines, bamboo, fire-hardened sticks and nails. If large fish or turtles are hunted it is wise to attach some sort of float to the end of the spear, connected by a line. If the creature proves too difficult to land, the spear is released, and the animal, allowed to exhaust itself towing the float around.

CHOP FISHING

The hunter wades into thigh-deep water at night with a machete, stick or club, carrying a torch. Fish are attracted to the light and clubbed. Several castaways may also hold an emergency blanket to reflect moonlight, instead of using a torch. Wear shoes. Shuffle along the bottom to frighten-off stingrays.

The sea cucumber.

POISON

The **sea cucumber**, when annoyed, produces filaments of a potent purple nerve toxin. The toxin irritates or kills the fish but does not contaminate their flesh for human consumption. The best way to utilize it is to cut in half and impale a sea cucumber on a long pole and poke it into places of concealment in the reef, shaking and twisting the pole to distribute the toxin. Working around tide pools at low tide, or along walls in the reef, the sea cucumber can be used to hunt for octopus, crabs and lobster, which are often difficult to detect or extract from their places of hiding in any other way. The sea cucumber can also be used to immobilize small fish trapped in a tide pool. Several cucumbers can be beaten (to irritate them), then tossed into the pool. The creatures affected soon come to the surface, gasping for air. The poison produces a reaction very similar to Rotone, a poison used by scientists to gather marine specimens. Chlorine bleach, muriatic or battery acid or any powerful acid or base, injected in small quantities under coral heads will cause all marine life to evacuate their hiding places. These chemicals also kill the coral, destroying that part of the reef, therefore this technique should be used only under survival conditions.

THE OCTOPUS

The octopus lives in caves, under ledges or in holes in the reef. It is extremely cautious, masters at camouflage, and it is rarely caught in the open during the day. The presence of an octopus lair can be inferred by the presence of broken crab shells (crab is their favorite food) or clam shells. In addition, as the octopus travels to and from its lair, its tentacles overturn small pebbles. A pink, photosensitive algae lives on the bottom of these pebbles and the pink color is a sign that the bottom has been disturbed.

If an octopus can be speared in its den, the spear should be quickly twisted to dislodge its grip and the creature pulled out. Any hesitation allows the octopus to spread its tentacles against the cave walls, making it all but impossible to extract.

It is often easier to force the octopus from its den before spearing it . The sea cucumber can be used as described above. The mortal enemy of the octopus is the moray eel which abounds on the reef. A small eel can be speared and pushed into the octopus' cave. This usually sends the octopus flying out.

KILLING AND CLEANING

The traditional way to kill an octopus is to bite it between the eyes, destroying its brain. One may also use a knife. A certain amount of care should be taken that the octopus does not bite you while you are killing it as they often have a venomous bite. Only the blue-ringed octopus, found in tropical waters, is actually deadly—one of the most venomous of all marine animals. This small creature, about 8 inches in length has bright blue markings on its mantle and they are quite distinctive. People occasionally catch them, handle them because of their beauty and, alas, later die.

Kill the octopus, remove the beak and viscera, beat the body mercilessly with (or on) a rock to tenderize it. This is really important, as the creature is tasty but incredibly tough. Octopus may be eaten raw, boiled for a few minutes and the tentacles sliced into thin rounds (to make it less chewy). It can also be sun dried, raw, like fish flesh.

THE SEA URCHIN

The sea urchin is one of the sleepers in the tasty food department. They are found everywhere on the reef. Urchins are echinoderms, and like their cousins, the starfish, they have five-fingered radial symmetry. This symmetry is evident, internally. The five radial fingers of bright orange roe or milt are extremely evident just prior to mating season, which occurs frequently. The eggs look like tiny eggs. The milt is much finer. The majority of urchins are female. The eggs, eaten raw, boiled or fried are extremely delicious. They are really tasty boiled quickly in coconut milk.

The creature is collected from the reef, inverted, the bottom part of the shell broken away and the guts washed out. The eggs are attached like fingers to the top of the shell. The urchin is extremely useful as bait. They can be smashed up, placed in a can (to keep them from being eaten) and used as trap bait. The eggs can be crumbled and wafted beneath coral heads to entice hidden occupants. They also make good bait for rats.

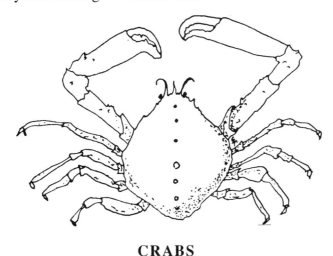

CRABS

Sea crabs are best caught in traps. One may also find them hiding under ledges in tide pools or lagoons and, if one has a diving rig, go get them. Small beach crabs (fiddlers) can be caught by hand (carefully), crushed and made into a broth. There usually isn't enough meat in them to mess with. Land crabs are usually quite delicious but aggressive. They may be eaten raw or boiled. The meat can be extracted from the shell and dried. If the day is hot, the crab may be dismembered and the leg meat partially dried in the shell, then extracted.

Food from the Island

BIRDS

Birds are particularly vulnerable at night when they come to roost. Those which are not nocturnal are usually reluctant to fly after dark for fear of collision with trees, etc. Rain not only increases this natural reluctance, it wets their feathers making it hard for them to fly. The preferred technique is to grab birds quietly and break their necks. The less fuss the better. If they are out of reach, a club or pole is the weapon of choice to knock them from their roosts. The hunting site should be selected during the day and, if possible, ground litter which will make noise when trod upon should be cleared. The important thing is to move quietly and not disturb the birds, for once they have become alarmed enough to fly, they will continue to do so for hours, or all night.

Some birds, such as the Cape dove, are nocturnal at the nesting site and can be caught by making a bonfire near the nests. The birds flutter around, attracted like moths to the light, and often fling themselves into the fire. This is an ancient technique used to capture shearwaters and petrels, and is still used in many parts of the world.

During the day, flesh-eating birds can be caught with a fishing hook and line. A small hook is embedded in a piece of bait large enough for the bird to swallow in one gulp. If the bait is too large, the creatures have a tendency to fly away with it to avoid competition with other birds. The bait is placed on a rock or log and the line led off a short distance Be sure to allow 3 to 4 feet of slack. The line does not have to be tended, but should be checked frequently.

Eggs and fledglings can often be found, and on low-lying, coral atolls, their nests are often concealed in ground litter or shrubs. Stand without moving or watch from a place of concealment. Chicks and fledglings are very sensitive to movement and instinctively freeze if you move. They are camouflaged and blend beautifully with their environment.

Tar balls, found on the beach, can be melted and smeared on branches where birds are seen to alight. Smaller birds are often trapped this way whch is used by many primitive people.

Some birds nest in burrows or holes. Probe for them with a stick but not your hand, as the holes sometimes contain crabs. Birds and other animals who hide in holes can often be flushed by lighting a small, smoky fire made of leaves, and fanning it into their burrows.

RATS

Most isolated places have a rat population, and they should not be shunned as food. Asians are very fond of rats, and they are sold in local market places. Westerners are disgusted by the thought of eating rats, because we associate them with garbage and disease, but as mentioned, a moment's thought makes it clear that there is neither garbage not disease on an uninhabited tropical island.

Rats are most easily caught using a baited bucket, sunk into the ground. The rats jump in to get the bait, but the smooth sides of the bucket make it impossible to climb or jump out. Coconut meat makes good bait and whatever you catch, rats or crabs, are edible. If no bucket is available, make a similar trap using a piece of plastic or an emergency blanket.

I personally prefer my rats sautéed, but if you don't have a good pan and a bit of garlic, I suggest that they be either boiled or spitted and roasted over a fire.

The Carolina hanging snare. Drawing by Rafael Monroy.

SNARES

Deserted areas sometimes harbor small animals such as rabbits or large ground birds, such as domestic chickens or turkeys, which have gone wild. There are a variety of ways to trap these creatures, but the easiest to remember is the **Carolina hanging snare,** frequently taught in U.S. Military survival courses. The trap can be set either as a head or foot snare on a trail or run. A bait-set can also be made at the base of a tree, or debris can be positioned to restrict the approach. The snare is made with a loop of line slipped with a bowline knot. The bent branch or sapling should be heavy enough to lift the animal out of the reach of rats and other predators. The loop either kills the animal by strangulation or prevents it from reaching and biting through the rope.

Another snare, useful for carrion-eaters is the baited trigger deadfall. Drawing by Rafael Monroy.

COCONUTS

Every tropical island in the world has coconut trees and they have always represented a staple part of the native diet. The top of green nuts are the softest and are more easily cut than mature nuts. A nail or other probe can be inserted through the eyes (it is necessary to make two holes, one to admit air, the other to emit the juice). Green nuts contain up to a quart of clear, delicious juice which, unfortunately has a slightly laxative effect. Most people find that they don't want to drink more than two nuts per day for this reason. Let your heinnie be your guide. The inside of a green nut contains immature meat called jelly, which is gelatinous and quite delicious. It makes a fine sauce for fish. Green nuts can be pared open with a knife or by using the several techniques described on the next page.

Mature nuts contain less liquid and it, too, is a laxative, but it has a pronounced coconut taste and is quite delicious. The meat is white and almost everyone knows what it tastes like. It can be shredded and mixed with flesh into a sort of stew.

When nuts fall from the tree, they are almost invariably devoured by rats or coconut crabs, but obviously some survive, or there wouldn't be any coconut trees on the island. The nuts that survive usually fall into debris where they are hidden or covered. When they sprout, the inside of the nut is completely filled by a white, delicious fiber called "cabbage." The sprout is also edible. It makes a fine salad and it can also be mixed with flesh to add variety to the meal.

The first problem is getting the nut out of the tree. A coconut pole, made out of whatever you can find, a knife, saw, junk metal hook, or rope loop is the tool of choice. Natives climb coconut trees hand-over-hand, either digging their toes into the trunk or using the edges of their feet. It looks easy, but so does ballet. I have never mastered it. Every survival manual mentions the "climbing loop," made from woven coconut husk or breadfruit bark fiber. The loop goes over the insteps and you hold on with the hands, hunching up both feet together. Then straighten out and repeat the process until you're up there. I have tried this a number of times and either failed immediately or gotten half way up, run out of both steam and courage, and then thanked a fickle God that I got down in one piece. Good luck!

Another method, which I have never seen used nor tried myself, is to make a fire around the trunk and burn the tree down. A coconut tree is both fibrous and full of moisture. It doesn't like to burn, but if you've got nothing else to do, why not give it a try? The advantage of taking the entire tree down is that you also get the leaves, for roofing material and the palm heart, in addition to the nuts.

Opening the coconut is another interesting process. I have seen natives open green nuts by pulling the fibers off with their teeth. I have always been very fond of my teeth, every one of them, and have maintained them at considerable expense. The inside of my mouth represents the complete history of dentistry in the 20th century, but if you want to go native, good luck.

The most popular and effective technique is to sharpen and fire harden a short, stout stick to strengthen the point. The blunt end is inserted into the ground at about a 30° angle. Hold the coconut in both hands, eyes down. Straddle the stick with the pointed end facing away from you. Raise the nut over your head and bring it smashing down on the point of the stick. Give the nut a twist to pry a piece of the husk away. Repeat until satisfied. I have watched skilled natives do this in about five seconds but I always held back, thinking that perhaps I would save my fingers for something more useful, such as typing. Finally I was goaded into giving it a try and found that it is a learnable technique that does not, in fact, require a finger sacrifice.

The third method, useful because it requires no tools, is to kneel in front of a rock with the nut, pointed end down, held in both hands. The nut is then pounded on the rock and the husk peeled away as the opportunity arises. The nut inside invariably cracks when this technique is used, so it is wise to have a container ready to receive the liquid. The draining of the nut, using this technique, is slow, so one nut is set aside to drain while others are opened.

The top 2 to 3 feet of a coconut tree contains a core called the heart. The fresh **palm heart** is extremely delicious, immensely superior to the canned variety. I consider it one of the gastronomic pinnacles of the vegetable world.

The coconut opening stick. Drawing by Rafael Monroy.

It is crisp, like a water chestnut, with a delightful, nutty flavor. Once the tree is felled and the top 2 to 3 feet separated from the trunk, the outer core is peeled back until a color change (the heart is ivory-colored) appears.

FINDING ABANDONED, CULTIVATED FOOD

An island may be deserted, but at one time natives may have come to harvest coconuts. These people often planted the classic island foods breadfruit, taro and bananas. Sometimes one finds mangos. Breadfruit is a round, rough-textured, green fruit, bigger than a softball and smaller than a basketball, which grows on a tree up to 30 feet tall. The tough, 3 to 9 lobed leaves are 1 to 3 feet long. They make a good plate or roof covering.

The breadfruit tree and its leaves. Drawing by Raoul Reys.

The breadfruit, knobby on the outside with a thick skin, has ivory-yellow flesh and black seeds. The fruit can be eaten raw and is supremely uninteresting to the palate. It may also be cooked by tossing it into the embers of a low fire, turning it until the husk is thoroughly charred. It may be cut into pieces and roasted next to the embers. Natives are fond of dipping the cooked breadfruit into a mixture of shredded, fermented coconut meat and juice. Discard the seeds.

The Taro plant. Drawing by Raoul Reys.

Taro looks like a large lily plant, with a single, heart-shaped leaf up to two feet long on a stalk up to five feet high, and a pale flower, a foot or more high containing a pale yellow spike. The huge leaf makes a fine hat. The plant likes moist, rich earth and prefers overhead forest cover. **Taro patches** are usually created by natives as the plant is not indigenous to waterless islands. Look around places where villages have been. Taro patches are usually created by digging a large pit, lining the bottom with rock (to hold moisture) and filling it with plant vegetation. Bananas grow in similar areas. The tubers and leaves of the taro plant are both edible, but must be boiled, to remove crystals, which irritate the mouth and throat.

Bananas, when no longer cultivated, tend to form dense patches and grow to great heights. The stalks are easily broken and the ripe fruit harvested. Bananas may be ripened by dipping in sea water and hanging until they turn yellow-green. The stalk may be cut three to six inches from the ground and hollowed-out. The bowl thus formed fills with a bitter liquid which, if drained two or three times, becomes drinkable and refills for several days. In many ways the banana is the "perfect food," rich in potassium, carbohydrates and oils. It may be cut into rounds and smoked over the fire, which slightly dries and preserves it. Banana leaves make good roofing material and are also used to wrap fish and meat for cooking on embers.

Face page: Distilling fresh water from sea water. Top: Sun shines through clear plastic, evaporating water from seaweed or other sea water-immersed debris. Water vapor collects on plastic, then drips into can. Bottom: Line pit with rocks. Allow sun to warm the pit. Add sea weed or wet debris after sundown. Cover pit with plastic or bottom of life raft.

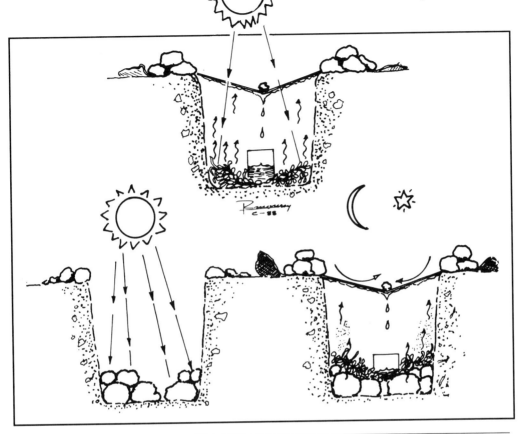

Water

The best way to make fresh water from sea water is with the solar still illustrated above (unless of course you have a desalinator). Dig a large, sloping pit, cover the bottom with wet sea-weed or debris and place a can or bucket in the center (top illustration). Cover the pit with clear plastic, place a weight at the center. Sunlight will evaporate the fresh water from the sea weed. It will condense on the plastic and drip into the can.

If you lack clear plastic but have an emergency blanket, about 3-4 p.m., line the pit with rock, then water-impregnated plant debris or seaweed (bottom illustrations). Just after sunset, add the scaweed, cover the pit with plastic, an emergency blanket or a life raft. Put a weight on the material above the can. The warm debris will emit water vapor which will condense on the cool plastic after sundown.

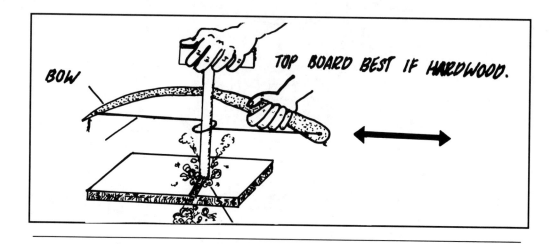

BOW

TOP BOARD BEST IF HARDWOOD.

Making a Fire

A magnifier has been included in the survival pack for making a fire. If you have no fire-making equipment, try the bottom of a broken bottle, found on the beach. This rarely works, but give it a try. Failing that, try one or several of the methods shown above. None of these techniques is "sure-fire", in damp conditions they take time and practice. That's the reason someone invented the match. Persistence is the motto for this job.

If you don't have matches or a magnifier, it is better to keep a fire going overnight. This is best accomplished with a pit made of closely packed stones, mortared with sand or debris. The bottom of the pit is lined with stones to act as a heat sink. A fire is started, a bed of embers built-up, then fresh fuel is added and the pit is covered to damp the flame. Air is allowed to enter the system at its base by making one or two small holes in the base of the pit wall. Primitive people who use this technique usually develop the habit of waking several times in the night to add fresh fuel. In the morning, the pit is uncovered and the ashes fanned away. The few remaining live coals form the base of a new fire.

Signals

Having reached a tropic island, the methodical survivor will neither starve nor die of thirst. Do not become anxious or depressed; help will eventually arrive. Be sure to have a signal fire and flag at the highest point of the island to attract assistance. The fire can be prepared in advance from sticks, debris and coconut frond spines. It is best to collect them just after a rain, so that the salt has been washed away. Allow them to dry before preparing the fire. Dig a pit to shield the flames from the wind. Place the material on a piece of plastic or hard debris to prevent permeation by ground moisture. Use shredded wood debris as tinder. Add tar balls and dried coconut meat to create smoke. Examine and turn the tinder daily to be sure it is dry. If you have any remaining rockets or flares, store them nearby as the highest place on the island is one of the best places to fire them.

A signal flag indicating distress consists of a flag showing a square and a ball above or below the square. This is a universal signal understood by all licensed Captains. Cloth, plastic or debris may be used. If cloth is used, make a support arm so that the signal can be seen in a calm. Find or clear a place on the beach and make as large a "HELP" signal as possible. A square and a circle may also be used, but private pilots may not understand this signal. If your camp is not adjacent to the signal, make an arrow pointing toward it.

An offshore view of rescue signals.

CHAPTER VIII: FOOD AND WATER

A sailor contains about 55-65% fluid (by weight)—7% of that is blood and an unknown quantity, beer. One would think that with so much liquid sloshing around in a sack of skin, a considerable amount could be spared. Unfortunately, the body does not like its chemistry tampered with even slightly. A body fluid loss of just 2% causes strong thirst signals and immediate discomfort. After a 10 % loss of fluid, a normal man can no longer stand. A 20% loss results in death.

Since there is extremely little water in a life raft equipment pack, the wise captain makes sure that extra water is taken aboard the survival craft. How much water? As much as possible. Five gallons of water per crewman, in plastic jugs also containing air, connected to the survival craft by stout lines would be ideal. This amount will sustain someone without supplement for 32 days if a proper survival strategy is adopted.

The Physiology of Water Loss

Think of the human body as a machine that runs well only at 98.6° F. and a surface temperature of about 92° F. When the air or water surrounding the body causes the skin temperature to fall below 92°F., the machine runs faster to keep the body warm. Above 92° F. It must dissipate heat.

The human machine runs all the time, even when the body is at rest. Like all idling motors, it generates a certain minimum amount of heat and waste products, which must be constantly removed. Heat is usually dissipated using body fluid as the carrier. In other words, the human machine is water cooled, and most of its waste products are carried off using water as the carrier.

Face Page: Art by Jim Sollers

SOURCES OF NORMAL FLUID LOSS

In order to keep the human machine functioning, water is dissipated as vapor in the breath, urine and sweat. A normal person exhales about a quart of water vapor every 24 hours. This amount is increased by labor. The elevated temperature resulting from labor, infection or dehydration causes panting and additional vapor loss.

The water in urine is required to carry off body wastes. The average normal person excretes about 1.5 pints of urine, but someone experiencing initial dehydration excretes about .75-1 pint per day. Since it is quite salty and full of toxins, it should never be drunk. When the intake of fluids is further reduced, urine volume decreases, but only slightly, not in proportion to the water deficit, and always at the cost of reduced kidney efficiency, making the sufferer feel a variety of symptoms, all unpleasant. In the final stages of dehydration, when body systems are failing, urine turns first bloody, then black, and dramatically decreases in volume, below about 4 oz. per day. This is a sign of kidney failure. Shortly thereafter, the sufferer lapses into a coma and never recovers.

Urine production increases (which of course means more water is lost) as the result of work. When there is insufficient water, hunger usually disappears. High quality survival rations, made from sugar and carbohydrates, actually make more water available to the body than is needed to digest them. Protein digestion produces less, but since fish flesh is mostly water, it, too, is a source of vital fluid. **It is a myth that food generally takes more water to digest than it produces.** Read more about this in chapter XIX.

Sweat is the major vehicle of heat dissipation and causes the greatest amount of fluid loss in warm climates. When the body is dehydrated, sweating decreases, but, like urine production, there is a certain minimum that must be produced. Tiny, almost microscopic beads of moisture are excreted from 2,000,000 sweat glands. Heat is carried off with it and evaporation further cools the body. An individual is not really aware of the sweat or of the fluid being lost. **Keeping the body cool with saltwater is therefore the best strategy to reduce sweat loss to a minimum.** Survival time may be increased significantly this way. Unfortunately, constantly wet skin increases the likelihood of saltwater sores.

A water ration of less than what the body needs results in depletion of body fluids. No strategy, such as drinking a little bit each hour or all of it at mealtimes, makes any difference. The body only cares that it gets enough and expresses this need as thirst. When it does not get enough water, the body first uses cellular fluid and plasma to maintain the proper heat dissipation rate. It eventually breaks down first fat, then muscle tissue, for the water and nutrients it contains. This explains the almost inevitable weight loss castaways experience, regardless of food consumption.

No method of "adapting" the body to reduced water intake or training it to ignore thirst has ever been discovered. Desert nomads, once thought to have reduced fluid requirements have absolutely the same physiology as you or me. Nomads are merely more capable of reducing unnecessary water losses than we are.

While thirst is how the body measures its water needs under normal conditions, the hardships of survival produce some failure of this mechanism. The body may be "thirsty" for various salts (discussed later). Sometimes sudden water ingestion, sufficient to rehydrate the body, produces nausea when it is drunk. In addition, the stomach of a castaway shrinks and cannot hold large amounts of water. Last but not least, foul-tasting water is often difficult to drink, even if it means the difference between life and death. Since the body itself is the best place for a survivor to store water, this is a problem of considerable concern. This is the reason why the introduction of water by enema should be considered, and why an enema kit is included on the survival pack list. Fresh or ill tasting (**but not salt**) water may be introduced through the bowel, a cup at a time, until no more is absorbed. **Taking saltwater by enema has the same negative results as drinking it.**

The Symptoms of Dehydration

(Read more about food and water deprivation in chapter XIX)

Severely dehydrated castaways eventually spend much of their time in a catatonic-like state. They experience auditory, olfactory and visual hallucinations which seem powerfully real. More than one castaway has jumped over the side to swim for a nonexistent beach, to find help, even to go and buy a newspaper. Sometimes they become violent and have been known to kill their mates. They must be restrained with force or tied down, but these clever madmen often find a way to silently slip their bonds and vanish over the side.

This report, by Lt. A.H. Rowlandson, survivor of the SS BRITANNIA adrift for five days on a float, is classic:

> Marks showed signs of exhaustion and it soon became clear that his mind was wandering . . . . He was able to picture a scene of his own fishing village and carried on conversations with boatmen around him. He was very anxious to swim ashore which he said he had often done from there before and I had to use force to restrain him on several occasions. . . . During the night Marks at last swam away from us and swam into the darkness. From: *Safety and Survival at Sea* by E.C.B. Lee and Kenneth Lee, © 1980., by permission of K.S. Giniger Co. New York and Greenhill Books/Lionel Leventhal, London (Pg. 93)

People on insufficient water rations suffer a series of body changes: their pulse and temperature rise, they breath faster, the thickened blood requires the heart to beat harder to maintain circulation. Circulation in the fine capillaries servicing the skin is highly reduced due to the thickened blood. This can result in "bedsores" from laying too long in one position on a hard surface. These sores, actually a form of gangrene, can result in severe damage to the affected areas. Poor circulation also causes tingling and/or numbness of the limbs, a loss of appetite, nausea, motor impairment, psychological instability, depression, and of course both mental and physical exhaustion.

The mouth and mucous membranes become severely desiccated, usually forcing the mouth to remain open, hastening dehydration. The membranes become "as dry as lizard skin," according to Dougal Robertson. He said, "This is why, when the water supply is so low that only a mouthful may be taken in the evening, it is such a pleasure to let the mucous membrane resume its identity and the mouth obeys the shut-up order."

The symptoms of water deprivation are vividly described by Nursing Sister Doris Hawkins, who endured an incredible 27 days adrift in the doldrums. The thirty foot lifeboat from the SS LACONIA originally contained sixty-eight persons, sixteen of whom survived.

> Our worst torture was thirst . . . . When we received our precious drop [a ration of two ounces], we took a sip, ran it around our teeth and gums, gargled with it and finally swallowed it. We repeated this until not a drop nor a drip was left clinging to the little biscuit tin from which we drank . . . . As we grew weaker and our mouths more and more dry, we only spoke when necessary. . . . Our nails became brittle and broke easily; many of us found our cuticles peeling away, and our nails became very pale. After a few days we all became a little light-headed and were unable to sleep, but dozed lightly and dreamed always of water, cool drinks, fruit—and of rescue. . . . Our tongues became hard and dry and our lips swollen and cracked. Many of us kept our teeth clean by rubbing them with a piece of cloth soaked in sea water. When we talked our mouths were curiously misshapen and our voices harsh and weak . . . . It was impossible after a few days to eat our biscuits or malted-milk tablets. The biscuits just blew out of our mouths as we chewed them and they just would not go down . . .   From: *Safety and Survival at Sea* , ibid.

Towards the third week at sea, I could not eat at all because I was devoid of saliva, and depended for life on my water ration. We ran out of water. We prayed for rain. The next morning we had a torrential downpour, lasting nearly six hours. . . . Our dried-up bodies took on new strength as we absorbed this life-giving water and drank as we had dreamed of doing for so long. That day I managed to eat two biscuits again, and two or three Horlick's [malted milk] tablets. From *Safety and Survival at Sea* , *ibid.* (Pg. 96)

As the body dehydrates, the human machine works harder, producing more heat and therefore increasing body fluid loss. In other words, one of the best ways to reduce unnecessary fluid loss is to drink enough in the first place and this must be remembered when deciding on the size of the water ration. A tiny water ration, designed to make the supply last as long as possible, may in fact be more wasteful and life-threatening than a larger one.

SUMMARY OF WATER REQUIREMENTS

There is no consensus about what is the precise amount of water a person needs to survive and extensive library research by this author has revealed nothing but conflict. The *Manual of Naval Preventative Medicine* recommends a minimum of a gallon of water per day to maintain health. Research done during WW II described in *Physiology of Man in the Desert* suggests a minimum requirement of about 1.5-3 quarts per day, depending on conditions. The *Search and Rescue Manual* produced for the U.S. armed forces suggests about 2/3 quart per day depending on conditions (see table on next page), and this seems to be a more realistic figure, in line with SOLAS suggestions of **600 ml. (20 oz.).** Steve Callahan states that he lived on about 1.25 pints per day, supplemented by occasional fluid from fish. In addition, it is clear that actual needs vary from person to person depending on body weight physiology, etc. As a result, there is no really fair way to determine what an individual needs to sustain life. The ration is therefore kept uniform to eliminate arguments about unfairness—even though that, too, may be unfair.

Problems of Ion Deficiency

The castaway's main problem is lack of adequate drinking water. But body fluid also contains sodium, potassium calcium, and magnesium chloride salts, which, when dissolved, exist as positively and negatively charged ions. If they are seriously depleted, death occurs. Vomiting and diarrhea, as induced by diseases such as cholera, cause death because essential ions, as well as water, are rapidly depleted. Vomiting from seasickness in a survival craft is equally life-threatening because both the water and the ions are difficult to replace. The motion of the survival craft is different than that of a boat or ship and sea-sickness may occur even in sailors who are never seasick.

Drainage of soluble ions into damaged, burned, ulcerated or infected areas is life-threatening if they are not replaced. Extra-cellular fluid, rich in ions, seeps into these tissues robbing the body core. The affected areas become swollen. This is because they are full of lost cellular fluid. Sunburn is a serious

TOTAL FLUID LOSS AT DIFFERENT TEMPERATURES
(of a slightly dehydrated person wearing clothes in the shade)

TEMPERATURE (°F)	FLUID LOSS (quarts/day)
90	3.0
85	2.3
80	1.9
75	1.7
70	1.5
60	1.4
50	1.3
40	1.3

From: *Physiology of Man in the Desert*, Pg. 293

TOTAL LOSS OF BODY FLUIDS PER DAY (24 hours)
(of a slightly dehydrated man in a raft at 85°F)

CONDITIONS (at 85°F)	FLUID LOSS (quarts/day)
No shade, wet	1.3
No shade, immersed	1.5
Shade, dry	2.4
No shade, dry	3.2

From: *Physiology of Man in the Desert*, Pg. 290

problem for the castaway. The same sunburn, acquired at the beach and considered only a minor annoyance, can be life-threatening in a survival craft.

The area affected by a sunburn is often massive, and far more plasma infiltrates it than is realized. The survivor's temperature rises, breathing rate increases, and even more vital liquid is lost through the breath. Tremendous amounts of soluble ions are concentrated near the damaged tissue. The injured person becomes thirsty, but this signal from the body is somewhat erroneous. What the body really needs, in addition to water, is soluble ions as are found in broth—or seawater.

In the survival craft environment, a considerable quantity of salt particles are ingested by breathing, licking the lips, etc., and it is seems unlikely that a castaway would lack sufficient potassium, calcium, iron and magnesium to maintain a healthy ion level. Sea water contains all of these salts. But Thor Heyerdahl, whose environment was similar to that of a castaway, said:

> On really hot days in the tropics you can pour tepid water down your throat till you taste it at the back of your mouth, and you are just as thirsty. It is not liquid the body needs then, but, curiously enough, salt. The special rations we had on board included salt tablets to be taken regularly on particularly hot days, because prespiration drains the body of salt. We experienced days like this when the wind had died away and the sun blazed down on the raft without mercy. Our water ration could be ladled into us 'til it squelched in our throats, but our stomachs malignantly demanded much more. On such days we added 20 to 40 per cent of bitter, salt seawater to our fresh water ration and found, to our surprise, that this brackish water quenched our thirst. We had the taste of seawater in our mouths for a long time afterward but never felt unwell, and moreover we had our water ration considerably increased. From: *Kon Tiki* (Pg 133)

When survival pack vitamins are purchased, be sure they contain minerals.

The Water Ration

There is no way to know how long a water supply must last or when it will be replenished. Most survivors spend less than three days adrift before being rescued. Others, described in this book, have spent months afloat. A rescue vessel may arrive at any moment. It might rain enough to fill every container an hour after the last drop is drunk. There also may be no rain for weeks, even though it is the heart of the rainy season. The uncertainty of the future encourages hoarding, but this natural tendency must be balanced by knowledge. It may seem prudent to issue a tiny ration, far below the body's minimum needs, but this is invariably a losing strategy.

From the discussion in this chapter, it is obvious that a ration of less than 1-1.5 quarts of water per day, depending on conditions, will cause a water deficit, resulting in fluid loss from the body core and eventually loss of fat and protein. A person cannot maintain good health indefinitely on this amount but 600 ml. or twenty ounces per day will prevent death for a long time if a person does not fall ill or develop extensive sores.

Since there is no way to know how long you will be adrift, there is absolutely no way to make a perfect plan for conserving water. The available supply, your location, the season, how much it has rained in the past weeks are all factors to consider. If a decision has been made to sail for land, and if water supplies are adequate, it is logical to divide the water by the number of days projected to make a landfall.

If water is in short supply, it is wise to drink nothing (or very little) for the first day to bring the body into a slight state of dehydration. This will cause the body to reduce fluid output to a minimum when drinking begins. Thereafter, start with 1.25 pints (600 ml.) of water per day, which should be increased if disturbing dehydration symptoms occur.

Keep in mind twenty ounces is not a sacred measure. The crew of the LUCETTE lived on 1/3 cup of water per day for six days and were still able to function. Every imaginable tiny quantity of water has been issued to castaways as a ration over the centuries. The pitiful survivors described in *Lost* (see Chapter II) were reduced to **a cup per week**. Others have been issued 2 ounces per day, 1/3 pint per day, etc. In all of these cases, a shocking reduction in the ability to function eventually occurred, frequently followed by death. Regardless of quantity, the size of the ration must be discussed with the crew and an agreement reached. Never make a unilateral decision regarding water rations.

WHEN TO DRINK

A drinking schedule for castaways is one of choice. The group should analyze the available supply and agree on how much and when to drink. It is best to spread the ration over the course of the day, if for no other reason than that it gives everyone something pleasant to anticipate and keeps the mouth lubricated, allowing it to close. Certainly, it is wise to drink before and after eating to promote digestion and to clear the mouth. Consuming morning, afternoon and evening rations of water and food also coincides with normal body biorhythms. The evening ration, taken after sunset, will help the castaways to sleep. A small ration should be issued 10 to 20 minutes before eating, to restore appetite and lubricate the palate. A few sips during the meal also hclp, followed by the balance of the ration for "dessert." It is unwise to issue a ration at night because the water may be spilled in the darkness.

Regardless of how the water is divided, everyone must get the same ration, unless illness indicates special treatment due to the imminence of death. Children are a special problem, and it is painful to watch them suffer. They have a more active physiology, but this is somewhat balanced by their lesser mass. The size of a child's ration must also be decided by the group. Everyone should drink at the same time, in view of the others, preferably from a container which holds the individual ration. In this way no one can thought to be taking more than their share. If one person drinks, everyone drinks. Pleas for more must, by necessity, fall on deaf ears.

If the group is large, one person must be assigned the task of guarding the water. Since water, for a castaway, means life itself, some sort of punishment must be imposed on anyone who steals it. Stealing water may very well be the equivalent of murder. Under desperate conditions, men have been killed for stealingit. This may seem like an unusually cruel punishment which I am certainly not suggesting, but the fact that murder is committed gives one a clear idea of how maddening chronic thirst is and how precious water can be. The logical punishment to impose on a water thief is a reduction of their ration.

WATER CONSERVATION

While it is impossible to reduce water requirements below minimum body demands, much can be done to eliminate additional losses. Any kind of heavy work, such as rowing, should be done in the cool of the night. One should relax in the shade as much as possible and further cool the body with seawater. The canopy should be doused with seawater as well. It is unwise to actually jump into the ocean to cool off because of sharks and the possibility of being unable to climb back aboard. But clothing may be dipped into the sea, then wrung out and worn, especially as a turban, trailed down onto the neck.

Wet clothing cools you off, reducing sweat prouction, but cold, wet clothing worn at night must be experienced only once to be fully appreciated. Clothing must therefore be allowed to dry before sunset, or the castaways must wrap themselves in emergency blankets, which do not absorb water.

Water can also be poured over the body, using the raft as a bath tub. A double floor, a canopy and (in addition to the canopy) a fly (an additional shade over the canopy) made from emergency blankets all insulate the body from the effects of heat or cold. An insoluble skin barrier such as sun block reduces radiation induced losses, but not as well as clothing.

Collecting   Water

Collecting rain is one of the primary life-sustaining activities of any castaway. When rain water becomes available, **drink it first**, in preference to packaged supplies. **Rain does not keep as well as sterile packaged water.** It may become foul-smelling,-looking and-tasting. The map-diagrams at the end of this chapter make it clear that there are few areas of the sea where it does not rain. Water may be collected by catching rain in clothing which is then wrung out into a container. Most raft canopies have been designed for rain collection and some rafts come supplied with an additional plastic sheet for this purpose, but a container for rain water is usually not provided. Empty tins, or whatever is available must be used. A survival pack containing several emergency blankets and a **collapsible jug** radically improve your chances of maximizing rain collecting efforts.

The quantity of rain collected is a direct function of catchment surface area. A strategy to maximize this area utilizing the efforts of all castaways must be devised and practiced before it rains. Some people should be assigned to holding water collection panels, others to collecting the run-off and storing it. Place the collector as high as possible to avoid contamination by salt spray.

Before a rain shower, wash the raft, clothing, and collecting panels with seawater to remove encrusted salt. Rinse the interior of the craft as well, for it is quite likely that bilge water, accumulated during the rain, may be drinkable or used as an enema even if it is slightly brackish. Secure all loose items before the shower so that they will not be lost in the excitement of rain collection.

LIQUID FROM FISH

Aside from rain, dew, desalinator production, or solar still distillate, the only water supplement available to a castaway is found in the body fluids of fish. This fluid is a beautiful balance of water and essential soluble ions. For this reason castaways who are short on water should actively fish as much as possible. But people who are severely dehydrated because of an insufficient water ration are usually too weak to fish, reducing their chance of survival.

Obtaining fluid from fish is a well-known technique, discussed in Chapter II (*The Bombard Story*) and was described in 1947 by Thor Heyerdahl, in his book, *Kon Tiki:*

> The old natives knew well the device which many ship-wrecked men hit upon during the war—chewing thirst-quenching moisture out of raw fish. One can also press the juices out by twisting pieces of fish in a cloth, or, if the fish is large, it is a fairly simple matter to cut holes in its side, which soon become filled with ooze from the fish's lymphatic glands. It does not taste good if one has anything better to drink, but the percentage of salt is so low one's thirst is quenched. (Pg 132)

COLLECTING DEW

Late in the afternoon, it is wise to thoroughly sponge the salt crust off of the survival craft so that evening and morning condensation will not be excessively brackish. This moisture can be sponged up and consumed.

SOLAR STILLS

More than one lucky survivor has thanked the man who invented the marine solar still, but they are expensive, don't always produce at their "rated" capacity, and become damaged by time. People often compare their price to the cost of a jug of water, and decide to take their risks. Sea conditions, clouds, and cold weather often reduce their efficiency. They were, until recently, just about the only way to "make" drinking water. Years ago, survival craft contained chemical packets which precipitated the salts from seawater but the price of these chemicals became excessive and they are no longer manufactured. One may occasionally find surplus desalting kits and these still function, but the yield-to-kit-weight is poor.

Solar stills evaporate fresh water from seawater, using sunlight, or temperature differences as the driving force. They function best in the backyard and they don't like cloudy days or rough seas. They have never been a popular item, they are expensive, and a number of manufacturers have stopped making them.

Thousands of solar stills were manufactured for life rafts during WW II and many of these are still sold as surplus. The solar stills Steve Callahan had were of this type and kept him alive. THESE UNITS ARE NOW TOO OLD and should not be purchased. I carried three in my survival pack. When I tested them, two of the three would not hold air and could not be fixed. The third produced up to a quart per day—floating in a swimming pool.

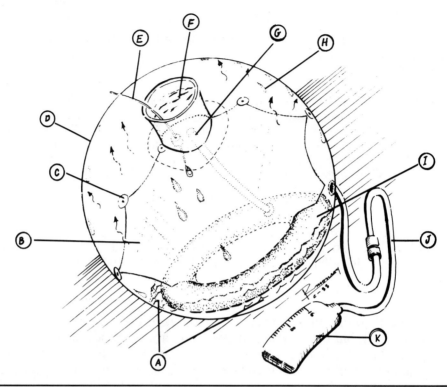

The "heart" of this still is a sea water-impregnated black wick (B), from which fresh water is distilled, using the sun's energy. Pure water vapor (arrows), evaporated from the wick condenses inside the balloon and runs to the bottom of the still (A), then drains through a tube (J) into a bag (K). The unit is first inflated through the reservoir (F), after which a half gallon (four pounds) of sea water, is poured through a tube (G), into a ballast ring (I) which keeps the unit upright. Additional water, added periodically to the reservoir then dribbles through a valve, aided by a "jiggle string" (E). It wets the wick, which is suspended by clips (C) inside the balloon. The floor of the still is semi-permeable, allowing passage of sea water to moisten the wick, but trapping air inside. If the sea is rough, sea water often drips from the wick onto the balloon surface, contaminating the distillate. Maximum production, determined under actual survival conditions indicates production of 30-16 ounces/day, depending on conditions.

Most solar stills are designed to operate while floating in the sea, but more than one castaway found that they worked better sitting on top of the raft. If solar stills are purchased for a survival pack, the wise captain buys more than the minimum number needed to sustain life and it might be cheaper to purchase a desalinater, discussed next.

The initial distillate from a solar still tastes strongly of the chemicals associated with manufacture and packaging. Later, the distillate becomes as tasteless as all distilled water and since it lacks minerals, it does not quench your thirst, even if the body utilizes it efficiently. For this reason, it is better to mix the distillate with a bit of rain water or dew. Some manufacturers recommend mixing a bit of the glucose tablet found in survival rations with the distillate.

Reverse Osmosis Water Purifiers

In the mid-1980's, Recovery Engineering, (1204 Chestnut Avenue, Minneapolis, MN 55403) developed a hand-operated seawater desalinator containing a synthetic, semi-permeable membrane. The membrane acts as a barrier against salt and other impurities, such as bacteria. Sea water is hand pumped against it under high pressure. A small amount of fresh water (10%) passes through. The remaining 90%, still under pressure, is recycled to the back side of the pump's piston. This clever technique makes pressures as high as 1,000 psi possible, utilizing hand power alone and resulting in 99% salt-elimination.

Recovery Engineering's *"Survivor 06"* is a 2.5 lb, 5" x 8" device which is rated to produce a cup of fresh water (0.24 L) in 13 minutes at 30 strokes per minute. Navy enlisted men in a life raft simulation, produced almost a half-gallon in 35 minutes. The promotional literature indicates a shelf life of four years without testing, and an operational life of 1,000 hours, but the primary mission of the unit is to operate with extremely high reliability and efficiency for 100 hours, during which time about 96 liters of water could be produced.

The pump is extremely rugged and has been tested under a wide variety of conditions. Since the membrane is organic, it does not deteriorate, and a biocide is provided to discourage bacteria from developing on the membrane after use. There is considerable reason to believe that the unit would function properly after many years of storage, even without testing.

On the other hand, the unit requires a considerable expenditure of effort to operate. A 30-minute test left me tired, although the unit did produce at its rated capacity. Eventually, I discovered that pumping faster than suggested was counter-productive. It required much more energy, and pumping very slowly resulted in little yield. If food was scarce, the survivors would weaken. They would find it increasingly difficult to produce water. Their water need would be further increased as a result of the energy expended to operate the pump. Children and/or injured crew would find it difficult to supply sufficient energy to meet their drinking needs and it would require a stronger person to help them.

On the third hand, the psychological advantage of knowing that there is a virtually inexhaustable water supply cannot be underestimated. In addition, it would allow the survivors to save their emergency water rations and this would pro-vide even further security.

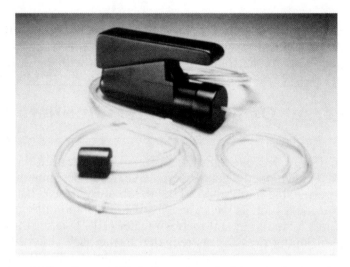

The Survivor 06 Desalinator. The bulb on the end of the tube is a pre-filter. The other end may be placed in the mouth or led into a container. Units with greater capacity are available.

I conclude that a desalinator is most effective in a short-term emergency situation, particularly for pilots, but does not eliminate the need for taking along as much water as possible during a boat abandonment. Having one aboard would represent tremendous security and allow the water ration to be considered more dispassionately.

CONCLUSIONS

While it is clear that a desalinator would radically change water consumption strategy, the suggestions below are based on the assumption that a desalinator has not been included in the survival pack.

1. Take a drink before abandoning ship if possible, but drink no water for the first 24 hours if it is in short supply. A slightly dehydrated survivor utilizes water more efficiently.
2. Discuss the size of the ration with the crew, giving them as much information as possible regarding physiological needs and your estimate of how long the supply must last. Even though you may be the captain, do not make a unilateral decision regarding the size of the water ration. Lead the group into making a joint decision regarding how much water to issue and the times of distribution.

3. If water is abundant, issue up to a quart per person per day. If water is scarce, issue 600 ml per person per day. A smaller ration is counter-productive, but may be necessary if the supply is extremely small. It is easier to begin with a small ration and increase it if dehydration symptoms occur.

4. Practice rain collection before it rains and collect every drop available. Be sure the night lookout wakes everyone in time to collect rain.

5. When water (from rain) is abundant and every container is filled, drink over a period of hours to become as satiated as possible.

6. Drink rainwater and save packaged water for emergencies.

7. Regardless of the water ration's size, issue it in small quantities several times per day. Use a measured container, if available, to insure fairness. Children and ill persons may be issued a larger ration but its size should be decided as a matter of policy and not given in an arbitrary, random fashion.

8. Always maintain and speak positively about the chances of obtaining more water from fish, rain, solar stills, etc. Never say anything which would lead others to believe they will die of thirst.

9. Labor and digestion increase water requirements. Consumption of sugars andcarbohydrates actually reduce water requirements.

10. Keep the body cool by wearing damp clothes or at least a wet turban, with a sail hanging onto the neck. Stay in the shade and rest when possible.

11. Fish as much as possible and utilize the juices of fish, turtles and sea birds.

12. Apply anti-motion sickness adhesive units (Transderm) as needed.

ABOUT DRINKING SEAWATER

Suggestions about drinking seawater are controversial with highly polarized believers on both sides. Unquestionably, seawater drunk in quantity at full strength over a period of time (more than three or four days) will result in death, caused by the dehydrating effects of the salty water and inflammation of the kidneys. One fact is well-known: it is much easier to start drinking seawater than to stop. Seawater is 3.5% salt, and 78% of that is sodium chloride. If seawater is consumed, keep in mind that it is three times as salty as body fluid and should be diluted at least 4:1 with fresh water to be advantageously utilized by the body. Read more about this subject at the conclusion of *The Bombard Story (see Chapter III)*.

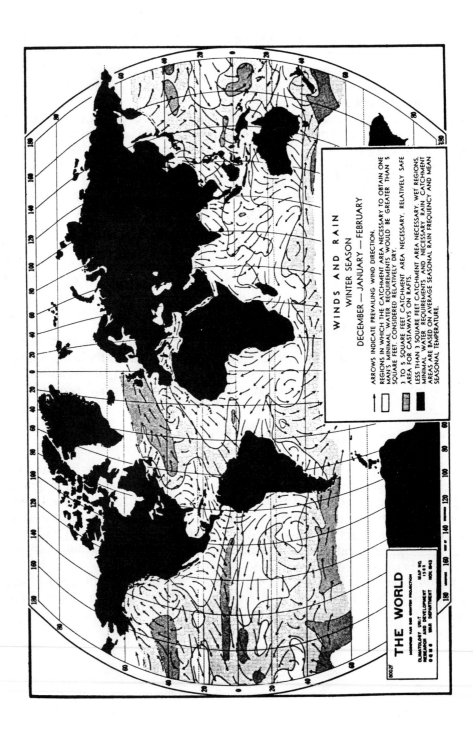

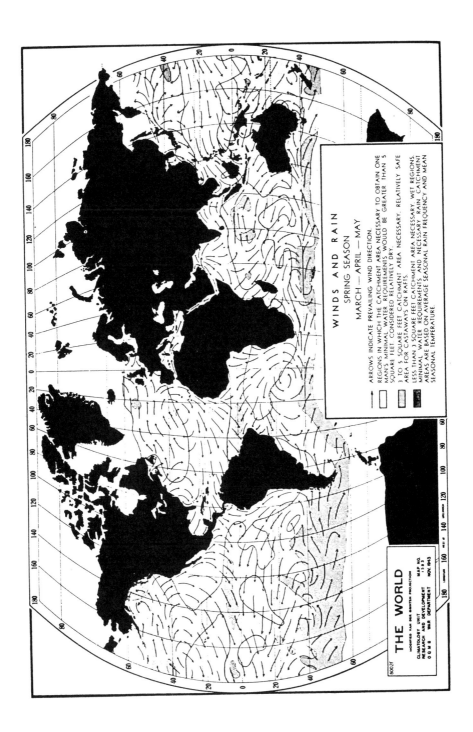

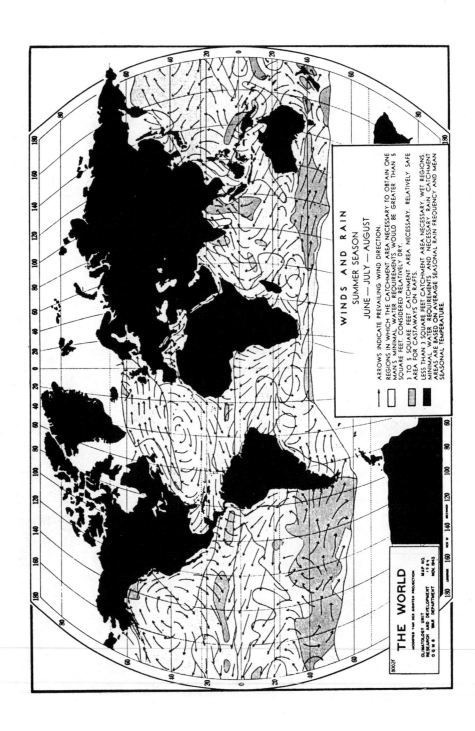

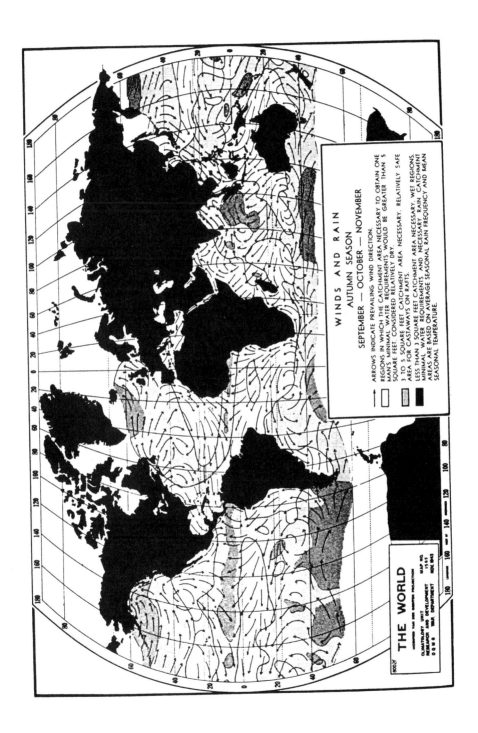

Food Rations

It is a well-documented fact that normal, healthy people can live as long as two months without food and, based on this data, one might conclude that the nature and extent of survival rations would be relatively unimportant. Unfortunately, most castaways don't know that they can live so long without food and the exhausted, dream-like state of starvation makes one feel that death is imminent. After a few days in a survival craft, the desire to eat and drink becomes so strong that even under test conditions, where people knew they had not been left to their fate, more than the allotted ration of food and water was consumed and in some cases people even stole from each other.

It should be clear from accounts in this book that castaways, assaulted with a variety of discomforts and few distractions, measure the passage of time by the number of hours, minutes and seconds to the next sip of water and morsel of food. Even the smallest morsel, a scrap which would have been contemptuously discarded under normal conditions, becomes a cherished prize.

Under survival conditions, hunger and food become an obsession, which is expressed by intense fantasies, endless discussion of tempting recipes and the multitude of delicious dishes which will be immediately consumed after rescue. It is therefore important to realize that survival rations are more than just something to stave off hunger. The availability of food becomes a tremendous comfort, even if the need for it is not critical.

Before WW II, food rations consisted of the famous (or infamous) ship's biscuit, and (if one were lucky) tins of condensed, sweet milk. The chief (and possibly only) virtue of the biscuit was that it stored well and lasted a long time if it was properly packed. If not, the biscuit quickly became moldy and/or infested with weevils. It was the habit of sailors, faced with an unending diet of ship's biscuit, to tap it gently on a hard surface for a few minutes, prior to consumption, to encourage the weevils to depart.

One can occasionally find ship's biscuit in gourmet (!) stores, where it is sold for its novelty value in fancy, colorful tins. I encourage you to buy some and savor this dry, incredibly hard, tasteless cracker, which reluctantly dissolves into the most marvelous glue in the mouth. In order to increase the "desperate survivor" fantasy, eat several of them without drinking any water, and don't brush after the meal. Today (fortunately) there are no nations which accept ship's biscuit as a survival ration, although sweet, condensed milk is still allowed in a few places. The milk is both nourishing and tasty, but it makes one thirsty and becomes extremely viscous in cold weather.

After WW II, the British government did an intense study and evaluation of wartime survival cases in an effort to determine the optimum type of food and the number of calories needed to survive. The Naval Life Saving Committee decided on a ration of **600 calories per day**, consisting of 100 grams of carbohydrates and a half-liter (a pint) of water per day. Trials showed that if this ration was provided for **five days**, the majority of people in a survival craft remained fit enough to take care of themselves.

Carbohydrates were preferred for several reasons. In addition to nutritional benefits, **carbohydrate digestion liberates water from food and reduces the cannibalization of body protein**. A high carbohydrate diet reduces urine output by as much as 200 ml per day. Since water conservation is of utmost importance in survival conditions, the reduction of urine output is extremely important. The survey also concluded that the best way to administer the ration was in the form of barley sugar or hard-boiled candy.

A Verkade ration.

About the same time as the British study, the Dutch Navy was considering the same question. They wanted a very compact ration of high nutritional value which kept well. They contacted the Royal Verkade factory, famous in the Netherlands as innovative biscuit-makers. Verkade designed a food tablet which provided 5,500 calories per kilogram, considered a ration sufficient to last one man for six days. The ration, really a sort of cookie, was rated to last five years.

As a result of these two studies, a compromise ration was developed consisting of 2/3 cookies and 1/3 compressed glucose (sugar). This reduced the caloric value of the unit to 5,000 calories, providing a daily intake of about 850 calories and this combination is almost universally accepted today by the majority of maritime nations. The glucose tablet is just that. There is nothing in the least creative about it, and I personally think it is best consumed dissolved in a cup of cappucchino, with a survival cookie and a slice of fresh lime on the side. If your life raft has a cappucchino machine and coffee in its equipment pack use them.

Tinned, Royal Verkade dessert cookies are excellent and are available in most American supermarkets. The survival cookie produced by them is both tasty and nutritious. It chews easily and can be crumbled and mixed with water, to be used as either a "sauce" for fish or for feeding to an injured crewman. If one would add a bit of icing or some cheese, it could be served at parties. One therefore wonders why Verkade would be content with something as uninspiring as a glucose tablet, when they could have produced an excellent hard candy (boiled sweet), or something which would have interested the palate.

The answer is that some people do not like boiled confections at all and get sick of hard candy, which is very sweet and cloying. As a result, the glucose tablet was developed, which, if not very appetizing, is at least not very disgusting. The tablet tastes less sweet than hard candy and, if nibbled, is not as chalky as it looks. In addition, a bit of glucose can be easily dissolved in water and fed to an ill, seasick, or injured crewman who cannot eat more substantial food or someone with dental problems (or who has lost their dentures).

Now lets talk about the cookie. The Royal Verkade cookie consists of: carbohydrates 73%, fats 23% and protein 4%. A similar cookie, of equal quality, made by Seven Oceans, contains: carbohydrates 64 %, protein 8 %, fats 22% and miscellaneous 6%.

Both companies fortify the cookie with vitamins. The dense, rectangular cookie has a mild, nutty flavor and each is packed in individual wax-paper wrappers. The rations are packed in 500 gram (2500 calories, 3 days ration for one man) and 1,000 gram (5,000 calorie, six-days ration) foil packages. The foil packs are further protected against damage by a water-resistant cardboard box which also contains instructions in several languages, printed on a plastic sheet. The packages, once opened, are not resealable. The ration, once wet, dissolves into mush. For this reason, the smaller 500 gr. (slightly more than 1 lb.) ration is more useful for boat-sized rafts. The containers are dated and have a rated shelf life of five years, after which they are replaced by survival craft certification centers. In fact, they often last twice as long without deterioration. These rations are quite inexpensive.

While the rations produced by these two firms are of the highest quality, many other companies produce a highly inferior product which they foist upon an unwitting public solely for the additional profit they can gain, utilizing fancy packaging and advertising. Some come in multicolored tins, others in nicely designed foil packs. In all cases, they are designed to meet the requirement of 5,000 calories per kg., so it is their quality, not their caloric content, which is in question.

One sample consisted of a coconut cookie which was rancid, tough, chewy, and indigestible. It was already spoiled even though it was less than six months old and purchased fresh off the shelf. Another was virtually insoluble and hard to swallow. The glucose in these rations consisted of: (1) a small, extremely hard tablet, the size of a large medicine capsule, which was not easily chewed; one might suck it, if one had any saliva with which to suck it; (2) a soft boiled sweet (ju-ju bead type) in a variety of flavors that was so sweet it was hard to eat even a few of them. It is therefore wise to **specify your choice of ration** at the certification center when your raft is repacked. You never know, you just might end up having to eat that stuff.

Selecting Survival Food

The simplest expedient when considering food for a survival pack is to buy as many Verkade or Seven Oceans rations as desired and place them in the survival packs. Should supplementary food items be desired, keep in mind that variety is the spice of life—do not just buy a huge quantity of one food item. Other cookies selected on the basis of personal preference can be purchased and packed in waterproof bags. They should be eaten at the end of the passage, since they invariably become stale within 4 to 6 months. Keep in mind that cookies with chocolate chips or cream centers frequently melt and spoil in the tropics.

Candy bars, especially those specially designed for hiking, are also excellent, just be sure you like their taste and select them on this basis. Chocolate bars, unless specifically made for survival, deteriorate rapidly, especially in the tropics. They get soft in the heat of day, then cool into an unpleasant-tasting mass at night. Avoid them.

As previously mentioned, boiled sweets, also known as hard candy, are quite acceptable as a supplement to survival rations, if you like them, but they must be purchased in a sealed tin, not a plastic bag. Hard candies are extremely hygroscopic, which means that they attract and hold moisture and the moisture spoils them. Tins prevent this. An extensive diet of hard candy is (as mentioned) extremely cloying.

Soups, condensed sweet milk and broth also appear on the survival pack list. These survival foods are ultimately not as efficient as the Verkade and Seven Seas rations, but many castaways just love them, and there is no question that they provide a pleasant break from a monotonous diet of survival rations. Since they are liquid, they can be fed to a debilitated person. Broth, rich in minerals, is especially good for seasick, feverish or burned castaways. All ordinary condensed soups are somewhat salty and one should be sure they are no-salt-added (low sodium) before purchase. Keep in mind that these items must be completely consumed after opening, since they become contaminated, even at sea, and are easily spilled.

Items like tinned meat, stews, tinned fish and mixtures like paté should never be added to a survival pack. They liberate little water upon digestion and do less to reduce urine production. These items may end up stuffed into a grab bag at the last moment. They should be reserved for times when water is plentiful, when foods high in protein and fat can be more easily assimilated.

"Hey! That's milk! And you said you were all empty, you
stinkin' liar!"

From *The Far Side* 1986 © Universal Press Syndicate,
reprinted with permission. All rights reserved.

Painting by Jim Sollers

CHAPTER IX: DISASTER IN COLD WEATHER

People interested in finding out about God and themselves are attracted in ever-increasing numbers to the Far North and South, because of the challenge and the austere beauty of these lands. The famous explorers of the 19th century went there for the same reason, but the days of the romantic explorer who relied on bravery and faith are gone, because most of those folks died relying on bravery and faith. Several centuries of cold weather marine exploration have proven again and again that the only way a voyager will live to see old age is by careful planning and preparation for the rigors of the trip.

For you, this means a strong boat, with not one but several high quality aids to navigation such as a Loran, Sat Nav or Omega, weather FAX, a radar and several depth sounders, top-of-the-line immersion suits for all crew persons, a top quality life raft, and a survival pack in excess of that suggested for tropic seas. In other words, you need cash to cruise safely in the far North—or, you can take a ride on a shoestring like Elmo Wortman—and take your chances. Sometimes, despite the risks, it may be more important to take your chances.

Almost Too Late By Elmo Wortman

Sudden disaster in the night is the sailor's greatest fear. Imagine being suddenly hurled from a sound sleep into the howling conditions of a subarctic disaster, ship-wrecked on a desolate island off southeastern Alaska during the dead of winter, with a disabled captain, a crew of children, without food, adequate clothing or even a knife—it sounds like the stuff from which films are made, too awful to be real.

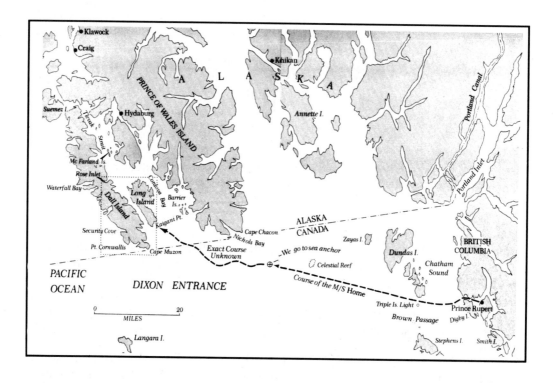

Chart of Dixon Entrance. from *Almost Too Late* by Elmo Wortman © 1981, by permission
of Random House

Elmo Wortman was a 50-year-old carpenter, disabled with rheumatism
and unable to work. Rather than just rot away on social security, he and his
four children—Randy, Cindy, Margery, and Jena, ages 12 to 16—decided to
live aboard their 33-foot ketch, HOME, which Elmo had built. The family
thought they could best stretch their meager income by living anchored off a
small islet near the west side of Prince of Wales Island in the southeastern part of
Alaska.

Living far from civilization they were able to supplement their regular
diet with fish and game. Their shrimp trap yielded several pounds daily and the
family had good luck catching snapper, cod, scallops and clams. Unfortunately,
Elmo's children needed their braces adjusted. Since he had no car, Elmo
Wortman decided to sail approximately 90 miles to Prince Rupert Island, British
Columbia, in February with the three youngest children, in order to visit a
Canadian Public Health Service dentist, because he could not affoard the cost of
American dental care.

One could easily say that Elmo Wortman was a fool for doing what he did. Who would cross a subarctic sea so minimally equipped? When considering the answers to these questions, one must certainly consider the alternatives for the Wortmans—to rot away on welfare in some ignoble hovel, robbed of the cries of the sea birds and the promise of the freedom which every hove-up, muddy anchor provides. Even children can understand these alternatives, perhaps they can comprehend them more clearly than adults. People with courage understand that the richness of life is measured day by day. Some might say it is better to risk all for freedom than to be safe and live the life of quiet desperation.

The route was across Dixon Entrance, a part of the "inside passage" open to the North Pacific Ocean. Wortman had traveled this route before and was aware of the risks:

> We didn't plan to be away very long, but in the turbulent waters of Dixon Entrance one's plans are often altered by a violent and unforgiving Mother Nature. . . . The mouth of Dixon Entrance opens wide to the violent storms and relentless swells of the North Pacific Ocean. From: *Almost Too Late* (Pg. 5)

That a disabled man would sail a tiny, homemade boat across a subarctic ocean in the dead of winter with a crew of young children was more than slightly unwise. Wortman, being low on funds, HOME lacked radar, Loran, and Omega. The radio direction-finding equipment operated poorly in bad weather and provided only the most approximate position. These circumstances led directly to the disaster which followed.

The voyage to the dentist was uneventful, and on February 13 (a decidedly unlucky date for the Wortmans), they departed Prince Rupert Island anticipating a quick run of 80 miles across open sea into the more sheltered waters of Cordova Bay. Unfortunately, Mother Nature had other plans.

Elmo Wortman was so badly disabled he could not steer. His children stood one-hour watches in rotation. In the middle of the night the wind increased and it started to snow. The boat was hove-to with a sea anchor but unfortunately a steadying mizzen sail was not set. The mizzen would have reduced the boat's tendency to yaw back and forth, reducing its drift. The seas became violent and visibility was reduced to less than a hundred yards. The children took turns standing watch. Everyone was seasick and wet, but the real problem had nothing to do with discomfort. It had everything to do with not knowing where they were and having no electronic navigation aid such as a Loran to assist them, aside from the RDF.

The storm continued into the next night. Huge waves swept over HOME and the boat began to take damage. Wortman's 16-year old daughter, Cindy, went on watch at 11 p.m. but no one was monitoring the depth sounder, the only electronic aid on the ship. Unfortunately the coasts in this area are steep-to and a depth sounder would have provided little warning of impending disaster. It would have required a sharp watch indeed to have escaped from the ensuing disaster using just a depth sounder. Visibility had become even more limited because of the violent seas and heavy snow. It was very dark but:

> Then, near midnight, a darker object appeared momentarily amid the jumble of sky and water. She waited for a replay so she could focus on it exactly. "Daddy, there's land! I know it's land!"...The stark terror of the scene forced down my nausea and shocked me awake. "My God! We're on the beach!" ibid. (Pg 31)

The surf was exploding against the rocky shore just 50 feet away. Beyond the narrow beach, a forbidding cliff rose hundreds of feet blotting out the horizon. In his haste to depart, Wortman motored over the sea anchor line which became entangled in the propeller. With the boat thus disabled, its destruction was assured.

A heavy anchor was dropped and this gave the terrified family a brief respite. They had no life raft. Their dinghy, a plastic, double hulled Sport-Yak was suitable only for two people and sheltered conditions. There was no possibility of using it in the maelstrom of waves and dark rocks. A few minutes later the boat struck. The family had no choice but to jump into the dark, freezing water and swim for their lives.

That they all reached the beach alive was a miracle, but it seemed as though an even more cruel fate awaited them. They were only partially clothed. Jena was naked from the waist down. The sea had sucked off even her underpants. Most of their shoes had been lost. They lay thus, among the ice covered rocks, with the howling wind and snow sweeping over their wet, freezing bodies, waiting for the dawn.

As the boat was sinking, they had hastily stuffed food and clothing into plastic garbage bags, hoping that the wind would drive the buoyant packs onto the beach. None of these bags were seen again. None of their survival equipment reached the shore. They had no chart. They had forgotten to take a knife. Elmo and Randy had matches, and they found a small can of gasoline washed up from the wreck, so they were able to make a fire. Exploring the beach, they found some flotsam from the wreck:

sail	50' of rubber tubing
rope ladder	three foam pads
pillowcase	plastic container
comb	pair of girl's shoes
pair of gloves	girl's vest
first-aid kit	2 oars
propane tank	roll of electrical wire
Japanese glass fishing float	the galley sink and counter
6' Sport-Yak, badly damaged	

Their food supplies consisted of:

6 apples, badly damaged	1 packet of spaghetti sauce
3 onions	1 jar Tang (mostly empty)
1 gal. corn oil	1 jar Cheez Whiz (mostly empty)

They found some mussels which they steamed open near the fire. A shelter was made from the sail and the foam pads were used as a bed. They later decided that more heat would be conserved if they just used the sail as a cover. The Sport-Yak was repaired by filling the interior with pieces of foam. The next morning they ate the apples and made a limited exploration of the shore, hampered by lack of clothing, snow, and freezing wind.

HOME had hit the southern end of Long Island, an uninhabited rock in the middle of Cordova Bay. A few miles of set one way or the other would have allowed the vessel to drift unimpeded up the Sound. Talk about bad luck. The nearest house was on Dall Island to the west. Prince of Wales Island, to the east, was farther away. Reaching the house was their only chance. It was located at the end of Ross Inlet less than twenty miles away.

By the next day they had managed to work their way around the tip of Long Island, where they found logs and built a raft, using the Sport-Yak as a sort of cockpit. Although hampered by falling snow and oppressed by a leaden sky, the family cast off and headed north on February 18, 1979, four days after their shipwreck. A southwest wind, favorable tide, and calm seas made it possible to paddle the raft two miles up the coast into the mouth of Kaigani Strait.

Their immediate prospects were hardly brighter than before. Elmo, a sick man at the beginning of the disaster, was severely cut and bruised in the shipwreck. His feet were badly frostbitten. Four days of brutal conditions had aggravated his rheumatism and further reduced his capacity. It was necessary for the children to do most of the work, and they, too, were suffering from frostbite.

Everyone had an insulated float coat with a hood, but not float pants. What a difference they would have made! The coats were very warm and saved them from immediate death, but there was not enough clothing to go around. Jena had to wear an upside-down sweater instead of pants. Elmo and Jena had lost their glasses. Without them, Jena was nearly blind.

The favorable wind deserted them, and with it the relatively warm southern breeze. The temperature fell below freezing. The only food they had was a diminishing gallon of corn oil, a packet of dried spaghetti sauce and two onions. Mussels and clams picked by Randy from the freezing water were their only other source of food. The house was still 18 miles away, up the Sound, against the prevailing wind. That small distance seemed immense.

Head winds defeated them for the next two days but the night of February 20th the wind dropped. The family was able to cross the Strait and travel five miles toward their goal. After a few hours of troubled sleep aboard the raft they continued north but were able to make only 1.5 miles against the wind. Head winds prevented their departure the next day. Both of the girls were now suffering the lassitude caused by starvation and hypothermia. Only Randy was able to forage along the beach for mussels and clams.

The wind rose against them again the following day and they were unable to travel. The next day was even worse. The wind had blown out their fire during the night and their gasoline supply was gone. It was necessary to use the corn oil as a starter fuel.

The wind dropped suddenly in the afternoon and the family cast off at once. They ran five miles up the Strait that night, surrounded by swirling snow. The next day at dawn, they saw a few small islands and an apparent indentation in the coast which they believed was Ross Inlct, just a mile away. Elmo and Randy decided to take the Sport-Yak and complete the short trip, returning later in the day with food. The two girls were left with all of the remaining provisions, which consisted of one onion and the remaining corn oil.

It soon became evident that their presumed position had been incorrect and that they were much farther from their goal than estiomated. A furious headwind and steep seas forced them to alternately drag the dinghy along the beach, then return to the sea and row around sections of steep cliffs. By nightfall, at the end of their strength, they reached Ross Inlet, only to find an impenetrable sheet of sea ice which thwarted their advance.

It was necessary to row ashore and proceed on frostbitten feet. Finally, in the middle of the night, having alternately walked and crawled for miles, they reached the house, exhausted and severely frostbitten. It was February 26. Eleven days had elapsed since the shipwreck. They knocked on the cabin door but only silence greeted them. No one was home.

The cabin was completely equipped and contained plenty of food but the CB radio didn't work. The two did not sleep well that night. Their frostbitten limbs began to thaw, causing excruciating pain:

> As the swelling in my feet reached its maximum, it was hard to recognize them as such. My toes protruded black and splayed wide like tits on a balloon. My ankles appeared only as dimples in the sides of an overstuffed sausage. ibid. [Pg. 148]

They cut the dead skin away with a scalpel, in many places to the bone which caused no physical pain, since the tissue was dead, but furthered their psychological anguish. The ordeal had damaged them so severely that they were unable to leave the cabin for thirteen days.

Imagine a father's agony, lying in relative comfort, knowing that his daughters were dying, less than five miles away:

> I knew that, barring massive infection in the dead parts of our feet, my son and I would live. I knew also that it was at the fatal expense of my two younger daughters.   ibid.

By the time Elmo and Randy had recovered enough to walk, they assumed the girls were dead. Elmo's only desire was to retrieve their bodies. They repaired a damaged skiff found near the cabin, wrote a note for the owners, gathered provisions, and with heavy hearts, departed into the freezing cold.

They returned to the desolate, forbidding place where the girls had been left—weak, cold, starving, protected from the Alaskan winter by a few folds of sail. As they approached the shore, grim thoughts oozed through Elmo's mind:

If their bodies were below the tide line, any number of small crustaceans would be feeding on them. If they were on the higher beach and uncovered, predatory animals and birds might have fed on their faces. ibid. (Pg. 186)

They spotted the sail on the beach and rowed ashore. Elmo approached the pathetic shelter:

"Girls, I've come to take you home." There was no movement, no sound, but as I stopped and bent to grasp the part of the sail covering Jena, the part over Cindy virtually exploded. And there was the skin-covered skeleton of what I had once known as my second daughter. The big blue eyes were sunken but shining. The face was smiling.
"Cindy, you're still alive!" I exclaimed with amazement, and pulled the cover from Jena. Her head turned slightly on a body that could not move. ibid. (Pg 187)

Despite the joyous reunion the family's suffering was not yet at an end. They still had to make the return voyage of five miles to the cabin. Cindy could walk but Jena had to be carried to the skiff. Only Randy was capable of rowing and the voyage lasted far into the night. They finally grounded the boat on the rocky beach beneath the house, 26 days after the ship wreck. Fifteen-year-old Randy had spent 13 hours at the oars.   Then,

. . . on feet with bare bone protruding where nails and ends of toes once were, he took his little sister on his back and, leaning forward , carried her surely and safely up the long, steep ramp to the cabin beyond. ibid. (Pg. 196)

Elmo lost large portions of both feet. Later he said he never had to cut his toenails again. Cindy had surgery and skin grafts on three toes. Randy and Jena made full recoveries. That summer all of the children had their braces removed. Their lives and their personalities returned to normal. The Wortmans had the psychological drive to be survivors. They were able to continue enjoying the azure sky, the jade green sea, and the fertile tidelands of their Northern home. Their sufferings became a memory, their future a reminder that life is beautiful and sometimes must be fought for with unremitting tenacity.

Hypothermia

Hypothermia means <u>a subnormal temperature of the body core, (the torso and the brain)</u>. This may be caused by cold wind or being immersed in cold water. The human body protects itself from death by hypothermia by reducing circulation to the limbs. The blood remaining there is not only very cold, it becomes acidified and toxic. Attempts to "promote circulation" by warming the feet or hands is therefore more likely to hasten the person's demise. The last thing one wants to do is introduce this blood to the core. Considering the numerous nasty ways that there are to die, hypothermia is relatively painless, since the victim usually falls asleep and lapses into a comatose state before death, which actually occurs because of heart failure or drowning.

Entering really cold water is a great shock to the body but it rarely kills directly. Some people, after falling overboard involuntarily aspirate seawater, if their heads slip under water, and others may drown after falling unconscious, but the majority of hypothermia victims die with little water in their lungs, from cardiac arrest.

Normal body temperature is 98.6° F. or 37°C. and if someone is immersed in water even slightly colder than this, they are going to die of hypothermia. Ocean water never gets warmer than 84°. The question, therefore, is not whether death from hypothermia will occur, but when. People floating in a tropic sea may live for more than eighty hours, but eventually they are as badly chilled as someone swimming in an Arctic ocean where death from hypothermia can occur in less than thirty minutes.

One does not actually have to be floating in water to suffer from hypothermia. Body heat may be drained by lying on the cold floor of a life raft that does not have an inflatable floor from wind chill or from wearing continuously wet clothing that does not trap and hold body heat. Under these circumstances hypothermia kills by reducing the ability to function. A languorous indifference permeates the mind, making it a supreme effort to perform simple tasks such as keeping the raft floats inflated.

Hypothermia is not the same as "thoroughly chilled." Being chilled implies that warm clothes and a hot cocoa will put the man back on his feet. This is not the case with hypothermia. Basic blood chemistry changes occur and body systems begin to fail. People frequently die from hypothermia so we are talking about a serious injury, requiring immediate hospital treatment.

Symptoms: Mild to Moderate. Severe shivering heralds the onset of hypothermia. A <u>fruity-acetone smell from the mouth</u>, inappropriate response, a stronger carotid pulse, compared to those in the limbs, confirms diagnosis. In many cases the person appears conscious but paralyzed and cannot help rescuers. They may arrive conscious but collapse shortly after rescue.   Cold paralysis of the hands, known as **"hand lock"** often occurs.

Symptoms: Severe. Apparent death. Vital signs, such as pulse or heartbeat may be so depressed as to appear completely absent. Blink reflex is suppressed. Breathing ceases. Loss of vital signs does not mean the person is dead, and every attempt to revive them should be made. People who actually die from hypothermia often feel unbearably hot in their last moments of life. Failing body systems allow warm blood, reserved in the body core, to suddenly flow outward, toward the skin, creating an illusion of heat; the victim tears off his clothes in desperation as he dies.

Core temperatures continue to fall for up to half an hour after a person is removed from the water. This is why people often die of hypothermia after they have been "saved." The limbs are the first areas affected by the cold. The head droops as the person becomes unconscious. This often results in drowning. Fat people live longer because of the insulating quality of the fat. Women get their "curves" from a fat layer which is less pronounced in men and, therefore, women survive longer than men. Adults live much longer than children because they have a smaller surface-to-mass ratio and therefore, have less surface exposed to the cold. Whites live longer than Blacks because of slightly less peripheral circulation, and Asians survive the longest , but I do not know why.

SYMPTOMS OF DECREASING BODY CORE TEMPERATURE		
Effects on the Body	**Body Core Temperature**	
	°C	°F
Temperature regulation of body fails	33	91
Shivering ceases, muscular rigidity, slurred speech	32	90
Drowsiness	29-31	83-88
Death	25	77

Tables often do not tell the entire story. The chance of reviving someone aboard a survival craft with a body core temperature of 83° F is slim. The table on page 251 also looks good, but so does the **"Sterns Rule of Fifty**," which states that in 50° F water, you have a 50-50 chance of living 50 minutes. Others state that in 70-80° water a person will become unconscious in

3-12 hours. On the other hand <u>people have been known to live longer than expected in cold water, so don't give up a search based solely on these tables. Forget those damned tables.</u> The wise person avoids testing any of these theories. Captains who fail to provide this gear are invariably judged morally and legally negligent (see Chapter XX).

    Treatment: There are two treatments for hypothermia: slow or rapid rewarming. **Rapid rewarming** (discussed later) is indicated for mild hypothermia victims, distinguished by their disoriented or amnesiac state. **Slow rewarming** is recommended for seriously affected victims, who are unconscious or appear "dead". Under survival conditions this means doing little more than trying to get them dry, covering them, particularly the body core, and applying mouth-to-mouth resuscitation.

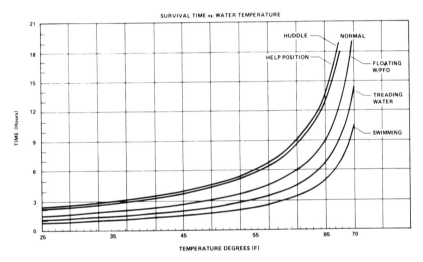

    This chart indicates that a swimmer's survival time can be a function of strategy, particularly in warmer water. Charts like this one should be used with a great deal of caution, particularly when deciding to call off a search based on "information" it provides. Many other variables contribute to survival time, including sea state, the victims dress, their stamina, and weight. From *USCG Seamanship Manual.*

REWARMING A COLD VICTIM

    The most effective way to restore body core temperature of a cold (not hypothermic), alert functioning individual depends on what is available at the moment of rescue.

Victims who are merely cold, but alert and shivering, may be warmed by manipulating and rubbing the skin. Other methods are:

1. Soaking in a warm bath or shower.
2. Applying hot, wet towels or water bottles to the body, neck, and groin.
3. Drinking hot, sweet, non-alcoholic drinks (not tea or coffee)
4. Inhaling steam vapor from a kettle. Use a towel as a hood (<u>very effective</u>).
5. Wrapping the victim's torso in survival blankets or a rewarming bag.
6. Now comes the one I've been waiting to tell you about all along. It makes writing this whole chapter worthwhile. Feel free to accuse me of complete chauvinism if you wish:

    Sandwich the victim between two hot, naked women (women are hotter than men) inside a sleeping bag or closely wrap with blankets. Give the women a stiff drink (to increase peripheral heat loss). Have them rub and chafe the victim's torso and make soft, sympathetic sounds. If the victim responds enough to take full advantage of the situation it is certain he will survive.

RAPID REWARMING PROBLEMS

In mild cases, where the victim remains conscious but is disoriented and shivering, rapid rewarming, including the ingestion of warm, sugary drinks and hot towels applied to the torso and neck, is recommended. The problem is that water heating facilities aboard a boat are usually inadequate to produce the large volume needed to be really effective. Should this be the case, it may be wiser to use whatever hot water is available on neck towels, hot steam, or warm enemas. The most effective technique available aboard a boat is the inhalation of steam from a kettle as mentioned above. This introduces warmth directly into the body core. The heat does not have to pass through the skin and fat layers of the body and is immediately effective. Warm enemas are also effective. The obvious technique, putting the feet in warm water is <u>incorrect and dangerous</u>. The extremities should be warmed last. In a survival craft, the "hot woman" warm-up technique (buddy warming) works well.

SERIOUS HYPOTHERMIA PROCEDURES

A serious hypothermia victim is identified by his/her arriving aboard unconscious, or in a state of severe disorientation and muscular rigidity followed by collapse. Unconsciousness or death may occur after he has been "saved," even if he has been able to talk you before collapse. In a hospital, rapid rewarming, supplemented by oxygen, IV treatment for damaged blood chemistry and possible attachment to a heart-lung machine would probably be used. In a survival craft, there is much to be said for the "do nothing" or "do little" approach. Wrap the victim in blankets and make him comfortable. Make no attempt to warm the limbs. If possible, give hot steam. Once the patient comes around enough to drink, hot sweet liquids should be forced (make them drink even if they are not thirsty).

TREATING AN APPARENTLY "DEAD" HYPOTHERMIA VICTIM

People who appear to be dead from hypothermia or hypothermia-induced drowning may sometimes be resuscitated even if they have no apparent vital signs. The reason is that body tissues, especially the brain last much longer when chilled. So do not give up. If respiration has ceased, apply mouth-to-mouth respiration but not cardiac massage (if the heart is beating). Continue these procedures as long as possible or until breathing returns (then stop). Never think of a hypothermia patient as lost until they are both warm and dead.

Alcoholic beverages should not be consumed by survivors after a rescue. Alcohol causes increased heat loss due to dilation of peripheral blood vessels. It has an anesthetic effect, which masks the cold. A small quantity of alcohol is usually considered a stimulant, but for someone badly chilled, it becomes a depressant, just what someone on the edge of death does not need. It usually makes them sleep—and they do not wake up.

On the other hand, there are critical moments, when action is required and alcohol can definitely put real punch in your afterburners. Survivors have often achieved sudden incredible strength and clear-headedness from a shot of liquor, or even after shave lotion.

COLD INJURIES

Cold injuries result from inactivity in below-freezing temperatures. For either the sailor or the castaway, it is far easier to prevent these injuries by good planning and proper clothing than to cure them once the injury has occurred.

Frostnip, resulting from moderate exposure to damp-cold results in an injury similar to sunburn. The nose, ears, and extremities become white, hard, and cold. The area later peels like a mild sunburn. In chilblains of the hands and trench foot, the skin becomes puffy, pale, numb, and clammy. The affected tissue is easily damaged, without the victim being aware. Trench foot got its name from the fact that soldiers are sometimes severely injured by having to stand for weeks or months in a wet, cold, muddy trench without being able to dry and massage their feet.

Hypothermia victims must be assisted aboard a rescue craft with a minimum of effort on their part. Sometimes a swimmer will float or cling to wreckage for hours, on the edge of death. The effort to scramble aboard a rescue craft may prove too great. The unfortunate swimmer in the photo above, barely alive, was assisted into a harness by the airman (upper right). The man nevertheless died of hypothermia two hours later. Photo by Andrew Besley/Royal Navy.

A victim of **frostbite** has frozen flesh, usually of the fingers, toes, ears and nose. The skin is hard, white and numb. When it defrosts, it becomes blotchy-red and very painful. If frostbite is mild, the sufferer recovers without major complications. If not, permanent circulatory damage and/or gangrene occurs.

The old method of slowly rewarming chilled areas or rubbing with snow in now considered improper treatment. The best method that a castaway has of rewarming cold-damaged skin is to <u>place it against a warm part of the body</u> such as under the armpit or between the legs, or against the chest or stomach of someone else. Warming the area with warm water works very well, and if nothing else is available, urine can be used.

Frostbite is not a deadly injury, but if gangrene results, either a serious penicillin therapy or amputation may be necessary. The best way to prevent all of these injuries (aside from not being exposed to the cold) is to exercise, manipulate and massage the affected areas. This may be more easily said than done, because, of the languor and indifference caused by hypothermia. If you cannot get into a warm shelter, the only way to prevent serious injury is by the methods described above.

Cold Weather Clothing

Dress for survival before abandoning ship. Be sure each castaway has a whistle and a light on their life jacket to speed their recovery if they end up in the water. Just a thermal, foam-filled, close-fitting life vest increases immersion survival time considerably. An immersion suit once kept a man alive for 27 hours in 37° F. Alaskan water. A man and wife team clad in immersion suits survived 44 hours afloat in 56°F. water. Stories about the incredible value of these suits abound. The same clothing which protects the survivor in the water is immensely more effective in sustaining core body heat on land. Elmo Wortman's family survived for weeks in the Alaskan winter mainly because they wore float coats.

All cold weather, marine clothing should be made of synthetic material or wool since they hold less water and dry faster than cotton. The layered look is definitely "in" among the best dressed castaways, beginning with thermal underwear and ending with the best quality immersion suit you can afford. Commercial vessels operating in cold water are required to have an immersion

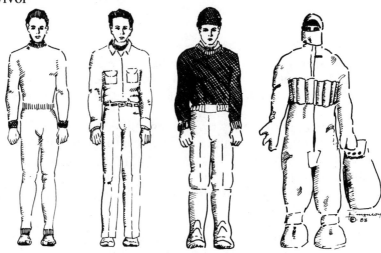

Dressing in layers traps insulating air between the clothing.

suit for every crewman since their ability to save lives is well documented. Be sure to have a warm hood, a high collar, insulated boots and a bib that goes under the crotch, as these are sources of considerable body heat loss.

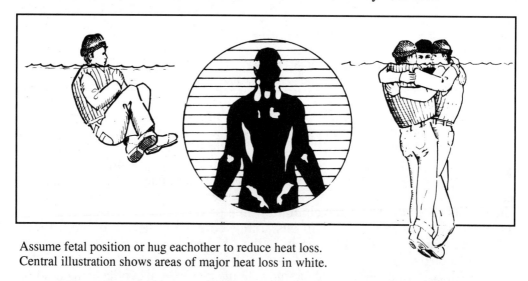

Assume fetal position or hug eachother to reduce heat loss.
Central illustration shows areas of major heat loss in white.

If one is unfortunate enough to end up in the water (rather than in a raft), assume a head-up, fetal position to preserve body heat. If several people are in the water, they should cling together to preserve body heat. Try not to swim or tread water, since this cools the body about 35% faster than remaining immobile. An immersion suit vastly increases your survival time in cold water.

IMMERSION SUITS

Immersion suits are basically bags made of a waterproof, buoyant, insulating material such as neoprene, with watertight seals at the entry and face to keep water out. An inflatable collar or cushion allows the wearer to float face-up. The gloves and boots are an uninterrupted part of the sleeves and pant legs, although some have removable gloves and wrist seals. In other words, an immersion suit is dry inside and, if the wearer is in the water, he is surrounded by his own miniature life raft. If he is in a life raft, survival time is vastly increased because of the protection from hypothermia which the suit offers.

On land an immersion or exposure suit with thermal clothing beneath it, offers weeks of protection against hypothermia. One fisherman floated in the Aleutian Sea for two days in an immersion suit, then spent ten days alone with no food and little water on a rocky islet—and lived. If you buy immersion suits, be sure that you and your crew practice putting them on—they aren't hard to don, unless something is happening, such as the boat sinking beneath you.

If space and/or funds are limited, a good quality wet suit (top and bottom) does excellent duty as an exposure garment. It not only traps and warms water should you fall in, it also provides an amazing amount of positive buoyancy. A wet suit can be worn like a pair of long underwear and has the advantage of keeping you warm during a rainy deck watch, even if you're wet. A suit which is fabric lined inside and out, is most comfortable.

If your vessel makes frequent voyages in cold weather, an insulated float suit (sometimes called an exposure or anti-exposure suit) with closures for the wrists and ankles, insulated gloves, and thermal boots should be available for every crewman. It may be worn in conjunction with a wet suit (somewhat bulky) or with thermal underwear and a comfortable, loose-fitting set of clothes such as a sweat suit. The disadvantage of these suits is that they allow the entry of water—but it becomes trapped between the body and the suit is warmed by body heat and offers a thermal barrier from the colder seawater. Their advantage is that they may also be used as foul weather suits, to work on deck, whereas the bulky immersion suit is not really designed for this purpose. An insulated float suit is far superior to a float coat and pants since the latter permits the greater circulation of water. On the other hand, there are many days when a float suit is too hot to wear on deck.

Quick action by Skipper Joe Lang, saved the lives of all aboard the LORA LEE. Lang salvaged the crew's survival suits just before the vessel capsized off Kodiac, Alaska. The suits kept the men alive until they were rescued by a USCG HH-3H helicopter. See *National Fisherman*, November, 1987. Art by Jim Sollers

FLOAT SUITS AND FLOATATION

The name "float suit" implies that the buoyant material in it is the equivalent of a life jacket or vest and that the wearer does not need additional flotation to survive in the sea. This is not true. The USCG COMMANDANT notice reprinted below says it all:

USCG COMMANDANT NOTICE 10470 (25 Aug '84)

"Recent Coast Guard tests involving various types of protective clothing and flotation devices demonstrated two potentially serious problems for Coast Guard personnel accidently immersed in rough seas. The first problem involved buoyancy requirements. Life-jackets or flotation garments which provide about 15 to 17 pounds of buoyancy (e.g. float coats and other Type III devices) proved inadequate to keep the test subjects comfortably afloat for periods exceeding approximately 30 minutes.

Although these devices have adequate buoyancy to keep one's head above water in calm seas, they could not provide flotation in rough seas. Even though the test subjects were physically fit, good swimmers, and experienced in rough water survival, they became exhausted in a short period of time, keeping their heads clear of the water while combating 4 to 6 foot swells and 2 to 3 foot wind chop. These subjects did not experience similar problems with garments or life jackets providing buoyancy greater than about 17 pounds, (e.g. inflatable life jackets, anti-exposure coveralls, wet suits, etc.). Coast Guard personnel who are not as physically fit or as competent in swimming skills as these test subjects could expect to have even more difficulty with rough seas.

Float coats or other Type III devices shall only be worn in non-hazardous conditions when the risk of accidently falling overboard is minimal or when the probability of rapid recovery is high. These recommendations are already incorporated in the Coast Guard Rescue and Survival Manual, COMDTINST M10470.10A Ch 5, par. B2 and Ch 7, par. C3, but they are restated in this Notice for added emphasis."

An immersion suit can save your life.

The fourth choice for cold water protective gear is a high quality flotation vest, layers of clothes and foul weather gear   If you think you're going to live for even twelve hours in really cold water floating in a vest and foul weather gear, your thinking has departed from the realm of logic and entered the world of fantasy. On the other hand, thermal clothing, foul weather gear and a vest offer considerable thermal protection in a life raft and are better than Bermuda shorts and a mint julep.

A Thermal Protection Suit, now a SOLAS requirement.

THERMAL PROTECTION SUITS

Thermal Protection Suits are a new, important step forward in the fight against death at sea. They are a bag-like affair, covering everything but the face, to be worn in rescue craft (or on land). Like emergency blankets, TPS' are designed to highly reduce body heat loss and evaporation. In addition, they are waterproof and therefore reduce the possibility of salt water sores since the skin is relatively dry. They are easily entered through a zipper-seal and can be easily removed in the water. A TPS is the ideal outer garment over other clothing worn in a survival craft. Thermal Protection Suits are compact to store and inexpensive. They are of major importance in any survival pack. **Carry at least one TPS for each crewman.**

Cold Weather Survival Craft

In addition to an immersion suit, only a quality life raft, with an insulated floor and a double canopy offers any protection from the cold. In ice conditions, a life raft is lighter and easier to lift than a life boat, so it is possible to carry it over ice flows, then put it back in the water. Life rafts made of neoprene and several other materials become brittle in extreme cold, so it is wise to examine the chart in Chapter III regarding material ratings for cold weather use. Many experts advise the use of natural rubber for cold weather adventures. The nitrogen/carbon dioxide mixture in life raft gas cylinders contain sufficient gas to inflate the raft, even in extreme cold conditions. Carbon Dioxide, as it expands, forms frozen crystals which block the cylinder exit orifice. The Nitrogen is added as a propellant. A raft rated to hold six men may not do so when they are dressed in immersion suits and bulky cold weather survival gear.

ABANDONING SHIP IN COLD WEATHER

In addition to the necessity of dressing for cold weather, it is important to avoid getting wet. That, of course, is a tall order in an emergency situation, with the waves and the dying vessel conspiring against you. If possible, jump directly into the life raft, onto the canopy, or lower yourself into the lifeboat, rather than jumping into the water and swimming to it.

Life rafts can be purchased with or without an inflatable floor, but anyone venturing into cold water should consider an inflatable floor mandatory. As soon as you enter the raft, inflate the floor! It offers considerable insulation from the freezing sea. Remove wet clothing as soon as possible and wring it out. Dry your body with special attention to the head. If you don't have a hat, make one out of spare clothing or a plastic bag. When not using them, keep your hands tucked beneath your arm pits. Sponge the raft as dry as possible, as soon as possible. Close the door and huddle together to conserve heat.

Northern seas are extremely unforgiving, but a well dressed crew, clad in immersion suits, with a good quality life raft, one or more EPIRBS and a survival pack stand an excellent chance of surviving. Be sure you point this out to your crew as soon as possible. Assign them tasks—establish a watch and bail-out routine. Extraordinary efforts to keep the survival craft dry must be made.

The Yacht ARIANDE, dismasted and abandoned, but riding high, found adrift in the Irish Sea after the Fastnet race. The entire crew could have survived if they had stayed aboard. After violating Rule No. 1, DON'T ABANDON SHIP 'TIL THE SHIP ABANDONS YOU, several crewmen died, including Frank Ferris, shown on pg. 254. Photo by Andrew Besley.

CHAPTER X: ABANDON SHIP!

Preparation for Disaster

It is impossible to defend your boat against every disaster or prepare for every emergency. Good planning and good equipment reduce risks, but a state of complete safety cannot be achieved. In short, there is an element of risk involved in messing around with boats, and if it's a safe hobby you want, try raising tulips. If you still must go to sea after this warning, then remember that the three P'S may (may) save you: PLANNING, PREPARATION and PRACTICE (for disaster).

Making a Disaster Contingency Plan

Sit down in an easy chair and ask yourself: What would I do if my boat suddenly started filling up with water? Break the problem into categories, such as: through-hull fitting failures; collision with a submerged object; holes; cracks; shaft leaks, etc—and plan accordingly. The first major problem is to find the source of the leak, a job which is often far harder than one would believe, particularly if the damage is already under water.

If the source of a leak cannot be found by the noise of in-coming water, it is often necessary to isolate sections of the boat, and examine them separately. This includes closing watertight doors, jamming mattresses into narrow places, etc, then looking for a water rise which indicates the section containing the leak.

If you are not intimately familiar with the location of through-hull fittings, make a diagram of their location in the log. Fittings are often the source of leaks, and fitting failure should be considered first, if a collision has not occurred. Attach wooden stoppers to each through-hull fitting so that they will be ready for instant use

Face Page: *Abandon Ship* by Steve Callahan.

Disassemble, lubricate, and examine through-hull fittings when the boat is hauled. Be sure the valves operate smoothly. Be sure hose clamps, particularly the screw parts, are in good condition. Examine hoses connected to through-hull fittings and replace worn ones. All of these procedures will reduce the chance of a failure and familiarize you with the condition and location of these potential sources of danger.

A variety of leak-stopping systems are available for purchase, or they can be created. If your boat is made of wood or glass, examine it and make a variety of thin, flexible plywood patches which can be used in different locations. Predrill fastener holes in the wood. Tape an excess quantity of cement nails to the wood, so that they are "at hand" when needed. Cement nails are tempered and drive better in an emergency than other types. Buy underwater epoxy in sufficient quantity to cover the largest patch. Keep the entire "kit" together in a bag. If a hole can be patched from the inside, do so, then shore up the patch to prevent its working loose.

When it comes to patching holes, remember that collisions with submerged objects often produce jagged holes with debris projecting into the hull, making an inside patch difficult to apply. Under those circumstances, it may be necessary to jam a pillow or other soft object into the hole to reduce the inflow. If the water can be slowed, an outside patch should be considered, but if the sea is rough, it may be better to concentrate on sending a MAYDAY.

Underwater fiber glass repair kits (containing glass cloth, impregnated with a resin that can be used underwater) are available, and they are good for patching cracks from the outside. They are less effective for inside repairs, since in-coming seawater pushes the material away from the crack. If you do not have such a kit, sail cloth, awning material, even foul weather gear material can be smeared with underwater epoxy and used. Heavy staples will hold the cloth in place while the epoxy hardens.

Making a Survival Plan

Soldiers are overtrained to operate their weapons so that they will respond properly during the stress of combat. The **overlearning** is a safety feature of the training. In the same way, the crew and passengers of cruise lines all participate in abandon-ship drills at the beginning of each voyage. Many long-time crew members have participated in these drills hundreds of times. They know their emergency drill jobs by rote. How many times have you participated in an abandon boat or man-overboard drill? A survival plan, which includes an Abandon-Ship Procedure List, station bills, survival pack(s), clothing bag, navigation equipment pack and water jugs, also includes practice. Repeated practice may be boring, but it is the only defense against error in the stressful moments of a sinking.

Naval and merchant marine vessels prepare **station bills** that identify the duties each person must perform in the event of a disaster. Boat crews should have similar lists, prominently posted. Be sure each crew member knows which jobs are theirs. A group discussion, entitled "How to Abandon Ship," with the entire crew present, should occur before leaving port. It is an essential minimum procedure which, by itself can save lives.

An **abandon-boat drill** should take place before every voyage into the blue water. Each person should practice the duties assigned to them on the station bill. They should simulate abandoning ship, which may include donning personal equipment such as life jackets, float or immersion suits, picking up the raft, examining the survival pack, learning how survival equipment operates and where to find the items which are required for survival. It may be valuable to create a booklet showing the layout of your boat and its emergency equipment, what the raft looks like inflated, how to board it, how to activate the EPIRB and use other equipment. Take the attitude that the captain might be killed or lost during the abandonment and that the crew will have to fend for themselves. Man-overboard drills are equally important and are discussed later.

Assessing the Damage

RULE No. 2: THE BUTTOCKS RULE

When a boat begins to sink, the captain faces a difficult decision: When should he order the crew to discontinue ship-saving efforts and begin abandonment procedures? If he abandons ship too soon, nagging doubts that more could have been done to save the vessel will always plague him, and, of course, life in a survival craft is by no means secure. In some cases, abandoned vessels have been found adrift, weeks and even months later. On the other hand, every minute spent attempting to save a doomed boat is a minute lost from the job of ensuring the safety of the crew—and in all likelihood a few minutes is all you've got.

I always use RULE NO. 2: WHEN WATER STARTS NUZZLING THE BUTTOCKS, STOP REPAIR EFFORTS AND START TRYING TO SAVE YOUR BUTT. You will notice that this particular part of the anatomy is mentioned several times in this book, possibly leading the reader to the conclusion that the author might have an anal fixation. Without addressing that issue, keep in mind that measurements using body parts are very ancient (the foot, for example). I have noticed that cold saltwater, when reaching the buttocks level, causes a certain cinching reaction, and this is a signal to which one should listen. If your boat is too big or too small for this rule to apply precisely, modify it.

What are some of the indicators that it's time to apply Rule No. 2? One of the big ones is an inability to find the leak, or, once found, an inability to stop it. A critical moment comes when the water level inside the boat threatens the batteries, and a decision to transmit a MAYDAY must come before that occurs. No batteries, no transmission. No transmission, and it's just you, your little EPIRB, your survival craft, and that great big sea. Regardless of what duties have been assigned to others, <u>it is the responsibility of the captain to be sure a distress message is sent before power is lost.</u>

Vital information to be broadcast includes: the boat's position, number of crew, type of survival craft, physical characteristics of the boat, and its hull number. If one radio is all that is available, one man can devote himself to calling. If there are two, the less-seasoned crewman should operate the VHF radio, which is simpler to use. The captain or radio operator sends a message on the high seas radio.

Radio contact with shore stations, the Coast Guard or other vessels should be made immediately (see Chapter XIV). Absolutely nothing increases your chances of survival as much as the transmission of vital data and <u>acknowledgement that the message has been received.</u> Remember, a distress message can always be cancelled should the vessel be saved. Never let pride embarrass you and cause you to delay sending a distress message. If you have a hand-held VHF, put it into a waterproof bag before abandoning the boat.

Once radio contact has been established and all survival equipment is ready for instant deployment, efforts to save the vessel may continue.

Caught in the Rigging by Jim Sollers Survivors of the MASTER CARL, a 75' crabber, struggle to free their life raft before the boat slides under. The MASTER CARL took on water, rolled over and sank during a storm in the Gulf of Alaska, less than ten minutes after the flooding problem was discovered. The survival craft was eventually blown to land. Two of the crew were killed in huge surf, which pitched the remaining survivors on the beach of Montague Island. Protected from hypothermia by their survival suits, the pair survived for two days before being found, despite being chased by bears. One of the survivors went back to sea, the other moved inland and bought a farm. Read about it in *National Fisherman*. November, 1988

Good Reasons to Abandon Ship

A good reason to abandon ship is when the threat of a capsize becomes apparent. Motorboats which are in trim before an accident, and sailing yachts which have heavy keels, usually sink without rolling over, provided that **ports and hatches have been secured prior to the knock-down.** Many a vessel has sunk because a hatch was left open, allowing the boat to flood when it was knocked down. Under all other circumstances, it is unnecessary to abandon the vessel before the decks are awash. But if the boat develops a list, or if it is forced over by wind and waves, the risk arises of being hit by the mast or superstructure as the boat rolls over arises. A sudden capsizing may also trap anyone working below. On large ships, a 20° to 30° list is usually the signal to abandon ship. On a boat, the captain must decide for himself when a list has become life-threatening.

Another reason to abandon your boat is when fire fighting equipment is exhausted, when explosion or flames threaten the lives of the crew or the survival equipment. If a fire has spread to the point where smoke and flames have enveloped the interior of a boat, a number of basic errors in preparation have already been committed which are virtually uncorrectable. The additional, ultimate error would be to lose someone to the flames. The risk of smoke inhalation injury, or of someone being lost below decks, must be weighed against the possibility of saving the boat.

The wrong reason to consider abandoning ship is that bad weather appears to be of an overwhelming nature. A boat can take considerable damage to its deck equipment and superstructure while the hull, engine and pumps remain intact. Even if the engine and pumps fail, it is often possible to keep a sound hull afloat by forming a bucket brigade. There is no pump quite as willing as a scared crew with buckets. Do not be panicked by the sights and sounds around you. Always remember Rule No. 1, **NEVER ABANDON SHIP UNTIL THE SHIP ABANDONS YOU.** Never deploy your life raft until it is needed.

In the days of steam, crews abandoning ship were in considerable peril that they would be caught in an explosion if they did not get clear of the ship before cold, inrushing seawater contacted the red-hot furnaces. In times of war, crewmen were often forced to abandon their ship-saving efforts prematurely and get clear of the vessel, because on-board explosives were exposed to the flames. Tanker crews often flee because of the explosive nature of their cargo and the fear of being surrounded by burning fuel. As a result of crews' fleeing from such doomed ships, a myth arose that people near a sinking vessel would be sucked down with her. This is not true. The only risk when a boat sinks is that someone will become trapped and dragged down by rigging or debris, and this is a good reason to get clear.

The complete abandon-boat procedure itemized below should take no more than three or four minutes—except for the time needed to dress. Try to give that order as early as possible. A great deal will now be said about just what to do in the event of a sinking. Keep in mind that the various lists below only apply under certain conditions. If your vessel explodes or sinks in one minute, there may only be time to inflate the life raft, grab the survival pack and get clear. So do not take these procedure lists so literally that someone goes down with the ship while trying to complete their assignment.

ABANDON BOAT PROCEDURE: THE SEVEN STEPS

1. Recogize that the boat is going down. Do not wait until it's too late to take effective action.
2. Inventory the equipment which will help you survive. Properly written Abandon-Boat Procedure List and station bills will define what must be done.
3. Seek shelter: the best shelter is your boat and it should now be evident that theboat should not be prematurely abandoned. Shelter also consists of the survival craft, clothing, immersion and exposure suits and life jackets.
4. Collect signals: signals represent your best chance of being saved. They include the hand-held VHF transceiver(s), an EPIRB, rockets, flares, smoke devices, strobes, flashlights, mirrors, etc.
5. Collect water: water, for a castaway, may represent life itself. Be sure a five-gallon jug, with an air space sufficient to make it float is attached to the raft , preferably one for each crewman.
6. Collect food: food consists of rations but also of equipment to produce food and water. This means rations and equipment in both the survival craft and the survival pack. A high quality survival craft, food and water, represent the best insurance a sailor can buy.
7. Be determined to "make it": the will to survive, discussed in Chapter II is as critical as good equipment. People die from disaster syndrome, even though adequate equipment and provisions were available. Strong leadership is essential to keep minds of exisitng problems or potential dangers. Create games or in other diversions to keep everyone busy and avoid disaster syndrome.

SAMPLE PROCEDURE LIST

The list below (Ship's Standing Orders) and the station bills which follow are samples for a small craft in typical conditions. You must make up and post your own list to suit the needs of your vessel.

STANDING ORDERS

ALL CREW MEMBERS MUST:

1. Be familiar with the vessel and the location of all emergency equipment, particularly their life jacket and emergency clothing.
2. Know your emergency station assignment, and be familiar with the duties listed on their station bill.
3. Participate in "man-overboard" and abandon-ship drills prior to the voyage.
4. Wear a a safety harness when working outside the cockpit. on deck.
5. Know the location and course of the vessel at the beginning of each watch.

ABANDON-SHIP PROCEDURE

PUT ON: Long underwear   Pants/shirt/cap
            Sweater   Float suit; life jacket
            Deck shoes or boots

Take a drink of water. Put a knife, flashlight, and spare food in your pockets.
Proceed to your station and complete the jobs listed on your station bill.
When all jobs are completed, inform the captain, then go to your lifeboat station

STATION BILL: LAUNCH CREW

The launch crew deploys the raft, survival pack(s), water jugs, and other essential items. The launch captain is the first officer and is first into raft. The following personnel are designated as the launch crew:

Launch Captain: JOHN BROWN
Launch Crew: MADELINE SMITH

1. Bring the following items to the cockpit:
   - The life raft. Be sure to untie the red painter line which is secured to the mast.
   - 4 blue water jugs tied on the port rail.
   - 1 blue survival pack in box next to raft.
   - 1 red survival pack in lazarette.
   - 1 signals pack—obtain from Jesse Halpman.
   - 1 navigation pack—obtain from the captain.
   - 1 man-overboard pole secured behind the cockpit.
2. Attach the red safety lines from these items to a strong point in the cockpit.
3. Upon the captain's orders, deploy life raft on the leeward side of the boat.
4. The launch captain then enters the raft.
5. The launch captain will transfer all emergency equipment to the life raft. Tie it down immediately.

STATION BILL: EQUIPMENT CREW

The equipment crew gathers extra equipment, the signals pack, food, emergency equipment and passes it to the launch crew.

Equipment Captain: JESSE HALPMAN

1. Take the green duffle located in the sail locker and fill it with:
   - 1 portable radio in waterproof pouch.
   - 2 spear guns in starboard cockpit locker.
   - The flare gun box located in the dinette locker
   - The ship's log and documents from the captain. Place in a waterproof bag.
2. Close the bag and give it to the launch crew.
3. REPORT TO THE CAPTAIN.

STATION BILL: SIGNAL CREW

Signal crew sends a distress message, gathers documents, determines the last position, and gathers charts and navigation equipment.

Signal Captain: CAPTAIN SMITH

1. Send out a distress message on:
    • VHF Channel 16
    • 6215.5 USB
    • U.S.C.G. emergency frequencies, 13,313 MHz USB
2. Update the position in the ship's log.
3. PLACE THE FOLLOWING ITEMS IN THE NAVIGATION BAG:
    • The chart, almanac, tables, and protractor.
    • Passports, documents, and valuables.
    • The VHF radio in a waterproof bag.
4. Give the bag and the sextant to: Jesse Halpman.

POSSIBLE PROBLEMS WHICH MAY BE ENCOUNTERED

The raft may inflate upside down. The dinghy may swamp. Most rafts can be properly positioned from the deck of the boat. Entering the water to right a survival craft should be a last resortt, since it exposes the swimmer possible to death by traumatic injury and hypothermia. To right a capsized raft, grab the painter in a crouched position, stand on the gas bottle, wait for a wave to help, then pull. Spring away from the raft as it falls.

A dinghy is at considerable risk during the time it is lying against a boat if the weather is bad. The dinghy may capsize or be damaged against the boat's side. If a dinghy with positive flotation capsizes the easiest way to bail it from the boat, using a bucket . But if the sea is rough it may be necessary to let it drift away from the boat and have someone bail it from the water. Be sure to wear a life jacket and safety line.

RAFT FAILS TO FULLY INFLATE

Rafts usually fully inflate or do not inflate at all. If this problem occurs, use the hand pump and pump up the upper ring (doughnut) first. The arch tube will begin to inflate as soon as the upper doughnut is full. A six man raft can be inflated in about three minutes by a scared man with a pump.

ABANDON THE BOAT

The survival craft is particularly vulnerable to capsize and equipment loss, particularly in the chaotic, first moments of abandonment before the survival effort is organized. It is therefore extremely important to <u>secure all equipment as it comes aboard</u>. All equipment should be secured at <u>all times</u>, fair weather or foul. Never, never leave anything lying around, because you <u>will</u> eventually lose it. Secure the spare water jugs or bags to the raft with long painter lines. They should contain an air bubble to keep them riding high. Securing emergency equipment takes priority over all other considerations, including most forms of first-aid (more about this later).

As soon as everyone is in the survival craft, let all of the painter line out, and get as far away from the boat as possible to prevent smashing against it. As has been indicated several times in this book, **it is extremely difficult for a survival craft to remain attached to a sinking boat,** but if possible, do so. It may be salvaged later and the wreckage is easier to spot than a tiny survival craft.

Bail and sponge the raft as dry as possible, and assign someone to keep it that way. If someone is terrified or panicky, assign them this job. Another good "job" to assign a panicked person is tending the sea anchor line, hauling in the slack and letting it out as the raft rides the waves. Keep them busy.

As soon as the survival craft separates from the boat, **stream the sea anchor.** This item may look insignificant, but deployment of the sea anchor considerably reduces the possibility of capsizing. Move all personnel to the windward side of the raft to act as ballast. Their weight on the windward edge will reduce the chance that it will be lifted and flipped by the wind. Haul the anchor in every few hours, to examine the line and anchor connection points for wear.

Everyone should take seasickness tablets or attach scopolamine adhesive units behind the ear as soon as possible The motion in the raft is different from that of a boat and even seasoned hands may become ill. Sea sickness causes both fluid loss and incapacity. It must be avoided.

When conditions permit, examine the contents of the equipment and survival pack. Carefully examine all signals and be sure you know how to operate them (see Chapter XVII). Make sure everyone knows where they are stored. As soon as you have examined the equipment, secure it. Never leave anything lying loose in a survival craft. It may be lost if the craft capsizes.

POSSIBLE PROBLEMS WHICH MAY BE ENCOUNTERED

Injuries incurred during an abandonment must be treated promptly, but it is even more important to secure the survival equipment, upon which everyone's life depends. The only possible exception might be to control bleeding in the case of a severe injury. In that case, circumstances will have to be your guide. If the injured person is in the water, slide him into the survival craft, face down until his hips rest on the floats or gunnel. Gently turn them over and complete the job of bringing them aboard. Treat crew who are not breathing with mouth-to-mouth resusitation and CPR. Treat bleeding victims with direct pressure to the wound, or a pressure point. Use a tourniquet only as a last resort. People who have a tourniquet applied to a limb often lose it due to inadequate blood supply. Treat burn victims by covering the burned area with Silvadene Cream, then a light gauze bandage. Read Chapter XI for more medical information.

CREW IN THE WATER

If crew are in the water and you are in the survival craft, use the throwing line and quoit to save them. If you must swim to help someone, be sure a line is attached from the craft to you. <u>Do not, under any circumstances, swim away from the craft without a safety line</u>. The survival craft is usually drifting much faster than is apparent, faster than you can swim, especially if you are assisting someone else.

KEEPING SURVIVAL CRAFT TOGETHER

If more than one survival craft is used in an abandonment, it is important to keep them together, if possible, by using as long a (stretchy nylon) connecting line as possible. By doing so, resources, navigation skills and the skill of the captain can be shared. Unfortunately, it is almost impossible to keep life-rafts together in bad weather, so supplies and equipment should be promptly divided. It may become necessary to suddenly cut the rafts apart in bad conditions.

There have been many instances where survival craft, equally equipped, have separated, with a resulting loss of one of the vessels. If the craft are life rafts, they should be connected by their painters and a **lazy back-up line**. Lifeboats (dinghies), if drifting in settled seas, may be similarly connected, and every attempt should be made to keep the craft together.

The Psychology of Survival

People are usually too busy to think of the future during an abandonment, but the full impact of their precarious state becomes evident soon thereafter. As Alain Bombard noted, fear and despair are as lethal as the dangers of the sea. It is just as important to treat the psychological injuries caused by a sinking as it is to treat physical wounds.

A disaster situation is a time for strong leadership, a quality not easily taught. In cases where military or commercial vessels sink, the mantle of authority not only rests with the captain and officers, it is a continuation of the authority which they had aboard ship. This is not necessarily the case aboard a boat, where the captain and crew are often friends, lovers, or at least close associates. Despite this close relationship, one must not underestimate the possibility of sudden stress-related personality changes and the need for discipline.

A good example is found in a life raft survival test, conducted in the North Sea, involving people who were knowledgeable about life raft survival, who were aware that they were participating in a simulation. The test was conducted well offshore, out of sight of land. The attending vessel disappeared over the horizon and, at that point, the test leader told the others that he had forgotten batteries for his portable VHF radio, the sole device for communication with the ship. This comment caused such immediate distress and even aggression among the persons aboard that the leader was forced to take the batteries from his pocket, insert them in the radio, call the ship, and terminate the test. There is nothing even remotely amusing about a life raft ride, even if it's a practice run.

In a real situation, where death is possible, passengers not only have to face the stress of the uncomfortable ride and hypothermia, they will undoubtedly face thirst, hunger, and a dreadful fear for their lives. The completely enclosed raft has no visual horizon and, unlike a boat, it constantly undulates. The result is usually seasickness, even among seasoned sailors who are rarely, if ever sick.

This is why motion sickness pills or (preferably) Transderm adhesive units should be used. From life-raft level, the complete ability of the sea to snuff you out becomes painfully apparent. It is hardly surprising that some people react harshly to this type of stress.

DISASTER SYNDROME

Disaster syndrome is not easily treated while in a survival craft because the conditions which caused it still exist. This is what the *National Search and Rescue Manual* has to say about it under the section titled "Urgency of Response:"

> It should be assumed that all survivors are incapacitated, capable of surviving only a short time, under great stress, experiencing shock, and requiring emergency care. Normally able-bodied, logical-thinking persons may be, as survivors, unable to accomplish simple tasks or to assist in their own rescue. Some may be calm and rational, some hysterical, and others temporarily stunned and bewildered. This last group will be temporarily passive and easily led during the first 24 hours after the incident. As shock wears off, most regain active attitudes. Those who remain passive die unless quickly rescued. This behavior, commonly known as "disaster syndrome" is characterized by an attitude of "I am not here and this is not happening to me."

Since the cause (the ongoing stress of the disaster) cannot be corrected, understanding and a sympathetic response to what otherwise would be considered extremely aggravating behavior is important. As indicated in the rescue manual quoted above, passive, withdrawn victims are most seriously at risk, particularly since they are indifferent and uncaring about their survival. They must be fed, given water, and encouraged to exercise and change position, to prevent the development of "bedsores," a form of gangrene.

WHO IS THE CAPTAIN?

Should a foolish captain become the commander of a survival craft? Custom says yes, but bad captains often create the disaster which has forced everyone into a survival situation. There are some famous cases, such as the MEDUSA disaster, in which large numbers of the ship's complement died, solely as a result of bad judgment by the leader. If you are a sailor on a government-operated vessel, with armed soldiers in attendance, there may be no choice but to obey. But in a non-military survival craft, group survival always outweighs all other considerations and there are no laws which designate the captain of the boat as the legal commander of the survival craft. If a lawsuit results from the disaster, let the lawyers sort it out in a dry, warm place.

There are situations where inexperienced captains have relied on more experienced crew, and this sensible attitude is a sign of leadership. There are instances where a group of castaways have found themselves adrift with a madman in command. People who followed such a person would be regarded as madmen themselves. Let it never be forgotten that in a boating survival situation, rule is by the consent of the group.

On the other hand, most captains are more experienced than their crew, and are the logical choice for survival craft commander. These people command by virtue of their ability, not their rank. The wise captain governs least, and achieves his goals by suggestion. Orders are reserved for times of emergency, when quick action counts.

THE WILL TO SURVIVE

This subject hardly need be discussed again here, but crew must be reminded that a negative attitude, feeling that all is lost is in itself the first firm step on the road to death. Those who have hope for the future consistently do better than the others.

WE'RE OK NOW AND TOMORROW WE MAY BE SAVED

When groups of people are subjected to physical hardship and chronic stress, psychologists have learned that those most likely to survive adopt a positive strategy and avoid depressing thoughts about the future. They concentrate on being as safe and comfortable as possible for the moment. Their attitude seems to be "I'm ok now, and maybe things will get better later". This is an essential attitude, and it is the responsibility of the captain to foster and encourage it.

Immediately after the abandonment promote awareness of your advantages by discussing what has been achieved:

A MAYDAY was sent and acknowledged. The EPIRB will soon bring help. A MAYDAY was not acknowledged but was probably heard. The survival craft is in good condition. We are not far from a shipping lane. Food, water and equipment seem adequate. We are drifting toward land. We will be reported missing by relatives and a search will soon be mounted. Everyone survived the accident and will definitely reach land. The great majority of survival craft are rescued in less than five days.

Never create doubt or agree with anyone who has negative comments such as: "we're all doomed," "that ship was our last chance," "it will never rain", "the sharks will get us all." Try to turn these gloomy comments aside with a joke if possible: "you're too bony for the sharks to eat." "A man destined to be shot by a jealous lover will never drown;" etc.

If in doubt, keep busy. Immediately put everyone to work doing something. If anyone is seriously panicked, assign them a redundant job, such as tending the sea anchor line or bailing. Fishing is another good activity to keep someone busy. If you are afraid they may injure the raft or themselves with a hook, just attach a weight to the line (without telling them) and have them to jig it up and down to attract fish.

Structure your time. Create a rotational watch system and assign duties. Be sure everyone feels as though what they are doing is an important contribution to the survival effort. Give everyone the chance to be the "captain" of something, to increase their feeling of self-worth. Crew should know when they have free time, when they must bail, fish, clean up, pump flotation compartments, when they will eat, drink and sleep. Assign people to prepare food, dry fish, tend the equipment. Encourage the survivors to play games. If cards are available, use them. If not, make them. Establish a "play period." Play word games such as "Twenty Questions," pantomime games, tell stories or read aloud. There is an eternal quality about the sea, where a day seems to be marked by nothing but the sunrise and sunset. After a few days adrift, people often feel as though it is their fate to drift forever. Highly structured time does much to alleviate this problem.

Keep a good watch. The chance of being rescued is very small if a good watch is not kept. This is particularly true at night. But keeping a watch is exhausting and easily neglected. Keep watches short, not exceeding two hours. Shorten them when conditions warrant. Never skip a watch. One delinquency can mean the collapse of the entire system, particularly if the castaways are near the end of their strength.

Exercise. Part of the lethargy associated with survival conditions comes from collapse of muscle tone. Isometric exercises, either alone or with a partner, pushups or situps should be done every day, if possible, for 5 to 15 minutes. The improved muscle tone and its psychological effect are worth the price of the fluid lost during exercise.

Maintain the Cohesive Unit. If the castaways are to survive, they must think and act as a cohesive unit. Even (especially) the weaker or less adept individuals should be drawn into the survival routine. Keep them busy at things they do best and be sure you mention how well they are performing their jobs. Build and strengthen self-confidence when possible. The captain should provide the group with his knowledge and skill, but not create a dogmatic, authoritarian atmosphere where he issues orders and expects a dispirited crew to respond. Always seek group support by asking, "are we all agreed?"

Rations. Be particularly clear about establishing times for eating and drinking. When one person eats or drinks, everyone does so. If a debilitated crewman needs an extra ration, say so out loud: "Jones need a bit extra today." Never let anyone (such as a parent) give their ration away. Everyone should be required to consume their ration if they can do so. Most life raft equipment packs contain a measuring cup. Each person's ration should be measured out in some way and consumed in view of the others. Do not let lingering doubts arise that someone was favored.

Discuss rations and be sure everyone decides times and quantities as a group. Avoid making unilateral decisions and subsequently having to defend your decisions as a lone voice.

CANNIBALISM

People can exist for months on very little food, and a determined, creative crew can usually find ways of obtaining nourishment from the sea, even if it is nothing more than small quantities of plankton. A wise captain, who has read this and other books and who has prepared for an abandonment with a good survival pack, will never need to consider cannibalism. Instances of it are extremely rare among castaways and talk of it should be discouraged immediately, as it is extremely demoralizing and an indication that the cohesiveness of the group is weakening. After all, a ship may find you tomorrow. On the other hand, it may be disgusting but is not immoral to eat a crewman who has died, since it is the obligation of everyone to sustain their own life if possible.

Never Give the Lady with the Green Eyes a chance. Never forget that lethargy and the apparently overwhelming power of the sea can dominate your thinking and paralyze your effort to survive. Keep reminding yourself and everyone else that they have a future. Spend time making plans and frequently discuss what you will do after reaching land.

IN EXTREMIS

Under extreme conditions, when food and particularly water are almost exhausted, the group should consider issuing an extra ration to one or several persons who will then be able to continue functioning, and performing essential duties such as inflating flotation cylinders, fishing, keeping watch, etc.

CHAPTER XI:
EMERGENCY MEDICINE FOR CASTAWAYS

DISCLAIMER

I am a captain, not a doctor. I know soldier's and captain's medicine, and some of my techniques are never used in the better hospitals. Out of necessity, I have learned to do what doctors did for thousands of years before the creation of labs or the invention of X-rays—diagnose from gross symptoms and treat accordingly. My diagnoses are guesses, but they are good guesses.

   If you are the ship's medic, you should learn a few basics of first aide which will make an injured person's chances of survival zoom upward. In a survival craft it may be impossible to consult a guide while handling an injury, so a fundamental knowledge of emergency procedures is essential. These include:

> How to Control Bleeding
> How to Take Pulse and Respiration Counts
> Treatment of Burns
> Preliminary Treatment of Orthopedic Injuries
> Cold and Exposure Treatment
> Basic Use of Dressings and Bandages
> Cardiopulmonary Resuscitation

CARDIOPULMONARY RESUSCITATION (CPR) WARNING

   Cessation of breathing and/or heart functions is the most imminently life-threatening condition someone can experience, and fast action is necessary to save life. This consists, as a minimum, of clearing the air passageway to the lungs, then introducing air. Simultaneously, or as soon as possible, a diagnosis should be made to determine the cause of the condition. Once it is clear that cardiac massage is not contraindicated, CPR is applied, in addition to artificial respiration. A big contraindication would be a chest injury with broken ribs which might be driven into the lungs by pressing on the chest. In this case only mouth-to-mouth reventilation should be used.

CPR can save lives, but it is also <u>extremely dangerous</u> if improperly performed. People who have practiced application of CPR on a conscious person sometimes forget that muscles relax when vital signs cease, and the chest is much more easily manipulated than during a demonstration. It is easy to break ribs, particularly the bottom tip of the sternum. The sharp ends of these broken bones can be driven into the lungs, causing considerable damage. Keep in mind that the object is to depress the sternum just an inch or two, not drive it into the chest.

CPR must be performed on a firm or hard surface, not the undulating floor of a life raft. Get something under the patient's thorax, even another crewman, if nothing else is available. Kneel next to the patient, place the palm of one hand over the lower portion of the sternum (breast bone), avoiding its lower tip. Place the second hand over the first. Lock the arms. Rock forward, so that at the end of the maneuver, your shoulders are above the patient's chest.

Remember, <u>this procedure does not require great force</u>. Repeat every second, not faster. If two people are available to help, one applies mouth-to-mouth <u>simultaneously</u>, while the other performs CPR. A single rescuer should perform CPR strokes for ten seconds, followed by two mouth-to-mouth inflations.

Symptoms and Signs of Improvement: Pupil reaction to light is positive, as opposed to a dilated, unresponsive reaction. The **carotid pulse** in the neck is a sensitive indicator, so any pulsing is positive. Return of skin color is positive, but warming skin which is still pale and lacking tone is negative. Faint breathing can be detected by placing a piece of cool metal, such as a knife blade, or a piece of glass in front of the nose. Slight frosting is a positive indicator.

Signs of death: Failure to respond within 15 to 30 minutes usually results in brain death. If the patient drowned in cold water, remember, keep working for at least 30 minutes or until the patient starts to warm up, but is still unresponsive. Don't consider them dead until they are <u>warm and dead</u>.

LEARN BASIC MEDICAL PROCEDURES

In addition to emergency procedures, the prudent mariner will familiarize himself with a few specific fields of medicine, particularly treatment of trauma and drug administration. The ship's medic must understand and be prepared to make basic diagnoses in the field of trauma and burns, give injections, clean wounds, tie off an artery and close wounds.

Prepare for medical emergencies by reading and taking courses. It is amazing how much you can do with a few drugs, medications and dressing if you know how to use them. Correspondingly, a medicine chest is only as good as the person who uses it. I have treated many ill, wounded and injured people in my time. All of my patients got well. None died. The reason was not that I was so good, it was because I only did what I knew how to do. Someone may need an appendectomy, but they're not going to get it from me.

Field medicine for the survival craft revolves around having a kit designed to cope with medical emergencies specifically associated with life raft survival. This means treatment of gross trauma, burns, and saltwater associated infections. If you or your crew have other known problems, add what you need to the kit. A survival medical kit usually contains items which have been set aside from the boat's medicine chest. The object is to have them in the survival pack, so they are not forgotten during an abandonment.

The secret of my success as a field doctor has been to "keep it simple" and use drugs when indicated to produce a cure or delay the need for surgery. I give an initial large dose of medication, as much as is allowed in the literature. This is followed by a prescribed regimen which means the patient must take more pills over a period of time.

I lecture the patient about the need to take the entire regimen of the drug and if I have the slightest suspicion that this is not being done, I make them take it in front of me, then threaten to continue the medication by injection. I show them a huge glass syringe with a harpoon-sized needle which I use for injecting sauces into meat. I tell them that the injection they will need is so copious and thick that it will require this type of syringe. We both invariably agree it would be better to continue with the oral medication.

INCREASE OF WATER INTAKE

One of the dilemmas of giving drugs in a life raft is that the patient will then need additional water to help his kidney excrete the drug and its metabolic by-products. Pain killers are particularly hard on kidney function. On the land this problem is solved by allowing the patient to drink his fill or making him drink. In the survival craft the patient's life must be weighted against the lives of the other survivors. How much more water is needed? I don't know, to the best of my knowledge no one knows and your guess is as good as mine.

SURGERY

Get your physician to show you a few procedures and get a few books. Look at the procedures in this book. Buy a pig's foot in the grocery and practice on it. This will give you the confidence to act if the need arises. Don't think of this as an insurmountable project. You can do it.

The text which follows has been written using my six years as experience as a combat medic and also information from the same texts I use at sea. It has been examined for accuracy by a select group of physicians. The procedures in this Chapter reflect what I would do for myself and my crew if forced to act as a doctor. Talk to your own doctor, get your own texts written by experts, and learn.

PROGNOSIS

It is an unfortunate reality that a seriously injured castaway does not, in general, have a good prognosis. Even something as minor as a broken hand can set the stage for gangrene and death. Large open wounds close slowly and infect easily. A wet, undulating, cold liferaft, limited fresh water, wet clothes, the inability to rest, constant contamination of wounds, breakdown of mucus membranes, weakening of immune system, and extremely limited medical equipment all contribute to a downward spiral that can only be reversed with the appearance of a nice, big, fat cruise ship.

Keep in mind that an injury of any kind in a survival situation is much more serious than on land, where help is available. No matter how minor a wound, it must be washed, covered with a salve, and dressed. Do not allow minor cuts to become infected, requiring medication and painful debridement.

Being in a survival situation places a great deal of stress on the body. Medical problems which existed before the accident will probably be get worse in a life raft. You will note in Chapter XIX, *The Yacht Spirit Affair* that one crew member's hemorrhoid problem contributed to his death.

GENERAL PRINCIPLES OF FIELD MEDICINE

Oral medication is a big part of field medicine because it is safer to administer. Oral mrdication gives positive results slightly slower than an equivalent intramuscular (IM) injection.

Prophylactic medicine, medication given as a preventative, is usually avoided in areas where medical help is readily available. Physicians are afraid that the individual may develop a drug allergy or that some micro-organism may develop a resistance to the drug. In a survival craft, the risk of being unable to control an infection once it is established outweigh these risks.

Debriding is usually required before dressing open wounds. This may mean light soaking and washing in clean ration water with a cloth, or it may require a local anesthetic and minor surgery. In a survival craft, constant movement of imbedded material aggravates the problem and it is better to remove it.

Minor surgery in a survival craft is usually limited to debriding a wound, opening a boil or similar infection, tying off an artery and closing a wound using butterfly strips or suture.

Dressing a wound open wounds must be covered with an antibiotic salve to protect it against saltwater contamination, dressed, then protected as much as possible from getting wet.

FACING THE POSSIBILITY OF DEATH

Part of the price of admission to the wild blue valleys of the sea is the risk one faces from accepting absolute freedom and absolute responsibility. If you have a real problem with accepting this risk, do not tempt the Lady with the Green Eyes. She will do her best to eat you. Always keep in mind that the price of admission to this world of unparalleled joy is the possibility of dying in it.

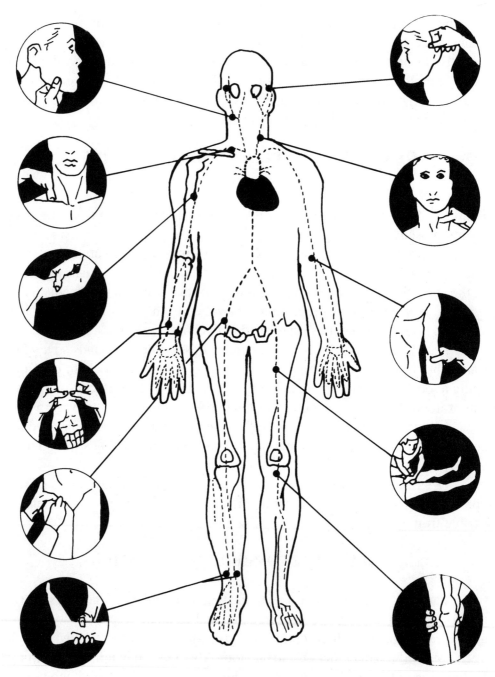

Pressure points useful for the control of bleeding. Drawing by Raoul Reys.

Treatment of Medical Emergencies

OPEN WOUNDS

Open wounds bleed externally. They are usually treated by quickly cleaning the area, then pressing a dressing over the wound. Once a dressing has been applied, it should be left on for at least a few hours or for a day because the blood clot protects the wound, and removal of the dressing can cause more bleeding.

Cuts across arteries **spurt blood**. Cuts across veins **ooze blood**. Arm and leg incisions which run parallel to the bone are usually less threatening and bleed less than others because there is less chance that arteries and veins are cut. Head wounds bleed copiously but may not be serious. Wounds in the buttocks or fatty areas may be deep but bleed very little and contaminate easily. Wounds to the fingers or hand may be small but can result in painful lesions which do not heal if left unattended.

If the wound is deep, it can be gently spread for examination. Pressure-point control or a tourniquet can be used if the wound is deep and dirty. Ragged wounds and/or those full of debris must be cleaned. Xylocaine can be injected into the subcutaneous layer in sites around the wound, every one to two inches, and also dripped onto the open tissue. Ragged edges and mangled tissue should be cut away.

TYPES OF OPEN WOUNDS

Incisions are caused by sharp objects, such as knives or flying glass. The wound usually has a clean edge and bleeds copiously. Minor incisions can be closed with direct pressure. The surrounding tissue may be wiped with antiseptic, then dried. They can be butterfly sutured closed, then covered with a dressing. Prophylactic medication is usually indicated when a wound is closed.

Avulsions are tears, such as a partially ripped-away ear. They usually bleed heavily but the bleeding is usually not life threatening and the panic associated with the blood should be treated psychologically. Direct pressure or a temporary pressure bandage can be applied to stop the bleeding. When the bleeding is controlled the area must be debride by paring away devitalized tissue, applying antibiotic ointment and a dressing. This should be done within a few hours of the accident. Disfiguring avulsions may be butterflied into place, then repaired ashore with plastic surgery if necessary.

Scrapes incurred during abandonment bleed lightly and are not serious in themselves, but they are usually very dirty and must be cleaned or debride. Scrapes are a nuisance on land but they are a serious problem in a life raft because they cannot dry, and are therefore a source for the entry of bacteria, ideal for the development of raw lesions. They must be covered with an antibiotic salve and dressed.

Penetrations, holes from thin, pointed objects, usually look minor but may be deep. Underlying organs or tissues may have been penetrated, and bacteria may have been introduced into the wound.

Grasp a small piece of gauze with a hemostat and dip it in clean water with a little soap. Probe gently into the puncture and wash it. If debris appears on the gauze, continue the washing. Small penetrations can be washed and wiped. Deeper ones must be irrigated with a syringe, using sterile water and a little soap. It may be necessary to poke the syringe into the puncture and squirt out debris. This procedure should be repeated several times.

Shrapnel or **splinters** are sometimes driven into a wound caused by accidents such as explosions or falling on debris. Combat medics learn a great deal about shrapnel. Small splinters or debris are annoying on land but are a real threat in a survival craft. They cause increasing pain and, if untreated, become open lesions or, worse, result in deep infection which can become general. Penetrating objects must be removed, and also the area from which they are removed must cleaned. This is not as easy as it would seem, since living tissue tends to close around penetrating objects and around the holes they create when removed.

Lacerations have ragged edges, caused by duller objects, such as rough metal or moving machinery. Torn tissue and bacterial contamination are usual complications.

TREATING OPEN WOUNDS

Nasty cuts, abrasions and more serious wounds which occurred during the abandonment should be treated with **prophylactic oral drug therapy.** Open wounds and wet conditions often lead to infection. Because survival craft wounds are often contaminated, they usually have to heal by "secondary union," which means they must be left somewhat open—not sutured, due to the high risk of sewing contamination into the wound.

Only "clean wounds" which can be treated within a few hours in settled conditions are candidates for healing by "primary union," meaning that the edges are brought together by suture or butterfly closures. Wounds can be pulled together using butterfly closures (a material similar to adhesive tape), and the closures can be easily removed if infection is detected.

ASEPTIC TECHNIQUE

Aseptic technique means creating bacteria-free conditions in and around a wound so that contamination is not further introduced. One may argue that a dirty wound is already contaminated, so why bother? The answer is that, while this may be true, the ensuing treatment is designed to clean the wound and prevent the transmission of contaminated material into deeper tissues.

Aseptic technique includes **sterilizing the skin** surrounding the injury with Betadine solution. First, roll up your sleeves and cover your hair so it won't drop into the wound. It is better to remove your shirt than to risk dragging it across the wound.

Cleaning the wound is essential prior to closing or dressing it. This may mean first washing the site with a gauze pad and surgical soap. The site is then dried and further cleaned, if necessary, with a hydrogen peroxide wipe. Never pour antiseptic into a wound as this damages the tissue. Betadine, another excellent antiseptic, is an instrument and skin sterilizing solution, never used inside wounds.

Debriding means removing both foreign matter and devitalized tissue from the wound site. This must always be done before the wound is closed or covered. Dead tissue should be considered as dangerous to the patient's health as foreign matter, for dead or dying tissue makes an ideal site for the development of infection. Ragged edges, loose flaps of skin overhanging a wound, and ragged or crushed subcutaneous tissue are all candidates for removal.

If the wound is clean and conditions permit, it should be closed immediately, and this is discussed later. If the wound becomes contaminated during the abandonment, or more than four hours elapses before treatment, it must be packed with Silvadene cream and allowed to heal by secondary union (fill up with scar tissue). Bleeding should be controlled. The wound is then covered with a loose dressing. Disfiguring scar tissue can be corrected with plastic surgery later. Your job is to keep the patient alive.

CONTROL OF BLEEDING DUE TO SEVERED ARTERIES OR VEINS

The human body contains about six pints of blood, and the loss of a few can kill or set the stage for death. The severing of a major artery can lead to death in just a few minutes, so **rapid control of bleeding** is important. **Shock** results from considerable loss of blood.

If a wound is "clean," control of bleeding can start immediately **direct pressure**. Direct pressure may be applied by pressing the dressing firmly over a cut until the bleeding stops. Pressure can be applied directly to the severed vessel

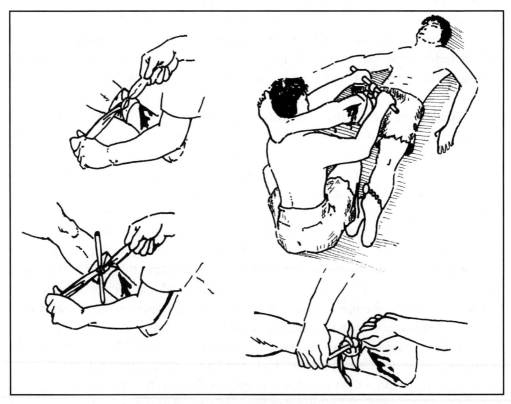

Applying a tourniquet. Drawing by Rafael Monroy.

or to the site of the wound. A surgical-gloved hand is ideal, not only because it is sterile, but because the smooth surface of the glove will not tear out the clot when pressure is released. Pressing with a dressing is the second choice. If nothing else is available, just use your finger or palm. If you suspect that shrapnel, chards, or other relatively large debris are in the wound, you should apply initial control at **pressure points,** remove the debris, <u>then</u> apply direct pressure at the wound site. This will prevent driving debris deeper into the wound. If a limb is injured, <u>elevate it</u>. Put it on your shoulder if necessary.

A **tourniquet** is extremely effective for controlling serious bleeding, but it can also be <u>extremely dangerous</u>. It completely stops the flow of blood to a limb and can cause extreme damage, loss of the limb, or death if used improperly. A tourniquet can be used for a minute or two, to stop bleeding just long enough to examine a wound for gross debris or to consider further strategy. Apply a tourniquet to tie off ruptured arteries or veins, then remove it, to restore circulation.

A tourniquet which is **too narrow** is dangerous and can damage muscles and nerves. Be sure it is at least two inches wide. If something like a belt or piece of rope is all that is available, pad the area with clothing. Use a piece of wood or screwdriver to tighten it.

TYING OFF BLOOD VESSELS

If blood spurts from a wound and the bleeding cannot be stopped with direct pressure, it may be necessary to tie off a blood vessel. Apply a tourniquet to stop the bleeding, wipe the wound, locate the source of bleeding, and sterilize the hemostat by soaking or wiping with Betadine solution. Clamp the severed vessel with the hemostat. Release the tourniquet.

Get your hands as clean as possible, using soap and Betadine. If you have gloves, use them. Create a sterile field. Peel open the suture (absorbable "gut"), lift it out with the clean hemostat, shake it loose, hold the bitter end with your fingers, and cut off about six inches of line. Place the remainder between two pieces of sterile gauze to be used for suturing. Hold the ends of the line in your hands. Loop it around the clamped vessel. Tie a square knot. Tie the first knot, right-over-left hand, then have an assistant use a hemostat to clamp the tie. Be sure the knot is clamped with <u>just the tip</u> of the hemostat. Tie a left-over-right hand knot to complete the square knot and snip off the ends.

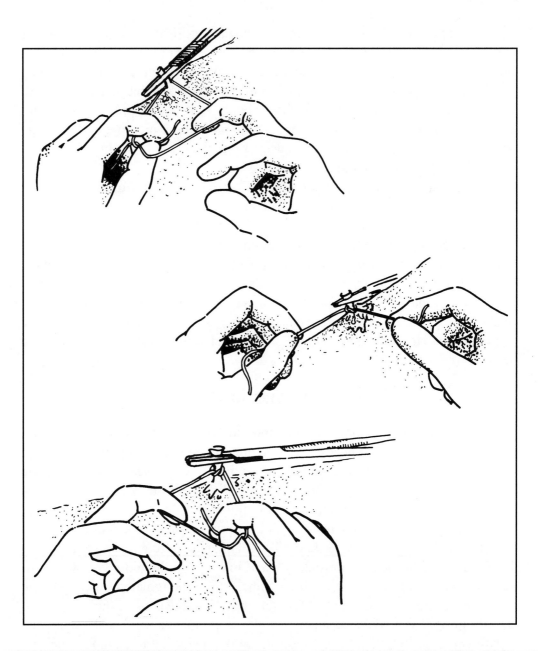

Tying off a blood vessel: (1) clamp the vessel with a hemostat; (2) make a right-over-left hand tie;
(3) clamp the knot; (4) make a left-over-right hand tie to complete the knot. Drawing by Rafael
Monroy.

SUMMARY OF BLOOD VESSEL TYING TECHNIQUE

1. Control bleeding.
2. Wipe the surrounding area clear of blood and debris with a gauze pad.
3. Clamp severed vessel with a sterile hemostat. Release tourniquet.
4. Try to create aseptic conditions: Wash the hands. Create a sterile field. If not already sterile, dip other instruments in Betadine.
5. Clamp the blood vessel with a hemostat.
6. Tie off the clamped vessel with **absorbable suture material**, using a square knot.
7. Clean wound with surgical soap and sterile water (ration water).
8. Paint the surrounding area with Betadine.

SHOCK

Description: (1) Sudden contraction of the vascular system from various causes, such as blood loss, toxic reaction to massive infection, hypothermia, or the pain of a trauma. (2) A term indicating a psychological injury, an inability to cope or respond properly to stress.

SYMPTOMS, TESTS, AND TREATMENT

Low blood volume (hypovolemic) shock usually follows extensive bleeding, including internal bleeding. If someone has lost a great deal of blood (a pint or more), assume hypovolemic shock will occur and act immediately, even before symptoms appear. By the time the classic symptoms of shock occur, the patient is in a true emergency situation that can result in death.

Symptoms: Considerable anxiety and restlessness, rapid pulse, nausea, thirst, weakness, cold hands and feet, cold, clammy skin, occasionally bluish finger and toe tips, rapid, shallow respiration or hyperventilation. The patient knows they are in deep trouble.

As the shock deepens, the patient may become comatose. Breathing slows, the breath begins to smell acidic, the pulse becomes rapid and thready, or disappears, pupils dilate (glassy-eyes). In the final stages, heart failure due to inadequate brain oxygen may occur. These symptoms plus obvious blood loss are usually sufficient evidence to indicate the patient is entering a state of shock.

Treatment: On land paramedics would administer IV fluids to replace lost blood volume. They would probably put the patient into anti-shock trousers, which are inflatable pants, designed to press the blood out of the limbs, into the body core. Just these two procedures would vastly increase the patient's chance of surviving. So would getting him to a hospital in about five minutes.

In a life raft very little can be done to prevent shock once a great deal of blood has been lost, but you must do what you can. The list that follows is a standard one for generalized gross trauma. Make no mistake, the list below is inadequate to deal with a problem that only a good IV set and an intensive care unit could turn around.

1. Lay the patient down.
2. Restore breathing if it has stopped.
3. Stop the bleeding.
4. Slightly elevate the victim's legs, put them on your shoulders if necessary.
5. Cover and keep person warm.
6. Remove dentures (if any), clear mouth.
7. Try to keep the patient warm. Use your own body if necessary to supply heat.
8. Make patient control breathing.
9. Remain near head to assist vomiting.
10. Give respiratory assistance, if necessary.

Placing a bag or cupping one's hands over the patient's nose and mouth for a minute or two often helps a hyperventilating patient regain control. Rebreathing used air somewhat reduces the carbon dioxide deficient/super-oxygenated condition of the blood which results from hyperventilation.

Prognosis: Shock, due to blood loss or internal hemorrhage, can only be treated on a first-aid basis in a survival situation, and prognosis is poor. The prognosis is much better for more moderately afflicted persons, who are not in an otherwise life-threatening situation. They may be treated with fluids and psychological therapy. Prevent shock by jumping on its causes fast.

OTHER TYPES OF SHOCK

Anaphylactic shock: This type of shock results from a **hypersensitivity reaction** to something like penicillin, jellyfish venom, or fish spine slime. Anaphylactic shock is characterized by a pronounced, rapid, violent onset.

Symptoms: Rapid pulse (90 to 110 beats per minute), respiratory difficulty including airway obstruction, bronchospasm, wheezing, local swelling and irregular heart rhythm. Look for a "sucking-in" of the skin between the collar bone, an indication of airway obstruction. The patient is usually very agitated.

Treatment: Survival craft treatment consists of an injection of **adrenaline** (**Epinepherine**). I am partial to the Ana-Emergency Treatment Kit which comes in its own little plastic container with instructions, two alcohol wipes, a syringe and two individual doses of Epinepherine (0.3 ml. each), and four antihistamine tablets (chlorpheniramine). In a hospital Epinepherine for shock is usually administered IV but this is a dangerous procedure in survival craft.

Epinehperine comes in many different containers including **Tubex cartridges** which contains the drug in a glass tube complete with a needle. You will need a tubex injector (very inexpensive) which holds the cartridge.

The IM injection may be repeated after ten minutes, then every 30 minutes, or as needed to suppress life-threatening symptoms. Two shots are usually enough. The antihistamine may be given again in four hours (or you may give Benadryl) if swelling or respiratory problems persist.

In very rare cases a patient may experience a very severe shock reaction to drugs, fish slime or venom. The most serious symptom which is treatable in a survival craft is swelling of the tongue and upper throat, blocking the airway, causing asphyxiation. In this case, in addition to an injection of Epinepherine, a plastic airway must be inserted in the throat.

Prognosis: Prompt medication vastly improves prognosis and most patients recover within twelve hours, although people with severe cases can die.

Bacteremia or septic shock in a survival situation results from massive infection by bacteria. It is usually associated with a burst deep abscess, improper surgical procedures, a tooth abscess, the inadequate drainage of pus, or suturing of a contaminated wound which becomes infected.

In the field, septic shock may result from uncontrolled infection such as gangrene. If a massive infection is not drained and debride, and the patient medicated, death is usually the result. The symptoms and signs of infection usually are quite evident before septic shock symptoms appear and the infection should be treated.

The symptoms of septic shock: Some of the symptoms of septic shock are typical of all forms of shock including: low blood pressure, elevated pulse, nausea, and vomiting. Elevated temperature; pink, warm, dry skin and diarrhea are almost always present as are diurnal fever "spikes," chills, tremors, skin eruptions, and a general malaise—all of which are extremely alarming.

When the breath begins to smell acidic, the heart begins to beat irregularly, the skin and eyes become jaundiced, and the patient becomes comatose, death is near and will occur most of the time in a lifeboat and up to 50% of the time even in an intensive care unit.

PSYCHOLOGICAL TRAUMA SHOCK

Disaster Syndrome, a hysterical reaction to a disaster situation, is a form of schizophrenia and is not treated like physical shock, although people often say "he's in shock." Disaster syndrome can be extremely life threatening, especially if the victim is not rescued promptly.

Symptoms: The patient, horrified by the situation, copes by saying subconsciously, "I'm not here, this isn't happening to me." Symptoms include a mild, inappropriate attitude, a vacant expression, and extreme docility. Others experience powerful auditory and visual hallucinations, and frequently believe they are elsewhere.

These people are extremely dangerous to themselves and may slip silently over the side to "buy a newspaper" or "get some groceries." They must be watched carefully and often tied down. You must be sure they consume their rations and are not exposed excessively to the elements, since they usually say nothing about their discomfort. Reasoning with them is usually ineffective.

Treatment: People experiencing disaster syndrome sometimes become completely catatonic and must be repositioned about every half-hour to prevent the development of "bed sores," a form of skin gangrene. The only way to cure this malady is to remove the sufferer from the disaster situation.

Prognosis: Prognosis is poor, with a high mortality rate. However, if the patient can be sustained until rescue, rapid recovery usually occurs.

Hysterical shock can also follow very painful, less life-threatening injuries, or can result from hysteria after an accident. This is a more mild form of shock and is rarely fatal.

BURN SHOCK

Burn shock is an early complication of a serious burn. The symptoms may appear immediately or hours after the accident. Huge amounts of body fluid immediately flood the wound site, robbing the body core. A considerable quantity of essential soluble ions such as sodium and potassium are lost, and the kidney shuts down to prevent further fluid and ion losses. The reduction or cessation of urinary output, dark or sediment-laden urine, is an ominous sign.

The patient should be urged to urinate immediately after the accident, so output can be monitored. Normal urinary output for a burn patient would be about four to five ounces (0.5 to 1 ml./kg.) every hour, and this liquid loss must be replaced by forcing fluids (drinking water). A significant drop, to as little as a half ounce, indicates trouble. Vomiting, rapid pulse, and sweating further confirm diagnosis. Since the lifeboat does not have an IV setup, the patient must force liquids orally. Sea water contains most of the ions lost. Burn shock is a serious complication and, if untreated, can result in death.

HEATSTROKE (SUNSTROKE)

Heatstroke is a type of shock caused by loss of blood volume due to severe dehydration. It has a potentially high mortality rate if untreated and a much lower mortality rate if treated. The victim gets hot, does not or cannot drink enough, suddenly stops sweating, then collapses into unconsciousness. The skin is dry, pink, and hot. Body temperature soars to as much as 108°F. (42.2°C.). Respiration is deep and rapid. Pupils dilate and contract. Other symptoms include twitching, convulsions, and vomiting. More serious victims lapse into deep shock.

Treatment: Cool the patient's body as rapidly as possible. Use sea water and wet towels. Fan the wet body and massage it to promote circulation. Give no drugs. Let the patient drink when he has stabilized.

PSYCHOLOGICALLY INDUCED SHOCK

Some elements of trauma-induced shock are **psychological.** A patient can become so agitated and upset because of pain and fear that they can induce a physical shock reaction. It is important to begin homing in on the patient's psychological state, even as you apply emergency techniques. Calm, sympathetic instructions to the patient can do much to help them help themselves, such as:

Look, Charlie, I know it hurts, but you're going to be okay, so stay calm. There are some things I want you to do. You've need to control your breathing. You're breathing too fast. Hold your breath for a moment, then try to breath normally, okay? That's much better. Are you feeling nauseous? Try to fight it down right now, but if you cannot hold it, let me know. I'll give you something for the pain as soon as you get over the nausea and weak feeling. Don't close your eyes. Keep your eyes open, do not doze off, etc.

Initially, give nothing by mouth. Demerol or morphine injections are frequently given to trauma victims to calm them and prevent pain induced shock. If the patient isn't bleeding profusely and internal injury is not suspected, a morphine injection is an option.

Fractures

Every bone in the body can be broken, and it is impossible to discuss all possibilities here. In a hospital, a broken bone is usually diagnosed, aligned and set using X-ray. In the field, many breaks are obvious, and others may be inferred by pain, swelling, deformity, and loss of function. In addition to pain and swelling, internal bleeding, which shows as a purple or yellow stain under the skin, increases the likelihood that a bone is broken.

In a survival craft it is impossible to properly set breaks, due to the vessel's undulating motion or lack of space and materials. Immobilization may be all that is possible.

Should this minimum treatment be all that's possible, straighten the limb by applying slight traction. Slowly apply increasing traction until you can manipulate the limb into as natural a position. Use the minimum force necessary.

Rough alignment of a broken limb is accomplished using the good limb as a model. If a leg is broken, look at the unbroken one. Sight over the big toe of the good limb. See where the line of sight hits the knee cap and make a pen mark on the good kneecap at this point. Make a mark on the knee cap of the damaged leg as a reference.

Use other references such as the alignment of the ankle bone and the crest of the hip. Arms are aligned using the little finger and elbow, elbow and shoulder. Fingers are about 10 to 15% out of alignment with the line of the forearm. Make pen marks on the good arm to make the job go faster when applying traction. Keep in mind that you are not trying to set the break, just realign the limb as much as possible for comfort.

Prior to manipulation, a local anesthetic of xylocaine 1% up to 20 cc may be administered (in several injections) into the fracture site, being careful not to inject into a blood vessel. The thing to remember about breaks, particularly if drugs are not available, is that there is usually a period of a few minutes after the accident when the area is in shock, is numb and the muscles have not yet become tense. If at all possible, this is the time to make the "set," or at least straighten and splint, thus avoiding the need for an injection. Xylocaine injections around a fracture site are a common procedure.

The limb or fractured area is **immobilized** with a splint. A broken leg may be bound to the other leg. An arm can be immobilized against the chest. Hand or wrist fractures can be immobilized with a raft paddle. Fingers can be splinted to pencils. Necks can be immobilized using a dinghy paddle or piece of wood. Broken collarbones are immobilized with a triangular bandage which pulls the shoulders back and reduces movement. The bad arm should be rested in a sling. If available, a cold pack can be used to reduce swelling.

Splint material is sold in rolls. It is ideal, but bulky, and for this reason is not included in the suggested survival pack med kit. Plastic arm forms are also available. Buy these for the boat's medical chest.

Always wrap a splint in cloth to pad the skin. Two or three pieces of wood or other material can be used as a splint, and they can be initially positioned with tape. Always leave fingernails and toenails exposed so that thcy can be examined for lack of circulation. If the bandage is too tight, extremities turn pale or blue and feel cold and insensitive.

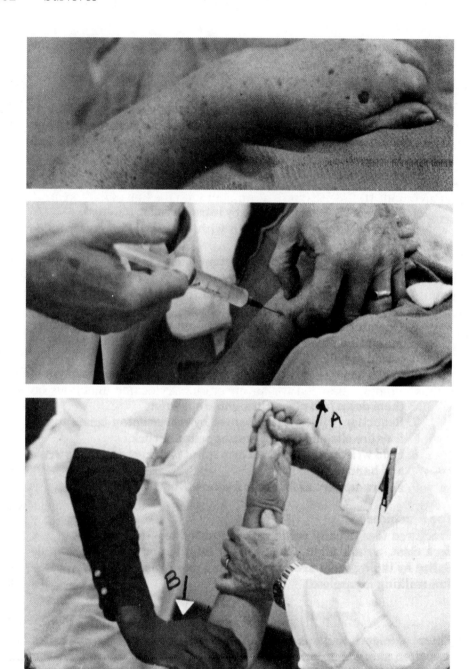

(1) Reduction of (Cole's) fracture of both arm bones near the wrist, often the result of a fall. (2) Center: Injection of Xylocaine. (3) A: Traction and B: counter-traction to align and reduce the break. From *Advanced First Aid Afloat* by Peter F. Eastman, M.D., © 1987 by permission of Cornell Maritime Press

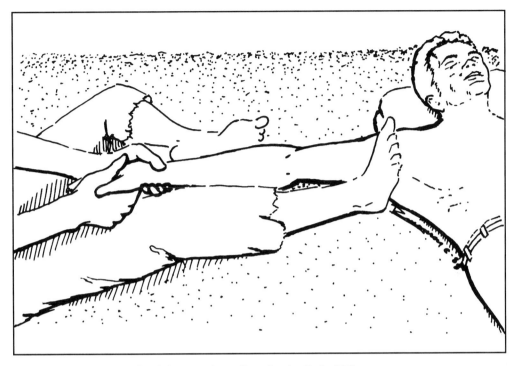

Applying traction.   Drawing by Rafael Monroy.

If this occurs, apply a slight traction and ease the bandage until circulation returns. Gently rub fingers or toes to promote circulation. After a few days it may be possible to gently manipulate them which helps reduce swelling. The injured limb should be elevated to retard swelling and to reduce internal hemorrhage due to small broken blood vessels. Cold packs also help.

Control of pain. An injection for pain is usually not needed unless the patient appears to be in intractable pain. Patients with simple fractures are good candidates for pain medication, meaning that the pain killers are safe to use. Pain killers are discussed later.

CRUSH INJURIES AND MULTIPLE FRACTURES

Crush injuries, such as occurs when limbs are caught between a vessel and a life boat, may produce multiple fractures, discoloration from broken blood vessels, and swelling. These injuries are not easily treated in a survival situation.

How to apply a triangular bandage: Align or set the broken arm, then splint it. Support the limb with the triangular bandage, as shown. Tie with a square knot on the <u>side</u> of the neck. Further immobilize the limb with a second cloth or belt. Drawing by Rafael Monroy.

Immobilize the area, control pain, and begin prophylactic medication. Keep a sharp watch for signs of infection. Massive infections resulting from such an injury <u>must</u> be opened or death may occur.

Compound fractures are caused either by broken bones projecting through skin or penetration by an object which breaks the bone, such as a bullet or shrapnel. These are very serious injuries which must be treated properly.

<u>Control bleeding first</u> at pressure points. Watch for **shock**. Deep contamination of the wound should always be suspected. Administer morphine if you have it. Administer local anesthetic prior to treatment if available. Begin use of oral antibiotics. Wash and debride. Remove bone fragments. Pare back sharp bone points.

If the break was caused by a penetrating object, gently spread the wound with the hemostat, or if it is large, spread with the fingers. Remove debris and pare back shredded or devitalized tissue. Do not probe further than you can see. Wash the wound and the bone with surgical soap. Disinfect it with hydrogen peroxide. Disinfect the surrounding skin with Betadine and shave it, if possible.

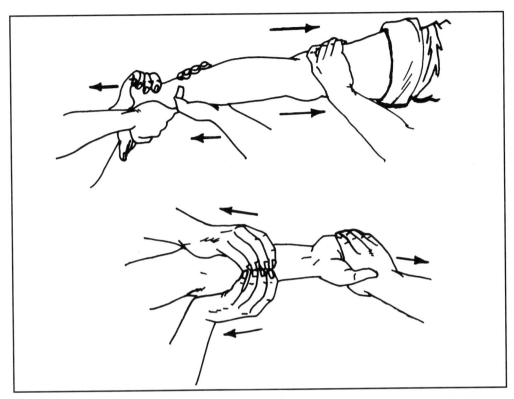

Aligning Fractures: Steady traction is applied by one person while the other presses the fracture into as natural a position as possible using the good limb as a model. This is obviously not a "set," as is done in a modern hospital but this was the way it was done in the days before x-rays. When aligning simple fractures, particularly of larger bones one can often feel the fracture slide into place. Injection of Xylocaine into and around the site is recommended. Drawing by Rafael Monroy.

Prepare splints and cloth dressing. Apply traction and allow the bone to slide back into the wound.

Align broken bones by repositioning and rotating limb. Use the good limb as a model. Allow the traction to ease <u>slowly</u> while manipulating the limb, to improve the set. Cover the wound with Silvadene cream-impregnated gauze. Administer oral painkillers or use a Demerol patch. Watch for indications of internal hemorrhage, which must be controlled at pressure points above the injury site.

BURNS

Skin is a vital organ, and like the kidneys, it removes waste. Also like the kidneys, the skin can withstand a certain amount of damage and continue to function. The remaining healthy tissue can compensate for the loss. But if 20 to 35% of a person's skin is lost, the remaining healthy tissue fails as an organ. In a hospital burn unit, various life-support techniques could be used to greatly increase the chance of survival, but in a survival craft, little more than control of pain and protection of damaged tissue are possible.

In addition to removing waste (in the form of sweat), the skin acts as a barrier against infection. When it is damaged, a huge "hole" in the body's defense system is created, and the risk of infection is an even greater threat than the loss of skin. In a survival craft every effort should be made to keep the burn as clean as possible and protect the area against microbial invasion with Silvadene cream. Silvadine creme is quite expensive but worth the price.

Burns are classified as first-, second-, third or fourth-degree. **First-degree burns** are **scalds**, and this usually includes typical sunburn. **Second-degree burns** result in **blisters**, but the subcutaneous tissue is basically undamaged, and the skin can repair itself, given time.

First- and second-degree burns should be immediately cold-packed, if possible, to reduce pain and further tissue damage. Even cool ration water on gauze can be used. These injuries can be covered with Silvadene cream-impregnated dressings to prevent infection, and they will heal even if extensive, although the risk of infection always exists. Pain can be controlled with oral medication.

Third-degree burns are called **full-thickness burns**, because the skin layer is entirely destroyed. Third degree burns are characterized by **charred tissue**. People with third-degree burns sometimes do not feel pain in the area of injury, since the nerves which signal pain have been destroyed. The destroyed area is an optimum route for infection. Wounds of this type must be closed by surgical grafting.

Fourth-degree burns often look the same as third degree, but deeper tissue, even bone is destroyed. Lightning produces a typical fourth-degree burn. The underlying, devitalized tissue produces septic shock which will eventually kill the patient unless removed, presumably in a hospital.

SEVERE BURNS

Emergency treatment for third-degree burns consists of the following procedures:

1. Control pain initially with morphine. See morphine warnings. When the patient is stabilized give oral Demerol. Switch to Vicodin as soon as possible.
2. Gently clean the injury with cool compresses of ration water and surgical soap. Debride charred or loose tissue.
3. Cover the area with Silvadene cream, then with Silvadene-impregnated dressings, then a loose bandage. Fingers and toes should be individually wrapped, to allow exercise, or thoroughly covered with Silvadene cream, then slipped into a surgical glove. Protect against moisture by isolating the dressed wound in a plastic bag. Air when possible, hopefully frequently. Inspect and freshen daily. Keep as dry as possible.
4. Begin prophylactic oral medication. Force fluids.

Control of Pain

Control of pain is an important part of medicine, and it is the most pressing item on the patient's agenda. The doctor's first priority, however, is to gain insight into all ramifications of the problem, prior to administering anything which would mask important information, change the patient's physiology, or endanger his life.

Pain is relative and subjective. There is no way I can tell you, '*this is enough pain for morphine, but that pain only requires Vicodin.*' In a hospital environment, this insight is conveyed to novices by those with experience. In text, this is not possible. Novices see experienced personnel standing by, apparently unmoved while a patient suffers, not realizing that sometimes inaction when medicating for pain may be a positive approach.

It is hard to refuse painkillers to a friend in pain, but the danger of administering painkillers to people entering shock must always be kept in mind. Morphine and Demerol accentuate the dangerous symptoms of shock, such as depression of respiration and lowering of blood pressure. In a survival situation, very little can be done to reverse the damage caused by hasty use of painkillers. On the other hand, quick use of pain killers can prevent a patient from entering pain-induced shock and do much to comfort him. If a patient does not appear to be internally injured and has not lost considerable blood, administration of a narcotic is an option.

Pain Medication and It's Uses

MINOR PAIN: NON-PRESCRIPTION DRUGS

Non-prescription drugs control minor pain such as first- and second- degree burns, strains and bruises. Non-prescription drugs have many advantages: they are readily available; they are cheap and can therefore can be replaced frequently; they store well and do not break down easily; they do a good job for minor pain. My favorite is **Ibuprofen**, you select yours.

Aspirin is not only effective to fight mild pain, it lowers temperature and reduces swelling. It stores well for long periods and does not break down easily. If you and your crew can handle aspirin, it is the drug of choice. **Dose**: 300 to 600 mg. (usually one to two tablets) every four hours. Peak serum levels for Ibuprofen and aspirin are reached in 30 to 40 minutes with a half-life of two hours.

MODERATE PAIN: VICODIN

Vicodin is the modern equivalent of the old emprine/codeine tablet found in the life raft survival packs of WWII sailors. Each tablet contains 5 mg. of codeine (a very small amount) and 500 mg. of acetaminophen which is the main ingredient in Tylenol. So you get the effect of Tylenol, then the boost of the codeine which kicks in later. Ask your crew if they have any reaction to codeine.

Personal experience indicates that Vicodin provides slow but effective relief for moderate pain and is a little easier on the stomach than the old emprine/codeine, with a peak of effectiveness in about 40 minutes (when the codeine kicks in) and a half life of about 90 minutes. Forty minutes is a long time. Your patient will need to take these tablets with a cup of water since codeine is hard on the kidneys.

Usual Dose: 1 tablet every six hours up to three in one dose.

Maximum Dose: 8 tablets in twenty-four hours.

A few comments from personal observation: Try to get the injured person to defecate as soon possible after taking these pills. Codeine usually causes constipation.

DRUGS FOR INTRACTABLE PAIN

Morphine sulfate is a derivative of opium and it is the most effective pain killer available for use against severe, intractable pain. Unlike Vicodin, morphine is a dangerous drug which, if used improperly, can kill. Those who enjoy its recreational qualities will often go to great lengths to get it, which might include robbing a survival pack. I once had a crew member suck all of the morphine out of a multi dose vial--and replace it with tap water. Even when used for emergency purposes, the patient always remembers the injection as a particularly pleasant ride. Correspondingly, physicians do not like to write script for it unless it is to be administered by licensed personnel in a controlled situation.

When someone asks a doctor for a morphine prescription, they immediately envision someone lying dead, with a needle in their arm, and next to them, a box with a prescription label showing the doctor's name and narcotics number. This is the approximate equivalent of a statement saying, "This corpse courtesy of friendly Dr. Smith." Physicians must write morphine prescriptions on tablets called "triples," which is a three part form. One part is for the doctor, one for the pharmacy, and one for the DEA.

Morphine and Demerol are "triples." Doctors are afraid of the DEA, whose firm policy is that it is better that some suffer in order to keep others from getting high. They are good at harassing doctors, particularly those who write triples for a drug kit. A drug kit is considered a "sachet," a supply for an accident which has not occurred. That is illegal. That is why doctors will immediately suggest Vicodin when you ask for morphine, and why they become nervous and avoid eye contact when you tell them that you would also like script for Demerol tablets.

Keep in mind that controlled drugs are only obtainable from a friendly doctor who knows and trusts you. When a stranger, possibly speaking a foreign tongue, appears in a doctor's office and asks for narcotics, the doctor immediately envisions his license with little wings on it, flying out the window. If you succeed in obtaining morphine, I recommend that you <u>never tell anyone you have it</u> and you keep it hidden, separate from other medical supplies or in the survival-pack medical kit covered with a plain wrapper.

General: Morphine exerts its primary effect on the central nervous system and peripheral tissues by blocking the firing mechanism of pain receptors. It is unquestionably the best narcotic for pain, with minimum impairment of bodily functions. <u>It combats pain-induced shock, but is contraindicated when a patient has entered shock</u>. It may be injected IV or IM, subject to a variety of contraindications and warnings. It is a short-duration, fast-acting drug injected IV, with a half-life of 1.5 hours. Peak serum levels are reached within 30 minutes, but the effect reaches a low level within two to three hours. Injected IM, peak serum levels are usually achieved in 30 to 60 minutes, with a more gradual decline of effectiveness.

Indications: To control severe trauma-related pain.

Contraindications: <u>Never administer to a patient who is in shock or suffering from hypothermia</u>. Never administer to someone who is comatose or showing signs of a head injury. Contraindicated for cardiac patients and asthmatics. For other warnings, read literature enclosed with the drug.

Adverse Reactions: Adverse reactions to normal doses are rare. The most serious adverse reaction is respiratory depression. It is rare that patients will require emergency treatment if the drug is used as recommended. Other, more common adverse symptoms include: nausea, vomiting, dizziness, urinary retention, anxiety, constipation, and interference with thermal regulation.

Warnings: Morphine is addictive and is a controlled substance. Do not separate the prescription label from the contents. Keep records of its use.

Dose: Morphine is sold in Tubex cartridges, which are recommended, 15 mg. (quarter grain) in 1 ml. of solution with a 1.25 inch, No. 22G needle. In combat, quarter grains are administered IM, for severe trauma such as gunshot.

The *Physician's Desk Reference,* recommends five to ten mg. IM, a little less than the combat dose, depending on severity of pain and body weight. A second, equal dose can be given an hour or more later. Subsequent doses must be given no more frequently than every four hours. **IV use**: two to five mg. per 70 Kg (154 lbs.) body weight, given slowly, administered every two to three hours.

Demerol tablets: Oral Demerol is similar in its effect to oral morphine. Its onset is more rapid than morphine tablets, and its duration is shorter. It is much less effective given orally than either morphine or Demerol given by injection, but it is safer to administer than injectable morphine and is less addictive. Most importantly, it produces less constipation than morphine. It may be administered as a switch to oral medication, approximately two hours after a morphine injection.

Indications: It is used against severe pain. Preoperative prophylactics. Postoperative control of pain.

Contraindications: Shock, hypersensitivity reaction, asthma and other respiratory disorders may result.

Warning: Some people are sensitive to Demerol. A 100-mg. dose can be dangerous. Use with caution.

Adverse effects: Smooth muscle spasm, suppression of the cough reflex, constipation, and depression. Common adverse reactions: nausea and dizziness.

Overdose: Dangers and treatment similar to that of morphine.

Dose: 50 to 150 mg. every three to four hours. **Children**: 0.5 mg./lb. of body weight.

How Supplied: 50 and 100 mg. tablets.

Infection

Prevention is better than cure, and this includes getting a tetanus shot or booster before a voyage. A gammaglobulin shot is also a big plus. Discuss your voyage with your doctor and ask if he recommends gammaglobulin. A good field doctor instills in his associates the need to guard against injury and to scrupulously clean those which do occur. Even a minor cut or a crushed finger can become serious, particularly if antibiotics are not available. Injuries while

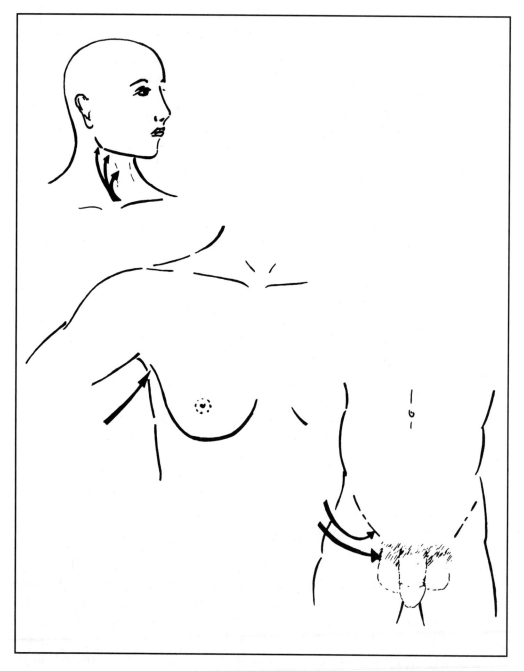

Location of major lymph nodes useful in diagnosing infection. Drawing by Rafael Monroy.

fishing are particularly dangerous, for the slimy, filthy condition of the hands and arms and the inability to get really clean make infection or an open lesion a likelihood. Landing a fish should be discussed in advance, with the prevention of injury in mind. Fish spines should be cut away as soon as possible, BEFORE you cut up the fish.

Sunburn is also a great danger because the damaged skin is susceptible to infection. Wearing pants and a shirt, if available, is important, even if it's hot. Water-resistant sunscreen should be applied where the skin is exposed to sunlight. Skin care in general should be emphasized. Ointment should be applied to chafed areas to prevent saltwater sores. Castaways should take turns massaging skin areas which have been in contact with survival-craft surfaces for long periods of time to prevent "bedsores," which are similar to and just as dangerous as saltwater sores. Airing the buttocks, rubbing them, spreading them apart, and exposing the area to sun and air is important.

SYMPTOMS OF INFECTION

Healthy people live harmoniously in a world surrounded by micro organisms, some of which, if they could, would invade the body and possibly kill you. Some of these organisms, including *Streptococcus*, actually live in or on the body of a normal person or in the nasal hairs and air passages. Natural defenses, such as nose, mouth and throat mucus, the skin, immune factors, and white cells in the blood deter these organisms from multiplying to the point where they cause illness. One can easily see that a dehydrated castaway with abraded skin, a throat "dry as lizard skin" and diminished resistance is a particularly good candidate for microbial invasion.

When these organisms invade the body, most of the fever, swelling, pain, etc., are not caused directly by them but by the toxins they produce and the reaction of the body to their presence. When microorganisms overwhelm local defenses, they use the lymphatic and/or the circulatory system as pathways to other sites of the body.

Lymph is a clear fluid, rich in fat and soluble ions. The liquid which one finds under a blister is lymphatic fluid. It travels through a tubular system similar to veins and drains fluid from peripheral tissues in cooperation with veins. The lymphatic system has only limited ability to fight against infection, and this is why invading organisms often use it to spread through the body.

The lymphatic centers of defense are in the **nodes**, each of which contains an artery, vein, and a number of lymph tubules. Lymph nodes produce cells which, like white blood cells, attack invading organisms. As a result, the nodes become inflamed, swollen, and tender and are a good indicator of infection, its virulence, and how fast it is spreading. A "sore throat," inflamed tonsils, painful "knots" in the neck, groin, or armpits are examples of inflamed lymph nodes. In a survival situation, where basic medical equipment is often not available, examination of lymph node sites frequently offers information which can contribute to a diagnosis.

Fever is an indicator of infection, but it is also an indicator of dehydration. If a dehydrated castaway is feverish, he may or may not need medicine, but he definitely needs a drink. An ancient technique that can be used when a thermometer is not available is to compare temperatures. Placing the back of one hand on the patient's forehead, the other on your forehead or the forehead of a healthy person. Normal temperatures can run from 97 to 99°F. Castaways, tend to have "normal" temperatures toward the high end of the scale because of dehydration, a slight fever is "normal" for them

Fever, chills, and sweats are all body reactions to the toxins produced by microorganisms. These <u>symptoms</u> are best controlled by aspirin (two tabs every two to three hours). Nothing works quite as well as aspirin, in my opinion, although some people are allergic to it. Unless one of your crew is sensitive to aspirin, use it.

Fever is caused by bacterial invasion, and the infection may be effectively treated with antibiotics. Viral infections also cause fever, chills, etc., but antibiotics are ineffective against them. Since you have no way of determining its cause, treat fevers as though they were of bacterial origin.

Infection increases the **pulse rate** (about 10 beats per minute per degree F. of fever). Another symptom of infection is changes in the rate, color, and smell of the urine. The urine of severely ill patients may be orange or smoky and full of sediment. If this is accompanied by developing jaundice (a yellow cast to the skin and whites of the eyes), the patient's prognosis is poor.

Blood pressure measurement requires a stethoscope and a sphygmomanometer. Since most survival craft lack these items a change in blood pressure can only be surmised, based on other indicators such as the strength and rate of the femoral pulse (in the thigh near the groin). **Low blood pressure with a rapid, bounding pulse** usually indicates **shock**. **High blood pressure,** is associated with **dehydration, infection**, and in some cases, **kidney**. These statements are somewhat simplistic because a change of blood pressure can have many causes. Be sure to read more about hypo- and hypertension in *The Merck Manual*.

Respiration: Normal respiration for an adult is 15 to 20 breaths per minute, for a child about 30, and babies about 40. People with a fever or respiratory illnesses, such as pneumonia, breath faster. In any event, rapid breathing is a sign of disorder and also indicates an accelerated loss of body fluid, through the breath.

Other important indicators of infection include the **appearance of the skin** (cool and pale indicating shock, warm and pink indicating infection, jaundiced indicating possible liver failure); the eyes (jerky movement, uneven or dilated pupils indicating cranial trauma); and the patient's **psychological state**. Someone who does not respond, responds in a passive manner, or inappropriately is afflicted with something, and in the absence of any other indicators, should be considered a victim of **disaster syndrome**, a life-threatening disorder.

TREATMENT OF INFECTION

Although a good survival doctor may have an educated guess upon which to base a diagnosis, he has absolutely no way of knowing which organism is causing an infection. Therefore medication selection is easy since we have just three antibiotics in our kit. The drug of choice for wounds and skin infections is Cephalexin which is a broad spectrum antibiotic particularly effective against *Staph* infections. Cipro and Flagyl are used in combination for unspecified internal infections which are diagnosed by fever, pain and swelling. All three drugs may be administered individually or in combination.

Combining antibiotics In a survival craft, drug combination is often an effective strategy because the identity and variety of infecting bacteria are unknown. Multiple organisms might be the cause of an abscess, or complicate a case of gangrene for example. If a serious infection is threatening the life of a patient, all three drugs could be administered at the same time.

In a survival situation **secondary infection** may be caused by filthy conditions and is not unusual. If Cephalexin does not appear to be doing its job curing skin infections, Cipro might be administered in conjunction with it.

When treating mucus membrane, respiratory or internal infections with Cipro, the recommended combination drug is **Flagyl**, which in addition to its medical properties has the financial property of cheapness. You can take both drugs together or if the infection is moderate and not threatening you might want to give Cipro first and wait for a day to see if you get results.

CIPRO TABLETS (FLOXIN)

Cipro (or Floxin) is an extremely broad spectrum synthetic antibacterial drug which is particularly well suited for use in a survival pack. It is quite stable and stores better at higher temperatures than many antibiotics. Cipro was a drug

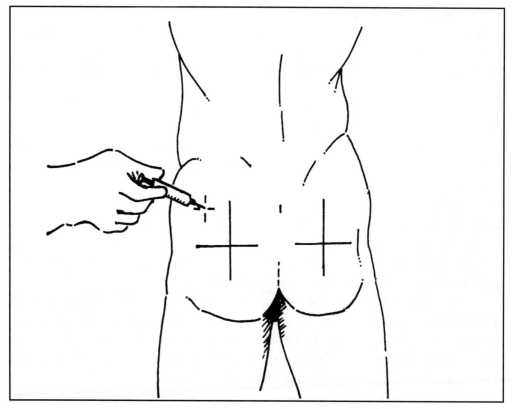

Injections are given in the buttock as shown, to avoid possible injury to the sciatic nerve. Drawing by Rafael Monroy.

of choice used by US forces during Desert Storm. If one could choose just one antibiotic for an emergency kit our vote would be for Cipro.

Cipro's major negative feature is its high price. Cipro is extremely potent and requires just two doses per day to achieve results. Relative to most other antibiotics including both penicillin and cephalexin, very few people are hypersensitive to Cipro.

Cipro is a broad spectrum, fast acting drug effective against mucus membrane and internal infections. It is also the drug of second choice against many organisms which are more sensitive to Cephalexin. Cipro is also effective against *E. Coli*, a fecal bacteria which usually ends up spread around the interior of survival craft. It is also broadly effective against urinary tract infections and digestive tract infections which cause diarrhea.

About 50% of each oral dose is lost through the kidney, but the remainder produces very high serum levels in the blood very quickly, something which was quite impossible using previous generation drugs. 500 mg. of oral Cipro given on an empty stomach produces approximately the same serum level in two hours as an injection of 400 mg. in one hour.

Warnings: (1) Patients taking Cipro may become more sensitive to sunburn. (2) About 3% of all users get typical mild hypersensitivity symptoms serious enough to warrant discontinuance of the drug, and an additional 1% have a more pronounced reaction. The most common symptoms include nausea, diarrhea, vomiting, tingling or itching of skin, or sudden development of a rash. If any of these symptoms occur, discontinue medication immediately. On the other hand, all antibiotics may cause indigestion and occasional dizziness, and these symptoms should not be confused with hypersensitivity reaction. (3) In addition, the drug destroys the flora of the intestine which may result in what is called "antibiotic associated colitis" whose temporary effects include intestinal pains and loose stool.

Emergency Treatment: The emergency treatment for a severe hypersensitivity reaction is the administration of adrenaline (Epinephrine) which is recommended for the medical kit.

Dose: This drug (Cipro) requires increased water intake (by how much we don't know).

Location of infection:	Unit	Frequency	Daily
Mucus membrane/respiratory tract:			
mild:	500 mg.	12 hr.	1000 mg.
severe:	750 mg.	12 hr.	1500 mg.
Urinary tract:			
mild:	250 mg.	12 hr.	500 mg.
severe:	500 mg.	12 hr.	1000 mg.
Diarrhea:	500 mg.	12 hr.	1000 mg.

Regimen: Take for two days after symptoms disappear.
Prophylactic: 250 mg. every 12 hours for two days unless symptoms develop.
Recommended Strength: 250 mg. bottle of 50 or 100

FLAGYL

Flagyl is much less broad spectrum than Cipro and is a previous generation drug, with much lower achieved serum levels. An infection responds much slower with Flagyl than with Cipro. Flagyl's most common use today is for the treatment of vaginal and urinary tract infections (but not in a survival craft). It is particularly effective against anaerobic (non-air breathing) organisms such as those which cause peritonitis and abdominal abscesses whereas Cipro is most effective against aerobic (air-breathing) bacteria. This is why Flagyl is useful in combination with Cipro.

Adverse effects: About 12% of all patients experience gastrointestinal discomfort when taking Flagyl. If alcohol is consumed while taking Flagyl it causes the most startling and dramatic hot flashes, nausea and headaches. Remember this if your survival craft has a bar.

In addition, a bad taste, furry tongue and slight dizziness are typical mild reactions which do not require discontinuance of the drug.

Warnings: The most common sign of moderate hypersensitivity is numbness in the limbs. Should this occur, discontinue treatment immediately. More serious hypersensitivity reactions are extremely rare and is treated with Epinephrine as is Cipro.

Dose:

Location of infection:	Unit	Freq.	Daily	Regimen
Amebic dysentery/liver absc.	750 mg.	8 hr.	1500 mg.	10-15 days
Deep tissue infections	500 mg.	6 hr.	4 gr. max.	7-10 days
Bone and joint infections	500 mg.	6 hr.	2 gr.	10+ days

Prophylactic: 500 mg. every 12 hours for five days unless symptoms develop.
Recommended strength: Flagyl comes in 250 mg. tablets. Buy 100.

CEPHALEXIN

This is an orally administered drug whose injectable counterpart is Cephalothin which is recommended for the ship's medical kit. Results arrive slightly more slowly with oral medication but it is safer to administer in a survival craft. In a hospital Cephalexin is often considered a drug of second-choice, because it is less effective than Penicillin-G when that drug works, but Cephalexin is a very broad-spectrum antibiotic and is effective against many organisms which are resistant to Penicillin.

Cephalexin is also safer to use than penicillin since it is much less likely to cause hypersensitivity reaction than penicillin. It is effective against our old enemy *Staphylococcus aurens*, which causes skin ulcers and boils.

Indications for use: Infections of the skin and immediate underlying tissues. Use against Carbuncles, furuncles, infected wounds, infected abrasions.

Dose and administration: **Prophylactic**: One capsule of 500 mg./8 hrs. To treat **infections**: initial dose of one gram (two caps), then 500 mg./6 hrs. Larger doses, up to four grams per day in equal doses, may be administered in serious cases. **Children**: 100 mg. per kg. per day in 4 doses.

Warnings and contraindications: Hypersensitivity reaction to the drug. Use caution if kidney impairment is suspected. A lower dosage can be administered if under these circumstances. Use caution if the patient has a history of penicillin hypersensitivity.

SKIN ABSCESSES

An abscess is a collection of pus, usually caused by bacterial invasion. Infection may be caused by an unclean needle or scalpel, or by bacterial migration from another site, via the lymph or circulatory system. A wide variety of organisms could be the cause. Abscesses can be located anywhere, and are somewhat controlled by antibiotics, but the field doctor is really only capable of positively diagnosing visible abscesses of the cutaneous and subcutaneous layers. The following discussion concerns only these types. Saltwater sores are discussed later in this chapter. Please note that there is only a gray distinction between abscesses (which are closed) and saltwater sores (usually open ulcers). In addition to the misery which abscesses cause, small blood vessels in the immediate area almost invariably become blocked, and this leads to **dermal gangrene**.

Furuncle (a boil) is an inflammation and swelling of the skin which becomes necrotic and pustuler often, but not always as the result of *Staphylococcus* infection. It contains **necrotic tissue** commonly called the "**head**" or "**core.**" Necrotic tissue looks like puss and varies in color from light yellow to light green, but is in fact fibrous, semi-solid, infected material which closely adheres to healthy tissue. It will not flow and is not easily removed. A boil may be lanced, but if the core is not removed, recovery will be slow or reinfection may occur.

Carbuncles are a cluster of furuncles. They develop more slowly than boils and are much more serious, often invading deep tissues, facilitating secondary infection by other microorganisms. Medication with all three antibiotic drugs is recommended although these infections are particularly resistant to drug therapy. Symptoms include fever, body pains, and malaise.

General: Poor state of health, numerous abrasions, inadequate water and mental anguish all predispose a castaway to abscess and skin-ulcer formation. These agonizing infections are in themselves not life-threatening, but they have the capability of undermining the health of an already weakened person and could become the deciding factor in a life-or-death situation. A small infection or "pimple" has an uncanny way of spreading in a body with weakened defenses. In some cases, new pockets of inflammation spread in an uneven, expanding circle from the original site and become carbuncles, encompassing silver dollar-sized areas which may invade deeper tissues. Infections of this size are truly life-threatening to a castaway and require surgery or death may result.

Carbuncles and furuncles frequently open spontaneously and drain. Drainage can be greatly assisted with warm wet packs and a little bactericidal soap. <u>Open abscesses are contagious to others and can also spread to other parts of the infected person's body</u>. A widely distributed, rash-like condition may appear anywhere on the patient's body, but particularly in the vicinity of the infection. Some of the small bumps subside; some open and ulcerate or heal slowly; others form small purple pustules which become sources of reinfection.

Symptoms: Heat, swelling, redness, tenderness at the site, inflammation of some major lymph nodes, and fatigue, disability. The site usually bulges, is discolored and tender. If surgical intervention does not occur, **gangrene** or **septic shock** become possibilities.

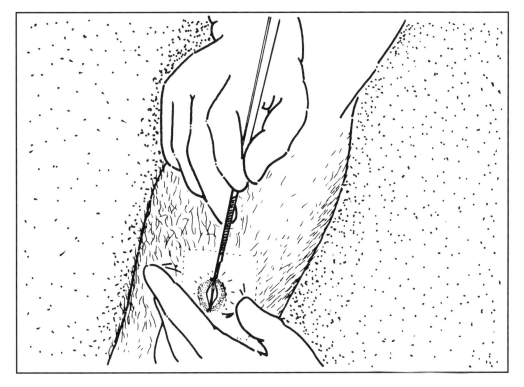

Opening a boil. The precision cut. Straddle wound with fingers and stretch the skin, extend cutting fingers, push down, draw back cutting fingers, and wrist to make a cut. You can rest the middle finger or the wrist on the patient to steady the cutting hand. Drawing by Rafael Monroy.

Treatment: Abscess development may be slowed by antibiotics surgical intervention is usually required to remove them. The risk of surgery is small compared to the large risk of further complications without surgery.

In minor cases such as that of a gum abscess or boil, proceed with **lancing** followed by an ointment/dressing (the gum incision is painted with Betadine but left undressed). The object is to keep the incision open, allowing the site to drain for several days. The area around the site is shaved, if possible, then bathed with Betadine solution to prevent the spread of infection.

Doctors usually do not give anesthetic other than of a topical nature to a patient prior to this type of surgery, reasoning that the pain of the injections will approximately equal that of the quick cut. Since you will be slower and less certain than the doctor and may have to install a drain after the cut, you might want to consider several xylocaine injections around the site. These injections swell and distort the area, but do not be dismayed. The injections are also extremely painful and you may be forewarned that the patient will scream or at least moan meaningfully.

Do not think of this surgery as a "lancing job," inferring a quick slash. Think of it as surgery, where small, precise cuts are made, using a No. 15 scalpel, as shown on the preceding page. Scissors, hemostat, and forceps are used to straighten edges or debride. Wear glasses to protect your eyes from pus.

The surgeon holds the scalpel like a pencil, with the handle resting in the web of the hand. He visualizes the depth and length of the cut. The thumb and first finger do the cutting, steadied by the middle finger or wrist which contacts the patient. The cut is made by extending the thumb and first finger, bringing the scalpel into contact with the skin, then pushing down and pulling the two fingers back at the same time. The wrist also moves back slightly. A quick cut does not have to be a sloppy cut. The other hand is used to stretch the skin tight.

If the infection is large, <u>consideration must be given to the cavity created by the drained pus</u>. It is an ideal site for further infection. Should there be a cavity, the site is irrigated, using a syringe without a needle containing tinned water. The site is then cleaned with antibacterial soap, using gauze as a sponge, followed by additional cleaning with hydrogen peroxide. The cavity is then packed with Silvadene-impregnated gauze. This is an extremely painful procedure and the patient is going to be quite unhappy. Drip Xylocaine into the wound before installing the gauze drain.

Two or three days later the packing may be removed. A Demerol tablet 30 minutes before the procedure is suggested. Remove the drain with one steady pull. Do not hesitate, as the removal is extremely painful and there is no practical way to reduce the burning pain other than to make it brief. Removal of the drain usually causes slight bleeding and that is good. Clean the area and soak the incision to keep it open. Wash and sterilize the site, then cover it with an ointment/dressing.

Surgical debriding of the site: It is essential to remember that the most common error made in this type of surgery is inadequate debridement, meaning that too little of the contaminated tissue is removed. In the field, this could be a major error. The drug supply is small, the patient will be considerably weakened and will resist a second painful episode under the knife.

Examine the site carefully and decide what must be done. If the abscess is small, like a typical "boil," a single cut will suffice. If it is more general, several connecting cuts may have to be made. The minimum objective of the cuts is to allow an adequate avenue for infected material to escape. It is important to prevent dead tissue from flopping back into place, cutting off exposure to air and preventing drainage. Trim it way. The area around an abscess is highly vascular, so the cut will probably bleed and drain. Guard against spurts. If bleeding persists, apply pressure to pressure points or sites at least an inch or two from the incision to prevent driving infection into surrounding tissue. Allow as much pus as possible to escape, irrigate inside, dry with gauze, and look inside the cavity to determine how much material must be removed.

If an abscess is decentralized, it may not be possible to simply remove all infected tissue. At least be sure that all pockets have been well exposed by the knife, facilitating drainage. If a cavity has been formed, irrigate and pack as previously described. <u>Never close a draining abscess with sutures or butterfly closures</u>.

If anesthetic has been used and the patient is not in too much discomfort, probe around in the wound with a gauze wipe attached to a hemostat. Wipe, pull, and cut away damaged flesh, particularly if it contains necrotic tissue which cannot be wiped or washed away. Lift the edge of the incision with a hemostat and pare back any dead material which is lying on lower, healthy tissue.

Anesthetic: The site of an abscess is extremely tender, and patients invariably scream or at least moan meaningfully during surgery if no anesthetic is available. This is nevertheless a job which must be done. At least administer several of the painkillers found in the life raft survival pack, if available, prior to treatment. Keep in mind that what you are doing is going to hurt someone else, not you, and you're doing it for their own good.

Preoperative procedures: If painkillers and anesthetics are available, give a 100 mg. Demerol tablet about twenty minutes before the operation. See Demerol warnings. Xylocaine, in shots of a 1-2 cc (shown on the syringe) are given in three to four sites around the infection, about a half-inch outside the most tender area. More injections can be given if the site is decentralized. This temporarily puffs up and deforms the area, but do not be dismayed. You can shoot a little anesthetic into the abscess but it is important not to shoot through it, spreading the infection to lower layers. After the initial cut has been made, Xylocaine can be dripped into the open cavity to further desensitize it.

Postoperative care: Cephalexin 500 mg., every eight hours for at least three days. Cover with a loose dressing, bathe the surrounding site with clean water and soap, several times per day. Soak away clots or scabs for three to four days to promote drainage. Pain is unfortunately concurrent with the treatment. Cover with a dry dressing or a gauze and Silvadene if the site cannot be kept dry.

Prognosis: It is amazing how quickly a patient feels better after an abscess is opened. They may even thank you, usually much later.

GANGRENE

Description: A very serious infection frequently caused by *Clostridia*, or by other organisms. Gangrene usually results from a crush injury, compound fracture, or penetrating wound with surrounding devitalized tissue. It can also result from a serious injury to a limb which will not stop bleeding. If a wound will not stop bleeding you must expose the severed vessel and tie off the blood vessel. If you opt to keep the tourniquet on the limb will be robbed of its blood supply and become a candidate for deep surgery or removal. Proper debridement and prophylactic medication drastically reduce the possibility of such an infection under most circumstances.

Symptoms: Gangrene is a galloping infection which arises six hours to three days after the accident and is characterized by its foul smell, gooey-brown appearance, abundant bubbles, severe pain, high fever, local tenderness and finally, delirium. A brownish serum exudes from the wound site. If you have allowed gangrene to develop, you haven't been doing your job. The underlying muscle may be initially pale and damaged-looking, then turn deep red and finally gray-green or mottled purple. Discoloration or gross swelling of the limb is rare. When gangrene has taken hold there is very little doubt about it. Do not let denial cloud your judgement and deter you from swift action.

Treatment: Fast action is essential. Delayed or inadequate treatment can result in death within one to three days of onset. An initial large dose of Cephalexin/Cipro/Flagyl should be given and maintained until the problem is under control. The wound should be anesthetized, thoroughly debride, and left uncovered or covered with a light gauze. Never use an ointment or Vaseline.

An injection of morphine (10 mg.) may be given for severe prior to and following surgery. Be sure the area blood supply is not restricted. Try to keep the wound-site at the same height as the body core, not elevated. Continue antibiotic medication. This is a touch and go crisis where the outcome is in question. Administer pain medication as needed. Failure to control gangrene may result in the need to amputate the limb.

Prognosis: The rapid onset, virulence, and spread of gangrene are its main dangers. This is a very stubborn infection requiring large amounts of antibiotics and swift surgical intervention. Prompt treatment greatly improves prognosis. Since the organisms which cause this condition are usually sensitive to air, opening the wound site and thoroughly debriding may completely reverse the problem. This must be done in any event. When debriding, remember, it is far better to take out <u>all</u> of the devitalized tissue. The prompt, massive use of antibiotics as indicated further improves the prognosis.

Suturing

The minimum approach is best for survival craft medicine, so if possible, avoid suturing. Clean the site around it with an alcohol wipe to remove body oils, shave off hair, then use sterile **butterfly closures** and/or sterile adhesive strips. Butterfly closures are also good for drawing a larger wound together for alignment purposes, prior to suturing. A tape or butterfly closure <u>must be kept clean,</u>

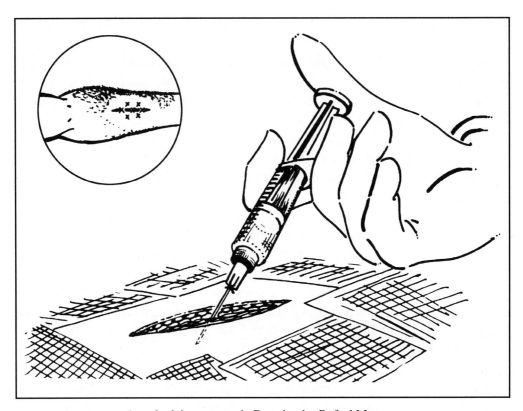

Anesthetizing a wound. Drawing by Rafael Monroy.

greaseless, and dry and that is its major disadvantage.

Sutures may be necessary to close deeper or longer wounds and the site may then be covered with Silvadene cream, then Silvadene-impregnated gauze dressing to deter contamination. If an incision wound has cut into deep tissue, it is necessary to close that tissue with absorbable suture, before closing the skin.

Anesthetic: Xylocaine (1% Lydocaine HCl) can be administered as a local or regional anesthetic. Injected around a wound site, it is relatively safe to use, cutaneously and subcutaneously. It is important, under all circumstances, to pull back the plunger of the syringe prior to injection to be sure that the anesthetic is not injected into a blood vessel.

Dose: Use the smallest effective dose possible to achieve results. Maximum dose for **adults**: 4.5 mg./kg. (about 2 mg./lb.), not to exceed 500 mg. Typically, a small cut, two to three inches long requires four to six ml of Xylocaine to numb it. A fracture may require 20 to 40 ml. **Children**: 75 to 100 mg. (1.5 to 2 mg./lb.). Injecting Xylocaine temporarily puffs up an area but this quickly passes.

Administration: Inject Xylocaine in 1 to 5 cc. doses, each at several different levels, to distribute the anesthetic. Start about a half inch under the skin and follow the numbness down slowly with the needle, injecting as you go to the depth desired. Effective radius from the injection site is one to two inches. Inject into the skin and muscle layers to be sutured or debride. Do this at several locations around the site, then drip xylocaine into the open wound. Make a few smaller injections into or through the wound. Wait about two minutes or until the wound is desensitized. Test for effectiveness with a probe.

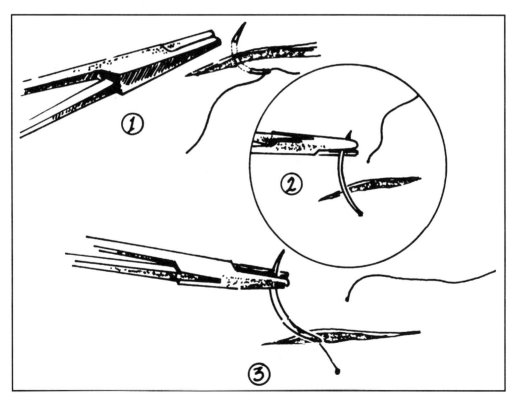

Placing the first suture: 1. The needle is gripped with the needle holder and pushed through both edges of the wound, using a rotating motion of the wrist. 2. With a similar rotating motion, pull the needle from the wound. 3. Draw the suture tight. Drawing by Rafael Monroy.

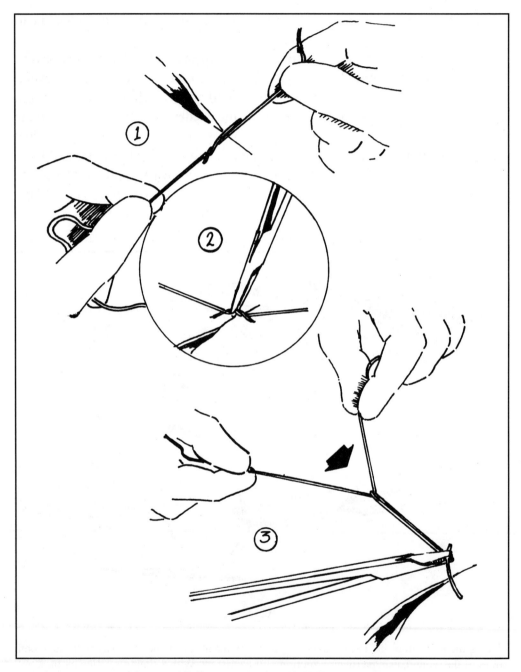

Tie several square knots to secure it. Drawing by Rafael Monroy.

Warnings: Do not use if the patient is in shock. Do not use as a pain-killer (as opposed to use as an anesthetic prior to surgery). Have adrenaline ready for emergency use in the event of <u>hypersensitivity reaction</u>. Use caution if the patient is debilitated by starvation, etc.

Suturing Technique: The **running suture** is easy, reminiscent in some ways of stitching a sail, and makes for fast work. It requires the minimum of technical skill, and the suture is easily removed when no longer needed. All of these features make it the preferred technique for inexperienced surgeons, but running sutures have some disadvantages that must be remembered. First, if a single knot opens, the entire ligature is lost unless the thread is clamped with a hemostat, which is then taped to the body. The running suture can create a puckering of the wound edges. The margins are excellent sites for the development of infection. If the puckering is serious, it makes a nasty scar. Proper technique and use of butterfly closures in conjunction with a running suture can do much to correct these problems.

First, the skin around the wound must be wiped with alcohol to remove body oil. If necessary, several butterfly closures can be used to align and close the wound prior to suturing. Have extra closures ready to make changes.

Place a single suture in the edge of the wound, farthest from your working hand. If you are right-handed start at the upper right. This is important and considered good technique. Skin is easy to penetrate on the "down stroke," but it often bulges on the "up stroke". Use the back of a scalpel or other blunt instrument or your thumb—don't not prick yourself during this procedure.

Continue the running suture toward you, keeping tension on the completed work with your fingers or a hemostat. When you have reached the end, keep pressure on the suture material with the hemostat, then place butterfly closures over the wound adjusting suture tension as needed. Tie the suture with several square knots, then reposition butterfly closures as needed.

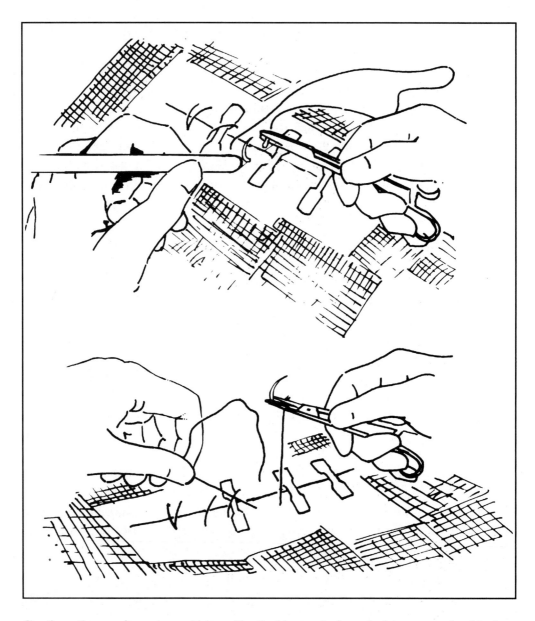

Continue the running suture. Above: Use the blunt end of a scalpel to prevent the skin from bulging. Below: Maintain tension on the suture with the free hand. The clamp the suture with the hemostat (not shown) to maintain pressure, allowing use of both hands to make the next suture. When the running suture is complete, readjust tension of all stitches before tying off. Drawing by Rafael Monroy.

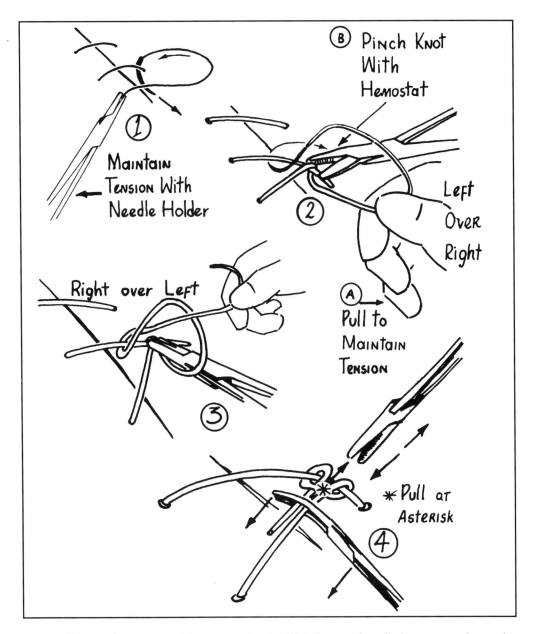

Tying-off a running suture with a square knot: (1) Adjust tension all along suture, then maintain tension with a hemostat. (2) Make a left-over-right tie and clamp with the tip of a hemostat to maintain pressure. (3) Make the reverse tie. (4) The "broken" knot is flipped Cover the knot with a butterfly closure to further prevent untying. Drawing by Rafael Monroy.

Common Survival Craft Related Disorders

ANEMIA

Anemia is a classic symptom of people who endure long passages in survival craft. Survival craft anemia is similar in some ways to Kwashiorkor, the classic disease of starvation resulting from chronic protein, vitamin, and mineral deficiency. In addition, as the result of water deprivation, red blood cells are broken down for their fluid, and this also induces anemia. Last but unquestionably not least, anemia is associated with kidney failure, resulting from lack of water. The two go hand in hand. Obviously, if the castaway had enough food and water, none of the problems associated with anemia would occur.

Cause: Red-cell deficiency, mineral and/or vitamin deficiency.

Symptoms of anemia: Weakness, vertigo, headache, seeing spots, drowsiness, irritability, low-grade fever, paleness of the lips and inside the of the eyelids..

Specific symptoms: Iron deficiency: smooth tongue and white finger and toe nails. Vitamin B_{12} deficiency: nails become ridged, concave and sometimes drop off; Cracking of the skin at the corners of the mouth.

Prevention: Take vitamin and mineral supplements. The oral iron tablets or vitamin/mineral tablets are the medication of choice.

DROWNING

People who survive drowning (and in some cases hypothermia) often have out-of-body experiences, see themselves floating underwater near their body or in the air, dispassionately watching the rescue. They "re-enter" the body when revived. This indicates a certain level of consciousness, even when the person appears dead, and this is why it is important to keep on encouraging them. They may just be unconscious and lack strong vital signs. Negative remarks may cause them to give up.

The maximum time which may elapse between drowning and revival varies according to conditions, but it is extremely rare to save anyone who has not been breathing longer than 26 minutes. People who drown in cold water last longest. Someone who drowns quickly lasts longer than someone who struggled because more oxygen is left in the blood. Never give up on a drowning victim until they are both <u>warm and dead</u>.

Even if vital signs are absent, keep applying mouth-to-mouth resuscitation, and if there is no heartbeat, apply cardiac massage. If by chance you have oxygen, put the tube in <u>your</u> mouth and breath enriched air into the patient's lungs. Slightly elevate the body to make water run out of the mouth. Suck water from the patient's mouth with your mouth. Be sure to check for dentures and remove them. Keep trying for at least 30 to 60 minutes, or longer if the victim remains cold. Death from drowning (based on experiences of those who have been revived) is one of the least painful and possibly slightly euphoric ways to die.

SALTWATER SORES

Description: An ulcerated cutaneous infection of the skin. Saltwater sores are thought to be the result of microbial invasion through abraded or otherwise damaged skin which has been further damaged by a constant saltwater environment, stress, and discomfort. It eventually involves subcutaneous tissue. The infected site may initially appear to be a small abscess, such as a boil. They also may open and ulcerate, with surrounding inflammation and a brown-black or honey-colored crust.

General: Saltwater sores are considered to be **staphylococcal infections**, but **streptococcus** may also be the cause. *Staphylococcus aureus*, a penicillin-resistant organism, is most commonly responsible for these infections. It often resides in human nasal hairs and is passed from one person to another by hand contact, contaminated clothing, etc. One may assume they are present in the survival craft. Abrasions incurred during abandonment, chafe burns, clothing irritations, and fish-spine pricks are all breaks in the skin's integrity which, because they are constantly wet, will not heal. They present an ideal entry for organisms residing on the skin's surface, which then choose their own site to develop. The infection usually occurs at the site of entry but may occur anywhere. Staph infections, as they heal, often form knobby, bacteria-containing purple or brownish discolorations around the scar site. The bacteria can become active again the next day, months, or years later. Surgical removal may be necessary in a hospital at a later time.

Symptoms and signs: A generalized rash, spread across the skin, which is sensitive to pressure and sunlight; a red inflammation of the skin, pea- sized if individual, or a series of infections, spread over a silver dollar-sized area. A "pimple" or boil which opens but refuses to heal, enlarges into an ulcer, becoming red and tender around the edges, often weeping a clear fluid which hardens into a honey-colored crust.

Prevention is by far better than cure but of course there is no absolute method of preventing a staph infection. These infections are stubborn, form pockets which resist medication, and are slow to heal. Topical ointments may prevent chafe or a minor skin-break from developing into a sore. Ointment may also ease the pain of these sores, but the infection, once established, is really subcutaneous and is not usually affected by topical medicine.

Prevention also includes **washing the body**, using the bacterial soap recommended for the med kit. This soap may be used with sea water. It might not make you feel clean, but it leaves a Staph-inhibiting film on the skin. When it rains, wash the body with the soap, rinse clothing and body in fresh water. Air dry when possible. Any form of staph rash is irritated by strong sunlight, so it is erroneous to think that "sunning" a saltwater sore will heal it.

General Treatment: Minor injuries should be cleaned, treated with **Silvadene cream**, then covered with a loose dressing. On land, where water can be heated, a **warm wet pack** can be applied, meaning warm fresh water on a cloth, for about twenty minutes at a time, three or four times per day, to gently debride the wound, to increase peripheral circulation, and promote healing. A little soap can be added to cleanse the wound. Very little can be done in a survival craft beyond covering with an ointment, although oral medication may be effective.

Drug Therapy: Early intervention with Cephalexin/Cipro may have an effect but these infections are very resistant to drugs.

Warnings: These sores are extremely painful and quite maddening but they **should not be squeezed**, as this only helps to spread the infection.

SEASICKNESS

Description: Dizziness, nausea, vomiting, and disorientation caused by excessive stimulation of the inner ear.

General: The precise mechanism of this disorder is not clear, and susceptibility varies from person to person. A moving horizon, motion, fumes, and anxiety are all contributing factors. The primary danger of seasickness is ion loss and reduction of body fluids caused by vomiting.

Symptoms and signs: Cyclic nausea and vomiting, usually preceded by drowsiness, yawning, hyperventilation, dizziness, and fatigue. Some people also suffer headaches. Vomiting causes muscular tremors and general malaise, although the person usually feels better immediately afterward.

Prophylactic and Treatment: It is extremely important to take prophylactic oral anti-motion medication, well before it is needed, preferably as soon as one enters the survival craft.

Anti-motion sickness pills are (hopefully) included in your survival-craft equipment pack. Unfortunately, when the nausea of sea sickness begins to occur, the muscle separating the stomach from the intestine (the pyloric valve) closes. The pill cannot reach the intestine to be absorbed and is therefore useless.

Anti-motion suppositories are more effective than pills, since the medication is absorbed by the lower intestine and not blocked by a closed pyloric valve. But suppositories work best when chilled. They get soft when warm and cannot be inserted in that state.

Transderm adhesive units, placed behind the ear are recommended on the survival pack list. The medication in Transderm (scopolamine, a form of belladonna) enters the blood stream in a small dose, slowly, through the skin and prevents seasickness very effectively. The single disadvantage of Transderms is that they must be worn for several hours before they become effective and it is possible for castaways to become sick during that interval.

After a two or three days, a Transderm adhesive unit can cause assorted unpleasant (but not fatal) symptoms, such as dilated pupils and hallucinations, so it is recommended that castaways switch to seasick pills after the nausea has disappeared. The Transderm unit is rated as effective for 72 hours.

Injectable Compazine, sold in two ml. (5 mg./ml.) disposable syringes is a rapid-acting, effective medication for motion sickness. A Compazine IM injection should be considered as indicated if an uninjured castaway feels nau-seous in the survival craft. An anti-motion pill or Transderm adhesive unit can be given an hour after the injection. If you buy injectable Compazine cartridges, consider adding a few to the survival pack med kit.

Reef-Related Disorders

CORAL CUTS

Coral cuts are no joke for the castaway, no matter how small. They are at best painful and slow to heal. A coral cut is really a laceration with underlying dead or bruised tissue, the kind of debris-laden wound which easily becomes infected, usually with *Staphylococcus*. Wash the wound and use an antiseptic, Betadine or peroxide, a boiled sea water soak, or a little ration water followed by a dry gauze dressing or clean cloth. Small injuries can be left undressed but should be kept clean. Make sure the wound gets plenty of air. If you have antibiotics, take them if an infection occurs.

JELLYFISH, ANEMONE, AND CORAL STINGS

Some jellyfish, certain corals, and all anemones are armed with stinging mechanisms which are used to immobilize food or protect against predators. The stinging organ is called a **nematocyst**, a cell containing a spiny, poison-filled dart, pressurized with fluid. A pressure-actuated trigger hair projects from the business end of the cell. The actual chemistry of the firing mechanism is not completely understood, but when most creatures brush against the trigger hair, the nematocyst explodes firing the dart. Nematocyst darts of jellyfish are con-nected to the tentacle by a thread. Small fish, brushing against the jellyfish's dangling tentacles are speared, then paralyzed by the fast-acting poison which consists of a variety of ammonium compounds. The paralyzed fish, tethered by the threads, is then drawn toward the jellyfish's "mouth."

Nematocyst stings are painful far out of proportion to the amount of venom injected. Severely afflicted victims have experienced twitching tremors, followed by cardiac arrest and death within minutes, from a combination of venom and pain-induced shock. More fortunate souls survive, but have to suffer through a recovery from the incredibly painful stings, which cause welts and eventually localized lesions resulting from a breakdown (necrosis) of skin tissue. The damaged tissue may become secondarily infected later. The welt first turns brown, then purple, and the discoloration may last for years. Severely afflicted persons feel pain through the entire area or limb, rather than in the immediate vicinity of the injury. Some experience muscle spasms and histamine reactions such as difficulty breathing.

Treatment: Initial treatment consists of alcohol, meat tenderizer, ammonia, or urine applied to the site. These liquids cause an immediate reduction of pain. <u>Do not attempt to remove the tentacles at this point</u>, because in doing so, more nematocysts are triggered causing additional injury. The best procedure is to trap them by powdering the site with talcum, flour, sand, or dirt which is allowed to dry for a minute or two. The site is then carefully scraped clean and allowed to dry. <u>Never rub the site, wash it with water or wet sand</u> as this will only activate any remaining nematocysts.

STINGRAY WOUNDS

The spine of a stingray is a marvelous weapon—long, razor sharp, indented with long, venom-filled grooves, covered first by a venomous mucous, then by a brittle integumentary sheath—which is easily broken and left in the wound. The spine is serrated so that tissue damage is substantially increased when the sting is pulled out.

Treatment: It is rare that anyone dies from the wound itself, but a castaway may be so debilitated from it that he may die from being unable to collect food and water.

Irrigate the wound thoroughly with a syringe (no needle) containing packaged ration water and a little soap, then frequent soaking of the site in water which has been heated if possible. Irrigation may have to be repeated if the wound begins to ooze. If it becomes clear that the wound is infected, surgery may be necessary.

SEAFOOD POISONING

Eating reef fish sometimes causes an illness called **ciguatera**. Ciguatera causes gastrointestinal inflammation in combination with neurological distress within 3 to 12 hours of consumption. It results from an odorless, tasteless, heat-resistant poison that does not often kill but can be extremely disabling. It also has the nasty quality of recurring months or even years later. It is a common illness on islands where the people depend on reef fish for food.

In some areas, such as New Caledonia, the illness is so common that most natives no longer eat reef fish. This approach is recommended for the castaway, who may survive the illness but die later as a result of the inability to gather food and water. Most cases are extremely mild and not reported. The serious cases end up in the hospital—and in the statistics. It is these statistics which make ciguatera so feared. In places like Polynesia, it is possible that 50% of the population has had some form of ciguatera during their lives.

The origin of this sweet little malady are micro-organisms called dinoflagellates, a planktonic protozoa, cousins of the little killers responsible for the red tide. They have been around for a long time and were doubtless the cause of the "rivers of blood," mentioned in the *Old Testament,* which were toxic to the fish, undrinkable, and stank (*Exodus 7:20-21*). Dinoflagellates exist at the same level on the food chain as coral polyps and algae. They are ingested by coral and algae eaters. The toxin, harmless to marine creatures, is concentrated in their flesh and in the flesh of fish that prey upon them.

Like the red tide, ciguatera comes and goes, and theories about its cause abound. The current one is that ciguatera and the algae with which it is associated arise on denuded surfaces of the reef, as is caused by ships hitting a reef, hurricane damage, dredging, etc. The new patches of algae are eventually overgrown and the malady then disappears. Fish from one area may be toxic while those from another are safe. Certain fish from one ocean are always poisonous while the same species are esteemed elsewhere as food. One fish from a catch may be poisonous and the rest not. Species known for years to be edible suddenly become toxic. Some well known reef species, such as triggerfish, considered poisonous when on the reef are not poisonous when found at sea.

The several Pacific varieties considered most likely to carry the poison are the red snapper, moray eel, sea bass, triggerfish, bonito, mackerel and barracuda. Some varieties of Caribbean grouper such as the spotted rockfish and the amberjack are also potential carriers. Coral grazers like parrotfish and surgeonfish are also suspect. Eating the **liver, intestines,** or **brains** of these fish is particularly dangerous, but there are at least 500 species which are known to carry the toxin, so identification is not the solution.

Tests: There are no quick tests to detect ciguatera, but it is known that cats vomit from eating poisoned fish's intestine. So if you have a cat, use it. Concentrate on catching shellfish, lobster, octopus, and crabs.

Symptoms: Different geographic areas produce different combinations of symptoms. Among the more notorious effects are diarrhea, itching, tingling of the extremities, numbness or burning sensation in the mouth and lips, muscle weakness, and reversing the sensations of hot and cold. It is rare that anyone dies. But the sickness lingers for weeks or even months, and recovery is slow. While you have it, you are sick as a dog and must be nursed. If you were alone, you would be in deep trouble.

Treatment: When symptoms arise, induce vomiting.

THE POISONOUS PUFFER

Any Pacific or Indian Ocean fish that inflates or has body spines such as puffers, porcupines, cowfish, or boxfish are considered toxic. The flesh of these fish is extremely delicious. Atlantic puffers are sometimes found for sale in Northeastern fish markets. They are safe to eat. The deadly Pacific puffer is esteemed as the epitome of gourmet cuisine by the Japanese. It sells in Japan for far more than lobster or fillet. Some delight in eating the delicate, slightly rubbery flesh as sashimi, carved into delicate patterns sliced razor thin on chilled plates. Most diners live to dine again, but some die after dinner.

Some Hawaiians believe that if the puffer's teeth are yellow, it is a certain sign that the fish is deadly, and if you like those odds, go for it! The toxin rests in the skin and internal organs, particularly the gall bladder, which is easily ruptured when the fish is caught and cleaned. The gall of a Pacific puffer is 25 times more potent than curare. Just a drop or two will kill off a whole Boy Scout troop. The liver is considered the most delicious—and the most deadly part to eat. It is against the law even to serve puffer liver in Japan.

The Pacific puffer is extremely delicious, but potentially deadly. Drawing by Rafael Monroy.

A few years ago, the celebrated Kabuki actor, Mitsugoro Bando, ate four delicious portions of puffer liver, then died. The poison is neurotoxic. Everyone has heard how the poisoning characteristically begins in the extremities and progresses slowly. Death is caused by asphyxiation. The diaphragm becomes paralyzed. The victim remains fully alert and aware of his impending demise.

VENOMOUS FISH

Scorpion and stonefish are both families of numerous species, all of whose members have poisonous spines. There are several types of scorpion fish. The best known is the lion or zebra fish (actually several species), which have long, extremely deadly spines that look like feathers. The fish is quite territorial and very aggressive about protecting its turf. Don't mess with this fish. It may not kill you but you will wish you were dead if it gets you. The lion fish is quite

The stonefish (upper) and scorpion fish. Drawing by Rafael Monroy.

beautiful and is sometimes kept as a pet in home aquariums. This is one pet, however, which should never be petted!

The venom of the stonefish is even more lethal than that of the scorpion fish. Stones are very sedentary, and their spines are short and purely defensive. They are beautifully camouflaged and look like a pile of debris. They live in shallow water and it is quite common for people to be stung by a stonefish they never saw. Do not wade around on the reef in bare feet.

The sting of either family, if it does not kill, may cause infection a few days to a week after the attack. One injured man responded well to 1,000,000 units of penicillin injected IM in five doses over a 16-hour period. This gives you some idea of the massive tissue damage caused by such an injury. The wound site turned black—then sloughed off, leaving a deep, draining cavity which took three months to heal. The affected hand remained weak, and the man's health was impaired for a long time thereafter.

The venomous lion fish: just brushing one of the spines causes instant searing, intense pain, sometimes followed by convulsions and cardiac arrest. The venom can cause the paralysis of a limb for weeks. It produces the most horrible, intense pain known to man. The pain alone can kill and the toxin leaves deep, permanent scars. Drawing by Rafael Monroy.

Cone shells, as their name implies, are cone-shaped and often brilliantly colored. When they are moving on the bottom (usually at night) the mantel completely covers the shell making it difficult to identify. Cones are small (one to four inches) and usually of interest only to shell collectors. They are not poisonous to eat but have a defensive system which makes them dangerous to handle. Most snails have radular teeth designed to scrape algae off of rocks. But cone shells teeth have been modified into spears, which are used to catch their prey. The spears contain poison. Most cones are not deadly to man, but being speared by one will ruin your whole day. If a cone is handled or perceives that it is being molested, it will spear the offending hand promptly (but fortunately not with lightning speed).

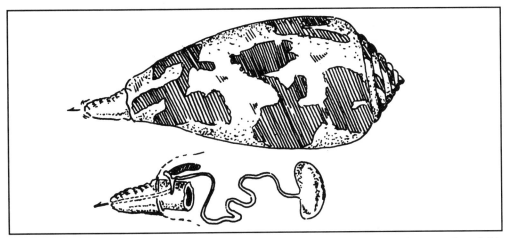

Venomous cone shell, (upper), showing shell without mantel. (Lower) Poisonous dart (left), projects from Cone's snout. Poison sac and connecting tube (right). Drawing by Rafael Monroy.

SHELLFISH POISONING

Dinoflagellates associated with toxin-producing algae cause shellfish poisoning in addition to ciguatera. The "red tide" is an example of an algal bloom, but the red tide is not always toxic, and sometimes shellfish become toxic without there being a red tide. The sudden appearance of dying gulls or other shellfish-eating birds or large numbers of dead fish washed up on the beach or dead shellfish is a more certain sign of shellfish toxicity.

Most shellfish poisoning occurs on the east and west coasts of North America, the British Isles, and Northern Europe. Few cases of Pacific reef shellfish poisoning have been reported, and the most common of the edible mollusks, the tridacna or giant clam, whose easily identified brilliant mantle, looking like wiggly lips, are eaten and esteemed throughout Polynesia.

Symptoms: Shellfish poisoning symptoms include a tingling or burning feeling in the lips, tongue and face with gradual progression to the extremities.

Treatment: There is no antidote and severely afflicted people die.

Chapter Summary

Success in treating medical emergencies at sea is more dependent on preparation and planning than skill or luck. Proper diagnosis, medication, and procedure cannot be snatched out of a hat—or picked up from a book—the way one would pop a telephone number out of a directory. It is the result of a fundamental understanding of the human body, its gross anatomy, and physiology.

If you are interested in this subject, there is no limit to what you can learn. If you are not interested, a certain fundamental knowledge still is necessary—this is one of those subjects which, like learning to read, is an essential tool for life. A captain who has not paid his dues by spending hours, days, or even weeks with his nose in a medical text is negligent, and this may well result in someone's death.

On the other hand, it is unrealistic to think that a simple admonishment will change the attitude of someone who is truly uninterested in emergency medicine or becomes queasy just thinking about the sight of blood. Still, these people can still familiarize themselves with the use of oral drugs and improve their lifesaving skills by taking a basic first-aid course.

Regardless of one's attitude, a complete survival med kit, including an emergency medicine text is considered a core item in a survival pack and is also standard equipment on a blue water vessel. Its contents may well include medications and equipment with which the captain is unfamiliar, but these items should not be omitted for this reason. Other members of the crew may be able to perform essential procedures if the captain cannot, and in addition, there may be time to read—and learn, before death occurs.

There is an agonizing uncertainty regarding the necessity to perform unpleasant, painful, or even dangerous procedures in a survival situation. Improper technique may result in death. Perhaps the situation is not as bad as estimated. Help may arrive at any time. Powerful forces of denial sometimes paralyze the field doctor's hand. I always ask myself, *"What will happen to the patient if he is not treated for two or three days?"* If I do not like the answer, it is time to act. I always try to remember that the procedure will hurt the other guy much more than me.

Over the years people have died after I refused to perform what I considered procedures beyond my ability or beyond the capabilities of the available equipment. Some of these people may have lived had I taken the risk and operated, but the moral and legal implications and the high risk of doing so stopped me. In other words, I was not only considering the patient's health and future well-being—I was considering mine. You should do the same.

Many people have seen dramatized versions of various extremely dangerous medical procedures performed by actors on TV and in the movies. In real life, the idea that you are going to put someone's guts back together with Mike Greenwald's handy dandy back-pocket med kit is absurd. Do what you can do—no more, and remember that life is not always just.

I would again like to remind you that I am a captain, not a doctor and that the contents of this chapter represent what I, myself, would do if I were shipwrecked or a castaway in some deserted spot, where professional help is not available. Techniques, drugs, and equipment change rapidly and there are other alternate approaches to the same problem. People who are allergic to certain drugs may require a different approach than is suggested here. All of this should be discussed with your doctor, who should advise you regarding drug use. He may prefer a totally different approach, which you should follow.

Recommended Medical Kit for Survival Craft

The "standard" **first-aid kit** (if there is such a thing on non-U.S.C.G.—Approved rafts) as is found in the standard "E-Pack," contains:

1. Pain pills
2. Motion sickness pills
3. Triangular bandage, safety pins
4. Assorted bandages and dressings
5. Antiseptic ointment
6. Burn ointment
7. Small scissors

All of these items, with the possible exception of the pain medication, could be purchased over-the-counter in any drug store. You can see that such a kit would just provide first-aid support for a few days until help arrives. If you think there is any possibility that you might be in a life raft longer than that, a supplementary kit added to your survival pack is recommended. A survival pack medicine kit contains prescription drugs which are essential to combat infection, in addition to supplementary over-the-counter medications

The medications listed for the emergency pack med kit represent a small part of a complete onboard medicine chest. These drugs should be packed at the top of the emergency pack, so that the kit may be easily accessed for normal use.

A prescription-drug medical kit is only as good as the person who uses it. When one makes up a kit, this must be kept in mind. It may be necessary to create a booklet to describe the use of each drug. The booklet should, of course, be packed in a waterproof bag. A wise captain will be thoroughly knowledgeable about the contents of the survival medicine pack and require the booklet only as a reference. Also include a small "medicine afloat" book to use as a guide.

The list below is intended for four persons. All items should be packed in waterproof packages and placed in a watertight box with a resealable lid.

Pain Killers
- 6 morphine Tubex cartridges, 1/4 grain
- 18 Demerol, 100 mg. tablets
- 24 Vicodin
- 2 Xylocaine, 1%, 50 ml. vial

Oral Antibiotics
- 50 Cipro, 250 mg. tablets
- 100 Flagyl, 250 mg. tablets
- 100 Cephalexin, 500 mg. tablets

Biocides

l/4 pt. Betadine solution
l/4 pt. hydrogen peroxide
24 alcohol wipes
l/4 pt. bactericidal soap containing isopropyl alcohol and chloroxylenol

Ointments

2 2-ounce tubes antibiotic cream
4 20-gram tubes Silvadene cream
2 bottle waterproof sun block

Dressings (individually packed)

1 triangular bandage
2 rolls gauze, two-inch wide butterfly closures
2 rolls adhesive tape
1 box Band-aids, mixed
2 medium trauma dressings
12 sterile gauze dressings, 4" x 4"
8 large gauze sponges
1 ACE bandage

Miscellaneous

1 orthopharyngeal airway
1 disposable shaving razor

Miscellaneous Drugs

6 ea. person Transderm patches
15 ea. person vitamin/mineral tablets
12 antihistamine (Benedryl) tablets
1 small bottle Ibuprofen
1 small bottle aspirin
2 kits Epinepherine injections (4 doses, 0.3 ml. each)

Sterile Equipment

2 sets sterile gloves
1 hemostat
1 needle holder
1 surgical scissors
1 fever thermometer
1 scalpel with 4 blades, #15
1 fine tweezers
  sterile sutures with needles:
  • 4 #0 monofilament
  • 3 #00 absorbable "gut"
  • surgical tweezers
  • 8 syringes, 6 cc./22G IM needles
  • 4 needles, #18, 2 inch

Non-Sterile Equipment

1 Tubex injector splint material

SPECIAL THANKS

The author would like to thank Captain Stephan Lewis, M.D., USN; Captain Alan M. Steinman, M.D., Chief of Preventative Medicinc-Clinical Branch, U.S.C.G.; and Phil Ronningen, pharmacist, for their review and editorial comments regarding Chapters VIII, IX, and XI.

CHAPTER XII: LIFEBOAT NAVIGATION

A DISCUSSION FOR THE EXPERIENCED NAVIGATOR

There is no limit to what you can learn about celestial navigation if you are interested, and lifeboat navigation is a particularly fascinating subject, for it pits man's brains (not his technology) against the sea. Unfortunately, most boat navigators tend to rely on electronic aids for navigation instead of devoting their efforts to improving the more reliable, but laborious, celestial techniques.

The information given here is only a sample of what the prudent master will know by heart. A fundamental knowledge of celestial navigation, understanding the celestial triangle, the circle of equal altitude and skill with the plot will, somewhere along the line, be translated into a longer life. If you are interested in further information, start with *The American Practical Navigator*.

With basic celestial navigation skills, the deck log (with the information suggested in this chapter), a sextant and a few basic navigation tools, an accurate position can be obtained at least once a day. Since most survival craft travel fewer than 60 miles per day, one position should suffice.

As was mentioned in Chapter III, life rafts usually go slowly from disaster to nowhere in an erratic way. Knowing where you are provides uncertain data on where you are going. Rafts often drift within sight of land only to have contrary winds and currents spring up and push them away. To row even five miles in a life raft is an absolutely exhausting job. It is hard to imagine exhausted, dehydrated survivors performing this feat. Luck and chance therefore play the dominant role in where the raft goes, although its speed may be influenced. Navigation may provide data which creates hope, but it can also create despair. Nothing would be more discouraging than to chart steady progress toward land, only to find, after weeks adrift, that a fickle current had turned the raft toward the open sea.

On the other hand, knowledge is strength, and knowing where you are may save your life. Knowing that you are approaching a shipping lane or are near land may encourage a change of strategy which leads to rescue. Lifeboats are capable of going in a direction other than downwind. Good strategy, based partially on navigation, may affect the outcome of a lifeboat adventure.

Face Page: Painting by Richard DeRosset

METHOD

The logical method of navigation for a lifeboat navigator to use is the method with which he is most familiar. The ship's sextant, chronometer (or digital watch), the **almanac, tables, chart(s), a pilot chart, dividers, protractor and a compass** should be stuffed into a bag and placed in the survival craft before abandoning the boat. Take the ship's log, or at least tear out the last few pages, so you can determine your last position. Celestial observations are then determined in the usual fashion, no easy job from a survival craft! A portable radio, even a cheap one, in a waterproof bag, is useful for providing the time and may also be used as a Radio Direction Finder.

The modern, electronic, waterproof wrist watch is quite sufficient for use as a lifeboat chronometer. If several crew members have watches, they should be synchronized at the beginning of the voyage, then checked daily for a few days to establish their rate of error. Each person should remember the error of their watch, and group resynchronization should take place weekly.

A navigation-emergency kit should be created and placed in the ship's lifeboat. It should contain the same equipment listed above, plus a decklog, discussed below. Charts should be waterproof, if available, or waterproofed with multiple coats of acrylic. A cheaper, plastic sextant can be included as lifeboat navigation is considered less accurate than a metal one. An old almanac can be used if cash is short; a section on how to update old editions is in the back. If an old almanac is used for the sun and stars, the tables may be torn apart, waterproofed with acrylic and the non-relevant sections discarded. If a kit cannot be created, at least have an Emergency-Navigation Equipment List attached to your Abandon Ship Plan.

THE DECKLOG

It costs nothing to make this log, and it may save your life. It should be added to your survival pack and contain the following information:

1. The lifeboat compass deviation card.
2. A summary of potential land falls (see below).
3. Notes on currents, winds, weather and pilot information for the season.
4. Specific notes and reminders from this and other books.
5. Abbreviated tables, especially sun declinations and GHA (at 1200 GMT) for the voyage month and the two months thereafter. Also include the correction table for Polaris.

6. The frequency, range and call sign for radio stations and
    beacons on the land masses selected for the potential
    land fall list and others which will provide good position data.
7. The CONVERSION OF ARC TO TIME and INCREMENTS AND
    CORRECTIONS section from an old almanac.
8. A copy of the survival pack list.

The Summary of Potential Land Falls should primarily list places relatively down wind from the yacht's intended course that are high and easily seen. Include latitude, longitude, notes about off-lying dangers and places for suitable landings. If the area is surrounded by reefs, make precise notes about the location of passes.

EMERGENCY NAVIGATION EQUIPMENT LIST

Position report	Radio
Sextant	Chronometer
Tables	Almanac
Protractor, 360°, plastic	Dividers
Decklog	Chart(s)
2 pencils with erasers	Pilot chart

STRATEGY

The first question to ask is whether to strike out for land or try to maintain position. If one has succeeded in sending a distress message (and received a reply), it is obviously wise to maintain position, by using the sea anchor or by sailing. This is also true if the disaster occurred in a shipping lane. If a major shipping lane is nearby (downwind), and land is far away, it may be wise to head for the lane, then sail along it. A longer route, along a shipping lane, may be wiser than the shorter route. If these options are not available the next question is "Where to go?"

A wise lifeboat captain will steer for a high, downwind land mass. It is better to head for a place that can be easily seen from a distance even if low-lying land is closer. The closer place may seem the obvious choice, but the danger and the potential demoralization of not finding the land in question should be considered.

If the lifeboat is not equipped with a complete navigation system, latitude sailing should be considered. This means reaching the latitude of the desired landfall while well offshore, then sailing due east or west to reach one's goal. This ancient technique is useful because it is easy to determine latitude (by meridian transit or by Polaris) if one has a sextant, but lacks tables.

While the decision of what to do is up to the captain, it is wise to present all of the data to the crew and explain the decision. If there is no clear-cut choice, or if the captain is undecided, it is better to let the crew decide by vote. Never choose hastily. Your strategy is the most important decision you will make. A bad one undermines the captain's authority and endangers the lives of the crew.

GOING FOR IT

Once the decision has been made to sail, the lifeboat log should be set up in a methodical fashion. Each page should be divided down the middle with one side for position data, such as celestial observations, speed-log entries, sunrise-sunset data etc.; the other is for dead reckoning data and other notes. The course should be laid and told to the helmsman. Every course change should be announced. A lookout should be assigned and a watch rotation system established.

THE CHIP LOG

A chip log should be made and used hourly. A chip log, sometimes called a Dutchman's log, is a piece of wood or plastic connected first to a bridle, then to a line. When it is thrown into the water, the bridle positions the chip to act as a sea anchor. In other words, the chip stays where it was thrown, and the boat sails away from it. The line is of a known length, and the time it takes to run out is used to determine speed. A nautical mile should be considered 6,000 feet for lifeboat purposes. If, therefore, the line is 60 feet in length, and it takes one minute to run out, the boat will travel 1.2 nautical miles per hour. Here's the formula:

$$\text{SPEED} = \frac{3{,}600 \text{ (The seconds in an hour) X Length of Line}}{6{,}000' \text{ (nautical mile) X Seconds of Elapsed Time}}$$

Since most of the data do not change, that is the 3600, the line length and the 6000-foot nautical mile, a constant can be created to simplify the calculation:

$$\text{CONSTANT} = \frac{3{,}600 \text{ Seconds X 60 feet of line}}{6{,}000 \text{ feet}} = 36$$

The constant, divided by the elapsed time, is the speed:

$$\frac{36 \text{ (the Constant)}}{30 \text{ Seconds}} = 1.2 \text{ knots}$$

The data from the chip log should be entered on the position data side of the page in a column. A total should be made every evening at sundown to determine the day's run.

A variety of other methods can be used to determine distance. Steve Callahan employed a typical approach:

I time the passage of seaweed between RUBBER DUCKY [his life raft] and the man overboard pole. Earlier I had calculated the distance to the pole to be about seventy feet, or 1/90 of a nautical mile. If it takes one minute for a piece of weed or other flotsam to pass between DUCKY and the pole, I am going 60/90 of a mile each hour or 2/3 of a knot, which works out to 16 miles a day. I make up a table for times from 25 to 100 seconds, 9 1/2 to 38 miles a day. I never do see a 38 mile day. From *Adrift* (Pg 104)

THE EFFECT OF WIND AND CURRENT

The wind and current marks on the pilot chart are based on a statistical average of weather over a long period of time. The Pilot Chart shows "normal" conditions. But lifeboats move at one to three knots. Drift and set become a larger component of True Course than would normally be the case. As a result, small variations from the norm produce large differences between the actual and tabulated drift and set. Pilot charts are therefore of only limited use to the castaway. Learn about wind and currents (Ch. XV).

Position based on celestial observations is the best method of determining drift and set. The corrected compass course and the speed based on the chip log readings produce a DR position. Any difference between the DR and the observed position may be attributed to drift and set. As the vessel approaches land increased celestial observations are the only defense against course errors due to drift and set. Ocean wind and current are often affected by the presence of a land mass. Frequent celestial observations and bearings on the land are the only defense against being swept past one's objective.

THE COMPASS

If a deviation card and a nautical chart showing variation are available, determine the course to be run in the normal way. If this data is not available take a sight of Polaris at night while on course or determine the azimuth of the sun during the day. If, for example, the sun's azimuth is 260° True and a compass bearing on the sun is 275°, the combined error and deviation is +15° and the correction is correspondingly -15 ° (15° west). This is applied to the calculated course.

USING THE SUN AND STARS AS A COMPASS

If you have included declinations in your decklog these will give direct azimuths (true bearings) to the sun at sunrise and sunset. Polaris gives a True north bearing and the vertical portion of the Southern Cross points to True south.

THE RADIO

A portable radio with a Marine/Aero band, or even an ordinary AM radio with an internal antenna, packed in a waterproof bag, an aero chart and a chip log may be all you need to make land. The frequency of the landfall station is tuned-in and the radio rotated through 360 degrees. When a "null" or lowest signal level is achieved, the narrow side of the radio is pointing at the station and the broad side, with the band and dials is at right angles to it. By sailing toward the station and noting distance run using the chip log, amazing accuracy can be achieved.

CELESTIAL OBSERVATIONS

If a full set of navigation equipment is available, position may be determined in the normal way. If only the sextant, and decklog (and presumably your wrist watch) are present, latitude may be determined with accuracy, by shooting the sun at noon (meridian transit), and Polaris at night.

POSITION BY MERIDIAN TRANSIT

When the sun is at its highest point in the sky (the transit), latitude is determined, using the typical "noon sight" formula: 90°- observed altitude +or- the declination. Since your decklog has only the declination for 1200 GMT it will be necessary to interpolate, using the next day's declination as a guide. The observed altitude is corrected for dip, semi-diameter and refraction.

Longitude at the moment of the meridian transit may be calculated by converting the time of the transit into arc (see below). One may assume dip to be -3' and semidiameter for the sun's lower limb to be +16'. The sun seems to linger for several minutes at its highest point, the transit, so it is advisable, for the sake of accuracy, to shoot it some time before and after noon at the same altitude. The time of the observations is averaged. This is the moment of the meridian transit.

DETERMINING POSITION BY MERIDIAN TRANSIT

In contrast to the formulae above, finding both latitude and longitude by meridian transit is, if anything, even easier than using other, more conventional methods, providing, of course, that you have the GHA of the sun at 1200 GMT. Since you recorded the sun's GHA at 1200 GMT in your decklog (if you were wise), you can calculate the precise moment of noon in Greenwich. For example, on December 31, 1988, the sun's GHA at 12 noon was 359°12'. So the meridian passage occurred a little later than 12 noon at Greenwich:

$$
\begin{array}{r}
360°\ 00 \\
-359°\ 12 \\
\hline
48'
\end{array}
$$

By following to its conclusion the fact that the earth rotates through 360° in 24 hours, you find that

$$1° \text{ of arc} = 4 \text{ minutes of time}$$
$$1' \text{ of arc} = 4 \text{ seconds of time}$$
$$48' = 4 \times 48 = 192 \text{ seconds of time}$$

So noon at Greenwich occurred 3 minutes and 12 seconds after 1200 GMT. Let us say your meridian passage occurred at 4 15 35 p.m. GMT. The difference between these two times is

$$
\begin{array}{r}
4\ 15\ 35 \\
-\ 00\ 03\ 12 \\
\hline
4\ 12\ 23 = 4 \text{ hours, 12 minutes, 23 seconds.}
\end{array}
$$

So this difference, 4 h 12 m 23 s, may be converted into arc:

$$
\begin{array}{r}
252 \text{ minutes} \div 4m = 63°\ 00' \\
23 \text{ seconds} \div 4' \quad = 00°\ 06' \\
\hline
63°\ 06'
\end{array}
$$

The same information can be obtained by using the CONVERSION OF ARC TO TIME table. You are therefore 63° 06' west of Greenwich.

Position Determination Using
Concise Tables for Sight Reduction

The remarkable *Concise Tables for Sight Reduction,* prepared by Rear Admiral Thomas Davies, USN (Cornell Maritime Press, 1984) is a complete celestial navigation system in a single slim 64 page volume, suitable for use in a survival craft without any other texts. It includes a complete four year repetitive almanac, although it is slightly more difficult to use than the *Nautical Almanac* . "Concise" is certainly the right word to appear in the title of this work. The concept is explained with one page of text and a single diagram. The procedure is explained in two and a half pages plus a sample work sheet. The rest of the 64 pages include tables sufficient to determine the azimuth and zenith distance of the sun, Aries and 38 navigation stars. The *Concise Tables* also include corrections for determining latitude by Polaris, an explanation for determining compass error/variation using Amplitudes as well as solutions for determining great circle distance, track and bearing. Not bad for a 64 page manual.

The *Concise Tables* are easy to use, requiring only the addition and subtraction of two digit numbers. The *Tables* assume that the user is an experienced navigator. There is absolutely no discussion about how to reduce a sight or make a plot and it is also assumed that the user knows how to determine declination, is familiar with the usual navigational terms such as GHA, LHA and Aries.

Regarding accuracy, Rear Admiral Davies claims that the Concise Tables are more accurate than *H.O. 229*, which this volume replaces, and eliminates *229's* major short-comings. Since it does not require a logarithmic solution, it is easier to use and it is certainly small enough to fit into a navigation survival pack, eliminating the need for components of the *Nautical Almanac* mentioned earlier as a suggested part of the deck log. The major short-coming of the *Concise Tables* is that it is not waterproof.

POLARIS

Polaris is a second magnitude star located within one degree of the Celestial North Pole. It never seems to move (much) and is useful as a determinnation of latitude from about 9° to 60°N., the heavens seem to revolve around it. The observed altitude of Polaris, plus or minus a correction, based on the table found in your decklog, provides latitude. If you have no decklog, a correction accurate to, let's say, 20 miles can be made by visual observation.

The constellations *Cassioppeiae* and The Big Dipper are used like the hands of a clock. More specifically, the trailing star in Cassiopeiae and in the Big Dipper form a nearly straight line with Polaris (see next page).

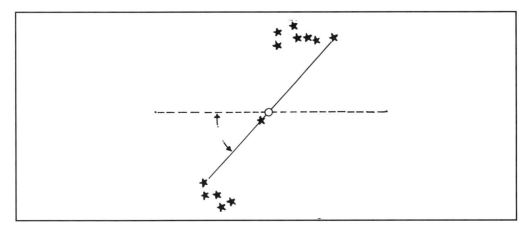

(1) When the line is horizontal, no correction. (2) When vertical, the maximum 56' correction applies.(3) The correction is + if the dipper is on top, - on the bottom.(4) Estimates of the correction are made by eye. Drawing by Rafael Monrot.

THE SOUTHERN CROSS

The Southern Cross is visible from about 10°N Southward. It becomes visible at about the latitude where Polaris is either invisible or extremely low on the horizon. The cross of the Southern Cross points to true South. Using Polaris or the Southern cross and a compass, True Course can be obtained.   The

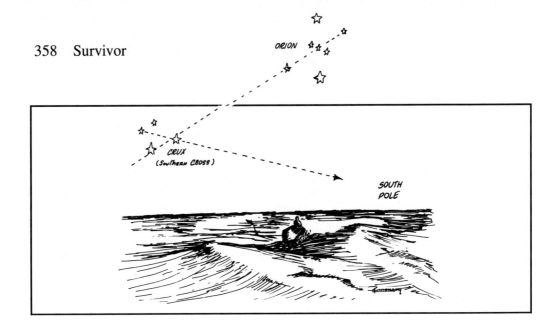

The Southern Cross

traditional survival craft technique is to stream a line behind the craft to indicate reciprocal course. The compass is then aligned with either Polaris or the Southern Cross and the True Course can then be read directly off the compass.

MAKING A NAVIGATION DEVICE

A crude navigation device can be made from a protractor, weight and some string. A chart compass rose can also be used. In the day, the sun's shadow is allowed to fall across the card as shown (next page). At night one sights Polaris and calls "mark" while a second observer reads the protractor at the weighted line. This gives the zenith distance of Polaris. Under ideal circumstances, 0.5° or 30 NM accuracy can be expected. If a protractor is not available, angles can be measured by lashing three pencils or other rigid objects together to form a triangle. The angle can be measured on the compass rose of a chart. It's a very crude technique.

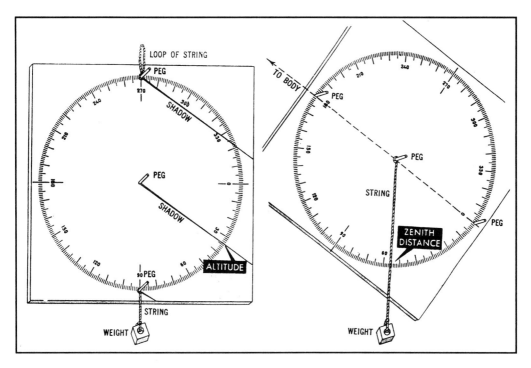

Using a compass card as an astrolabe. Left: Insert a match or pin as a peg at the center of the card. Read Altitude from peg's shadow. Right: Hold card by center peg. Use the two pegs shown as a sight. Read Zenith Distance where string indicates.

DETERMINING DISTANCE-OFF BY FORMULA

The formula to determine visible distance off is $1.15\sqrt{H}$, where H is the known height (in feet). For example, an object at sea level can be seen 2.7 miles away, if eye level is 5.5' above sea level $1.15\sqrt{5.5}=2.7$. If an island has a height of 500' and its top has just become visible over the horizon, it can be seen $1.15\sqrt{500} = 25.7$ miles plus the 2.7 miles of eye height or 28.4 miles away.

While this method of determining distance-off is quite accurate, distant objects are often obscured by haze or smog. If the land mass is clearly above the horizon when it becomes visible, application of the distance-off formula should not be used.

CHAPTER XIII: LAND FALL

Signs of Land

Early signs of land can often be inferred from clouds: A motionless, fixed cloud, either in a clear sky or when surrounded by other, moving clouds, often hovering above land. A light green color on the daytime cloud cover indicates sunlight reflected from a lagoon or reef. A loom off low clouds at night may indicate a settlement, but a streak of light, pointing in the direction of the sunset or the sunrise may be a phenomena called zodiacal light. In northern latitudes, look for a light tint, or loom, on low cloud during the day or on a moonlit night which may be light reflected from ice fields. Layers of cold, dry northern air and warm, moist air can cause refraction abnormalities which make objects visible that are actually much farther away than estimated. Objects occasionally appear upside down, have a washed-out or distorted appearance.

Changes in water color occur as one approaches a continental shelf. The water turns light green, due to the growth of algae or a mixture of green, brown and yellow suspended particles carried to sea as run-off, or the outflow of a river. Great rivers such as the Amazon, discolor the sea for a tremendous distance. If the color of the water is milky, it is may be the result of fish spawning, not an indication of land.

Watch for **an increase of bird activity** around the craft. Coastal-based marine birds fly from the land at dawn and to it at dusk, but during the day they fly a random, hunting pattern. Look for species which do not venture far from land (see Chapter XV). Do not be fooled by tiny land birds which arrive exhausted (during the day) at the survival craft. If you can touch them, they are disoriented and near death. Eat them or use them for bait. Such an occurrence is a sign that no land is nearby—for if it were, the birds would be there. It is very likely that they have been blown off a migratory route and are as lost as you.

If the wind is light, a reversal of direction at dawn and dusk due to the **land effect** may be felt 20 to 30 miles from shore. The breeze flows toward the land from late morning until just after sunset, then away from the land during the night until dawn.

The land effect may also carry land odors many miles offshore, especially smoke. The strong smell of vegetation from a beach, forest, or jungle is particularly evident after dark. Pollution, such as smog, also travels on light breezes from the land.

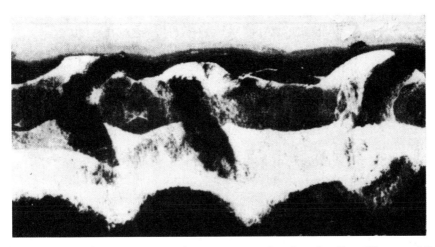

Rips disturb the normal wave pattern and cause waves to break early. From*Waves and Beaches*
by Willard Bascom © 1980 by permission of the author.

Increasing signs of fresh flotsam, such as flowers, green leaves,
fruit, dead insects or animals are signs of land, but dead birds, kelp, Sargassum,
driftwood, cut wood or floating garbage, especially styrofoam items, are not.
These items (except, of course, the birds) last much longer than one would
think, may have been dumped from a ship or traveled far from land.

Sometimes the sound of surf can be heard for a great distance. If so, it
should chill the blood. If surf can be heard before the land can be seen, it must
be heavy surf indeed and you're in deep trouble.

CURRENTS

When the wind is blowing toward the shore, the general prevailing current is toward land, then parallel to the coast or around an island.. It is much
stronger at the edges of an island (strongest on the right side in the direction of
flow in the Northern Hemisphere, left in the Southern), where the water, ob-
structed by the land flows around it. On the sheltered side, the general current is
away from land, but there are usually important counter-currents which run toward shore. These are found on the left side of the island (back to wind) in the
Southern Hemisphere, the right in the Northern. If it becomes apparent that a
survival craft will miss an island, the back-current may carry you into the lee
and/or toward land.

The Wind and Water Near Shore

Rip currents and rip tides, caused by underwater obstructions or sandbars, are most common when surf runs parallel to the beach. The waves tumble over the shallow bar which retards its return to sea. The water rushes along in a trough, between bar and beach, looking for an exit. Where it finds one, a rip occurs. Rips usually flow at right angles to shore and are most common on gradually sloping bottoms or where underwater rocky ledges exist. They are usually intermittent, more active with the running tide and fan out from a point near land to a width of a half mile or more at their seaward end. Most of the time a back-current, or eddy, is encountered immediately after a rip current.

Since rips are formed by a bar, one or more spots, shallow enough to stand, often exist on either side of the rip or inside the bar, even though the water from the bar to the beach may be much deeper. The shallows are indicated by lighter-colored water.

Indications of rip currents are: smooth, oily-looking patches or flat water, agitated with small wavelets, with breaking water on either side. Streaks of discolored water caused by beach sediment also indicate the presence of a rip current. Areas where a part of a breaker consistently starts ahead of the rest of the wave usually indicate the unseen presence of a rip counter-current, although an underwater obstruction may also cause a wave to break in shallow water. Rip currents result in more severe breakers and should be avoided.

LOCAL CURRENTS

Local currents are usually influenced by the tide. They run into and out of bays, but a river's outflow is usually just diminished, rather than reversed by an incoming tide. When an incoming tide overcomes an outflow, a tidal bore, or standing wall of water is sometimes created. These are extremely dangerous and must be avoided. Tidal current in general is about two knots, but it can be much greater close to estuaries and rivers. **Wind** also influences current, and the few feet of water in which the raft travels always moves in the direction of a strong wind. If it becomes apparent that a tidal current is setting against you, it may be possible to forestall its negative effect by anchoring, sailing or rowing until the tide changes.

Waves have an uncanny way of bending around islands and irregular coast lines. Waves tend to travel roughly parallel to underwater contours, so they bend, and align themselves with the beach as they approach it. It sometimes seems as though a calm lee does not exist. Having successfully worked your survival craft around the windward side of an island, it is dismaying to find surf where none should be. Should these conditions occur and the surf appears to be dangerous, it may be possible to anchor or remain on station using oars to await changes caused by the land effect. These include the offshore breeze near sundown or the calm period just after sunrise.

Undertow or backrush occurs close to shore and is a great danger in the final moments of a landing. In reality, undertow is a highly overworked word, and the people using it are really describing one of a variety of phenomena. They think they are referring to some sort of current which will suck them under, but this does not exist. They may be talking about the **orbital motion** of the wave, which first bashes a swimmer against the bottom, then pops him to the surface. They may be referring to the few feet of **backrush** from a receding wave which runs down the beach, pulling people with it. Backrush can pull a person back into the breakers, which may kill him, but it cannot pull anyone under water.

Nevertheless, since everyone else uses the word, we will call these collective events undertow. Undertow pulls at clothing more than bare skin, particularly loose-fitting clothes, which, in addition, retain a great weight of water, but bare skin is often abraded by contact with the shore. This is another of those unresolvable, two-pronged dilemmas. More than one castaway has reached land, only to be pulled back by a hungry sea. It is instinctive to try to stand in shallow water, but it is extremely difficult to stand in an undertow. The best strategy is to keep swimming, as much on the surface as possible, in order to take advantage of the shoreward flow of surface water. If anything such as rocks project from the beach, one can grab them and hang on. After the backrush recedes, crawl out of the water, then give thanks that a fickle Neptune decided to turn you loose.

As a wave approaches the shore, its base makes contact with the seabed and this retards the wave-bottom's forward motion. The top keeps moving at the original speed, but the bottom falls farther and farther behind. A specific series of events occur as the wave approaches the beach: When the slope of the seabed is gradual, a wave may break several times before hitting the shore. Its steepness, speed and force dissipate slowly. But when the slope of the seabed is steep, the wave breaks close to shore and it is considerably higher than the prevailing swell, possessing incredible power. Waves reflected off shoals or reefs produce very dangerous seas when they encounter incoming waves. The **pyramid seas** produced have tremendous power.

Waves resulting from a long, unobstructed fetch (having traveled a great distance) may be of irregular heights and be separated by different distances, but the time **interval** between them remains relatively steady. Search for the wave interval around you and use this knowledge to coordinate the landing.

When a wave breaks, its top falls forward, toward the land. As a result it is extremely difficult to see breakers from their seaward side or judge their height—until you are in them. Indirect inferences must be made. Judge a wave by irregularities in its crest. Big, breaking waves have rougher tops when seen from seaward. Look for patches with smoother tops and steer toward them.

Long lines of surf travel farther up the beach than short waves of irregular breadth. It is possible to travel behind the long ones with more security. Wind and surf have a tendency to bend toward the land, so the surf line usually parallels the beach. When it does not, a strong 'longshore current may cause rebounding waves that run back out to sea at an angle to the prevailing breaker line. These waves get steeper near the shore and must be considered when attempting a landing. Beaches exposed to heavy surf often end in heavily eroded foothills. Look for long strips devoid of vegetation which can be seen from a great distance. Listen for the booming sound of heavy surf.

In Northern waters, when the sea bottom within a few miles of shore is less than (approximately) 75', kelp beds often occur. These beds act as a buffer against surf and if a survival craft can enter a kelp bed the likelihood of a safe landing is greatly increased.

LANDING THROUGH SURF

It is not easy to land safely on a breaking beach, even in a fast outboard, let alone with an engineless survival craft. Castaways, particularly if they are in a weakened condition, are at extreme risk in this type of landing. It is, of course, preferable to look for a sheltered beach, and every effort should be made to do so. Look for irregularities on the coast which may offer a lee. Villages are usually located near a suitable landing. Villages often become visible suddenly if they are at the end of a bay, estuary or behind an islet. Keep watch for them, even if the area seems uninhabited.

Before making the approach, secure all items in the survival craft and be sure a long line (the painter) is attached to the boat so that it may be pulled up the beach. Put on long-sleeved clothes, if available, and make foot-and-hand coverings, particularly in coral areas.

Some authorities recommend wearing life jackets; and others claim that the jackets get in the way. If the surf is high and it appears as though the beach is steep-to (with a considerable undertow), it is wiser to wear the jackets.

LANDING THROUGH SURF WITH A DINGHY

Trying to land a survival dinghy through surf can get you killed. If (as is likely) the dinghy overturns, it becomes a lethal weapon which can roll over and crush luckless castaways. In heavy surf, it may be wiser to jump clear of the overturned dinghy and swim for shore. More about that later.

SURF MECHANICS: The wave pattern remains normal until the water shoals to a depth of less than 1 wave-length. (1) As bottom drag increases, wave-length shortens, wave height increases. (2) Contact with the seabed causes the bottom of the wave to be retarded. At a depth of 1.3 the wave height the wave starts to break. (3) The top of the wave moves so far ahead of the bottom that a foam line appears. Undertow increases. (5) The remains of the wave run up the beach and are called *uprush*. Drawing by Rafael Monroy.

The best strategy for a landing through surf depends on which type of survival craft is making the attempt. A survival dinghy or inflatable boat should have a sea anchor ready to drop as the shore is approached. Hang back a short distance behind the breaker line and wait for the right opportunity. Keep the boat end-on to the waves and use the sea anchor or a long line to accomplish this. Keep the boat from drifting into the breakers with oars.

People talk about trying to pick the "big wave" of a group, but wave patterns are random. On the other hand, the time **interval** between crests is generally regular, so strategy is based on **timing**, not "picking the big one."

Once the decision has been made, trip the sea anchor with a tripping line, attached to its pointed end, but leave it in the water. It can be deployed in the event that a breaking wave threatens to overwhelm the craft. Get the craft moving just before the crest of the selected wave passes. Put all of your energy into keeping just behind the crest. It can be fatal to fall too far behind. The wave ahead, after breaking on the beach, creates a backwash (undertow), which can unexpectedly delay the landing. Then, the next wave arrives and falls upon the luckless castaways. If you have oil, stream it when the craft gets moving.

Row the craft as far as possible up the beach. Resist the temptation to jump out until after the boat has actually grounded. If it capsizes, **get away from it** before it rolls over and kills you. The succeeding waves will push the boat farther up the beach. Even though everyone will be exhausted after the landing, it is important to save the survival craft and its contents. These items may be useful later, and the survival craft can be used as a shelter.

LANDING THOUGH SURF IN A LIFE RAFT

Since a life raft is not as maneuverable as a survival dinghy, a different landing strategy must be adopted when landing in surf or with an onshore breeze. Both the raft and its ballast bags travel with the flow of water toward the beach. The ballast bags are useful during the landing because they prevent capsize and cushion the float chambers from damage, but there is always the danger that the bag will snag on objects projecting from the sea bed resulting in a capsize. As a result there is a great likelihood of a capsize during the final approach, and this should be anticipated. The bags also make the life raft very slow, it is not really possible to "make a run through the surf". Cutting the bags away radically changes the stability of the craft. It may make the life raft more maneuverable, but it also makes it much more likely to capsize prematurely.

Strategy: Since this section discusses landing through surf, presumably on a windward shore, it is assumed that the wind and waves will carry the raft and its occupants onto the beach or at least very close to it. As the craft approaches the beach, a sea anchor should be deployed, using as much line as possible. It is important that the sea anchor remain on or near the surface at this time so that it does not snag on the bottom. An empty water bottle or other flotation device may be secured to the anchor's mouth for this purpose. All items in the raft should be well secured, as they may be useful in the ensuing land survival effort. The raft and its contents will probably wash up on the shore.

Once a landing site has been chosen, the raft's canopy should be cut away so that the passengers will not be trapped if the raft capsizes. The material and anything else available should be used as body covering to prevent abrasions from contact with the seabed if the raft capsizes.

A decision must be made regarding life jackets. Many authorities recommend them and of course they could definitely save lives if the castaway were injured during the approach or swept away. They also offer some protection against pounding on coral or rocks. On the other hand, the strategy of swimming through surf (in the event that the raft capsized) precludes the wearing of life jackets.   The physical condition of the survivors (whether they are strong enough to swim) must be considered. As the surf line is approached, everyone should position themselves at the seaward side of the raft and grasp the lifelines.

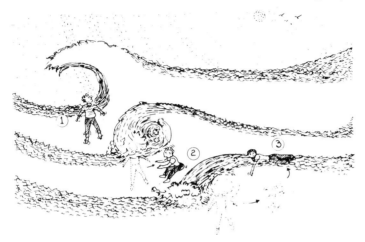

Body surfing technique. Drawing by Raoul Reys.

If you have elected to abandon your dinghy, or if the raft capsizes and it is necessary to swim through surf, one of two strategies must be adopted. If the castaway has body surfing experience this technique may be attempted. The swimmer treads water, facing the waves. When a wave is selected, preferably a low one with considerable breadth, the swimmer turns toward the land and swims madly, to gain momentum, as the wave approaches. When the crest hits, the arms are extended, as though one were diving. Kick madly. Keep the shoulders hunched, the stomach sucked in, the back slightly bent (not arched). If the wave is smooth, ride it out. If it starts to break, reverse with the arms and allow the breaker to sweep past. Repeat as necessary. The advantage of body surfing is that it requires less energy than swimming.

It is easy to see, from the description above, that someone not experienced in body surfing can get themselves killed this way, principally by getting caught in a breaker and pushed down onto the seabed. The second method, safer but slower, is to swim toward shore, preferably using a side stroke so that the waves to seaward can be watched. When a breaker is about 10 to 15 feet away, take a deep breath and dive as far as possible using three or four good strokes. Resurface when the wave has passed. When the water gets shallow, dive and assume the fetal position, protect the head with your hands, to minimize injury from contact with the bottom.

Landing through surf is a terrifying experience. Fear and exhaustion are the survivor's greatest enemies. Marshal your energy. If you are swimming, rest when tired. Use the "dead man's float", resting face down, raising the head occasionally to breathe.

When approaching the shore, select a wave, allow it to pass and swim madly after it, following it onto the beach. Beware of the backrush. Do not attempt to stand until the water is less than knee deep. Crawl if necessary.

LANDING ON A WINDWARD SHORE

Cliffs are usually visible from afar and, in addition, the waves hitting them have a particular booming sound which carries for a great distance. It's blood-chilling, and the message is very clear. It's the sound of God calling in your cards. As soon as it becomes apparent that the craft is approaching cliffs, every effort should be made to delay or alter the approach. This includes use of the sea anchor, sails, if available, and oars.

If there is no way to avoid landing among cliffs, look for boulders near shore which may offer a lee, visible as a slick of calm water on the boulder's shoreward side. With luck, and a considerable effort, it may be possible to land there.

The second choice, far down the list, is any sort of ledge. The third choice, even farther down the list, is to head for a rocky projection, upon whose sides the waves do not break directly. It is possible that survivors may be able to scramble above the waves. Needless to say, a successful landing on such a place depends a great deal on luck. In a letter, Dougal Robertson commented:

> The only successful landing among cliffs in a heavy surf (to my knowledge) was achieved by a yachtswoman who remained within an inflatable survival raft with the canopy firmly closed until it was all over. She was thrown about, capsized and righted a time or two, but finished right way up on a rock shelf where she emerged and scrambled to safety. I do not know the science of this maneuver, but success is not a bad guide.

The wind near cliffs is tricky and full of surprises. When there is an onshore breeze against a cliff, a pocket of high pressure forms. In settled conditions, light variables may occur close to shore. In strong winds, a gusty offshore breeze may spring up close to shore, creating a miserable cross swell.

When an offshore wind blows over a cliff, a reverse, onshore flow is created, possibly extending as far offshore as the height of the cliff. Beyond the onshore flow, a pocket of calm is found, sometimes extending offshore as far as two or three times the cliff height.

Rocky beaches: If you must land on a rocky beach, look for a place where the wave runs well up the shore. Avoid areas where the waves explode into white spray. If you are capsized from a dinghy close to shore, get away from it as it may crush you. Hold onto a life vest, jerry can or the oars. If you are in a life raft, stay with it as long as possible and try to use it as a cushion. If you end up swimming in shallow water, remember that there is usually a considerable undertow off a rocky beach. Do not do not try to stand up unless the water is less than knee deep. Watch the sea, dive when breakers approach and try to hold onto rocks to prevent being sucked seaward.

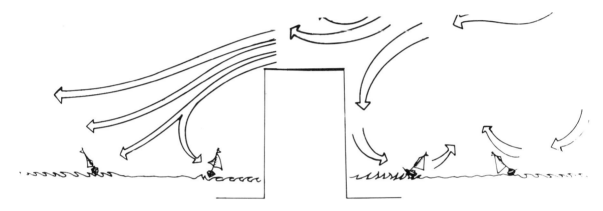

Wind flow near cliffs. Drawing by Raoul Reys.

CROSSING A REEF

Being tossed onto a coral reef is really dangerous, so every effort should be made to reach a sheltered landing or look for some sort of pass. Do not just look ahead but to both sides as well. It is quite common for a pass to exist between two overlapping reefs, and the pass is therefore not visible from directly ahead. Some coral atolls are completely surrounded by unbroken reefs, but the majority have at least one pass.

It is important to wear clothes and foot-coverings. A head covering and a life jacket are also recommended. If there are items which can be used to cushion the body from contact with the reef, they should be divided among the castaways, so that they know what to grab if the craft capsizes. If the survival craft is a raft, every effort should be made to stay with it, as the raft itself is the best available cushion, but **do not tie yourself to it.** If you are separated from the craft and washed across the reef, search for it before striking out for shore. It is much safer to stay with even a swamped craft and maneuver toward the land very slowly than to swim.

Some reefs extend unbroken from the shore, but the majority are separated from the land by a bay or lagoon. The reef itself is extremely hazardous to walk upon, as it is sharp, and contains spiny urchins and eels. Castaways who receive cuts or abrasions bleed, and this attracts sharks. This is another reason why it is essential to clothe the body as much as possible. Swim rather then walk whenever possible. Use your life jacket to buoy your body. If there are currents inside the reef, do not struggle against them, continue toward the land in a slow, methodical way.

Sharks are cautious, curious animals which can be temporarily intimidated by agressive behavior. Swim toward shore using the side stroke, and avoid splashing as much as possible. If a shark seems to menace you, swim toward it, shout, make aggressive motions. If you must hit it, remember that a shark's body is as hard as a rock, and the skin is very rough. You may abrade or cut you hand on it, and the blood will incite the shark. Use something beside your hand as a weapon.

Headlands, if they are steep-to, create confused seas, unpredictable breakers and swirling currents which are heavily influenced by the tide. Do not land on them. If the surf is hitting a headland at an angle it is likely that some sort of a lee, often a beach, will be found just around the point and this is an ideal landing spot. Sometimes headlands are convoluted and form bays. Try for the sides of the bay; the surf is less dangerous there, rather than at the head of the bay. Landing at the head is dangerous, for wave action becomes compressed by the confines of the bay, undertow is severe and the surf is usually heavy. Work toward landing in the shelter of the point, as mentioned above.

LIFEGUARD OR BEACHPATROL SIGNALS

Internationally understood landing (lifesaving) signals, are used by on-shore beach patrolmen, life guards and coast guards. Ships officers, while directing a rescue, may also resort to their use. Learn them.

This is the best place to land: (1) A white light at night or a gun fired three times at intervals of one minute means "you have been seen." This signal may be combined with orange smoke. Red rockets or hand signals may also be used (2) The vertical motion of a white flag (up and down) during the

"This is the best place to land." Drawing by Rafael Monroy.

day, used alone or combined with a green light, a green rocket or a horn sounding the letter "K" (- . -) indicates "This is the best place to land." At night car lights and a green light waived up and down may be used. A white light is occasionally used if a green one is not available (3) A horizontally waved white flag, possibly combined with a red rocket or the signalling of the code letter "S" (. . .), either alone or combined with a light or sound signal means "Landing here is unsafe" (4) A horizontally waived white flag, placed in the ground, followed by the life guard walking away with a second white flag means "Do not land at this place, a more favorable location is in this direction." This may be combined with, or supplemented by, a horizontally fired red rocket and a white rocket aimed in the favorable direction, sound or light signals "S" (· · ·) followed by "R" (. – .) for "go to your right" or "L" (. – . .) for "go to your left".

"Landing here is very dangerous." Drawing by Rafael Monroy.

CHAPTER XIV: RADIO TRANSMISSIONS AND SURVIVAL

Emergency Communications

IMPORTANT GENERAL INFORMATION

Since a boat fills with water from the bottom up as it sinks, it is essential to mount radio equipment as high as possible. The best place is on a bracket attached to the overhead. A boat's main batteries are usually located near the engine, beneath the waterline. The smart captain therefore connects the radio(s) to a <u>separate battery</u>, mounted as high as practical, as close as possible to them. This battery should be capable of at least 30 minutes of full-power transmission. A car battery rated at 40 to 50 amps fulfills this need. The transmission battery should be connected to the ship's main supply, but a **one-way, protective diode** must be installed between the two systems to protect the transmission battery from being inadvertently drained, as would occur if the main system went under water. In addition to functioning as an emergency energy source, a separate transmission battery will also protect the radio(s) from damage caused by accidental sudden power reduction in the main system, as is caused when the boat's engine is started.

Most boat antennas are mounted on the main mast,or the backstay is used as a long wire antenna. If this is the case, the prudent captain carries a backup antenna or have one permanently mounted on the deck or mizzen mast. If you lose your mast, just about the last thing in the world you want to lose with it is the ability to call for help.

Most radios, particularly powerful SSB equipment, are very sensitive to low input voltage. Input voltage is, of course, a function of the battery state, but the size of the power cable is also extremely important. Radios may perform properly when the batteries are fully charged and connected to a charger, but they may produce a garbled signal (known as FMing) underway if the power input cable is too small, particularly when the batteries are not fully charged.

Every SSB should receive input power via heavy battery cables for this reason. In addition to the strength of the transmitter, the radiated power of a radio signal is determined by antenna type. A small, coil-loaded whip antenna, typical of many found on boats, may actually decrease the radiated power of a signal. Dipole and long wire antennas increase the radiated power, but one must understand their use to take advantage of them. Consult your local antenna doctor and select a good one, or two.

Regardless of type, it wise to turn your radios on periodically, to be sure they are operating properly and to drive off moisture. Like all modern electronic equipment, radios like to be left on continuously. Turning them on and off frequently shortens their life.

Antenna, ground, and power cable connections should be inspected and cleaned regularly. A poor ground connection (to an SSB radio) will tremendously shorten the radio's effective range. When a radio is not in use, it is extremely smart to disconnect the antenna cable, and, in addition, connect the center prong of the cable to a ground. This provides some protection from lightning damage.

THE VHF RADIO

Marine emergency radio signals may be generated by three types of radios: VHF, SSB, and EPIRB. Most boats are equipped with VHF (Very High Frequency) transceivers which operate in the 156 MHz frequency range at a maximum of 25 watts. Most people think their VHF is capable of transmitting 25 to 50 miles. This is incorrect. The VHF is, with some exceptions, an electronic line-of-sight apparatus, which means that if the antenna of the receiving station is below the electronic horizon, the signal will not be heard. Powerful, land-based government stations with sophisticated antennas can reach further, but aboard a boat, the only way to increase the range of your VHF is to raise the antenna height. As a rule of thumb, **you may anticipate a nominal range of 20 NM when transmitting an emergency message to a USCG facility**.

You can see that the VHF, as a safety device, works much more effectively near shore, particularly where the nearby land (and therefore the receiving antennae of shore stations) is high. At sea, the chance of a VHF MAYDAY transmission reaching another vessel is not great, particularly if you are far from a shipping lane.

The advantage of a VHF radio is its low price and ease of operation. As a handy-dandy little radio, for use 'longshore or in port, it's great. As an emergency device, its use is very limited.

THE SINGLE SIDEBAND TRANSCEIVER (SSB)

The SSB (single sideband) radio is a long range device which operates in the 2 to 30 MHz range. An SSB radio is considerably more powerful than a double sideband or AM transmitter operating on the same frequency and with the same power.

The reason is that the double sideband radio generates the entire voice signal, while the SSB transmits only the harmonics of the upper (USB) or lower (LSB) portion of the signal. All of the output power is concentrated in this small portion of the signal. The other station's receiver takes this portion of the signal and adds the rest to make understandable speech. This is the reason why an SSB transmission sounds garbled when heard on an AM radio.

Unlike VHF transmission, an SSB signal bounces off the ionosphere and can travel around the world. When the signal is generated from the antenna, most of it heads toward the sky and begins bouncing between the ionized layer of air and the earth. A small portion of the signal is radiated horizontally and can be received slightly beyond line-of-sight distances, like the VHF. Signals between 2 to 6 MHz also contain a ground wave component which travels parallel to the earth, beyond the horizon, making them particularly ideal for emergency transmissions. Beyond this range, a receiving station must receive the skywave signal. The "skip" distance at which the "first bounce" returns to earth is a function of the frequency. A signal generated in the 22 MHz-range may be clear 2000 miles away but inaudible 75 miles from the antenna.

A transmission on 2182 kHz (2.182 MHz), the international distress frequency, may be clear 75 miles away but you may be absolutely positive that a speech transmission on this frequency will not be heard 2000 miles away. Nominal range on this frequency is 300 NM.

The skip distance, in addition to being influenced by the wavelength, is also a function of the height of the ionized layer above the earth, which varies with the season and the time of day. The sunspot cycle and the pathway of the signal (east-west or north-south) and weather conditions also affect the clarity of the signal. Since there are so many variables, it is not possible to make up a little chart of frequency-to-skip distance which would tell one the optimum frequency to use for any station. Selecting the right frequency is therefore a bit of an art.

"Ham" operators usually subscribe to magazines which supply this data, and a big part of their fun is trying to transceive over long distances with little power, by careful selection of frequency and use of a good antenna. If you are up to your knees in cold saltwater, it is unlikely that you will share their interest. As a result, the wise captain, when making a long distance voyage should develop a day-to-day strategy based on his location and what he thinks is his best chance of being heard in the one or two minutes he will have to complete his transmission.

Basically, the choice is between local- and long-range communication. Obviously, a vessel 75 miles away, able to receive transmissions in the two to six MHz frequency range, will be able to render assistance quickly. Most SSB marine radios are capable of transmitting a very strong signal over this distance, regardless of conditions, most of the time . This is the reason why a low frequency (2182 kHz) has been chosen as the primary international distress frequency. On the other hand, there may not be anyone nearby, they may not be listening or they may not speak your language. Transmissions in the 8 to 12 MHz range, on frequencies guarded by the USCG or commercial radiotelephone stations always have someone standing by at the mike, but it is more of an art to hit their antenna with a strong signal.

I certainly hope the last two or three paragraphs have made you realize that one just cannot jot down a few notes from this or any other book, go to sea and hope to slam a MAYDAY into someone's ear at the flick of a switch. One must not consider the SSB a box that sends out signals. It is an instrument, like a violin, which can be played badly or well. If you want to be the King of the Airwaves you have to work at it, as does every professional "Sparks" in every merchant vessel's radio room.

SELECTING A STATION

The best way to select an optimum emergency frequency is to listen. Listen daily, at your leisure. Do not wait for the moment when the salt sea is waist heigh inside the boat to get your act together. Generally speaking, frequencies which you receive loud and clear will correspondingly provide good transmission at that time. If you adopt this strategy, long-term natural phenomena such as the sunspot cycle and seasonal changes need not be considered. If, for example, 22 MHz is nonfunctional because of reduced sun spot activity, no one will use 22 MHz and the frequency will be silent.

The optimum frequency changes during the course of the day. Higher frequencies are most effective during daylight, particularly when the sun is high in the sky. Lower and lower frequencies must be utilized as the middle of the night approaches. The time after sunrise and before sunset, when the sun's rays stream across the sky are the most unstable periods for transmission.

Higher frequencies, 16 to 22 MHz, are most effective for transmissions to stations 1,000 miles or more away. As a result, one station may be in daylight, the other in the dark. Should you elect to make an emergency transmission in this frequency range, it is important that neither station is caught in the hour before and after sunset and sunrise. Ideally, the weaker station should transmit at high noon to a more powerful station whose local time is 8 p.m. Generally speaking, the quality of transmission in this range is less consistent, and that is the reason why no distress frequencies have been allocated in it.

Emergency Transmissions: 2.182 MHz

THE RADIOTELEPHONE ALARM SIGNAL AND 2182 KHZ

A **radiotelephone automatic alarm** is an apparatus attached to the ship's main SSB transceiver (not the VHF), which responds to the international radiotelephone alarm signal on 2182 kHz. It also can generate the alarm signal when the ship is in distress and feed it to the transmitter. Once you have heard the auto alarm signal, you will never forget it. It consists of a two-tone (sinusoidal), alternating signal. One tone has a frequency of 2200 Hz and the other 1300 Hz. The signal length is 250 milliseconds with a silent interval of 10 milliseconds, repeated continuously for up to one minute. It is required SOLAS. equipment on all merchant vessels over 300 tons gross. If the vessel does not have an auto alarm, a qualified operator must listen for emergency signals 24 hours per day (fat chance of that!), unless engaged in message traffic. The auto alarm also generates the alarm signal, which it then transmitted. It has an effective range even greater than that of voice. The auto alarm functions all of the time, and is especially effective during the three-minute silent period, on the hour and half-hour, when no other radio traffic is initiated.

Emergency Transmissions: 4 to 22 MHz Range

The emergency frequencies in the four to six MHz range are 4125 kHz and 6215.5 kHz. In addition, it is legal to use any frequency in any band to attract attention in the event of an emergency. In this frequency range I have always been partial to 6215.5 kHz. This is close to the ship-ship frequency 6222 kHz, popular with deep-sea fisherman. The signal has a better range during the day but, admittedly, is not as completely reliable at night as 4.125 MHz.

SHIP-SHIP CALLING FREQUENCIES

The hailing frequencies at the top of the next page are used by ships to call each other as well as for distress and safety traffic. Most coast guard stations also guard these frequencies. As a result, there is a great likelihood that a distress message on these frequencies would be heard:

4125 kHz	12392 kHz
6221.5 kHz	16522 kHz
8257 kHz	22062 kHz

FREQUENCIES RESERVED FOR EMERGENCY TRAFFIC

FREQUENCIES RESERVED FOR EMERGENCY TRAFFIC	
FREQUENCY	**USE**
500 kHz	Radiotelegraph alarm, distress, safety & hailing frequency
2182 kHz	International ship distress frequency
3023 kHz	Mobile-Land search and rescue frequency
4125 kHz	Supplementary distress and safety frequency
5680 kHz	Aero-aero/land search and rescue frequency
6215.5 kHz	Supplementary distress and safety frequency
8364 kHz	Survival craft-aero/ship communication frequency
121.5 MHz	Aero/ship/EPIRB emergency and distress frequency
123.1 MHz	Emergency and distress frequency (aux to 121.5)
156.8 MHz	VHF (Channel 16) calling and distress frequency
243 MHz	Military ship-air emergency/distress/EPIRB frequency
406 MHz	COSPAS-SARSAT EPIRB uplink frequency

Sending an Emergency Transmission

After (if) the alarm signal is generated, the following information is broadcast by voice:

1. MAYDAY repeated three times.
2. The words "This is" followed by:
3. The name and call sign of the vessel.
4. Position in latitude and longitude.
5. Nature of the distress.
6. Number of souls aboard.
7. Assistance required.
8. Other pertinent details.

Once you have heard a MAYDAY, like the radiotelephone alarm signal, you will never forget what one sounds like. In addition to the details, there is a certain something in a person's voice when death is imminent. A MAYDAY message goes something like this:

MAYDAY, MAYDAY, MAYDAY, THIS IS THE YACHT WASP, THE YACHT WASP, THE YACHT WASP, WHISKEY ROMEO X-RAY 4434. MAYDAY POSITION: 24°30' NORTH, 161°21' WEST, WE ARE ON FIRE. FOUR SOULS ABOARD. WE ARE ON FIRE AND ABANDONING SHIP. WE HAVE A YELLOW LIFE RAFT AND AN EPIRB. THIS IS OUR LAST TRANSMISSION.

After the distress message is sent, a silent period (at least one minute) follows, to allow a response. The message is then repeated. This assumes, of course, that there is time to do so. Once the signal has been received (and acknowledged), if time permits, it is also wise to provide the following information:

> The size, color and type of vessel in distress
> The name of the captain or owner and a next-of-kin
>   (name and phone number)
> The names of the crew
> Any other information about the survival craft

In addition, if abandonment is not immediate, the rescue vessel may ask the distressed vessel to transmit a short count (1,2,3,4,5,5,4,3,2,1), or a long count (1 to ten to one), followed by call letters, to permit direction-finding stations to determine the vessel's position. This request may be repeated frequently. If the vessel must be abandoned, but there is some possibility that the it may remain afloat for awhile, the transmitter is locked into the "transmit" mode, either by locking the telegraph key in the "down" position, or adhesive taping the mike button in the "send" mode. Some radios can also be set in a "tune" mode to accomplish this. This is done to transform the radio into a direction-finding station to assist search and rescue craft.

Large ships, particularly passenger ships, have radio rooms which are manned 24 hours per day. Other vessels receive most of their radio communications via satellite radiotelephone (INMARSAT), or transmit and receive message traffic at prearranged times. Most ships have a loudspeaker in the wheelhouse, connected to the auto alarm device. If an alarm signal is sensed by the apparatus, the speaker is activated at that time. A voice transmission is of course not sensed as an emergency signal, so, in reality, a voice MAYDAY transmission has an extremely small chance of being heard on 2182. It is also worth noting that 2182, an extremely low frequency for voice transmissions by modern standards, is full of static. The noise from an open speaker on this frequency is extremely irritating and no one, unless required, listens to it.

If your boat does not have an auto alarm apparatus, you may be successful on 2182 kHz close to a coast guard listening station, 50 to 300 NM away, depending on atmospheric conditions. It is much wiser to spend your precious time transmitting on other frequencies.

Emergency Transmissions to Coast Guard, "Ham" and Commercial Stations

A list of all Coast Guard frequencies, U.S. and foreign, may be found in the *List of Radio Determination and Special Service Stations*, produced and sold by the International Telecommunications Union. If you have not forearmed yourself with this information, telephone the nearest U.S.C.G. base, prior to a voyage and obtain this information.

In general, the Coast Guard monitors ship-ship hailing frequencies and responds to the call NOVEMBER CHARLIE GOLF (NCG), MAYDAY or SECURITY transmissions. They use powerful beam antennas and may ask for a slow count to align them. They also listen to duplex hailing frequencies. Be sure you have all essential information ready before calling the Coast Guard. Be sure the information required by a MAYDAY is available, including the call sign of your radio station, the registration number of the vessel, etc.

TRANSMISSIONS TO RADIOTELEPHONE STATIONS

Distress messages may be transmitted to commercial radiotelephone stations, but, as mentioned above, a good "Sparks" routinely listens to the selected stations, talks to them and learns their ways. It is important to remember that most commercial radiotelephone stations operate on duplex channels. This means that they talk on one frequency and receive on another. Their transmitters are crystal controlled, and they usually do not have the ability to switch frequencies. So your radio must be equipped to transceive in the duplex mode to meet their requirements.

Big American stations, like Whiskey Oscar Mike (receive near Ft. Lauderdale, Florida, transmit in Ojis, Florida), Whiskey Oscar Oscar (Ocean Gate, New Jersey), Kilo Mike Iroquois (Point Reys, California) and Whiskey Lima Oscar (Mobile, Alabama) have truly awesome equipment, antennas which cover four to five acres, diesel-electric locomotives to power their transmitters and extremely qualified old-timers who know their business at the mike. Other stations, in Third World countries or on remote islands, are often not so well endowed. They may not be listening when they should, they may not speak your language or they may have switched to a different frequency. Regardless of who or where the station is located, their "Sparks" loves to talk (that's his job), and he can give you more good advice about how to send a MAYDAY in two minutes than anyone else. Call him.

The *List of Coast Stations* contains information on most licensed radio stations in the world. It is sold by the International Telecommunications Union, Place des Nations, CH1211, Geneva 20, Switzerland. The characteristics of the station's signal, its frequencies, hours of transmission, language of communication, etc., are all listed. *Coast Stations,* the *Manual for Use by the Maritime Mobile and Maritime Mobile-Satellite Services*, and *List of Radio Determination and Special Service Stations* are available by mail (at considerable cost, but their price list is free). The volumes are required texts for the long-distance cruiser.

EMERGENCY TRANSMISSIONS TO "HAM" STATIONS

Hams love to help vessels in distress. If you are receiving a ham station loud and clear and are sinking, feel free to blast right through any non-emergency traffic with your message. In addition, Hams have maritime mobile "nets" that perform countless services for mariners. In order to conduct a non-emergency conversation on an amateur frequency you are required to be a licensed amateur radio operator. If you are in distress or have a medical emergency, this requirement is waived. A sample of the available nets are below. Keep in mind that the frequencies listed below may vary a few Hertz one way or the other if the "normal" frequency is in use. For information: Downwind Marine, 2819 Canon St., San Diego, CA 92106, 619-224-2733.

NAME OF NET	FREQUENCY	TIME	DAYS
Pacific Maritime Mobile Net	14313	1700Z	Daily
Pacific Maritime Net	21404	2300Z	M-F
Baja Net (California-Mexico)	7238.5	1600Z	Daily
Sonrisa Net	3963.5	1430Z	Daily
South Pacific Net	21404	2300Z	M-F
Pacific-Indian Ocean Net	21407	0100Z	Daily
Hawaii P.M. Net	7290	0100Z	M-F
USA/Australia Net	14280	0500Z	M-F
South African Net	14320	0630Z	Daily
Mediterranean Net	14313	0900Z	Daily
Barbados Cruising Net	14265	1030Z	Daily
Southeast Asia Net	14320	1200Z	Daily
Coast Guard Maritime Mobile Net	14313	16-1700Z	M-F
Northwest (Pacific) Marine Net	3990	1900Z	Daily

Special Case Emergency Signals

REQUEST FOR SILENCE

Ship-ship frequencies, including emergency channels, are often crowded with message traffic. If it is necessary to obtain silence for emergency purposes, the signal to be transmitted by the distressed vessel or the controlling station is SILENCE MAYDAY. The signal SILENCE DISTRESS is used by other stations to impose silence. This signal is repeated as often as necessary to obtain results. When you no longer need silence, the signal given is SILENCE FINISHED or SEELONCE FEENEE (French) is repeated three times.

RECEIVING A DISTRESS MESSAGE

A distress message, when received by a boat with a low-power transmitter, should be logged immediately, but not acknowledged for a few minutes, in the hope that a ship with a more powerful transmitter will take command. Should that not occur, a response should be transmitted to the vessel in distress:

> MAYDAY, MAYDAY MAYDAY,
> ARCTIC CHALLENGER, ARCTIC CHALLENGER, ARCTIC CHALLENGER
> THIS IS SUNDANCER, SUNDANCER, SUNDANCER,
> WHISKEY ROMEO X-RAY 6792. RECEIVED MAYDAY.

If you feel it necessary, you may also ask for further information regarding:

> Number and type of survival craft
> Type of emergency radio equipment in the survival
>   craft and their working frequencies
> Name and phone number of the owner

The message is then rebroadcast on your frequency of choice, preferably directly to the USCG on one of their operating frequencies.

RELAYING A DISTRESS MESSAGE

If you wish to relay a distress message which you have received, the following signal sequence is used:

1. The words MAYDAY RELAY repeated three times.
2. The words "This is" followed by the name and call sign of your vessel, both repeated three times.
3. The message, exactly as it was received.
4. The working frequency of the distressed vessel and whether it is upper or lower sideband.
6. The word OUT.
7. The name and call sign of your vessel.

Here is an example:

MAYDAY RELAY, MAYDAY RELAY, MAYDAY RELAY.

THIS IS SUNDANCER, SUNDANCER SUNDANCER, WHISKEY ROMEO X-RAY 6792.

WE HAVE RECEIVED THE FOLLOWING TRANSMISSION FROM THE RESEARCH VESSEL, "ARCTIC CHALLENGER," ROMEO VICTOR 334:

"MAYDAY, MAYDAY, MAYDAY. THIS IS THE RV ARCTIC CHAL-LENGER ROMEO VICTOR 334. WE HAVE HIT AN ICEBERG AT 70°21 NORTH, 15°45 WEST. 63 SOULS ABOARD. WE ARE SINKING AND REQUIRE IMMEDIATE ASSISTANCE. WE STAND BY 6215.5 USB. OUT."

THIS IS SUNDANCER, WHISKEY ROMEO X-RAY 6792, OVER.

URGENCY AND SAFETY TRANSMISSIONS

Urgency transmissions concern the safety of the vessel or someone on board. This includes medical emergencies and reports that your vessel is damaged or without power but not sinking. In this case, your message, consisting of the vessel's name, call sign, position, nature of difficulty, etc., is preceded by the words PAN PAN, repeated three times.

IMPORTANT NAVIGATION, SAFETY OR METEOROLOGICAL WARNINGS

If you find it necessary to transmit important navigation or meteorological warnings, the message is transmitted on a distress frequency and is preceded by the words, "SECURITY, SECURITY, SECURITY," followed by your ship's name, call sign and the message. In international waters, SECURITY is pronounced "SECUR-E-TAY." This would be a typical SECURITY message:

SECURITY, SECURITY, SECURITY
THIS IS SUNDANCER, SUNDANCER, SUNDANCER, WHISKEY
ROMEO X-RAY 6792. WE HAVE SIGHTED A LARGE
WATERSPOUT, LOCATED NEAR FOWEY ROCK, HEADING
WEST AT ABOUT 20 MILES PER HOUR.

Radio Help for Medical Emergencies

You may obtain medical assistance by radio through the DH MEDICO program. The DH stands for Deadhead, an old railroad term meaning "a free ride." As this implies, assistance, including the telephone call, is free. DH MEDICO is a global, 24 hours a day assistance program which was started in 1921 and has saved thousands of lives. The U.S. Public Health Service handles these requests when forwarded by the Navy, Coast Guard and commercial radiotelephone stations. Virtually every maritime country in the world has a DH MEDICO program. If you must contact a MEDICO doctor who is not proficient in English, a section of The Code of Signals, reprinted in *The Ship's Medical Chest and Medical Aid at Sea,* allows you to communicate in international phonetic code.

CALLING FOR ASSISTANCE

DH MEDICO assistance can be obtained through commercial radiotelephone stations, Ham operators, or U.S. Coast Guard stations. The general call NOVEMBER CHARLIE GOLF (NCG) may be used. The message, if urgent, may be preceded by the word PAN PAN, repeated three times. The general call, CHARLIE QUEBEC (CQ) should not be used if possible.

PREPARING EMERGENCY MEDICAL INFORMATION FOR TRANSMISSION

Before calling for emergency medical advice, it is essential to make a thorough examination of the patient and write up a synopsis in the log which will subsequently be read to the DH MEDICO doctor. His reply, which should also be logged becomes a legal document. Here is an example of a typical transmission:

"I have a 31-year-old male who has been sick for five hours. He has no history of previous illness. His pulse is 95. His temperature is 37° C. He is sweating and has pain in the kidney area. The pain is severe and is increased by hand pressure. His bowels are regular, he is nauseous but is not vomiting. Over."

"Does the pain radiate to the groin and testicle? Does the patient have pain when urinating? Are his urinary functions normal? Over."

"Yes, the pain radiates to the groin and testicle. Yes, the patient has pain when urinating. He is voiding small quantities frequently. Over".'

"My probable diagnosis is kidney stones. Give a 10-milligram injection of morphine, subcutaneous injection. Let him drink water freely. Apply a hot water bottle to the kidney region. How long before you make port? Over."

"I understand. I expect to make port in three days. Over."

"You may give the patient morphine every six hours for pain, if needed. Have the patient see a doctor when you arrive in port. If his condition deteriorates, call us again and we will consider medical evacuation by helicopter. Over."

"I understand. Roger. Thank you for your help."

THE IMPORTANCE OF KNOWING YOUR POSITION

A vessel's position may be indicated four ways: (1) by latitude and longitude; (2) by a speed, time, and course from a latitude and longitude; (3) by a bearing and distance-off a well-known object; and, (4) by loran lines. Of the three, latitude and longitude are the best, for they tell the story without the possibility of confusion.

Long distance cruisers usually plot their position several times per day and the prudent ones also log the latitude and longitude. But in an emergency there may be no time to plot the present position, and so they might say:

"At 1400 hours Zulu we were at 24°31 North, 161°30 West. Our course has been 285° True at 8 knots for 3 hours."

You can see how a message of this type could cause confusion. It would be better to say:

"Our position is 24 miles, 285° true from 24°31 North, 161°30 West."

Boat operators who work 'longshore usually do not think in terms of latitude and longitude. They usually give bearings like this:

"This is the LAUGHING LADY, we're three miles East of Fowey light."

In an emergency situation it is better to phrase the message like this:

"This is LAUGHING LADY, Whiskey Delta Tango 4434. Our position is nine zero degrees magnetic, three miles from Fowey Rock."

Since transmission of your last position is of ultimate importance in a disaster, the conscientious master makes a point of logging his position hourly, or at the end of every watch.

Emergency Position Indicating Radiobeacon (EPIRB)

An EPIRB is a small radio transmitter which emits a homing signal when it is activated. It is the marine equivalent of the Emergency Locater Transmitter (ELT), which is standard equipment on commercial aircraft. **In addition to a life raft, an EPRIB is the most essential piece of survival equipment you can possess**. It sends your chances of a prompt rescue zooming upward, and a prompt rescue is the equivalent of lives saved. Without it, your disaster may go unnoticed for weeks or months.

The EPIRB in common use by most U.S. boats, called an A or (usually) **B-class EPIRB**, generates a signal on 121.5 and 243 MHz. These are aircraft emergency frequencies monitored by all commercial (121.5 MHz) and military (243 MHz) aircraft as well as by satellite (in most Northern hemisphere areas). An A or B EPIRB generates a 50- to 100-milliwatt, continuous signal of a duration determined by battery size, usually at least 48 hours, if, of course, the battery is not old and expired.

EPIRB DETECTION BY AIRCRAFT

Like a VHF radio, an EPIRB generates a line-of-sight signal. The range at which an aircraft can receive an EPIRB signal is therefore a function of its altitude. Low-flying aircraft, at an altitude of, say, 10,000 feet can detect the signal at a distance of 115 NM. Modern jets, crossing an ocean at 35,000' would be capable of receiving a signal at a distance of 215 NM. Like merchant ships, civilian aircraft follow great circle routes from point to point. Their paths are shown on aero charts.

Aero charts are particularly useful for the castaway, since they show these routes and because they are much more compact than nautical charts. They also indicate the frequency and call sign of aero beacons, heights of dominant mountains and point-to-point distances.

THE SEARCH AND RESCUE SATELLITE SYSTEM

In addition to aircraft, EPIRB and ELT signals are received by low polar orbiting **COSPAS/SARSAT satellites** which complete an orbit in about 105 minutes. The advantage of a low polar orbiting satellite is that it "sees" the entire globe every 12 hours, but, since so much area is covered, contact time with any one spot is quite short. To improve response time, at least three satellites are in continuous orbit. This satellite array permits **an average detection time of about one hour at mid-latitudes and even less in the higher latitudes**, where a hostile survival environment makes quick response more important. Several satellite passes are necessary to determine the transmitter's position.   This takes an average time of **two hours**, but may require **six hours** in the worst case.

SARSAT stands for Search and Rescue Satellite-Aided Tracking and COSPAS is the same thing in Russian. Correspondingly, some of the satellites have been produced and are operated by the U.S., others by Russia. We will call all of them SARSATs. The SARSAT system is an international project funded and operated by Canada, France, the U.S.A. and Russia. A number of other nations are either in the process of joining the consortium or are studying the system's effectiveness. Since its inception in 1982, the system has been credited with saving more than 1000 lives. Considering how much money has been spent by these same nations to develop the technology of mass destruction, it is an irony that so very much money has been spent to save so few.

The location of a transmitting distress beacon is determined by the Doppler-shift technique. As the satellite rushes toward the transmitter, the frequency of the signal seems higher. As it passes over or adjacent to the beacon, the signal seems to be "on frequency," and as the satellite moves away, the frequency seems to decrease. This is analogous to the changing sound of a train whistle as the train rushes past. This information and the time of its receipt are down-linked from the satellite to the nearest ground station, called a **Local User Terminal** (LUT).

MAJOR SHORT-COMING OF THE SYSTEM

Signals generated on 121.5 and 243 MHz are down-linked from the satellite immediately. The satellite has no signal memory or storage capacity. As a result, the satellite must "see" both the emergency transmitter and a ground station simultaneously, otherwise the signal is lost. The new 406 MHz system, not yet fully implemented, will have global capacity.

Note that there is absolutely no coverage of the Southern hemisphere. Some parts of the North Atlantic and Pacific are not covered. The Indian Ocean has no coverage at all. Distressed vessels transmitting emergency signals in these areas would have to rely on aircraft to receive their signal. If the disaster occurred beyond satellite coverage and more than 200 NM from an aircraft route, the chance of of the signal being detected would be extremely remote.

OTHER SHORTCOMINGS OF THE SYSTEM

EPIRB signals (121.5 & 243 MHz) are extremely low powered and can be contaminated with random noise, harmonic interference from data transmitters, from voice transmissions and solar storms. When strong interference exists, the emergency signal may be suppressed below the threshold of the signal processor. Identification of individual signals on 121.5 and 243 MHz is also slowed by the presence of simultaneous broadcasts, and this is a very common problem, since emergency beacons are often accidently activated and continue to function for days at a time. In addition, killer storms often produce simultaneous disasters resulting in multiple transmissions.

EMERGENCY BEACON CHARACTERISTICS

Frequency	121.5 & 243 MHz	406 MHz
Transmitter Power	50-100 Milliwatt	5 Watt
Transmission Life	48 hours minimum	48 hours minimum
Duty Cycle	Continuous	1 to 1.5%
Modulation Type	AM-Amplitude modulated	PM- Phase Modulated
Message	Analog	Digital
Signal Repetition	Continuous	about 0.5 sec./ 50 sec.
Location Accuracy	10-20 KM	2-5 KM
Coverage	See chart	Global

SEARCH AND RESCUE MISSION CONTROL

Each of the participating countries has a **Mission Control Center** which forwards information to local **Rescue Coordination Centers** where the decision on how to best handle the problem is made. When survivors have been located, a data marker, usually in the form of a radio beacon, but occasionally a smoke signal (if rescue is imminent) is dropped to mark the area. Other aircraft or surface vessels are routed to the survival craft after it has been located.

THE EPIRB

All EPIRBs are waterproof and have an on-off switch, a test switch and an "in operation" indicator light. Others come with a variety of options, including speech mode, for talking to SAR vessels. Most (Types A and B) transmit on both 121.5 MHz and some also generate a 243 MHz signal at the same time. EPIRBS are manufactured with a variety of batteries, each with a specified shelf life. Some use conventional batteries, but others have "long life" batteries which last 5-10 years. The unit usually continues to function after the battery expiration date, but it should nevertheless be returned for a new battery and recalibration after expiration. If a boat has one EPIRB, it is usually stored in the survival pack, rather than the raft, so that it is easily accessible for testing and use. An EPIRB (as well as a radar reflector) can be used to help guide rescue craft in the event of a medical emergency. If cash permits, a second unit containing a long life (ten year) lithium battery can be packed in the raft.

Class A EPIRBs are required aboard all ocean-going vessels that travel more than 20 NM from harbor. They can be manually activated but must also be able to float free in the event of a sudden sinking, automatically extend their antennas and begin transmission. They are therefore more versatile than class B units but cost more.

Class B EPIRBs are for voluntary carriage by non inspected vessels such as pleasure craft and fishing boats. It is not mandatory that the unit float, but a flotation collar is usually (not always) provided if it does not. These units begin automatic transmission if floating, but the antenna must be manually deployed. Both A and B class units transmit on 121.5 and 243 MHz.

PROPER USE OF AN EPIRB

An EPIRB has a short antenna which must be deployed or extended prior to use. The unit is activated by removing the switch guard and turning the unit on . Some EPIRBs come with a flotation collar and the unit will function floating in the water if no other option is available.

An EPIRB should be activated and left "on" to effect rescue. Turning the unit off periodically to save the battery destroys the effective reception of the signal and the homing capability of SAR vessels.

OTHER TYPES OF EPIRBS

Class C EPIRBs are VHF/FM transmitters which operate on channels 15 and 16. Class C EPIRBs generate a 1.5 second alert signal on channel 16, followed by a 15 second homing signal on Channel 15. Both signals are similar to the international two-tone alarm signal described earlier in this chapter. Like all EPIRBS, Type C's transmit line-of-sight distances, but neither commercial aircraft nor satellites are equipped to receive their signals. Considering their short range, about 2.5 miles from a life raft (plus the range of the receiving vessel, based on antenna height), they may be considered lake or 'longshore units, to be used within 20 NM of a USCG facility. The fact that few captains (other than USCG officers) know what a class C EPIRB sounds like further reduces their utility.

THE 406 EPIRB

The 406 MHz EPIRB, not yet available for private vessels in the United States, is an up grading and considerable improvement over existing models. It transmits a signal which can be stored by SARSAT, then downlinked when in view of an earth station, so the system has global capacity. Position of 121.5 and 243 MHz signals are determined by earth-based computers. The "406" signal position is computed by the satellite. Several satellite passes are necessary to provide a position fix with an accuracy of about 20 km.

The 406 generates a periodic emergency signal which is about ten times more powerful than the older models, making the signal easier to discriminate from background noise. Each unit can be individually programmed with a ship identifier code, and this makes it easier for the Rescue Coordination Center to respond appropriately. The 406 can also be programmed by the ship's navigator to provide digital information regarding last charted position, making it easier to respond swiftly in the event of simultaneous emergency signals. The major disadvantage of the 406 is its price, which is five to seven times the cost of the existing units.

A TYPICAL EPIRB RESCUE

The rescue of the crew of the trimaran ATLANTA, off the coast of San Diego in January, 1988 is a classic case of castaways being saved by an EPIRB. The 42-foot multihull capsized in hurricane force winds and 50' seas. The two persons aboard, Joe and Jan DeJulius took their EPIRB and swam out of the overturned hull. They sat on the trimaran's cross-beam, lashed by huge 53° F. seas, then activated their recently serviced EPIRB.

Because of the bad weather and their exposed position on the overturned hull, the EPIRB antenna was under water so often the signals were not recognized as such by SAR computers until the seas calmed, two days later. At that point, radio dishes at USAF bases in Alaska and at Scott Air Force Base picked up the down-linked signal.

Unknown to the DeJulius' they had been spotted by a USCG Falcon jet, which homed on their EPIRB signal at 2 a.m.. A second Falcon jet returned at wave-top level at first light, dropped smoke markers and told them, through a powerful loud-speaker, that help would arrive within an hour. Shortly thereafter, a USCG Dolphin helicopter, using the USCG 210 Cutter RESOLUTE as a refueling platform, located the couple and winched them aboard. The DeJulius' survival suits and EPIRB saved them after a 66-hour ordeal in the cold Pacific. Read more about this rescue in Chapter XIX.

Receiving Weather Warnings by Radio

Listening for weather warnings is an essential part of being a prudent mariner. The National Bureau of Standards provides this information and time signals on 5, 10 and 15 MHz through its stations, WWV and WWVH. WWV, in Fort Collins Colorado broadcasts North Atlantic and North Pacific (East of 140 W.) weather warnings at 8,10 and 12 minutes after the hour. WWVH in Hawaii broadcasts weather warnings for the North and South Pacific at 47, 49 and 50 minutes past the hour. These are powerful stations that can usually be heard. Set an alarm to ring a few minutes before the announcement, so that your receiver can be turned on and stabilized before the message, which is given in a concise manner, is transmitted. It is wise to record their message, then write down the part which pertains to you.

A full list of stations which broadcast weather is found in the *List of Radio Determination and Special Service Stations*, and in the US government publication *CFR Title 46*. Included in both is a list of USCG High Seas broadcasts.

Illustration from *Rage to Survive* by Jaques Vignes © 1975, by permission of
William Morrow & Co., Inc.

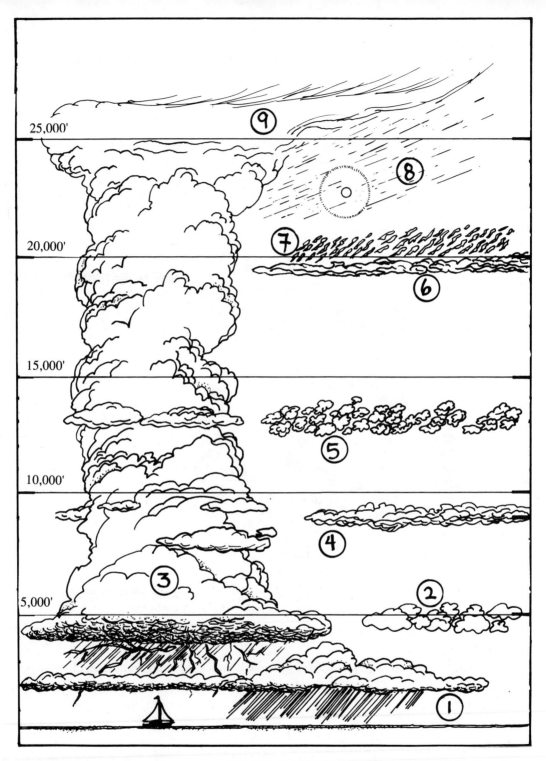

(1) Nimbostratus rain clouds, a low, sold gray layer often accompanied by "scud" (2) Cumulus, puffy "trade wind" clouds (3) Cumulonimbus "thunderheads" (4) Stratocumulus (5) Altocumulus (6) Altostratus, white puffs, possibly becoming a solid layer, heralding rain or snow (7) Cirrocumulus "mackerel sky" (8) Cirrostratus "torn gauze strips," may cause sun halo (9) Cirrus "mare's tails" blown with high wind or "anvil head" on a thunderhead top

CHAPTER XV: OCEANS AND SURVIVAL

Predicting   the   Weather

I am one of those sailors who thinks that dark clouds, high winds and short, steep seas are a prediction of bad weather. I confess to listening to my bones, watching for an ominous cross-swell, noticing that the sea birds have disappeared. I started messing around, like a fool, with small boats in the days when a High Seas, SSB receiver was too big and power-consumptive to carry aboard a boat. I had a 125-watt AM transceiver, full of tubes and heaters, as big as a backpack, that dimmed the lights, even on "receive." As a result, it was necessary to rely on the same sensory data which sailors used for millennia to make predictions.

For a long time, before I learned how to use an aneroid barometer, I sailed with one made from shark liver. A small amount of finely chopped shark liver was added to a pop bottle full of shark oil. The bottle was hung by a cord from its neck. I suppose the bits of liver had air trapped in them which expanded or contracted, depending on barometric pressure. On a good day, the liver remained in a layer near the bottom. When the bits of liver began to rise, it was a sure sign of a blow. My bones, the shark oil barometer and the rising gale were what I called a prediction. My predictions were not much worse than one I received from a port captain. I asked what he thought the weather would be. He stepped up to the window, binoculars in hand, looked out and said, "Bueno, bueno, muy bueno."

One day, while just about in the middle of the Atlantic Ocean, the liver in the shark oil barometer rose in an ominous column. Shortly thereafter, I sailed through my first hurricane. After that, I decided that it might be best if I learned a bit more about weather prediction. I bought a High Seas radio (they became much smaller after the invention of the transistor). Confusion still reigned, but there was sometimes less of it.

The well-found bluewater cruiser should be armed with a FAX or at least a high seas receiver, a tape recorder and a barometer A weather forecast should be recorded, then replayed several times. Most of the time these reports accurately describe what is happening around you. Sometimes you will be fighting to reef, in your own postage stamp-sized piece of hell, while elsewhere all is allegedly delightful. Sometimes a predicted low will suddenly intensify, trapping the unwary. Sometimes a fast-moving front will create line squalls, catching everyone unaware. Only the great, well-developed, killer storms are tracked with a high degree of accuracy. So the weather report, the cross-swell, your bones, your instincts, the falling glass and the rising gale must all be given consideration.

In a survival craft, it is rare that a barometer or a radio is available. Predictions must be based on the same information that sailors used for thousands of years before the invention of these instruments. In addition, there is very little that can be done to avoid whatever weather is sweeping toward you. So the main points of interest for a survivor are: where am I being taken, is a storm coming and when will it rain? The following description of weather patterns has these needs in mind.

What is Weather?

The interrelationship between the atmosphere and the sea is endless. Heat from the atmosphere drives currents of the ocean, which in turn release heat, creating winds and weather. Changing atmospheric patterns affect current flow which, in turn, determines how much heat is released to the air—which determines cloud cover. Clouds, caused by atmospheric cooling, affect how much heat is given up by the sea. The changing temperatures associated with the seasons, day and night and sun spot activity also contribute to a turbulent, swirling atmosphere. It's a complex, not very stable (or predictable) system, fully capable of reversals, convulsive jerks—of being every mean thing it can be.

CONVECTION CELLS AND RAIN

Vertical wind patterns are caused by heating and cooling at the interface between the air and sea. The surface of the earth (both land and water) is always warmer than the upper atmosphere. Air warmed and humidified at the surface rises and cools, condensing at 2-5,000 feet into puffy little **cumulus clouds.** They are quite dynamic, constantly changing shape and appear to be fast-moving because they exist in a layer at low altitude. Often called cotton clouds, cotton candy or **Trade Wind clouds,** cumulus are associated with settled weather. When the air in the cloud has cooled sufficiently, it sinks back to earth. The system is called a **convection cell,** and in settled weather, these cells operate over vast areas.

How a cumulonimbus convection cell developes. Drawing by Rafael Monroy.

When the air is calm and moist, a cumulus cloud often grows and rises. The underside becomes flat and dark with moisture. Rain frequently begins to fall, and the cloud is now called a **cumulonimbus** or **thunderhead**. A cumulonimbus cloud sucks up surface moisture, which cools as it rises, finally condensing into **rain.**

When the surrounding air is warm, moist and unstable, a cumulonimbus cloud may rise in a towering column to as much as 65,000 feet. At that height it hits the stratosphere where the cloud's condensation is blown away, creating the famous **anvil-head pattern.** The column is a fully developed cumulonimbus cloud, but the wispy anvil-head, blown away by high winds, is a **cirrus** top. Powerful up and down drafts, thunderstorms, hail, shifting winds and **rain** are associated with towering cumulonimbus clouds.

Sailors who are short of water often chase these clouds, which is a merry sport if you're not dying of thirst. Since they typically move at about 25 mph, an actual chase is impossible. The vessel must be placed on a collision course to be successful. The best way to chase thunderheads is to observe a cloud from afar and determine its direction of movement by bearings and the slant of rain. Local winds vary around these formations and are an unreliable indicator of the cloud's track.

A dark, tubular "**roll cloud**" usually forms beneath the forward edge of a thunderhead. If the cumulonimbus cloud is producing rain, it will be visible just behind the roll cloud. This cloud is visibly turbulent and is sometimes quite scary. Much can be told about the trouble to come from the nature of the roll cloud and the agitated state of the sea beneath it. It's one of those natural phenomena which tells you immediately just how scared to be. When you can see the sea beneath the roll cloud, you are about one to two miles away and the face will arrive in about three minutes.

A thunderhead can reach a diameter of five to ten miles and affect the wind four to six miles from its edge. Wind flows toward it until about a mile from the face, then one encounters light variables. As the "nose" of cold air beneath the cloud approaches, the wind increases, sometimes going from a calm to as much as 50 knots in a few seconds, blowing from the cloud. Rain, if there is any, follows almost immediately. Within a minute or two the wind drops, usually by at least half, and, as the rain decreases, it becomes quite calm.

If the cloud produces lightning, its distance-off can be determined with great accuracy. Since sound travels at a bit more than 1,000'/sec., the number of seconds between the flash and the bang can be multiplied by 1,000' to give distance.

DOWNBURSTS

Downbursts are, if anything, more common and nastier than line squalls. They are at their worst when they are clear weather phenomena, but, like line squalls, they often give warning with **curtains of rain**. No one completely understands what causes downbursts, but they seem to be severe downdrafts of cold, dense air from very high altitudes. They are invariably **associated with towering cumulonimbus clouds**, a relatively stable barometer and otherwise stable winds. It is not uncommon to see the wind go from a calm to 64 knots in a minute. The fact that they last from a few seconds to a few minutes does nothing to mitigate their destructiveness. A downburst is undoubtedly what sank the PRIDE OF BALTIMORE, and many other vessels have fallen victim to them. In the case of the PRIDE, a line of dark clouds rapidly approached, Captain Elsaesser ordered sails to be taken in and started to bear off the wind. Before he could accomplish either, the winds increased from 30 to 90 knots in about 20 seconds and caught the ship. The PRIDE rolled over, filled with water and sank in less than two minutes.

CLOUDS AND THEIR MEANING

Clouds are man's oldest weather predicting tool. They are by no means a certain indicator of what is to come—but then, nothing is. **cirrus clouds,** sometimes called **mare's tails,** for example, are high clouds and often herald an approaching depression, but they can also mean nothing more than a possible increase in surface wind. In some areas cirrus clouds mean bad weather, in others, good weather. We are interested only in clouds that are rather reliable indicators of what is to come. The others have been omitted from this discussion.

Clouds are classified into low, medium and high, depending on the altitude of their bases. Cumulonimbus are, for example, classified as low cloud, even though their tops may reach the stratosphere.

HIGH CLOUDS

In addition to cirrus, **high, wispy cirrostratus clouds** look like torn veils or wind-blown strips of gauze. They are sometimes quite thin and transparent, consisting entirely of ice crystals, causing a haze or halo around the sun. They usually approach from the west to northwest in the northern hemisphere (N) or east to southeast in the southern hemisphere (S), precede the front by as much as 1,000 miles (24 to 30 hours of warning) and are aligned with the direction of the advancing front. Keep in mind that cirrostratus clouds indicate change and are not an automatic sign of rain or bad weather. **If cirrostratus clouds are not continuous and do not increase, the front center will pass to the south (Northern Hemisphere).**

MEDIUM CLOUDS

Altostratus are one of the most reliable heralds of rain. They are a gray, featureless, layer of mid-level clouds which cover all or most of the sky. They are created when warm air flows up over cold air. Sometimes they become dense enough to produce rain by themselves, although the rain, if light, may evaporate in the cool, dry air beneath the cloud before it reaches the sea. If the cloud layer progresses and thickens, **rain or snow is soon to follow.** Prudent mariners consider altostratus an indicator of rain or snow, poor visibility and high seas to come.

LOW CLOUDS

In addition to cumulus and cumulonimbus, **nimbostratus** are low-level clouds which arrive as a gray, featureless layer, completely obscuring the sun from which prolonged rain usually follows. They are not much good as weather predictors, because they are the cloud a prediction is supposed to predict. A nimbostratus layer usually extends hundreds of miles horizontally and 3,000 to 6,000 feet vertically. Near the center of a depression nimbostratus clouds may extend up to the highest part of the atmosphere.

Nimbostratus clouds are often accompanied by **fractostratus** clouds also called **scud.** The upper portion of a nimbostratus cloud contains ice crystals and these are necessary to form rain. As the cold rain falls from the cloud and hits warmer air, some of it evaporates and scud is formed.

Scud looks like very low wisps of cotton and, if the wind is high, it takes on a torn appearance. Scud, associated with nimbostratus cloud, has no particular meaning, other than the possible confirmation of wind. But sometimes scud appears as if by magic and is associated with **line squalls.**

HORIZONTAL MOVEMENT OF AIR

The wind pattern near shore is affected during the morning and evening hours when the land is experiencing rapid temperature change. This is called the **land effect.** Wind flows toward the land in the morning as it heats up, causing rising thermals. As the land cools off in the evening, it cools the air above it, causing it to condense, shed its dew, and flow like water down the hills and out to sea. The land effect is important to castaways. Read more about it in Chapter XIII.

The offshore sea temperature remains relatively constant, varying slowly with the seasons. As a result, major wind systems prevail over the oceans. They are powerfully driven by rotational effects and resist local phenomena. Ocean currents in the few feet of water upon which a survival craft floats are affected by all but the lightest breezes. In prevailing conditions, the survival craft will crab toward the right or left of the wind direction as a result of **Ekman layer phenomena** (explained on page 399), and this will not be apparent by visual observation. Even though current diagrams may, for example, show a westward flow, a contrary breeze and wave pattern will do much to nullify the prevailing current's effect on survival craft drift.

Since the earth rotates, one would expect the winds to seemingly flow from the east. Several physical forces create distortions. The wind wants to flow in a straight line, but the earth's motion makes it appear as though it had a curved trajectory in the same way that the sun appears to rise and set. This is why a rocket's path seems to be curved, even though the vehicle is moving in a straight line.

The **Corilois effect** is a description of the effects of angular momentum on wind patterns. **The Corilois force acts at right angles to the wind and is in direct proportion to its velocity.** In the Northern hemisphere, the force appears to come from the right side (and from the left, below the equator), facing the wind. This is why the wind appears to flow in a clockwise direction in the Northern Hemisphere and counterclockwise in the south. The **Ekman phenomena**, also caused by angular momentum, powerfully drives ocean currents.

The charts which follow show world wind patterns during summer and winter. The important thing to remember about wind charts is that they are merely descriptive of a general pattern. If one released a balloon, it is highly unlikely that it would follow the smooth pattern depicted on the chart. Planning a precise landfall using a pilot chart as a guide will usually result in disappointment.

The great ocean wind systems (with the exception of the monsoon) are circular in movement, moving around a high of cool, dry air. Wind spirals outward from a high in a clockwise direction (Northern Hemisphere), and counterclockwise into a low. So storms or hurricanes (an intense low pressure cell containing high winds) rotate in a **counterclockwise** direction in the Northern and **clockwise** in the Southern hemispheres.

"Here comes another big one, Roy, and here — we — gooooooowheeeeeeeooo!"

From *The Far Side* 1985 © Universal Press Syndicate, reprinted with permission. All rights reserved.

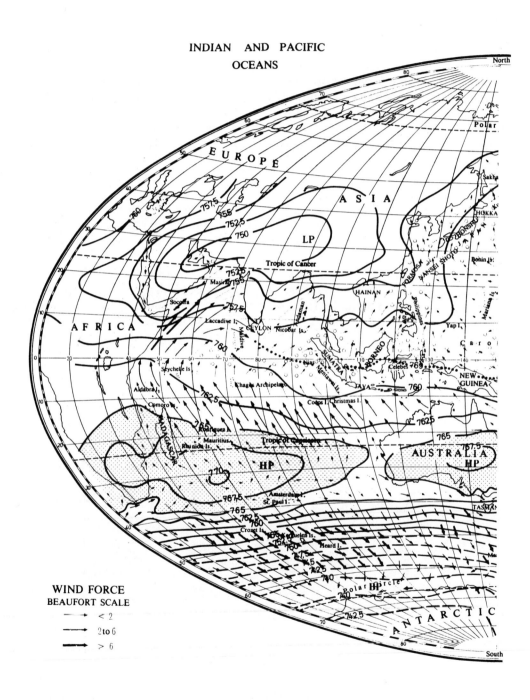

INDIAN   AND   PACIFIC
OCEANS

WIND FORCE
BEAUFORT SCALE
    →   < 2
    ⟶   2 to 6
    ➤   > 6

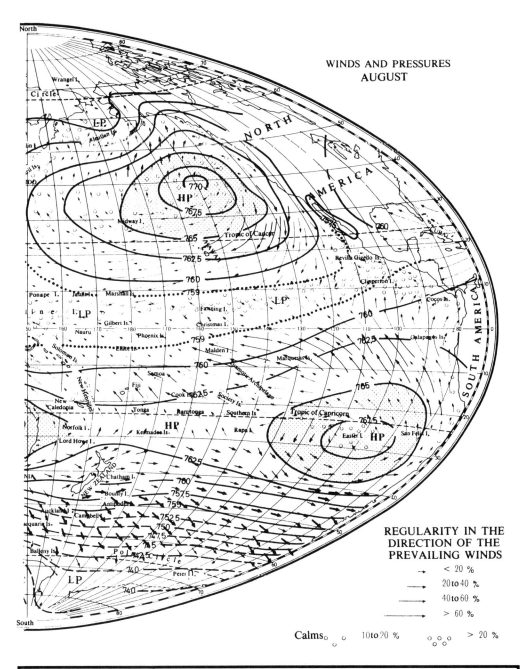

WINDS AND PRESSURES
AUGUST

REGULARITY IN THE
DIRECTION OF THE
PREVAILING WINDS

→   < 20 %
⟶   20 to 40 %
⟶   40 to 60 %
⟶   > 60 %

Calms ○ ○   10 to 20 %   ○ ○ ○   > 20 %

From: *Descriptive Regional Oceanography* by P. Tchernia (originally from Schott, 1935-44).
Courtesy of Museum National D'Historie Natuerelle, Laboratoire d'Oceanographie Physique.

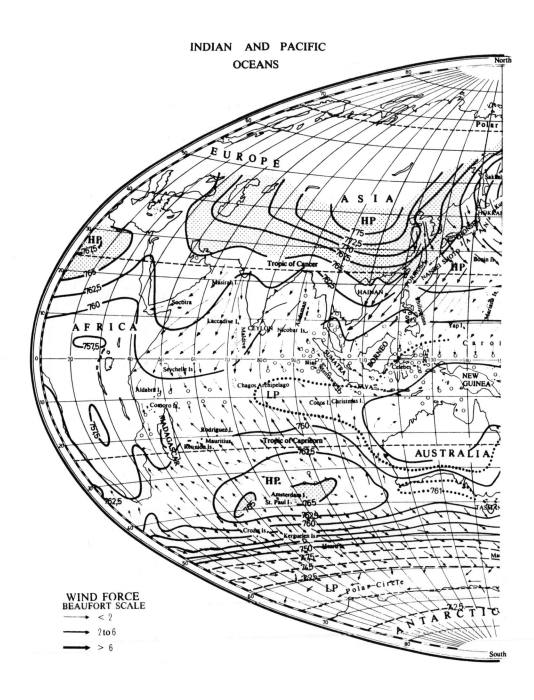

INDIAN   AND   PACIFIC
OCEANS

WIND FORCE
BEAUFORT SCALE
⟶ < 2
⟶ 2 to 6
⟶ > 6

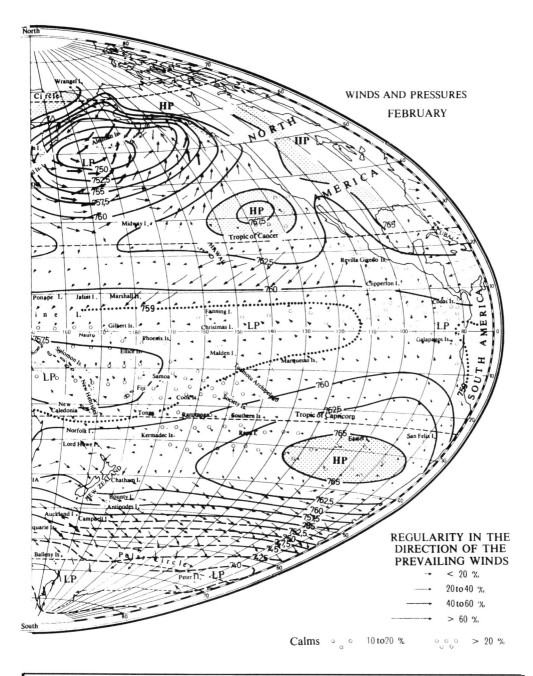

WINDS AND PRESSURES
FEBRUARY

REGULARITY IN THE
DIRECTION OF THE
PREVAILING WINDS

→   < 20 %
→   20 to 40 %
→   40 to 60 %
→   > 60 %

Calms   ∘ ∘   10 to 20 %   ∘ ∘ ∘   > 20 %

From: *Descriptive Regional Oceanography* by P. Tchernia (originally from Schott, 1935-44).
Courtesy of Museum National D'Historie Natuerelle, Laboratoire d'Oceanographie Physique.

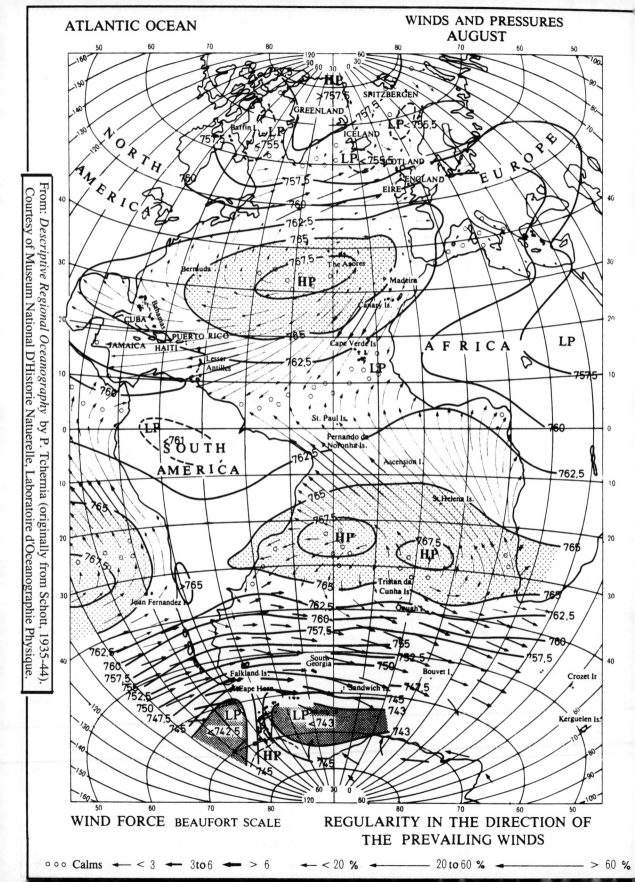

ATLANTIC OCEAN

WINDS AND PRESSURES
AUGUST

From: *Descriptive Regional Oceanography* by P. Tchemia (originally from Schott, 1935–44).
Courtesy of Museum National D'Historie Natuerelle, Laboratoire d'Oceanographie Physique.

WIND FORCE BEAUFORT SCALE

REGULARITY IN THE DIRECTION OF
THE PREVAILING WINDS

∘∘∘ Calms   ← < 3   ← 3 to 6   ← > 6   ← < 20 %   ← 20 to 60 %   ← > 60 %

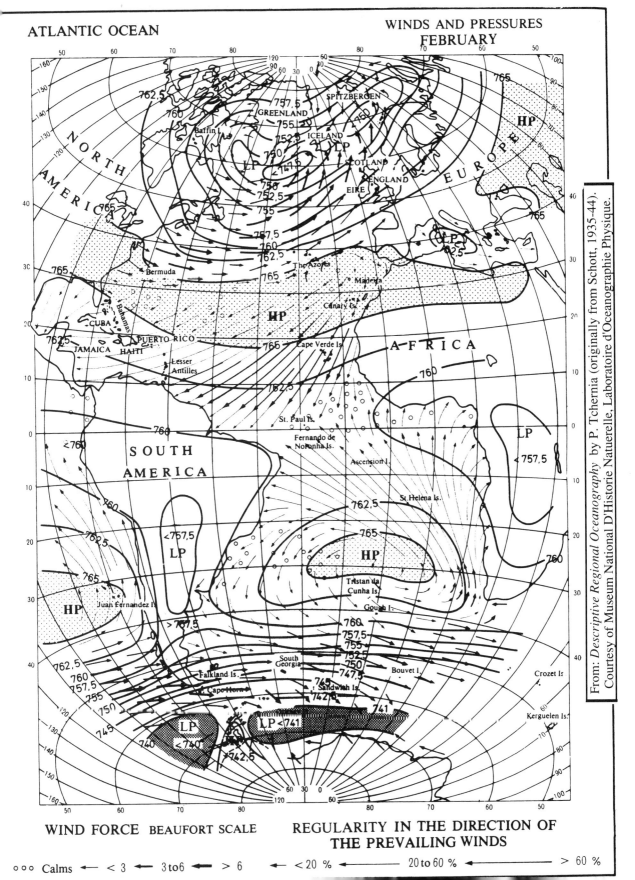

ATLANTIC OCEAN

WINDS AND PRESSURES
FEBRUARY

WIND FORCE BEAUFORT SCALE

REGULARITY IN THE DIRECTION OF
THE PREVAILING WINDS

○ ○ ○ Calms ← < 3 ← 3 to 6 ← > 6   ← < 20 % ← 20 to 60 % ← > 60 %

From: *Descriptive Regional Oceanography* by P. Tchernia (originally from Schott, 1935-44).
Courtesy of Museum National D'Historie Natuerelle, Laboratoire d'Oceanographie Physique.

FRONTS

Since a shipwreck survivor usually does not have a barometer or weather report, he must rely solely on knowledge and his senses to forecast the weather. Researching wind, current, and seasonal patterns before a voyage is considered normal procedure. Understanding weather patterns in the vessel's cruising area is important. So is data derived from the senses. These include a sense of humidity and temperature, and an awareness of swell patterns and cross swells. The wise captain, having both knowledge and a current weather report can do much to prevent inclement weather from overwhelming his vessel, so a certain minimum amount of advice to boat owners experiencing severe conditions is included in this section. The discussion below has been designed to give the castaway the most general, reliable advice around which his strategy can be planned. Survival craft are not fast enough to avoid bad weather, but a basic understanding of how weather is generated can indicate what is to come.

The sloping convergence between two air masses of different densities and temperatures is called a **front**. A warm front has warm, moist, low pressure air behind it and a cold front's passage brings dry air, lower temperatures, and high pressure. The term "front" is an old one, associated with war, and this aptly describes what is happening at the face of a front. A front is a place of rapid temperature and pressure change, rising thermals and strong, shifting winds. Strong fronts are usually confined to the areas from 30° north or south of the equator, to the poles, but this is certainly not a rule. Fronts are strongest in winter, when cold polar air spirals into warmer latitudes.

Rapidly advancing cold air, since it is more dense, undermines slower-moving, warm, lighter air. The slope of advance is rapid, downward, and about four times as steep as a warm front, making cold fronts appear to be rising walls of cloud. A warm front, advancing on a weakened mass of slower, cool air is pushed upward, on top of the denser mass. The clouds appear to lower.

COLD FRONTS

Cold fronts are more severe in the temperate and higher latitudes than in the tropics. Above 38° North and South (particularly from 50 to 60° N and S), they can be real killers. Sometimes a particularly potent cold front will reach as far south as Miami (25°N), occasionally bringing snow. The first indications of a cold front are a towering wall of **cumulonimbus**, advancing (seeming to rise)

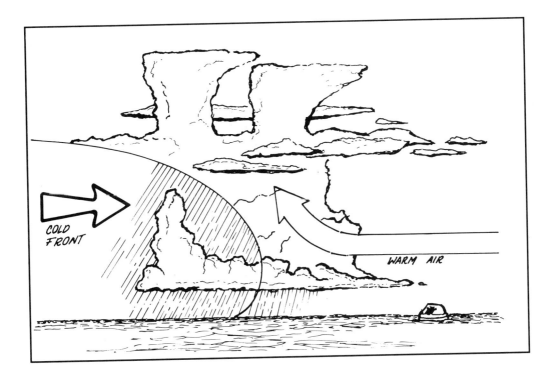

The cross-section of a cold front. Drawing by Rafael Monroy

with the wind. When the dark, solid mass of **nimbostratus and Stratus clouds** can be seen at the base, the front is not far away. The air ahead of the front is warm and moist; behind it, it is cool and dry. Regardless of where the prevailing wind is coming from, the local wind will shift (sometimes as much as 90°) and come from the face of the front as it arrives. The frontal passage results in high pressure, gradually decreasing wind, and eventually a brilliant, cloudless sky, which is found in the center of a high.

    In the Northern Hemisphere, cold fronts (in contrast to actual depressions) usually move in a broad, curved sweep toward the east or South-east. In the Southern hemisphere, a cold front sweeps toward the east or northeast. A cold front advances 12 to 50 mph. Its speed and therefore its intensity can be judged by the speed with which the clouds advance. Cold fronts and their associated highs are more pronounced in winter than in summer. The sequence of events preceding the passage of a cold front are described on the next page (the direction of the pattern is reversed in the Southern Hemisphere).

COLD FRONT SEQUENCE, NORTHERN (N) HEMISPHERE

The wind backs 12 to 15 degrees and freshens. The sky begins to darken with altostratus clouds, then nimbostratus. The wind increases and it begins to rain. As the face of the front arrives, the wind veers northwest to north. Squall activity increases. Heavy rain often flattens seas but wind-against-current creates a steep, vicious chop. When the front passes, the torrential rain ceases, the gusty wind slowly backs (counterclockwise) and moderates. Squalls continue. Sea state varies locally. Visibility improves. Lower temperatures, clearing, and steady wind follow, slowly decreasing in velocity,. Cumulonimbus and finally cumulus clouds appear.

SUMMARY OF EVENTS ASSOCIATED WITH A COLD FRONT		
Before front	**During Passage**	**After Passage**
Weathe: rain, thunder	heavy rain, thunder, and sometimes hail.	heavy rain, then showers then fair.
Clouds: altocumulus or altostratus, then nimbostratus, and squalls	nimbostratus and scud	lifting clouds. culumonimbus or cumulus
Wind: increasing backs, freshens (N) veers, freshens (N)	sudden clockwise shift NW-W (N) SW-SSW (S) very squally	gusty, backing (N) veering WSW (S)
Temp.: steady	sudden drop	slow drop
Visibil.: poor	poor, then better	good except in rain

LINE SQUALLS

An intense cold front may be preceded by a phenomena called a line squall, which can be extremely dangerous if one is caught unprepared. In some cases, a series of intense disassociated squalls advance, paralleling each other within a narrow zone of extreme instability. This is called line squall which arrives 40 to 300 miles ahead of the front. It is a truly vicious phenomena, extremely fast-moving (up to 70 mph), and contains most of the wind and rain normally found in the front itself. A line squall is a sort of shock-wave, caused by sudden forward surges of a rapidly advancing cold front. Line squalls form, approach and disburse suddenly, leaving a swath of damaged boats behind to be further dismembered by the approaching front.

Line squalls usually contain rain, sometimes hail, and are therefore visible on radar. Visually, a typical line squall seems to be a wall of boiling black cloud, rising from the sea. Even if you never saw one before, or never heard the name "line squall," you would know you were in trouble when you saw one of these.

Sometimes a clear-weather line squall comes seemingly out of nowhere and assaults the boat. Since most line squalls contain rain, a few minutes warning is provided by (1) thin, sparkling sheets of rain appearing to be generated by insignificant, but dark, thin lines of scud, easily distinguished from the slight showers generated from cumulus clouds. When (2) disturbances on the ocean become visible, the front is two to three miles away and will arrive in

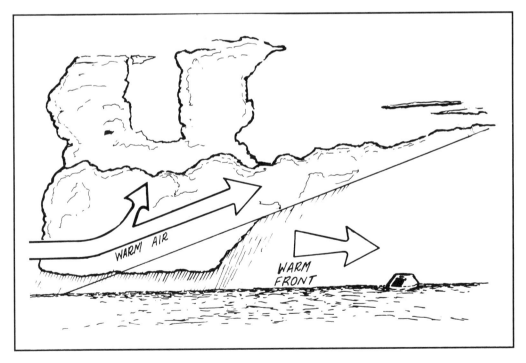

Cross-section of a warm front. Drawing by Rafael Monroy.

less than one minute. When you see these two warnings, act decisively. Do not procrastinate or it might bc your last procrastination. Be prepared to drop sail and motor into the wind, or drop the mainsail and run with the jib. Line squalls rarely last more than a few minutes, but those are invariably memorable ones.

WARM FRONTS

Warm fronts are usually less intense and less clearly defined than cold fronts. They usually arrive behind the clear, settled weather of a weakening high. Their arrival is announced by high, wispy **cirrostratus clouds.** Altostratus clouds are an even more certain indicator of a warm front. Following the altostratus, dark **nimbostratus** clouds appear, thick enough to block out the sun, and it starts to rain. If the front is windy, torn wisps of **scud** form beneath the nimbostratus. A low ceiling, rising temperatures and protracted, continuous rain prevails, sometimes for 24 hours, until the face of the front arrives. In the Northern Hemisphere, warm fronts usually occur on the east side of lows and are followed by cold fronts. They do not advance as rapidly as cold fronts, usually moving 12-18 mph.

Warm front sequence is as follows: cirrostratus followed by altostratus; moderate to heavy rain (or snow) showers or thunderstorms; lowering sky and (usually) continuous rain (or snow) associated with a low ceiling of stratus or nimbostratus clouds and scud; a gradual decrease or cessation of rain as the face of the front passes and the appearance of departing cumulonimbus (anvil-head) clouds; warm air, mist, fog, drizzle, stratocumulus, stratus, and nimbostratus clouds.

SUMMARY OF EVENTS ASSOCIATED WITH A WARM FRONT

	Before Front	During Passage	After Passage
Weather	no rain	continuous rain	light drizzle
Clouds	cirrostratus/ altostratus	nimbostratus and scud	lifting ceiling, then cumulonimbus, then warm and damp
Wind	increasing	clockwise shift, decreasing	steady
Temperature	steady or rising	steady rise	little change
Visibility	good	poor, mist, fog	fair, mist, fog

Frontal   Systems

A frontal system has a **center of low pressure,** which slowly rotates counterclockwise (N) and consists of a fast cold front chasing and eventually overtaking a slower warm front. The space between the two "arms" is therefore full of warm, moist air. As the cold front catches up, it slows, partial overlapping or **occlusion** occurs, and the low ceases to intensify. Shifting winds, cross-seas, and squalls are particularly in evidence in the area where the occlusion occurs. As the occlusion continues, the low loses its punch, slows up and may become stationary. A frontal system, even if it has not reached even gale magnitude, moves along a track. It has a more dangerous side, while the other side is called "navigable".

In most cases, rain is associated with frontal systems, but if the system has become completely occluded, the castaway usually finds himself in a world of unbroken, low cloud, thunder and lightning; warm, moist air; variable breezes; lumpy seas, and—**little rain.**

PREDICTING THE TRACK OF A FRONTAL SYSTEM

	Low Passes to North	Passes Overhead	Passes to South
(N)	wind backs almost SE	backs almost East	backs beyond East to NE
(S)	wind veers to NE	veers almost East	veers beyond E to SE, S

BUYS BALLOT'S LAW

Buys Ballot's Law is a mariner's rule of thumb for determining the direction of a high or low center. In the Northern Hemisphere, if a mariner faces the wind, the center of low pressure is slightly behind his right shoulder. A high is slightly ahead of his left shoulder. In the Southern Hemisphere, the low is behind his left shoulder and the high ahead of the right one. This rule applies when the high or low is still several hundred miles away. As it gets closer, the words *slightly behind* (meaning about 115°) should be changed to *aligned with* (about 90°). So, as a depression (for example) approaches in the Northern Hemisphere, it is off the sailor's right shoulder.

Overleaf: A fully developed frontal system whose low pressure center is at the left center of the following page (pg. 412). An overhead view of the same system is shown at the top of the next page (pg. 414). Illustration by Raoul Reys

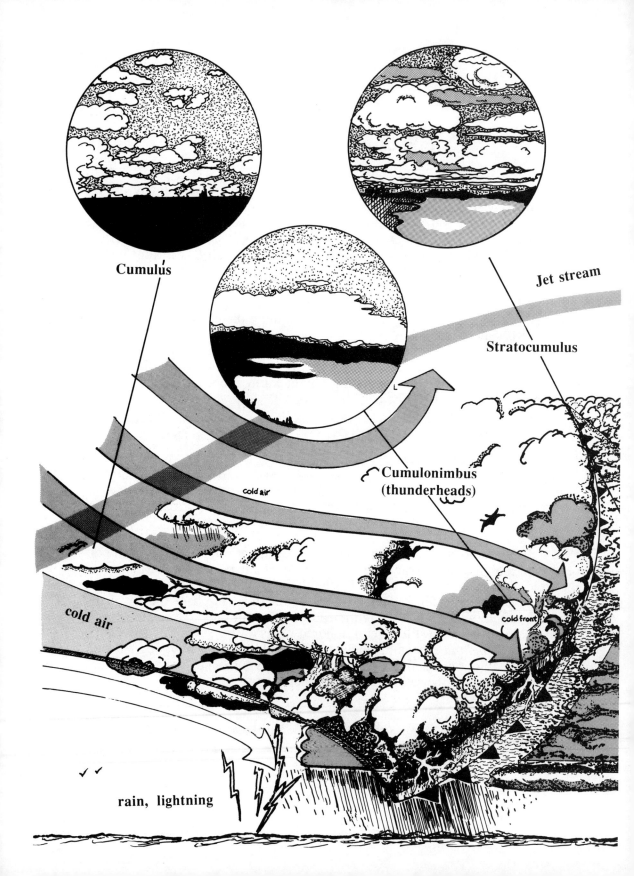

Cumulus

Jet stream

Stratocumulus

Cumulonimbus
(thunderheads)

cold air

cold air

cold front

rain, lightning

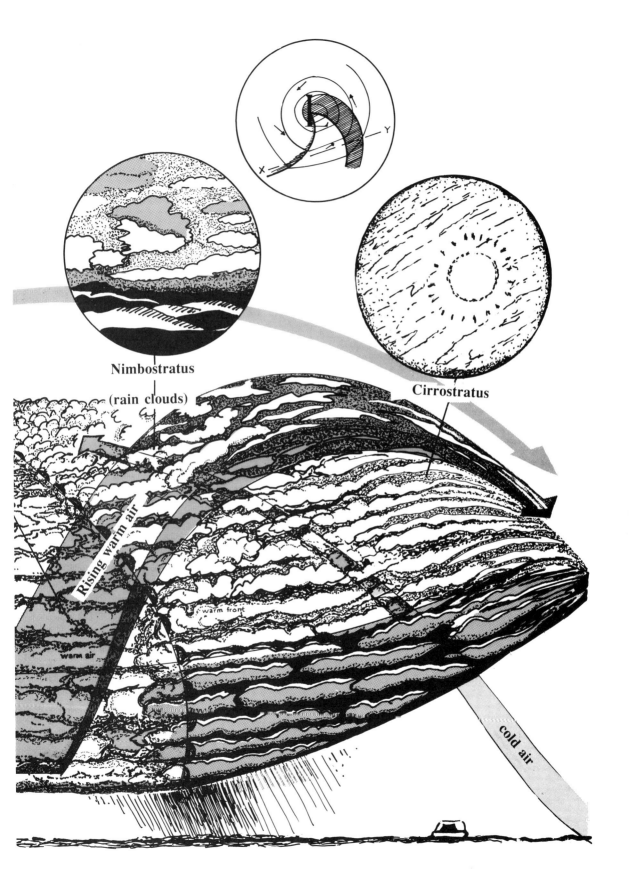

Nimbostratus

(rain clouds)

Cirrostratus

Rising warm air

warm front

warm air

cold air

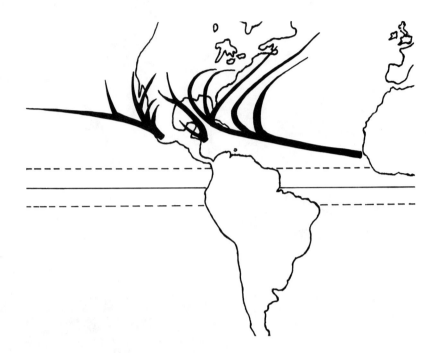

Killer Storms

Killer storms are intense, circulating, low-pressure systems, depressions which are a regular part of normal weather phenomena. In latitudes above 30° N. they may occur any time, but the most violent ones are usually associated with high latitudes, winter or early spring. Someone with a sense of humor named them "temperate" lows, and in many instances, they are, in fact, temperate. But severe temperate lows can be real killers.

Lower-latitude storms are different. Tropical lows (hurricanes or typhoons), occur in the summer months and usually originate between 8° and 15° N. or S. of the equator. Because tropical hurricanes usually generate around islands, occur in warm weather and areas of heavy boat traffic, they cause boatmen the greatest loss of life and are most feared.

Low-pressure systems usually contain warm, moist air and this is true of tropical depressions, such as hurricanes. They seem to materialize out of warm, tropic seas (above 78°F/27°C), large clusters of towering cumulonimbus clouds, which are in turn are associated with warm, moist air. Hurricanes (called

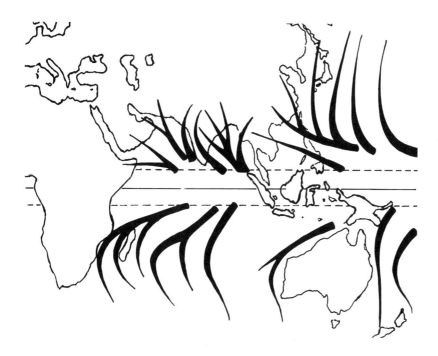

Typical Hurricane Paths. Drawing by Rafael Monroy.

Typhoons in some areas) are hot, humid storms, typical of low pressure. First warning of a hurricane is the absence of puffy, cumulus, trade wind clouds and the appearance of extremely high (50,000 feet) cirrostratus sheets which may cast a halo around the sun. They may be visible several hundred miles from the hurricane and indicate its axis. An increasing swell, usually an ominous cross swell running contrary to local conditions, begins to arrive from the direction of the storm center. Long, settled swells indicate a distant storm. A short, steep, broken swell indicates its approach.

A tropical hurricane consists of a series of intense line squalls, which reach hurricane strength within 10 to 40 miles of the eye. The squalls spiral into the eye, which is 10 to 30 miles in diameter. The "eye" is a huge column of dry, warm air, reaching to the stratosphere, cooling as it rises, giving its heat as fuel to the storm.

I first visited the center of a hurricane in 1970 in a 39-foot Belize built sloop named FIREWITCH. This was a 75-mph storm, a relatively mild one by hurricane standards, but still no row around the lake. In it, the seas raged but the sun was brilliant, and the air quite clear. The raging winds suddenly dropped, and I seized the moment to rush on deck to put more gaskets on the sails. The sky was clear but the brilliant sun offered little comfort. The seething, towering wall of clouds around me made it overwhelmingly obvious that there was more trouble to come.

In sharp contrast, other eye visitors, who experienced more violent storms and lived to tell about it, have described calm winds but towering pyramid seas, assaulting the vessel from every direction and an unbroken wall of clouds. Certainly, Joseph Conrad's account in *Typhoon,* is a description of the depression eye as it is best known. One is never happy in the eye of a hurricane, even if the sun is shining.

Hurricane squalls reach storm strength near the eye with gale winds extending 100 to 300 miles from it. The worst winds and seas in a hurricane are located quite close to the eye. If a vessel can avoid being swept into it, the worst conditions will pass within a half day.

TEMPERATE STORMS

Higher latitude, **"temperate" storms** have cold centers, caused by the descent of cold, polar air. Warm surface air is sucked into the stratosphere. The low is caused by this sucking phenomena. Temperate lows are much more common in some areas than others, and you can learn more about that from a pilot chart. The worst weather is somewhere in the forward portion of the dangerous semicircle, along the line of the dissociated, partially occluded front. Tremendous wind sheer effects are experienced in this area, with the wind on the warm side blowing toward the center, while storm winds on the cold side blow in the opposite direction. The killer conditions are much more sustained and widely distributed than in a tropical hurricane.

A long-distance cruiser, able to pick his season, may be able to significantly reduce the risk of being caught in a hurricane or cyclone, but killer temperate latitude storms are less predictable and usually have much larger diameters than hurricanes. They may have a gale-force diameter of 2,000 miles, while hurricanes generate gale winds over a diameter of 250 to 600 miles. The monstrous waves generated by the temperate-zone storm, not to mention the considerable winds, may batter a vessel for two or three days. Temperate storms are therefore more dangerous and harder to avoid than hurricanes.

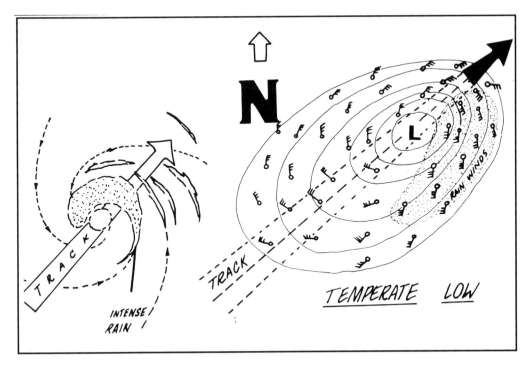

A temperate (high latitude) storm and a hurricane showing their most dangerous areas.

GENERAL BAD-WEATHER STRATEGY

If it becomes clear that your vessel is about to experience bad weather, a defensive strategy will do much to ensure survival:

1. Secure all ports and hatches. Cover ports with protective material.
2. Drain the bilge and be sure the pumps are ready for action.
3. Get as much non-essential deck gear as possible below and stow everything.
4. Rig storm sails for instant use.   Put extra lashings on the dinghy.
5. Rig lines near the deck to which safety harness leads can be clipped.
6. Bring your log up to date and include a clean position fix.
7. Get on the radio and give someone (a Ham, a commercial operator, etc. your position, course and speed. Tell when you will next contact them.
8. Bring your emergency equipment into a state of readiness. Be sure your flashlights have strong batteries.
9. Make some food and coffee. Put it in a place easily reached from the cockpit—you may be up there for some time.
10. Have everyone dress for disaster, as discussed in Chapter X.

STORM STRATEGY BASED ON PLOTTING INFORMATION

Regardless of type, a storm revolves around its center. The direction or path of the depression is its axis, and the system is divided into two hemispheres, also called semicircles. The **dangerous semicircle** contains winds and seas whose strength is supplemented by the foreword movement of the storm, so a hurricane with 70 kt. gusts, moving at 25 kts will seem to have winds of 95 kts.

In the navigable semi-circle, winds are decreased by the forward motion of the storm. A storm with a 70 kt. wind and a 25 kt. forward movement will have an apparent wind of 45 kts in the navigable semi-circle. Keep in mind, however, that sailing in either semicircle is no trip to the store.

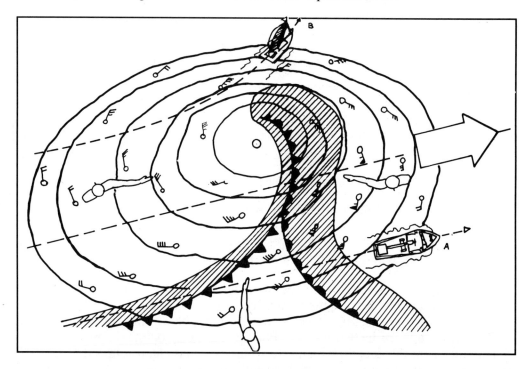

Using Buy's Ballot's Law to estimate location of storm center. The unlucky Captain of vessel A will catch the full force of the wind, augmented by the forward speed of the storm. He will be overtaken by both the warm and cold fronts of the occlusion and catch the worst rain and cross-seas. The lucky Captain of vessel B will miss most of the rain, the front faces and experience less wind, since the forward speed of the front diminishes apparent wind.

BUYS BALLOT'S LAW AND STRATEGY

Plotting transmitted storm-center data is important, but as a depression approaches, this data becomes less reliable. First, there is a lag time between bulletins; second, a storm does not, in fact, follow a straight path, it changes direction frequently, following a zig zag path. As a result, the mariner must apply Buys Ballot's law and create his own defense. The direction of the storm should be plotted and the vessel driven away from the center, hopefully into the less dangerous, navigable semicircle, or, preferably, run for port. Never try to cross the track of a revolving storm to gain the less dangerous semicircle. Think of how annoyed you would be if, having sailed into the hurricane's path, you were dismasted or lost power.

When it is time to heave-to (or lie ahull), it should be done so that the wind pushes the vessel away from the center, rather than into it. In general, a vessel caught in the dangerous semicircle in the Northern Hemisphere should put the wind at a 45° to the starboard bow (port bow in the Southern Hemisphere) and make as much way as possible. If necessary, heave to on a starboard tack, stream a sea anchor and oil. If the vessel is in the navigable semicircle, run with the wind on the starboard quarter (135° relative bearing) in the Northern hemisphere or port quarter in the south. Use Buys Ballot's law to determine your position relative to the storm center.

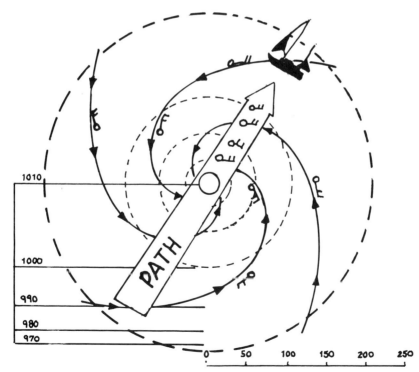

Vessel positioned directly in hurricane's path. The wind direction remains relatively steady, while the barometer drops.

If wind direction remains relatively steady while the barometer continues to pump and drop, the center is heading directly for you. At that point, even though every cell in your body wants you to head directly away from the center, apply Buys Ballot's law: head the vessel toward the navigable semicircle, presumably by keeping it at right angles to the path of the storm. Initially, this means a broad reach, eventually bringing the wind onto the beam (remembering that when facing the wind, the center of the depression is off the right shoulder). Use the chart on the previous page to indicate tendency of direction for tropical depressions or pilot chart storm track data for temperate depressions.

OCEAN CURRENTS

Ocean currents as shown on pilot charts (and the current charts found on pages 422-426) depict the average current force on ships, averaged over 50 years. Like the surface winds shown on pilot charts, this is a statistical average and in no way guarantees that what is shown on the chart will occur in the future. On the other hand, current direction is generally reliable, although special circumstances can cause it to cease or even reverse direction. El Niño, for example, causes current shifts, and the Gulf Stream will sometimes cease to flow for a few days after a protracted norther.

Evidence that one has entered or left a current system will usually be indicated by water temperature change. For example, when leaving the cold Humbolt Current, warmer temperatures indicate the presence of the equatorial countercurrent and a change of set from west-northwest to east. The Gulf Stream, moving toward the east (in the central part of the Atlantic) is warmer and deeper colored than the surrounding water which is traveling north-northwest. Dougal Robertson said,*"I have found ocean currents to be the most reliable of natural phenomena at sea and are seldom entirely absent where recorded."*

Various forces affect the direction of surface current flow. The eastward rotation of the the earth has a tendency to make the seas pile up on eastern shores, creating powerful, consistent currents such as the Gulf Stream. Another force, one which affects survival craft is the **Ekman layer phenomena**, which states that, theoretically, surface currents run at a 45° angle to the wind. In reality, the few feet of water occupied by a survival craft will drift at an angle of about 30° to the right of the wind's direction (N) or 30° to the left (S) and the set will be about 1/30th of the wind's velocity.

Like the Coriolis effect, the Ekman phenomena is more pronounced at the higher latitudes. Along the equator (10°N to 10°S), both wind and current have a tendency to flow west.

Like the Corilois effect, the Ekman phenomena is more pronounced at the higher latitudes, and along the equator (10°N-10°S) both wind and current have a tendency to flow west.

Regional currents: While global winds and currents can be generally described, boats and survival craft in particular are affected by powerful local currents such as the Humbolt Current or Gulf Stream. It is not possible to discuss them all, but it should be mentioned that many of them (including the Gulf Stream) are generated by prevailing winds. When a contrary wind arises, short, steep seas are usually created, accompanied by a cross-swell. The winds do much to nullify surface currents and, in addition, if they prevail for several days, current flow may be highly reduced for several days thereafter.

"And the next thing I knew, the whole ship just sunk right out from under me. So what's the deal with you? ... You been here long or what?"

From *The Far Side* 1986 © Universal Press Syndicate, reprinted with permission. All rights reserved.

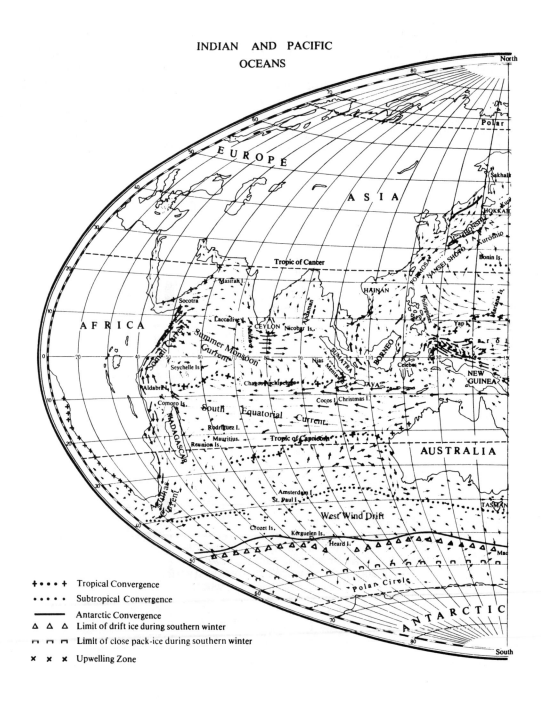

INDIAN   AND   PACIFIC
OCEANS

+ • • • +   Tropical Convergence

• • • • •   Subtropical Convergence

————   Antarctic Convergence

△ △ △   Limit of drift ice during southern winter

⊓ ⊓ ⊓   Limit of close pack-ice during southern winter

✕ ✕ ✕   Upwelling Zone

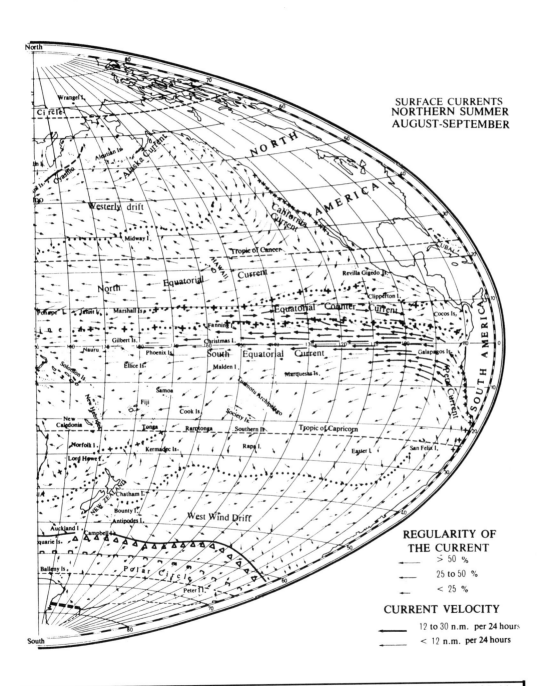

SURFACE CURRENTS
NORTHERN SUMMER
AUGUST-SEPTEMBER

REGULARITY OF
THE CURRENT

⟶   > 50 %

⟶   25 to 50 %

⟶   < 25 %

CURRENT VELOCITY

⟶   12 to 30 n.m. per 24 hours

⟶   < 12 n.m. per 24 hours

From: *Descriptive Regional Oceanography* by P. Tchernia (originally from Schott, 1935-44).
Courtesy of Museum National D'Historie Natuerelle, Laboratoire d'Oceanographie Physique.

INDIAN   AND   PACIFIC
OCEANS

+ • • • + Tropical Convergence
• • • • • Subtropical Convergence
───────── Antarctic Convergence
△ △ △ Limit of drift ice during southern summer
⊓ ⊓ ⊓ Limit of close pack-ice during southern summer
× × × Upwelling Zone

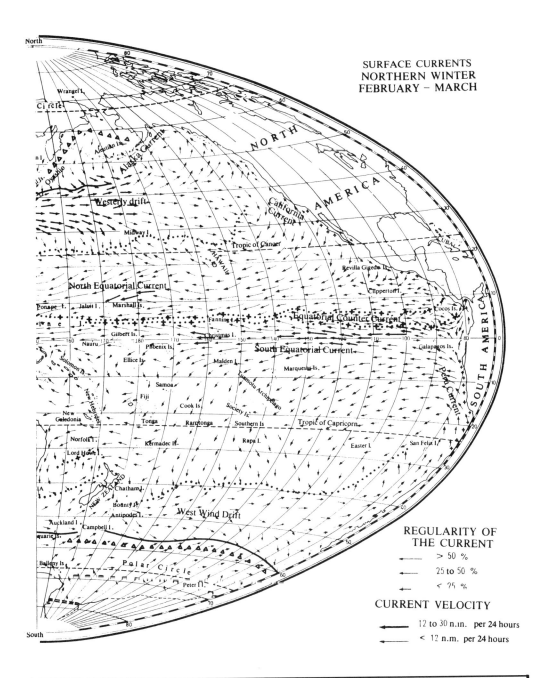

SURFACE CURRENTS
NORTHERN WINTER
FEBRUARY – MARCH

REGULARITY OF
THE CURRENT

> 50 %

25 to 50 %

< 25 %

CURRENT VELOCITY

12 to 30 n.m. per 24 hours

< 12 n.m. per 24 hours

From: *Descriptive Regional Oceanography* by P. Tchernia (originally from Schott, 1935-44).
Courtesy of Museum National D'Historie Natuerelle, Laboratoire d'Oceanographie Physiqu

ATLANTIC OCEAN: SURFACE CURRENTS — FEBRUARY

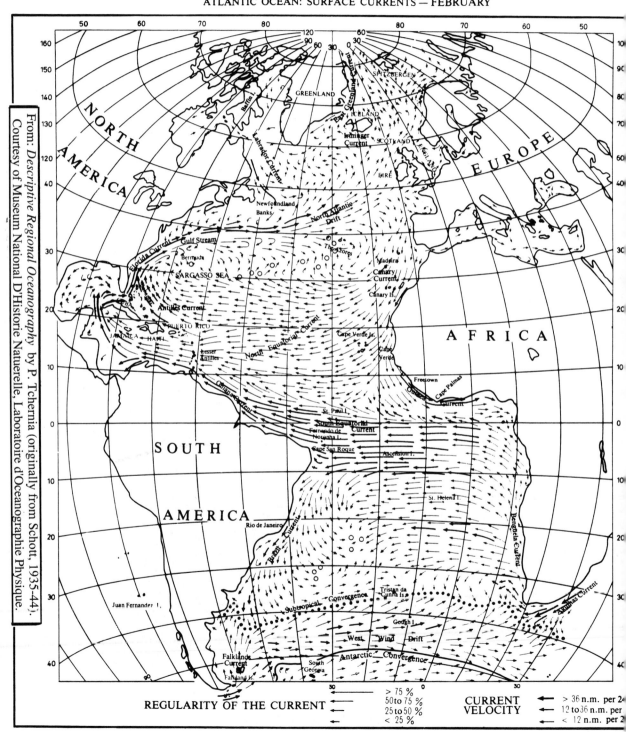

From: *Descriptive Regional Oceanography* by P. Tchernia (originally from Schott, 1935-44). Courtesy of Museum National D'Historie Naturelle, Laboratoire d'Oceanographie Physique.

REGULARITY OF THE CURRENT

> 75 %
50 to 75 %
25 to 50 %
< 25 %

CURRENT VELOCITY

> 36 n.m. per 2
12 to 36 n.m. per
< 12 n.m. per 2

Illustration by Karen Harrod

Birds Encountered at Sea

A great deal has been written about inferring proximity to land by the presence (or absence) of certain birds. Certainly, if large numbers of **coastal birds, such as pelicans, gulls, and skimmers** are seen arriving in the morning from one direction, then heading that way toward dusk, a strong inference about land can be made. But offshore species may travel hundreds of miles from land to feed, even during the mating season. Migratory sea birds, such as the **wandering albatross,** spend years at sea, and circumnavigate the Antarctic Continent before landing to mate. **Shearwaters** travel enormous distances, but do so at a leisurely pace, roaming far from their "migratory path" in search of food. Deep ocean birds, like **terns, gannets, boobies and frigates** spend months at sea, hunting, but return at night or even more frequently when rearing young.

Even migrating land birds "on course" are often carried off their normal path by the wind. Migratory birds also become lost, confused by bad weather, and fly over wide areas, eventually perishing in great numbers. Trying to determine position from a lost bird would be foolish indeed! In general, the migratory paths of birds vary from flock to flock, making precise predictions impossible. Migratory pathways, shown on charts, are often based on incomplete information. Migratory charts have been created to help the public get a general idea about migratory routes, not to help survivors find position based on bird sign. Last but not least, when terrestrial birds fly toward a vessel and attempt to land upon it, it may be inferred that they are lost, at the end of their strength, and that there is no land within many miles.

Having warned the castaway about not putting undue faith in birds, it is now time to firmly state that one of the first, definite signs of land is an increase in bird activity. The birds to watch for are the coastal birds mentioned above and described later in this chapter, all of whom leave the land in the morning and return to it at night, spending the day flying random hunting patterns in search of food.

The tropic bird. Art by Rebecca Thomson.

Bird Classification

Birds have been grouped by the marine areas they frequent, just like life rafts. Keep in mind that some birds which normally frequent coastal waters, for example, may have migratory paths which take them far from land. A blue heron, for example, once landed on my deck—1,000 miles from land. Single sightings, such as this one, are not an indicator that land is near.

Sea birds, frequently called **midocean birds**, spend most of their lives flying far offshore, coming to land only for the purpose of rearing young. These include the **albatrosses, petrels, fulmars, kittiwakes, shearwaters, tropic birds, phalaropes and some terns.**

Offshore birds may fly far out to sea in order to feed, but they return to the land at night or periodically. These include **gannets, boobies, skuas, frigates** and other **terns.**

Coastal birds are sea birds with localized habits associated with land. They stay close to land except when migrating and feed near shore. They nest or roost at night. These include such birds as **gulls, ducks, herons, pelicans, and cormorants.**

Land birds, may inhabit the shore and even fly a few miles offshore but they sleep ashore and have feet which are well adapted for walking.

IDENTIFYING BIRDS

The illustrations in this chapter have been designed to help the castaway identify various bird families, but not specific species. The descriptions have been written in a similar vein. It is not important to know which variety of bird one had for lunch, it is sufficient to say, "humm-mm, that was a tasty boobie!" The castaway is therefore urged to base identification on head and beak shape and general body configuration, rather than on size and plumage.

BIRDS AS FOOD

Oceanic birds concentrate in areas where food is most abundant and are, in turn, a potential food source for the castaway. But catching a sea bird at sea is strictly a matter of luck, not cunning or strategy. If your life depends on catching a sea bird, you are in deep trouble. Read more about catching them at

Food from the Skies, by Steve Callahan

Brown pelicans with flock overhead. Drawing by Rebecca Thomson

sea in chapter V and on land (where your chances are greatly improved) in chapter VII. Modern man is used to eating domestic fowl such as turkey, chicken and duck. Wild fowl are often thought to be fishy or gamy in taste and are often distained. Yet sea birds have been exhaustively hunted for food in earlier times, and a variety of species, such as the great auk, have become extinct because of it. All birds are edible even though some may smell and taste strongly of fish. Edible parts that should not be neglected include the brain, organs, and eyes. The small green gall bladder, attached to the liver, should be removed. It tastes bitter and will strongly taint the flesh if broken. The flesh of sea birds may contain bioluminesent substances as the result of their eating small sea-creatures which in turn feed on luminescent plankton. The luminescence is non-toxic.

A bird's fat is found just beneath the skin and is attached to it. Because it is easier than plucking, remove a captured bird's skin by pulling it off inside-out, like a glove. The fat can then be sucked from it. Bird blood is very nutritious, although some people find it disgusting. The amount of disgust probably varies in direct relation to how hungry one is. A good way to consume the blood without waste is to pull off the creature's head and drink from the stump. As is true of most animals, bird flesh keeps better if it has been bled. In earlier times people used to hang birds in much the same way as meat is hung and aged today. This is not a safe procedure in a survival craft since there is no way to kill microorganisms by cooking. It is undoubtedly best if a bird is consumed within 24 hours.

The forewings and legs of birds do not contain much meat, but they make fine bait. The Bailey's (see Chapter IV), found that trigger fish would fight so tenaciously over a wing stump that they could be lifted from the water, still clinging to the meat. The large feathers of the wings and tail should be saved, since they can be made into lures.

All oceanic birds live on marine organisms and it is possible that a captured bird may have partially digested sea food in its stomach. The stomach contents may be eaten, and some castaways find it particularly tasty.

Sea Birds

For the sailor, there is something about sea birds that stirs the heart. Their wild freedom, their beauty and the vibrancy of their calls cannot help but strike a sympathetic cord. I have a special feeling for the tropic bird, which often descends to fly within a few feet of the surging rail. Clothed in a spectral whiteness, its piercing black eyes seemingly alive with insight, its high, pure call, so human in quality—one feels communication is imminent, that suddenly the secrets, the wisdom of the tropic bird will be revealed.

There is nothing quite so amazing to behold as the flight of large sea birds during bad weather, soaring like bullets above the waves, seeming to enjoy the very weather which causes the mariner so much grief. On fair days, they look so fragile and alone, condemned, it would seem, to flying without rest above the cruel ocean, sort of an avian Flying Dutchmen fated to a short, hard existence. Yet their life has its rewards: the ecstasy of flying, the clean, sweet air, total freedom and, in the end, a quick death. Then consider the lot of men, struggling in teeming warrens, breathing an atmosphere poisoned by their own wastes, doomed, it would seem, to a long, miserable life. If I could vote, I'd vote for the life of the tropic bird.

These creatures are in fact superbly adapted to the marine environment, which is abundant with food and free of predators. All they have to do is keep flying—sometimes for years at a time. Large sea birds, are expert gliders. Land birds, such as eagles, use rising thermals to gain great altitude without beating their wings, but most sea birds are low-flying. They use the updrafts created when surface wind hits a wave. This is undoubtedly the reason why dense populations of sea birds, particularly the tube-nose birds are found in the windy southern oceans which support about 25% more bird species than oceans in the Northern Hemisphere. Gliding birds need a strong wind in which to glide.

Sea birds use different components of wave-generated wind variances to achieve their goals. They seem to understand Buys Ballot's Law and skate away from revolving storms. When the clouds are lowering and the birds have suddenly disappeared, it's time to reef. Sea birds also protect themselves from high winds by flying in the troughs of waves. The wind is slowed by drag in the troughs, and the wave becomes a sort of hill which provides a lee. Large sea birds glide effortlessly for astonishing distances in the few inches of "ground effect," an area of greater lift between the bottom of their wings and the water, where the air is temporarily condensed by their passage. Continuous gliding is difficult for small, light-weight birds. They must flutter their wings.

A typical large sea bird gliding sequence begins up to 50 feet above a wave crest. The bird then establishes a long glide parallel to the wave, eventually descending into the calmer air above the trough. When altitude becomes critical, the bird increases the angle of glide to gain speed, then climbs, almost to the point of stalling, until it reaches the updrafts above the wave crest. It uses these powerful updrafts to reestablish its original position.

It is calms, rather than high winds, which represent a great danger for large sea birds. They are gliders and burn up too much energy flapping their wings. It is often necessary for them to land and await the return of the wind. At these times they are particularly vulnerable to the castaway. Many such birds prefer landing on a floating object, such as a survival craft, particularly if they are heavy with food. It is difficult for them to take off from the sea in light wind.

THE TUBE-NOSES

This is the most numerous Order (Procellariiformes) of the true sea birds, and includes the wide-ranging **albatrosses, fulmars, petrels, prions and shearwaters**. They are all called **tube-noses**, a very inelegant name for such classy creatures, but the tubular shape of their nostrils is one of their most obvious similarities. The **albatross** and the **fulmars** are scavengers; the **shearwaters** eat small fish, squid, and crustaceans taken near the surface; **petrels** are also surface-feeding birds, but they eat smaller creatures such as krill; **prions**, sometimes called whale birds because of their eating habits, consume, still smaller creatures on the zooplankton level, straining them from planktonic blooms with specially adapted bills—like blue whales.

The **wandering albatross,** sometimes called a "**goonie,**" is the largest flying creature on earth, now that we have eliminated the North American condor. It has an awesome wing-spread of up to 12 feet and weighs up to 27 pounds. Its cousin, the royal albatross, is just a bit smaller. A few other species migrate north of the equator. One, *D. irrrorata*, nests on Hood Island in the the Galapagos. Others nest on small islets west of Hawaii. Because they are gliding birds, Albatrosses do not do well in calms and are never seen in the doldrums.

Albatrosses will fly for days at a time behind sailing ships, feeding on garbage and sea creatures brought up in the wake, gaining lift from the wind disturbed by the vessel. These beautiful, graceful and tireless gliders are famous in myth and legend. This is the creature mentioned in the *Rhyme of the Ancient Mariner*. The Ancient Mariner killed one, using a cross-bow, and this brought bad luck. Albatrosses, fulmars, and storm petrels were thought to be the reincarnation of men lost at sea. If so, there are some hunters out there with extremely bad karma, for all of these birds, in their prefledged state, have been collected by the millions for their oil and meat. If you can get your hands on an albatross (extremely unlikely), do not worry about what the Ancient Mariner had to say. Kill it and eat it.

The albatross is the very symbol of the midocean wanderer, spending years at sea before returning to land in order to breed. Very little can be inferred from seeing them, except that the area is rich with marine life. Most albatross' nest in the Antarctic regions and rear a single chick, which takes as much as nine months. The chick hatches at the onset of the viscious Antarctic winter and spends most of its time in a state of semi-hibernation in its rudimentary nest. The parents return to feed it three to five times per week.

Most albatrosses glide too fast to take live food from the sea while flying, although they are sometimes able to take floating debris on the wing. Most land on the water and swim toward their prey. They also dive short

Head Shapes of the Fulmar family

distances after squid which they have first observed from the air, then stalked, with their heads under water. Albatross' also eat carrion and offal. Most sea birds, having no contact with man, show little fear of his approach. This makes them vulnerable to the castaway. The albatross is a big, strong bird with a vicious beak that can do much damage. Grab it as soon as possible, to avoid serious lacerations or having your eyes pecked out.

The fulmar in flight. By Rebecca Thomson.

The **fulmar** (18" long x 45" wing span) is often mistaken for a common gull, but their tubular nostrils identify them as a separate order. They vary in color from gull white to a blue-gray. Fulmars have increased dramatically in numbers over the last 200 years because they have become adept at scavenging offal discarded far at sea, first by whalers, then, later, by fishermen.

The **giant fulmar** is either white or mottled chocolate brown, depending on species, with a wing span of up to seven feet. These creatures venture far out to sea, and the white ones are sometimes confused with a young wandering albatross. The two are quite similar in appearance, except for different beak shapes.

Storm petrels at sea. Art by Rebecca Thomson

Like the albatross, these birds spend years at sea and some call them the "little albatross." Even during the breeding season, they may be found up to 600 miles from land. They and the seagull are beautiful, but the beauty conceals both birds' voracious character. Both of these creatures will fight viciously over food and their greed knows no bounds. Great numbers of fulmars inhabit all seas with the exception of the Polar Oceans.

The **antarctic petrel**, also called the **Cape pigeon**, is the most numerous bird of the Southern Ocean. It looks much like a pigeon or magpie, but the tube nose identifies it as a member of the fulmar family. It is a scavenger and appears almost as if by magic when offal is thrown from a ship. Like all fulmars, the Cape pigeon is an opportunist, screaming and voracious when feeding, mercilessly attacking weak or wounded birds, tearing at floating carcasses, but normally feeding on krill and zooplankton. It has difficulty walking, lands only to breed and rear young, then returns to sea.

The **storm petrels**, smallest of the tube-noses, look so fragile and dainty that it is hard to accept the fact that they, too, are hearty birds which inhabit the farthest reaches of the cruel sea. They are solitary creatures at sea, but occasionally gather in flocks, brought to the area by food. In such a flock they are sometimes called "**Mother Carey's Chickens.**" They are considered by some to be an ill omen, because they often fly near shipwrecks and vessels in distress, ready, it is believed, to collect the souls of drowned sailors. Storm petrels do hover close to ships wakes, or the disturbed water surrounding a dying ship to gather the planktonic material churned up.

Wilson's (storm) petrel, hardly bigger than a sparrow, breeds by the millions on the Arctic and Antarctic ice. It is always inspiring to seeing this tiny speck of life fluttering daintily in the few inches of calm air above an otherwise raging sea. They are found in large numbers flying above plankon concentrations, as are found in the Humbolt Current and on the Newfoundland Banks. Their presence in large numbers should encourage the castaway to do a little plankton fishing himself. They and other varieties of storm petrels are found in every ocean, and their absence is an indicator that the area is particularly poor in seafood.

The storm petrels are, like all tube-noses, consummate gliders, but their technique is unique. They spend much of their time fluttering within a few inches of the sea, where the wind velocity is reduced by surface drag. As a result, the storm petrel must reduce its stall speed to the minimum and it accomplishes this in the same way as an aircraft does, by lowering its landing gear. In this case the gear are its feet, which seem to be walking on the water, but are in fact being used to achieve lateral stability.

Various types of **shearwaters** are found in almost every ocean. Some have migratory routes of an incredible 20,000 miles in length. The parents alternate on the nest and, when freed from this duty, fly as far as 600 miles in search of food. They are opportunists and will follow food fish migrations for thousands of miles when not rearing young.

Countless shearwaters have been caught by mackerel fishermen, and the birds are willing to try for small pieces of trolled bait. Shearwaters are too clever to be taken with a lure. These birds have sharp eyes, so a small, well-concealed hook must be imbedded in the bait.

Shearwater in flight. By Rebecca Thomson .

Kittiwakes are gulls, a family not normally known as mid ocean birds. Their smaller size and more delicate bills distinguish them from other gulls. Kittiwakes are true pelagic birds and are rarely seen near land, except during the breeding season, which runs from April to July. They inhabit the North Atlantic, up to the Arctic ice, ranging South into the Sargasso Sea. They are well known in Europe and even inhabit the Western portion of the Mediterranean Sea.

Kittiwakes. Drawing by Rebecca Thomson.

The graceful flight of **the tropic bird** and its spectacular tail streamers make it hard to believe it is related to boobies and gannets, clumsy creatures that make every landing look like a crash landing. There is nothing quite like seeing a tropic bird, flying almost at arm's length, master of all it surveys, calling, calling with a high-pitched trill. The call carries dramatically and can often be heard before the creature is seen.

Their long-tail streamers, sometimes called "marlinspikes" are most sensuous, and the male and female stroke each other with them while in flight, during the mating season. The tropic bird mates for life and unerringly returns to its nest again and again every year. When not engaged in areal hanky-panky, the tropic bird spends its time fishing for squid, diving beneath the sea surface for a few seconds at a time.

Phalaropes. Art by Rebecca Thomson.

Phalaropes look like shore birds and, when 'longshore, have habits similar to wading birds. They look out of place at sea, as though they were migrating, but when not breeding (summer), they become true mid ocean creatures. They swim in a distinctive, very buoyant fashion which makes them easy to distinguish. They are completely fearless of people and can be approached very closely, making them a potential food item. **Wilson's phalarope** is the least pelagic of the family, does not migrate over water and very seldom ventures far from shore. It spends its summers in North America, as far south as California. The rest of the year is spent on the east and south east coasts of South America.

The Magnificent Frigate in flight. Art by Rebecca Thomson.

Offshore Birds

These are all birds of tropic seas, capable of flying hundreds of miles from their breeding grounds. Unlike the tube-noses, they are capable of hunting in windless conditions, such as the Doldrums and the Sargasso Sea. Their breeding cycle is more varied than that of the tube-noses. It is more dependant on variations in food supply and weather which occurs in warmer climates.

THE FRIGATE OR MAN O' WAR BIRD

If it's hard to believe that the tropic bird is a relative of the boobie, it's equally hard to think of the **magnificent frigate** as a close relative of the pelican. There is just the slightest chance that a castaway will ever get his hands on a frigate, for they are wholly adapted to life in the air, never alight on the water, and land only to breed and rear their young. Frigate's legs are atrophied and virtually useless for walking. They neither walk nor swim voluntarily, and their plumage is not waterproof.

The frigate is a consummate glider and although it has a wing span of only eight feet it is much lighter than an albatross and is by far the better glider. For this reason it is possible for the frigate to fly in relatively windless areas which are not inhabited by the tube noses.

The frigate is called the **Man O' War bird** because it is a pirate. It delights in pursuing other sea birds that have made a catch, harassing and tumbling them in flight until they disgorge their meal. The frigate then, with the greatest of ease, dives for the jettisoned morsel, catching it in mid air. It is extremely rare that a frigate attacks another bird which is not carrying a meal, and if an error is made, it is soon recognized. Ornithologists speculate that the angry cry of the pursued bird is slightly different if they are full of fish. When not acting as pirates, frigates are also capable of catching their own fish.

In addition to being an annoyance, the frigate nests near other sea birds, particularly boobies and terns. They not only molest these birds as they return to their nests, they also devour their eggs and young when the opportunity arises, picking them from the nests while in flight, sometimes even stealing an egg from beneath the breast of a nesting bird. Frigates even have the audacity to snatch food from the mouths of parent birds engaged in feeding. If it were not for the slow development and high mortality of young frigates, they would be the scourge of the seas.

GANNETS AND BOOBIES

These birds have long, narrow wings, long pointed beaks and webbed feet. They are similar looking, but the gannets are larger, almost twice as heavy and prefer cold water, while the boobie is a creature of tropic seas. They are otherwise very similar and might be considered close cousins. They are beautifully adapted for hunting underwater and make spectacular dives. Gannets dive as deep as 30' but boobies stay closer to the surface. These birds swallow their prey beneath the surface, presumably to avoid detection by frigate birds. Since these birds dive for food, they have a tendency to fly higher than the tube-noses and often cruise at 200 to 300 feet. When a fish is spotted, they fold their wings and come plummeting down, occasionally braking to check their speed.

Boobies. By Rebecca Thomson.

Unlike pelicans, who arch their necks prior to impact, boobies and gannets enter the water straight as an arrow. They are capable of catching and eating four to six pounds of fish, after which they must flap madly and "run" on the water to take off.

Gannets and boobies are heavy birds and have comical faces because, unlike other sea birds, they have their eyes in front, rather than on the sides of their heads. This permits binocular vision, important when diving for food. They are superb flyers, but are like a fish out of water on land. Their landings at the nest sight can only be called remarkable, and it is amazing that more birds are not killed attempting to land. Belly landings, collisions with other birds and even end-over-end tumbles are most common.

During the mating season, these birds build nests in inaccessible areas near the sea. Most species prefer cliffs. They usually lay in the Spring, but the season varies depending on species and food supply. The nests are made from seaweed, and the sight of a gannet with its bill full of seaweed is a certain indicator of land. The chicks of these birds require immense amounts of food, and the parents take turns feeding them. The adult birds hunt during the day, return to the nest when gorged or before nightfall. After the mating season these birds, like the tube-noses, wander far out to sea and assume random hunting patterns over schools of small fish, particularly anchovies, sardines and flying fish.

Boobies (and gannets) are particularly unafraid of man. Early sailors, who slaughtered tens of thousands of these birds for food, named them thus, obviously thinking that any creature trusting of man was indeed a boobie. On the nest they stand their ground, and at sea, they often land on a castaway-laden survival craft, to preen and stare in amazement at the strange creatures they have encountered.

Skua, or "sea-eagle." By Rebecca Thomson.

Skuas are robber birds, like the frigates, built to cause trouble and are sometimes called **sea hawks**. They are related to gulls and look like them, except for their dark plumage. When not nesting, they are extremely wide-ranging, fly far from land and have even been found 80 miles from the South

vour carrion. Skuas nest in the far North or South, but spend years at sea without returning to land. They can sometimes be caught by laying out bait and grabbing them as they approach.

Terns. By Rebecca Thomson.

Landlubbers think of **terns** as land birds, but ocean sailors know them equally well. Terns are little birds, just a handful of feathers, weighing a few ounces. Most of them are coastal birds who never venture into midocean. The **arctic tern** is famous for long distance migration, from its northern breeding grounds to the South Polar ice. When not breeding it can be found anywhere over the South Atlantic or Pacific Oceans.

The round trip migration, about 22,000 miles, circumnavigates Antarctica, takes eight months and averages more than 100 miles per day. This bird neither dillys nor dallys during the trip to Antarctica. It presses on, rarely feeding or landing while enroute. It sheds its worn flight feathers immediately after arrival on the southern ice, then becomes a midocean bird, roaming the trackless sea.

While nesting (northern summer), the Arctic tern becomes a coastal dweller for about two months. During this brief time it breeds and fledges several chicks. It breeds in gregarious colonies, from the Arctic to as far South as Maine and Britain. Terns are fiesty little creatures and vigorously defend their young against all comers. After the breeding season, it's back to sea.

Other types of terns either do not migrate or migrate over a more limited distance. They feed from lakes or bays, often migrate over land or near shore and are considered land birds.

Terns feed on small marine creatures, particularly fish and shrimp. Since some are seen offshore, a tern flying with a fish in its mouth would be an inference about both the proximity and direction of land.

Coastal Birds

Gulls are famous for following fishing boats and have developed an uncanny ability to distinguish between fishing vessels and pleasure craft. They are considered coastal birds, but gulls are extremely adaptive and opportunistic. They have a piratical sort of camaraderie. They scream over food and attract their friends. They appear to fight viciously over anything edible, but seldom injure each other during the fight, yet they would think nothing of driving an injured gull away from food.

Gulls are perfectly willing to fly farther out to sea if the squid are running; scavenge a beach at low tide; pick at the carcass of a whale; steal chicks from another bird's nest; gorge on garbage, lizards, turtles or mice, penetrate far inland when the food is there, as noted in the *Book of Mormon* or compete for popcorn and hot dogs with the pigeons at the zoo. Gulls are even willing to eat their own young, if food is scarce. Their adaptability makes them increasingly successful, but does nothing to dispel their notoriety as the most evil of creatures, cannibals, scavengers, thieves, and ruthless predators.

Gulls normally range up to 30 miles offshore or to the 100 fathom line. **Sighting gulls is a sign that land is nearby**, but it is important to be sure the creatures are not fulmars, with their tubular nostrils. The only truly pelagic midocean gull is the kittiwake.

Pelicans, by contrast, can only but be described as the honest farmers of the sea. They are fishermen of lakes and bays, although they, too, are willing to fly farther offshore if the fish are there. They will scuffle over scraps at a bait

The common gull.

dock and for the best perches, but are otherwise just plain hard working fishermen, not voracious competitors, as are fulmars and gulls. A pelican's bill will hold an incredible 3.5 gallons of water, and when it is full, the bird cannot raise its head. If there are fish inside, it must let the water slowly trickle away, so as to not lose its catch. During this time, pelicans are often harassed by other smaller marine birds who land on the pelicans' head, hoping that scraps or injured fish will escape. Pelicans and cormorants are found within sight of land. Cormorants, although fishing birds, spend most of their time on land, and are often seen drying their wings in a tree perch or on a piling.

Herons and **egrets** are wading birds which feed in bays and lakes. They seldom venture far from shore except when migrating. Some of them migrate great distances over water. If one is seen at sea, this is not a sign of land, since these birds occasionally become disoriented and wander far from shore.

The Blue Heron. Art by Rebecca Thomson

Land Birds

Land birds, when migrating, follow established **flyways** which sometimes parallel the coast and sometimes span oceans. The ocean crossings are usually routed to take advantage of islands where the birds can rest. Migrating birds use a variety of sensory data to guide them, including stars, the sun and land shapes. When bad weather obscures this information, these birds often land, if land is available, and wait for conditions to improve. If a storm should catch them over water, these poor creatures may wander aimlessly for days. When the weather clears, they get their bearings and resume the migration, but the lost time and extra exertion often deplete fat reserves to the point where they perish before reaching their goal.

Ducks and geese are famous migrating birds whose flyway usually parallels the coast. If flights of these creatures are sighted, an inference of land can be made.

CHAPTER XVI: SIGNALS

History of Pyrotechnic Signals

Pyrotechnics originated centuries ago in China, and, for hundreds of years, they were considered little more than an amusement. Even the rockets used by the British against Napoleon's forces produced more spectacle than damage, and "the rocket's red glare," mentioned in the US national anthem, is followed shortly thereafter by a reminder that the fort subsequently refused to capitulate. Those rockets were inaccurate because no-one had mastered the problem of how to stabilize the spin of a rocket in flight, although the secret of stabilizing bullets (by rifling the gun barrel) was understood 250 years ago.

It wasn't until 1960 that the modern marine signal was developed by Hansson in Sweden. Prior to that, ships carried a supply of rockets which looked much like ancient Chinese fireworks, including a long stick attached to the tail, which somewhat stabilized spin. The fuse was ignited by the famous "light blue touch paper," and the rule was "touch fuse with light blue paper and stand clear!"

These signals, in addition to being erratic, were extremely sensitive to moisture. To make matters worse, the concept of internationally recognized signals was not developed until after the sinking of the TITANIC. The officers of that doomed vessel fired dozens of distress rockets, clearly visible to a nearby ship, but the captain of that ship thought the TITANIC was celebrating an event and offered no assistance.

In 1960, Hansson applied the breakthrough in spin mechanics theory, developed during WW II and produced the **Ikaros distress rocket**. The stabilization stick was eliminated and a delay train fuse was ignited by a manually detonated primer cap, giving the signalman time to either get both hands on the device or move away from it. The Ikaros was packaged in a moisture-resistant tube, which also acted as the launcher. The entire unit was sealed in a plastic package to further waterproof it. Improvements in packaging, reliability, brilliance, duration and shelf life have been made since then.

Pains-Wessex Schermuly, an old English firm long committed to the production of rescue equipment,.is prominent in the American pyrotechnic market because of the quality and reliability of their signals. Pain held one of the

Face Page: *Man in Distress.* Courtesy of Pains-Wessex Schermuly.

earliest patents for marine distress signals and Schermuly originally developed the line thrower in 1897, a revolutionary idea for its time. These men were among the first to recognize the need for extremely rugged, easily operated firing mechanisms which could be triggered by injured sailors, and people wearing gloves. The hand flare shown on the first page of this chapter is a Pains-Wessex design. In addition to conventional marine signals, Pains-Wessex makes an excellent self-contained **line-throwing rocket,** with a 250-meter range, suitable for ship-to-shore, ship-ship, and overboard operations

A hand-held marine rocket can deploy a variety of signals, including:

1. **Red meteors** for distress.
2. **Blue meteors** for pilot signals.
3. **Red parachute flares** for distress.
4. **White meteors** for warning of collision.
5. **White parachute flares** for illumination.
6. **Green meteors and parachutes** for signalling.
7. **Maroons**, which give off a loud bang and bright flash.
8. **Colored stars**, usually fired as two-star groups (The French use a red, two-star group for distress.) Colored stars are frequently used from shore to assist beach landings of lifeboats.

QUALITY

When companies began manufacturing modern distress rockets, some disreputable firms, managed by the same types who build shoddy life rafts, started producing inferior signals. Some standards were set by the USCG and they are still in force today. But the language of the USCG recommendations and the loopholes in the code allowed much latitude. As a result, many signals manufactured in the U.S. today are comparable with earlier technology, such as the original Ikaros rocket, manufactured twenty-eight years ago.

The SOLAS convention recommendations of 1974, which also proved insufficient, were rewritten in 1983 and implemented in 1986. Many nations, particularly the seafaring ones, signed the SOLAS recommendations into law. The US did approve SOLAS recommendations for certain categories of ships, but not for boats.

The SOLAS recommendations include the precise color, brightness, duration, minimum altitude, descent rate, immersion resistance, ruggedness requirements, minimum operating temperature ranges, etc. A SOLAS signal must also be deployable at a low angle, so that it is useful under low cloud. As a result, a signal built to SOLAS standards is superior—and you pay for that.

Steve Callahan makes the following editorial comment:

On the other hand, some non-SOLAS signals are also of good quality, though generally less bright or having a shorter burn time. Then the question is, if you're going to spend $40, do you buy <u>one</u> Pains-Wessex parachute signal that burns 40 seconds at 30,000 candela at 1000 feet <u>or two</u> Olin parachutes that burn at 10,000 candela for 25 seconds at 1000 feet plus a meteor or a hand-held. A signal pistol with numerous flares takes up as much space as a few hand launched parachute signals. I prefer numbers since I have experienced failures in both types of flares.

Rule No. 3

Anything that attracts attention to your survival craft is a signal. If a signal works, it's good enough, and more than one lucky survivor has successfully signaled to an oncoming ship by waving a shirt. Of course, the usual reason WHY a person waves his shirt is because he has nothing better with which to signal. This brings us to Rule No. 3 (You remember Rule No. 1 Don't Abandon Ship, etc, and Rule No. 2, The Buttocks Rule). **RULE No 3: SIGNALS ARE LIKE BLESSINGS, YOU CANNOT HAVE TOO MANY OF THEM.** More than one desperate castaway has had ship after ship pass by, heedless of their signals, until the signals were all gone. In addition, pyrotechnic signals, particularly old ones, often don't work.

It's easy, if you're a desperate castaway, to curse the lookout who does not see your signal. Without a doubt, many ships (and boats) barrel along on autopilot, with inadequate watch (if any), trusting their fate (and yours) to a variety of gadgets proven beyond a doubt to be inadequate; in clear violation of international law and convention, captained by a fool as innocent of criminal negligence as any happy, drunken idiot on the highway.

That's their part of it. Your part is: (1) Being fool enough to mess around with boats in the first place; (2) Ending up in a situation where you must rely on someone else's eyesight and alertness to save your heinnie and, maybe (3) Neglecting your signals bag, which, under certain circumstances is far worse than neglecting your lover, who may forgive your neglect. Cheat on a signals bag, and it will repay you in kind.

There are several ways to classify signals: day or night, cheap or expensive, and effective or useless. Let's start with the useless ones.

USELESS SIGNALS

A useless signal is one that doesn't work. These include flashlights with dead batteries, as are found in equipment packs that have not received their annual inspection, or flares which are packed where you can't find them, or in an open bag in a damp locker, where they deteriorate. Old signal pistol shells have a tendency to deteriorate and a telltale sign is corrosion around the primer cap. The wise captain places his signals in a heavy duty, waterproof container.

"Off-the-shelf" life raft equipment packs are woefully short of pyrotechnic signals. Some contain none. Others have three each red hand and orange smoke signals. Old signals (as are found in rafts which have not been inspected for years) and even those within expiration date have a distressingly high failure rate. This is another reason to have plenty of signals in your pack. The USCG conducted an Approved Pyrotechnics test on marine signals in 1985. The results were shocking:

TYPE SIGNAL	TESTED	FAILED	
12 mm meteor shells (fresh)	36	9	25%
12 mm meteor flares (3 yrs. old)	50	21	42%
Red hand flares (fresh)	41	5	12%
Red hand flares (3 yrs. old)	29	15	51%

Other tests have been conducted with similar or even more dismal results. **Survival Technologies Group**, St. Petersburg, Florida, conducted tests on red hand flares alleged to meet USCG water immersion requirements. All of them failed. They now sell only signals manufactured to SOLAS specifications. Rocket deployed parachute signals are particularly susceptible to age-related failure. I have tested numerous rockets 2-3 years out of date—and seen the majority of them fail.

STRATEGY

A ship's lookout thinks his job is to warn of impending collision. He spends far more time monitoring dials and making log entries than watching relentlessly, night after night, month after month for someone's flare. If you want to be rescued, you're going to have to play his game, not yours. Your flare has to be up there long enough for the lookout to get around to seeing it. If the look-out is looking out and your rocket-deployed parachute signal is launched from two miles away, he will see it instantly, if it is within his field of vision.

Flares seen at different distances

At six miles, the lookout will see it, but it will no longer illuminate the whole sky as it does at a range of two miles. It will definitely seem to be a flare, but it will no longer dazzle the eyes. It may take several moments for meaning to register.

At eight miles, the flare must not only register, the lookout must also convince himself that the flare is real. At ten miles, a signal is a rather quiet cry for help. If the lookout catches sight of it at the end of its burn, he may convince himself that it was a mote in the eye, an illusion. After all, he just cannot amble over and have a look. If he wants to make something of it, it usually means waking the Captain. One way to convince him, if sufficient signals are available, is to fire signals at regular intervals, and that takes plenty of signals.

Beyond ten miles, only the superstructure of the largest ships can be seen from a castaway's eye height of three feet above sea level. So a flare has a useful range of ten miles or less, for practical purposes, regardless of its rated range or altitude. At that distance, a rocket- deployed parachute flare will start its burn well above the horizon.

DANGERS

A signal is even more than useless if it blows your head off. The USCG says old signals, particularly rockets, can do this and I believe them, although I personally have tested hundreds of old rockets and never had one blow up. But it's clear that the propellent could pack quite a wallop if it went off all at once, rather than in a controlled burn. Once more, the castaway is caught on the horns of a dilemma: Flares are expensive and then there's RULE #3 (Flares are like blessings). My theory is to keep them, use the new ones first and protect the hands, chest and face when using them.

DIAMETER	——- U. S. C. G. REQUIREMENTS—-			VIS.RANGE
	ALTITUDE	BURN TIME	BRIGHTNESS	
(in mm)	(in feet)	(in seconds)	(in candela)	(in NM)*
12	250	6	10,000	22
25	375	8	30,000	30
* seen from a ship's bridge 50' above sea level				

The chief virtue of **boat type signal pistol shells** (as distinguished from the larger 37 or 38 mm pistol signal) is that they are cheap. Their spec sheets are impressive, hinting at more bang for less bucks.

This is a case where the facts do not really tell the true story. The visible range assumes the observer is watching for and anticipating the signal and that atmospheric conditions are optimum. If you think that a lookout on a ship 30 NM away is looking for your signal, you are steering into fantasy.

The truth about a 12 or 25 mm pistol-launched meteor flare is: it goes up, it comes down. It does not linger to make conversation with the moon—or to catch a lookout's eye. The meteor reaches an impressive altitude and, let's admit, 10,000 (or 30,000) candela is nothing to sniff about. But a meteor signal is always brightest when seen from directly beneath (the bang sounds reassuring as well); it's brightness diminishes amazingly at a range of three or four miles—it just looks like a pinpoint of not very bright red light. A pinpoint.

DAY SIGNALS

Day signals consist of orange **smoke signals**, dye packets, the heliograph, and signal flags. **Orange smoke** is a potent signal, but not when even a moderate breeze is blowing; it whips the smoke away. Smoke is particularly useful for attracting aircraft. The USCG requires a minimum one minute burn, SOLAS requires three minutes. Cannisters of smoke, designed to be activated, then thrown overboard, are also available and sold to SOLAS specifications.

A Pains Wessex smoke signal. Remove cap and pull tab to operate. Cutaway shows (1) firing pin and (2) solid smoke fuel. Illustration by Rafael Monroy

Castaway using dye marker and orange smoke as a day signal.

DYE MARKERS

Dye packets are most useful for attracting the attention of aircraft. The iridescent green dye spreads rapidly through the water, creating a 2-600 sq. yd. patch depending on the amount of dye, indicating the castaway's location, which can be seen for miles from the air. A dye packet is both inexpensive and has a long shelf life. It may be attached to a life jacket (along with a light, heliograph and whistle), to make a swimmer more visible to SAR helicopters.

This photograph, taken in the English Channel shows how the Bailey's raft and dinghy looked during their ordeal. A pair of foul weather pants lofted on an oar were far more visibile than either the dinghy or raft. From *Staying Alive* by Maurice and Maralyn Bailey.

DISTRESS FLAGS

A distress flag consists of a square surface (cloth, wood, etc.) on which are displayed a square and a ball. A common one would be an international orange field showing a black ball and square. It is usually used between vessels or for identification from the air. Needless to say, a rescue craft would have to be rather close to see this signal which is, in addition, visible only in daylight.

THE HELIOGRAPH

The heliograph is a signal device made from a mirror. It is used during daylight to flash sunlight at rescue vessels. Almost every life raft equipment pack contains one. Do not let its toy-like appearance fool you. It is a fundamental piece of rescue equipment whose virtue is further enhanced by its low price. Learn to use this tool.

The typical survival heliograph is made from a polished piece of stainless steel, the size of a G.I. hand mirror. More expensive versions are made from weight-saving metalized plastic. The mirror has an eye hole bored at its center around which have been scribed, on its shiny side, several circles, and a set of cross hairs. A reflective foresight with a hole in it is attached to the mirror by a short cord.

A heliograph may seem like a primitive device, and that is its virtue. It functions when wet, never deteriorates and, unlike flares, is reusable. It is more visible than orange smoke on a windy day and can be seen from a great distance. Last but not least it may be your last, but not least, signal device, when all others have been expended.

OPERATION

The heliograph mirror is held close to the eye, and the foresight is extended in front of it, aimed at the rescue vessel. The mirror is tilted so that the sun's reflection from the mirror falls upon the foresight. The device is properly aimed when (1) a reflection of the mirror's cross hairs can be seen on the foresight and (2) both the foresight and the hole in the mirror align with the rescue vessel. Once the mirror is aligned, it should remain aimed at the vessel. Movements of the raft, and slight hand movements appear as flashes to the observer. Newer models have an illumination grid mounted in the eye hole. Sunlight is reflected from the mirror onto the hand. The mirror is brought up to the eye and manipulated so that the hand, used as a foresight, is aimed at the target. The hand is then removed. A bright spot in the grid becomes the foresight.

RANGE

Heliograph signals are visible for incredible distances. Aircraft flying at 30-35,000 feet have been able to spot heliograph flashes. Even if an aircraft is not visible, aim the heliograph in the direction of its sound. Aim it at ships, even if they are partially below the horizon. A heliograph is a line-of-sight instrument. If you can see the other vessel, there is an excellent chance your heliograph signal will be visible—if anyone is watching.

APPLICATION

In addition to use on a survival craft, heliographs may also be attached to life jackets. This makes a swimmer much more visible to searching aircraft. A heliograph, a whistle, and a waterproof light vastly increase the survival chances of a man overboard, particularly if an air search has been initiated. A heliograph should also be standard equipment in the boat's tender (dinghy).

A heliograph is easy to operate, but the wrong place to learn is while floating in a life jacket. It is therefore wise to keep a spare heliograph handy and encourage the crew to amuse themselves with it while underway. Begin practice by aiming at nearby objects such as buoys.

Heliograph made from a can lid.

IMPROVISED HELIOGRAPHS

Any flat, shiny surface, such as a can lid or a piece of reflective plastic can be made into a heliograph by punching a hole in its center. A foresight can be made from a spoon or a knife. If no foresight is available, hold the heliograph a few inches from the face and sight the rescue vessel through the hole. The sun's rays will pass through the hole, fall on the face and be reflected onto the back of the signal device. Move the mirror around until the spot of reflected light falls on the hole. The heliograph is now aligned with the rescue craft.

Even improvised heliographs work well and can be seen for great distances. I made one from a can lid and flashed it (from the top of a 7-story building) at a boat 15 miles away with positive results. The range of a heliograph in survival craft-ship encounters is, of course a function of height-of-eye on the ship. A lookout on a ship's bridge 50 feet above sea level can see the flash of a heliograph (at sea level) $1.15 \times \sqrt{50} = 8$ NM.

USE AT NIGHT

A heliograph will function using moonlight, but a moon-lit, sparkling sea diminishes its effectiveness. If no other signal devices are available, why not give it a try? A heliograph, reflecting moonlight at the water acts as a fish lure (as does a reflective emergency blanket).

NIGHT SIGNALS

Night signals consist of meteor flares, red hand flares, rocket deployed parachute flares, signal pistol parachute flares, strobe flashers and a signal flashlight. Extremely bright chemical lights are available as life jacket lights and they may be used as a substitute for a flare, once the ship is alerted to the presence of the survival craft and has begun a search operation. Some boats carry white rocket-deployed illumination signals for collision-avoidance purposes, and this is a good idea if funds allow.

USCG and SOLAS requirements for illumination pyrotechnics are quite different, and it is clear that (in this case) he who goes with SOLAS is going to get the better stuff. As usual, the better quality costs more. The table below illustrates the point about quality:

DEVICE	U.S.C.G REQUIREMENTS Altitude	Burn	Bright.	SOLAS Altitude	Burn	Bright.
Red Parachute*	1,000'	25 sec.	10,000 cd	1000'	40 sec	30,000 cd
red hand flare	——	2 min.	500 cd	——	1 min	15,000 cd
*Hand launched rocket deployed type.						

Red hand flares are technically visible at a distance based on height-of-eye of the ship's lookout (50 feet = 8 NM, for example). This is once more a fact which obscures rather than reveals the truth, for it would take an especially alert look-out to spot (and identify) a hand flare at this distance. A red flare, periodically hidden by waves, could be mistaken for boat running lights, dipping below the horizon, an assumption easy to make.

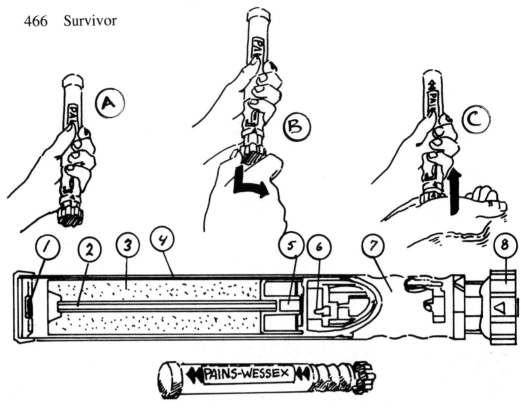

A cut-away of the Pains-Wessex hand flare and how it is used. TOP, left-to-right: A. Grasp handle. B. Rotate striker. C. Hit striker with palm. BOTTOM: (1) igniter pellet (2) center tube (3) flare composition (4) steel tube (5) rimfire cap (6) syriker pin (8) striker.   By Rafael Monroy.

  The longer burn of a hand flare (relative to that of a parachute signal) is its biggest advantage. It not only gives the lookout more opportunity to spot and identify a survival craft, it helps a vessel, alerted to the presence of castaways, to spot the precise location of the craft in the darkness. One would think a half-blind myopic could see such a bright signal, but poor visibility and a steep swell make the task more difficult.

  The 15,000 candelas of illumination held at arm's length do a wondrous job of showing the bright canopy of a life raft. But again, the brightness is far more apparent when viewed at arm's length. Several other factors, of which the castaway is usually unaware, contribute to the survival craft's difficulty. The swell and motion of the craft tend to obscure a burning hand signal, giving it an irregular, winking appearance. It's maddening trying to gauge the bearing and range of such a signal. In addition, the survival craft skates along with the wind, the strength of which is not felt by the lookout on the ship's bridge. The helmsman on the search ship is usually running a bearing taken on a flickering point of light, seen several minutes ago, unaware that the raft is rapidly slipping off downwind.

PARACHUTE FLARES

The most effective parachute flares (and the most expensive) are deployed by hand-launched rockets which carry the parachute and flare to 1,000'—theoretically visible for 44 NM, but most effective at 10 miles or less. The updated Ikaros and the Pains-Wessex rockets burn for 40 seconds at 40,000 candela and are deployed at 1,150'. SOLAS rockets come in a waterproof plastic case, appx. 11" x 2" with pictorial instructions and written instructions, often in in several languages.

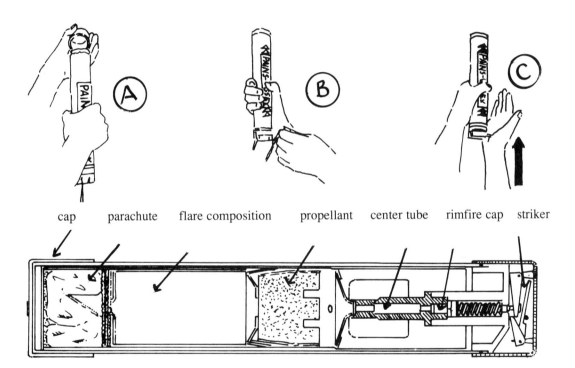

cap   parachute   flare composition   propellant   center tube   rimfire cap   striker

Cut-away illustration and sample launching instructions found on a rocket-deployed Pains-Wessex parachute signal. TOP, left to right: A. Remove seal and cap. B. Remove bottom seal and cap. Pull safety pin. C. Push striker mechanism with palm.

People pop these things off on the 4th of July and seldom think about the potential destructiveness of the flaming monster in their hand, an arm's length from their eyes. Surprisingly, very few accidents occur, which is a credit to the manufacturers.   Nevertheless, protect yourself as much as possible from potential burns and/or shrapnel from a hand-launched rocket.

Hand-launched rockets should be fired with the back to the wind, so that smoke and flame are carried away from the face (if a sea anchor has been properly deployed, the raft door will be facing down wind). Hold the signal in your strong hand, aimed straight upward in a calm or 15-30° (from the vertical) in a breeze, to minimize wind-induced altitude loss. The recommended posture for launching a rocket is shown later in this chapter. Pistol launched parachute signals, in my opinion, fall in the same category as 12 and 25 mm meteor flares.

DANGERS FROM MISHANDLING

If a rocket doesn't fire after 10-12 seconds, jettison it. **<u>Do not look down the tube to see what's wrong</u>**. Never aim a rocket at anyone. At close range they can be really mean. Wear protective clothing. Never launch a rocket facing the wind. Smoke and flames may be blown into your face.

When firing the signal, hold the flare with locked arms, head against chest, eyes closed, holding your breath. Wear protective clothing if possible. Be sure the rocket burn is not directed at the survival craft.

THE STROBE FLASHER

The hand held strobe flasher is undoubtedly your cheapest, biggest bang for the buck. A good parachute flare puts out 30,000 candelas. but a good strobe flashes 300,000 candelas and does so for hours, depending on battery size. Emergency strobes are waterproof and their batteries can be replaced without servicing. Unlike flares, strobes are reusable. Unfortunately, a strobe is not an officially recognized distress signal, and they are often found on fishing floats, floating targets, NOAA drift buoys, etc. Under normal circumstances ships have a tendency to stay away from them, so a strobe must be used in with other, universally recognized distress signals.

THE SIGNAL LIGHT

A signal light is a waterproof flashlight with an intermittent button to facilitate signalling. Because of its low power, it isn't much of a signal, but it may be all you've got. The usual signal is S.O.S. (SAVE OUR SOULS), ···/ - - - /···

EMERGENCY RADIOS

The **EPIRB**, a castaway's best friend (after his life raft!), is discussed in Chapter XIV. In addition, a portable VHF radio (and spare batteries) packed in a waterproof case can do much to save you. Visible ships may be hailed on channel 16 and when none are visible, the radio can be left on "listen," particularly when near shipping lanes, with very little battery demand. The advantage of a VHF is that an unalert lookout, trusting to God and the radar auto alarm to prevent collision, may hear your distress message, even if he did not see your signal or radar image. In addition, a ship's VHF aerial is usually mounted higher than the bridge, so a distress message may be heard even though the survival craft is beyond line-of-sight.

A **radar reflector** is one of those "big bang for the bucks" devices, since it is inexpensive and never wears out. It operates day and night and is only ineffective in high seas. It provides an extremely good return image, which can be seen at a distance relative to the height of the oncoming ships radar antenna. If the ship's antenna is at 60 feet, the range will be 12NM. An oncoming vessel's radar alarm may be a more untiring and faithful lookout than a human. In addition, a reflector can be seen by radar from a SAR aircraft. A reflector made from shiny material is much more visible than a flag, and also provides an extremely good reflection when hit with a searchlight beam. Be sure you have a collapsed, lightweight reflector in your survival pack. The ideal place for a radar reflector is on a man overboard pole, towed by a survival craft.

CHAPTER XVII: THE SURVIVAL PACK

Rub a dub, dub
Four men in a tub
Two deck apes,
The captain and cook.
If you like to eat
As much as they do,
Check your survival pack
Or it might be you—
—In the stew.

It must be clear from the stories you have read in this book, that many boats, when they sink, do so very quickly. In their haste to abandon ship, castaways sometimes forget critical items, such as food, water, fishing equipment, knives—simply because in the confusion—they just forget. The terror of the disaster and the short time available make it important to have some sort of survival pack ready for instant use. The pack is supposed to contain a mini-environment, sufficient to sustain life for an indefinite period of time.

There are several different ways to increase the chances that your survival craft and your emergency equipment end up in the same place at the same time. Certainly the most obvious is to pack the most critical (core) items, the EPIRB(s), water-maker, medical kit, and signals pack in the survival craft itself, being absolutely sure that the items are well-secured, to prevent their loss in the event of a swamping or capsize. If a life raft is your survival vehicle, it may not be possible to add what you consider all essential equipment and still close the raft's container. In that case one may consider the possibility of obtaining a larger raft container. Many life raft certification centers have cannisters available.

Another option is to pack core items in a small, strong bag, which is attached to a short line which runs to a strong point on the raft. The raft and the pack are jettisoned at the same time, or float up from the wreck together if the sinking was extremely sudden. A second, larger supplementary pack containing the remainder of the survival equipment, plus water jugs and other items, can be loaded after the survival craft is launched.

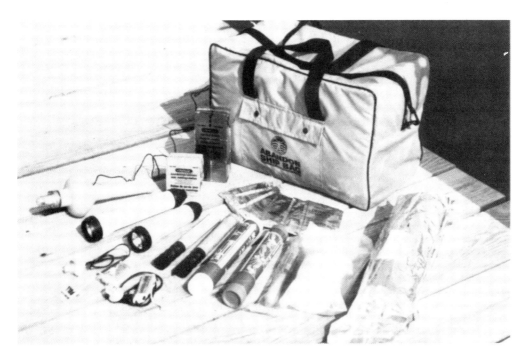

Survival Technologies "core" size Survival Pack Container with positive Flotation

TYPE OF CONTAINER

Some life raft equipment packs are soft, made out of strong synthetic cloth and plastic fasteners. A soft survival pack or packs have the advantage of being lighter, and they conform to their storage space. On the other hand, the contents of a soft pack can be damaged if sat or stepped upon, and the pack must be protected from this as well as exposure to the elements. A hard pack offers better protection for its contents and may keep them dry, if the unit is waterproof. If the survival craft is a dinghy or lifeboat, the hard pack may be used as a seat or built in as a seat.

Regardless of what type of material is used as a container, it is important that the pack is buoyant or at least doesn't sink like a stone. This may be accomplished by making the pack watertight, but the individual items within the pack should be in waterproof containers. The air trapped in them should provide positive buoyancy, even if the pack itself does not. Some people prefer to use clear waterproof freezer bags for this purpose and the advantage is that bags are cheap, take up a minimum of space. Others, who have spent time in survival craft, recommend using hard plastic refrigerator containers or heavy wide-mouth bottles with screw-cap tops, and these have several advantages: they protect their contents from being crushed, they are easily resealed. They are less fragile than bags, and they can be used to store rainwater or food. You may want to use a combination of bags and containers in your pack. Regardless of what you use, be sure all items are <u>easily inspected</u>.

Weight is always a consideration when creating a survival pack, the limiting factor being the ability of <u>the weakest person</u> to lift and deploy it. Several packs may be required to meet your needs, and if this is the case, the food, water, etc., should be divided so that some will survive, even if one of the packs is lost.

Even if all items in a survival pack are in waterproof containers, it is just good procedure to protect the pack itself from exposure to water. This may mean using rubberized rafting bags, placing the pack in a deck-mounted storage box or a large plastic container. Some people prefer to store it in a locker or lazarette, which protects against moisture and gets the pack out of the way, but this procedure often separates the survival craft and pack, increasing the possibility that the two will not end up together when needed.

CREW DRILLS

Crew have different capabilities, and it may not be possible to explain in detail how absolutely everything (such as the surgery kit) works. Nevertheless, everyone should be able to operate the EPIRB and signals and should be advised about the other items in a general way. If possible, open the survival pack and show its contents, explaining their use. Make an explanation booklet, if necessary, by photocopying and pasting up literature about the equipment, especially the core items: the EPIRB, water-maker, and signals. Include a copy of the pack contents list. Remind the crew that there is very little water in the pack and raft. Show them the location of the emergency water supply and other survival equipment not contained in the pack.

CREATING A SURVIVAL PACK

There is no such thing as a perfect survival pack. Many factors help determine what is best for you. A minimum kit, containing core items, water and food, may suffice for some voyages, an extremely sophisticated and expensive pack may be necessary for others. You may decide that the area through which you will be traveling is well-protected by the Coast Guard or Life Saving Service. Perhaps core items and a second, spare EPIRB and/or survival suits will be all that is needed. It may be best to ask oneself, "what is the worst-case situation I may experience?" The answer may well be "a few hours to a few days in a life raft in warm water and summer weather"—or something very different.

Keep this in mind when examining the proposed pack items in the following list. You will doubtless find items missing which you think should have been included or others which seem both expensive and useless.

Survival Pack: Four Persons

Contents to supplement life raft equipment pack.
Approximate Weight: 40 lbs.

SUGGESTED TOTAL		CORE PACK

FOOD

10	food rations, 3 man-days each, life raft type in 500 g. units	4
8	survival candy bars	4
24	oz. glucose sweets (sour balls)	
8	soup, 10.5 oz., salt-free (beef bouillon and chicken noodle)	2
8	cans 3.14 oz. ea. sweetened condensed milk	
32	vitamins, chewable	
16	packs (sachets) water, 125 ml. ea.	16

EQUIPMENT

1	collapsible jug, 20 liter, bladder with nylon cover	
8	survival blankets	
1	nylon mesh bag, 30" X 45"	
4	towels, small	
1	collapsible bucket, 2.5 gals.	
2	eating utensil sets	
1	spear gun, short, double rubber	
1	ea. spare spear, rubbers	
3	spare heads, detachable type.	
1	*Sea Survival, a Manual*, by Dougal Robertson, in waterproof bag or life raft survival manual, *SEA JAY* (Elliot Life Raft), waterproof, (alternate book)	1
1	literature and/or a notebook and pencils in a plastic container	
1	pack playing cards, plastic	
3	pr. panty hose, support, heavy (for plankton seines) and wire loop	

1	measuring cup with handle	
1	Barracuda mask (eye goggles)	
6	solar stills or desalinator(s	all
100	feet ea. nylon line (1/4, 3/16, 3/8) and sail twine	
1	magnifier	
1	sea anchor (spare), Icelandic, non-rotating, cone-type	1
2	tubes silicone seal	
2	box matches, wind- and waterproof	

TOOLS

1	can opener	
1	sharpening stone	
1	screwdriver	
1	pliers, stainless steel with wire cutter	1
4	assorted hose clamps, up to 1.5" diameter	
1	trail ax or hatchet with lanyard	
4	needles and heavy, waxed nylon thread	
1	double-edged, commando-type knife, about 7" with nylon sheath	1
1	heavy-duty stainless combination knife	1
2	sets life raft patching clamps	1
1	pr. shears	

FISHING EQUIPMENT

275	yards 50 lb. test monofilament fishing line	all
100	yards codline	
10	yards wire leader, 75 lb. test, plastic-coated	all
26	hooks, stainless steel, barbed (for mahi-mahi)	all
12	hooks, barbed, medium	all
24	hooks, small (for trigger fish)	all
3	hooks, #0, gaff size, stainless steel	all
8	sinkers, 1/4 oz.	all
4	lures, assorted	all

SIGNALS (To supplement signals in equipment pack)

1	heliograph	1
10	red rockets, parachute	
6	orange smoke signals	3
8	red hand flares	6
3	dye markers	
1	strobe flasher and spare batteries	1

1	radar reflector, collapsible	
1	high quality, underwater flashlight with batteries	1

RADIO EQUIPMENT

2	EPIRBs	1
1	VHF hand-held radio transmitter, spare batteries	1

NAVIGATION EQUIPMENT (see Chapter XIII)

1	compass and deviation card	1
1	aero chart of the area, waterproofed	
1	marine chart of the area	1
1	aero protractor	1
1	deck log	1
1	emergency navigation pack	

CLOTHING BAG
Contents to be based on area of travel and may include for each person:

1	ea. thermal protection suit
1	pair thermal underwear, synthetic material
1	synthetic or wool.shirt
1	pair pants, heavy and loose-fitting
2	pair socks, synthetic material or wool
1	set foul weather gear or float gear
1	pair boots, rubber
2	pair underwear, cotton, heavy material

FOR COLD WEATHER

1	immersion suit (best choice), wet suit, or insulated float suit and booties
1	pair gloves, synthetic, insulated
1	air matress for uninsulated floors

MONEY AND DOCUMENTS   ALL

ABANDON SHIP MEDICAL EQUIPMENT KIT   1

Comments About Suggested Survival Equipment

COMMENTS BY DOUGAL ROBERTSON

"What are the size of these packs? They may need another raft to carry them! I think a spare sea anchor of good quality, oil for troubled waters, and an oil distribution bag to fit the sea anchor would be necessary additions to the pack. Parachute type sea anchors would not be as efficient as cone type, especially in high seas.

A urine bottle saves a great deal of agony to boil-covered survivors and keeps the raft in a sanitary state (good for morale!). The mesh bag (or possibly the spare Icelandic sea anchor) makes a good storage for dried fish, allowing them to be hung up to air."

COMMENTS BY STEVE CALLAHAN

"I stress a couple of concepts: Raw materials and tools allow survivors the most flexibility to adapt to their circumstances. Basics like plastic sheet, string, and knives can be used to fashion a lot of specialized equipment. In the raft or "core" pack, put only essentials. In the survival pack, put items which need maintenance or may be required for use aboard the boat. Other packages, to be ready for instant use include water jugs, immersion suits, etc."

AUTHOR'S COMMENTS

FOOD

Since people are able to live for a long time without food, one might ask why rations and other foodstuffs sufficient for 65 to 70 days have been included in the survival pack. The reason is because sufficient food and water offer great reassurance to people in a desperate situation. Think of how nice it would be to tell your frightened crew, *"Look! We have enough food and water for months!"*

In addition to hard rations, a certain amount of liquid food (milk and broth) has been included in the recommended pack. It may be fed to the injured or sick more easily than hard food. In addition, if you have purchased quality emergency rations, they will dissolve in these liquids, to make a sort of gruel, which can fed to a patient or eaten by someone who has lost their dentures.

EQUIPMENT

The collapsible jug is just for water storage and may be eliminated if other containers are included in the pack. Survival blankets are the cheapest, most compact item capable of offering some protection from hypothermia. In addition, they have a variety of uses which make them valuable. Two thermal blankets are sufficient to completely wrap one person. The mesh sack, such as a dive bag, can be used to store loose items, preventing their loss in the event of capsize, among its many uses. The bucket is included as a bailer and has many other uses. Some sort of survival manual is strongly recommended. It must be waterproof, as is the *Sea-Jay* booklet, or packed in a safe, dry container, such as a wide-mouth jar, with other items which must remain dry. The dive mask can be used for examining the bottom of the survival craft, or for diving. The magnifier is intended for starting fires

Tools: Aside from standard tools, an ax or hatchet is recommended for killing turtles or for defense against sharks.

SIGNALS

The "heart" of a survival pack consists of signals and water. Keeping in mind Rule No. 3 (signals are like blessings; you cannot have too many of them), the signals bag recommended here is considered a minimum. Take as many additional signals, including expired flares, as you can manage. Keep in mind that signals, including electronic ones, have a high failure rate and those which do function may not be seen by the ship's lookout. A single flare, seen briefly by an unalert or disbelieving lookout may bring no response. A series of signals, fired at intervals of one or two minutes may be much more effective, but they, too, may bring no response. It is not unusual for a castaway to be passed by three, four, or more vessels, before being sighted. All of this suggests the need for a hefty signals bag containing a variety of different attention-attracting devices. Some signals, such as the parachute flares, an EPIRB and a VHF radio are expensive. Hard decisions about how to invest your money must be made. Other signals, such as the heliograph, radar reflector and strobe flasher are cheaper. There is a natural tendency to buy the low-priced items and neglect the others, but a signals bag of this type is incomplete. Buy what you can afford.

RADIO EQUIPMENT

One or more A or B class EPIRBs are the heart of any survival pack, despite their shortcomings. In many areas of the world they are sufficient to activate the global SAR network. Even in areas where A or B class EPIRBs are as ineffective as uplink transmitters, it is possible that a passing aircraft will hear the signal. The new 406 MHz EPIRB should prove much more reliable, activating a SAR response regardless of the transmitter's location. EPIRBs, like all electronic equipment, sometimes fail, and this is why a second unit should be considered.

EPIRBs are now manufactured with long-life batteries (ten years or more) and these may be stored in a raft equipment pack. This is an ultimate way to be sure your EIPRB ends up with you in the survival craft. A second unit can be stored in the survival pack so that it is easily accessible, should it be needed.

A hand-held VHF radio provides possible contact with nearby vessels or with SAR craft, attracted by your EPIRB signal. Think of how absolutely delightful it would be to climb into your survival craft, turn on your emergency VHF, send a MAYDAY and get an immediate response. Boats traveling in or near shipping lanes or near land vastly increase their chance of a quick rescue if a MAYDAY is sent and acknowledged. Generally speaking, any station sending a VHF transmission you can hear will also be able to hear your signal.

CLOTHING BAG

Thermal protection suits, basically waterproof sacks made from material similar to emergency blankets, are the recommended minimum for the clothing bag and are now mandatory equipment for SOLAS-type rafts. If other clothing items are lost in the abandonment, thermal protection bags may well be all that stands between a castaway and death from hypothermia. On the other hand, thermal protection suits are insufficient protection for emergencies in waters which are not tropical or semi-tropical. The clothing bag may appear to be a bulky, expensive nuisance, but the clothing recommended will not only protect against hypothermia, the recommended materials (wool and synthetic cloth) greatly contribute to keeping skin dry and reduce the chance of developing skin sores.

COLD WEATHER CLOTHING

Many factors must be considered when selecting cold-weather emergency clothing, including cost and available space for storage. If you have the cash and the space, exposure suits are items which quite frequently mean the difference between life and death. A well-made, well-equipped survival suit, may also be considered a PFD.

Medical Equipment: Even if you personally cannot stand the idea of treating someone medically, it is still wise to carry a good med kit containing prescription drugs. Someone else in the crew may be able to use the kit, even if you cannot. When showing the kit, I usually do not mention that it contains controlled substances, since this might offer someone an unnecessary temptation.

Comments:

Nothing improves your chance of surviving a boat disaster as much as the three P's: Planning, Preparation and Practice. Planning includes the creation of a survival pack list, where to store it and where to deploy it. Selection of the right survival craft is also important. Planning also includes assigning abandonment jobs to each crew member, based on their abilities. Station Bills (see Chapter X) act as reminders, and the crew can refer to them during an emergency.

You will notice that the suggested survival pack, like the equipment pack inside a life raft, contains very little water. Water greatly increases the size and weight of a survival pack. Our suggested pack is already quite heavy and already contains a variety of water-making devices. The wise captain stores a supply of water in jugs as close as possible to the place where the survival craft will be launched. The jugs should have lanyards attached so that the jugs can be tied to the survival craft strong point, then tossed into the sea.

CHAPTER XVIII: MAN OVERBOARD!

The best way to prevent death at sea is to prevent the accident from occurring in the first place. An overboard fatality may be blamed on a misstep, bad weather, even drunkenness, but if the path to disaster is followed to its ultimate source, negligence by the owner/captain is usually the cause, and that includes allowing drunken fools to cavort about. Failure to have or maintain safety equipment, or lax procedure, eventually results in an accident, which is then blamed on crew carelessness.

Among the most common failures: lack of deck traction pads in slippery, hazardous places; old, fatigued life lines; short stanchions; old or improperly designed stanchion pads; lack of a jack line to which safety harness leads can be connected; failure to string extra life lines in bad weather; lack of an overboard pole; no abandon boat or overboard drills and, most common of all, failure to establish safety rules. These are invariably the real causes of death.

The Risk of Loss and Difficulty of Recovery

There is a relationship between wind speed and sea state, but larger waves occasionally sweep the decks even of large ships. In general, you may anticipate at least one mini-rogue wave, 1.5 times the height of the average highest 10% of all other waves encountered. So if seas are running 6 feet on the average, with some waves 9' in height, it is extremely likely that a 12-13 feet wave will come to visit about every hour. That is the kind of wave that eats unwary crew. Anyone working outside the cockpit should be required to wear a harness. A safety harness clipped to a jack line should be lying in the cockpit, ready to use, one for each side of the boat. Several more harnesses should be "ready for action." Foremost among those to wear one should be the captain, who will then be teaching by example. Some high-quality Type III vests have built-in harnesses, and these are ideal.

Face Page: *Man Overboard!* Painting by Richard DeRosset.

Retrieval of a man lost overboard looks much easier from an armchair than it does from the cockpit on a dark and stormy night, with the wail of your lost friend's cry ringing in your ears. It is incredible how hard it is to see a human head sticking out of the water, even on a tranquil bay in daylight.

I once sailed with some friends on Biscayne Bay (Miami). The day was hot and sunny, the bay calm, the winds quite light. The boat was not making more than three or four knots. One of the girls wanted to drag behind the boat at the end of a line. She jumped overboard, but missed the line. The pleasant conditions lured me into a false sense of security. I made a leisurely turn to pick her up. By the time I turned the boat around the girl was nowhere to be seen. A cold stab of fear shot through me. I had to force it down so as not to panic the others. I told them to get up on the cabin top and look for her. She was spotted eventually, far away. I never told her how close she had come to death that warm, sunny day. What would her chances have been in the open sea, with a 20-knot breeze and an appropriate sea-state?

The difficulty of seeing someone in the open sea must really be experienced to be appreciated. Tie a weighted rag (to act as a sea anchor) to an empty gallon milk jug. The jug will represent a human head. I like to take a marking pen and put a face on the jug to enhance its realism. When everyone is sailing along, having a good time, suddenly throw the jug over the side and cry "Man overboard!" Assign someone to watch the jug. Try to recover it. This is a fun game with a jug, and it's amazing how often you miss the jug. One sailor insisted on using his wife instead of the jug, every time they sailed. She didn't like it from the start, and it went straight down hill from there. One day, after he insisted, as usual, she finally jumped overboard, swam to shore, went home, then divorced him. Stick to the jug.

Because it is so very difficult to see a swimmer, random searching has virtually no chance of succeeding. Only a preplanned, systematic search procedure, backed by a certain minimum amount of equipment will work.

Boat Safety Features

LIFELINES

Most (but not all) boats have lifelines, but since there are no regulations concerning them, lifeline systems are often designed around aesthetic, rather than safety guidelines. Small boats frequently have short stanchions. I have seen boats with stanchions just 10 inches high. They would be ideal for a crew

How far could a human head be seen in this picture?

whose average height was 24 inches. Marine catalogs show standard stanchion height to be 26 inches, which would catch the average man just above the knee, yet it is clear (measure yourself) that a 30 inches stanchion would catch the average person closer to the waist, making it much harder to fall overboard.

The great majority of lifelines are fabricated using cold molded (sometimes called swaged) terminals. All cold-moulded fittings have a life, after which they fail. Any terminal that has the slightest crack or is leaking rust is a deteriorated terminal, awaiting only the right opportunity to fail in some spectacular way. Someone falling on a lifeline secured by a cracked terminal would be just the right opportunity for the wire to pull free. Old, deteriorated lifelines (or safety equipment) may be more dangerous than none at all, because of the false sense of security they provide.

Most boat stanchions provide holes for two sets of lifelines, one at the top and a second set slightly more than halfway from the bottom. The essential third set, six inches from the deck is almost never found, yet many a sailor has fallen on a wet, heaving deck, slipped beneath the lifelines, struggled to hold on to the toe rail, only to be sucked away by the hungry sea.

JACKLINES

Jacklines run fore and aft along (or near) the decks and are attached to hefty strong points at either end of the boat. Safety harness leads are clipped to them, allowing the wearer to walk the entire length of the boat in safety. Jacklines should be able to take the full shock of a 180-pound man coming up suddenly at the end of a six foot lead, a shock-load of about 1,000 foot-pounds.

TRACTION PADS

Raw teak decks are a pain to maintain, but they provide the absolute best traction when wet. Plastic and shiny paint look great in port, but are accidents waiting to happen when wet. Modern, anti-slip matting glued to a plastic deck works really well, but the older textured fiberglass is slippery when wet and also slippery when dry and salty. Walnut shells, mixed with paint produce an excellent non-skid surface. The wise captain makes sure that critical areas, such as around the mast and the forward portion of the foredeck have excellent, non-slip surfaces and/or guard rails where necessary.

Personal Safety Gear

It is extremely rare to see boaters wearing safety equipment of any kind. If one looks through boating magazines, it is unusual to see even harnesses being worn by deck crews on racing boats, even though risks which could result in an overboard situation are taken regularly. Should an accident (or fatality) occur, the correct place for the blame will be on the captain's head.

The majority of drownings occur on inland waterways, within a few feet of safety. People who die offshore almost always go into the water without their Personal Floatation Device (PFD), despite the fact that one was available to them prior to the accident.

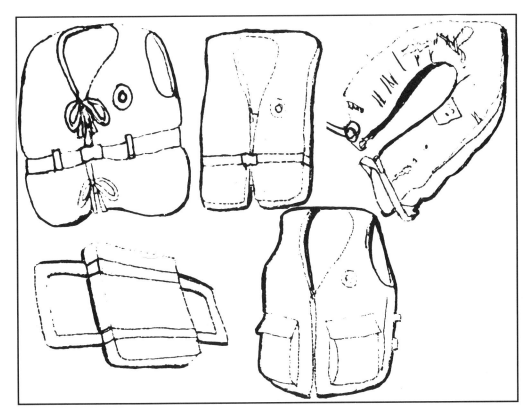

Typical Type I-V Flotation Devices. Left to right, top to bottom: Type I,II, IV, III and V.
Drawing by Raoul Reys.

    Far more people die after being lost overboard than as the result of sink-
ings. There are more powerboat than sailboat fatalities in this category, presumably because a power boat's wheel house is enclosed, and that last frantic cry for
help is not heard above the noise of the engines. Losing someone overboard can
be even more horrifying than having to abandon ship. Desperate visions race
through one's head of the poor soul struggling for life in the open sea, alone,
cold, frightened, bait for the sharks, or, ultimately, the crabs. Good Lord, what
does one tell the man's wife, his children, his parents? How many lives will be
damaged because you had no overboard equipment, were lax about life jacket
and safety harness requirements, or didn't practice man overboard drills? Make
no mistake, your chances of finding someone lost overboard range from not
good to lousy. If you are the captain, that person's death is your responsibility.
God may protect fools, drunks and sailors (not necessarily in that order) but
nothing will save a swimmer, except equipment and practice.

LIFE VEST DESIGN

The human body is naturally buoyant in water but the behind is more buoyant than the head. The buttocks tend to float, while the head sinks. Constant movement of the hands is necessary to keep a swimmer from floating in a butt up, face down position. This struggle is very exhausting, as anyone who has tried to tread water for perhaps thirty minutes knows. A good life jacket corrects these problems by adding sufficient buoyancy to the chest. A flotation collar or "pillow" keeps the head from slipping under water. A good vest not only positions the wearer face-up, it gets the face as high above water as possible, provides a significant degree of thermal insulation, and has an assortment of straps and "snugs" to prevent slipping of the device in a seaway.

CLASSIFICATION OF PERSONAL FLOTATION DEVICES

Type I Offshore Jacket
Type II Near-Shore Buoyant Vest
Type III Flotation Aide

Type IV Throwable Devices
Type V Special Use Devices

Children's vests: Children have (for their size) larger heads than adults and children's vests are specially designed with this in mind. Many have either extra thick collars or a sort of pillow to support the head. The wise captain carries at least one child's vest or one for every ten adult vests or as many as necessary.

THE OFFSHORE JACKET

It's easy to understand that the buoyancy of a life jacket is what keeps one afloat. An Offshore Type I jacket, with 22 to 35 lbs. of buoyancy, obviously does a much better job of keeping you afloat than 8 lbs. On the other hand, it's much easier to get casual wearers to don a smaller, more compact vest, with less flotation, so the location, as well as the amount of buoyant material is critical.

Without question, the Type I jacket, provides the most flotation and unfailingly positions the wearer, even if he is unconscious, in the face-up position. They are reversible, easy to don and they get the face and shoulders out of the water. A good, snug-fitting Offshore jacket also provides some insulation against the effects of hypothermia. But a PFD is only useful if it is worn, and it is virtually impossible to get anyone to wear an offshore jacket, unless the vessel is obviously in deep trouble. In addition, Type I's are huge and hard to store aboard a typical boat.

This Fastnet racer died as the result of a succession of errors, as is so often the case. He broke his collar bone, prior to abandonment and could not properly don his inflatable vest. While in the raft, the problem was not corrected. A German coaster spotted the raft, came along side and dropped a scramble net. The uninjured crew climbed aboard, but the injured man had difficulty and was swept away. This type of "dead man's float" also results when the head slips out of a vest lacking crotch straps. Photo by Andrew Besley.

A flotation device functions only as long as it remains attached to a swimmer's body. If the securing straps are old, worn, of cheap construction or have fasteners which slip, the vest is likely to slip off, particularly when the wearer becomes exhausted. Do not neglect examining these straps when purchasing a flotation device and <u>be sure you know how to operate them for optimum fit</u>. Crotch straps prevent people from slipping down, out of their jackets.

THE STANDARD TYPE II "NEAR-SHORE" PFD (MAE WEST

Boat owners usually buy cheap, less bulky, Type II life jackets, formerly called "Mae Wests" because they reminded flyers of that actress' exceptional natural endowments. They are similar in size and shape to the Type V aircraft inflatable vest when it is inflated (also called the "Mae West" for the same reason). Typical cheap Type II's are inadequate, suitable only for Coast Guard courtesy inspections and keeping the Marine Patrol off your case. Type II's are called "near-shore vests," and there is an implication that an accident near shore is less serious than one "offshore," whereever that is, but this argument hardly bears examination. I spent five hours floating in a Mae West (in sight of land) and still marvel that I have a neck left to support my head.

The Mae West was an early design in personal flotation devices and, in its day, it was great. Thousands or maybe tens of thousands of people have had their lives saved using this device. Its big improvement over earlier equipment is that it was designed to keep the head from falling forward, into the water, a common occurrence when suffering from hypothermia.

The Mae West positions the wearer on his back in a semi-horizontal position and is supposed to turn a debilitated or unconscious castaway face up. It does not do this consistently. Because the wearer is positioned more or less horizontally, the head is just inches above sea level. Every passing wave provides an excellent opportunity to get a mouthful of salt sea. That's when things are going well. If one has bought a real "bargain," only the narrow strap and thick collar connect the Mae West to the swimmer. The strap has a tendency to ride up (or the swimmer slips down), and when that occurs, the vest floats free of the torso, so that the victim floats in a vertical position with all of the strain on the neck. All the skin is chaffed off the neck and the sufferer, whose mouth is mere inches above the water, is half-drowned with every passing wave. Eventually, fatigue takes its toll fighting these conditions, and the jacket slips off the wearer's head, allowing him to drown.

The Mae West provides no thermal insulation for the body core and is not designed to fight hypothermia in any way. Last but not least, wearing a Mae West is like wearing two loaves of bread on your chest and a deli-sized salami around your neck. It is hard to get people to wear them, except when a crisis occurs. Since flotation devices only save lives if they are worn, the Mae West has become the runt of the litter. A runt is what you get for ten bucks.

TYPE III PFD'S: FLOTATION VESTS

Type III flotation aid, as sports vests are classified, have a multitude of advantages over the Mae West, including better positioning, thermal protection, and wearing comfort. They are not an ultimate solution, as is the Type I heavy-duty, Offshore jacket, but it is relatively easy to get crewmen to wear a Type III and this makes them invaluable. Some are **hybrids** with inflatable collars, making it possible to cushion the head and increase buoyancy. Others have **crotch flaps** to conserve body heat.

In a Type III vest, buoyancy is distributed so that the wearer floats in a slightly backward, upright position, with the shoulders (or maybe armpits) awash. These few extra inches of freeboard (between the mouth and the sea) do much to reduce the ingestion of saltwater.

The better-quality Type III vests have closures which snug the vest against the body, providing added thermal insulation. A high collar can be snugged against the neck, further reducing heat loss. A good vest will increase survival-from-hypothermia time by as much as 70% (see Chapter IX). In addition, a good vest has pockets, which can be stuffed with survival equipment such as a heliograph, dye marker, pocket-type flares, and a whistle. Small strobe flashers can be attached to the outside of the vest or dropped in a pocket, for use in the event of a nighttime accident. Some people also carry a small, portable VHF in a waterproof pouch, which can be used (in the water) to direct SAR craft, or can be homed in on, if the SAR vessel has a directional VHF antenna.

The Mae West may be adequate to keep the Marine Patrol from writing you a violation ticket, but the wise captain provides his crew with buoyancy vests. They are much more comfortable to wear and if the captain puts his on as the boat departs, it is easy to convince the others to do so as well.

Consumer Reports (July 1988 issue) printed the results of an exhaustive study, in which people of different sizes wore different Type III vests, both in a pool and in a lake, where waves were generated by a speed boat, to simulate ocean conditions. The report, part of which is printed on the next pages, is a reminder that all PFDs are not the same, and that care should be taken when investing in them. *Consumer Reports* term "breathing margin" refers to the vest's ability to keep the head 6-12 inches above water. The term "ride up" refers to the tendency of most vests to allow the wearer to "slip down," out of the device. *Consumer Reports* also noted that all of the jackets required effort to remain vertical, especially if hit from the rear by a wave, although the best models just required slight head or body movements.

Ratings of Type III life jackets

Listed in order of estimated quality, based on combined test results for all body builds considered. Dashes in performance columns denote lack of data because jacket could not be made to fit securely on tester. Except as noted, all are available in bright, highly visible colors. Unless otherwise indicated, prices are list; * indicates that price is approximate; + indicates that shipping is extra. ⒹＤ indicates that model has been discontinued.

Better ◄——————————► Worse

Brand and model	Price	Sizes[1]	Medium female					Medium male					Comments
			Breathing margin	Face up/face down	Vertical position	Stability on back	Resists ride-up	Breathing margin	Face up/face down	Vertical position	Stability on back	Resists ride-up	
Americas Cup 100W	$80	S/M,L,XL	⊖	⊜	⊜	⊜	⊜	⊜	⊜	⊜	○	○	—
Mustang MV3114	66	S,M,L,XL	◑	⊜	⊜	⊜	⊜	○	⊜	⊜	⊜	⊜	C,D
Omega Pullover PV-50	39	M,L/XL	⊜	⊜	○	⊜	⊜	⊜	⊜	⊜	⊜	○	C,H,J
Safeguard Seafare 505	38	S,M,L,XL	◑	⊜	⊜	⊜	⊜	⊜	⊜	⊜	○	⊜	C,D,K
Stearns SBV6777	40	S,M,L,XL	○	⊜	⊜	⊜	⊜	⊜	○	⊜	○	⊜	C,D
Americas Cup 305	67	S,M,L,XL	⊖	⊜	○	⊜	⊜	⊜	●	⊜	⊜	⊜	C
Cypress Gardens CSM	25*	S/M,L/XL	○	◑	⊜	⊜	○	○	◑	○	○	○	L
Ⓓ Sears Helmsman Cat. No. 63150	[2]	Universal	◑	⊜	●	⊜	○	⊜	⊜	○	⊜	○	P
Ⓓ Sears Helmsman Cat. No. 63134	[2]	Universal	◑	⊜	⊜	⊜	○	○	○	○	⊜	◑	E,P
Mustang MV3100	38	S,M,L,XL	◑	⊜	○	○	⊜	○	⊜	●	⊜	⊜	E
Stearns SBV6900	27	Universal	◑	○	○	○	⊜	○	⊜	⊜	○	⊜	—
Apco GPA	14*	Universal	○	⊜	●	⊜	⊜	○	◑	◑	○	◑	—
Sears Helmsman Cat. No. 63131	12+	Universal	○	⊜	⊜	⊜	⊜	◑	◑	◑	○	◑	—
Cypress Gardens CA3	17*	Universal	◑	⊜	○	⊜	⊜	○	◑	◑	○	◑	B
Ⓓ Omega Rally-Stripe RS50	49	S,M,L,XL	○	◑	⊜	⊜	⊜	◑	◑	●	◑	◑	M
Kent A2	18	Universal	◑	⊜	○	⊜	⊜	◑	○	◑	◑	○	—
Sears Helmsman Cat. No. 63147	18+	S,M,L	○	⊜	○	⊜	⊜	◑	◑	◑	⊜	◑	B,E
Cypress Gardens EA3	15*	Universal	○	⊜	⊜	○	⊜	◑	◑	◑	◑	○	—
Stearns SSV2135	33	M,L,XL	—	—	—	—	—	⊜	○	○	◑	◑	A,E,G
Cut'n Jump WO223	20	S/M,L/XL	●	○	●	○	●	◑	◑	○	○	●	E,N
Cut'n Jump WO236	26	S/M,L/XL	●	◑	○	●	◑	◑	◑	●	◑	●	E,I,O
Stearns SBV2126	20	S/M,L/XL	◑	●	●	○	○	○	◑	◑	○	◑	F
Ⓓ Americas Cup 809	26	Universal	●	⊜	⊜	●	●	●	●	◑	●	●	B,E,F,M
Stearns WJM9147	69	S,M,L,XL	●	○	◑	⊜	◑	◑	○	⊜	◑	◑	A,E,G
Stearns SSV2128	20	S/M,L,XL	●	◑	○	◑	◑	◑	◑	⊜	◑	●	B,E,F
Stearns SBV2125	16	Universal	●	●	●	◑	◑	◑	●	●	○	●	E,F

[1] S = small; M = medium; L = large; XL = extra large. Universal models can be adjusted to fit chest sizes from 30 to 52 in.
[2] Not listed in current catalog.

KEY TO COMMENTS

A—Trapped almost 1 gal. of water; could hinder wearer's emergence from water.
B—Difficult to adjust for fit in water.
C—Drawstring or belt fits under rib cage and prevents jacket from riding up.
D—Exceptionally comfortable.
E—Closes with zipper only, a possible problem if zipper disengages.
F—Secured with laces running through rings; laces slipped loose in our tests, worsening fit and aggravating ride-up.
G—Cannot be adjusted for fit, a shortcoming that caused excessive ride-up in our tests.
H—Pullover design; difficult to put on in water.
I—Not available in bright, highly visible colors, judged a serious deficiency.
J—Model number is for medium size. Large/extra-large size is designated PV-60.
K—Model number is for medium size. Small size is designated 503; large, 507; extra-large, 509.
L—Model number is for small/medium size. Also tested was large/extra-large model CLXL, but that has been replaced by model CVLX, which is cut differently around the neck.
M—Model number is for small/medium size.
N—Model number is for small/medium size. Large/extra-large size is designated WO224.
O—Model number is for small/medium size. Large/extra-large size is designated WO237.

Performance table on next page

Performance of Type III life jackets on different body sizes

Brand and model	Breathing margin	Face up/face down	Vertical position	Stability on back	Resists ride-up	Breathing margin	Face up/face down	Vertical position	Stability on back	Resists ride-up	Breathing margin	Face up/face down	Vertical position	Stability on back	Resists ride-up	Breathing margin	Face up/face down	Vertical position	Stability on back	Resists ride-up	Breathing margin	Face up/face down	Vertical position	Stability on back	Resists ride-up
						Slight female					Large male					Large female					Husky male				
Americas Cup 100W	⊖	⊖	●	⊖	⊖	⊖	⊖	⊖	⊖	⊖	⊖	⊖	⊖	⊖	○	⊖	⊖	⊖	⊖	⊖					
Mustang MV3114	○	⊖	⊖	⊖	⊖	○	⊖	⊖	⊖	⊖	○	⊖	⊖	⊖	●	⊖	○	⊖	⊖						
Omega Pullover PV-50	⊖	⊖	⊖	⊖	⊖	○	⊖	○	⊖	⊖	⊖	⊖	⊖	⊖	○	⊖	⊖	⊖	⊖						
Safeguard Seafare 505	⊖	⊖	⊖	○	⊖	⊖	○	⊖	⊖	⊖	⊖	⊖	⊖	⊖	○	⊖	⊖	⊖	⊖						
Stearns SBV6777	⊖	⊖	⊖	○	⊖	○	○	⊖	⊖	⊖	⊖	⊖	⊖	⊖	○	●	⊖	⊖	⊖						
Americas Cup 305	⊖	○	⊖	⊖	⊖	○	⊖	⊖	●	⊖	⊖	⊖	⊖	⊖	●	⊖	⊖	●	⊖	○					
Cypress Gardens CSM	⊖	⊖	⊖	⊖	⊖	○	⊖	⊖	⊖	○	⊖	⊖	⊖	⊖	●	⊖	○	⊖	○	○					
Sears Helmsman Cat. No. 63150	⊖	○	⊖	○	○	○	⊖	○	⊖	⊖	○	⊖	⊖	○	○	⊖	○	⊖	○	○					
Sears Helmsman Cat. No. 63134	○	⊖	⊖	○	●	⊖	⊖	⊖	⊖	⊖	⊖	⊖	⊖	○	○	○	○	○	⊖	○					
Mustang MV3100	⊖	⊖	⊖	⊖	●	○	⊖	⊖	⊖	⊖	●	⊖	⊖	⊖	○	⊖	○	○	○						
Stearns SBV6900	⊖	⊖	○	⊖	⊖	⊖	⊖	⊖	⊖	⊖	⊖	○	⊖	○	●	○	●	○							
Apco GPA	—	—	—	—	—	⊖	⊖	○	⊖	⊖	⊖	⊖	●	○	⊖	⊖	⊖	⊖	⊖						
Sears Helmsman Cat. No. 63131	⊖	⊖	○	⊖	⊖	○	○	○	⊖	⊖	⊖	⊖	⊖	●	⊖	⊖	○	○	○	⊖					
Cypress Gardens CA3	⊖	⊖	⊖	⊖	⊖	○	⊖	⊖	⊖	⊖	●	⊖	⊖	⊖	○	⊖	○	○	○	⊖					
Omega Rally-Stripe RS50	—	—	—	—	—	○	⊖	○	⊖	⊖	○	⊖	⊖	⊖	●	⊖	○	●	●	⊖					
Tent A2	—	—	—	—	—	○	○	⊖	○	⊖	⊖	⊖	⊖	○	⊖	⊖	○	⊖	○	○					
Sears Helsman Cat. No. 63147	⊖	⊖	●	⊖	⊖	○	⊖	⊖	⊖	⊖	⊖	○	⊖	○	○	⊖	⊖	○	⊖						
Cypress Gardens EA3	—	—	—	—	—	○	○	○	⊖	⊖	⊖	○	⊖	⊖	⊖	○	○	●	●						
Stearns SSV2135	—	—	—	—	—	⊖	⊖	○	⊖	⊖	⊖	⊖	⊖	⊖	⊖	⊖	○	●	●						
Cut'n Jump WO223	⊖	⊖	⊖	⊖	●	⊖	⊖	⊖	⊖	●	⊖	⊖	●	⊖	●	⊖	●	⊖	●						
Cut'n Jump WO236	⊖	⊖	⊖	⊖	⊖	○	○	⊖	○	⊖	⊖	●	⊖	●	⊖	●	⊖	●	⊖						
Stearns SBV2126	⊖	●	●	●	●	⊖	⊖	●	⊖	○	⊖	●	⊖	●	⊖	●	⊖	●	●						
Americas Cup 809	⊖	⊖	⊖	⊖	⊖	○	⊖	⊖	●	⊖	●	⊖	⊖	⊖	●	⊖	●	●	●						
Stearns WJM9147	●	⊖	⊖	⊖	⊖	○	⊖	○	⊖	●	⊖	⊖	●	⊖	●	○	⊖	●	●						
Stearns SSV2128	—	—	—	—	—	⊖	○	○	⊖	●	●	⊖	⊖	⊖	●	●	●	●	●						
Stearns SBV2125	—	—	—	—	—	⊖	⊖	○	●	⊖	●	○	⊖	⊖	●	●	●	●	⊖						

Copyright 1988 by Consumers Union of United States, Inc., Mount Vernon, NY 10553. Reprinted by permission from *CONSUMER REPORTS*, July 1988.

TYPE IV PFD'S: FLOTATION CUSHIONS

Flotation cushions make you legal but not safe. They are just to sit on or to throw to a swimmer, prior to jettisoning of the overboard pole. They cannot really be worn, and I have never met anyone who would care to estimate how long a swimmer might successfully cling to one. A number of them, thrown one at a time into the water prior to the jettisoning of the pole, do provide a trail to the swimmer. Since they have little windage, they may (may) drift more slowly than the pole and give an additional bit of information to the SAR craft. They are useful in dinghies and in outboards, but a captain who thinks he is solid because he has a flotation cushion for each passenger is sailing in fairyland.

TYPE V INFLATABLE FLOTATION DEVICES

There are a number of inflatable devices available and their chief advantage is that they are easy to wear. Some are even contained in a pouch that may be worn on the belt. Most may be gas-inflated from a small gas bottle, which is activated with a lanyard. In addition, all of them have an orifice for manual inflation by mouth. Really high-quality vests, not necessarily USCG-approved, are sold as safety equipment for divers, water skiers and fishermen. They look something like commercial airline PFDs. These units are expensive, but they are made of extremely tough material (several layers of laminated synthetic cloth), and are therefore less subject to failure.

The negative features of Type V's are that they have similar flotation characteristics to Type II's when inflated and are usually not designed to support the wearer for long periods. One popular vest contains, for example, just eight pounds of buoyancy and is not sold as a PFD. They may require manual inflation, regular recertification to be legal, and they do not deal with hypothermia.

SAFETY EQUIPMENT FOR PFD'S

Every PFD should have **retroreflective panels, a light or strobe** and a **plastic whistle** attached to it by a short lanyard. The piercing call of a whistle can be heard much farther than a scream and requires less energy. It also produces a longer, much more directional signal than a scream. If a PFD had a whistle, a swimmer would not need a high IQ to know he should stick it in his mouth and blow long and hard.

A variety of ways to wear a Type IV cushion.

A waterproof light, clipped to the part of the PFD that remains highest above sea level is just about the only life insurance an overboard victim has at night. A small strobe flasher is ideal (but expensive). A WW II type "c-cell" waterproof life jacket light is ok.

A small heliograph is your biggest bang for the bucks, only in daylight, of course, and only if the user has a firm idea of how it operates and had the chance to practice before the accident. Small plastic heliographs are now available with instructions printed on them and these are the best for this use.

Dye markers are also potent and cheap. Since the swimmer drifts with the wind, a dye slick is created, visible from a great distance by SAR aircraft. In addition, the slick usually becomes long enough to stretch over the crest of a wave, making it visible when the swimmer's head is hidden by the crest. Buy two for each PFD—they're cheap.

Standard lifeboat pyrotechnic signals are too bulky for attachment to PFD's, but small, pocket-sized red meteor signals (sets of three), packaged in plastic are a nice addition.

Man Overboard Equipment

A man overboard pole vastly increases the chance of recovering lost crew and aside from PFDs, is the primary, essential piece of overboard emergency equipment. It should float at least six feet above sea level, and a ten foot pole is ideal. A **sea anchor,** strobe light, radar reflector, and horseshoe preserver should be connected to the pole (see illustration) so that everything goes into the water together. The sea anchor is absolutely essential, otherwise the pole will drift faster than a swimmer can swim, making it impossible to catch up with the pole. Learn your pole's <u>relative drift rate</u>—while practicing. The horseshoe preserver should have a whistle, heliograph, and personal light attached to it. One or more dye packets are an added plus. Overboard poles may be purchased in marine stores and the more expensive ones have a saltwater-activated strobe flasher at the top, which greatly aids nighttime recovery. This type of pole is ideal. The strobe is up high, where it can be seen from a considerable distance. Many overboard pole rigs include a floating strobe, which is visible only on the crests of waves. Fortunately, the bright loom of the floating light reflects off the pole and flag, making it more visible at night. There is no reason why a boat should lack this safety equipment.

The entire strategy of SAR for an overboard victim is based on the assumption that an overboard pole (often called the **datum marker** by the Coast Guard) has gone into the water in the immediate vicinity of the accident. To facilitate this, the pole should be mounted as close to the helm as possible. If no one else is on deck, the helmsman or person on watch will have instant access to the pole. A mizzen mast is a great place to mount it. Many sailors mount it aligned with the backstay. Powerboat operators should mount the pole as close as possible to the wheel house door, with a second one on the fly bridge, if it is used as a steering position. The pole should be secured in a quick release mount. Some captains trail (astern) a polypropylene (floating) line from the pole, so that a swimmer can pull the pole overboard, without assistance. Poles rigged like this are sometimes connected to inexpensive, battery operated burglar alarms, which are activated when the pole goes overboard.

The flag at the top of the pole should be furled inside a tube or bag, affixed to the mast, etc., so that it unfurls automatically when the pole is tossed overboard. Modern overboard flags have support arms that keep them extended, even if there is no wind. But with the wind blowing, it is obvious that there are

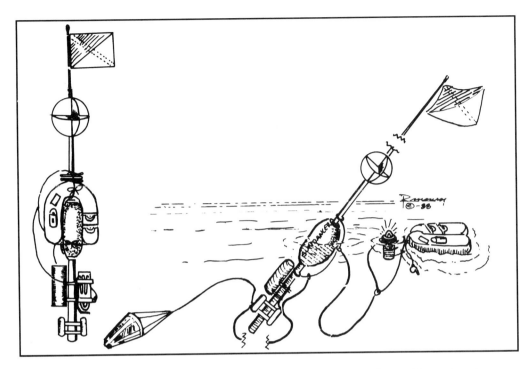

Man overboard pole, with radar reflector, floating strobe, sea anchor and horseshoe ring.

three directions where the flag cannot be seen: upwind, downwind and into the sun. A light-weight, shiny radar reflector, mounted half way up the pole solves this problem and would make the pole visible to radar two to five NM away. In addition, if the vessel has radar, the reflector will provide constant distance data.

The overboard pole will support itself in the water but will not support a person. A horseshoe preserver or throwing ring is necessary for this purpose. A fifteen to thirty feet polypropylene line (which floats) should attach the float to the pole via a snap shackle. The shackle can be unclipped from the pole and attached to a lifeline, thrown from the boat if necessary. The whole affair, including the swimmer, may then be hoisted aboard using a spare halyard (more about that later).

Prior to leaving port, everyone should be familiar with the overboard pole, the equipment attached to it and the procedure which will be followed in the event of an accident. Select a search pattern from those in this chapter and show the crew how a search is conducted. Crew should be assigned station bills and shown where their emergency SAR equipment is located. This information will clarify the whole procedure and also give the swimmer more determination, based on hope.

When someone falls overboard, proceed based on your options (unless you are alone). First, cry, loud and clear, "man overboard!" Then, either commence a crash stop or jettison the pole if a crash stop is not an option. If there is the option of getting flotation cushion(s) into the water faster than the pole, fling them in and get on with it. If the boat can't be stopped quickly, glance at the compass and be sure you know the course and the bearing back to the swimmer and <u>write it all down.</u> Consider which search pattern to use.

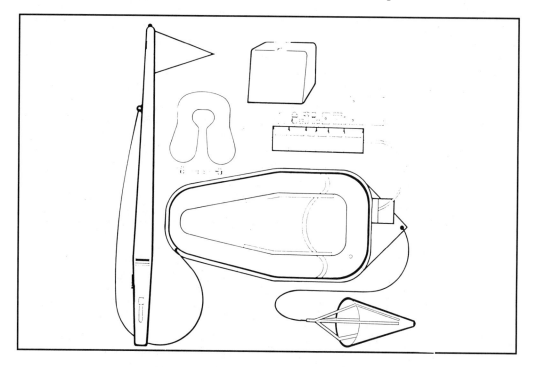

A M.O.M. deployed

MAN-OVERBOARD MODULES

These self-contained units consist of a lanyard-activated, inflatable man overboard pole, topped with a light, which is driven by a seawater-activated battery. A one-man self-inflating survival platform is attached to the pole. It gets the swimmer out of the water, reducing his chance of death by hypothermia. A survival equipment pack is attached to the platform. The survival pack usually contains one or more emergency blankets, a signals kit, flashlight and, if desired, an EPIRB. An optional device allows the unit to be automatically jettisoned by operating a switch in the cockpit. These units have several huge vantages: they are easily jettisoned by an inexperienced crew and they are self deploying. The negative feature of these devices is they are expensive and must be serviced yearly, like a life raft.

BOAT-CONNECTED RECOVERY DEVICES

A boat moving at seven knots will travel 100 feet in 8.5 seconds. If someone fell overboard, and it took the crew just four seconds to throw a life ring with a 100 foot line, the swimmer would be 48 feet away at that time. A ring tossed that distance has a flight-time of three seconds and in the interval the boat moves another 35 feet. If the line didn't foul and the ring landed right in the swimmer's hands, he would have not more than one to two seconds to get it on before the lanyard became taught. This is an indication that a boat-connected recovery device, particularly if it is the only throwable floatation on board, creates a false sense of security.

On the other hand, if the line were made of polypropylene, it would float. When recovery was attempted, the swimmer would have an excellent chance of grabbing the line (and ring) as it dragged behind the boat. A person wearing a life ring, Life Sling or flotation collar which is already attached to the boat by a line is well positioned for recovery.

A packaged self-inflating, throwable lifebuoy.

If you decide to have a boat-connected recovery device on board, it is probably best to buy a packaged unit, rather than making your own. The reason is that the heaving lines of purchased equipment have been machine wound to prevent fouling. In addition, the complete unit is packaged, reducing the chance that properly coiled line will become unlayed due to handling or misuse.

RECOVERY RADIOS

Oceanographers, pirates, and spooks know that the only good way to find objects floating in the sea is with a directional beacon. Oceanographers tracking drift buoys, people who recover millions of dollars worth of air-dropped cocaine, and NSA agents retrieving subsurface listening devices mark these packages with a radio beacon. Is your heinnie worth less? A recovery radio system is the Cadillac of personal recovery devices. At night or during bad weather it may be the only life-saving device that does the job. As usual, they are expensive. These are VHF or UHF frequency radios, so range varies with antenna height, say six to nine miles for a typical boat.

Several companies sell man overboard alarms. One boat-mounted receiver is activated by a manually operated personal transmitter, carried by each crew member. Another type employs a transmitter driven by a saltwater activated battery. It can be attached to a pole, a life jacket, or worn on the belt. A directional receiver on the boat is required to track it. These are highly reliable devices and may greatly decrease response time, particularly if the castaway was alone on deck.

Rescue without a Search

If you have your act together, there is a great likelihood that someone lost overboard will be retrieved immediately, without a search. Among the factors which vastly increase your chances are a PFD (worn by the victim) with a whistle, dye marker, light, and heliograph attached. Equally important is a man overboard pole with a horseshoe ring and strobe. If you can get the pole into the water within 20 seconds after the accident, the swimmer will be close enough to the pole to swim to it and don the horseshoe ring. Be sure to assign someone to watch the swimmer, and do nothing else. If you can keep him in sight, all you have to do is turn around and pick him up. The next question is: how to turn around? Some people favor the crash stop, and others prefer a turning maneuver.

THE CRASH-STOP FOR SAILBOATS

If a boat can be maneuvered quickly, there's nothing quite like the crash-stop to save the day. If the vessel is under sail, this means instantly turning into the wind and letting the sails luff, allowing the swimmer time to reach the boat. A second alternative is a 360° turn, approaching the swimmer upwind.

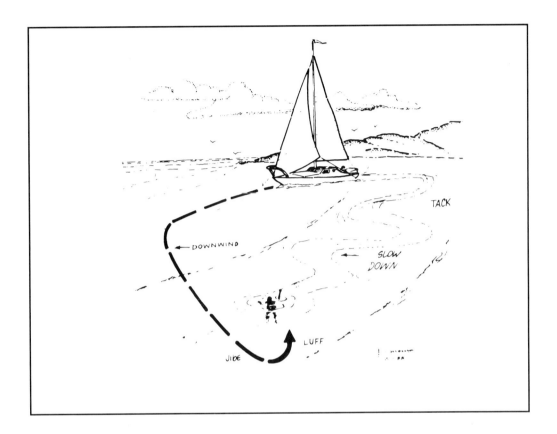

The crash stop for sail boats.

THE CRASH-STOP FOR POWERBOATS

The vessel should be turned toward the side that the victim fell from, to avoid catching him with the prop. Never try to back down on a swimmer, since you may suck him into the prop. Turn toward the victim's side, put that engine into reverse while maintaining "ahead" on the outboard engine.

Turn toward the victim, bring the vessel into the wind, come alongside, then create a lee with the last bit of momentum. DO NOT BACK DOWN.

IF THE MOTOR IS USED ON THE APPROACH. . .

Always make the approach upwind, with the final part of the maneuver in neutral. If the attempt is unsuccessful, allow the vessel to drift down wind, away from the swimmer, and repeat the approach, rather than trying to maneuver with the victim alongside, possibly catching him with the prop. Ideally, the boat should be brought abeam, upwind of the swimmer with the last of its momentum, then turned off the wind, so that the vessel drifts down on the swimmer, providing a lee. Shallow-drafted vessels drift rapidly with the wind and may drift over a swimmer. Use caution.

Turning maneuver for vessels under power, regardless of wind direction. Time from moment of accident to first turn is the same for each leg. Two 60° turns are made.

TURNING MANEUVERS

Unlike the crash-stop, a turning maneuver is something you can practice and perfect. The maneuver always consists of creating some sort of triangle whose final leg leads back to the swimmer. Instinct makes one want to put the wheel hard over immediately, but this rarely produces the desired effect, which is to return to the point of the accident. To do this, it is essential that you start counting the seconds it takes to make the first turn. Count one, one thousand, two one thousand, etc. and repeat this procedure, at the same speed, for the other legs of the maneuver.

With a power boat, the usual procedure is to create an equilateral triangle (60° turns), counting the seconds from when the man went overboard as the first leg. The vessel makes the final legs without altering speed, noting the time, so that the legs are of equal length. When the swimmer is spotted, the vessel is then slowed to creeping speed and maneuvered into the wind.

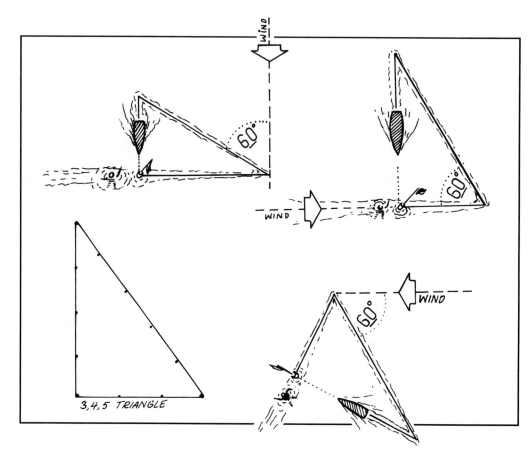

The 3/4/5 right-triangle maneuver

Sailboat Captains who have missed the opportunity for the crash stop usually opt for a turning maneuver, using the wind as a guide. Since most sailboats cannot sail at less than 45° to the wind, a 3/4/5 (30°/60°/90°) right triangle is created. The time between the accident and the first turn is the "3." The boat is then hauled to a beat of 60° off the wind, and this is the "5" leg. If the time between the accident and the first turn was 30 seconds, the second leg would be 5/3 X 30 or a timed run of 50 seconds. The final leg, a 30° turn, always off the wind (usually down wind), is 4/3 of "3." If "3" was 30 seconds, the last leg would be 40 seconds.

Man Overboard Search Strategy

For plotting purposes, 6000' will be considered a nautical mile.

Any search has a focal point (**the "datum"**), and yours is the overboard pole. The entire strategy discussed in this section is based on having and promptly jettisoning a pole, so that it and the swimmer are within a mile of each other.   If a boat is travelling at six knots, it will take ten minutes to cover a mile. If the pole was thrown over the side within one minute, it would be located within 600 feet of the swimmer. If your swimmer reaches the pole, your only job is to find the pole and retrieve him. If not, even if the pole has a sea anchor, it will probably drift at a different rate than a man. Some poles are specifically designed to prevent this, but if it is not mentioned in the sales literature, you may be assured a pole without a sea anchor will drift faster. If it was dropped quickly, it is likely that the swimmer will be to windward of the pole. Boats conducting the search under power begin at the pole. Sail boats begin by beating to windward.

The search patterns below have been devised for the slower speed and reduced visibility of a boat, as opposed to the greater speed and height-of-eye aboard a ship or aircraft.

VISUAL CONSIDERATIONS

At any given moment, there is just a slight chance that a swimmer's head will be visible above the waves. This period decreases as the sea state increases. As a result, there is an extremely small chance that someone sweep-scanning the sea will notice a castaway. So sweep-scanning is out. One must steadily scan a sea-sector, at an angle which is fixed in relationship to the vessel. Using this strategy, the swimmer's head will eventually pass slowly through the visible arc, greatly increasing his chances of being seen.

The minimum optimum number of lookouts (including the captain) is three. We are assuming that the helmsman's eye is at six feet above sea level and those of the others are at ten feet. Higher is better.

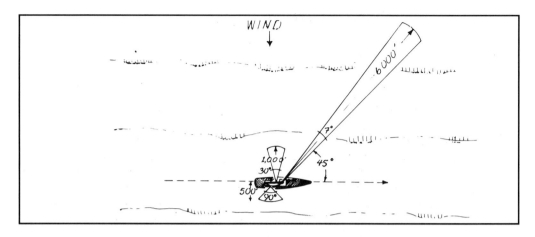

Optimum lookout visual deployment. Illustration by Rafael Monroy

1. The helmsman, who both steers and searches a wide area (90°) to port which has already been searched, within 500 feet of the vessel.
2. The second observer, positioned on the coach roof, steadily scans the opposite side abeam, over an arc of 30° and a distance of 1,000'.
3. The third look-out scans the unsearched side, over a distance of 6,000' (about onethird of the way to the horizon), holding the binoculars (7 X 50 with a 7° angle of vision) steady at a 45° to the bow. This person should be positioned as high as possible (such as on the coach-roof or at the spreaders).

Using this technique, if every leg is separated from every other leg by 1,000 feet, every foot of water within the search area will have been scanned at least two times with the unaided eye and many times (depending on pattern, with the binoculars.

Search Patterns

A search technique should be simple, both in theory and execution, but the wrong place to learn it is while searching. Review the two patterns shown on the following pages and choose the one most suitable for your vessel. Learn that procedure thoroughly, and learn to use the tables which accompany it. Practice it several times at sea, using both the book and personal notes entered in the ship's log. Over-learning is essential. There are many details presented here. They have been included to make the job easier, but they will confuse you instead, if you do not practice. It's easy to make an error while under pressure.

RETRIEVAL PROBABILITY

Retrieval probability is a function of many factors. Sea state, area to be searched, emergency equipment possessed by the swimmer, and availability of lookouts are the biggest factors. The probability of finding someone decreases rapidly as the hours slip by. If the overboard pole was jettisoned promptly after the accident and is therefore considered a reliable center for the search, a small, intense search pattern covering a total area of a square mile or less can be made. If it took some time to get the pole into the water, distance between the man and the pole increases and the area which must be searched increases exponentially (Area equals 3.14 times the distance squared). If the seas are rough, a tighter pattern, with less distance between the legs will be necessary, in contrast to the patterns described below, which are for moderate seas.

The ability of a vessel to hold course during a search is an important factor. The Coast Guard favors a sector search for swimmers, but they use heavily built, fully powered vessels handled by trained experts. A sail boat with a small engine, incapable of driving the vessel to windward on a straight course, might be better off using the parallel search pattern suggested for low power vessels.

THE SECTOR SEARCH

The sector search has many advantages and is the pattern of choice if (1) the vessel has sufficient power to motor into the wind and (2) the pole was dropped promptly, so the area to be searched is relatively small. The length and separation of the legs are easily modified to suit the sea state. The search is more visually coordinated with less dependence on precise navigation. The most intense area searched is near the pole. If the initial search is not successful it is easy to expand the search area by increasing the length of the legs, without having to abandon the pattern.

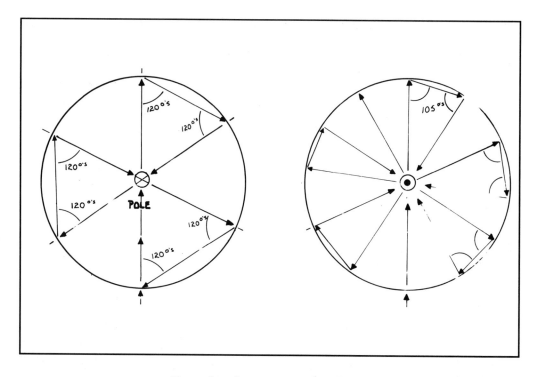

Six- and twelve-sector search patterns.

The **six-sector search** is particularly easy to use, since it segments the area around the pole into six equilateral triangles. Although the sector search breaks the area into equilateral triangles, it should be noted that the actual search consists of a **long leg** and a **short leg**. The long leg is always a diameter of the search "circle" with the pole at the center and the short leg is the length of a radius. The long leg begins at the edge of the search area, runs toward the pole and past it. The vessel is then turned right 120° and run for half the distance of the long leg, along the distant edge (circumference) of the "circle." This is the short leg. The vessel is then turned right 120° once more, and another long leg is run. Slight alterations of running time must be made to compensate for the effects of wind and sea.

If the time between the accident and the jettisoning of the pole is known, an optimum search radius can be determined. If the time is short, say less than two minutes, the initial search pattern can begin with eight-minute long legs and four-minute short legs, modified for the effects of wind and sea. This results in a completed six sector search in 36 minutes. If the vessel was moving at high speed during the accident, it may be necessary to reduce speed and increase running time, to improve the chance of detection.

A second important variable to consider when determining the length of legs of a sector search is the sea state. If the sea is rough, a twelve sector search which covers the same area twice as thoroughly (but takes longer) may yield better results. Should a twelve sector search be initiated, 105° right turns are made and the short leg distance becomes one quarter of the long leg, but the pattern is otherwise the same.

THE EXPANDING SQUARE

This is a good pattern for fully powered vessels, especially if the moment of the accident is not precisely known. The expanding square search is simple to implement, but a plot must be made and this takes the navigator away from the search for those precious moments. It has the advantage of starting the search at the pole, which (presumably) is where the swimmer is located. Its negative feature is that if the accident occurs late in the day, it may not be possible to complete the search. If that is the case, there are two options: use the expanding square technique assuming that the swimmer is less than a mile from the pole, or increase the size of the legs to 1,500 or 2,000 feet.

Sail boats that beat to windward exceptionally well or have a sufficiently powerful motor can also use this technique, by placing the wind on a corner of the square, with it blowing diagonally across the search pattern. One side of the square then becomes a beat at a 45° angle to the wind. The search vessel returns to the floating pole and begins a timed run in an expanding square, starting on a course of choice, such as N, E, S, W or NE, SE, SW, NW, etc. depending on sun glare, wind conditions, etc. The effects of wind on time/distance must be considered when plotting. Set up a search pattern which has one corner pointed at the sun, so that glare will not interfere with the lookout's job.

TIME TO COMPLETE A 1 NM EXPANDING SQUARE SEARCH

SPEED (KTS.)	TIME IN HOURS		
	17 NM	15.5 NM	11.7 NM
4	4.3	4.0	2.9
5	3.4	3.1	2.3
6	2.9	2.6	2.0
7	2.4	2.2	1.7
8	2.1	1.9	1.5
9	1.9	1.7	1.3
10	1.7	1.6	1.2
11	1.5	1.4	1.1

EXPANDING SQUARE SEARCH: LENGTH OF LEGS

LEG NUMBER	LENGTH OF LEG IN FEET		
	1,000'	1,500'	2,000'
1	1,000	1,500	2,000
2	1,000	1,500	2,000
3	2,000	3,000	4,000
4	2,000	3,000	4,000
5	3,000	4,500	6,000
6	3,000	4,500	6,000
7	4,000	6,000	8,000
8	4,000	6,000	8,000
9	5,000	7,500	10,000
10	5,000	7,500	10,000
11	6,000	9,000	10,000
12	6,000	9,000	
13	7,000	10,000	
14	7,000	10,000	
15	8,000	10,000	
16	8,000		
17	9,000		
18	10,000		
19	10,000		
20	10,000		
TOTAL COURSE	102,000'	93,000'	70,000'
NAUTICAL MILES	17.0	15.5	11.7

TIME REQUIRED FOR THE EXPANSION OF EACH LEG IN MINUTES

SPEED IN KNOTS	1000'	1500'	2000'
4	2.5	3.8	5.0
5	2.0	3.0	4.0
6	1.7	2.5	3.3
7	1.4	2.2	2.9
8	1.2	1.9	2.5
9	1.1	1.6	2.2
10	1.0	1.5	2.1
11	0.8	1.4	1.8

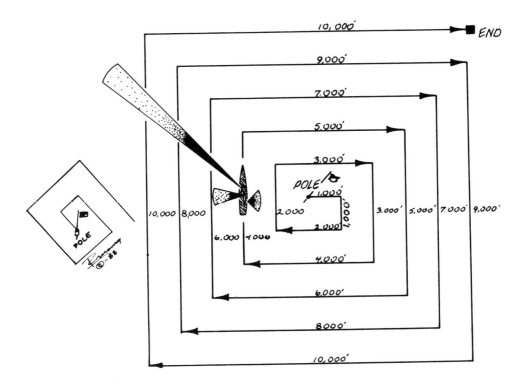

A 6000' expanding square pattern. Total distance run: 17 NM. Inset at left shows pattern of second search.

So if a boat were moving at an average speed of 5 kts., the first and second legs of the 17 NM square would take 2 minutes, the third and forth, four minutes, the fifth six, an additional two minutes, etc.

This is a good pattern for a sail-driven boat. The method described here is a modification of the classic parallel search pattern, shown below, where the long legs run up and down wind. The advantage of the classic pattern is that the visibility of a swimmer is optimized, since they are more likely to be silhouetted against the sky instead of against other waves.

Our modification of the parallel search orients a low-powered boat to commence an off-the-wind search. It begins by beating to windward at 45° on the port tack for 1.4 NM. If the vessel cannot beat at 45°, it can run 1.8 NM at 55°, then tack and broad-reach to "start search."

Illustration shows advantage of up and down wind long legs.

THE TIME IT TAKES TO REACH "START SEARCH"		
SPEED	**45°**	**55°**
4 kts	21 mn	27
5	16.8	21.6
6	14	18
7	12	15.4
8	10.5	13.5
9	9.3	12
10	8.4	10.8
11	7.6	9.8

As was true for the expanding square, there may be insufficient time to complete the parallel search if the accident occurred late in the day. In this case, it is possible to start a little closer to the pole (say 5,000' away) to complete the pattern before sundown, or, as with the expanding square, one may also increase the distance between the parallel lines. A parallel track search with 1,000' separation between legs (4 NM square) has a course of 23.6 NM. With a 1,500 separation, the course is 18 NM and with a 2,000' separation, a 13.7 NM course is run.

TIME REQUIRED TO COMPLETE A 1 NM PARALLEL TRACK SEARCH

	LENGTH	OF	COURSE
SPEED(KTS)	23.6 NM	18 NM	13.7 NM
4	5.9 hrs.	4.2 hrs.	3.4 hrs
5	4.7	3.6	2.5
6	4.0	3.0	2.3
7	3.4	2.5	1.9
8	2.9	2.3	1.6
9	2.6	2.0	1.5
10	2.4	1.8	1.4
11	2.1	1.6	1.2

How to enter a parallel search using the wind as a guide. The search vessel, upon reaching "start search," a position to windward, is brought onto the opposite tack and sailed with the wind on the beam for 2 NM. The boat is run downwind for 1,000' , then jibed onto a port tack.

Night-Time   Procedures

If the victim has a light, it is possible to conduct a search in the normal way. It may be even easier to spot his light than the head of a daytime swimmer. Should he have a light, the search is conducted in the normal way, using the strobe connected to the pole as your focal point. If he has no light, there is

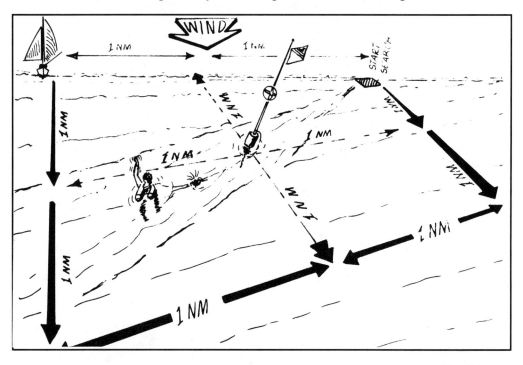

A parallel search using the wind to determine headings.Total distance run: 23.6 NM

virtually no chance that you will locate him in the dark. It is undoubtedly wisest to stand by near the pole, showing as much illumination as possible, particularly masthead lights, in the hope that the swimmer will be able to see them, and reach the vessel. If not, the search is begun at first light. When discussing SAR strategy with your crew, it is important to mention this, so that someone floating in the darkness will understand that they must be prepared to wait 'til first light. They must know that their best strategy is to rest quietly, allow blood circulation to slow and conserve body core heat.

Bringing the Swimmer Aboard

As the vessel makes its approach, throw the swimmer a life ring or similar device with a line attached and be sure he puts it on. Do not attempt to simply haul him aboard without first assuring a positive connection between him and the boat. It is amazing how hard it is to board a wet, waterlogged, exhausted swimmer, who may be injured and/or further exhausted in the rescue attempt. A swimmer suffering from hypothermia may be unable to assist himself. In that case, someone connected to a safety line must dive in and help.

If you fail to board him and have neglected to connect him to the boat with a line, you may not get a second chance. I was once about 40 NM off the Cape Verds and had a Nigerian fisherman <u>right in my hands</u>, but he did not speak English (or French or German or Mogreb) so he did not put on the ring and dropped it when I grabbed him. He was immensely heavy in his wet gear, the night was dark and stormy with confused seas, our ship's boat rolled like a pig in the swell, and I could not hold him. He slipped away. We never found him again. The sea does not like to give anyone a second chance.

While the search is being conducted, decide how you plan to secure and lift the swimmer. If you just throw him a line, which he secures around his chest, it is possible that you will break his back or a few ribs while hauling him aboard. A Life Sling, an improvised sling made from a blanket or well-made horseshoe preserver is better, secured to a stout piece of line at least 30' long, preferably polypropylene floating line.

If the search is a long one and the victim is expected to be in a state of hypothermia, it may be necessary to have a crewman standing by to jump overboard and assist the victim. Under those circumstances, the victim should be assisted as much as possible, minimizing all efforts to help himself. Should this be the case, prepare the rescuer—you do not want a second person lost over the side! Ideally, he should be dressed in a wet suit, Offshore Type I life jacket with survival equipment, a harness, mask, and flippers. Connect him with a line to a strong point on the boat, and be sure to tend it and the line connected to the sling, to prevent fouling in the prop. He can then swim to the victim, place a harness or sling, etc., on him and assist, getting him aboard.

One method of boarding a swimmer. Choose your own—in advance.

BOARDING

The best way to get a man out of the water into the boat is different for each vessel; the sling line can be led from the sling to a halyard, a block on the boom bail, or the fly bridge, then down through a deck block to a winch or block-and-tackle. Decide in advance.

Prepare another piece of line (one on each side) to be used as a step, positioned so that the swimmer can get his foot into it, located at the spot selected for boarding. Once his foot is in place, help him, if necessary, but there is less chance of injury if he is able to climb aboard himself (assuming he is not in a state of hypothermia). If this is not possible, only apply as much lifting force as is needed to assist him. Don't winch him up like a sack of coal; he may swing free and smash against the lifelines, injuring himself.

EMERGENCY MEDICAL PROCEDURES

For the treatment of hypothermia, see Chapter IX. For the treatment of injury, see Chapter XI. If the victim is not breathing, apply cardio-pulmonary resuscitation.

EXAMINATION AFTER RESCUE

Unless the retrieval is quick and easy, it is wise to strip the victim and examine thoroughly for cuts or discolorations that may have resulted from the fall or retrieval. People who are suffering from hypothermia should have their wet clothes cut away, to avoid exercizing the limbs, which should remain cold. Someone suffering psychological trauma from an overboard accident may not realize that they are injured. If they complain of a sore neck, or a discoloration or bruise is detected there, immobilize against the possibility of a broken neck.

Wait for a patient to recover enough to feel pain. Then gently press the ribs to be sure none are broken. This is the most common type of recovery injury. If he has pain there, immediately listen to his lungs to detect gurgling sounds caused by a rib piercing the pleural cavity. Use a stethoscope or your ear. Do not give pain killing drugs until you are sure the person is safe from shock. Shine a light into the eyes and be sure the pupils react normally and are equal in size. If he can sit up, have him close his eyes and touch his fingers together, to check for cranial trauma. Give him a hot, sweet drink but no alcohol. Wrap him in a blanket, a space blanket or a thermal protection suit.

Let the victim rest or sleep, but assign someone to keep a watch. Listen for irregular breathing or gurgling sounds. If you hear them, sit the person up and call for medical advice by radio (see Chapter XVI). Established safety procedures and good equipment could have prevented the mess in the first place.

CHAPTER XIX: SEARCH AND RESCUE

Search and Rescue Organization

A distressed sailor sees the Coast Guard appear when he needs them but has no insight into the planning and organization necessary for a search to be successful. First, SAR is a global organization, but each nation handles its part of the job as it sees fit. For example, in Great Britain the job is divided between the military, which operates SAR aircraft, and ocean vessels, while the Royal National Life Boat Institute (RNLI), privately funded and operated, conducts coastal rescues. The tale of the Penlee lifeboat disaster which follows, gives some idea of the RNLI's dangerous job.

In the United States, SAR is a part of the military, split between the Coast Guard and the Air Force. Americans also have a volunteer, quasi-military SAR organization, the Coast Guard Auxiliary, but unlike the Brits, they are never asked to make rescues under highly hazardous conditions. That is a job for the military. The Coast Guard patrols all maritime areas and navigable waterways, the Air Force covers the rest. The two work together, and have rapid access to additional equipment and personnel from other branches as needed. Highly specialized computers and satellites are also used by the coast guard for searching. If you are within their jurisdiction, and can successfully signal them, this entire infrastructure is available to save your vessel and the lives of your crew. There are about 10 million American boaters and they require 70,000 to 90,000 USCG SAR responses every year.

Face page: Among the most daring air rescues ever performed by the USCG: Aircraft Commander Lt. Cdr. Thomas Walters and pilot Lt. John Flipowicz maneuver USCG HH3F Pelican #1467 at sea level, during a raging storm in Shelicoff Strait (near Kodiak, Alaska) in order to snatch two immersion suit-clad fishermen from the icy sea. Their vessel, the 48-foot F/V LAURA had taken on water and was awash in 50-knot winds, 80-knot gusts and 30-t o 40-foot seas. The chopper rescue basket and hoisting cable were lost during the initial attempts to lift the two large fishermen, who were further weighted by water in their immersion suits. Despite the night, bad weather, extreme cold, and quarter-mile visibility, Lt. Flipowicz dropped the chopper into the trough, allowing the lucky survivors to be hauled aboard by three other Coast Guardsmen, HS-3 John Holcomb, AT-2 Donald Nolan, and AM-3 Antonio Juan. The chopper, having hovered over the disaster for hours, was so short of fuel that Lt. Cdr. Walters was forced to make a night landing on an unlit, uninhabited islet off the coast of Alaska. Painting by Richard DeRosset

Lost with all hands: Last photo of the Penlee Lifeboat SOLOMON BROWNE (above), being launched before her tragic loss. The 47 foot Royal National Lifeboat SOLOMON BROWNE, manned by eight volunteers, was launched from the tiny village of Mousehole during the night of December 19, 1981, to rescue crew from the doomed 1,400 ton coaster, UNION STAR. The UNION STAR, on her maiden voyage from Holland to Ireland, lost power eight to nine NM offshore in force 10 to 11 winds and huge seas. The vessel eventually dragged ashore at Tater-Dhu, near Lands End, GB. Although the loss of power was reported to the Falmouth CG by radiotelephone at 6:05 p.m., the skipper, Mike Morton, initially refused help from the nearby Ocean Tug NOORD HOLLAND, stating he was unable to do so without authorization from the main office. By the time the NOORD HOLLAND offered assistance under Lloyd's Open Form of Salvage, huge seas, "the biggest in living memory," defeated every attempt to pass a tow cable. Captain Morton clearly failed to realize the gravity of the situation. He failed to send a MAYDAY, declare distress or ask for assistance, the magic words which galvanize a rescue effort. The ensuing confusion and red tape delayed the launching of rescue craft until too late. Photo by Andrew Besley.

Wreck of the UNION STAR. Photo taken the morning after the disaster. The stricken vessel was less than a mile offshore when Lifeboat Captain Trevelyan Richards, threw red tape to the winds and told Captain Morton he was coming to take off all hands, which included four crewmen, the captain, his wife and two young daughters.

Photographer Andrew Besley said:

I arrived at the lifeboat station at 8:15 p.m., just after the SOLOMON BROWNE had been launched. By the time I drove to Tater-Dhu, The UNION STAR was in 40 foot breakers, less than a mile away and rapidly coming ashore. A Sea King helicopter tried to drop a line, but the 115-knot wind whipped it away. Then the lifeboat came in and pushed her nose against the ship's side. Suddenly the lifeboat went hard astern as a huge wave towered above it. The lifeboat very nearly made it through that wave, but was lifted up and hurled onto the coaster's deck. It then slid off, slowly, stern first. It drifted, broadside to the seas, and sent a final, garbled message that it had taken off four survivors. Then its lights went out and I lost it in the darkness

About thirty minutes after the loss of the SOLOMON BROWNE, the UNION STAR ran aground and rolled over, with the loss of all hands. Part of the SOLOMON BROWNE was discovered by divers the following month.   Photo by Andrew Besley

The body of Captain Richards, coxswain of the Penlee lifeboat SOLOMON BROWNE, discovered the next morning by the Wessex helicopter. This stark photo certainly commemorates all brave men who have died in the service of humanity. Captain Richards and his crew were buried at Paul Church in the village of Mousehole on Christmas eve.
Photo by Andrew Besley

One can imagine the dilemma of Captain Richards, calling for release by telephone from the Ship Inn at Mousehole. A bitter, pitch black winter night had already fallen. The windows of the Inn were covered with spume. A killer storm was shrieking in the background. The imminent doom of the UNION STAR must have been quite apparent to a man such as Captain Richards, a fisherman who knew that piece of coast so well. There were his shipmates waiting—men who trusted him from a tiny village where everyone knew everyone and their parents. They waited to go out and cheat the Lady with the Green Eyes if they could. One can imagine the whole thing, like a train running out of control down a track. Captain Richards and his crew understood the risk. They knew that Fate had already tipped the scales against them. Perhaps they foresaw the death that every sailor sees in his secret dreams. But who among them could say, *"No, it's too late, let them perish."*

The R.N. Lifeboat from St. Ives returning with injured castaways—at night, in terrible weather—as usual. Photo by Andrew Besley

Securing Assistance

There are a variety of ways to signal for help, and they are discussed in the chapters on Signals and Radio Transmission. Keep in mind that the huge organization just mentioned is designed to react swiftly only to certain stimuli, which includes various <u>emergency radio transmissions</u> and visual signals seen by other vessels or from shore. These methods of communication, <u>if received and understood</u> usually bring swift help.

Other stimuli bring a more sluggish response. Ambivalent messages, such as those sent by the captain of the UNION STAR, can cause tragic delays. Telling a friend to "call the coast guard if I'm not in by Wednesday," will certainly not result in an instant massive search, even if the friend has good information. Such reports are greeted with a certain amount of doubt and confusion, whether or not it is well justified. It may be <u>weeks</u> before the hue and cry is actually raised. In other words, if you need The Man quickly, you have to play his game. That means sending a distress signal and <u>having it received</u>, then <u>being sighted</u> by someone in a rescue craft. A pair of human eyes must actually see you for you to be saved, so there is the human element, implying human failures and the element of chance.

Keep in mind that a search and rescue operation is usually a last, desperate attempt to save someone, with no guarantee of success under the very best of circumstances, regardless of equipment. Being well prepared for an emergency vastly increases your chance of survival, but sometimes Lady Luck and the Lady with the Green Eyes gang up against you.

Equipment is lost or fails. Radio messages are garbled or misunderstood. Bad weather conceals you. The monotony of a long search is awesome. A weary searcher's attention is sometimes diverted. Never consider yourself "saved" until you are hauled aboard a rescue craft.

Do not forget that that responsibility for saving your life and the lives of your crew is ultimately yours. Do not place ultimate faith in electronic gizmos or assume good radio equipment makes you "as good as saved". The EPIRB-COSPAS/SARSAT system has huge holes in its coverage and for inexplicable reasons, it often takes far longer to fix a position than one might think, with less accuracy than advertised. Numerous false signals or multiple signals in the same vicinity confuse searchers and slow their response.

If the weather is bad, the men in SAR craft must be extra cautious, devoting more of their attention to staying alive and less to looking for survivors. Any sort of search has definite elements of risk, and I have been on a few which were absolutely, truly, terrifying. Survivors know their own terror but sometimes do not realize the courage needed by rescuers to save them. Night is a very hazardous time for low-level search by aircraft or helicopter. Without night signals, a survivor would have little chance of being seen. In the end, it's man against the sea, and even with all his fancy equipment, man does not always win.

Assistance for Disabled or Distressed Vessels

Barges and some dinghies are made specifically to be towed. Boats usually aren't. Towed vessels can be run aground by the tow, damage can occur if hull speed is exceeded, tow cables can tear out deck fittings, cables break, and people can get maimed and killed in the most gruesome ways. These risks are well known to the Coast Guard, but are usually not apparent to the boater until they happen. This does not mean a boat cannot be towed, but a tow should never be requested or accepted if the vessel can free itself or reach shelter unassisted. Sailing vessels with disabled engines, which are still able to sail, should do so, and if becalmed, should wait for wind. Be patient. After all, if you wanted to go fast, why did you buy a boat? Sail or drift toward your destination as far as possible. Anchor if necessary. If you can reach the entrance of the harbor, it is likely that a private vessel will come along and give you a tow to the dock.

There is a difference between a **disabled** and a **distressed** vessel. A disabled vessel needs a tow, probably from a friend, the Coast Guard Auxiliary, or a commercial operator. A distressed vessel, meaning one which is sinking, on fire, aground in breakers, or experiencing a medical emergency, needs the Coast Guard. If your vessel is disabled, it is very likely that the Coast Guard will assign a commercial operator to assist you, at considerable cost to you. On the other hand, think carefully before you declare distress, for the manpower, equipment, and cost of saving you may be far, far greater than your estimate, and it is possible that a frivolous claim to the Coast Guard will be charged to your vessel. Read more about obtaining assistance by radio in Chapter XIV and with the use of other signals in Chapter XVI.

The Coast Guard, upon receiving a distress message, performs the marine equivalent of **triage**, meaning that they assess the problem and assign it a priority, based on what else is happening at that moment. If you are not in immediate danger, you may have to wait. If you are in immediate danger you also may have to wait. In any event, you are going to have to wait 'til help arrives, and that interval should be spent as profitably as possible, improving your situation, or at least trying to prevent it from becoming worse. In the case of a grounding, this usually means dropping one or more anchors in deeper water. These should be buoyed, since it may be necessary to cast off the anchor line quickly during the rescue. If a dinghy is not available, the anchor can be swum out, using cushions, life jackets, etc, to float the anchor.

If you are assisted by the Coast Guard, in addition to their assistance, they will usually perform a vessel safety inspection. As a minimum, you had better have a life jacket or flotation device for everyone aboard, and the Coast Guard likes everyone to be wearing them upon arrival, and the captain had better be sober.

The 41 foot Utility Tow Boat. Photo courtesy of USCG San Diego.

SURFACE RESCUE EQUIPMENT AND TECHNIQUES

The two coastal and offshore workhorse vessels of the USCG are the 41' Utility Tow Boat (UTB) and the 44' Motorized Life Boat (MLB), sometimes called a "surf boat". The UTB is more common and is used for typical rescues. The MLB is designed for rough weather, working in or near breakers, departing through a breaking inlet. Many are equipped with fire-fighting equipment. The MLB is designed to withstand a capsize and is self-righting (in about 8-10 seconds, long enough for your entire life to flash before your eyes), but Coast Guard personnel do not enjoy the inverted position, even though the boat was designed to recover from it.

The Motorized Lifeboat doing its thing. Although designed to be self-righting, a capsize destroys the vessel's extensive electronics system. Photo: USCG San Diego

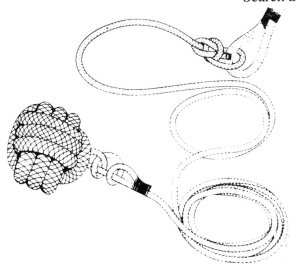

The Monkey's fist and messenger attached to a line.

If a surface rescue craft cannot reach you directly, because of rough weather or shallow water, they may either send a lifeboat, life raft or inflatable rescue craft to assist you. If that is not possible, they may float a line to you from up-wind, use a heaving line, or fire a line to your vessel using a line throwing rifle (the old Springfield '03, used in WW I). The projectiles weigh 13-15 ounces, so <u>don't get in their way or try to catch them.</u> At night, an illuminated projectile is sometimes used. The projectile is connected to a light **shotline**, with a breaking strength of 100 or 350 lbs. The lighter line is used for greater range, up to 550'. The projectile is not as accurate as a bullet, so much closer ranges are preferred. The projectile is supposed to be fired <u>over</u> rather than <u>at</u> the vessel, but mistakes sometimes occur.

The **messenger** is attached to the shotline, and the crew of the distressed vessel pulls it aboard. A **towing cable** or **hawser** is attached to the end of the messenger and is pulled aboard and made fast to the boat's cleat(s).

Towing is dangerous business. People have been killed and horribly maimed, often with virtually no warning, during a towing operation. I met a man who had stood on the fordeck of a vessel being towed. The towing cleat of the tow boat pulled out, hurtled toward the tow at cannonball speed, struck him in the head, blinded him, destroyed his nose and sense of smell. So we are not

If it is necessary to remove the occupants of the distressed vessel, the SAR craft may send over an **unmanned life raft**, attached by a bridle.

talking about small accidents or cut fingers here. You may be an experienced captain with a good vessel and properly mounted cleats. Very little is usually known about the other guy or his boat. If possible, board the disabled vessel, and examine the towing cleats. After all, it's just your life that's at stake.

Some consideration should be given to the **psychological state** of the captain and crew of the disabled vessel. What may seem like a minor annoyance to you (breaking down and needing a tow, or a fire which has been extinguished), may be extremely stressful to less experienced sailors. They may be unable to perform simple tasks, such as attaching the tow cable properly, or maneuvering their vessel. It may be necessary to leave an experienced crewman aboard their vessel.

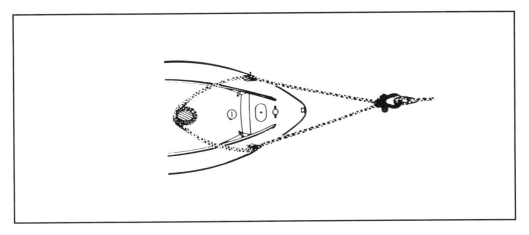

A towing bridle with back-up lines.

("Do you agree to accept all liability and pay for any damages incurred during this tow, regardless of cause?") and this may have standing in court, depending on circumstances, but courts sometimes do not recognize contracts made under duress and a distressed vessel (in contrast to a disabled vessel) is under duress. All of this is mentioned to make you aware that there are grave risks involved in being a "Good Samaritan," even if you feel morally compelled to render assistance.

Towing puts incredible strain on the tow line and the cleats or bits to which it is attached. The most dangerous type of strain is the intermittent type, called **shock loading**, associated with rough seas or improper cable length. The tow line becomes slack, the tow boat accelerates, until brought up short by the tow cable. Every time the process repeats itself, additional fatigue weakens the materials. The line can break, or the cleat to which it is attached can tear out. In either event, the line and/or the cleat goes hurtling toward the area where it is attached to the other vessel. A standard 2.75 inch towing cable, used on a 41 to 44 foot SAR boat has a tensile strength of about 285,000 lbs. The bollards on those vessels are designed to hold an even greater force, so if a failure occurs, either the cable will break or the cleat of the towed vessel will pull out, often taking bow pulpits, chocks and headstays with it. Just the broken cable alone can tear your head off.

For these reasons, if you are being towed:

1. Keep people away from the area near the towing cleat(s).
2. <u>Never</u> let them get between the towing cleats and the other vessel.
3. Attach the tow line to a strong point which is low, far forward and near the centerline, preferably to cleats or bollards. Use a bridle if possible.
3. Always lead tow lines through **fairleads,** to prevent torn-out cleats from hitting the other vessel.
4. Be sure cleats are bolted through back-up plates, which distribute strain to the deck. Never attach a tow line to a cleat which is not through-bolted.
5. If the forward cleats are not strong enough to take the strain of a tow, lead the line to the base of the mast, if it is strong, or make a bridle, carrying the strain through the bow fairleads, to several well-secured cleats as far forward as possible.
6. Have everyone don life jackets. Bad things occasionally happen without warning while towing.

APPROACHING A DISABLED VESSEL

The parallel approach is used in good weather. The tow boat approaches from astern, passes the tow line by hand and stops ahead of the disabled vessel, to allow them time to make fast the tow line.

Crossing the "T" is used in heavy weather or windy conditions, where the boats drift at different rates. The tow boat crosses the disabled vessel's bow, preferably in an upwind direction. The line is passed just before the vessels bows cross. Sometimes the rescue vessel will approach from a 45 degree angle, and the line is passed just before the bow of the distressed vessel is passed.

The back-down approach is sometimes used when it is necessary for a single crewman to both pass the line and pay it out, to prevent its becoming tangled in the prop. Never pass the line with stern-way on. This is an approach for well-powered vessels that maneuver and accelerate quickly.

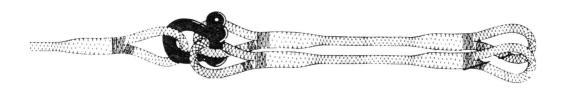

A towing bridle, two legs. From: *Boat Crew Seamanship Manual, U.S.C.G.* (Pg 12-35)

ASSISTING A GROUNDED VESSEL

The first rule to remember when assisting a grounded vessel is <u>do not run aground yourself</u>. Consider beach contours and refer to your chart before making the approach. Decide on a minimum control depth and do not venture into water which is shallower. Allow yourself a safe margin and stick to your decision. If you have enough fuel, keep your engine running at all times. Steep and rocky shores are extremely dangerous, since a depth sounder may not provide a warning of the imminence of danger. Sea state, visibility, capability of crew and condition of your vessel are also considerations. Always listen to your own fears. Your first consideration is the safety of <u>your crew and vessel</u>. Don't create two disasters for the Coast Guard to sort out. Lay offshore and transmit for assistance, if you think a rescue may endanger your vessel.

In addition to the risk of grounding, the moment of **passing the tow line** is one of <u>great danger</u>. If a vessel is grounded on an open coast, it is usually pounding, and God help anyone that gets caught beneath it or between it and another vessel. This is a good place to use a heaving line, if you have one. A cable, connected to the tow boat, loaded into a dinghy, can be paid out as the dinghy moves toward the grounded vessel. It is far wiser for the person in the dinghy to deliver the line via messenger, using a **heaving line and monkey's fist.** Don't get too close to the grounded vessel as you may be swept beneath it. If a grounded boat is full of water and/or sand, ask yourself "Why?" before attempting a tow. Don't tow a sinking boat off the beach.

Floating a line to the disabled vessel is an option, if the disabled vessel is aground and the water is shoal. This approach often works better in theory than reality, because cross-currents, tidal set and other variables affect the course of the drifting line, and this is true even though both wind and waves are directly onshore. If this approach is attempted, a man-overboard pole may be used as a float, and this will reduce the need for grappling at sea surface level for the line, as would occur if the line were attached to an empty fuel can.

Dropping an anchor for the grounded vessel may be sufficient assistance to get her free, and in any event, it will keep the distressed vessel from broaching or getting pushed farther aground by the waves. Broaching, which in this case means being thrown onto the beach broadside to the waves, often breaks the back of a boat which is grounded. A short chain leader can be used to protect against rock, but this is otherwise a job for long lengths of stretchy nylon line. Occasionally a grounded vessel with a deployed anchor (whose line has been winched as tight) can be broken loose from the ground by running past the grounded boat with another vessel, throwing a big wake.

Anchoring and dropping back toward the grounded vessel offers the safety of being anchored in sufficient water to prevent a second grounding. The tow boat's winch can also assist the engines to get the other vessel unstuck. On the other hand, boats anchored on an open coast pitch and roll unmercifully and this increases the risk of injury.

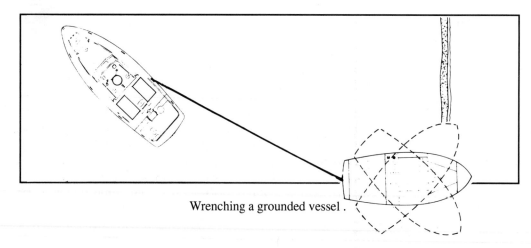

Wrenching a grounded vessel .

Never pull a grounded vessel at low tide. If steady pressure fails to free a grounded vessel, it may be stuck in mud or sand. The tow boat may try to **wrench it off**, as shown on the previous page. Keep steady pressure on the tow cable at all times.

DEPLOYING THE TOW CABLE

A heavy, nylon line, such as an anchor line, makes a good towing cable since it stretches, allowing dissipation of strain. If a heaving line is used to pass the tow cable, be sure it is supple and, if not, wet it before use. Be sure to warn the disabled vessel before heaving the weighted monkey's fist, and aim the throw so that the fist passes <u>over</u> their boat, well above head height. I once heaved a lead-loaded monkey's fist to someone who tried to catch it. The monkey's fist hit him in the head and knocked him right out of the boat! This fortunately occurred in the days before people sued Good Samaritans.

The tow boat must prepare the cable before the approach, so that it will run out smoothly and is not underfoot or otherwise a danger to the crew. As soon as the line is made fast to the disabled vessel, it should be paid out <u>under strain at all times</u>. Never allow a belly to form in the line. It may pass beneath the disabled vessel, catch in the prop or rudder, which may be ripped out, sinking the disabled vessel when the line comes taught. Assign a crewperson to watch the cable for chafe and slack, and be sure they are located off to the side, a safe distance from the towing cleats   Remember, <u>do not let them get between the towing cleats and the other vessel</u>. If slack develops, be sure to supervise its taking-in to prevent tangles and injuries.

If you are towing another vessel:

1. Make a **towing bridle** to distribute the strain to several cleats. Be sure to run the bridle through fairleads. Apply power <u>slowly</u> to avoid shock loading. Get the tow moving, <u>then</u> come to course.
2. Adjust the length of the tow line so that it maintains steady tension.
3. Establish communication with the other vessel, preferably by VHF radio. Be sure to contact them about every twenty minutes.
4. Adjust speed of the tow so that it does not exceed or even get close to the towed vessel's hull speed. <u>Be sure</u> neither boat starts to **yaw**. This can be <u>extremely dangerous</u> and cause a <u>sudden</u> capsize. If the towed vessel starts to yaw, reduce speed or have them rig a **sea anchor**.
5. Pad the area between you and the tow cleats with seat cushions, a hatch cover, etc. to protect you in the event of a line failure. Do what you can.

6. If the disabled vessel is a sail boat, have them furl their sails to avoid having them sail up on you.
7. Be sure <u>everyone is wearing a life jacket.</u>
8. Remove unnecessary personnel from the disabled vessel if necessary.

TECHNIQUES TO AVOID

1. Never run a line around a vessel's cabin to effect a tow.
2. Never run a bridle or line around the hull of a disabled vessel.

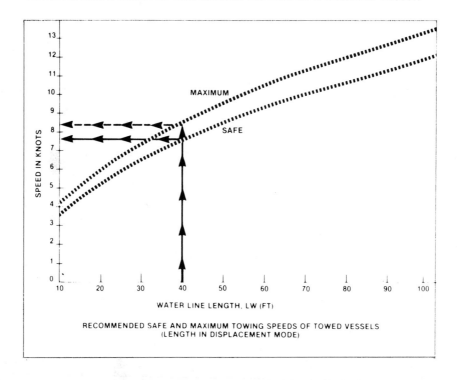

Maximum Safe Towing Speeds for Displacement Hulls. From: *Boat Crew Seamanship Manual, USCG* (Pg 12-39)

PREVENTING SHOCK LOADING

Offshore or heavy weather towing cable lengths are expressed in terms of **wave lengths**. A towed vessel is said to be **in step** with the tow when the cable, speed, etc. are correct. A minimum separation of two or even three wave lengths may be necessary to achieve a state of constant tension. This may require a tow line of 500 feet or more. The longer the nylon tow cable, the more it acts as a spring, preventing shock loading by stretching. A proper tow line length places the vessels on the crests and in the troughs at the same time. If the tow is rushing down a crest while the towboat is climbing another, dangerous slack can occur in the towing line, or the towed vessel may rush forward and climb into the tow boat's cockpit! Yes, it does happen and more frequently than you would imagine. A sea anchor or dragged loop of line reduces the tendency of the tow to yaw or overtake.

SIGNS OF DANGER WHILE TOWING

(1) **Yawing** of either vessel, as mentioned, can cause a <u>sudden</u> capsize which occurs without other warning. (2) A bow-down attitude of the towed vessel or a list. (3) Excessive movement of the tow line over sharp or rough objects causes chafe. It may be necessary to wrap a rag or piece of leather around the cable at this point, to act as a **chafe-preventer**. Movement or deformation of towing cleats is very serious.

TOWING A SINKING VESSEL

Towing a sinking vessel is tricky and dangerous. Sinking boats under tow sometimes capsize or sink <u>suddenly</u>. Every effort should be made to re-move non-essential personnel before the tow begins and, if anyone must remain aboard, be sure they are wearing a life jacket and are prepared to enter the water. Be sure a towboat crewman stands by <u>with an ax</u>. Place a piece of wood or chopping block on the deck where the cut is to be made. Order him to chop the cable or let it slip, <u>just after the vessel sinks</u>. Keep some way on the sinking vessel Do not let the tow cable get slack and catch in the prop. If the water is shallow enough, you may want to buoy the line, so the vessel may be found and recovered later.

On the other hand, if the vessel is not holed in the bow, towing may al-low water to run off the stern or reduce its in-flow, so the tow may help keep the distressed vessel afloat. A sinking boat may tow well at first, then start to yaw as it fills. Be prepared to reduce speed. Boat yard operators and the police are wary of sinking vessels because they sometimes sink right in the middle of ev-erything. As you approach the harbor, decide whether to try for the haul-out or drive the sinking vessel onto the beach. If you fear that a sinking is imminent, declare MAYDAY and hope someone will come along with a pump. High tide is a good time to beach a boat, and temporary repairs can be made when the tide is out. Beaching a boat at low tide often ensures further destruction when the tide comes in.

APPROACHING THE DOCK

A towed vessel is not easily maneuvered against a dock and the approach is a dandy time for all kinds of accidents to occur. The captain of the disabled vessel may not be aware of this, so it is up to the tow captain to decide how to best handle the approach. Many unforeseen variables await one at the dock. It may be full, too short for both vessels, or someone, not realizing your problem, may zoom ahead of you and take your place. The disabled vessel should have an anchor ready for instant use in case it is necessary to suddenly slip the cable. All fenders on both vessels should be ready for instant use. If you are not well versed in docking a tow, it may be <u>far wiser</u> to have the disabled vessel anchor rather than risk an accident near the dock.

The greatest dangers during an approach are crush and tear injuries to limbs which have been caught in lines, between the dock and the vessel, etc. As they say, shit happens. Be sure unneeded people are either below or seated near the centerline, to avoid injury. Use seasoned hands for the dangerous jobs.

As the two vessels approach the dock, shorten the tow line to one boat-length. <u>Try to make an upwind approach</u>, bleeding off speed slowly, to avoid slack. Never attempt a downwind approach in a strong wind. If down wind is the only option, it may be wiser to have the disabled vessel anchor, then drift down on the dock. If a light breeze is blowing toward the dock, it is often practical to come to a stop parallel with and just off the dock, allowing the wind to complete the job. If the wind is blowing off the dock, it may be better to approach slowly, then pass the tow cable to a dockhand. Make every maneuver slowly, so that the tow can align with the path of the tow boat. Be sure both the disabled vessel and the tow know who will slip the tow cable and who will issue the command. Both boats should have someone standing by the cable. It must be taken in as soon as it is released to avoid its tangling in the prop.

Twin screw tow boats, or vessels attempting to maneuver a much smaller vessel may want to bring the disabled vessel alongside (**hip tow**) for the final approach, since more maneuverability is attained in this configuration. Keep in mind that when hip towing, it is the **after spring line,** rather than the bow and stern lines which does the pulling. Prior to approaching the dock with a hip tow, practice maneuvering both vessels at low speed. The hip tow causes drag on that side, making the tow boat turn in that direction. It may be necessary to steer both vessels at the same time (two helmsmen), to achieve rudder control. At low speed, during the final approach, this extra drag, etc., may cause sudden loss of rudder control, and it is better to know about this before hitting the dock.

DEWATERING

Sometimes boats leak or fill slowly, allowing time for SAR units to come alongside and dewater with an unit called an "educitor", a suction device attached to a fire pump. I always call it an "educator", providing a learning experience not soon forgotten. It is also possible for the Coast Guard to provide a **dewatering pump** packed in a waterproof barrel. It can be lowered by helicopter or transferred from surface craft boat to boat, tossed into the water at the end of a cable, to be pulled aboard by the crew of the distressed vessel, or air-dropped. Sinking boats often need a helicopter deployed pump, and this operation is more dangerous with sailboats, because of their rigging.

Operating Instructions for the USCG Dewatering Pump

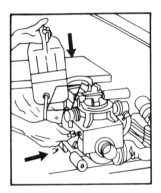 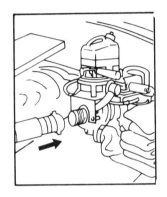 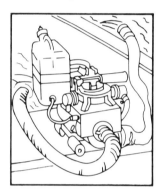

(L) The pump is fueled from a plastic container. Connect the feed line. (M) Connect the intake hose and place the strainer end in the bilge. (R) Connect the outlet hose and drain overboard.

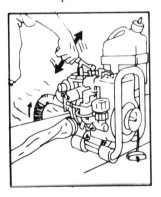 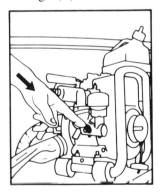 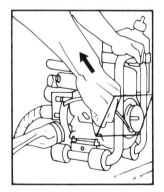

(L) Prime the pump using the hand operated priming pump attached to the frame. (M) Choke the motor to start. (R) Pull-start, then release choke.

When a helicopter is ready to drop a pump, the Coast Guard prefers to lower a lanyard to someone on deck, then drop the pump in the water. This eliminates the possibility of accidently dropping the heavy pump on someone's head. It takes two people to pull the dewatering pump assembly on deck and if there is any reason this is not possible, be sure you make this fact known, either by radio, hand signal, or by refusing the lowered lanyard. When an aircraft makes a drop, they approach upwind, if possible, or from abeam, drop the pump short of the vessel, then pay out a long messenger line which is (hopefully) dropped across the vessel. The boat's crew pulls in the messenger, then the leader and finally the pump.

A standard dewatering pump operates at 140 gallons per minute. The power plant is a gasoline driven Briggs and Stratten 3-HP motor. Inside the barrel, one finds: a container of gasoline, two lengths of hose, the pump, a set of instructions. The pump must be fueled, the hose installed, the strainer end placed in the bilge. A hand operated bilge pump attached to the unit's frame is used to prime, then the motor is started. The instructions for doing this job are best reviewed in an armchair, rather than in knee-deep water, so I have reproduced them here.

Coast Guard SAR Aircraft

The C-130 Hercules aircraft is the Guard's lumbering giant, selected for its great range and hauling capacity. It can make a whole lot of unhappy people really happy, by spewing a virtually inexhaustible supply of lifesaving equipment from its huge maw. If a vessel foundered more than 700 to 1,000 miles from the nearest Falcon base, the Hercules would be called upon to conduct the search.

The Falcon jet (HU 24A Guardian, shown on the facing page) is the Guard's medium-range, fast response vehicle, with a 2,000 NM range, 4.25 hour endurance (with a 45 minute reserve), and a speed of 350 KTS. It has an onboard computer which is highly integrated with the aircraft's Rockwell-Collins avionics, allowing the jet to fly a variety of search patterns on auto pilot. That permits the flight crew to maximize their time searching, rather than flying the aircraft. Officially, a Falcon on stand-by is supposed to be airborne in not more than 30 minutes, but it is not unusual for the crew to be briefed and aloft in half that time. All models have surface search radar, effective for finding ships and possibly for sensing radar reflectorsaboard life rafts, but not swimmers.

Overleaf: Lowering the dewatering pump by Richard DeRosset

The Falcon "Guardian" Jet. Courtesy of USCG Group, San Diego

Later models also carry infrared scanners, which could locate a group of castaways by their body heat, even at night. A drop hatch is used to deploy dewatering pumps, Navy seven-man life rafts, and an assortment of smoke and datum markers.

HELICOPTERS

Any sort of helicopter operation in close proximity to a vessel is a tense moment for the aircrew and dangerous for everyone, including those awaiting rescue. Another SAR craft is almost invariably assigned to fly guard over the rescue craft to render assistance in the event of a crash, and this procedure should serve as a reminder that there is considerable risk to rescue personnel at this time. Material from the doomed vessel, flailing rigging or loose line may be sucked into the helicopter's blades. Every effort is made to keep the helicopter a

(continued on page 544)

The HH52A helicopter carries a crew of three, has a speed of 80 to 106 KT. and a range of 300 NM. It can carry three survivors, in addition to its crew. It is the Guard's fast-response vehicle and is also used for surf patrol. USCG, San Diego photo

Face Page: "Bomber" Trench, aboard an RAF Nimrod successfully drops a replacement life raft to crew of a transatlantic racer (bottom of photo) which foundered in bad weather 600 NM offshore. The boat's life raft, although damaged, kept the two crew afloat long enough for them to activate their EPIRB, which was heard by a transatlantic Pan Am jet at 30,000 feet. An RAF Nimrod was launched, picked up the EPIRB signal and flew "down the beam". By the time "Bomber" made his drop, the raft had deflated to the point where it could not support both men. Note the messenger line, above the parachute, which is paid out after the raft is jettisoned. "Bomber" laid the mesenger right in this lucky survivor's hands   A ship later picked them up.   Photo by Andrew Besley, taken from a RAF Nimrod aircraft.

safe distance above the distressed vessel, and this is why a basket hoist is lowered. The survivors are winched aboard. If the weather is bad, the rising and falling of the vessel may make the basket seem to plunge into the sea, then zoom upward into the air. At the critical moment, the winchman will prevent this.

If a helicopter rescues people from a life raft, the down draft from the chopper's blades may undermine and flip it, <u>particularly if the raft's ballast pockets are small</u>. It may be wise to fill the raft with seawater, to give it added weight. In some cases, a loaded raft becomes increasingly unstable as the crew are winched aboard and the last man suddenly finds himself—blown away.

The **HH3F Pelican** is a twin-turbine craft with two pilots and two crew. Its speed is 110 to 142 Kts. with a range of up to 850 NM and is the Guard's longest-range rotary wing aircraft to date. It is the replacement for the venerable HH52A. So if your accident occurred more than, say, 375 to 400 NM from shore, it will be necessary for a fixed-wing aircraft to be deployed or the HH3F must refuel, hovering in the air above a moving Cutter; it is too heavy to land on its deck. The HH3F can carry 10 to 15 survivors, although it has in fact lifted more. See the Pelican at work on pages 545-546.

THE HH65A DOLPHIN

The Dolphin (see photo on the next page)is a short range recovery vehicle like the HH52A and has a range and speed similar to it, but this is where the similarity ends. It is a state-of-the art machine, about as different from the old, thrundering Coast Guard Sikorsky amphibious helicopters as a 747 is to a DC-3. The Dolphin, made in France, looks different, with its streamlining and rotor blade inside the tail assembly, but is its major improvement over older craft lies in its highly integrated avionics package. It automates routine communications, navigation and mission management. The Dolphin can fly a variety of automated search patterns, integrating data from position-finding devices, altimeter, datum marking transmitters, etc, allowing the chopper crew to spend their time searching, rather than fighting to stay in the air. The Dolphin is equipped with several types of radar, and can also carry other sensors and night-vision devices, all of which optimize its time in the air. The on-board computer will automatically initiate a maneuver to return to the spot where a castaway was sighted, descend and hover, maintaining position, using a radar altimeter to maintain altitude, while the flight crew prepares to hoist.

The HH65A Dolphin, hoisting one of six crewman after their fishing vessel sank 60 NM SE of Banrneqat, NJ. Note brilliant retro-reflective tape on life vests. Also note lack of life raft and immersion suits. Their rescue is further proof that God protects fools, drunks and sailors, not necessarily in that order. (See photo on pg. 555) *AP Wide World* Photo

Overleaf-HH3F Pelican doing what it does best—rescuing large numbers of people, far offshore. The doomed 482-foot KOMSOMOLETS MIRGIZII, a Russian bulk carrier, was bound for Cuba with 10,292 tons of flour, which shifted in bad weather. The photo was taken just before she capsized. Thirty-seven crewmen were rescued by USCG helicopters. *AP/Wide World Photo*

HELICOPTER LIFTING DEVICES

It is extremely difficult to lift survivors directly from a sailboat, because of its mast and rigging. In some cases, the boat captain may consider cutting away the mast to facilitate rescue, but this is a dangerous procedure, not recommended and, if not done properly, can result in more casualties and risk. It is best to await the decision of the rescue commander who must decide on how best to save you. Rescue Commanders often opt to drop a weighted line to the boat crew. The helicopter then moves away from the distressed vessel's rigging, paying out line as it goes, then the basket is lowered. The boat crew pulls it aboard. The chopper then climbs, paying out line and hovers above the boat. The basket is then hoisted. Another option is to use the boat's life raft, which is allowed to drift down wind, attached to the distressed vessel by a line. A single ill person, or several people at a time can go in the raft, which can be tended from the boat. If the on-scene Rescue Commander deems it necessary, a crewman will be lowered onto the distressed vessel to assist the crew. A metal basket, lowered on a metal cable, generates static electricity, so <u>always allow the basket to ground on the hull or in the water before touching it.</u>

In any event, it is important to:

1. Secure loose objects, such as clothing, line, cushions, etc.,which may be swept into the helicopters blades.
2. Be sure everyone is <u>dressed for survival</u> and is wearing a life jacket.
3. Include the survival pack when abandoning ship. Something might go wrong. You might be out there longer than you anticipated.

TYPES OF HOISTS

The basket hoist is the preferred device for lifting, especially in bad weather. It is easy to enter. It has positive flotation, and will not sink. As a result, it is possible for the winchman to allow the cable to go slack for a moment, and the basket will ride the swell, permitting a survivor to enter. Get in, tuck hands under thighs and chin against chest, <u>be sure no part of you is hanging out</u>, including head or hands, grit your teeth and—away-y we go! Do not try to grab the helicopter as the basket approaches it, the basket might bounce against the hull, crushing your hand. Stay in the basket until the winchman tells you to get out. <u>Do not try to help him</u>.

The Stokes Litter is lowered for an injured or sick crewman. It is not very practical for use with boats, because it requires a rigging-free flat area upon which to lower the litter.

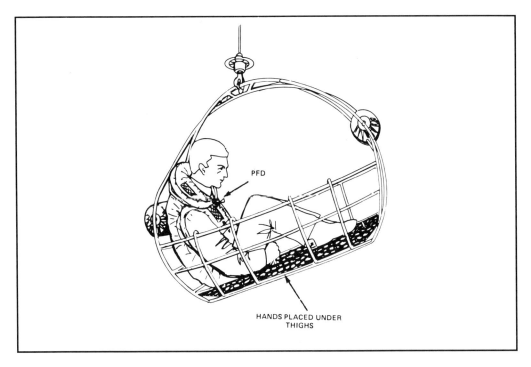

PFD

HANDS PLACED UNDER
THIGHS

The Basket Hoist. Courtesy of USCG San Diego Group. Also see photo on pg. 555

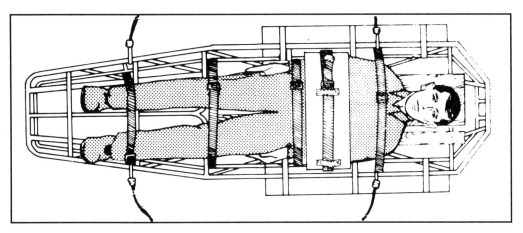

The Stokes Litter.

AMVER Alert

The Automated Mutual-assistance Vessel Rescue Program (AMVER) is a computerized, world wide rescue system, utilizing volunteer non-military participating vessels. Coast Guards of participating nations transmit distress information to the AMVER center. The course and position of participating vessels are computer-maintained. Should a disaster occur, the nearest vessels are diverted to the scene of the accident. Sixty nations participate in this program which is operated solely for the benefit of humanity. Tankers, passenger ships, even sailing vessels can and have been diverted to search for castaways. I was once diverted to sail a five-day, expanding box search for a downed balloonist off the coast of Africa. I never found him, and he was never seen again. One does not always win in SAR. All one need do to participate in the AMVER program is to file a sail plan and make periodic position reports, which may be sent by radio-transmission to AMVER Center. Most vessels are routed to the scene of a disaster by INMARSAT radiotelephone. Other vessels respond on hailing frequencies, described in Chapter XIV.

A Classic Rescue

The killer storm which ripped through Southern California on January 17-18, 1988, was one to remember—the kind that comes only a few times each century, causing millions of dollars in damage—a storm that takes its tole in blood. It intensified suddenly out of an ordinary gale, with little warning. The NOAA weather report, transmitted the previous day, predicted gale winds, rain showers and 20-foot seas, not the 65 to 70 m.p.h. winds and 40- to 50-foot seas which arrived with amazing suddenness. As a result, many boats were caught at sea, unprepared for what was to come.

It blew so hard in San Diego that even the puddles were breaking. The STAR OF INDIA tore loose from the dock, taking a good piece of the pier with it. A USCG-Motorized life boat pitchpoled at the sea buoy, but fortunately did not drive in far enough to hit the seabed. The coxswain looked rather white and tight-lipped as the boat tied up. A number of boats in the anchorage dragged, and no one would go get them—too dangerous to operate. That was in the harbor. At sea, men were dying, and the air was alive with the sound of distress messages.

Three fishing boats, the CATHRYN, the KITTY LEE, and the APACHE BRAVE, were lost with all hands. They had been seen fishing at 12:45 p.m. At 4:30 p.m., passengers aboard the cruise ship TROPICAL, passing through the same area, saw a single man clinging to debris. The ship passed so close that it was possible to see his face and hear his cries, but by the time the TROPICAL turned around, he was nowhere to be found.

The CATHRYN had no survival equipment or life raft. The owner of the KITTY LEE, Ronnie Rowe, was alone on board. The vessel had no survival equipment or life raft. It is believed that it was Rowe who was seen from the TROPICAL. The APACHE BRAVE was an 86-foot, well-found, well-equipped commercial fishing vessel. An empty life raft and part of the bow were found the next day. The four crew were never seen again.

The hue and cry was definitely raised. Few men of the USCG-San Diego Group would sleep that night. Every available vessel capable of withstanding the storm was out searching, and the search included looking for the source of an EPIRB signal, picked up by COSPAS/SARSAT and down-linked to Scott Air Force Base in Illinois and another station in Kodiak, Alaska. Both stations reported the location of the signal to Coast Guard Search and Rescue Control Center, Long Beach, California.

During the small hours of the morning, the RESOLUTE, a USCG 210-foot cutter, sent the following message to the SAR command center in Long Beach, California:

FROM: USCGC RESOLUTE

SUBJECT: DISTRESS SITUATION REPORT #1

1. SITUATION:

    A. EMERGENCY LOCATER TRANSMITTER TRANSMITTING AT POSITION 30-57N 119-37W DISCOVERED BY FALCON JET AM 20JAN88.

    B. AT 0418 LOCAL TIME OVERHEARD CG FALCON #2130 NOTIFY AIRSTATION SAN DIEGO THAT THEY HAD SPOTTED SMALL VESSEL AT 30-57N, 119-37.5W SUSPECT PERSONS ON BOARD. VESSEL DRIFTING WITHOUT LIGHTS. COAST GUARD FALCON #2130 DROPPED ILLUMINATED DATUM MARKING BEACON AT LOCATION.

    C. 0425LT RESOLUTE NOTIFIED LONG BEACH SAR COORDINATION CTR OF TRANSMISSION PARA. 1B.

    D. AT 0451LT HAVE BEEN DIRECTED TO DESIST FROM PWI [search for missing fishing boats}, POSITION 105NM WSW SAN DIEGO AND PROCEED 270 DEGREES TRUE AT BEST POSSIBLE SPEED. RESOLUTE AT 0500 LT POSITION 31-07.8N, 117.33.1W.

    E. ON SCENE WEATHER: WIND 024 DEG TRUE 20 KTS, VIS 10NM, BAR. 30.27 RISING, SEAS 030 DEG TRUE 3FT, SWELL 340 DEG 4-6FT.

2. ACTION;

    A. 0500LT DIVERTED TO SIGHTING OF 20FT VESSEL WITH POSSIBLE PEOPLE ON BOARD. 0530LT EMERGENCY LOCATOR POSITION PLOTTED 264 DEGS TRUE 12 KNOTS TO INTERCEPT 20FT VESSEL LOCATED 110NM FROM RECENT 0500 POSITION.

3. FUTURE ACTION:

    A. CONTINUE BEST POSSIBLE SPEED COURSE 264 DEGS TRUE UNTIL 630LT, ESTIMATED TIME OF ARRIVAL OF HH 65 [Dolphin helicopter] FOR REFUELING. UPON COMPLETION OF REFUELING INTEND TO PROCEED TO POSITION 30-57 N, 119-37W AT 16 KTS. UPON ARRIVAL WILL CONDUCT AN EXPANDING SQUARE SEARCH FOR 20FT VESSEL.

For Joseph and Jan DeJulius, it had also been a long night and an even longer couple of days. Enroute from Puerto Vallarta, Mexico to Catalina Island, the storm had fallen upon them like a cat. Their 40-foot trimaran ATLANTA was a well-built and equipped for the blue water. She carried extensive good-quality survival equipment, and before the vessel capsized, the DeJulius' donned their Sterns survival suits.

The DeJulius' climbed onto the overturned hull, activated their EPIRB, but could do little more after that than stay with the wreck. They clung to life in that way for two days. At one point, Joe removed his survival suit and tried to dive into the inverted hull to retrieve supplies. This was a <u>big mistake</u>. He became badly chilled by the cold water and had to re-enter his survival suit while wet. From this point on, his condition deteriorated rapidly.

Lt. Craig Britton had already made numerous air sorties since the storm had hit. He flew toward the coordinates provided by Scott Air Force Base and soon picked up an EPIRB signal on 121.5 MHz, a surprisingly strong signal considering the transmitter had already been operating continuously for more than two days.

At 2 a.m., Jan DeJulius was standing on the cross-arm of the capsized ATLANTA. She saw two bright lights heading their way. *"The jet passed right over us. I started waving and blowing my whistle like mad."* Lt. Britton made another four passes over the area, coming in low enough to illuminate the scene with the jet's landing lights. He then transmitted the message reported by the RESOLUTE, and headed back to base.

Shortly after sunrise CG Falcon #2130 returned to the scene, screamed in directly over the capsized vessel, turned, dropped a illuminated smoke marker, then made another pass and told the DeJulius', through a powerful 700 watt PA system that help was on the way. By this time, Joe was in a state of serious hypothermia. He thought they were at a bus stop and the damn bus was late.

A Coast Guard Dolphin helicopter from San Diego was dispatched soon after Lt. DeGroot first sighted the wreck. Since the Dolphin is a short range helicopter, it did not have the endurance to make an adequate search, in addition to the round trip. The plan was to rendezvous with the cutter RESOLUTE to refuel.

FROM: USCGC RESOLUTE

SUBJECT: DISTRESS SITUATION REPORT #2 OPEN 20FT VESSEL

1. SITUATION:

    A. 0642LT CG HELICOPTER #6332 ONBOARD AND REFUELING.

B. 0707LT COAST GUiARD FALCON #2130 REPORTED SIGHTING OVER-TURNED 50FT TRIMARAN WITH 2 PERSONS ABOARD, ONE STANDING, ONE SITTING. PERSONS ON BOARD APPEAR IN GOOD CONDITION AND WEARING MUSTANG SUITS. TRIMARAN POSITION 31-02.8, 119-36.4W

C. ON SCENE WEATHER: WIND 024 DEGS TRUE 20 KTS ,VISIBILITY 10NM BAROMETER 30.27 RISING SEAS 030 DEGS TRUE, 3FT SWELL 240 DEGS TRUE, SEAS 4-6 FT.

2. ACTION TAKEN: 0726LT CG6532 BRIEFED AND LAUNCHED. ETA 35 MIN.

3. FUTURE PLANS:

A. COAST GUARD FALCON No. 2130 REMAINING ON SCENE UNTIL CG6532 ARRIVES. ON-SCENE ENDURANCE 2.5 HRS.

B. PROCEED TO POSITION AT MAX SPEED ETA 1300LT 20JAN. WILL PRO-VIDE ASAP ALL INFO RECEIVED WHEN PERSONS ON BOARD ARE RECOVERED AND DEBRIEFED.

Long before sunrise Lt. Cdr. Pat Gregory (USCG, age 38) and Capt. Bill Elliott (USAF age 32), pilots of Dolphin CG #6332, knew they would be putting in a long day. Briefed about the mission at 4:30 a.m., minutes after the initial Falcon confirmation, the two men considered their risks, inspected their craft in the chill darkness, then departed before 5 o'clock to rendezvous with the RESOLUTE. These are men who make instrument departures under conditions where visibility is measured in yards, to conduct searches at low level in fog at night, or in bad weather. It may be necessary for one of them to swing down on a wire to snatch people off a dying ship, or jump from a helicopter into the open sea to help a swimmer. It's a job for men with a strong sense of ethics, who have a good working relationship with their God—whom they just might be talking to, face-to-face, rather suddenly. It was Gregory and Elliot's plan to cheat the Lady with the Green Eyes, if they could. Angry clouds and gusty winds, the last vestiges of the waning storm, slowly gave way as they flew into the darkness.

An HH65A Dolphin helicopter hoisting crewman Scott Jeffery, survivor of THE PRIDE OF BALTIMORE, May 20, 1986. *AP/Wide World* Photo.

Lt. Cdr. Gregory landed the Dolphin on the RESOLUTE shortly after sunrise, refueled and arrived over the wreck ready to hoist at 8:06 a.m. While the helicopter maneuvered to pick up the survivors, the Falcon jet circled overhead to keep watch on the helicopter. Jan DeJulius was still in good condition, despite her two-day ordeal, although her skin was bruised and also irritated by body wastes which had accumulated in the suit. Her husband, however, was nearly dead from hypothermia. He could not stand and had become very disoriented and confused. He struggled against his wife as she
tried to help him into the lifting basket. Hampered by breaking waves which washed across the wreck, the bad footing on the cross-arm netting, and her husband's struggles, it took fifteen minutes of intense effort to get him aboard. Then Jan, another lucky survivor, was hoisted from the wreck.Jan recalled,*"When they hoisted us aboard, they asked us how we were by name. They'd read the hull numbers during one pass and knew all about us!"*

By the time Joe DeJulius was hoisted aboard, his body core temperature had dropped to 87 °F and his heart had started beating irregularly (**thermal fibrillation**). The Dolphin took them directly to the University of California San Diego, Medical Center, where Joe was placed in intensive care. That evening, he ate his first meal, scrambled eggs, two hamburgers, four milk shakes, and a half-gallon of orange juice—a clear sign of recovery. The Lady with the Green Eyes had been cheated once again.

The Yacht SPIRIT Affair

Everyone who laid eyes on the Yacht SPIRIT thought she was an exceptional boat. She was *"basically sound and well constructed"* as reported in the survey and it wasn't just her strong hull, built over steam-bent oak frames on 12 inch centers that made her so. It wasn't her good diesel or even the fact that she was well-equipped. There was just something about the SPIRIT that said "I'm going places. Are you coming?"

The SPIRIT was a double-ended ketch built in 1954 by Irving Dgiese. She was 42-feet long including the bowsprit, 38.8 feet on deck, 12.3 feet in the beam—the classic dimensions of many boats that have tasted the blue water, neither too large nor too small. She grossed just over 18 tons. By the time Ray and Ellen Jackson bought her in 1974, she had already proved herself a strong and capable vessel through many thousands of miles of bluewater cruising.

After her purchase, the Jacksons spent a year outfitting the vessel for an extended cruise of the South Pacific. They were the kind of people who devoured a challenge, down to the last detail. They lived and breathed the year of effort and were totally involved in every aspect of it. Everything that could make the vessel ready for the adventure was done, including the installation of a new Perkins diesel and a new galley. The safety equipment included an Avon six-man life raft and a survival pack, extensive even by today's standards, purchased from Wave Traders. It contained more than 70 items, including an EPIRB, solar stills, rations, tools, fishing gear, a raft patch kit, medical supplies, and a survival manual.

SPIRIT was hauled in Sausalito, California, and serviced by some of the area's best men. Everyone, including the crew who sailed aboard her during her last days, thought she was a fully found vessel, thoroughly equipped. Her

The SPIRIT under full sail.

sudden loss and the subsequent tragic ordeal of her crew is a reminder that even the best preparation does not guarantee protection from all the mean things the Lady with the Green Eyes can do.

The Jacksons sailed the SPIRIT beneath the Golden Gate Bridge in September of 1975, and eventually cruised her through the Pacific for 8,000 miles, until the boat arrived in Hawaii on a voyage intended to return her to Sausalito. She had been well-maintained during the cruise, and had been hauled, inspected and painted in Tahiti. During the last part of the voyage, Ray hurt his back, so the Jacksons decided to have a paid crew deliver her, including Ellen Jackson's brother, Jim Ahola.

Jim was in his early 20s, had sailed with the Jacksons during the voyage and was very protective of the boat, but had less sailing experience than Bruce Collins who was hired as captain. Collins had attended USC before taking a leave of absence to go blue-water cruising. A third crewman, Durel Miller, was also an experienced sailor, in his early 30's.

Prior to departure, two young ladies, Camilla (Cammy) Arthur and Nancy Perry, decided to join the crew. Camilla had been Jim Ahola's girlfriend and they had known each other for many years. The two women had gone to live in Hawaii but had changed their minds about staying there and decided to return to the mainland. When Jim learned Camilla was in Hawaii, he immediately contacted her. Nancy and Cammy wanted an adventure and decided to seek passage on the SPIRIT.

Neither woman had any sailboat experience, and a transpacific crossing is no trip to the store, hardly the place for an introduction to sailing. Ray Jackson spoke to them about the realities of the trip and its difficulties, but they could not be dissuaded and in the end. Ray gave his consent.

On September 12, 1976, the SPIRIT left Ala Wai harbor on its final voyage. In addition to the boat's life raft, a second, virtually identical one was aboard, a six-man offshore model with an uninsulated floor. Its presence on board was a coincidence. It was being returned to its owner in Sausalito as a favor. Ray Jackson, the SPIRIT's owner, was there to see them off. After the boat left the dock, he ran down the beach to get a last glimpse of it as it disappeared out to sea.

The passage was easy, almost boring from the start. The winds were lighter than usual, and it was necessary to motor for days at a time. The vessel was well-provisioned, and it was a good opportunity to listen to music and get a tan. Despite the settled conditions, the girls were frequently sick and could only offer minimal assistance as crew, but the men could easily handle the boat. The voyage was going well.

The SPIRIT at anchor in French Polynesia. Courtesy of Ellen Ahola

After about a week, on September 27th, the wind picked up to 20- to knots, with 10- to 15- foot seas. The SPIRIT rose to the occasion, maintaining a pace of six to eight knots, under a single jib. The conditions seemed alarming to the less seasoned crew members, but the captain and most experienced crewman, Durel Miller, thought the weather was "just fine, perfect". During the morning watch, Nancy Perry was seasick, lying in a troubled sleep in the aft cabin. She dreamed someone was knocking on the cabin door and when she opened it, there stood a scruffy, red-haired man with a stringy beard, dressed like a *"Telegraph Avenue hippy."* *"Hi,"* he said. *"I'm your Angel of Death."* She slammed the door in his face.

Shortly thereafter, completely without warning, BANG! With a shuddering crash, the SPIRIT was knocked almost upside down. Durel Miller, who was steering, was washed overboard, but grabbed or became tangled in the mizzen rigging, which dragged him back aboard as the vessel righted. He could see some visible signs of disaster, including a possible hole in the bow, broken lifelines, a missing twenty feet of bulwark and starboard rail. Bruce Collins had just finished eating. He was relaxed, thinking about taking a morning sextant shot. He suddenly found himself sitting on his head—on the inverted cabin overhead, while loose objects rained around him like falling shot. Jim, Cammy, and Nancy were asleep. Nancy awoke to find herself completely under water, with the vessel going down. She had to swim from the aft cabin because the water was already too deep to stand.

When SPIRIT rolled on her beam ends, iron pigs, weighing 280 pounds used as internal ballast, lying loose beneath the floorboards, broke free and smashed about destroying the boat's SSB radio, narrowly missing Bruce Collins. With the radio gone, no distress message could be sent. The life rafts were intact, but where was the survival pack? It had been attached to the missing section of the starboard bulwark and had vanished without a trace. The captain started to go below to gather food and equipment, but the sight of the in-rushing water made him change his mind. In the two minutes which had elapsed since the accident, the boat had filled to the point where he thought that she might capsize at any second. She was settling by the stern so fast there was no other option but to abandon ship immediately, into the two Avon life rafts.

Bruce Collins, Jim Ahola, and his girl friend, Cammy Arthur, got into one raft, Durel Miller and Nancy Perry took the other. By the time the second raft was launched, the SPIRIT's cabin top was awash. The raft and its occupants narrowly escaped being pulled under with the doomed vessel. In less than 5 minutes they had been hurled from a sound sleep into cold, wet life rafts, more than 750 miles from land, in a trackless part of the North Pacific Ocean.

The rafts never capsized, but Bruce said, *"A big wave would just fold the whole thing up. Fold us flat up, the three of us. Just fold as far as it could, crush us in between, then spring us back open when it went by."* There was no mistaking the fix they were in. Their lives clearly hung by a thread.

Shock and confusion reigned. What had happened? No one knew. Maybe the vessel hit a cargo container or a whale. She was traveling in a submarine operating area, perhaps a sub had hit her—and not stopped. Perhaps she had been smashed by a rogue wave. No one ever determined the cause of the disaster. The life rafts were tethered together, and the meager items, salvaged from the wreck, were redistributed. Durel Miller had been heavily dressed at the moment of the disaster. He generously gave most of his clothes to the others, who had swum naked from the dying hull. An inadequate amount of clothing, a blanket, and a partially filled container (2.5 gallons) were all they had been able to find. The life raft equipment packs were opened and the invariable, extremely humble contents distributed as equally as possible. Each raft contained:

1 first-aid kit	6 pts. water	1 raft knife
1 patch kit	1 flashlight	2 parachute flares
3 hand flares	2 paddles	1 bailer
1 tin opener	1 cup	1 air pump
1 quoit		

There wasn't an ounce of food in either equipment pack and no fishing kit. Water was in shockingly short supply. In addition to the six pints in the raft equipment pack, Bruce Collins' raft carried the single partially filled jug, salvaged from the wreck. There was no way to divide it without another container. Their disappointment was even more bitter when they realized that the precious EPIRB was also missing. It had been in the lost survival pack. Eleven hours after the sinking, the painter connecting the two rafts suddenly broke and they drifted apart for good.

Durel Miller was an experienced sailor and, although he had never been shipwrecked, he had read stories about boat disasters and was somewhat mentally prepared for the ordeal. Nancy Perry was just twenty one years old and a complete stranger to the sea. She was already weakened physically by seasickness, psychologically by the immensity of their misfortune. She was not able to withstand the suffering.

The raft containing Durel Miller and Nancy Perry before the painter (left quadrant) broke. Note how the raft blends with the waves, making it difficult to see, even at a short distance.

After 12 days, she began to experience **disaster syndrome**, catatonic withdrawal and hallucinations. *"Who's driving?"* she would ask. *"No one's driving,"* Durel would reply. *"No one's driving?"* she replied, incredulously. Sometimes Nancy thought she was in a house with a refrigerator. She accused Durel of hoarding food. *"I know you have that banana. At least you could give me half!"* She said she wanted to jump overboard, then swim toward the bottom until she drowned. She thought they were in a space ship, with Durel driving, and complained he was doing a lousy job. She muttered around the clock, held one-sided conversations. *"I know how to get home,"* she told Durel. *"All we have to do is go out the door and through the long tunnel of trees. We'll come out near that movie theater in San Rafael."*

As her physical condition deteriorated, she lost a shocking forty three of her 113 pounds, a loss of about 2 pounds per day, and approached a 50% weight loss from which few ever recover. Her catatonia deepened. It was hard for Durel to get her to move, to dry her constantly wet skin, or to exercise. Because she did not move or change positions, pressure sores developed and eventually became huge, painful lesions which made her mutter and moan in a comatose state.

Durel Miller lost 55 pounds in the 22 days they were adrift, but his heavier physique and better psychological state resulted in far less serious physical injuries. His legs and toes became ulcerated and even today his toes bear the scars. When he first saw the ORIENTAL FINANCIER, she was the size of a sugar cube on the horizon. Durel fired a parachute flare which not only failed to deploy, but it also burned a hole in the raft, deflating one of the buoyancy tubes. He fired a second parachute flare which worked, then ignited two hand flares and waived with Nancy's foul-weather jacket.

The ORIENTAL FINANCIER was a brand-new container ship, French owned, Liberian registered, with a Chinese crew from Hong Kong. At 4:30 p.m., the second engineer, having just come off watch, decided to stroll to the bridge to stretch his legs. The day was wonderfully clear, and through the ship's binoculars, he could see what he thought was an orange fishing float, bobbing on the horizon. He gave the glasses to the bridge officer to take a look. Then they saw the flares.

Durel Miller said the action on the ORIENTAL FINANCIER looked like a Chinese fire drill. The ship sounded its horn and circled twice, to slow down. Crewmen ran around shouting orders, shouldering each other aside. When they were close enough, heaving lines were dropped to the two lucky survivors.

If ever a man had a lousy night, October 18, 1976, was one which Ray Jackson will never forget. The parents of Camilla Arthur and Nancy Perry had called, asking about their daughters. Regular radio communications with the vessel had suddenly ceased, leaving an ominous silence. His calls to the Coast Guard four days before had initially been reassuring. The Coast Guard had talked to other captains who had just arrived and they reported light winds and a slow passage. Do not worry, The SPIRIT just needed a few more days. But those days had come—and gone. To make matters worse, his marriage was falling apart. He had just had a fight with his estranged wife, Ellen, the sister of crewman Jim Ahola. Most important, the SPIRIT was, beyond all reasonable doubt, overdue. An old friend invited Ray to dinner. It was an opportunity to set all of his cares aside for the evening and Ray gratefully accepted.

Around midnight, another friend, with whom Ray had been staying, called to say there was an urgent message from the Coast Guard. *"What's happened?"* Ray asked. *"They didn't say,"* was the reply. Ray went into the bedroom to make the dreaded call. A few minutes later, his host heard him sobbing into the telephone, *"What happened?"* Ray was saying, *"She went down? She couldn't have gone down. Missing? Who's missing?"*

Over in Emeryville, on the other side of San Francisco Bay, Lt. Jim Hartley, USCG, was getting ready for bed when Coast Guard Search and Rescue Center, San Francisco called with the bad news. Two survivors had been rescued from a wreck, and three were missing. Jim was wanted back at the office right away, and would get no sleep that night. By dawn, he had received a computer projection of the area to be searched, based on the position of the first raft, and had ordered the launching of five Coast Guard, Navy and Air Force planes, deployed the USCG cutter CAMPBELL, a Navy frigate (name unknown), the COOK, a Navy destroyer escort, and diverted several AMVER ALERT Merchant Marine ships, including the SS MAINE, to the search.

Three frustrating days later, the hue and cry reached a crescendo and Lt. Hartley pulled out all the stops, deploying 17 planes, including a U-2 reconnaissance aircraft that photographed the area from 54,000 feet. A tiny orange dot was seen in one photo. Based on this information, the search parameters narrowed. By the sixth day, the search had covered an incredible 196,000 square miles and in the end, over 52 air sorties were made. God knows what it all cost—many millions of dollars—but then, SUCCESS.

Awakened from a stupor by the sound of aircraft engines, Bruce Collins looked out the raft door to see a Coast Guard C-130 Hercules aircraft making a low pass overhead. While he waited for the Cutter CAMPBELL, Bruce took a few photos, then drifted off to sleep. Perhaps his ability to conserve energy was one of the reasons he was still alive after four weeks of little water and no food. Jim and Cammy suffered greatly from lack of food and water. It had rained, but the canopy of the life raft had deteriorated and the run-off from it was so foul tasting, the two found it impossible to drink.

Bruce Collins, shortly before the deaths of Jim and Cammy. Photo by Jim Ahola

Bruce drank the runoff and also added saltwater to his ration, usually about 3:1, fresh to salt, but the others were not convinced this would work. They rationed water severely, drinking on the average less than a pint each per day. Even on this severe ration, the water did not last. It ran out after twelve days. The three had held up well until then, and Jim had taken pictures of them with his underwater camera, but at this point, his health started to decline. After two days with neither food nor water, it rained.

The initial runoff from the deteriorating canopy was so foul tasting that Cammy and Jim again refused to drink. They thought it might be poisonous, but Bruce Collins reasoned that Avon would not put anything on the water collecting surface that could kill. He drank it. Then, when rain had washed the canopy, the others drank their fill. They were able to collect and save 2.5 gallons, but the ordeal had left its mark.

All three were very feeble, emaciated, and covered with saltwater sores. Jim Ahola's condition deteriorated rapidly. He began hallucinating, reprimanded Bruce for not hailing a passing truck, blamed Durel for the loss of the vessel. He became angry that they had not been rescued. His hemorrhoids, which had started bothering him after the first week, popped out and began to bleed. He pushed them back in, but then he started to have diarrhea and bled continuously through the rectum, draining precious body fluid. He insisted on cleaning it up himself, and became further weakened by the work. On the nineteenth day, he awoke from an exhausted sleep. Cammy and Bruce tried to talk to him. He gasped a few times but remained incoherent. His face had assumed the mask of death and it was extremely evident that the end was near. They all dozed off again and when Bruce awoke, Jim was dead. After rigor mortis set in, they pushed his body into the sea.

The effect of Jim's death was devastating to Cammy. Her depression, of course, increased, but, in addition, the saltwater sores which had plagued her went wild, consuming her body. Two days later, Bruce and Cammy began talking about the probability of their own death. Cammy had experienced a shocking weight loss and was extremely feeble. They cried, then fell asleep in each other's arms. When Bruce woke up, Cammy was dead. He pushed her body into the sea.

Bruce cried and blamed Cammy's death on himself, but afterward, his mind became exceptionally clear. He couldn't rewrite the past, ahead lay the future. There had to be some meaning to the tragedy; perhaps he could find it. To give up now might imply that he had lost his love of life, and this was not true.

When the lifeboat crew of the CAMPBELL saved Bruce Collins and took his raft in tow, they were surprised to find a calm, very philosophical man—another lucky survivor, who was less emotional about his rescue than they themselves.

Further bad luck plagued Ray Jackson. He and his wife divorced. Another boat in which he was a partner, the BLANQUITA, was lost with all hands. Ray later became an executive officer aboard a Greenpeace vessel .

Bruce Collins flew to England, where he advised the Avon company about his adventure and how to improve their rafts He then enrolled in the University of Southern California to work on his M.B.A. He now owns a boat yard, north of San Francisco. He said it took him ten years to regain the 65 to 75 pounds he lost. I asked him if he'd had enough of the sea and he said *"Oh no, that's my whole life."*

Nancy Perry got married and lives in Hawaii. She did not reply to my inquiry and, after all the pain she suffered, perhaps she views this tragic moment of her past as a memory, seen reluctantly, dimly, through dusty glass.

Durel Miller was one of the founders of The School of Ocean Survival in Orange County. He's a shipwright, still an Old Salt. The tragedy troubled him most of all, swirled through his memory for years. He regained all of his lost weight and more. He finds it difficult to refuse food, because of his ordeal, and once remarked, *"I'll never be hungry again."*   Friends say he sometimes has a far-off look and perhaps, like so many, he was changed forever by the bitter sea which, when it takes you, never lets you go.

The USCG Cutter CAMPBELL approaching Bruce Collin's raft with a C-130 Hercules aircraft flying guard. Blurred object (right) is survivor's finger. Photo by Bruce Collins.

"I don't mean to exacerbate this situation, Roger, but I think
I'm quite close to bursting into maniacal laughter and
imagining that your nose is really a German sausage."

From *The Far Side* 1986 © Universal Press Syndicate,
reprinted with permission. All rights reserved.

CHAPTER XX: SURVIVAL AND THE LAW

Injury, Disability, and Loss of Life

Before the 19th century, fair treatment of seamen was an individual matter and varied from captain to captain. Horribly injured sailors were usually put ashore at the end of a voyage, with no further thought being given to their welfare. Men were often cheated out of their wages and discharged without a penny in ports far from home. Safety equipment expressly designed to save sailors lives did not exist.

The idea that sailors had rights was slow to be born. Looking back at history, some might say that of all the so-called "free men" in the world—sailors, particularly those pressed into military service—were treated not much better than slaves. Yet these were poor men in a brutal age, where poor men everywhere were usually treated worse than animals; in fact, work animals would have died if they had received treatment considered normal for the poor.

The revolution in the American Colonies was just one expression of the revolution in individual rights which spread through the Western world. By the end of the nineteenth century seamen had acquired some rights, although they were tenuous and God help the sea lawyer who tried to remind the captain what those rights were.

Prior to the Jones Act, the marine lawscape going back to the English Merchant Shipping Act of 1876 could be summarized like this:

1. A vessel's owner is liable for a crewman's maintenance, wages and cure, if he is injured or became sick while in service of the ship.

2. An injured seaman could seek indemnity for injuries incurred because of unseaworthiness of the ship or failure to maintain it or its equipment.

3. Beyond maintenance, wages, and cure, a seaman could not recover for injuries caused by negligence of another crewman or officer.

4. Same as #3 but read "negligence of the master."

THE JONES ACT (Section 33 of the Merchant Marine Act, U.S. Congress 1920) amended earlier legislation and undercut items #3 and #4. It has its counterpart in British Admiralty law, and most other maritime nations of the world have enacted similar legislation. The Jones Act allowed seamen to recover damages for virtually any shipboard injury caused by negligence. The Jones Act was horribly written, and the flood of cases arising from it became a trackless sea of litigation. The well-known professors of law, Grant Gilmore and Charles L. Black Jr., said in their book, *Law of the Admiralty*, *"The Supreme Court should have struck it down as an offense to due process."*

For many years the United States Code prefaced the Act with a seventy-page Commentary, which included diagrams intended to help guide an attorney through the Act's perilous reefs. Later editions (1958) dispensed with the Commentary. Apparently the editors felt that one would be adrift in the Jones Act, regardless of assistance. They did add 307 pages of case law annotations, and an additional 241 pages were added in the next edition. Possibly the editors felt that, since reason was useless, blind example might suffice.

The Jones Act was extremely broad-based legislation, intended to address a variety of maritime matters. The part we are concerned with deals with the entitlement to compensation for the injury or death of seamen. Essentially the Act guaranteed hospitalization and compensation for permanent disability, loss of future wages, and/or services. In addition, wages had to be paid for the extent of the voyage. That meant that if the man was injured in the course of a voyage, he would be paid for the entire voyage, but if the ship sank, the wages stopped at that point, because the voyage stopped at that point. Prior to the Jones Act, the court distinguished between injury caused by the owners, the captain, or other crew members   The Jones Act made it possible to bring suit for damages caused by negligence, as long as the injury occurred in service of the vessel. This included injuries incurred 'longshore, if they were service related.

The Jones Act was a mess, but those who benefited from it were reluctant to see it replaced, presumably because they didn't think they could get a better deal. As a result, the U.S. Supreme Court as well as an astonishing number of state and local courts have been making marine legislation by their decisions instead of being guided in decision-making by written law. The process has not been smooth. One commentator regarding the patchwork of decisions, called it *"the devil's own mess."*   There has never been what could be called a consensus about it among the Chief Justices and "progress" has been very much a matter of two steps forward, one step back, and one step sideways.

Nevertheless, it has been established that:

1. The owner's duty to furnish a seaworthy ship is absolute and not satisfied by mere diligence.
2. The definition of "seaworthiness" is broad.
3. Both a civil and a Jones Act claim can go simultaneously to court.
4. Admiralty (Federal) law applies over state law only when State law is inconsistent with Federal law.

Jones Act (Admiralty) cases can be decided by a state or federal court. Many injured sailors, feeling that they will be more fully compensated, choose to pursue the matter of restitution in a civil court, believing that a jury will award more compensation than a judge. For this reason, item #3 (above) is more important than it seems.

During the 60 years of legal war which followed the Jones Act, the Supreme Court greatly expanded the liability of owners for injuries suffered by seamen in the course of their employment. This gradual revolution corresponded to the revolutionary expansion of product liability litigation in which manufacturers have been held strictly liable (without regard to fault or negligence) to those who suffer loss because of defectively manufactured goods.

DAMAGES RECEIVED FOR ILLNESS, MAINTENANCE DURING RECOVERY, AND FOR DEATH.

The Jones Act has been around for a long time and one of the reasons is that it is favored by the Merchant Seamen's and 'longshoreman's unions. They know that the Jones Act offers a high degree of protection for their members. The chance that an injured sailor will receive some sort of compensation is high, and in some ways the Jones Act provides protection similar to disability compensation, although one must go to court to get it.

In addition to the Jones Act, a number of civil suits brought in state civil courts, some for negligence, some for product liability, have been won by sailors or their heirs in recent years. In one case, the judge decided that negligence rendered the vessel unseaworthy because of missing survival gear. He based his conclusion not on law, but on a USCG directive which suggested that an exposure suit and a life raft seat were minimum requirements for seamen working in cold waters. In another case, a crewman badly injured by a defective winch was awarded a judgment greater than the value of the vessel, despite the fact that the owner was a corporation with the vessel as its sole asset. The actual, rather than the legal, owners or their insurers had to pay.

What all this should tell you is that you, as a boat owner, are liable for any sort of voyage-related accident, regardless of who was at fault. The court doesn't care that messing around with boats is known to be dangerous and just might kill someone. The inherent risk of death associated with small-boat sailing is not recognized as a legal defence. The good intentions of the owners, their efforts to make the vessel as seaworthy as possible, is not an issue. Whether the injured crewman contributed to the injury may be irrelevant.

Damage awards may be smaller if you were completely prudent and provided the best safety equipment money could buy, but there will be an award, based on the cost of recovery, the extent of injury, the loss of future earnings, pain and suffering, if the person died slowly. It sometimes includes compensation for loss of companionship (consortium). This is the reason why having either boat insurance or a good bankruptcy lawyer is important.

On the other hand, what we would call "criminal negligence" is not an issue in these suits, and punitive damages are seldom awarded, much to the annoyance of many plaintiffs. Someone whose son died because the owner of a vessel was too cheap to buy a life raft might consider him a murderer (which he is), and wish to punish him, but the court does not concern itself with this issue. As a result, boat (and ship) owners are relieved of the pressure associated with fighting criminal negligence or even homicide charges, and in this way, the Jones Act and assorted civil laws benefit them as well as their employees.

The Yacht SPIRIT Suit

The rescue of the SPIRIT survivors by no means ended the affair. The boat and its crew were from California, a most litigious state. Nancy Perry and the mother of the deceased Camillia Arthur threatened suit against a variety of people and corporations, some connected in only the most remote way with the accident. Included, among others, was the boat's original designer, who had died years before the accident. The firm which installed the boat's motor was cited as was the surveyor who had examined the vessel prior to its departure from Sausalito, more than a year before the disaster. This caused many people not really involved in the accident a great deal of anguish. They feared it would be necessary to hire attorneys and pay them to prepare a defense.

Various accusations were made against them, but little could be proved during the discovery phase of the suit, and the Coast Guard report stated that the cause of the sinking was unknown. Most parties were never served. The matter was either dropped or settled out of court. The C.J. Henry Company, who had repacked one of the Avon life rafts—settled for less than $200. The company that carried the insurance policy on the SPIRIT settled out of court for the extent of the insurance, about $70,000. Apparently they decided that the deaths of the two young people, the injury of Nancy Perry and the ghastly photos, taken during the disaster, would sway any jury, even though there was no proof that the boat owners were negligent in the moral sense.

The suit then focused on the Avon life raft company, whom the plaintiffs believed were negligent because the life raft lacked sufficient equipment to sustain life. This was ironic in its way, for the other two survivors, Durel Miller and Bruce Collins, gave testimonials for Avon which were used in advertising. The suit was entered as a product liability case, which essentially means, would an "ordinary consumer" of this product consider that it functioned properly when manufactured, or did it ,in fact, contribute to the accident. To put it in legalese:

> The manufacturer of a product is liable for injuries a proximate cause of which was a defect in its design . . . which was reasonably foreseeable by the Defendant . . .
> A product is defective if. . . it failed to perform as safely as an ordinary consumer of would expect when used in a manner reasonably foreseeable to the Defendant . . .
> In determining whether the benefits of the design outweigh the risks, you may consider, among other things, the gravity of the harm which can be caused by the design, the likelihood that such design could cause damage, the feasibility of a safer alternative . . . and the adverse consequences to the product and the consumer that would result from an alternate design.   From Judge Pfotenhauer's instructions to the jury

Avon, the defendant, said it was obvious that its products had functioned properly, for the two rafts remained afloat until the survivors were rescued. W. Robert Buxton, attorney for the Plaintiffs, said there was no question about that. He contended that the equipment pack lacked sufficient items needed to sustain life. He showed advertisements for Avon rafts that used phrases such as "complete safety equipment," "Designed and manufactured as if your life depended on them," and "Comforting assurance for all cruising yachts," yet it was nowhere mentioned in these ads or in other literature that supplementary equipment might be needed for a bluewater cruise.

To make matters worse, Mr. Buxton contended, the raft lacked an EPIRB to attract help, solar stills to produce water, a heliograph, rations, or a fishing kit. The "medicine kit" lacked seasickness pills and an effective saltwater sore salve. The flares became wet and inoperable. The raft had a single floor which leaked. The patch kit would not work on wet material, and no plugs or clamp-type patches were supplied. An inflatable air mattress, which would have acted as a double floor, was not retrofitted when the raft was serviced at an Avon station. As a result, the castaways were cold and could never get dry. This contributed to hypothermia, the development of saltwater sores and death.

The instruction card was made of paper and disintegrated before it could be read. Also, the card was totally inadequate and did not provide sufficient information, the whose nature was developed by expert testimony. Omitted was information about drying the skin, exercise, and the fact that one can live for up to 60 days without food.

In addition, the raft canopy, designed to be used as a water collector, had been painted with a florescent substance which deteriorated, flaked off and fouled the runoff. These flakes tasted so disgusting that Camilla Arthur and Jim Ahola would not drink the foul-tasting water, fearing it was poisonous. But the paint was not poisonous; the Avon company knew about the problem from previous episodes, did nothing about it, and did not warn the consumer that the paint was nontoxic. This, the plaintiffs contended, also contributed to Camilla and Jim's demise.

The attorney for Avon, Douglas Moore, was particularly hampered by the fact that the suit was for product liability. He was unable to offer as evidence the fact that Avon's equipment pack, while miserable, was similar to those of most other companies and that no one, (then or now), packs either an EPIRB or solar stills in a raft equipment pack unless it is specifically requested.

In addition, some of the equipment listed in the sales literature, was in fact missing from the pack. This made a finding for the plaintiff a virtual certainty. It also muddied the question about whether a normal consumer would consider the additional items (the EPIRB, etc.), essential.

Mr. Moore tried to make it clear that one of the "adverse consequences to the product and the consumer that would result from an alternate design" was a much higher cost for the life raft, a price most consumers would not pay (then or now). He explained that the normal use for an Offshore raft was close to home, or in an offshore race, where supervised help was close at hand. It was mentioned in testimony by Avon that the great majority of survivors are found within a few days, making the extra gear (and its extra cost) unnecessary. In addition, there were no legal requirements regarding the contents of Offshore life raft survival packs that existed in American law (then or now). The equipment pack, prepared in England, conformed to the "E pack" requirements recommended by the British Board of Trade. The Defense also tried to make it clear that the SPIRIT's owners, certainly possible "ordinary consumers" of the life raft, were aware that the equipment pack was minimally equipped and had provided an extensive supplementary survival pack, which was unfortunately lost when the vessel sank.

To make matters worse for Avon, there wasn't a single sailor on the jury and the judge admitted he had *"less than zero knowledge"* about sailing. Since sailors are usually the "ordinary consumers" of a life raft, one might think that only sailors should have been jurors. What a sailor would expect to find in a life raft equipment pack might be different from that of a landlubber. Bruce Collins and Durel Miller said they expected to find an EPIRB and were sorely disappointed when it could not be located (it was in the lost survival pack). But they did not expect to find much equipment in the raft and they were not surprised at the contents of the equipment pack. One could certainly call them "ordinary consumers." On the other hand, perhaps what a landlubber might decide—that a raft must not only float but also provide food, water, and equipment sufficient to sustain life (since it is called a "life raft")—is reasonable.

The trial began on September 15, 1980, and lasted an exhausting seventeen days. The stark photos, taken during the life raft ordeal were shown, as well as a TV video tape of Nancy Perry on "To Tell the Truth." The surviving Avon six-man Offshore life rafts used by the survivors were inflated and their contents examined. In addition to the testimony of the survivors, relatives, owners and heirs, and several expert witnesses were called. It is beyond the scope of this book to cite them all. Among them was Commander Stephan B. Lewis, MD, who was working for the Clinical Investigation Center, Naval Regional Medical Center, Oakland, California. He and other colleagues had written extensively about the physiological and psychological effects of life raft survival conducted with the cooperation of two Naval Reserve Aviators who drifted for 56 days from San Francisco to Hawaii.

The summary of information given by Dr. Lewis (which follows) consists of testimony taken from the public record which has been <u>freely</u> edited for brevity. Let it be clear that we are interested in the educational value of Dr. Lewis' statements, rather than his precise words. The legalese has been completely edited out, so the following is not to be considered a transcript.

Q: Doctor, let me come back to the paper you wrote on the raft experiment that you just described. What were the names of the two people involved?
A: The two gentlemen were Gore and Sigler.

Q: How did you get involved?
A: I was an assistant to the director. . . of the Clinical Investigation Center in Oakland [California] at that time. . . I became involved as a co-investigator to explore this rather unique opportunity of seeing two eager individuals willing to risk their lives at sea to test the concepts of their [new] survival craft. . . .

Q: What year did this experiment occur in?
A: This was 1974.

Q: Did they go from here [San Francisco] to Hawaii or from Hawaii to here?
A: They went from here, from the Farallon Islands, where their raft upended and they lost much of their gear with the exception of the minimum essential items for survival. By naval navigation strategy they were able to navigate in their raft from the Farallon Islands to Waikiki Beach.

Q: Were they reprovisioned?
A;   No, sir.

Q: Prior to them leaving here, did you doctors spend some time with these two men in their preparation for the trip?
A: We weighed them, measured skin fold thickness, and talked to them a good deal about what their motivating factors were for attempting this relatively high risk operation.

Q: What were the areas of concern?
A: The key to the thing was they could go without food for about 60 days given the fact they were of average weight, average height, and the amount of fat they had beneath their skin fold appeared normal. It would be about half a centimeter.

Q: You doctors told them they could go for about 60 days without food?
A: That is correct. But we cautioned them that. . . this statement was given with the proviso, the warning, that they must consume a minimum amount of water each day. This minimum amount of water was about 600 milliliters, which is a little over a pint of water per day per person . . . [an] absolutely minimum requirement.

Q: Did they also have, I think you mentioned, hard candy, or rations of some sort?
A: Yes, that is correct. . . we knew from the standpoint of storage, resistance to spoilage, that carbohydrate, hard candy, was the easiest for them to include in their provisions. The quantity is what concerned us since our calculations indicated a need for 37 pounds of sucrose [sugar]. They elected to take considerably less than that. So it was a way of keeping their mouths from being parched, and it did provide some energy, but that was a relatively insignificant amount.

Q: Did they have a radio onboard?
A: That is correct.

Q: . . . could they talk back and forth?
A: No. It was a signal . . . The airplanes flying the route from San Francisco to Honolulu [would receive the signal] and we were informed as to their progress.

Q: Did they have a solar still?
A: Just one that, when things were working right, gave them about two liters or a little over two quarts of fresh water per day.

Q: Out of the one solar still?
A: That is correct.

Q: And did the raft that they went in have a double bottom or an inflatable bottom?
A: It did have a double bottom.

Q: Did they have clothing with them?

A: . . . they were told that the wind-chill factor was an extremely hazardous problem, that if they were wet, combined with a 20-30 mph wind, or a 40 mph wind, that in rather warm temperatures the chill factor could simulate the same effect as freezing cold with no wind, and that relatively minor exposure could result in great hazards to their life because of the wind-chill effect.

The other area of concern was muscle activity. We were concerned that with prolonged isolation in a raft their muscles would become flabby and ineffective if they were thrown overboard or be required to swim for safety.. . . We suggested a series of isometric [exercises] throughout the day to break up the boredom and add some discipline and routine during their 56 days at sea. . . That means tensing the muscle without moving the extremity. They were able to put their backs against one wall of the raft and their feet against the other end, and just put a constant tension on their lower extremities. By doing push-ups they could maintain upper extremity tone of their muscles.

Q: Can you describe the clothing they took with them?
A: We suggested multi-layers of clothing. This would be the thermal underwear, use of wool clothing and then a protective covering over that which would be water repellant.

Q: You spoke earlier about how long you can survive with the minimum amount of food, provided you drink so much water. What was the value of talking to them about that before they left?
A: I think there is a great deal of anxiety about food in our society and people feel if we don't eat something everyday we are endangering our lives with starvation. In actual fact ... every person is physically well-equipped to tolerate 60 days of starvation as long as water intake is adequate.

Q: How about mentally?
A: Mentally, if you knew that, then you should be able to accommodate to that length of deprivation. . .

Q: And what if you don't know it?
A: Some people could become extremely anxious and consider their ill feelings to be due to starvation. . .

Q: And is that the reason you talked to these people about that, these aspects?
A: Yes, that is correct. They looked like cadavers when they were removed from the raft. Their bones were extremely prominent. They looked very much like a person coming from a prisoner of war camp where people starved to death. But they knew that was the way they were supposed to look and that the fat stores, when depleted, would create this very gaunt, very sallow, very ill appearance, but this was a normal, expected physiological effect of being without food. . .

Q: And what was the weight loss per man?
A: One individual lost 47 pounds. The other individual approximately 57 pounds.

Q: Were they Nancy Perry's size?
A: No sir. They were . . . about 160, 175 pounds [before the voyage].

Q: When they got off the raft . . . did they have saltwater sores?
A: No. They were in top physical condition. The only unusual finding was a white line in their fingernails, which would go along with the fact that they had not ingested protein during this period.

Q: . . . did you make any overall conclusions about survival at sea ?
A: Yes. It would appear, with a reasonable amount of knowledge of the hazards and the procedures that each individual must follow while at sea, that survival for two months would be expected to cause no undue physical or mental [permanent] hardship.

Q: Can [this information] be printed on three or four pages, five by seven?
A: Yes.

Q: Now, in addition to the information, is survival . . . also dependent on any other factors?
A: Yes. The problem, as you all know, with fever, people lose weight very much more quickly than they do without fever. With each degree 9centigrade0, the caloric demands would go up as high as 10 to 20 percent. Thus, a person who is severely infected, has vomiting, has diarrhea, has fever, then the rate of fat loss is greatly accelerated. So the 60 days could easily equate to 25 days . . . . It is conceivable that the drain on the body stores of energy might be increased two- or threefold because of severe stress, infection, fever, diarrhea and vomiting.

Q: Could it be less than that?
A: Yes. . . the wind-chill factor could certainly cause problems.

Q: How about sitting on a single piece of canvas with water maybe 10 to 15 degrees below body temperature?
A: That [would] really present problems.

Q: Did [Gore and Sigler] have space blankets?
A: They did have space blankets. They did in fact use each other's body heat by sleeping the head of one man to the feet of the other and reduced the radiation of heat from the individuals . . . .

Q: Did you talk to them about when you should drink water or how much at one time?
A: We suggested . . . about seven ounces of water three times per day.

Q: Now, are there any other general conclusions as to survival at sea that you recall right now that came out of this?
A: The most amazing thing . . . is the fact that these men became impotent and it took

nine weeks of replenishing this weight loss before they were able to have normal sexual function . . . We were able to ask Nancy Perry when her period returned after her ordeal at sea and it was five months until her menses returned to normal cycle . . .

Q: Doctor, without water, how long could you live?
A: I would guess five to eight days before dehydration would result in coma and death [with no infection, etc.]. . . .

Q: Doctor, let me show you these pictures [photos of Nancy Perry's sores] . . . can you show the jury [where the injury is located]? . . . What is necrosis?
A: This is analogous to bedsores which elderly people suffer if left unattended and unrotated in a hospital bed for a long period of time. The pressure prevents adequate blood supply on the subcutaneous tissues. The skin breaks down and an infection begins. Now the organisms that arise in these wounds are, in this case, . The staphylococcus organism exudes enzymes that literally destroy the tissues . . .

Q: So [fat necrosis occurred] on each side of the buttocks?`
A: Right. In addition, there is a surgical scar over each buttock where the Japanese surgeon invaded the areas and debride [excised] the wound, to remove . . . this tissue which contained these organisms.

Q: We have had testimony that there was absolutely no food supplied with the so-called survival kit on the raft. . . Of what importance, medically, would having some hard candy or food of some sort be . . .?
A: . . . the hydrogen content of the carbohydrate in the metabolic pathway will generate water.

Q: You mean, if you eat hard candy you generate water?
A: Yes, and the carbohydrate, in addition to supplying some energy, would reduce what we call ketogenesis. . . . these are molecules which cause the kidney to release water, badly needed water, into the urine. . . . In the interest of reducing urine production to the minimum amount, carbohydrate would be of all possible energy sources, the preferred one.

Q: Now, what importance would fishing gear have for survival on a raft?
A: [This] would be less optimal than carbohydrate but certainly preferred to that of total starvation.

Q: As to saltwater sores, what kind of salve would be helpful?
A: For minor skin problems, in this country we use an ointment called Neosporin.

Q: Are the saltwater sores that have been described in the deposition, and that Nancy had, minor skin irritations?
A: No. . . . They were of such a degree and of such devastating nature that hospitalization with intravenous antibiotics and surgical debridement would be the only approach to adequately treat these people and, of course [these potentially life-saving measures on the high seas] was totally denied to them.

Q: At the inception, though, of the sores, if you were able to dry out, would that help?

A: Yes. Had they known that survival required dryness . . . they would have, I think, remained free of infection. . . Gore and Sigler were in fact immersed the first day out, but they were able to organize their raft in such a way that they remained perfectly dry throughout the voyage and had no such skin lesions.

Q: Cammy [and Nancy] in the last couple of days had some hallucinations. Is there any medical significance to hallucinations in a situation as has been described to you?

A: Yes. The sequence I think for both goes like this: The amount of circulating fluid was inadequate because of the fever and inadequate water intake. The infection was a major problem that was consuming both women. The heart rate will increase as the water loss and infection become more advanced, and in the presence of high fever due to staphylococcal organisms, release of exotoxin, blood pressure can become extremely low, and, in that circumstance, the pulse becomes thready, barely palpable, and with this sequence, the blood supply to the brain is extremely marginal . . . resulting in delusions and hallucinations, leading ultimately to coma and in Cammy's case, to death, and in Nancy Perry's case to the brink of death. Due to the pickup and the excellence of the medical officer on the ship, she was given IVs [and antibiotics] and she broke the cycle of dehydration and spread of infection.

Q: Can you describe in terms of the physical process what happens in a person's body when they are on a minimum amount of water or perhaps just a little less and no food over a period of time.

A: One begins a rapid weight loss . . . we will lose as much as 2-3% of our body weight [within 24 hours] as we become ketotic. . . This means the body will metabolize its own fat [for energy], and as we burn our fat the body will release a lot of water to compensate for the ketones in the urine. The breath will become fruity. The ketones released from the lungs smell aromatic . . .. if you continue starvation. . . the ketones are consumed by the brain, and oftentimes they such individuals have a feeling of unreality, of being distant from the level of consciousness they had when in a fed state. The amount of fat loss can be considerable . . . The standard is a 70-kilogram man and about 15 kilograms of the 70 is fat. So we predominantly store our energy for starvation in the form of fat. The second is muscle, which is about the same order of magnitude. Carbohydrate, on the other hand is only one kilogram and that is rapidly lost within 12 hours of starvation. The striking thing is the loss of fat from certain areas. For a woman, breast tissue, facial fat, are often mobilized early on, along with [fat beneath] the skin overlying the triceps . . . . The effect is a very gaunt appearance because the bony prominences which are normally well-insulated by this fat, become extremely prominent. . .

The muscle becomes steadily less because that is the last barrier between you and death. So the fat will be utilized almost 80, 90 percent, then the muscle goes . . . the muscles of the arms are utilized just prior to death [from] starvation.

Q: What was [Nancy Perry's] weight loss on her ordeal?

A: She was approaching the 50% [loss]. Somewhere between 60, 65 pounds would be the absolute minimum. But her problem was complicated by infection.

Q: And in Cammy's case, were there any dissimilarities, save the fact that she did die?

A: I think Cammy weighed considerably more and lost less weight than Nancy. . . I suspect her death was related to dehydration, infection and the despondency over the death of her friend, Jim Ahola.

During the cross-examination, the defense pointed out that Gore and Sigler were specially prepared for their ordeal, had specialized clothing and equipment to use, and knew that their voyage was being monitored. They therefore had a number of psychological advantages which a typical life raft survivor could not expect. The SPIRIT survivors were poorly clothed, and it was this lack which hurt them, not the lack of a double floor. In addition, Gore and Sigler caught just a single fish in 56 days at sea, so the question of the fishing kit providing adequate food was extremely moot.

The defense pointed out the fact that it would have been impossible to supply 18.5 pounds each of candy for the six-man rated raft. He pointed to the fact that Nancy Perry, like Gore and Sigler, recovered completely from her ordeal, except for the scars. He pointed to the fact that Nancy Perry and Durel Miller had consumed about nine gallons of water during the ordeal and had two gallons left when they were rescued, so their water consumption was in fact considerably more than the minimum 600 ml per day needed to live. He reminded Dr. Lewis of his own testimony, that despair was a major factor in the death of Camillia Arthur, and this was not Avon's fault.

In the summation, the plaintiff's attorney, Mr. Buxton, said:

Now, this is a product liability case. What is the product? The product is not just a raft. It is a life raft. And what was brought out in testimony, there are two phases or two aspects of a life raft. One is that you have got a platform that blows up when you pull the lanyard and there is something to get off the sinking yacht into. That is the platform. That is the raft. The second phase is the 'life' part of the life raft, or the survival equipment. That is, the second part of surviving a shipwreck after you get into the raft is being picked up before you die, before you suffer so terribly, or before you almost die.

Now these rafts did fine in the first aspect. They blew up. That was a platform for them to get into. And they floated for 22 and 28 days. There is no criticism of that. There cannot be. The five people in the raft were darn lucky that they had rafts that blew up.

But in the second aspect of what a life raft is supposed to do, Avon failed miserably. They failed in the survival aspect. They were really tragically inadequate for long term survival. And long term survival has been testified to as more than four or five days. . .

Mr. Hubner [an expert] said that yacht owners have no idea what is in the raft. They come in, they just buy a raft with the survival pack, and it is the advertised survival pack, and it is advertised suitable for cruising, they come in, and, okay, I will buy it, and they put it on their boat. And Mr. Hubner said they all buy it and they expect it to save their life.

Mr. Buxton further contended that each of the missing or defective items, as well as the items purposefully not included, constituted a defect in the design which lead to injury and loss of life. It was not enough that prudent sailors carry a survival pack. Sometimes a boat sinks so quickly the pack is lost, as happened in this case and then the castaways must turn to the contents of the raft for survival. The castaways might drift for weeks, with nothing but the raft contents to sustain them before the hue and cry was raised. Again, this happened here.

He then addressed the question of pain and suffering:

> Now, it is four years after this incident happened. And I will ask you to recall the anguish, the obvious anguish with which Bruce, Durel and Nancy spoke of their time on the rafts. . . .

He briefly showed a slide, taken on the raft, showing Cammy and Jim just before their deaths (not shown, by request of the family), then commented on it:

> That was ten seconds. They lived through that for 22 days, of little or no sleep, adrift at sea, no food, always cold, always wet, always thirsty, no hope, terrible sores, but you can't do that. You have to try it here in the courtroom.
>
> So I leave it to your good sense and the good judgment to award an amount that will justly compensate both Nancy and Cammy for that terrible, terrible suffering.

They say a picture is worth a thousand words, but in this case it was undoubtedly worth much more.

Douglas Moore, for Avon , replied:

> Three people survived because of these life rafts and two died because the sailboat, 38.8' long sunk out in the Pacific ocean in very significant seas. . . yet the same waves that sunk or were responsible for sinking of this parent vessel did not sink the two life rafts.

It was clear, he contended, that the owners were aware that the equipment pack was designed for short-term survival, and that was why they had provided a separate survival pack. It was impossible for Avon to provide equipment sufficient to sustain life under every possible condition. He contended that the EPIRB had just come on the market, was not a standard retrofit on older rafts and was not supposed to be packed with the raft for reasons of safety. In addition, the public would not bear the expense of adding all the suggested equipment to a survival pack. All of the added gear would make the unit unacceptably heavy. He said that the much-discussed pin-hole that kept everyone wet was probably caused during the disaster and could not be laid at Avon's door. In any event, it was normal for life raft castaways to be constantly wet and cold, a condition of existence in a life raft.

There was nothing, Mr. Moore contended, to show that Camilla Arthur died from defects in the raft. The evidence indicated that Jim Ahola died from medical complications and Camilla Arthur died from illness, from despair, and from refusing to drink foul-tasting water, the same water Bruce Collins had drunk without ill effects. In addition, Bruce Collins had lived for more than a week after the other two died and only ran out of water a day and a half before being rescued.

In the end, the jury found for the plaintiffs, awarded Nancy Perry $45,000 and Camillia's mother $70,000. This sum was in addition to the settlement made with the insurance company that carried the SPIRIT's policy. Keep in mind that attorney's fees were paid from the award and might have been as much as 40% of the total. We may possibly surmise, regarding the size of the award, that the jury decided Nancy Perry's injury and suffering, while considerable, was not permanently disabling. Camilla Arthur was very young and her earning ability had not been established. In addition, there was very little to prove financial loss to her mother and perhaps the $70,000 was awarded for the anguish and loss of consortium. After the trial, the judgement was set aside, that decision was appealed and set aside. A new trial date was set, but at that point the case was settled out of court.

Conclusion

Neither Avon nor anyone else producing life rafts apparently took this case very seriously, for the equipment packs of today are little different from those of 20 years ago. Some of the glaring defects, revealed at the trial, such as the instruction card made of paper, were corrected. Other "standard" items, such as double floors are considered deluxe models by many companies, including Avon, but at least you can buy them if you pay the extra cash. Equipment designed to sustain life has vastly improved since the loss of the SPIRIT, and if it were "standard equipment" the chance of survival would be greatly increased. Why, then, has so little changed?

The main reason is of course that the manufacturers have not been compelled to change by law (there is none) nor have they been sued into a sense of caution. Yet it is not possible to blame them alone. They are caught in a dilemma, in a competitive economic squeeze where the consumer is extremely resistant to price increases. All raft manufacturers would unquestionably be delighted to add extra equipment to their life raft, just as long as everyone else was required to do the same. In conclusion, nothing will improve the safety of a life raft like clear legislation.

There is a growing body of increasingly sophisticated equipment in our complex world and it is clearly quite impossible for an "ordinary user" to be completely familiar with all of it. This is particularly true of safety equipment or the parts of machinery which protect the user. A car, for example, contains many safety systems which are not really understood by the average man. We are not asked by auto manufacturers to buy "optional, heavy duty" brakes nor, should they fail, does the burden of proving that better brakes should have been "standard" fall upon us. We have consumer protection agencies which do that for us.

Unfortunately, the sailor's "consumer protection agency" the USCG has been asleep at the switch when it comes to one of its primary functions, saving lives at sea. It is unfortunate that the USCG, instead of Avon, could not have been sued for the injuries and loss of life among the crew of the SPIRIT.   This is not to say that the Coast Guard is not quick to respond with rescue craft when the hue and cry is raised. They do that very well. The problem is that in many cases, particularly those of boats lost far at sea, the hue and cry is usually not raised promptly and the castaways, such as those from the SPIRIT, must rely on the gear in their life raft, a raft purchased at great cost. It is no more reasonable to expect an "ordinary user," the sailor, to be intimately familiar with his survival equipment than it is to expect a driver to comprehend the details of a brake cylinder.

In 1987, on the CBS Evening News, Dan Rather narrated a segment highly critical of the popular Type II life jacket we call the "Mae West." *Consumer Report* is also critical of these devices, as is the *National Transportation Safety Association*. Articles noting the inadequacies of USCG-approved equipment have appeared in the many boating magazines over the last ten years. The consumers agency which sailors depend upon to protect them, the USCG, has not assumed its responsibility and this has, without question, translated itself into needless deaths.

SAFE HARBOR

So now the many tales of doom and disaster are done. Prior to publication, I gave a copy of this manuscript to my mother. The next day, she came up behind me and hit me over the head with it. *"Why did you do that?"* I asked. *"If I knew all this before, I would have never let you go,"* she joked. If she had succeeded in stopping me, it would have been my loss.

If I had remained ashore, I might have been sensible, worked hard, and become rich (maybe). I would have never known the joy of green islands, smelled the land breeze rich with the scent of flowers and damp earth, or heard the cry of the tropic bird. I would not have fought with, loved, and hated the Lady with the Green Eyes. In short, despite my wealth (if that happened), I would have been forever poor, having been sensible but too timid to sail toward my dreams. Take risks, but be prepared. Always live the life of adventure.

Michael Greenwald
Aboard SUNDANCER
San Diego, 1989

Bibliography

Adolph, E. F., *Physiology of Man in the Desert*, Hafner Publishing Co., New York, 1947, '69 (reprint), LC 79-76440

Angel, Nicolas, *Capsize,* W.W. Norton & Co. New York, 1980, translation, ISBN 0-393-039264-7, originally published by Pen Duick, Paris, 1979

Bailey, Maurice and Marylin, *Second Chance*, David McKay Co, New York, 1977, ISBN 0-679-50752-3

Bailey, Maurice & Maralyn, *Staying Alive*, David McKay Inc., New York, 1974, ISBN 0-679-50458-3, originally published as *117 Days Adrift,* Nautical Publishing Co. Ltd., Lymington, England 1974

Bascom,Willard, *Waves and Beaches*, Doubleday/Anchor Books, Garden City, NY, 1980, ISBN 0-385-14845-3

Bascom, Willard, *The Crest of the Wave,* Harper and Row, Publishers, New York and Fitzhenry & Whiteside, Ltd., Toronto, 1988, ISBN 0-06-015927-8

Berkow, Dr. Robert, et. al, *The Merck Manual of Diagnosis and Therapy*, Merck Sharp & Dohme Research Laboratories, Division of Merck & Co., Rahway, NJ, 1899, fifteenth edition, 1987

Bateman, James A.,*Trapping*, Stackpole Books, Harrisburg, PA, 1973, '79, ISBN 0-8117-1743-7

Bodin, Svante, *Weather and Climate*, Blanford Press, Poole, England, 1978, ISBN 0-7137-0858-1

Bombard, Alain, *The Bombard Story,* Grafton Books, London, 1986, ISBN 0-246-13038-5, translation, originally published 1953, Andre Deutsch Ltd., Editions de Paris, Paris

Budassi, S. A. & Barber, J. *Emergency Care*, C.V. Mosby Co., St. Louis, MO, 1984, ISBN 0-8016-0453-2

Bureau of Medical Services, *Ship's Medicine Chest and Medical Air at Sea*, USGPO, Washington, 1978, HEW No. (HSA) 78-2024

Callahan, Steve, *Adrift*, Houghton Mifflin Co., Boston, 1986, ISBN 0-395-38206-8

Clark, John R., *Shark Frenzy,* Grosset & Dunlap, New York, 1975, ISBN 0-448-13336-9

Cloudsley-Thompson, J. L., *Man and the Biology of Arid Zones*, Edward Arnold Ltd, Publishers, London, 1977, ISBN 0-8391-1192-4

Coote, Jack H., *Total Loss*, Adlard Coles, Ltd., Publishers, London, 1985, ISBN 0-299-11684-1

Couper, Alastair, *Atlas of the Oceans*, Van Norstrand Reinhold Co., New York, 1983, ISBN 0-422-21661-0

Dennis, Felix, *Man Eating Sharks*, Castle Books, Secaucus, NJ, 1976, ISBN 0-7064-0554-4

Dodge, Bertha S., *Marooned*, Wesleyan University Press, 1979, ISBN 0-8195-5031-0

Edgerton, M. T. *The Art of Surgical Technique*, Williams & Wilkens, Baltimore, 1988, ISBM 0-683-02749-2 pbk, illustrated by Florence J. Kabir

Edwards, Peter, MD, *Advanced First Aid Afloat*, Third edition, Cornell Maritime Press, Centerville, MD, 1987, ISBN 0-87033-376-3

Fales, Dan, *Onboard Electronics (EPIRBS)*, Motor Boating & Sailing Magazine 7/87

Fisher, J. & Lockley, R. M., *Sea Birds*, Houghton Mifflin Company, Boston, 1954, LC 54-9568

Freiberg, M. & Walls, J. G., *The World of Venomous Animals*, T.F.H. Publications, Neptune City, NJ, 1984, ISBN 0-87666-567-9

Gilmore, G. & Black, C. L., *Law of the Admiralty*, The Foundation Press, first edition, 1957, revised 1975

Halstead, B. W., *Dangerous Marine Animals*, Cornell Maritime Press, Centreville, MD, 1980, ISBN 0-87033-268-6

Harrison, Peter, *Seabirds*, Houghton Mifflin Co., Boston, 1983, ISBN 0-395-33253-2

Helm, Thomas, *Dangewrous Sea Creatures*, Funk & Wagnalls, Publishers, 1976, ISBN 0-308-10225-8

C. J. Hendry Co., *Survival Manual*, C.J. Hendry Co., San Francisco 1977, 1972, 46CFR 160.051, 1972, '74

Heyerdahl, Thor, Kon Tiki, Rand McNally, Chicago, 1950, translation. Now published by Simon & Schuster Co. Inc, Anglewood Cliffs, NJ

IMCO, *International Convention for Safety of Life.At Sea, 1974*, IMCO, London, 1975, ISBN 92-801-1036-5

IMO, *Global Maritime Distress and Safety System*, IMO, London, 1987, ISBN 92-801-1216-3

Ingle, R. M. & Smith, F.G., *SEA TURTLES*, University of Miami Press, Coral Gables, FL, 1949

Johannes, Robert Earl, *Words of the Lagoon*, Univerwsity of California Press, Berkeley, CA, 1981, ISBN 0-520-03929-7

Johnston, Robin Knox, *Sea School, Part V: Safety on Board*, Yachting World

Korper, Jon, *Three California Sailors Survive 8 Days Adrift in a Life Raft*, SOUNDINGS, 5/87

Lee, E.C.B. & Lee, Kenneth, *Safety and Survival at Sea*, W.W. Norton, New York 1971, '80, and K.S. Giniger Co., New York, Greenhill Books/Lionel Leventhal, London, et al., ISBN 0-393-03242-6

Lewis, Dr. Stephan, *Adaptation to Low Calorie Diets*, Am. J. Clin. Nutr.,1975

Lockley, R. M. *Ocean Wanderers*, Stackpole Books, Harrisburg, PA, 1974, ISBN 0-8117-1133-1, also published by David & Charles, Newton, Abott, Devon , GB

Lockley, Ronald M., *Seabirds of the World*, Facts On File Publications, New York, 1983, ISBN 0-87196-249-7

Marquez, Gabriel, *The Story of A Shipwrecked Sailor*, Alfred A. Knopf, New York, 1986, ISBN 0-394-54810-8   translation, as told by Luis Velasco

Mea, Chris, *Bird Migration*, Facts on File Publications, New York, ISBN 0-87196-694-8

Menard, H. W. et al , *Ocean Science*, W.H. Freeman & Co., San Francisco, ISBN 0-7167-0014-X

Michaelmore, Peter, *Alone in the Shark-Filled Sea*, Readers Digest, 10/87

Morris, Lynda, *Anatomy of A Life Raft*, Cruising World Magazine, Newport RI, 3/86

Mundell, Gary & Folstad, Rick,*Castaway*, Cruising World Magazine, Newport RI, 9/87

Nelson, Bryan, *Seabirds*, A & W Publishers, New York, 1979, ISBN 0-89479-042-0

Newell, G. E. & R. C., *Marine Plankton*, Hutchinson Educational Press, London

Pepe, Lt. Cmd. Dennis & Andreeva, Lana L., *COSPAS/SARSAT, EPIRBs And IMO/FGMDSS*, NMEA News, Mar/Apr 86, published by NOAA & NESDS

Raymont, John, *Plankton and Productivity in the Oceans*, Pergamon Press, New York, 1963, LC 62-11561

Rebel, Thomas P., *Sea Turtles*, University of Miami Press, Coral Gables, FL, 1974 (rev) ISBN 0-87024-217-2   Revised from 1949 ed by Ingle

Ricketts, Calvin and Hedgpeth, *Between Pacific Tides*, Stamford University Press, Stamford, CA, 1939,'85, ISBN 0-8047-1229-8

Ristori, Al, *The New Survival Suits*, Fins and Feathers, Reston, IL 3/87

Robertson, Dougal, *Sea Survival, a Manual*, Praeger Publishers, New York, 1973, ISBN 0-275-52760-3

Robertson, Dougal, *Survive the Savage Sea*, Granada Publishers Ltd., London, 1985, ISBN 0-246-12509-8

Rolls, B. J. & Rolls, E. T., *Thirst*, University of Cambridge Press, Cambridge 1982, ISBN 0 521 229189

Rousmaniere, John, *Fastnet Force 10*, W.W. Norton Co., New York, 1980, ISBN 0-393-03256-6

Rudloe, Jack, *Time of the Turtle*, Alfred A. Knopf, New York, 1979, ISBN 0-394-40968-X

Russell, Findley E., *Poisonous Marine Animals*, T.F.H. Publications, Neptune City, NJ, 1971, first edition 1965 by Academic Press, London

Sanderson, Ray, *Meterology at Sea*, Stanford Maritime Ltd., London, 1986, ISBN 0-540-074-055

Silverberg, Robert S., *The World Within The Ocean Wave*, Weybright & Talley,. New York, 1972, LC 71-186561

Snivley, William, *The Sea of Life*, David McKay Co., New York, 1969, LC 72-82952

staff, *Life rafts Part I, II*, Latitude 38, Sausalito, CA, Vols 28,29

Staff, *Offshore Rescue*, Latitude 38 , Sausalito,CA, Vol. 14

staff, *Tragedy of the SPIRIT Part I, II*, <u>Latitude 38</u>, Sausalito, CA, Vol 8,9, letters Vol. 11

Stokes, Ted, *Birds of the Atlantic Ocean*, Country Life Books, Feltham, Middlesex, 1968, illustrated by Keith Shackelton

Tchernia, Paul, *Descriptive Regional Oceanography*, Permagon Press, Elmsford, NY, 1980, ISBN 0-08-020925-4   with plates

Teal, J. & M. *The Sargasso Sea*, Little, Brown & Co., Boston, 1975, ISBN 0-316-84351-3
        Art by Leslie Morril

Thompson, Thomas, *Lost*, Antheneum Publishers, New York, 1975, ISBN 0-689-10634-3, as told by Bob Tininenko

Titcomb, Margaret M., *Native use of Fish in Hawaii*, University Press of Hawaii, 1952 ISBN 0-87022-797-1

Trimmer, John W., *How To Avoid Huge Ships*, self-published, Seattle, WA, 1983, ISBN 0-88100-019

Trumbull, Robert, *The Raft*, Henry Holt & Co., New York, 1942

Unden, J.E. *Safety At Sea*, A/S Nordisk Gummibaadsfabrik, Denmark, 1/85, ISBN 87-980088-1-1

Van Dorn, William G., *Oceanography and Seamanship*, Dodd, Mead & Co., New York, 1974, ISBN 0-396-06888-X, illustrated by Richard Van Dorn

Van Keith, I. & Van Loan, D. *Sailing with Ham Radio*, Paradise Cay Publications, Sausalito, CA, 1987, ISBN 0-939837-17-x

Vaucher, Charles, *Sea Birds*, Olivier & Boyd, Publishers, Edinburgh and London 1960

Vignes, Jaques, *The Rage to Live*, William Morrow & Co., Publishers, New York, 1976, translation, ISBN 0-688-02992-2, originally published by B. Arthaud, Paris, 1973

Wortman, Elmo, *Almost Too Late*, Random House, New York, 1981, ISBN 0-394-50935-8

INDEX

A

Abandon boat:
  drill 267
  in cold weather 262
  orderly 275
  problems 274
ABLE TASMAN 149
Abrasions 297
Abscesses, skin 322
Adrenaline, use for shock 317
Advanced First Aid Afloat 284
AFRAN DAWN M/V 18
Ahola, Jim, loss of 558
Air movement-land effect 398
Aircraft rafts 80
Albatross 436
Alcohol, use of 251
Almost Too Late, Elmo Wortman 241
American Practical Navigator, 349
AMVER 550
  alert 563
  SPIRIT rescue 563
Anaphylactic shock 292
Anemia 333
Anesthetic:
  for closing wounds 327
  for opening an abscess 325
Angle of Death 559
Antibiotics 315
APACHE BRAVE, loss of 551
ARAKAKA 50
Arch tube, defined 73
Arctic tern 448
Arthur, Camillia, death of 558
Aseptic technique 298
Aspirin 308, 314
ATLANTA , loss of 552
AURALYN, loss of 130
Avon Life Raft Company, defendants 572

B

Back-down approach, when towing 530
Bacteremia or septic shock 293
Bad-weather strategy 417
Ballast
  bag 69
Bananas 210
Basket hoist 549
Beebe, Dr. William 173
S.S. BENALDER 61
Bioluminescence 170
Birds:
  as food 204
  sea 433
  catching at sea 169
Bishop, David L. 173
Black, Charles L. Jr. 569
BLANQUITA, loss of 566
Bleeding, control of 287
Blood pressure 314
Blood vessels, tying off 288
Blue-footed Booby 138
Boarding ladder 67
Boat-connected recovery devices 497
Body core temperatures 250

Bombard, Alain:
  attacked by swordfish 49
  medical problem 50, 51
  psychological preparation 52
"Bomber" Trench 541
Boobies 445
Breadfruit 209
Breathing, restoration of 295
Broaching 35
Broad-spectrum antibiotics 315
Buddy warming 252
Burns 305-7
  shock 306
  treatment 307
Butler, Bill & Simone 79-80
Butterfly closures 327

Buxton, Robert W. 572
Buys Ballot's Law 411
        and strategy 419

C

C-130 Hercules aircraft 540
C.J. Henry Company 571
Calling for assistance 383
CAMPBELL, USCG Cutter 563
Cannibalism 148, 281
Cannister 88
Canopy:
        life raft 72
        lighting 72
Capacity, life raft 87
Cape Pigeon 439
Capsize 35, 145
Captain as the authority figure 54
Captain's authority 278
Carbohydrate digestion 235
Carbon dioxide/nitrogen mixture 66
Carbuncles 322
Cardiogenic shock 294
Cardiopulmonary Resuscitation 295
Carolina hanging snare 206
Caroline Island 191
CATHRYN, loss of 551
Celestial observations 354
Cephalexin 320
Cephalothin 320
Certification, life raft 86
Chafe, life raft 89
Children's vests 486
Chip log 352
Cigutera 194, 338
Cirrostratus clouds 410
Clamp, for life raft repair 89
Clark, George 173
Clothing bag 478
Clothing, cold weather 255
Cloud types 397
Clouds and their meaning 397
Coastal life rafts 78-80
Coconut crabs 194
Coconuts, as food 206

Code of Signals 383
Cold front 406
        sequence 408
Cold injuries 253
Cold weather clothing 479
Cold weather survival craft 262
Cold weather, abandoning ship 262
Colin Archer 141
Collins, Bruce 558
Collision:
        ability to stop, ships 19
        altering course, speed 21
        with cargo container 24
        course 21
        fog 28, 30
        in heavy weather 24
        logs 25
        nighttime 27
        running lights 28
        ships 18
        tugs-in-tow 23
        VLCC 29
        whales 25
Communications, emergency 372
Compass, for emergency navigation 353
Compass, sun and stars 354
Cone shells 343
Consice Tables for Sight
        Reduction 356
Consumers Report
        (July, '88) 489
        life jackets 583
        vests 490, 491
Control of pain 308
Contusions 298
Convection cell development 395
        and rain 394
COOK, USN Frigate 563
Copepod 171
Copperization 85
Coral cuts 337
Cordova Bay 243
Corilois effect 399
CORIOLIS, R/V 196
Cork float 82
COSPAS/SARSAT 386, 551
        short-comings of system 523

Cousteau, Jaques-Yves 183
Crabs 203
        coconut 194
Crash stop
        for power boats 499
        for sail boats 498
Crew drills 472
Crossing the "T" towing approach 530
Crush injuries 303
Culpepper Island 133
Cumulonimbus or thunderhead 395
Cumulus clouds 394
Currents 364
Currents, affecting a landing 363

D

Damages received, insurance. 570
Datum 503
        marker 494
Davison, Ann 81
Day pack 99
Debriding , 284, 299
Deck log 350
Dehydration 104, 217
DeJulius, Joseph & Jan 552
Demerol 310
Dermal gangrene 322
Desalinator 80, 227-9, 474
Despair 148
Deviation card, lifeboat compass 350
Dew, collecting 225
Dewatering 537
DH MEDICO 383
Diatome 169
Dinghy:
        as a lifeboat 94
        selection of 96
        survival pack 99
Dinoflagellates 170
Direct pressure, to stop bleeding 287
Disabled or distressed vessel,
        differences 524
Disaster Syndrome, 43, 53, 278, 294,
        314, 562
Disaster, preparation 265

Disease, theory of 313
Dislocations 305
Distance off by formula 359
Distress
        flags 461
        message , relaying 381
Distress message, on Station Bill 268
Dixon Entrance 242
Docking a tow 536
Doldrums 138
Dolphin 544
Dolphin-fish 151
Dorado 151
        catching 154
DOROTHEA, loss of 97
Dougal's Kitchen 114
Downbursts 396
Dreams of food 50
Drinking schedule 222
Drinking water, in equipment pack 74
Drogue 75
Drowning 333
Dutchman's log 352
Dye markers 460
Dysentery 137

E

"E" pack 74, 573
EDNAMAIR   111
Egrets 450
Ekman layer phenomena 398, 420
Elastomers, characteristics of 84
Electronic aids 40
Emergencies, medical help by 383
Emergency
        Position Indicating Radio Beacon
        (EPIRB) 385-7
        transmissions to "Ham"
        stations   380
Emergency transmissions
        to coast guard, "Ham" and
        commercial stations 379
Emergency blankets:
        as canopy 104
        use and construction 103

Emprine/codeine 308
EPIRB 122, 385, 469, 553
    A and B Class 385
    C Class 389
    design 388
    detection by aircraft 385
    406 MHz 389
    short-comings 387
    typical rescue 390
    uses 388
Equipment pack 74
Equipment requirements, SOLAS 93
Expanding square search 507
Explosions, causes 34
Exposure or anti-exposure suit 257

F

F/V LAURA, loss of 517
Fabric, life raft 83
Fairleads, use of, when towing 530
Falcon jet (HU 24A Guardian) 541, 553
Fat necrosis 578
Feeding frenzy, inducing 153
Fever, as indicator of infection 313
Fiberglass repair kit 266
Fire:
    extinguishers, types 32
    making, on land 212
First-aid kit, standard 'E' Pack 345
First degree burns 306
Fish:
    "attack" 105
    killing and cleaning 159
    traps, reef 198
    venomus 340
Fishing:
    chop 201
    with poison 201
Flare:
    dangers 458
    hand, instructions 466
    parachute 467
    rocket deployed, dangers 468
    quality of 454
    seen at different distances 457, 458

Flashlight, emergency 73
Flipowicz, Lt. John 517
Floats 81
Float suits USCG warning 259
Floating a line, to distressed vessel 532
Flotation chambers 72
Fluid loss, sources of 216
Fluids, in human tissue 215
Flying fish 151
Flyways, bird 451
Floatation devices 492
Flotsam, as indicator of land 362
Food, minimum for survival 576
    starvation hallucinations 579
Fourth-degree burns 306
Fractostratus 398
Fracture:
    alignment 301
    mouldable splint material 300
    multiple 303
    setting a broken limb 301
    traction 301
Frequencies for emergency
    transmission 375, 377
Frigate or Man o' War Bird 445
Frontal systems 411
Frostbite 255
Frostnip 253
Fulmar family, head shapes 437
Fulmar 438
Furuncle (a boil) 322

G

Gaff 116, 156
Gangrene 317, 322, 326
Gannets and Boobies 445-7
Givens Buoy life raft 9, 68, 70
"Goonie" bird 436
Gore and Sigler 574
Gorges 157
Green Turtle 161
Grounded vessel, assisting 531
Gulf of Lyons 144
Gulls 449

H

Hallucinations 124
    caused by deprivation 218-9, 579
Ham
    nets 380
    operators 374
    radio license 55
Hand lock 250
Hand pump 65
Hasson 453
Hartley, Lt. Jim 563
Hawkins, Sister Doris 218
Hawksbill turtle 161
Hawser 527
Headlands, dangers of, while landing 370
Heat stroke 296
Helicopter:
    lifting devices 549
    Dolphin HH65A 545
    HH3F 545
    HH52A 543
    hoisting PRIDE OF BALTIMORE
        survivor 555
Heliograph 462
    made from a can lid 464
Hemorrhoids 565
Hercules aircraft 540
Herons 450
Heyerdahl, Thor 171
High clouds 397
Hip tow 536
HOME, loss of 242
Horizontal movement of air 398
Hurricane, 415, 419
    approach 7
    Caribbean 7
    and killer storms 6
Hybreds, life jackets 489
Hydrostatic release mechanisms 66
Hypersensitivity reaction
    to antibiotics 316
Hypothermia:
    protection 103, 145, 249, 256
    symptoms of 250
Hypovolemic shock 290

I

Ikaros distress rocket 453
Immersion suits 257
Incisions 298
Identifying birds 430
Inflatable floor 84, 103
Inflatable Boat as a lifeboat 101
Inflatable splints, for treating shock 292
Injection, giving 315
INMARSAT 378
Inspection, life rafts 86
Internal ballast, dangers 37
Internal sleeve, of Coastal raft 79
Internal-Governmental Maritime
    Consultative Organization 92
International Convention for the
    Safety of Life at Sea
        (SOLAS) 1974,1983 92
International Telecommunications
    Union 380
Intravenous injection (IV), defined 315
Ion deficiency 219
ISLAND PRINCESS, loss of 8

J

JACK JR., loss of 20
Jacklines 484
Jackson, Ray and Ellen 556
Jerk spear 116
Jones Act, United States Code 568-9

K

Kidney failure 314
Killer whales 107-8
Kilo Mike Iroquois 379
Kittiwakes 441
KITTY LEE, loss of 551
KOMSOMOLETS MIRGIZII
    loss of 546-7
Kon Tiki 171
Krill 171
KRITER IV, loss of 11

L

L' HÉRÉTIQUE (THE HERETIC) 44-51
Lacerations 298
Lancing, an abscess 323
Land effect 398
       indicator of proximity of land 361
Land, signs of 361
Landing
       among cliffs 368
       on rocky beaches 379
Lanyard, defined 65
Last Voyage 82
Launching a rocket signal 468
Law of the Admiralty 569
Length of legs, search pattern 508
Lewis, Dr. Stephan B. 574
Life-dinghy 98
Lifeboat, St. Ives 522
Lifejackets:
       Type II PFD 488
       Type III PFD 488
       Type IV PFD 492
       Type V 489
Life raft:
       capacity rating 71
       deterioration, due to sunlight 105
       fabric 84
       function 64
       inflation 65
       inflation faliure 65, 275
       inspection, 86
       metalized canopy 73
       operational life, 90
       packaging 87
       patch 127
       relief valves 66
       second hand 90
       self-righting 69
       types 63
Line squalls 408
Line-throwing rocket 454
Lion fish 342
Liquid, from fish 224
List of Coast Stations 380
List of Radio Determination and

Special Service Stations 379, 390
Litter, Stokes 549
Long Island 245
Lost, by Thomas Thompson 53
Low clouds 398
LUCETTE, loss of 107
Lures and bait 157

M

Mackerel 151
Mae West's PFD 488
Magnificent Frigate 444
Mahi-mahi 151
Man O' War bird 445
Man overboard poles 494
Man overboard modules 496
Manual for Use by the Maritime Mobile
       and Maritime Mobile-Satellite
       Services 380
Mare's Tails 397
Maritime mobile "nets," HAM 380
Mask of death 58, 565
MASTER CARL, loss of 269
MAYDAY 377
Meatball surgery 284
Medication, oral 284
Medium clouds 397
Merchant Shipping Act of 1876   568
Merchant Shipping Notice,
       regarding sea water consumption 52
Merck Manual, 284
Messenger line 527
Metalized canopy 73
Meteor flares, color code 454
Military antishock trousers 292
Milk fish 151
Miller, Durel 562
Mistral 143
Mizzen masts 39
Mollusks, raft damage 91
Moore, Douglas 573
Morphine 309
"Mother Carey's Chickens" 440
Motorized Life Boat (MLB) 551, 526

Mouth-to-mouth ventilation 295
Mundell, Gary 189

N

Nafcillin 318
NAPOLEON SOLO, loss of 118
Navigation:
>   device, making 358
>   equipment 78, 350
>   equipment list, emergency 351
>   effect of wind and current 353
>   emergency kit 350
>   errors 31
>   lifeboat 349
>   safety warnings (radio) 383
>   texts 350
Necrotic tissue 322
Nematocyst 337
Net, plankton 173
Nimbostratus 398, 410
NJORD, loss of 141

O

Occlusion 411
Octopus, catching and killing 202
Oil, to calm seas 37
Old boats 142
Ooze 170
Operational life, life raft 90
Orange smoke 459
Orca 107
ORIENTAL FINANCIER 562
Overboard
>   poles 494
>   procedure 496
>   visual considerations 503
>   examination after recovery 515
>   medical procedures, on recovery 515
Overdue reports 523

P

Packaging, life raft 87

Pain, control of 308
Pains Wessex 452-3
>   hand flare 466
Painter, defigned 65
Palm heart 208
Palmer, Jack 44
Parachute flares 467
Parallel approach, when towing 530
Parallel search
>   using the wind 512
>   time to complete 510
Paralyzer, spear head 155
Patch kit 89
Patch
>   life raft 127, 266
Pelagic fish 151
Pelicans 449
Penicillin 317
>   for gangrene and tetanus 319
>   Nafcillin 318
>   procaine and benzathine 317
Penicillin-G potassium 319
Perry, Nancy 558
Personal Flotation Devices (PFD),
>   classification 486, 492
PETRAL, loss of 190
Petrel 439
Phalaropes 443
Physiology of life raft survivors 575
Physiology of water loss 579
Phytolankton 169
>   as food for castaways 173
Pistol launched flares 458
Pitchpoling 35
Plankton 169
>   seine, use by Bombard 48
Plants and trees, on islands 193
Plastic whistle 492
Plessz, Catherine 141
Plugs, life raft 88, 89
Poisoning, seafood 338
Polaris 357
Portholes and hatches, dangers 37
>   securing 270
Position:
>   for emergency transmission 384
>   by meridian transit 354

Postural vital signs, shock 290
Precision cut, surgical 323, 324
Pressure points, to control bleeding 287
PRIDE OF BALTIMORE, survivors,
        hoisting 555
Primary union of wounds 298
Prince Rupert Island 243
Prophylaxis medicine 284
Prophylaxis oral drug therapy 298
Psychological advantages 580
Pulse rate 314
Punctures 298
Pyramid seas 373
Pyrotechnics, origins 453

Q

Quoit, throwing 276

R

Racing fever 12
Radar 27
Radar reflector 27, 469
Radio:
        calling for assistance 383
        emergency navigation device 354
        installation for emergencies 372
        recovery radios 498
Radiotelephone alarm signal,
        2182 KHZ   376
Raft canopy, defective material 573
Raft deterioration, due to sunlight 105
Rage to Survive 141
Ratings, life raft 87
Rations 84
        British and Dutch studies 236
Rats, as food 194, 205
Rebounding waves 373
Recovery radios 498
Reef, crossing in survival craft 380
Reincarnation of men lost at sea 436
RELIANCE, loss of 82
Relief valves 66
Rescue Coordination Centers 388
Rescue, probability 523

RESOLUTE, USCG Cutter 553
Respiration 314
Retrieval probability 505
Retroreflective tape 71, 545
Retroreflective panels 492
Rewarming:
        cold victim 251
        hypothermia victim 252
RHINOCEROS 3
Right Boat, The 39
Right-triangle maneuver 502
Righting an inverted raft 66
Rip currents and rip tides 363
Roll cloud 396
Row, Ronnie, loss of 551
Royal National Life Boat Institute 517
Rowing, a rubber dinghy 133
Rowlandson, Lt. A. H. 218
RTL-TIMEX, loss of 11
RUBBER DUCKY III 119,221
RULE No. 1   140, 270
RULE No. 2   267
RULE No. 3   455
Rules of the Road 19
Running lights, interpretating 29
Running suture, surgical 328

S

S.S. BENALDER 61
Sachets, water 72
Sailboat racing, dangers of 11
Sailboat towing bridle 529
Salt water:
        boils 114,147
        drinking 52
        sores 334
        sores, caused by sunburn 105
SAR organization 517
SARSAT 386
Satellite, SAR 386
Sat/Nav 31
Schiltz, Lucien 141
Scorpion fish 341
Scud 398
Sea:

anchor, defined 14, 76, 142, 275
    Viking 77
    birds 433
    cucumber 201
    hawks 447
    sickness 336
    urchin, as food 203
    water, consumption, comment by
        D. Robertson 52
    drinking 43, 46, 229, 565
Search and Rescue Mission Control 388
Search, focal point 503
SEAWISE GIANT 29
Second Chance (1977) 130
Second degree burns 306
Second-hand rafts 90
Secondary union of wounds 298
Sector search 505
Securing assistance from USCG 523
SECURITY message 383
Self-righting life raft 68
Septic shock 293
Seven Oceans rations 237
Sextant 40
Shark, 49, 138
    attack 124
    attack, Bombard 186
    attack, Dougal Robertson 186
    attack, Steve Callahan 186
    bull 180
    capabilities 175
    encountered while landing 381
    grabbing 159
    Great White, 180
    hammerhead 187
    mako 184
    Moby Dick 184
    repellant 185
    "Rogue" 178
    tiger 180
    tiger, attack 185
    whaler 182
    white Tip 183
Shearwaters 440
Shellfish poisoning 343
*Ship's Medical Chest and Medical Aid at
    Sea* 383

Ship, sudden turns 21
Ship-ship calling frequencies 376
Shock 290
Shock loading 529
    prevention 534
Shotline 527
Short count. for radio direction 378
SIBONY, loss of 78-9
Signal light 469
Signaling, strategy 456
Signals, from land 213
    night 465
    pyrotechnic, requirements 465
    useless 456
SILENCE MAYDAY 381
SILENCE, request on radio 381
Silvadene Cream 321
Single Sideband Transceiver (S.S.B.) 373
SITREP (situation report) 552
Skin:
    abscesses 322
    damage, caused by dampness 579
    as indicator of infection 314
Skip distance, radio waves 374
Skuas 447
Smoke signals 459
Snares 206
Solar stills 127, 225
SOLAS Convention, 1974, '83   91
    equipment requirements 93
SOLOMON BROWNE, loss of 518
Southern Cross 357
Sear fishing
    near land 199
    tide pools 200
Spear gun 155
Spears, emergency 156
SPIRIT
    loss of 556
    under full sail 557
SS LACONIA, lifeboats from 218
Standing orders 272
Staphylococcal skin damage 334, 578
STAR OF INDIA 551
Starvation, effects of 124, 126, 129
Station bills, sample 267, 272
Sterile field, creation of 299

Sterilizing the skin 299
Sterns Rule of Fifty 250
Stingray wounds 338
Stings 337
Stone fish 341
Storm strategy, based on plotting 418
Storm petrel 440
Strobe flasher 469
      life jacket signal 492
Strong point, life raft 65
Sunburn, danger of 105, 311
Sunstroke 296
Surf mechanics 374
Surf:
      landing through 373
      with a dinghy 375
      with a life raft 376
      swimming through 378
Surface currents 422
Surface rescue equipment
      and techniques 526
Surgical debriding
Survival craft, keeping together 276
Survival platforms 82
Survival pack:
      creating 472
      equipment 477
      food 84, 476
      radios 478
      weight 472
      type of container 471
Survival, psychology of 277, 279
Survival Technologies Group 456
Survivor compensation 570
Sutures 327
Sweat reduction 216
Switlik Parachute Co. 69, 71, 76-7, 468
      coastal raft 78-9
Swordfish attack 50
Symptoms of infection 313

T

Tangvald, Peter 97
Taro 210

Terns 448
Tetanus 317
Tetraodotoxin 340
THE SEVEN STEPS 271
*The Ship's Medicine Chest and Medical
      Aid at Sea* 284
Thermal protection suits 103, 261
Thermal fibrillation 556
Third degree burns 306
Thirst *Adrift* 124
      mechanism 217
Throwing line 497
Tininenko 54
      Linda, death of 59
TITANIC, loss of 1, 39
TOKA MARU II 117
Torroidal ballast chambers 70
Tourniquet 287
Tow
      cable deployment 533
      docking 536
      hip 536
Towing
      bridle 524, 527, 530, 533
      cable 527
      hazards of 524, 527, 530
      a sinking vessel 535
      in step 534
Toxic shock 294
Traction pads 484
Trade wind clouds 394
Transmissions to radiotelephone
      stations 379
Transmissions, urgency and safety 382
Traps
      crab, lobster 198
      fish 158
      the leaf sweep 199
Treatment for hypersensitivity
      reaction 317
      of infection 315
Trigger fish 123, 125, 134, 137, 151
      catching 153
Trimming with body weight 100
TRITON, Loss of 53, 54
Tropic bird 442
TROPICAL 551

Tube-noses 436
Tug-in-tow, running lights 24
Tuna 151
Turning maneuvers 501
Turtle 133, 139
        catching 166, 167, 195
        eggs 168
        green, hawksbill 161
        loggerhead 163
        meat, cooking 167
        Ridley 164
Types of wounds 297

U

Undertow or backrush 372
UNION STAR, loss of 518, 519
Urgency and safety transmissions 382
Urine:
        consumption, warning 216
        color and smell 314
Use of a heliograph 462
Utility Tow Boat (UTB) 526

V

Visual deployment of search lookouts 504
VHF radio, as safety device 373
Valise 88
Venemous fish 341
Verkade rations 236
Vessel overdue reports 523
Vignes, Jaques 141
Viking Life Saving Equipment
        Company 70
Visibility, from bridge 22
Vitamin C 137

W

Walters, Lt. Cdr. Thomas 517
Warm fronts 410
Warnings, by radio 383
Watch keeping 280
Watch, as navigation tool 350

Water:
        conservation 223
        color, indicating land 361
        collecting on land 211
        consumption 133
        lack of, on islands 193
        loss, physiology 215
        loss, charts 220, 221
        ration 104, 124
        requirements, summary of 219
        in urine 216
Waterproof compartments 39
Weak link 65
Weather
        Caribbean "Norther" cycle 7
        predicting 393
        warnings, by radio 8, 390
WEOLMI 306 140
Wet suit 257
WOM, KMI and WOO (radio stations) 379
Will to survive 43, 53, 192, 279
Wilson's (storm) petrel 440
Wilson's phalarope 443
Wind flow near cliffs 380
Wind-chill factor 576
Windward shore, landing on 378
Wortman, Elmo 241
Wounds:
        closing 327
        treating 298
        types 297
Wrenching a grounded vessel 533
WWV and WWVH 390

X-Y-Z

Yawing, danger of when towing 533
Zooplankton 169

About the Artists

Steve Callahan is author/illustrator of the international best-seller, *Adrift*. He lives in Ellsworth, Maine. His contribution to this book as both editor and artist is another reminder that Steve is a man of many talents. In addition to his literary and artistic skills he is a boat builder, teacher and designer. His long involvement with the sea, *"the place of utter freedom and utter responsibility"* includes 40,000 miles of blue water sailing, a number of ocean passages and a solo of the North Atlantic.

Richard DeRosset is a Navy combat and official USCG artist. His paintings hang in many institutions, including the Smithsonian and the Aerospace Museum. He lives with his wife in La Mesa, California. Captain DeRosset spent five years in the Navy, including a tour in Viet Nam aboard U.S. Navy assault boats as coxswain. He has spent more than fifteen years at sea, was Captain of the tanker PACIFIC TROJAN and crew of the F/V PETREL, which burned and sank 75 miles off California, during the night of May 21,1977. He and his crew were rescued by a USCG helicopter, which hoisted him off a hatch cover.

Rafael Monroy was born in Havana and fled with his family when Fidel Castro came to power. He was a combat illustrator and photographer for the U.S. Marines and served a six year tour of duty, which included service in Lebanon. He received numerous decorations and citations for his service. He now lives with his wife and child in San Diego and established his own design studio. He is also a student at the La Jolla Fine Arts Acadeny.

Jim Sollers has come to be known as the 'disaster artist of the *National Fisherman*' and has commemorated many marine tragedies of the twentieth century. He is a free-lance illustrator and lives in Portland, Maine. Jim was the first art director of *Small Boat Journal* and has illustrated numerous books and magazines, including *Sail* and *Cruising World,* in addition to the *National Fisherman.*

Rebecca Thomson is an experienced mariner, aircraft pilot and adventuress. She lives in Arvada, Colorado. Captain Thomson has made many ocean crossings under power and sail, crossed the Atlas mountains by mule and travled extensively in Africa and the Near East. She has participated in disaster relief efforts in several third world countries. A skilled artist in a variety of mediums, Rebecca Thomson has illustrated several books, including *The Cruising Chef Cookbook,* and numerous magazine articles.

The joy of having sailed far and eaten well linger in the mind long after the bitter, hard times have been reduced to laughter. Only the essence of the moment, the lust for life and the joy of it all remain, islands in the minds eye, more green and scented than anything dreams can bring.

The Cruising Chef Cookbook

By Michael Greenwald

An Encyclopedia of Knowledge for Lovers of Fine Food and the Sea

The Cruising Chef Cookbook is the most extensive and complete sailor's cookbook ever written, a hefty 420 pages, containing hundreds of solid tips and sound advice by Captain Greenwald, who is also a Paris-trained chef. Included are over 300 delicious recipes, each <u>created by the author</u> in the galleys of small cruisers during his eighteen years of ocean voyaging. Over 85,000 sailors have turned for advice to *The Chef*, which is sold in chandleries and nautical book stores all over the world. No-where else will you find such an extensive explanation of the pressure cooker, the sailors best friend. Many of Europe's great, classic recipes have been modified for pressure cookery, a faster, fuel efficient technique, resulting in superb cuisine. Here's an example:

Yacht Atria Spicy Beef Casserole Serves Four

This easy-to-make delight is an especially good way to prepare an interesting meal from canned ground beef, although it is much better with fresh meat. All of the ingredients, including the noodles are pressure cooked together in the same pot at the same time—for just <u>five minutes</u>.

1. Cover the bottom of the pressure cooker with 3 tsp. cooking oil
2. Mix and add to the pot:

1 lb canned or browned fresh beef	1 lg. onion, sliced
1 can (10 oz.) tomato sauce	4 cloves garlic
1 tbl. Worchestershire sauce	2 eggs, beaten
1 green pepper (optional)	1 tbl. mustard (or more)
6 tbl. catsup	
2 cups broad noodles, on top of everything:spread-out.	

3. Pressure cook five minutes after the jiggle. Bon Appetite!

Hundreds of Tips for the Galley Chef

Extending the life of fruits, vegetables
Preparing cans for ocean cruising
Growing salads at sea
Purchasing and stowing beer and wine
Proper provisioning for a cruise
Selection of pots and pans
Clean-up with little water

Ways to improve tinned soup
Tips for stowage and storage
The trash problem—what to do
Buying bulk food
Menu planning
Baking: pan and pressure cookery
Soups for all weathers

Short Stories and Interesting Anecdotes

At last there was a light. We thought at first that it was a star on the horizon. Then, as it grew brighter, we thought that it might be a ship on the rim of the sea, which would come toward us, unfolding itself from a point of light, and go rushing past, leaving us a little sad, as though at the parting of a friend. But the light did not move and finally we knew it was not a ship. . . .

We thought then that perhaps it was a fishing boat, working with lights, rolling in the heavy seas. but finally we knew that it was a beacon, though far away. . . and we watched for the rocks and the submerged wreck which would kill us in the darkness. We stared ahead, into the night, but it was hard and cold, like a stone and we did not know how to touch it, so we looked at the beacon, which bloomed like a flower, far away, and we watched it through the binoculars, hoping somehow to bring it nearer.

Then, through the glasses, we could see a glimmer of foam at the tower's base, the sea lacing its fingers through the fingers of the shore, and we could hear the dull boom of breakers, not from the shore but from abeam of us. We knew, then, the location of the wreck and that we had passed it. Something was gone from our minds, a weight which we had not known was there. But it was gone and we knew it was fear.

Then we passed the light and in our human way cared no more about it, but looked, instead, into the night, searching for some deep pool of silence in which to drop the hook. As we passed into calm water, the hatch was thrown back and Rebecca popped her head out. *"Care for a cup of soup, my love?"* From: *The Cruising Chef Cookbook*

The Dolphin Book Club Says . . .

So much more than a batch of recipes. Greenwald is talking about food, but he's really writing about cruising. . . Greenwald has so obviously "been there" and has such zest that you read him as though he were an old friend. . . This book makes you dream just a bit.

Beautifully illustrated with birds and fish from a dozen seas, live studies from the Everglades to the Cape Verdes, light-houses in lonely places, old sailing boats that still earn their keep and a few fish traps lying on beaches lost in time. *The Cruising Chef Cookbook* is sure to become a prized possession for those who love fine food and the sea —$14.95 from your chandler or **Blue Horizons Press**, Box 60778, San Diego, CA 92106